Lecture Notes in Artificial Intel

Subseries of Lecture Notes in Computer Sci

Edited by J. G. Carbonell and J. Siekmann

Lecture Notes in Computer Science

Edited by G. Goos, J. Hartmanis and J. van Leeuwen

Berlin
Heidelberg
New York
Barcelona
Hong Kong
London
Milan
Paris
Singapore
Tokyo

Hiroki Arimura   Sanjay Jain
Arun Sharma (Eds.)

Algorithmic Learning Theory

11th International Conference, ALT 2000
Sydney, Australia, December 11-13, 2000
Proceedings

Springer

Series Editors

Jaime G. Carbonell, Carnegie Mellon University, Pittsburgh, PA, USA
Jörg Siekmann, University of Saarland, Saabrücken, Germany

Volume Editors

Hiroki Arimura
Kyushu University, Department of Informatics
Hakozaki 6-10-1, Fukuoka 812-8581, Japan
E-mail: arim@i.kyushu-u.ac.jp

Sanjay Jain
National University of Singapore, School of Computing
3 Science Drive 2, Singapore 117543, Singapore
E-mail: sanjay@comp.nus.edu.sg

Arun Sharma
The University of New South Wales
School of Computer Science and Engineering
Sydney 2052, Australia
E-mail: arun@cse.unsw.edu.au

Cataloging-in-Publication Data applied for

Die Deutsche Bibliothek - CIP-Einheitsaufnahme

Algorithmic learning theory : 11th international conference ;
proceedings / ALT 2000, Sydney, Australia, December 11 - 13, 2000.
Hiroki Arimura ... (ed.). - Berlin ; Heidelberg ; New York ; Barcelona ;
Hong Kong ; London ; Milan ; Paris ; Singapore ; Tokyo : Springer, 2000
(Lecture notes in computer science ; Vol. 1968 : Lecture notes in
   artificial intelligence) ISBN 3-540-41237-9

CR Subject Classification (1998): I.2.6, I.2.3, F.1, F.2, F.4.1, I.7

ISBN 3-540-41237-9 Springer-Verlag Berlin Heidelberg New York

Springer-Verlag Berlin Heidelberg New York
a member of BertelsmannSpringer Science+Business Media GmbH
© Springer-Verlag Berlin Heidelberg 2000
Printed in Germany

Typesetting: Camera-ready by author
Printed on acid-free paper   SPIN: 10781103   06/3142   5 4 3 2 1 0

Preface

This volume contains all the papers presented at the Eleventh International Conference on Algorithmic Learning Theory (ALT 2000) held at Coogee Holiday Inn, Sydney, Australia, 11–13 December 2000. The conference was sponsored by the School of Computer Science and Engineering, University of New South Wales, and supported by the IFIP Working Group 1.4 on Computational Learning Theory and the Computer Science Association (CSA) of Australia.

In response to the call for papers 39 submissions were received on all aspects of algorithmic learning theory. Out of these 22 papers were accepted for presentation by the program committee. In addition, there were three invited talks by William Cohen (Whizbang Labs), Tom Dietterich (Oregon State Univeristy), and Osamu Watanabe (Tokyo Institute of Technology).

This year's conference is the last in the millenium and eleventh overall in the ALT series. The first ALT workshop was held in Tokyo in 1990. It was merged with the workshop on Analogical and Inductive Inference in 1994. The conference focuses on all areas related to algorithmic learning theory, including (but not limited to) the design and analysis of learning algorithms, the theory of machine learning, computational logic of/for machine discovery, inductive inference, learning via queries, new learning models, scientific discovery, learning by analogy, artificial and biological neural networks, pattern recognition, statistical learning, Bayesian/MDL estimation, inductive logic programming, data mining and knowledge discovery, and application of learning to biological sequence analysis. In the current conference there were papers from a variety of the above areas, refelecting both the theoretical as well as practical aspects of learning. The conference was collocated with Pacific Knowledge Acquisition Workshop and Australian Machine Learning Workshop, thus providing interesting interaction between the above communities.

The E. M. Gold Award is presented to the most outstanding paper by a student author, selected by the program committee of the conference. This year's award was given to Gunter Grieser for the paper "Learning of recursive concepts with anomalies."

We would like to thank the program committee members, Naoki Abe (NEC, Japan), Mike Bain (Univ. of New South Wales, Australia), Peter Bartlett (Australian National Univ., Australia), Shai Ben David (Technion, Israel), Rusins Freivalds (Univ. of Latvia, Latvia), Nitin Indurkhya (Nanyang Tech Univ., Singapore), Roni Khardon (Tufts University, USA), Eric Martin (Univ. of New South Wales, Australia), Yasu Sakakibara (Tokyo Denki Univ., Japan), Takeshi Shinohara (Kyushu Inst. of Tech, Japan), Frank Stephan (Univ. of Heidelberg, Germany), Osamu Watanabe (Titech, Japan), and Akihiro Yamamoto (Hokkaido Univ., Japan) and the subreferees (listed separately) for spending their valuable time reviewing and evaluating the papers.

We would also like to thank Eric Martin (Univ. of New South Wales) and Eric McCreath (University of Sydney) for local arrangments, and the ALT Steering Committee consisting of Peter Bartlett, Klaus P. Jantke, Phil Long, Heikki Mannila, Akira Maruoka, Luc De Raedt, Arun Sharma, Takeshi Shinohara, Osamu Watanabe, and Thomas Zeugmann for providing the management of the ALT series.

December 2000

Hiroki Arimura
Sanjay Jain
Arun Sharma

Referees

Nader Bshouty
Nadav Eiron
Toshiaki Ejima
Koichi Hirata
Hiroki Ishizaka

Satoshi Kobayashi
Takeshi Koshiba
W. S. Lee
Seishi Okamoto
Wolfgang Merkle

Tetsuhiro Miyahara
Noriko Sugimoto
Jun Takeuti
Takashi Yokomori

Sponsoring Institutions

School of Computer Science and Engineering, The University of New South Wales

Supporting Organizations

IFIP Working Group 1.4 on Computational Learning Theory
Computer Science Association (CSA)

Table of Contents

INVITED LECTURES

REGULAR CONTRIBUTIONS

Statistical Learning

Inductive Inference

ILP

Complexity

Neural Network and Other Paradigms

Support Vector Machines

Extracting Information from the Web for Concept Learning and Collaborative Filtering (Extended Abstract)

William W. Cohen*

WhizBang! Labs - Research
4616 Henry Street, Pittsburgh PA 15213

Abstract. Previous work on extracting information from the web generally makes few assumptions about how the extracted information will be used. As a consequence, the goal of web-based extraction systems is usually taken to be the creation of high-quality, noise-free data with clear semantics. This is a difficult problem which cannot be completely automated. Here we consider instead the problem of extracting web data for certain machine learning systems: specifically, collaborative filtering (CF) and concept learning (CL) systems. CF and CL systems are highly tolerant of noisy input, and hence much simpler extraction systems can be used in this context. For CL, we will describe a simple method that uses a given set of web pages to construct new features, which reduce the error rate of learned classifiers in a wide variety of situations. For CF, we will describe a simple method that automatically collects useful information from the web without any human intervention. The collected information, represented as "pseudo-users", can be used to "jumpstart" a CF system when the user base is small (or even absent).

1 Introduction

A number of recent AI systems have addressed the problem of extracting information from the web (*e.g.*, [15,17,12,1]). Generally, few assumptions are made about how the extracted information will be used, and as a consequence, the goal of web-based extraction systems is usually taken to be the creation of high-quality, noise-free data with clear semantics. This is a difficult problem, and in spite some recent progress, writing programs that extract data from the web remains a time-consuming task—particularly when data is spread across many different web sites.

In this paper we will consider augmenting concept learning (CL) and collaborative filtering (CF) systems with features based on data automatically extracted from the web. As we will demonstrate, extracting data for learning systems is a fundamentally different problem than extracting data for, say, a conventional database system. Since learning systems are tolerant of noisy data, novel approaches to extracting data can be used—approaches which extract lots of noisy data quickly, with little human cost.

---

* The work described here was conducted while the author was employed by AT&T Labs - Research.

H. Arimura, S. Jain and A. Sharma (Eds.): ALT 2000, LNAI 1968, pp. 1–12, 2001.

Here we propose a simple general-purpose method that takes as input a collection of web pages and a set of instances, and produces a set of new features, defined over the given instances. For example, consider a learning problem in which the instances are the names of musical artists. The generated feature $g_{classical}$ might be true for all instances that appear in a web page below a header element containing the word "classical". Other generated features might be true for all instances that appear on particular web pages, or that appear in particular tables or lists. When this "expansion" process is successful, adding the new features to the original dataset can make concept learning easier: *i.e.*, running a learning system on the augmented dataset will yield a lower error rate than running the same learning system on the original dataset. Analogously, the same features might make it easier to learn the concept "musical artists that William likes"; this suggests that the performance of a collaborative music-recommendation system might also be improved by the addition of these new features.

To a first approximation, one can think of the expansion method as generating features based on a large number of automatically-generated extraction programs. Most of the features proposed will be meaningless, but a few might be useful, and if even a few useful features are proposed the concept learning system may be able to improve the error rate.

Below we describe will briefly describe this expansion method, and summarize a few relevant experimental results for some sample CL and CF tasks. More information on these results is available elsewhere [7,8].

2 Generating features from the web

The method used for adding features to examples is motivated by a semi-automatic wrapper generation procedure, which is described elsewhere [6]. The expansion method takes as input a set of HTML pages $\mathcal{P}$, and a set of instances $\mathcal{X}$. In the case of collaborative filtering, $\mathcal{X}$ would be the set of entities for which recommendations should be made—for instance, a set of musical artists, for a music recommendation system. For concept learning, we will assume that $\mathcal{X}$ includes both the training and test instances.[1] The result of the expansion process is to define a number of new features $g_1(x), \ldots, g_n(x)$ over the instances $x \in \mathcal{X}$.

The expansion method procedes as follows. First a set of pairs $\mathcal{E}$ is initialized to the empty set. Then, for each page $p \in \mathcal{P}$, the following steps are taken.

First, the HTML markup for p is parsed, generating an HTML parse tree T_p. Each node of this parse tree corresponds either to an HTML element in p, or a string of text appearing in p. We use $text(n)$ to denote the concatenation (in order) of all strings appearing below the node n in T_p—that is, the text marked up by the HTML element corresponding to n. We use $tag(n)$ to denote the tag of the HTML element corresponding to n.

---

[1] Thus the approach described here is really a method for *transduction* [22] rather than induction.

Table 1. A simple HTML page and the corresponding parse tree.

> **Sample HTML page** p:
> \<html>\<head>...\</head>
> \<body>
> \<h1>Editorial Board Members\</h1>
> \<table> \<tr>
>   \<td>Harry Q. Bovik, Cranberry U
>   \<td>G. R. Emlin, Lucent
>   \</tr>\<tr>
>   \<td>Bat Gangley, UC/Bovine
>   \<td>Pheobe L. Mind, Lough Tech
>   ...
>
> **Parse tree** T_p:
> html(head(...),
>   body(
> n_1:   h1("Editorial Board Members"),
>   table(
>   tr(td("Harry Q. Bovik, Cranberry U"),
> n_2:   td("G.R. Emlin, Lucent")),
>   tr(td("Bat Gangley, UC/Bovine"),
>   td("Pheobe L. Mind, Lough Tech")),
>   ...

Table 1 shows an example HTML page p and the corresponding parse tree T_p. The tree is shown in a functional notation, where the tag of a node n becomes the functor of a logical term, and the subtrees of n become the arguments.

Next, the HTML parse tree is adjusted and analyzed. In adjusting the tree, for each node n that has K_{split} or more children corresponding to line-break (\
) elements (where K_{split} is a parameter) new child nodes are introduced with the artificial tag *line* and with child nodes corresponding to elements between the \
 elements. Conceptually, this operation groups items on the same line together in the tree T_p under a *line* node, making the tree better reflect the structure of the document as percieved by a reader. In analyzing the tree, the *scope* of each header element in T_p is computed. The scope of a header is all HTML elements that appear to be below that header when the document is formatted.

Next, for each node $n \in T_p$ such that $|text(n)| < K_{text}$, the pair $(text(n), position(n))$ is added to the set $\mathcal{E}$ of "proposed expansions". Here $position(n)$ is the string "$u(p)tag(a_0)...tag(a_l)$" where $u(p)$ is the URL at which the page p was found, and $a_0...a_l$ are the nodes encountered in traversing the path from the root of T_p to n (inclusive). Using Table 1 as an example, assume that u is the URL for p, and s is the string *html_body_table_tr_td*. Then this step would add to $\mathcal{E}$ pairs like ("G. R. Emlin, Lucent", us) and ("Bat Gangley, UC/Bovine", us). This step would also add many less sensible pairs as well, such

Table 2. Benchmark problems used in the experiments.

	#example	#class	#initial features	#pages (Mb)	#features added
music	1010	20	1600	217 (11.7)	1890
games	791	6	1133	177 (2.5)	1169
birdcom	915	22	674	83 (2.2)	918
birdsci	915	22	1738	83 (2.2)	533

as ("Editorial Board Members",us'), where $s' = html\_body\_h1$).

For CL (but not CF), an additional set of pairs are added to $\mathcal{E}$. For each node $n \in T_p$ such that $|text(n)| < K_{text}$, each header node n_h such that n is in the scope of n_h, and each word w in $text(n_h)$, the pair $(text(n), w)$ is added to $\mathcal{E}$. For example, in Table 1, the node n_2 is in the scope of n_1, so the pairs added to $\mathcal{E}$ would include ("G. R. Emlin, Lucent", "Editorial"), ("G. R. Emlin, Lucent", "Board"), and ("G. R. Emlin, Lucent", "Members"), as well as many less sensible pairs such as ("G. R. Emlin, Lucent Harry Q. Bovik, Cranberry U", "editorial").

Finally, $\mathcal{E}$ is used to define a new set of features as follows. Let $sim(s, t)$ be the cosine similarity [20] of the strings s and t.[2] Let $\mathcal{T}$ be the set of positions and/or header words appearing in $\mathcal{E}$: that is, $\mathcal{T} = \{t : (y, t) \in \mathcal{E}\}$. For each $t \in \mathcal{T}$ a new feature g_t is defined as follows:

$$g_t(x) = 1 \text{ iff } \exists(y, t) \in \mathcal{E} : sim(name(x), y) \geq K_{sim}$$

Here $name(x)$ is the natural-language name for x. For example, if x is an instance with $name(x) =$ "G. R. Emlin", then the pairs computed from the sample page might lead to defining $g_{editorial}(x) = 1$, $g_{board}(x) = 1$, and $g_{us} = 1$.

3 Experimental results for CL

To apply this technique, we need each instance to include some commonly used natural-language "name" that identifies the instance—$e.g.$, the title of a movie, or the name of a person. We also need to supply the expansion method with some set of relevant web pages—preferably, pages that contain many lists and tables that correspond to meaningful groupings of the instances, and many header words that meaningfully describe the instances.

Four benchmark CL problems satisfying these conditions are summarized in Table 2. In the first benchmark problem, $music$, the goal is to classify into genres the musical artists appearing in a large on-line music collection. In $games$, the name of a computer game is mapped to a broad category for that game ($e.g.$, $action$, $adventure$). In $birdcom$ and $birdsci$, the name of a species of North

---

[2] We follow the implementation used in WHIRL [5].

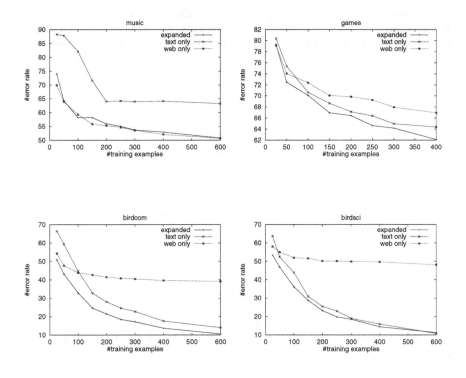

Fig. 1. Error rate of RIPPER on the four benchmark problems as training set size is varied.

American bird is mapped to its scientific order. In *birdcom* the species name is the common name only, and in *birdsci* the species names is the common name concatenated with the scientific name (*e.g.*, "American Robin—Turdus migratorius"). Each dataset is naturally associated [9,8] with a set of data-rich web pages, and in each benchmark problem, the initial representation for an instance is just the name of the instance, represented as a "bag of words". The first columns of Table 2 summarize the four benchmark problems, listing for each problem the number of examples, classes, features, and associated web pages, and the total size of all web pages in megabytes. The final column indicates the number of new features introduced by the expansion process.

Figure 1 shows the result of running the rule-learning system RIPPER [3,4] on the four problems. We used various sized training sets, testing on the remaining data, and averaged over 20 trials. Three representations were used for each dataset: the original representation, labeled *text only* in the figure; arepresentation including only the features g_t generated by the expansion process, labeled *web only*; and the union of all features, labeled *expanded*. To summarize, average error rates are generally lower with the expanded representation than with the original text-only representation.

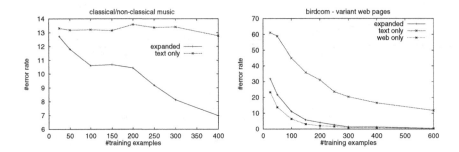

Fig. 2. Two problems for which expansion provides a dramatic benefit: a two-class version of *music*, and a variant of *birdcom* with automatically-collected web pages.

The reduction in average error associated with the expanded representation ranges from 25% (on *birdcom*) to 2% (on *games*). We note that on these problems, the possible improvement is limited by many factors: in the *bird* benchmarks, the initial term-based representation is already quite informative; in the *games* and *music* benchmarks, many examples are not usefully expanded; and in all benchmarks, the large number of classes leads to a "small disjunct problem" [14] which limits the learning rate. Figure 2 shows the learning curve for a version of the *music* problem where the only classes are *classical* and *non-classical*, and where instances not mentioned in the set of web pages were discarded. For this problem the reduction in error rate is a more dramatic 50%. A second dramatic reduction in error is also shown on another problem: a version of *birdcom* in which the web pages used for expansion were collected by automatically crawling an the web from an appropriate starting point. Assuming that the automatically spidered pages would be, on average, less useful than the manually chosen ones, we halted this crawl when 174 bird-related pages had been collected—somewhat more than were available in the original set of pages. The automatically-crawled pages also differ from the set of pages used in the previous experiments in that they contain many instances of bird names organized phylogenically—that is, using the same classification scheme that the concept learner is attempting to discover. The leads to a huge improvement in generalization performance.

4   Experimental results for CF

We also applied this expansion method as a preprocessor for a CF system. In CF, entities are recommended to a new user based on the stated preferences of other, similar users. (For example, a CF system might suggest the band "The Beatles" to the user "Fred" after noticing that Fred's tastes are similar to Kumar's tastes, and that Kumar likes the Beatles.) Using actual user-log data, we measured the performance of several CF algorithms. We found that running a CF algorithm using data collected by automatically expanding the set of instances against a set of relevant web pages was nearly as effective as using data collected from real users, and better than using data collected by two plausible hand-programmed web spiders.

In our experiments, we explored the problem of recommending music. The dataset we used was drawn from user logs associated with a large (2800 album) repository of digital music, which was made available for limited use within the AT&T intra-net for experimental purposes. By analyzing the log, it is possible to build up an approximate record of which musical artists each user likes to download. We took 3 months worth of log data (June-August 1999), and split it into a baseline training set and a test set by partitioning it chronologically, in such a way that all users in the training and test sets were disjoint. We constructed binary preference ratings by further assuming that a user U "likes" an artist A if and only if U has downloaded at least one file associated with A. We will denote the "rating" for artist A by user U as $rating(U, A)$: hence $rating(U, A) = 1$ if user U has downloaded some file associated with A and $rating(U, A) = 0$ otherwise. There are 5,095 downloads from 353 users in the test set, 23,438 downloads from 1,028 users in the training set, and a total of 981 different artists.

In evaluating the CF algorithms, we found it helpful to assume a specific interface for the recommender. Currently, music files are typically downloaded from this server by a browser, and then played by a certain "helper" application. By default, the most popularly used helper-application "player" will play a file over and over, until the user downloads a new file. We propose to extend the player so that after it finishes playing a downloaded file, it calls a CF algorithm to obtain a new recommended artist A, and then plays some song associated with artist A. If the user allows this song to play to the end, then this will be interpreted as a positive rating for artist A. Alternatively, the user could download some new file by an artist A', overriding the recommendation. This will be interpreted as a negative rating for artist A, and a positive rating for A'. Simulation with such a "smart player" can be simulated using user-log data: to simulate a user's actions, we accept a recommendation for A if A is rated positively by the user (according to the log data) and reject it otherwise. When a recommendation is rejected, we simulate the user's choice of a new file by picking an arbitrary positively-rated artist, and we continue the interaction until every artist rated positively by the test user has been recommended or requested. We define the *accuracy* of a simulated interaction between a CF method M and a test user U, denoted $ACC(M, U)$, to be the number of times the user accepts a recommendation, divided by the number of interactions between the user and the smart player.

We used several CF algorithms. Two of the best performing were *K-nearest neighbor* (K-NN), one of the most widely-used CF algorithms (e.g., [13],[21] and a novel algorithm called *extended direct Bayesian prediction* (XDB). XDB algorithm was motivated by considering the optimal behavior for CF given a single positive rating, i.e., a single artist A_i that user U is known to like. Assuming that users are i.i.d., the probability that U will like artist A_j is simply $Pr(rating(U', A_j) = 1 | rating(U', A_i) = 1)$ where the probability is taken over all possible users U'. This probability can be easily estimated from the training data. XDB employs with a simple *ad hoc* extension of this "direct Bayesian" recommendation scheme to later trials. Consider an arbitrary trial t, and let $B_1, ... B_{t-1}$ be the artists that have been positively rated by U. XDB always recommends the artist maximizing the scoring function

$$\text{SCORE}(A) = 1 - \prod_{j=1}^{t-1}(1 - Pr(rating(U', A) = 1 | rating(U', B_j) = 1))$$

We evaluated these CF algorithms on two types of data. The first was that baseline training set, containing user ratings inferred from the user logs. The second type of data was derived automatically from the web using the expansion algorithm of Section 2: specifically, each derived feature $g_t(x)$ is handled as if it were a user u who rates an artist x "positive" exactly when $g_t(x) = 1$. These "pseudo-users" can be either added to set of "real" users, or else can be used lieu of "real" users. Notice that in the latter case, the recommendation system requires no user community to make recommendations—only a set of relevant web-pages. The web pages used in these experiments were collected automatically by a heuristic process [8] in which commercial web-search engines were used to find pages likely to contain lists of musical artists.

As an additional baseline, we also hand-coded two recommendation systems based on data collected from a large on-line music database, `Allmusic.com`. One hand-coded system relies on genre information, and the second relies on lists of "related artists" provided by domain experts. Details of their implementation are given elsewhere [8]; briefly, the hand-coded systems use standard CF heuristics to look for genres (or lists of related artists) that correlate with a user's positive ratings, and makes recommendations based these well-correlated sets of objects.

Results for these experiments are shown in Figure 3. The first graph compares a K-NN CF system trained only on "pseudo-users" with the genre-based recommender, the related-artist recommender, and the baseline K-NN recommender (trained on the user data). We also show results for K-NN trained on a subset of the baseline dataset including only 100 distinct users. The second graph repeats this comparison using the XDB algorithm. To summarize, the performance of the system trained on "pseudo-users" is much better than either hand-coded recommendations system, but still worse than CF using the baseline dataset. For K-NN, training on "pseudo-users" leads to a system that is statistically indistinguishable from the 100-user dataset.

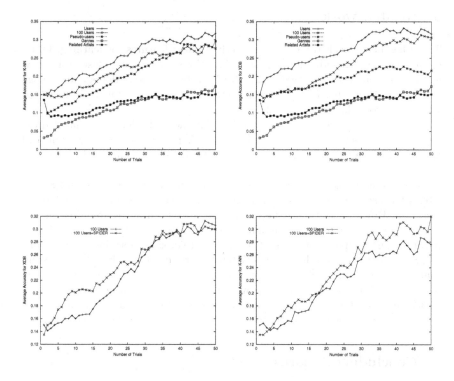

Fig. 3. CF performance with "pseudo-users". In the top pair of graphs, performance of pseudo-users instead of "real" users; in the bottom pairs of graphs, performance of a system that is trained on 100 "real" users, with and without the addition of "pseudo-users".

The last two graphs of Figure 3 show the result of combining a 100-user training set with "pseudo-users" obtained from the web. The results are intriguing. For both K-NN and XDB, adding pseudo-users so the undertrained CF systems leads to a small but statistically significantly improvement. However, augmenting the complete user dataset with "pseudo-users" did not improve performance for either K-NN or XDB: in both cases, performance on the combined dataset is statistically indistinguishable from performance on the baseline training dataset alone. This suggests that the best use for web data in CF may be to "jump start" a recommendation system that does not yet have a substantial user population.

On this dataset, the baseline CF systems far outperform random guessing, or recommending the most popular artists. Although XDB tends to perform somewhat better than K-NN, the difference is not statistically significant.

5   Related work

There has been much prior work on deriving new features for learning. Often called "constructive induction", most of this prior work involves constructing new features by combining old ones (*e.g.*, [19,16]) or by exploiting domain knowledge (*e.g.*, [11]). Here, in contrast, new features are found by exploiting unlabeled web pages from the same domain.

There has also been prior work on learning methods that use unlabeled examples as well as labeled ones (*e.g.*, [18]). In this paper, however, the additional input to the learning system is not a set of unlabeled instances, but a set of documents that may mention the labeled instances.

This paper is most closely related to previous work of Collins and Singer [10], who also consider constructing features based on occurances of labeled instances. However, in their experiments, instance occurances are found in free text, not in structured documents, and the constructed features are based on a natural-language parse of the text around an reference to an instance. Collins and Singer demonstrate that the extracted features can be exploited by a system that uses "co-training" [2] to exploit the new features. This paper extends the results of Collins and Singer by showing the utility of features extracted from structured HTML documents, rather than parsed free text, and also shows that more conventional learning methods can make use of these extracted features.

6   Concluding remarks

We have described a automatic means for extracting data from the web, under the assumption that the extracted data is intended to be used by a concept learner or collaborative filtering system. In particular, new features for a CL system (or new "pseudo-users" for a CF system) are derived by analyzing a set of unlabeled web pages, and looking for marked-up substrings similar to the name of some labeled instance x. New features for x are then generated, based on either header words that appear to modify this substring, or the position in the HTML page at which the substring appears.

These new features improve CL performance on several benchmark problems. Performance improvements are sometimes dramatic: on one problem, the error rate is decreased by a factor of ten, and on another, by half. Further experiments [7] show that these improvements hold for many different types of concept learners, in a wide range of conditions.

For CF systems, "pseudo-users" derived automatically from web data can improve the performance of undertrained CF systems. Perhaps more interestingly, CF systems based solely on "pseudo-users" have substantially better recommendation performance than hand-coded CF systems based on data provided by domain experts. These results suggest that collaborative filtering methods may be useful even in cases in which there is no explicit community of users. Instead, it may be possible to build useful recommendation systems that rely solely on information spidered from the web.

Acknowledgements

I thank Wei Fan for his contributions to the work on collaborative filtering.

References

1. Naveen Ashish and Craig Knoblock. Wrapper generation for semistructured Internet sources. In Dan Suciu, editor, *Proceedings of the Workshop on Management of Semistructured Data*, Tucson, Arizona, May 1997. Available on-line from http://www.research.att.com/~suciu/workshop-papers.html. 1
2. Avrin Blum and Tom Mitchell. Combining labeled and unlabeled data with co-training. In *Proceedings of the 1998 Conference on Computational Learning Theory*, Madison, WI, 1998. 10
3. William W. Cohen. Fast effective rule induction. In *Machine Learning: Proceedings of the Twelfth International Conference*, Lake Tahoe, California, 1995. Morgan Kaufmann. 5
4. William W. Cohen. Learning with set-valued features. In *Proceedings of the Thirteenth National Conference on Artificial Intelligence*, Portland, Oregon, 1996. 5
5. William W. Cohen. Integration of heterogeneous databases without common domains using queries based on textual similarity. In *Proceedings of ACM SIGMOD-98*, Seattle, WA, 1998. 4
6. William W. Cohen. Recognizing structure in web pages using similarity queries. In *Proceedings of the Sixteenth National Conference on Artificial Intelligence (AAAI-99)*, Orlando, FL, 1999. 2
7. William W. Cohen. Automatically extracting features for concept learning from the web. In *Machine Learning: Proceedings of the Seventeeth International Conference*, Palo Alto, California, 2000. Morgan Kaufmann. 2, 10
8. William W. Cohen and Wei Fan. Web-collaborative filtering: Recommending music by crawling the web. In *Proceedings of The Ninth International World Wide Web Conference (WWW-2000)*, Amsterdam, 2000. 2, 5, 8
9. William W. Cohen and Haym Hirsh. Joins that generalize: Text categorization using WHIRL. In *Proceedings of the Fourth International Conference on Knowledge Discovery and Data Mining*, pages 169–173, New York, NY, 1998. 5
10. Michael Collins and Yoram Singer. Unsupervised models for named entity classification. In *Proceedings of the Joint SIGDAT Conference on Empirical Methods in Natural Language Processing and Very Large Corpora (EMNLP99)*, College Park, MD, 1999. 10
11. S. Donoho and L. Rendell. Representing and restructuring domain theories: A constructive induction approach. *Journal of Artificial Intelligence Research*, 2:411–446, 1995. 10
12. J. Hammer, H. Garcia-Molina, J. Cho, and A. Crespo. Extracting semistructured information from the Web. In Dan Suciu, editor, *Proceedings of the Workshop on Management of Semistructured Data*, Tucson, Arizona, May 1997. Available on-line from http://www.research.att.com/~suciu/workshop-papers.html. 1
13. William Hill, Lawrence Stead, M. Rosenstein, and G. Furnas. Recommending and evaluating choices in a virtual community of use. In *Proceedings of ACM CHI'95*, pages 194–201, 1995. 8
14. Robert Holte, Liane Acker, and Bruce Porter. Concept learning and the problem of small disjuncts. In *Proceedings of the Eleventh International Joint Conference on Artificial Intelligence*, Detroit, Michigan, 1989. Morgan Kaufmann. 6

15. Nicholas Kushmerick, Daniel S. Weld, and Robert Doorenbos. Wrapper induction for information extraction. In *Proceedings of the 15th International Joint Conference on Artificial Intelligence*, Osaka, Japan, 1997. 1
16. Christopher J. Matheus and Larry A. Rendell. Constructive induction on decision trees. In *Proceedings of the Eighth International Workshop on Machine Learning*, Evanston, Illinois, 1989. Morgan Kaufmann. 10
17. Ion Muslea, Steven Minton, and Craig Knoblock. Wrapper induction for semistructured, web-based information sources. In *Proceedings of the Conference on Automated Learning and Discovery (CONALD)*, 1998. 1
18. K. Nigam, A. McCallum, S. Thrun, and T. Mitchell. Learning to classify text from labeled and unlabeled documents. In *Proceedings of the Fifteenth National Conference on Artificial Intelligence (AAAI-98)*, Madison, WI, 1998. 10
19. Giulia Pagallo and David Haussler. Boolean feature discovery in empirical learning. *Machine Learning*, 5(1), 1990. 10
20. Gerard Salton, editor. *Automatic Text Processing*. Addison Welsley, Reading, Massachusetts, 1989. 4
21. U. Shardanand and P. Maes. Social information filtering: algorithms for automating 'word of mouth'. In *Proceedings of ACM CHI'95*, 1995. 8
22. Vladimir Vapnik. *Statistical Learning Theory*. Wiley and Sons, New York, 1998. 2

The Divide-and-Conquer Manifesto

Thomas G. Dietterich

Oregon State University
Corvallis, OR 97331, USA
tgd@cs.orst.edu
http://www.cs.orst.edu/~tgd

Abstract. Existing machine learning theory and algorithms have focused on learning an unknown function from training examples, where the unknown function maps from a feature vector to one of a small number of classes. Emerging applications in science and industry require learning much more complex functions that map from complex input spaces (e.g., 2-dimensional maps, time series, and strings) to complex output spaces (e.g., other 2-dimensional maps, time series, and strings). Despite the lack of theory covering such cases, many practical systems have been built that work well in particular applications. These systems all employ some form of divide-and-conquer, where the inputs and outputs are divided into smaller pieces (e.g., "windows"), classified, and then the results are merged to produce an overall solution. This paper defines the problem of divide-and-conquer learning and identifies the key research questions that need to be studied in order to develop practical, general-purpose learning algorithms for divide-and-conquer problems and an associated theory.

1 Introduction

The basic supervised learning task is to find an approximation h to an unknown function f given a collection of labeled training examples of the form $\langle x, y \rangle$, where x is a fixed-length vector of features and $y = f(x)$ is a class label or output value (e.g., drawn from a small number of discrete classes or an interval of the real line). In the theory of supervised learning, these training examples are assumed to be produced by independent draws from some underlying probability distribution.

However, when we look at current and emerging applications of machine learning, we find the situation is much more complex. The x values—instead of being fixed-length vectors—are often variable-length objects such as sequences, images, time series, or even image time series (e.g., movies, sequences of aerial photos taken over several years). The y values may be similarly complex sequences, images, or time series. Let us consider a few examples.

Example 1: Text-to-Speech. A famous demonstration of machine learning is the problem of mapping spelled English words into speech signals, as in the NETtalk system (Sejnowski & Rosenberg, 1987). Each training example is an English word (e.g., "**enough**") along with an aligned phonetic transcription (e.g.,

H. Arimura, S. Jain and A. Sharma (Eds.): ALT 2000, LNAI 1968, pp. 13–26, 2001.
© Springer-Verlag Berlin Heidelberg 2001

"In^-f-") and an aligned stress transcription (e.g, "0>1<<<"). This is a case in which both the x and the y values are variable-length sequences.

Example 2: Grasshopper Infestation Prediction. We have been studying the problem of predicting future infestations of grasshoppers in Eastern Oregon based on a map of the adult grasshopper population in the previous year and the daily weather during the fall, winter, and spring (Bunjongsat, 2000). In this case, each training example is a two-dimensional population map coupled with a time series of daily weather maps, and the output is another two-dimensional map.

Example 3: Fraud detection in transactions. Many applications of machine learning involve analyzing time series of transactions (e.g., telephone calls, insurance claims, TCP connection attempts) to identify changes in behavior associated with fraudulent activity (Fawcett & Provost, 1997). This can be formalized as a problem of mapping an input sequence of transactions to an output sequence of alarms.

Example 4: Finding all volcanoes on Venus (Burl, Asker, Smyth, Fayyad, Perona, Crumpler, & Aubele, 1998). Many visual applications involve scanning images to identify objects of scientific interest (volcanoes, bacteria) and estimate relevant properties (location, volume, age). In this case, the input is a two-dimensional map of pixels and the output is a two-dimensional map of detected objects (and their predicted properties).

To solve these kinds of complex problems, practitioners have applied variations on the venerable "divide and conquer" schema. Viewed abstractly, every divide-and-conquer method consists of three steps: (a) divide (divide the original problem into subproblems), (b) conquer (solve the subproblems, possibly recursively), and (c) merge (merge the subproblem solutions into a solution for the original problem).

To apply this schema in machine learning, the x and y values are decomposed into "windows" or "regions", individually classified, and then merged to provide a classification decision for the original problem. For example, in the NETtalk task, the problem of predicting the entire phoneme sequence (and stress sequence) is divided into the subproblem of predicting each individual phoneme. To predict $y(i)$, the ith phoneme (and stress) of a word, a 7-letter window of the input, from $x(i-3)$ to $x(i+3)$, is used to extract a set of input features. To map an entire word from text to phonemes, we must separately predict the phoneme and stress of each letter and then concatenate them.

Similarly, for the grasshopper task, one approach is to define a grid of cells and try to predict the grasshopper population within each cell using as input the previous year's population and weather in that cell and neighboring cells. To construct a prediction map for each year, a prediction is made within each cell and then those predictions are concatenated to get the whole map.

In both of these examples, the merge step was a trivial concatenation, but more sophisticated versions of both problems employ complex merge steps. For example, in our decision tree text-to-speech system (Bakiri & Dietterich, 2000), we developed a "recurrent" classifier that constrained the allowable predictions for each subproblem based on the predictions of other subproblems. Specifically, we scanned each word from back-to-front, and the results of earlier predictions were used as input features to constrain subsequent predictions. This strategy enabled us to correctly pronounce word pairs such as "photograph" and "photography", even though they differ only in the last letter.

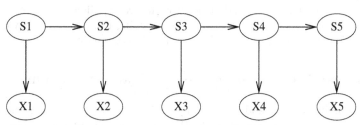

Fig. 1. Belief network representation of a hidden Markov model.

One of the most well-developed "merge methods" is based on Markov modeling (Bengio, 1999; Jelinek, 1999). Figure 1 shows a belief network representation of a hidden Markov model (HMM). Each of the hidden nodes S_i (except S_1) stores a transition probability distribution of the form $P(S_i|S_{i-1})$, and each observed node X_i stores an emission probability distribution of the form $P(X_i|S_i)$. An HMM is a stochastic finite state automaton that can be used to generate or recognize strings. To generate a string, state S_1 is chosen according to $P(S_1)$, and then the first output X_1 is chosen according to $P(X_1|S_1)$. Then the second state S_2 is generated according to $P(S_2|S_1)$ and so on. Only the X_t's are observed in the training and test data.

We can view the HMM as a divide-and-conquer method in which the base classifier is represented by $P(X_i|S_i)$ (which can be inverted by Bayes theorem to give $P(S_i|X_i)$, which assigns a class label S_i to the observed value X_i) and the merge method is represented by $P(S_i|S_{i-1})$. To merge a series of individual decisions, standard belief propagation methods can be applied to find the most likely sequence of states $S_1, S_2, \ldots, S_n$ that could have generated the observed data $X_1, X_2, \ldots, X_n$.

In speech recognition, for example, the problem is to map a speech signal into an English sentence. In this application, the hidden states of a hidden Markov model describe the temporal structure of English (i.e., what words can follow what other words, what phones can follow what other phones), and the emission probabilities can be viewed as naive Bayesian classifiers (or gaussian mixture classifiers) for deciding which phone generated each frame. One of the great virtues of the hidden Markov model is that both the base classifier and the merge step are trained jointly. This is in contrast to most other divide-and-conquer methods, where the base learning algorithm is trained independently of the merging process.

In recent years, many groups, particularly in speech recognition, have explored hybrid architectures where some other classifier (e.g., decision tree, neural network) is used in place of the emission probabilities of the HMM (Lippmann & Gold, 1987; Franzini, Lee, & Waibel, 1990; Bengio, De Mori, Flammia, & Kompe, 1992; Bourlard & Morgan, 1993). This permits a richer model of local interactions than the usual naive Bayes model, and that has led to success in such applications as online handwriting recognition (Bengio, Le Cun, & Henderson, 1994), molecular biology (Haussler, Krogh, Brown, Mian, & Sjölander, 1994; Baldi & Brunak, 1998), and part-of-speech tagging (Màrquez, 1999; Màrquez, Padró, & Rodríguez, 2000), as well as in speech recognition.

2 Research Issues in Divide-and-Conquer Learning

When applying a divide-and-conquer approach, there are six key design decisions that must be made: (a) output scale, (b) input scale, (c) alignment of outputs and inputs, (d) decomposition of the loss function, (e) base learning algorithm, and (f) merge method.

The output scale is the size of the regions or segments into which y is divided. For example, in our text-to-speech research (Bakiri & Dietterich, 2000), we chose to predict individual letters. But perhaps predicting pairs of letters would have been more effective, since some pairs of letters have highly predictable pronunciations (e.g., "st", "ck", and so on). Although we ran hundreds of experiments, we did not run this particular experiment. In our grasshopper study, we chose to predict the presence or absence of infestation in grid cells that were 10km on a side. Was this the correct size? We did not have time to test other grid sizes, so we do not know.

The input scale is the size of the input "window" that will be supplied as input to the base level classifier. In the original NETtalk system, Sejnowski and Rosenberg employed a 7-letter window. Bakiri (1991) performed an exhaustive series of experiments and found that a 15-letter window gave the best results. In our grasshopper domain, the input scale was a 30×30km square region, but other sizes may have been better.

The third decision involves how to align the output windows with the input windows. In the NETtalk domain, Sejnowski and Rosenberg manually inserted silent phonemes into the output phoneme string so that there was a direct 1:1 correspondence between input letters and output phonemes. But in many applications, the outputs and inputs are not pre-aligned. Lucassen and Mercer (1984) and Ling (1997) have both studied automatic alignment mechanisms for speech generation. Similarly, speech recognition systems typically employ forced Viterbi alignment to align the output words and phones with the input windows. Starting with a small set of aligned data, they train an initial HMM. Then this HMM is applied to unaligned data to find the most likely assignment of the given output words and phones to the input windows. This alignment is assumed to be correct, and it is then used as additional input data for training a new HMM.

The fourth decision involves how to decompose the overall loss function into a loss function that can be applied in the base case. The loss $L(\hat{y}, y)$ is the penalty incurred when the learned mapping h predicts $\hat{y} = h(x)$, but the true answer is $y = f(x)$. For example, in the grasshopper prediction task, the loss suffered when we fail to predict a grasshopper infestation is the cost of the resulting crop damage, and the loss suffered when we predict an infestation (rightly or wrongly) is the cost of spraying pesticides. This loss function decomposes perfectly into loss functions for any particular output scale, because the total loss over the entire region is the sum of the loss at each location. Such perfect decomposition means that the global loss function can be minimized by minimizing the local loss function using the base learning algorithm.

Unfortunately, in most complex learning problems, the loss function does not decompose so simply. Consider, for example, the problem of speech recognition. Here the goal is to identify the entire sentence correctly, so a loss of 1 is incurred if any word in the sentence is wrong (with a loss of 0 if no words are wrong). However, this does not decompose perfectly into a loss function for classifying each phone. In fact, as long as the maximum likelihood path through the HMM passes through the correct sequence of words, it does not matter whether every phone was correctly classified individually.

The loss function in fraud detection problems depends on the financial losses incurred by the fraudulent activity. This in turn is related to the amount of time between the start of fraudulent behavior and the time when the learned classifier raises an alarm. There is also typically a high cost to false alarms as well. This loss function is difficult to decompose into loss functions for the individual windows because only the *first* alarm in an episode matters.

The loss function for detecting volcanoes on Venus is also complex. If a volcano is detected in a slightly incorrect position, this is not a serious error. But detecting the same volcano at adjacent positions is an error (because each volcano should be detected only once), and so is the failure to detect a volcano at all. Hence, the definition of "correctly detecting a volcano" is not purely local—it depends on the results of several classification decisions in the neighborhood of the true volcano location. An additional complicating factor is that the training data (expert-labeled maps of "training regions" on Venus) is believed to contain volcanoes that were missed by the experts—inter-expert agreement is not very high.

The fifth decision involves choosing (or designing) the learning algorithm for solving the "base case" of the divide-and-conquer schema. Traditionally, standard machine learning methods have been applied here. However, many of the assumptions underlying those methods are violated in the divide-and-conquer setting: the training examples are no longer independent and identically distributed (iid) and the objective is not to maximize the percentage of correct classification decisions but instead to provide the most useful information to the merge step.

The merge method is perhaps the most important of these six decisions. This is the choice of how to merge the solutions of the individual subproblems to produce a solution to the overall problem. In the literature, many methods have been applied including simple concatenation (as in NETtalk), feeding the outputs through a second "merge" network (as in Qian and Sejnowski's (1988) protein structure prediction system), learning a recurrent classifier (as described above), and employing hidden Markov models (as described above) to find the most likely merged solution.

These six design decisions provide an agenda for machine learning research on divide-and-conquer problems. The goal of this research will be to study each of these design decisions, understand how the decisions interact, and develop methods for making them automatically.

In this paper, we will not address all six of these problems. Instead, we focus only on the input scale, the output scale, and the merge method.

3   Factors Affecting the Design of Divide-and-Conquer Systems

We begin with an analysis of the main factors that influence the choice of output scale, input scale, and merge method. The most important factor is the extent to which neighboring $y(i)$ values are correlated even after accounting for the information provided by the predictor x values. To make the discussion concrete, suppose that we are classifying each pixel of an image into one of two classes based on the measured red, green, and blue intensities of each pixel (the x values). Suppose the output scale is a single pixel, so $y(i)$ refers to the class of one pixel and $x(i)$ is a vector of the red, green, and blue intensities. Consider the conditional joint probability distribution $P(y(1), y(2)|x(1), x(2))$ of two adjacent pixels. Suppose that this can be perfectly factored into $P(y(1)|x(1)) \cdot P(y(2)|x(2))$. Figure 2(a) shows a belief network for this case. In this case, we can choose the output scale to be one pixel (i.e., $y(i)$), because the only way that $y(i)$ and $y(j)$ are correlated is through the correlations of $x(1)$ and $x(2)$.

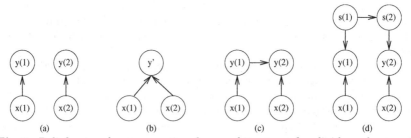

Fig. 2. Belief networks representing four architectures for divide-and-conquer systems.

However, now suppose that there is some additional correlation between $y(1)$ and $y(2)$ that cannot be accounted for by the correlation between $x(1)$ and $x(2)$.

In this case, the joint distribution $P(y(1), y(2)|x(1), x(2))$ does not factor. There are at least three ways to handle this. First, we can increase the output scale to include both $y(1)$ and $y(2)$ (and the input scale to include $x(1)$ and $x(2)$). This is equivalent to defining a new output variable y' which takes on four possible values corresponding to the four possible labels of $y(1)$ and $y(2)$ (see Figure 2(b)).

Second, we could apply the chain rule of probability and write the $P(y(1), y(2) | x(1), x(2))$ distribution as $P(y(1)|x(1)) \cdot P(y(2)|x(2), y(1))$ (where we have also assumed that $y(1)$ does not depend on $x(2)$.) This suggests a recurrent solution in which we first predict the value of $y(1)$ using $x(1)$, and then use this predicted value along with $x(2)$ to predict $y(2)$ (see Figure 2(c)).

The third approach is to model the relationship between $y(1)$ and $y(2)$ as a hidden Markov model (see Figure 2(d)), using hidden states $s(1)$ and $s(2)$.

This simple analysis shows that there is a tight connection between the choice of the output scale and the choice of the merge method. If we are merging the individual decisions via an HMM, we can use a smaller output scale (Figure 2(c) and (d)) than if we are merging by concatenating the independent classifications (as in Figure 2(b)), because the HMM captures the correlations between the y values that would otherwise need to be captured by a larger output scale.

The analysis also suggests that if the input scale is too small, the output scale may need to be larger or the merge step may need to be more complex. The reason is that if the input scale does not capture all of the correlations among the $x(i)$ values, then there will be "induced" correlations among the $y(i)$ values. For example, if $y(1)$ depends directly on both $x(1)$ and $x(2)$, but the base classifier ignores $x(2)$, then this will create an added dependency between $y(1)$ and $y(2)$ (because $y(2)$ depends on $x(2)$).

A second factor affecting the choice of input and output scale is the amount of noise in the $x(i)$ and $y(i)$ values. Large noise levels (for a fixed amount of input data) require high degrees of smoothing and aggregation. This is a consequence of the well-known bias-variance tradeoff. Noisy training data leads to high variance and hence, to high error rates. The variance can often be reduced by imposing a smoothing or regularizing process. In temporal and spatial data, it is natural to apply some form of temporally- or spatially-local smoothing, since we normally assume that the underlying x and y values are changing smoothly in space and time. One way of imposing local smoothing is to use a larger output scale. Consider again the example from Figure 2(b), where we introduced a new variable y' that took on four values $\{00, 01, 10, 11\}$ corresponding to the four possible pairs of labels for $y(1)$ and $y(2)$. We can impose spatial smoothing by constraining y' to only two possible values $\{00, 11\}$. In other words, the larger output scale is constraining $y(1) = y(2)$. A similar constraint can also be imposed through the merge techniques shown in Figure 2(c) and (d). These constraints can be made "soft" through Bayesian methods. For example, rather than banning the 01 and 10 values for y', we can just impose a penalty for using them by assigning them lower prior probability. In addition to building a smoothness constraint into the model, we can also impose smoothness by preprocessing the data to smooth the y values prior to running the base learning algorithm.

If there is noise in the input data, then this usually requires a larger input scale, so that the base classifier can aggregate a larger number of inputs to overcome the noise. Again, we can also consider smoothing the input data prior to running the base classifier (e.g., by modelling the process by which noise is added to the data as a Markov random field (a 2-D Markov process) and then finding the maximum aposteriori probability estimate of the true data given the observed data).

A third fundamental issue influencing the choice of the merge step is the direction of causality. In standard supervised learning and in learning belief networks, there is a growing body of evidence that suggests that learning is most efficient (statistically) when the model being fit to the data matches the direction of underlying causality. In such cases, the model can usually be parameterized using a small number of parameters, and consequently, less data is needed to fit those parameters.

Let us consider the direction of causality in the three merge methods sketched above. If we treat $y(1)$ and $y(2)$ as in Figure 2(b) or (d), we are assuming that there is no particular direction of causality between them. If we employ a recurrent method, we are assuming that a label for $y(1)$ is chosen first, and then it is used to help choose a label for $y(2)$. This direction of causality is typically more appropriate for time-series data than for spatial data or biological sequence data. This suggests that the choice of merge method in a particular application should depend primarily on domain knowledge about the likely direction of causality in the problem.

4   An Experimental Study

We now describe an experimental study of the tradeoff between using a large input scale with a simple merge method and using a small input scale with the more complex HMM merge method. To generate the training and test data, we employed a hidden Markov model of the kind shown in Figure 1. In this data, each S_i is a boolean class variable that is observed in the training data and hidden (and hence, predicted) in the test data. Each X_i is a vector of 10 boolean variables $(x_{i,0}, \ldots, x_{i,9})$ generated by a simple Naive Bayes model (i.e., there is a separate probability distribution $P(x_{i,j}|S_i)$ that generates each $x_{i,j}$ depending on the value of S_i), and these are observed in both the training and test data. We will choose the transition probability distribution $P(S_{i+1}|S_i)$ and the output probability distributions $P(x_{i,j}|S_i)$ to be stationary (i.e., the same for all values of i).

Given that we have generated training data according to this HMM, we wish to compare three learning algorithms. The first algorithm is "optimal" in the sense that it learns an HMM of exactly the same structure as the true HMM that generated the data. It is trivial to directly learn the HMM, because all of its random variables are observed in the training data. To classify test examples using the learned HMM, we must apply the forward-backward algorithm to compute $P(S_i|X_1, \ldots, X_N)$ for each S_i. The forward-backward algorithm can be viewed as a combination of two separate algorithms. The forward algorithm processes the sequence from left-to-right, and for each i, it can be viewed as computing $P(S_i|X_1, \ldots, X_i)$, which is the probability of the ith class label given the sequence seen so far. The backward algorithm processes the sequence from right-to-left, and for each i, it can be viewed as computing $P(S_i|X_{i+1}, \ldots, X_N)$. At each node i, these two probability distributions can be multiplied together and appropriately normalized to obtain $P(S_i|X_1, \ldots, X_N)$. (Note: This is a non-standard description of the forward-backward algorithm. The reader is referred to (Baldi & Brunak, 1998; Jelinek, 1999) for more rigorous and detailed descriptions.)

The second algorithm is just the forward part of the forward-backward algorithm. The reason to study this method is that it is similar to the kind of "recurrent" algorithm that Bakiri and Dietterich employed in the text-to-speech task. The results of classifying X values earlier in the sequence are used as inputs to classify later values.

The third algorithm applies the standard Naive Bayes classifier to predict each S_i independently. In other words, it assumes that each pair (X_i, S_i) is generated independently from the same distribution according to the probabilities $P(S_i)$ and $P(x_{i,j}|S_i)$. We will call this third algorithm, iid-Bayes, and we will allow it to use wide input windows as follows. An input window of width 3 uses X_{i-1}, X_i, and X_{i+1} to predict the value of S_i. Since this is a Naive Bayes classifier, it does this by learning probability distributions of the form $P(x_{k,j}|S_i)$, for all j and all $k \in \{i-1, i, i+1\}$.

In our experiments, we choose the distribution $P(S_i|S_{i-1})$ to have a symmetric form such that the class changes with probability δ and remains the same with probability $1 - \delta$. When $\delta = 0.5$, this means that the individual (X_i, S_i) pairs are generated independently and identically. But when δ is small, adjacent values of S_i are highly correlated.

Our experiments consisted of 100 trials. In each trial, we applied the HMM to randomly generate a training set and a test set, each containing 10 sequences of length 50. The probability distribution $P(S_1)$ was the uniform distribution.

Figure 3 shows the results of varying δ across a range from 0.01 to 0.50 while using a window size of 1 for iid-Bayes. We see that when $\delta = 0.5$, the three algorithms give the same performance, but as δ becomes small, the methods that explicitly model the dependency between the S_i values perform much better. The forward-backward algorithm gives the best results, of course, but the forward algorithm does quite well. The lesson of this experiment is that it is a mistake to ignore the dependencies between adjacent windows!

Figure 4 shows the results of varying the window size of iid-Bayes. When δ is very small, iid-Bayes can obtain excellent performance by using a very wide window. The reason, of course, is that the wide window captures the correlations between adjacent S_i values indirectly by exploiting the resulting correlations between the X_i values. However, when δ approaches 0.5, these large windows perform poorly, because now they are overfitting the data. Furthermore, the larger the window, the greater the opportunity for overfitting, and hence, the

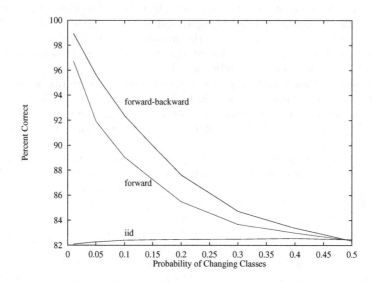

Fig. 3. A comparison of the percentage of correct predictions on the test data for the forward-backward algorithm, the forward algorithm, and the iid-Bayes(1) algorithm for different values of δ.

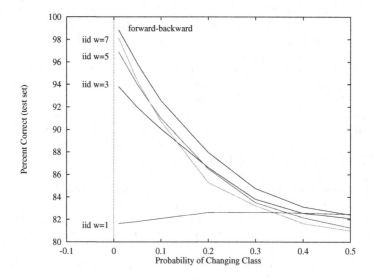

Fig. 4. Test-set performance of iid-Bayes for different input window sizes compared against the forward-backward algorithm.

worse the performance. Hence, we can see that a window size of 7 gives the best iid-Bayes performance for δ from 0 to 0.08. A window size of 5 gives the best performance for δ from 0.08 to 0.19. A window size of 3 gives the best performance for δ for 0.19 to 0.42. And for $\delta > 0.42$, a window size of 1 gives the best performance.

The lesson of this experiment is that the proper choice of input scale depends on the strength of correlation between adjacent S_i values, even when that correlation is a first-order Markov process. Another lesson is that there is an overfitting cost to using wide windows when they are inappropriate.

We performed a third experiment to see what happens when the temporal dependency model in the HMM is incorrect. We took each training example and re-ordered the individual (X_i, S_i) pairs to have the following order: (X_1, S_1), (X_{26}, S_{26}), (X_2, S_2), (X_{27}, S_{27}), ..., (X_{25}, S_{25}), (X_{50}, S_{50}). However, the HMM learning algorithm still applied the (now incorrect) HMM from Figure 1 to fit the data.

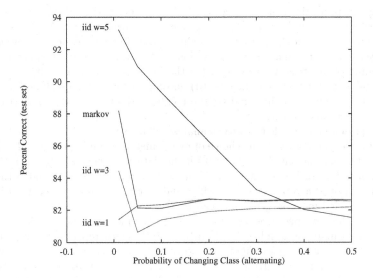

Fig. 5. Comparison of HMM and iid-Bayes on shuffled data, where the HMM model does not correctly capture the sequential dependencies in the data.

Figure 5 compares the performance of this incorrect Markov model with the iid-Bayes model for various settings of δ. We see that now iid-Bayes with a window size of 5 is able to do much better than the HMM, because a window size of 5 is large enough to capture the dependencies between S_i and S_{i-2} and S_{i+2}, whereas the first-order HMM cannot capture these dependencies. Notice that the first-order HMM gives essentially the same performance as iid-Bayes with a window size of 1 with the exception of very small values for δ. At these very small values for δ, there is a non-trivial correlation between S_i and S_{i+25}, so even a first-order HMM can capture some useful information. It is interesting that iid-Bayes with a window size of 3 also captures some of this information, but because of overfitting, it performs uniformly worse than the HMM.

This simple experimental study shows that if you have a correct model of the temporal dependencies in sequential data, then the HMM (forward-backward) approach to divide-and-conquer problems is the best method to apply. Sliding window methods that rely on a wide input window and a trivial merge step perform almost as well, but the window size must be adjusted depending on the strength of the temporal correlations. Finally, if you have an incorrect model of the temporal correlations, then the HMM method is much less robust, and the sliding window iid-Bayes approach gives superior results.

5   Concluding Remarks

Emerging applications of machine learning require algorithms that can learn mappings from complex input spaces to complex output spaces. A natural approach to solving such problems is to employ some form of divide-and-conquer. However, there are many difficult decisions that must be made in designing a divide-and-conquer learning system: (a) the input scale, (b) the output scale, (c) alignment of inputs and outputs, (d) decomposition of the loss function, (e) the base learning algorithm, and (f) the merge method. These design decisions interact in complex ways.

We presented a simple theoretical analysis which suggests that the input and output scales interact with the choice of merge method. Our experimental study verified this for the simple case in which the data was generated by an HMM. If we applied an HMM classifier, the input scale and output scale could both be 1. But if applied a Naive Bayes classifier and merged by simple concatenation, then we needed much larger input scales.

Researchers in speech recognition have had the most experience with learning complex mappings, and their HMM-based techniques appear very promising for explicitly representing temporal constraints. However, our study also showed that if the assumptions of the model (e.g., of first-order Markov interactions) is wrong, then HMM-based methods will perform very poorly, while large input windows are more robust. This is consistent with work combining neural networks (and wide input windows) with HMMs to overcome some of the modeling shortcomings of HMMs. It will be interesting to see how well other learning algorithms, such as tree- and rule-learning methods, can be combined with HMM-based merge procedures.

I hope this paper will encourage machine learning researchers to mount a systematic attack on the problems of divide-and-conquer learning. We are in the midst of a machine learning revolution, as the learning algorithms developed over the last 20 years are becoming widely applied in industry and science. However, many of the new applications of machine learning are complex, and require divide-and-conquer methods. Rather than continue the current trend of constructing ad hoc divide-and-conquer systems, we need to study these complex problems and develop learning algorithms specifically tailored to them. One can imagine a divide-and-conquer toolkit in which it would be easy to (a) describe the temporal and spatial structure of complex input and output data, (b) represent the global loss function of the application, and (c) automatically construct and train a divide-and-conquer architecture. As machine learning moves beyond simple classification and regression problems, complex divide-and-conquer methods are one of the most important new directions to pursue.

Acknowledgements

I wish to thank Dragos Margineantu for many conversations which helped refine the ideas presented in this paper. The author gratefully acknowledges the support of NSF grant 9626584-IRI.

Bibliography

Bakiri, G. (1991). Converting English text to speech: A machine learning approach. Tech. rep. 91-30-2, Department of Computer Science, Oregon State University, Corvallis, OR.

Bakiri, G., & Dieterich, T. G. (2000). Achieving high-accuracy text-to-speech with machine learning. In Damper, R. I. (Ed.), *Data Mining Techniques in Speech Synthesis*. Chapman and Hall, New York, NY.

Baldi, P., & Brunak, S. (1998). *Bioinformatics, the Machine Learning Approach*. MIT Press.

Bengio, Y. (1999). Markovian models for sequential data. *Neural Computing Surveys, 2*, 129–162.

Bengio, Y., De Mori, R., Flammia, G., & Kompe, R. (1992). Global optimization of a neural-network hidden Markov model hybrid. *IEEE Transactions on Neural Networks, 3*(2), 252–258.

Bengio, Y., Le Cun, Y., & Henderson, D. (1994). Globally trained handwritten word recognizer using spatial representation, convolutional neural networks, and hidden Markov models. In Cowan, J. D., Tesauro, G., & Alspector, J. (Eds.), *Advances in Neural Information Processing Systems*, Vol. 6, pp. 937–944. Morgan Kaufmann, San Francisco.

Bourlard, H., & Morgan, N. (1993). *Connectionist Speech Recognition: A Hybrid Approach*. Kluwer.

Bunjongsat, W. (2000). Grasshopper infestation prediction: An application of data mining to ecological modeling. Tech. rep., Department of Computer Science, Oregon State University. MS Project Report.

Burl, M. C., Asker, L., Smyth, P., Fayyad, U., Perona, P., Crumpler, L., & Aubele, J. (1998). Learning to recognize volcanoes on Venus. *Machine Learning, 30*(2/3), 165–194.

Fawcett, T., & Provost, F. (1997). Adaptive fraud detection. *Knowledge Discovery and Data Mining, 1*, 291–316.

Franzini, M., Lee, K., & Waibel, A. (1990). Connectionist Viterbi training: a new hybrid method for continuous speech recognition. In *International Conference on Acoustics, Speech, and Signal Processing*, pp. 425–428.

Haussler, D., Krogh, A., Brown, M., Mian, S., & Sjölander, K. (1994). Hidden Markov models in computational biology: Applications to protein modeling. *Journal of Molecular Biology, 235*, 1501–1531.

Jelinek, F. (1999). *Statistical methods for speech recognition.* MIT Press.

Ling, C. X., & Wang, H. (1997). Alignment algorithms for learning to read aloud. In *Proceedings the Fifteenth International Joint Conference on Artificial Intelligence (IJCAI-97)*, pp. 874–879.

Lippmann, R. P., & Gold, B. (1987). Neural classifiers useful for speech recognition. In *IEEE Proceedings of the First International Conference on Neural Networks*, Vol. IV, pp. 417–422.

Lucassen, J. M., & Mercer, R. L. (1984). An information theoretic approach to the automatic determination of phonemic base forms. In *Proceedings of the International Conference on Acoustics, Speech, and Signal Processing, ICASSP-84*, pp. 42.5.1–42.5.4.

Màrquez, L. (1999). *Part-of-speech Tagging: A Machine Learning Approach Based on Decision Trees.* Ph.D. thesis, Department de Llenguatges i Sistemes Informàtics, Universitat Politecnica de Catalunya.

Màrquez, L., Padró, L., & Rodríguez, H. (2000). A machine learning approach to POS tagging. *Machine Learning, 39*(1), 59–91.

Qian, N., & Sejnowski, T. J. (1988). Predicting the secondary structure of globular proteins using neural network models. *Journal of Molecular Biology, 202*, 865–884.

Sejnowski, T. J., & Rosenberg, C. R. (1987). Parallel networks that learn to pronounce English text. *Complex Systems, 1*, 145–168.

Sequential Sampling Techniques for Algorithmic Learning Theory

Osamu Watanabe

Dept. of Mathematical and Computing Sciences, Tokyo Institute of Technology
Tokyo 152-8552, Japan
watanabe@is.titech.ac.jp

Abstract. A *sequential sampling algorithm* or *adaptive sampling algorithm* is a sampling algorithm that obtains instances sequentially one by one and determines from these instances whether it has already seen enough number of instances for achieving a given task. In this paper, we present two typical sequential sampling algorithms. By using simple estimation problems for our example, we explain when and how to use such sampling algorithms for designing *adaptive* learning algorithms.

1 Introduction

Random sampling is an important technique in computer science for developing efficient randomized algorithms. A task such as estimating the proportion of instances with a certain property in a given data set can often be achieved by randomly sampling a relatively small number of instances. *Sample size*, i.e., the number of sampled instances, is a key factor for sampling, and for determining appropriate sample size, so called concentration bounds or large deviation bounds have been used (see, e.g., [9]). In particular, the Chernoff bound and the Hoeffding bound have been used commonly in theoretical computer science because they derive a theoretically guaranteed sample size sufficient for achieving a given task with given accuracy and confidence. There are some cases, however, where these bounds can provide us with only overestimated or even unrealistic sample size. In this paper, we show that "sequential sampling algorithms" are applicable for some of such cases to design *adaptive* randomized algorithms with theoretically guaranteed performance.

A *sequential sampling algorithm* or *adaptive sampling algorithm* is a sampling algorithm that obtains instances sequentially one by one and determines from these instances whether it has already seen enough number of instances for achieving a given task. Intuitively, from the instances seen so far, we can more or less obtain some knowledge on the input data set, and it may be possible to estimate an appropriate sample size. Recently, we have proposed [7,8] a sequential sampling algorithm for a general hypothesis selection problem (see also [6] for some preliminary versions). Our main motivation was to scale up various known learning algorithms for practical applications such as data mining. While some applications and extensions of our approach towards this direction have been

H. Arimura, S. Jain and A. Sharma (Eds.): ALT 2000, LNAI 1968, pp. 27–40, 2001.

reported [1,4,19], it has been also noticed [3,5] that sequential sampling allows us to add "adaptivity" to learning algorithms while keeping their worst-case performance. In this paper, we use some simple examples and explain when and how to use sequential sampling for designing such adaptive learning algorithms.

The idea of "sampling on-line" is quite natural, and it has been studied in various contexts. First of all, statisticians made significant accomplishments on sequential sampling during World War II [21]. In fact, from their activities, a research area on sequential sampling — sequential analysis — has been formed in statistics. Thus, it may be quite likely that some of the algorithms explained here have been already found in their contexts. (For recent studies on sequential analysis, see, e.g., [10,11].) In computer science, sequential sampling techniques have been studied in the database community. Lipton and Naughton [16] and Lipton etal [15] proposed adaptive sampling algorithms for estimating query size in relational databases. Later Haas and Swami [20] proposed an algorithm that performs better than the Lipton-Naughton algorithm in some situations. More recently, Lynch [17] gave a rigorous analysis to the Lipton-Naughton algorithm. Roughly speaking, the spirit of sequential sampling is to use instances observed so far for reducing a current and future computational task. This spirit can be found in some of the learning algorithms proposed in machine learning community. For example, the Hoeffding race proposed by Maron and Moore [18] attempts to reduce a search space by removing candidates that are determined hopeless from the instances seen so far. A more general sequential local search has been proposed by Greiner [12].

All the above approaches have more or less share the same motivation. That is, they attempts to design "adaptive algorithms" that can make use of the advantage of the situation to reduce sample size (or in more general, computation time) whenever such reduction is indeed possible. We believe that some of these approaches can be formally discussed so that we can propose *adaptive* learning algorithms with theoretically guaranteed performance.

This paper has some overlap with the author's previous survey paper on sequential sampling [22]. Due to the space limitation, we will omit some of the technical discussions explained there.

2   Our Problem and Statistical Bounds

In this paper, we fix one simple estimation problem for our basic example, and discuss sampling techniques on this problem or its variations. Let us specify our problem. Let D be an input data set; here it is simply a set of instances. Let B be a Boolean function defined on instances in D. That is, for any $x \in D$, $B(x)$ takes either 0 or 1. Our problem is to estimate the probability p_B that $B(x) = 1$ when x is given at random from D; in other words, the ratio of instances x in D such that $B(x) = 1$ holds.

Clearly, the probability p_B can be computed by counting the number of instances x in D for which $B(x) = 1$ holds. In fact, this is only the way if we are asked to compute p_B *exactly*. But we consider the situation where D is

Batch Sampling
begin
   $m \leftarrow 0$;
   for n **times do**
      get x uniformly at random from D;
      $m \leftarrow m + B(x)$;
   output m/n as an approximation of p_B;
end.

Fig. 1. Batch Sampling

huge and it is impractical to go through all instances of D for computing p_B. A natural strategy that we can take in such a situation is random sampling. That is, we pick up some instances of D randomly and estimate the probability p_B on these selected instances. Without seeing all instances, we cannot hope for computing the exact value of p_B. Also due to the "randomness nature", we cannot always obtain a desired answer. Therefore, we must be satisfied if our sampling algorithm yields a *good approximation* of p_B with *reasonable probability*. In this paper, we will discuss this type of approximate estimation problem.

Our estimation problem is completely specified by fixing an "approximation goal" that defines the notion of "good approximation". We consider the following one for our first approximation goal. (In the following, we will use $\widetilde{p_B}$ to denote the output of a sampling algorithm (for estimating p_B); thus, it is a random variable and the probability below is taken w.r.t. his random variable.)

Approximation Goal 1 *(Absolute Error Bound)*
For given $\delta > 0$ and ϵ, $0 < \epsilon < 1$, the goal is to have

$$\Pr[\; |\widetilde{p_B} - p_B| \leq \epsilon \;] \; > \; 1 - \delta. \tag{1}$$

As mentioned above, the simplest sampling algorithm for estimating p_B is to pick up instances of D randomly and estimate the probability p_B on these selected instances. Figure 1 gives the precise description of this simplest sampling algorithm, which we call *Batch Sampling* algorithm. Here only the assumption we need (for using the statistical bounds explained below) is that we can easily pick up instances from D uniformly at random and independently.

The description of Batch Sampling algorithm of Figure 1 is still incomplete since we have not specified the way to determine n, the number of iterations or sample size. Of course, to get an accurate estimation, the larger n is the better; on the other hand, for the efficiency, the smaller n is the better. We would like to achieve a given accuracy with as small sample size as possible.

To determine appropriate sample size, we can use several statistical bounds, upper bounds of the probability that a random variable deviates far from its expectation. Here we explain the Hoeffding bound [13] and the Chernoff bound [2] that have been used in computer science. (In practice, the bound derived from the Central Limit Theorem gives a better (i.e., smaller) sample size. But the Central Limit Theorem holds only asymptotically, and furthermore, the difference is within a constant factor. Thus, it is omitted here (see, e.g., [9,22]).)

For explaining these bounds, let us prepare some notations. Let $X_1, ..., X_n$ be independent trials, which are called *Bernoulli trials*, such that, for $1 \leq i \leq n$, we have $\Pr[X_i = 1] = p$ and $\Pr[X_i = 0] = 1 - p$ for some p, $0 < p < 1$. Let X be a random variable defined by $X = \sum_{i=1}^{n} X_i$. Then its expectation $E[X] = np$; hence, the expected value of X/n is p. The above three bounds respectively give an upper bound of the probability that X/n differs from p, say, ϵ. Below we use $\exp(x)$ to denote e^x, where e is the base of the natural logarithm.

Now these two bounds are stated as follows. (In order to distinguish absolute and relative error bounds, we will use symbols ϵ and ε for absolute and relative error bounds respectively.)

Theorem 1. *(The Hoeffding Bound)*
For any ϵ, $0 < \epsilon < 1$, we have the following relations.

$$\Pr\left[\frac{X}{n} > p + \epsilon\right] \leq \exp(-2n\epsilon^2), \quad \Pr\left[\frac{X}{n} < p - \epsilon\right] \leq \exp(-2n\epsilon^2).$$

Theorem 2. *(The Chernoff Bound)*
For any ε, $0 < \varepsilon < 1$, we have the following relations.

$$\Pr\left[\frac{X}{n} > (1 + \varepsilon)p\right] \leq \exp\left(-\frac{pn\varepsilon^2}{3}\right), \quad \Pr\left[\frac{X}{n} < (1 - \varepsilon)p\right] \leq \exp\left(-\frac{pn\varepsilon^2}{2}\right).$$

By using these bounds, we calculate "safe" sample size, the number n of examples, so that Batch Sampling satisfies our approximation goals. Here we consider Goal 1, i.e., bounding the absolute estimation error. It is easy to prove that the following bounds work. (The proof is easy and it is omitted here.)

Theorem 3. *For any $\delta > 0$ and ϵ, $0 < \epsilon < 1$, if Batch Sampling uses sample size n satisfying one of the following inequalities, then it satisfies (1).*

$$n > \frac{1}{2\epsilon^2} \ln\left(\frac{2}{\delta}\right). \quad (2) \qquad n > \frac{3p_B}{\epsilon^2} \ln\left(\frac{2}{\delta}\right). \quad (3)$$

This theorem shows that the simplest sampling algorithm, Batch Sampling, can be used to achieve the Approximation Goal 1 with a reasonable sample size. Let us see how the above (sufficient) sample size grows depending on given parameters. In both bounds (2) and (3), n grows proportional to $1/\epsilon^2$ and $\ln(1/\delta)$. Thus, it is costly to reduce the (absolute) approximation error. On the other hand, we can reduce the error probability (i.e., improve the confidence) quite a lot without increasing the sample size so much.

3 Absolute Error vs. elative Error

For another typical approximation goal, we consider the following one.

Approximation Goal 2 *(Relative Error Bound)*
For given $\delta > 0$ and ε, $0 < \varepsilon < 1$, the goal is to have

$$\Pr[\, |\widetilde{p_B} - p_B| \leq \varepsilon p_B \,] \; > \; 1 - \delta. \tag{4}$$

Here again we try our Batch Sampling algorithm to achieve this goal. Since the Chernoff bound is stated in terms of relative error, it is immediate to obtain the following sample size bound. (We can get a similar but less efficient sample size bound by using the Hoeffding bound.)

Theorem 4. *For any $\delta > 0$ and ε, $0 < \varepsilon < 1$, if Batch Sampling uses sample size n satisfying the following inequality, then it satisfies (4).*

$$n \; > \; \frac{3}{\varepsilon^2 p_B} \ln\left(\frac{2}{\delta}\right). \tag{5}$$

The above size bound is similar to (3). But it does not seem easy to use because p_B, the probability what we want to estimate, is in the denominator of the bound. (*Cf.* In the case of (3), we can safely assume that $p_B = 1$.) Nevertheless, there are some cases where a relative error bound is easier to use and the above size bound (5) provides a better analysis to us. We show such examples below.

We consider some variations of our estimation problem. First one is the following problem.

Problem 1 *Let $\delta_0 > 0$ be any constant and fixed. For a given p_0, determine (with confidence $> 1 - \delta_0$) whether $p_B > p_0$ or not. We may assume that either $p_B > 3p_0/2$ or $p_B < p_0/2$ holds.*

That is, we would like to "approximately" compare p_B with p_0. Note that we do not have to answer correctly when $p_0/2 \leq p_B \leq 3p_0/2$ holds.

First we use our sample size bound (2) for Approximation Goal 1. It is easy to see that the requirement of the problem is satisfied if we run Batch Sampling algorithm with sample size n_1 computed by using $\varepsilon = p_0/2$ and $\delta = \delta_0$, and compare the obtained $\widetilde{p_B}$ with p_0. That is, we can decide (with high confidence) that $p_B > p_0$ if $\widetilde{p_B} > p_0$ and $p_B < p_0$ otherwise. Note that the sample size n_1 is $2c/p_0^2$, where $c = \ln(2/\delta_0)$.

On the other hand, by using the sample size bound (5), we can take the following strategy. Let $n_2 = 48c/p_0$, the sample size computed from (5) with $\varepsilon = 1/2$, $p_B = p_0/2$, and $\delta = \delta_0$, where $c = \ln(2/\delta_0)$ as above. Run Batch Sampling with this n_2 and let $\widetilde{p_B}$ be the obtained estimation. Then compare $\widetilde{p_B}$ with $3p_0/4$. We can prove that with probability $1 - \delta$, we have $p_B > p_0$ if $\widetilde{p_B} \geq 3p_0/4$ and $p_B < 3p_0$ otherwise.

Comparing two sample size n_1 and n_2, we note that $n_1 = O(1/p_0^2)$ and $n_2 = O(1/p_0)$; that is, n_2 is asymptotically better than n_1. One reason for this difference is that we could use large ε (i.e., $\varepsilon = 1/2$) for computing n_2.

Next consider the problem of estimating the product probability. Instead of estimating one probability p_B, we consider here a sequence of probabilities

$p_1, ..., p_T$, where each p_t is defined as the probability that $B_t(x)$ holds for instance x randomly chosen from its domain D_t. Now our problem is to estimate their product $P_T = \prod_{t=1}^{T} p_t$ within a given absolute error bound. That is, the following problem.

Problem 2 Let $\delta_0 > 0$ be any constant and fixed. For a given ϵ_0, obtain an estimation $\widetilde{P_T}$ of P_T such that

$$\Pr[\ |\widetilde{P_T} - P_T| \leq \epsilon_0\ ] > 1 - \delta_0. \tag{6}$$

This is a simplified version of the problem solved by Kearns and Singh in [14] for approximating an underlying Markov decision process, and the following improvement is due to Domingo [3].

We may assume that, for each t, $1 \leq t \leq T$, it is easy to pick up instances from D_t uniformly at random and independently. Thus, by using Batch Sampling, we can get an approximate estimation $\widetilde{p}_t$ of each p_t. Here again we use sample size bounds for two approximation goals.

The strategy used by Kearns and Singh in [14] is essentially based on the bound (2) for Approximation Goal 1. Their argument is outlined as follows.

1. Check whether there is some t, $1 \leq t \leq T$, such that $p_t < \epsilon_0$. (We can use the condition discussed above.) If $p_t < \epsilon_0$, then we can simply estimate $\widetilde{P_T} = 0$, which satisfies the requirement because $P_T \leq \epsilon_0$.

2. Otherwise, for some ϵ specified later, compute the sample size n_1 for achieving Goal 1 with Batch Sampling. (We use δ_0/T for δ.) Then for each t, $1 \leq t \leq T$, run Batch Sampling algorithm with sample size n_1 to get estimate $\widetilde{p}_t$ of p_t.

3. From our choice of n_1, the following holds with probability $1 - \delta_0$. (We also have a lower bound inequality, which can be treated symmetrically.)

$$\widetilde{P_T} = \prod_{t=1}^{T} \widetilde{p}_t \leq \prod_{t=1}^{T} (p_t + \epsilon).$$

But since $p_t \geq \epsilon_0$, we have

$$\prod_{t=1}^{T} (p_t + \epsilon) \leq \prod_{t=1}^{T} p_t \left(1 + \frac{\epsilon}{\epsilon_0}\right) = \left(1 + \frac{\epsilon}{\epsilon_0}\right)^T \prod_{t=1}^{T} p_t = \left(1 + \frac{\epsilon}{\epsilon_0}\right)^T P_T.$$

Then by letting $\epsilon = \epsilon_0^2/(2T)$, we have the desired bound, i.e., $\widetilde{P_T} \leq P_T + \epsilon_0$.

4. Finally, the total sample N_1 size is estimated as follows, where $c = \ln(T/\delta_0)$.

$$N_1 = T \cdot n_1 = T(c(2T)^2/2\epsilon_0^4) = c(2T^3/\epsilon_0^4).$$

On the other hand, the argument becomes much simpler if we compute sample size n_2 using the bound (5) for Approximation Goal 2. (Since the first two steps are similar, we only state the last two steps.)

3. From our choice of n_2, the following holds with probability $1 - \delta_0$.

$$\widetilde{P_T} = \prod_{t=1}^{T} \widetilde{p_t} \leq \prod_{t=1}^{T} p_t(1+\varepsilon) = (1+\varepsilon)^T \prod_{t=1}^{T} p_t = (1+\varepsilon)^T P_T.$$

Then by letting $\varepsilon = \epsilon_0/(2T)$, we have the desired bound.

4. Recall that we are considering the situation such that $p_t \geq \epsilon_0$ for every t, $1 \leq t \leq T$. Hence, the total sample N_2 size is estimated as follows.

$$N_2 = T \cdot n_2 = T(c \cdot 3(2T^2)/\epsilon_0 \epsilon_0^2) = c(12T^3/\epsilon_0^3).$$

Note that $N_1 = O(T^3/\epsilon_0^4)$ and $N_2 = O(T^3/\epsilon_0^3)$. That is, N_2 is asymptotically better than N_1.

4   Adaptive Sampling for Bounding the Relative Error

In the previous section, we have seen some examples such that we can design an asymptotically better algorithm by bounding the relative error (instead of the absolute error) in the approximation problem. On the other hand, for computing the size bound (5), we need to know p_B or its appropriate lower bound, which is not easy in some cases. Even if we can use a lower bound p_0 for p_B, the actual p_B may be usually much larger than p_0, and we almost always have to use unnecessarily large sample sets. For example, for solving Problem 2 in the previous section, we may assume that $p_t \geq \epsilon_0$ for all t, $1 \leq t \leq T$, and thus we could determine the sample size bound $N_2 = O(T^2/\epsilon_0^3)$. But if every p_t, $1 \leq t \leq T$, is much larger than ϵ_0, then this sample size is unnecessarily big.

One way to avoid this problem is to perform presampling. By running our sampling algorithm, e.g., Batch Sampling, with small sample size and obtain some "rough" estimate of p_B. Although it may not be a good approximation of p_B we can use it to determine appropriate sample size for main sampling. This is the strategy often suggested in statistics texts, and in fact, this idea leads to our "adaptive sampling" techniques. Note further that we do not have to separate presampling and main sampling. On the course of sampling, we can improve our knowledge on p_B; hence, we can simply use it. More specifically, what we need is a stopping condition that determines whether it has already seen enough number of examples by using the current estimation of p_B.

Lipton etal [15,16] realized this intuitive idea and proposed adaptive sampling algorithms for query size estimation and related problems for relational database. Our approximate estimation of p_B is a special case of estimating query sizes. Thus, their algorithm is immediately applicable to our problem. (On the other hand, the proof presented here is for the special case, and it may not be used to justify the original adaptive sampling algorithm proposed by Lipton etal [17].)

Figure 2 is the outline of the adaptive sampling algorithm of [15]. Though it is simplified, the adaptive sampling part is essentially the same as the original

Adaptive Sampling
begin
    $m \leftarrow 0;\ n \leftarrow 0;$
    while $m < A$ **do**
        get x uniformly at random from D;
        $m \leftarrow m + B(x);\quad n \leftarrow n + 1;$
    output m/n as an approximation of p_B;
end.

Fig. 2. Adaptive Sampling

one. As we can see, the structure of the algorithm is simple. It runs until it sees more than A examples x with $B(x) = 1$.

To complete the description of the algorithm, we have to specify the way to determine A. Here we use the Chernoff bound and derive the following formula for computing A.

Theorem 5. *For any $\delta > 0$ and ε, $0 < \varepsilon < 1$, if Adaptive Sampling uses the following A, then it satisfies (4) with probability $> 1 - \delta$.*

$$A > \frac{3(1+\varepsilon)}{\varepsilon^2} \ln\left(\frac{2}{\delta}\right).$$

Furthermore, with probability $> 1 - \delta/2$, we have

$$sample\ size \leq \frac{3(1+\varepsilon)}{(1-\varepsilon)\varepsilon^2 p_B} \ln\left(\frac{2}{\delta}\right). \tag{7}$$

Compare the sample size given by (5) and (7). Since ε is usually small, the difference is within some constant factor. That is, the sample size of this Adaptive Sampling algorithm is almost optimal; it is almost the same as the best case where the precise p_B is given. Therefore, if our target algorithm is designed with the bound (5) for Goal 2, then we can add "adaptivity" to the algorithm without (drastically) changing the worst-case performance of the algorithm. For example, consider the previous Problem 2 of estimating the product probability P_T. We can modify the second strategy by replacing Batch Sampling with Adaptive Sampling. Then new sample size N_3 becomes (with some small constant $c' > 0$)

$$N_3 = c' \cdot c(12T^3/(p_0\epsilon_0^2)),$$

where $p_0 \geq \epsilon_0$ is a lower bound for $p_1, ..., p_T$. In the worst-case (i.e., $p_0 = \epsilon_0$), $N_3 = O(T^3/\epsilon_0^3)$, which is the same order as N_2. On the other hand, if the situation is favorable and p_0 is large, say, $p_0 > 1/2$, then N_3 gets decreased and we have $N_3 = O(T^3/\epsilon_0^2)$. That is, we could add "adaptivity" to our new strategy without changing the worst-case performance.

Now we explain the outline of the proof of Theorem 5. In the following discussion, let t denote the number of execution of the while-iterations until

Adaptive Sampling halts. In other words, the algorithm has seen t examples and then the while-condition breaks. (In the following, we simply call this situation "the algorithm halts at the tth step".) Note that t is a random variable that varies depending on the examples drawn from D. Let $\widetilde{m}_t$ and $\widetilde{p}_t$ denote the value m and m/n when the algorithm halts at the tth step.

Since the while-condition breaks at the tth step, it holds that $A \leq \widetilde{m}_t$. On the other hand, $\widetilde{m}_t < A + 1$ holds because the while-condition holds before the tth step. Hence we have $A/t \leq \widetilde{p}_t < (A+1)/t$. Here in order to simplify our discussion, we assume that $\widetilde{p}_t \approx A/t$. In fact, we will see below that t is larger than $1/(\varepsilon^2 p_B)$ with high probability; thus, the difference $(A+1)/t - A/t \,(= 1/t)$ is negligible compared with the error bound εp_B. Now assuming $\widetilde{p}_t \approx A/t$, it is easy to see that $\widetilde{p}_t$ is within the desired range $[(1-\varepsilon)p_B, (1+\varepsilon)p_B]$ (i.e., $|\widetilde{p}_t - p_B| \leq \varepsilon p_B$) if and only if

$$\frac{A}{(1+\varepsilon)p_B} \leq t \leq \frac{A}{(1-\varepsilon)p_B}.$$

holds for t. Therefore, the theorem follows from the following two lemmas. (Recall that t is a random variable, and the probabilities below are taken w.r.t. his random variable. The proof outlines are given in Appendix.)

Lemma 1. $\Pr[\, t < A/((1+\varepsilon)p_B)\,] < \delta/2.$

Lemma 2. $\Pr[\, t > A/((1-\varepsilon)p_B)\,] < \delta/2.$

Notice that the sample size bound (7) is immediate from Lemma 2.

5   Adaptive Sampling for General Utility Functions

We have seen two ways for estimating p_B within either an absolute or a relative error bound. But in some applications, we may need the other closeness conditions, or in more general, we might want to estimate not p_B but some other "utility function" computed from p_B. Recall the difference between the sample size n_1 and n_2 we have seen at Problem 1. One reason that n_2 is asymptotically smaller than n_1 is that we could use a relatively large ε for computing n_2, and we could use a large ε because Approximation Goal 2 was suitable for Problem 1. Thus, the choice of an appropriate approximation goal is important.

To see this point more clearly, let us consider the following problem.

Problem 3 *Let $\delta_0 > 0$ be any constant and fixed. Determine (with confidence $> 1-\delta_0$) whether $p_B > 1/2$ or not. Here we may assume that either $p_B > 1/2+\sigma_0$ or $p_B < 1/2 - \sigma_0$ holds for some σ_0.*

This problem is similar to Problem 1, but these two problems have different critical points. That is, Problem 1 gets harder when p_0 gets smaller, whereas Problem 3 gets harder when σ_0 gets smaller. In other words, the closer p_B is to $1/2$, the more accurate estimation is necessary, and hence the more sample is needed. Thus, for solving Problem 3, what we want to estimate is not p_B itself but the following value:

$$u_B = p_B - \frac{1}{2}.$$

More specifically, the above problem is easily solved if the following approximation goal is achieved. (In the following, we use $\widetilde{u_B}$ to denote the output of a sampling algorithm for estimating u_B. Note that u_B is not always positive.)

Approximation Goal 3 *For given $\delta > 0$ and ε, $0 < \varepsilon < 1$, the goal is to have*

$$\Pr[\, |\widetilde{u_B} - u_B| \leq \varepsilon |u_B| \,] > 1 - \delta. \tag{8}$$

Suppose that some sampling algorithm satisfies this goal. Then for solving the above problem, we run this algorithm to estimate u_B with relative error bound $\varepsilon = 1/2$ and $\delta = \delta_0$. (We are also given σ_0.) Then decide $p_B > 1/2$ if $\widetilde{u_B} > \sigma_0/2$ and $p_B < 1/2$ if $\widetilde{u_B} < -\sigma_0/2$. It is easy to check that this method correctly determines whether $p_B > 1/2$ or $p_B < 1/2$ with probability $> 1 - \delta_0$ (when either $p_B > 1/2 + \sigma_0$ or $p_B < 1/2 - \sigma_0$ holds).

Now we would face the same problem. There may exist no appropriate lower bound of u_B, like σ_0. Again sequential sampling algorithm is helpful for solving this problem. One might want to modify our previous Adaptive Sampling algorithm for achieving this new approximation goal. For example, by replacing its while-condition "$m < A$" with "$m - n/2 < B$" and by choosing B appropriately, we may be able to satisfy the new approximation goal. Unfortunately, though, this naive approach does not seem to work. In the previous case, the stopping condition (i.e., the negation of the while-condition "$m < A$") was monotonic; that is, once $m \geq A$ holds at some point, this condition is unchanged even if we keep sampling. On the other hand, even if $m - n/2 \geq B$ holds at some point, the condition may be falsified later if we keep sampling. Due to this nonmonotonicity, the previous proof (i.e., the proof of Lemma 1) does not work.

Fortunately, we can deal with this nonmonotonicity by using a slightly more complicated stopping condition. In Figure 3, we state an adaptive sampling algorithm that estimates u_B and satisfies Approximation Goal 3. Note that the algorithm does not use any information on u_B; hence, we can use it without knowing u_B at all.

Theorem 6. *For any $\delta > 0$ and ε, $0 < \varepsilon < 1$, Nonmonotinic Adaptive Sampling satisfies (8). Furthermore, with probability more than $1 - \delta$, we have*

$$sample\ size \lesssim \frac{2(1 + 2\varepsilon)^2}{(\varepsilon u_B)^2} \ln\left(\frac{1}{\varepsilon u_B \delta}\right).$$

We give a proof sketch. The proof outline is basically the same as the one used in the previous section. Again let t be a random variable whose value is the step when the algorithm terminates. For any $k \geq 1$, we use $\widetilde{u_k}$ and α_k to denote respectively the value of u and α at the kth step. Define t_0 and t_1 by

Nonmonotonic Adaptive Sampling
begin
    $m \leftarrow 0; \ n \leftarrow 0;$
    $u \leftarrow 0; \ \alpha \leftarrow \infty;$
    while $|u| < \alpha(1 + 1/\varepsilon)$ **do**
        get x uniformly at random from D;
        $m \leftarrow m + B(x); \quad n \leftarrow n + 1;$
        $u \leftarrow m/n - 1/2;$
        $\alpha \leftarrow \sqrt{(1/2n)\ln(n(n+1)/\delta)};$
    output u as an approximation of u_B;
end.

Fig. 3. Nonmontonic Adaptive Sampling

$$t_0 \ = \ \min_k \{ \ \alpha_k \leq \varepsilon|u_B| \ \}, \quad \text{and} \quad t_1 \ = \ \min_k \{ \ \alpha_k \leq \varepsilon|u_B|/(1 + 2\varepsilon) \ \}.$$

Since α_k decreases monotonously in k, both t_0 and t_1 are uniquely determined, and $t_0 \leq t_1$.

We first show that if $t_0 \leq t \leq t_1$, that is, if the algorithm stops no earlier than the t_0th step nor later than the t_1th step, then its output $\widetilde{u}_t$ is in the desired range. (The proof is omitted; see [22].)

Lemma 3. *If $t_0 \leq t \leq t_1$, then we have $|\widetilde{u}_t - u_B| \leq \varepsilon|u_B|$ with probability $> 1 - \delta/(2t_0)$.*

Next we show that with reasonable probability the algorithm halts between the t_0th and t_1th step. It is easy to see that Theorem 6 follows from these lemmas. (The proof of Lemma 4 is given in Appendix. On the other hand, we omit the proof of Lemma 5 because it is similar to Lemma 2.)

Lemma 4. $\Pr[\ t < t_0 \ ] < \delta(1 - 1/t_0).$

Lemma 5. $\Pr[\ t > t_1 \ ] < \delta/(2t_0).$

6   Concluding Remarks

We have seen some examples of sequential sampling algorithms and the way they are used for designing adaptive algorithms. For our explanation, we have used a very simple probability estimation problem and its variations, but there are many other interesting problems we can solve by using sequential sampling algorithms. For example, we have originally developed sequential sampling algorithms for selecting nearly optimal hypothesis [8], and some extension of our hypothesis selection technique has been also reported in [19].

Although only a simple utility function is considered, we may be able to use various functions defined on one or more estimated probabilities. For example, estimating the entropy or some pseudo entropy function by some sequential sampling technique is an interesting and practically important problem. In our general sampling algorithm [8], we have only considered utility functions that can be approximated by some linear function, because otherwise sample size may become very large. Since the entropy function does not belong to this function family, we need to find some way to bound sample size to a reasonable level.

Acknowledgments

This paper is based on a series of joint works [6,7,8] with Carlos Domingo and Ricard Gavaldà. I have learned a lot from these talented researchers. In particular, I thank Carlos for supplying me with information on related works for preparing this manuscript. I would like to thank Professor Akahira and Professor Lynch for discussion and giving me pointers to related works. This work is supported in part by Grant-in-Aid for Scientific Research on Priority Areas (Discovery Science), 1999, the Ministry of Education, Science, Sports and Culture.

References

1. J. Balcazár, a personal communication. 28
2. H. Chernoff, A measure of asymptotic efficiency for tests of a hypothesis based on the sum of observations, *Annals of Mathematical Statistics* 23, pp.493–509, 1952. 29
3. C. Dominogo, Faster near-optimal reinforcement learning: adding adaptiveness to the E3 algorithm, in *Proc. f 10th Algorithmic Learning Theory Conference* (ALT'99), Lecture Notes in Artificial Intelligence 1720, Springer-Verlag, pp.241–251, 1999. 28, 32
4. C. Domingo and O. Watanabe, Scaling up a boosting-based learner via adaptive sampling, in *Proc. f Knowledge Discovery and Data Mining* (PAKDD'00), Lecture Notes in Artificial Intelligence 1805, Springer-Verlag, pp.317–328, 2000. 28
5. C. Domingo and O. Watanabe, MadaBoost: a modification of AdaBoost, in *Proc. f 13th Annual Conference on Computational Learning Theory* (COLT'00), Morgan Kaufmann, pp.180–189, 2000. 28
6. C. Domingo, R. Gavaldà, and O. Watanabe, Practical algorithms for on-line selection, in *Proc. f the First Intl. onference on Discovery Science*, Lecture Notes in Artificial Intelligence 1532, Springer-Verlag, pp.150–161, 1998. 27, 38
7. C. Domingo, R. Gavaldà, and O. Watanabe, Adaptive sampling methods for scaling up knowledge discovery algorithms, in *Proc. f the Second Intl. onference on Discovery Science*, Lecture Notes in Artificial Intelligence , Springer-Verlag, pp.–, 1999. 27, 38
8. C. Domingo, R. Gavaldà, and O. Watanabe, Adaptive sampling methods for scaling up knowledge discovery algorithms, *J. nowledge Discovery and Data Mining*, to appear. (Also available as a research report C-136, Dept. f Math. and Computing Sciences, Tokyo Institute of Technology, from www.is.titech.ac.jp/research/research-report/C/) 27, 37, 38
9. W. Feller, *An Introduction to Probability Theory and its Applications* (Third Edition), John Wiley & Sons, 1968. 27, 30

10. B. K. Ghosh and P. K. Sen eds., *Handbook of Sequential Analysis*, Marcel Dekker, 1991. 28
11. B. K. Ghosh, M. Mukhopadhyay, P. K. Sen, *Sequential Estimation*, Wiley, 1997. 28
12. R. Greiner, PALO: a probabilistic hill-climbing algorithm, *Artificial Intelligence*, 84, pp.177–204, 1996. 28
13. W. Hoeffding, Probability inequalities for sums of bounded random variables, *Journal of the American Statistical Association* 58, pp.13–30, 1963. 29
14. M. Kearns and S. Singh, Near-optimal reinforcement learning in polynomial time, in *Proc. f the 16th Intl. onference on Machine Learning* (ICML'98), Morgan Kaufmann, 260–268, 1998. 32
15. R. J. Lipton, J. F. Naughton, D. A. Schneider, and S. Seshadri, Efficient sampling strategies for relational database operations, *Theoretical Computer Science* 116, pp.195–226, 1993. 28, 33
16. R. J. Lipton and J. F. Naughton, Query size estimation by adaptive sampling, *Journal of Computer and System Science* 51, pp.18–25, 1995. 28, 33
17. J. F. Lynch, Analysis and application of adaptive sampling, in *Proc. f the 19th ACM SIGMOD-SIGACT-SIGART Symposium on Principles of Database Systems* (PODS'99), ACM Press, pp.260–267, 1999. 28, 33
18. O. Maron and A. Moore, Hoeffding races: accelerating model selection search for classification and function approximation, in *Advances in Neural Information Processing Systems*, Morgan Kaufmann, 59–66, 1994. 28
19. T. Scheffer and S. Wrobel, A sequential sampling algorithm for a general class of utility criteria, in *Proc. f the 6th ACM SIGKDD Intl. Conference on Knowledge Discovery and Data Mining*, ACM Press, 2000, to appear. 28, 37
20. P. Haas and A. Swami, Sequential sampling, procedures for query size estimation, *IBM Research Report*, RJ 9101 (80915), 1992. 28
21. A. Wald, *Sequential Analysis*, John Wiley & Sons, 1947. 28
22. O. Watanabe, Simple sampling techniques for discovery science, *IEICE Trans. Info. & Systems*, E83-D (1), 19–26, 2000. (A preliminary version is available as a research report C-137, Dept. f Math. and Computing Sciences, Tokyo Institute of Technology, from `www.is.titech.ac.jp/research/research-report/C/`) 28, 30, 37

Appendix

Here we give proof outlines for Lemma 1 and Lemma 2.

Proof of Lemma 1. We would like to estimate the above probability, and for this purpose, we want to regard the B value of chosen examples as the Bernoulli trials and to use the statistical bounds of the previous section. There is, however, one technical problem. These statistical bounds are valid for fixed number of trials, i.e., examples in this case. On the other hand, the number of examples t itself is a random variable. Here we can get around this problem by arguing in the following way.

Let $t_0 = A/((1 + \varepsilon)p_B)$. Then our goal is to show that the algorithm halts within t_0 steps with high probability. Now we modify our algorithm so that it *always* sees exactly t_0 examples. That is, this new algorithm just ignores the while-condition and repeats the while-iteration exactly t_0 times. Consider the situation that the original algorithm does halt at the tth step for some $t < t_0$.

Then we have $\widetilde{m_t} \geq A$ at the tth step, where $\widetilde{m_t}$ denotes the value of m at the tth step. Though the algorithm stops here, if we continued the while-iteration after the tth step, we would clearly have $\widetilde{m_{t_0}} \geq A$ at the t_0th step. From this observation, we have

$$\Pr[\ \widetilde{m_t} \geq A \text{ for some } t < t_0\ ]$$
$$\leq\ \Pr[\ \widetilde{m_{t_0}} \geq A \text{ in the modified algorithm }].$$

On the other hand, the modified algorithm always sees t_0 examples; that is, it is Batch Sampling. Thus, we can use the Chernoff bound to analyze the righthand side probability. By our choice of $mhtz$ and A, it is easy to prove that the righthand side probability is at most $\delta/2$. Thus, the desired bound is proved. The reason that we could argue by considering only the t_0th step is because the stopping condition "$m \geq A$" is *monotonic*.

Proof of Lemma 2. Let $t_1 = A/((1 - \varepsilon)p_B)$. We want to bound the probability that the algorithm does not halt after the t_1th step. Note that this event implies that $\widetilde{m_{t_1}} < A$. Thus, it suffices to bound $\Pr[\ \widetilde{m_{t_1}} < A\ ]$ by $\delta/2$, which is not difficult by using the Chernoff bound. Here again we consider the modified algorithm that sees exactly t_1 examples.

Proof of Lemma 4. In order to bound $\Pr[t < t_0]$, we first consider, for any k, $1 \leq k < t_0$, the probability P_k that the algorithm halts at the kth step.

Note that the algorithm halts at the kth step if and only if $|\widetilde{u_k}| \geq \alpha_k(1+1/\varepsilon)$. Thus, we have

$$P_k\ =\ \Pr\left[\ |\widetilde{u_k}| \geq \alpha_k\left(1 + \frac{1}{\varepsilon}\right)\ \right]\ \leq\ \Pr[\ |\widetilde{u_k}| > |u_B| + \alpha_k\ ],$$

because $\alpha_k > \varepsilon|u_B|$ since $k < t_0$.

This means that $P_k \leq \Pr[\widetilde{u_k} > u_B + \alpha_k]$ if $\widetilde{u_k} \geq 0$, and $P_k \leq \Pr[\widetilde{u_k} < u_B - \alpha_k]$ otherwise. Both probabilities are bounded by using the Hoeffding bound in the following way. (Here we only state the bound for the former case. Also although we simply uses the Hoeffding bound below, precisely speaking, the argument as in the proof of Theorem 1 is necessary to fix the number of examples. That is, we first modify the algorithm so that it always sees k examples.)

$$P_k \leq \Pr[\ \widetilde{u_k} > u_B + \alpha_k\ ]$$
$$= \Pr[\ \sum_{i=1}^{k} X_i/n - \frac{1}{2} > p_B - \frac{1}{2} + \alpha_k\ ]$$
$$\leq \exp(-2\alpha_k^2 k)\ =\ \frac{\delta}{k(k+1)}.$$

Now summing up these bounds, we have

$$\Pr[\ t < t_0\ ]\ \leq\ \sum_{k=1}^{t_0-1} P_k\ \leq\ \delta\left(1 - \frac{1}{t_0}\right).$$

Towards an Algorithmic Statistics

(Extended Abstract)

Peter Gács*, John Tromp, and Paul Vitányi**

Abstract. While Kolmogorov complexity is the accepted absolute measure of information content of an individual finite object, a similarly absolute notion is needed for the relation between an individual data sample and an individual model summarizing the information in the data, for example, a finite set where the data sample typically came from. The statistical theory based on such relations between individual objects can be called algorithmic statistics, in contrast to ordinary statistical theory that deals with relations between probabilistic ensembles. We develop a new algorithmic theory of typical statistic, sufficient statistic, and minimal sufficient statistic.

1 Introduction

We take statistical theory to ideally consider the following problem: Given a data sample and a family of models (hypotheses) one wants to select the model that produced the data. But a priori it is possible that the data is atypical for the model that actually produced it, or that the true model is not present in the considered model class. Therefore we have to relax our requirements. If selection of a "true" model cannot be guaranteed by any method, then as next best choice "modeling the data" as well as possible, irrespective of truth and falsehood of the resulting model, may be more appropriate. Thus, we change 'true' to "as well as possible." The latter we take to mean that the model expresses all significant regularities present in the data.

Probabilistic Statistics: In ordinary statistical theory one proceeds as follows, see for example [3]: Suppose two random variables X, Y have a joint probability mass function $p(x, y)$ and marginal probability mass functions $p(x)$ and $p(y)$. Then the (probabilistic) *mutual information* $I(X; Y)$ is the relative entropy between the joint distribution and the product distribution $p(x)p(y)$:

$$I(X;Y) = \sum_x \sum_y p(x,y) \log \frac{p(x,y)}{p(x)p(y)}. \tag{1}$$

Every function $T(D)$ of a data sample D—like the sample mean or the sample variance—is called a *statistic* of D. Assume we have a probabilistic ensemble of

---

* Address: Computer Science Department, Boston University, Boston MA 02215, U.S.A. Email: gacs@bu.edu. The paper was partly written during this author's visit at CWI.

** Address: CWI, Kruislaan 413, 1098 SJ Amsterdam, The Netherlands. Email: {tromp, paulv}@cwi.nl

H. Arimura, S. Jain and A. Sharma (Eds.): ALT 2000, LNAI 1968, pp. 41-55, 2000.

models, say a family of probability mass functions $\{f_\theta\}$ indexed by θ, together with a distribution over θ. A statistic $T(D)$ is called *sufficient* if the probabilistic mutual information

$$I(\theta; D) = I(\theta; T(D)) \tag{2}$$

for all distributions of θ. Hence, the mutual information between parameter and data sample is invariant under taking sufficient statistics and vice versa. That is to say, a statistic $T(D)$ is called sufficient for θ if it contains all the information in D about θ. For example, consider n tosses of a coin with unknown bias θ with outcome $D = d_1 d_2 \ldots d_n$ where $d_i \in \{0, 1\}$ ($1 \leq i \leq n$). Given n, the number of outcomes "1" is a sufficient statistic for θ: the statistic $T(D) = \sum_{i=1}^{n} d_i$. Given T, every sequence with $T(D)$ "1"s are equally likely independent of parameter θ: Given k, if D is an outcome of n coin tosses and $T(D) = k$ then $\Pr(D \mid T(D) = k) = \binom{n}{k}^{-1}$ and $\Pr(D \mid T(D) \neq k) = 0$. This can be shown to imply (2) and therefore T is a sufficient statistic for θ. According to Fisher [4]: "The statistic chosen should summarise the whole of the relevant information supplied by the sample. This may be called the Criterion of Sufficiency ... In the case of the normal curve of distribution it is evident that the second moment is a sufficient statistic for estimating the standard deviation." Note that one cannot improve on sufficiency: for every (possibly randomized) function T we have

$$I(\theta; D) \geq I(\theta; T(D)), \tag{3}$$

that is, mutual information cannot be increased by processing the data sample in any way. All these notions and laws are probabilistic: they hold in an average sense. Our program is to develop a sharper theory, which we call *algorithmic* statistics to distinguish it from the standard *probabilistic* statistics, where the notions and laws hold in the individual sense.

Algorithmic Statistics: In algorithmic statistics, one wants to select an individual model (described by, say, a finite set) for which the data is individually typical. To express the notion "individually typical" one requires Kolmogorov complexity—standard probability theory cannot express this. The basic idea is as follows: In a two-part description, we first describe such a model, a finite set, and then indicate the data within the finite set by its index in a natural ordering of the set. The optimal models make the two-part description as concise as the shortest one-part description of the data. Moreover, for such optimal two-part descriptions it can be shown that the data will be "individually typical" for the model concerned. A description of such a model is an algorithmic sufficient statistic since it summarizes all relevant properties of the data. Among the algorithmic sufficient statistics a simplest one (the algorithmic minimal sufficient statistic) is best in accordance with Ockham's razor principle since it summarizes the relevant properties of the data as concisely as possible. In probabilistic data or data subject to noise this involves separating regularities (structure) in the data from random effects.

Background and Related Work: At a Tallinn conference in 1973, A.N. Kolmogorov formulated this task rigorously in terms of Kolmogorov complexity (according to [14, 2]). This approach can also be viewed as a two-part code separating the *structure* of a string from meaningless *random* features. Cover [2, 3] interpreted this approach as (sufficient) statistic. Related aspects of "randomness deficiency" (formally defined later in (11)) were formulated in [9, 10] and studied in [14, 17]. Algorithmic mutual information, and the associated non-increase law, were studied in [11, 12]. Despite its evident epistimological prominence in the theory of hypothesis selection and prediction, only some scattered aspects of the subject have been studied before, for example as related to the "Kolmogorov structure function" [14, 2], and "absolutely non-stochastic objects" [14, 17, 15, 18], notions also defined or suggested by Kolmogorov at the mentioned meeting. For the relation with inductive reasoning according to minimum description length principle see [16]. The entire approach is based on Kolmogorov complexity [8] (also known as algorithmic information theory). For a general introduction to Kolmogorov complexity, its mathematical theory, and application to induction see [7].

Results: We develop the outlines of a new general mathematical theory of algorithmic statistics, in this initial approach restricted to models that are finite sets. A set S is "optimal" if the best two-part description consisting of a description of S and a straightforward description of x as an element of S by an index of size $\log |S|$, is as concise as the shortest one-part description of x. Descriptions of such optimal sets are algorithmic sufficient statistics, and the shortest description among them is an algorithmic minimal sufficient statistic. The mode of description plays a major role in this. We distinguish between "explicit" descriptions and "implicit" descriptions—that are introduced in this paper as a proper restriction on recursive enumeration based description mode. We establish new precise range constraints of cardinality and complexity imposed by implicit (and hence explicit) descriptions for typical and optimal sets, and exhibit for the first time concrete algorithmic minimal (or near-minimal) sufficient statistics for both description modes. There exist maximally complex objects for which no finite set of less complexity is an explicit sufficient statistic—such objects are absolutely non-stochastic. This improves a result of Shen [14] to the best possible.

Application: In all practicable inference methods, one must use background information to determine the appropriate model class first—establishing what meaning the data can have—and only then obtain the best model in that class by optimizing its parameters. For example in the "probably approximately correct (PAC)" learning criterion one learns a concept in a given concept class (like a class of Boolean formulas over n variables); in the "minimum description length (MDL)" induction, [1], one first determines the model class (like Bernoulli processes). Note that MDL has been shown to be a certain generalization of the (Kolmogorov) minimum sufficient statistic in [16].

To develop the onset of a theory of algorithmic statistics we have used the mathematically convenient model class consisting of the finite sets. An illustration of background information is Example 3. An example of selecting a model parameter on the basis of compression properties is the precision at which we represent the other parameters: too high precision causes accidental noise to be modeled as well, too low precision may cause models that should be distinct to be confused. In general, the performance of a model for a given data sample depends critically on what we may call the "degree of discretization" or the "granularity" of the model: the choice of precision of the parameters, the number of nodes in the hidden layer of a neural network, and so on. The granularity is often determined ad hoc. In [5], in two quite different experimental settings the MDL predicted best model granularity values are shown to coincide with the best values found experimentally.

2   Kolmogorov Complexity

We assume familiarity with the elementary theory of Kolmogorov complexity. For introduction, details, and proofs, see [7]. We write *string* to mean a finite binary string. Other finite objects can be encoded into strings in natural ways. The set of strings is denoted by $\{0,1\}^*$. The *length* of a string x is denoted by $l(x)$, distinguishing it from the *cardinality* $|S|$ of a finite set S. The (prefix) Kolmogorov complexity, or algorithmic entropy, $K(x)$ of a string x is the length of a shortest binary program to compute x on a universal computer (such as a universal Turing machine). Intuitively, $K(x)$ represents the minimal amount of information required to generate x by any effective process, [8]. We denote the *shortest program* for x by x^*; then $K(x) = l(x^*)$. (Actually, x^* is the first shortest program for x in an appropriate standard enumeration of all programs for x such as the halting order.) The conditional Kolmogorov complexity $K(x \mid y)$ of x relative to y is defined similarly as the length of a shortest program to compute x if y is furnished as an auxiliary input to the computation.

From now on, we will denote by $\overset{+}{<}$ an inequality to within an additive constant, and by $\overset{+}{=}$ the situation when both $\overset{+}{<}$ and $\overset{+}{>}$ hold. We will also use $\overset{*}{<}$ to denote an inequality to within an multiplicative constant factor, and $\overset{*}{=}$ to denote the situation when both $\overset{*}{<}$ and $\overset{*}{>}$ hold.

We will use the "Additivity of Complexity" (Theorem 3.9.1 of [7]) property (by definition $K(x, y) = K(\langle x, y \rangle)$):

$$K(x, y) \overset{+}{=} K(x) + K(y \mid x^*) \overset{+}{=} K(y) + K(x \mid y^*). \tag{4}$$

The conditional version needs to be treated carefully. It is

$$K(x, y \mid z) \overset{+}{=} K(x \mid z) + K(y \mid x, K(x \mid z), z). \tag{5}$$

Note that a naive version

$$K(x, y \mid z) \overset{+}{=} K(x \mid z) + K(y \mid x^*, z)$$

is incorrect: taking $z = x$, $y = K(x)$, the left-hand side equals $K(x^* \mid x)$, and the right-hand side equals $K(x \mid x) + K(K(x) \mid x^*, x) \overset{+}{=} 0$.

We derive a (to our knowledge) new "directed triangle inequality" that is needed below.

Theorem 1. *For all x, y, z,*

$$K(x \mid y^*) \overset{+}{<} K(x, z \mid y^*) \overset{+}{<} K(z \mid y^*) + K(x \mid z^*).$$

Proof. Using (4), an evident inequality introducing an auxiliary object z, and twice (4) again:

$$K(x, z \mid y^*) \overset{+}{=} K(x, y, z) - K(y) \overset{+}{<} K(z) + K(x \mid z^*) + K(y \mid z^*) - K(y)$$
$$\overset{+}{=} K(y, z) - K(y) + K(x \mid z^*) \overset{+}{=} K(x \mid z^*) + K(z \mid y^*).$$

$\square$

This theorem has bizarre consequences. Denote $k = K(y)$ and substitute $k = z$ and $K(k) = x$ to find the following counterintuitive corollary:

Corollary 1. $K(K(k) \mid y, k) \overset{+}{=} K(K(k) \mid y^*) \overset{+}{<} K(K(k) \mid k^*) + K(k \mid y, k) \overset{+}{=} 0$. *We can iterate this: given y and $K(y)$ we can determine $K(K(K(y)))$ in $O(1)$ bits. So $K(K(K(k))) \mid y, k) \overset{+}{=} 0$ and so on.*

If we want to find an appropriate model fitting the data, then we are concerned with the information in the data about such models. To define the algorithmic mutual information between two individual objects x and y with no probabilities involved, rewrite (1) as

$$\sum_x \sum_y p(x, y)[-\log p(x) - \log p(y) + \log p(x, y)],$$

and note that $-\log p(s)$ is the length of the prefix-free Shannon-Fano code for s. Consider $-\log p(x) - \log p(y) + \log p(x, y)$ over the individual x, y, and replace the Shannon-Fano code by the "shortest effective description" code. [1] The *information in y about x* is defined as

$$I(y : x) = K(x) - K(x \mid y^*) \overset{+}{=} K(x) + K(y) - K(x, y), \tag{6}$$

where the second equality is a consequence of (4) and states the celebrated result that the information between two individual objects is symmetrical, $I(x : y) \overset{+}{=} I(y : x)$, and therefore we talk about *mutual information*. [2] In the full paper [6] we show that the expectation of the algorithmic mutual information $I(x : y)$ is close the the probabilistic mutual information $I(x; y)$—which corroborates that

---

[1] The Shannon-Fano code has optimal expected code length equal to the entropy with respect to the distribution of the source [3]. However, the prefix-free code of shortest effective description, that achieves code word length $K(s)$ for source word s, has both about expected optimal code word length and individual optimal effective code word length, [7].

[2] The notation of the algorithmic (individual) notion $I(x : y)$ distinguishes it from the probabilistic (average) notion $I(x; y)$. We deviate slightly from [7] where $I(y : x)$ is defined as $K(x) - K(x \mid y)$.

the algorithmic notion is a sharpening of the probabilistic notion to individual objects.

The mutual information between a pair of strings x and y cannot be increased by processing x and y separately by some deterministic computations, and furthermore, randomized computation can increase the mutual information only with negligible probability, [11, 12]. Since the first reference gives no proofs and the second reference is not easily accessible, in the full version of this paper [6] we use the triangle inequality of Theorem 1 to give new simple proofs of this information non-increase.

3 Algorithmic Model Development

In this initial investigation, we use for mathematical convenience the *model class* consisting of the family of finite sets of finite binary strings, that is, the set of subsets of $\{0,1\}^*$.

3.1 Finite Set Representations

Although all finite sets are recursive there are different ways to represent or specify the set. We only consider ways that have in common a method of recursively enumerating the elements of the finite set one by one, and which differ in knowledge of its size. For example, we can specify a set of natural numbers by giving an explicit table or a decision procedure for membership and a bound on the largest element, or by giving a recursive enumeration of the elements together with the number of elements, or by giving a recursive enumeration of the elements together with a bound on the running time. We call a representation of a finite set S *explicit* if the size $|S|$ of the finite set can be computed from it. A representation of S is *implicit* if the size $|S|$ can be computed from it only up to a factor of 2.

Example 1. In Section 3.4, we will introduce the set S^k of strings whose elements have complexity $\leq k$. It will be shown that this set can be represented implicitly by a program of size $K(k)$, but can be represented explicitly only by a program of size k.

Such representations are useful in two-stage encodings where one stage of the code consists of an index in S of length $\pm \log|S|$. In the implicit case we know, within an additive constant, how long an index of an element in the set is. In general S^* denotes the shortest binary program from which S can be computed and whether this is an implicit or explicit description will be clear from the context.

The worst case, a recursively enumerable representation where nothing is known about the size of the finite set, would lead to indices of unknown length. We do not consider this case. We may use the notation

$$S_{\text{impl}}, S_{\text{expl}}$$

for some implicit and some explicit representation of S. When a result applies to both implicit and explicit representations, or when it is clear from the context which representation is meant, we will omit the subscript.

3.2 Optimal Models and Sufficient Statistics

In the following we will distinguish between "models" that are finite sets, and the "shortest programs" to compute those models that are finite strings. Such a shortest program is in the proper sense a statistics of the data sample as defined before. In a way this distinction between "model" and "statistics" is artificial, but for now we prefer clarity and unambiguousness in the discussion.

Consider a string x of length n and prefix complexity $K(x) = k$. We identify the *structure* or *regularities* in x that are to be summarized with a set S of which x is a *random* or *typical* member: given S (or rather, an (implicit or explicit) shortest program S^* for S), x cannot be described much shorter than by its maximal length index in S. Formally this is expressed by $K(x \mid S^*) \overset{+}{>} \log |S|$. More formally, we fix some constant

$$\beta \geq 0,$$

and require $K(x \mid S^*) \geq \log |S| - \beta$. We will not indicate the dependence on β explicitly, but the constants in all our inequalities ($\overset{+}{<}$) will be allowed to be functions of this β. This definition requires a finite S. In fact, since $K(x \mid S^*) \overset{+}{<} K(x)$, it limits the size of S to $O(2^k)$ and a set S (rather, the shortest program S^* from which it can be computed) is a *typical statistic* for x iff

$$K(x \mid S^*) \overset{+}{=} \log |S|. \tag{7}$$

Depending on whether S^* is an implicit or explicit program, our definition splits into implicit and explicit typicality.

Example 2. Consider the set S of binary strings of length n whose every odd position is 0. Let x be element of this set in which the subsequence of bits in even positions is an incompressible string. Then S is explicitly as well as implicitly typical for x. The set $\{x\}$ also has both these properties.

Remark 1. It is not clear whether explicit typicality implies implicit typicality. Section 4 will show some examples which are implicitly very non-typical but explicitly at least nearly typical.

There are two natural measures of suitability of such a statistic. We might prefer either the simplest set, or the largest set, as corresponding to the most likely structure 'explaining' x. The singleton set $\{x\}$, while certainly a typical statistic for x, would indeed be considered a poor explanation. Both measures relate to the optimality of a two-stage description of x using S:

$$K(x) \leq K(x,S) \overset{+}{=} K(S) + K(x \mid S^*) \overset{+}{<} K(S) + \log |S|, \tag{8}$$

where we rewrite $K(x, S)$ by (4). Here, S can be understood as either S_{impl} or S_{expl}. Call a set S (containing x) for which

$$K(x) \stackrel{+}{=} K(S) + \log |S|, \qquad (9)$$

optimal. (More precisely, we should require $K(x) \geq K(S) + \log |S| - \beta$.) Depending on whether $K(S)$ is understood as $K(S_{\mathrm{impl}})$ or $K(S_{\mathrm{expl}})$, our definition splits into implicit and explicit optimality. The shortest program for an optimal set is a *algorithmic sufficient statistic* for x [3]. Furthermore, among optimal sets, there is a direct trade-off between complexity and logsize, which together sum to $\stackrel{+}{=} k$. Equality (9) is the algorithmic equivalent dealing with the relation between the individual sufficient statistic and the individual data sample, in contrast to the probabilistic notion (2).

Example 3. The following restricted model family illustrates the difference between the algorithmic individual notion of sufficient statistics and the probabilistic averaging one. Following the discussion in section 1, this example also illustrates the idea that the semantics of the model class should be obtained by a restriction on the family of allowable models, after which the (minimal) sufficient statistics identifies the most appropriate model in the allowable family and thus optimizes the parameters in the selected model class. In the algorithmic setting we use all subsets of $\{0, 1\}^n$ as models and the shortest programs computing them from a given data sample as the statistics. Suppose we have background information constraining the family of models to the $n + 1$ finite sets $S_k = \{x \in \{0, 1\}^n : x = x_1 \ldots x_n \& \sum_{i=1}^n x_i = k\}$ ($0 \leq k \leq n$). Then, in the probabilistic sense for every data sample $x = x_1 \ldots x_n$ there is only one single sufficient statistics: for $\sum_i x_i = k$ this is $T(x) = k$ with the corresponding model S_k. In the algorithmic setting the situation is more subtle. (In the following example we use the complexities conditional n.) For $x = x_1 \ldots x_n$ with $\sum_i x_i = \frac{n}{2}$ taking $S_{\frac{n}{2}}$ as model yields $|S_{\frac{n}{2}}| = \binom{n}{\frac{n}{2}}$, and therefore $\log |S_{\frac{n}{2}}| \stackrel{+}{=} n - \frac{1}{2} \log n$. The sum of $K(S_{\frac{n}{2}}|n) \stackrel{+}{=} 0$ and the logarithmic term gives $\stackrel{+}{=} n - \frac{1}{2} \log n$ for the right-hand side of (9). But taking $x = 1010 \ldots 10$ yields $K(x|n) \stackrel{+}{=} 0$ for the left-hand side. Thus, there is no algorithmic sufficient statistics for the latter x in this model class, while every x of length n has a probabilistic sufficient statistics in the model class. In fact, the restricted model class has algorithmic sufficient statistics for data samples x of length n that have maximal complexity with respect to the frequency of "1"s, the other data samples have no algorithmic sufficient statistics in this model class.

Example 4. It can be shown that the set S of Example 2 is also optimal, and so is $\{x\}$. Typical sets form a much wider class than optimal ones: $\{x, y\}$ is still typical for x but with most y, it will be too complex to be optimal for x.

For a perhaps less artificial example, consider complexities conditional to the length n of strings. Let y be a random string of length n, let S_y be the set of strings of length n which have 0's exactly where y has, and let x be a random element of S_y. Then x is a string random with respect to the distribution in which 1's are chosen independently with probability 0.25, so its complexity is much less than n. The set S_y is typical with respect to x but is too complex to be optimal, since its (explicit or implicit) complexity conditional to n is n.

It follows that (programs for) optimal sets are typical statistics. Equality (9) expresses the conditions on the algorithmic individual relation between the data and the sufficient statistic. Later we demonstrate that this relation implies that the probabilistic optimality of mutual information (1) holds for the algorithmic version in the expected sense.

One can also consider notions of *near*-typical and *near*-optimal that arise from replacing the β above by some slow growing functions, such as $O(\log l(x))$ or $O(\log k)$ as in [14, 15].

3.3 Properties of Sufficient Statistics

We start with a sequence of lemmas that will be used in the later theorems. Several of these lemmas have two versions: for implicit and for explicit sets. In these cases, S will denote S_{impl} or S_{expl} respectively.

Below it is shown that the mutual information between every typical set and the datum is not much less than $K(K(x))$, the complexity of the complexity $K(x)$ of the datum x. For optimal sets it is at least that, and for algorithmic minimal statistic it is equal to that. The number of elements of a typical set is determined by the following:

Lemma 1. *Let $k = K(x)$. If a set S is (implicitly or explicitly) typical for x then $I(x : S) \overset{+}{=} k - \log |S|$.*

Proof. By definition $I(x : S) \overset{+}{=} K(x) - K(x \mid S^*)$ and by typicality $K(x \mid S^*) \overset{+}{=} \log |S|$. $\qquad\square$

Typicality, optimality, and minimal optimality successively restrict the range of the cardinality (and complexity) of a corresponding model for a datum x. The above lemma states that for (implicitly or explicitly) typical S the cardinality $|S| = \Theta(2^{k - I(x:S)})$. The next lemma asserts that for implicitly typical S the value $I(x : S)$ can fall below $K(k)$ by no more than an additive logarithmic term.

Lemma 2. *Let $k = K(x)$. If a set S is (implicitly or explicitly) typical for x then $I(x : S) \overset{+}{>} K(k) - K(I(x : S))$ and $\log |S| \overset{+}{<} k - K(k) + K(I(x : S))$. (Here, S is understood as S_{impl} or S_{expl} respectively.)*

Proof. Writing $k = K(x)$, since

$$k \overset{+}{=} K(k, x) \overset{+}{=} K(k) + K(x \mid k^*) \tag{10}$$

by (4), we have $I(x : S) \overset{+}{=} K(x) - K(x \mid S^*) \overset{+}{=} K(k) - [K(x \mid S^*) - K(x \mid k^*)]$. Hence, it suffices to show $K(x \mid S^*) - K(x \mid k^*) \overset{+}{<} K(I(x : S))$. Now, from an implicit description S^* we can find $\stackrel{+}{=} \log|S| \stackrel{+}{=} k - I(x : S)$ and to recover k we only require an extra $K(I(x : S))$ bits apart from S^*. Therefore, $K(k \mid S^*) \stackrel{+}{<} K(I(x : S))$. This reduces what we have to show to $K(x \mid S^*) \stackrel{+}{<} K(x \mid k^*) + K(k \mid S^*)$ which is asserted by Theorem 1.   □

The term $I(x : S)$ is at least $K(k) - 2\log K(k)$ where $k = K(x)$. For x of length n with $k \stackrel{+}{>} n$ and $K(k) \stackrel{+}{>} l(k) \stackrel{+}{>} \log n$, this yields $I(x : S) \stackrel{+}{>} \log n - 2\log\log n$.

If we further restrict typical sets to optimal sets then the possible number of elements in S is slightly restricted. First we show that implicit optimality of a set with respect to a datum is equivalent to typicality with respect to the datum combined with effective constructability (determination) from the datum.

Lemma 3. *A set S is (implicitly or explicitly) optimal for x iff it is typical and $K(S \mid x^*) \stackrel{+}{=} 0$.*

Proof. A set S is optimal iff (8) holds with equalities. Rewriting $K(x, S) \stackrel{+}{=} K(x) + K(S \mid x^*)$ the first inequality becomes an equality iff $K(S \mid x^*) \stackrel{+}{=} 0$, and the second inequality becomes an equality iff $K(x \mid S^*) \stackrel{+}{=} \log|S|$ (that is, S is a typical set).   □

Lemma 4. *Let $k = K(x)$. If a set S is (implicitly or explicitly) optimal for x, then $I(x : S) \stackrel{+}{=} K(S) \stackrel{+}{>} K(k)$ and $\log|S| \stackrel{+}{<} k - K(k)$.*

Proof. If S is optimal for x, then $k = K(x) \stackrel{+}{=} K(S) + K(x \mid S^*) \stackrel{+}{=} K(S) + \log|S|$. From S^* we can find both $K(S) \stackrel{+}{=} l(S^*)$ and $|S|$ and hence k, that is, $K(k) \stackrel{+}{<} K(S)$. We have $I(x : S) \stackrel{+}{=} K(S) - K(S \mid x^*) \stackrel{+}{=} K(S)$ by (4), Lemma 3, respectively. This proves the first property. Substitution of $I(x : S) \stackrel{+}{>} K(k)$ in the expression of Lemma 1 proves the second property.   □

3.4   A Concrete Implicit Minimal Sufficient Statistic

A simplest implicitly optimal set (that is, of least complexity) is an implicit algorithmic minimal sufficient statistic. We demonstrate that $S^k = \{y : K(y) \leq k\}$, the set of all strings of complexity at most k, is such a set. First we establish the cardinality of S^k:

Lemma 5. $\log|S^k| \stackrel{+}{=} k - K(k)$.

Proof. The lower bound is easiest. Denote by k^* of length $K(k)$ a shortest program for k. Every string s of length $k - K(k) - c$ can be described in a self-delimiting manner by prefixing it with k^*c^*, hence $K(s) \stackrel{+}{<} k - c + 2\log c$. For a large enough constant c, we have $K(s) \leq k$ and hence there are $\Omega(2^{k-K(k)})$ strings that are in S^k.

For the upper bound: by (10) all $x \in S^k$ satisfy $K(x \mid k^*) \stackrel{+}{<} k - K(k)$ and there can only be $O(2^{k-K(k)})$ of them.   □

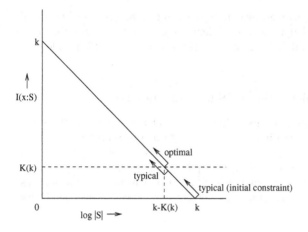

Fig. 1. Range of typical statistics on the straight line $I(x : S) \overset{\pm}{=} K(x) - \log |S|$.

From the definition of S^k it follows that it is defined by k alone, and it is the same set that is optimal for all objects of the same complexity k.

Theorem 2. *The set S^k is implicitly optimal for every x with $K(x) = k$. Also, we have $K(S^k) \overset{\pm}{=} K(k)$.*

Proof. From k^* we can compute both k and $k - l(k^*) = k - K(k)$ and recursively enumerate S^k. Since also $\log |S^k| \overset{\pm}{=} k - K(k)$ (Lemma 5), the string k^* plus a fixed program is an implicit description of S^k so that $K(k) \overset{+}{>} K(S^k)$. Hence, $K(x) \overset{+}{>} K(S^k) + \log |S^k|$ and since $K(x)$ is the shortest description by definition equality ($\overset{+}{=}$) holds. That is, S^k is optimal for x. By Lemma 4 $K(S^k) \overset{+}{>} K(k)$ which together with the reverse inequality above yields $K(S^k) \overset{\pm}{=} K(k)$ which shows the theorem. $\qquad \square$

Again using Lemma 4 shows that the optimal set S^k has least complexity among all optimal sets for x, and therefore:

Corollary 2. *The set S^k is an implicit algorithmic minimal sufficient statistic for every x with $K(x) = k$.*

All algorithmic minimal sufficient statistics S for x have $K(S) \overset{\pm}{=} K(k)$, and therefore there are $O(2^{K(k)})$ of them. At least one such a statistic (S^k) is associated with every one of the $O(2^k)$ strings x of complexity k. Thus, while the idea of the algorithmic minimal sufficient statistic is intuitively appealing, its unrestricted use doesn't seem to uncover most relevant aspects of reality. The only relevant structure in the data with respect to a algorithmic minimal sufficient statistic is the Kolmogorov complexity. To give an example, an initial segment of $3.1415\ldots$ of length n of complexity $\log n + O(1)$ shares the same algorithmic sufficient statistic with many (most?) binary strings of length $\log n + O(1)$.

3.5   A Concrete Explicit Minimal Sufficient Statistic

Let us now consider representations of finite sets that are explicit in the sense that we can compute the cardinality of the set from the representation. For example, the description program enumerates all the elements of the set and halts. Then a set like $S^k = \{y : K(y) \leq k\}$ has complexity $\overset{+}{=} k$ [15]: Given the program we can find an element not in S^k, which element by definition has complexity $> k$. Given S^k we can find this element and hence S^k has complexity $\overset{+}{>} k$. Let

$$N^k = |S^k|,$$

then by Lemma 5 $\log N^k \overset{+}{=} k - K(k)$. We can list S^k given k^* and N^k which shows $K(S^k) \overset{+}{<} k$.

One way of implementing explicit finite representations is to provide an explicit generation time for the enumeration process. If we can generate S^k in time t recursively using k, then the previous argument shows that the complexity of every number $t' \geq t$ satisfies $K(t', k) \geq k$ so that $K(t') \overset{+}{>} K(t' \mid k^*) \overset{+}{>} k - K(k)$ by (4). This means that t is a huge time which as a function of k rises faster than every computable function. This argument also shows that explicit enumerative descriptions of sets S containing x by an enumerative process p plus a limit on the computation time t may take only $l(p) + K(t)$ bits (with $K(t) \leq \log t + 2 \log \log t$) but $\log t$ unfortunately becomes noncomputably large!

In other cases the generation time is simply recursive in the input: $S_n = \{y : l(y) \leq n\}$ so that $K(S_n) \overset{+}{=} K(n) \leq \log n + 2 \log \log n$. That is, this typical sufficient statistic for a random string x with $K(x) \overset{+}{=} n + K(n)$ has complexity $K(n)$ both for implicit and explicit descriptions: differences in complexity arise only for nonrandom strings (but not too nonrandom, for $K(x) \overset{+}{=} 0$ these differences vanish again).

It turns out that some strings cannot thus be explicitly represented parsimonously with low-complexity models (so that one necessarily has bad high complexity models like S^k above). For explicit representations, there are *absolutely non-stochastic* strings that don't have efficient two-part representations with $K(x) \overset{+}{=} K(S) + \log |S|$ ($x \in S$) with $K(S)$ significantly less than $K(x)$, Section 4.

Again, consider the special set $S^k = \{y : K(y) \leq k\}$. As we have seen earlier, S^k itself cannot be explicitly optimal for x since $K(S^k) \overset{+}{=} k$ and $\log N^k \overset{+}{=} k - K(k)$, and therefore $K(S^k) + \log N^k \overset{+}{=} 2k - K(k)$ which considerably exceeds k. However, it turns out that a closely related set ($S^k_{m_x}$ below) is explicitly near-optimal. Let I^k_y denote the index of y in the standard enumeration of S^k, where all indexes are padded to the same length $\stackrel{+}{=} k - K(k)$ with 0's in front. For $K(x) = k$, let m_x denote the longest joint prefix of I_x^k and N^k, and let

$$I_x^k = m_x 0 i_x, \quad N^k = m_x 1 n_x,$$
$$S_{m_x}^k = \{y \in S^k : m_x 0 \text{ a prefix of } I_y^k\}$$

Theorem 3. *The set $S_{m_x}^k$ is an explicit algorithmic minimal near-sufficient statistic for x among subsets of S^k in the following sense:*

$$|K(S_{m_x}^k) - K(k) - l(m_x)| \stackrel{+}{<} K(l(m_x)),$$
$$\log|S_{m_x}^k| \stackrel{\pm}{=} k - K(k) - l(m_x).$$

Hence $K(S_{m_x}^k) + \log|S_{m_x}^k| \stackrel{\pm}{=} k \pm K(l(m_x))$. Note, $K(l(m_x)) \stackrel{+}{<} \log k + 2\log\log k$.

The proof is given in the full paper [6]. We have not completely succeeded in giving a concrete algorithmic exlicit minimal sufficient statistic. However, we show [6] that $S_{m_x}^k$ is *almost always* minimal sufficient—also for the nonstochastic objects of Section 4.

4   Non-Stochastic Objects

Every data sample consisting of a finite string x has an sufficient statistics in the form of the singleton set $\{x\}$. Such a sufficient statistics is not very enlightening since it simply replicates the data and has equal complexity with x. Thus, one is interested in the minimal sufficient statistics that represents the regularity, (the meaningful) information, in the data and leaves out the accidental features. This raises the question whether every x has a minimal sufficient statistics that is significantly less complex than x itself. At a Tallinn conference in 1973 Kolmogorov (according to [14,2]) raised the question whether there are objects x that have no minimal sufficient statistics that have relatively small complexity. In other words, he inquired into the existence of objects that are not in general position (random with respect to) every finite set of small enough complexity, that is, "absolutely non-random" objects. Clearly, such objects x have neither minimal nor maximal complexity: if they have minimal complexity then the singleton set $\{x\}$ is a minimal sufficient statistics of small complexity, and if $x \in \{0,1\}^n$ is completely incompressible (that is, it is individually random and has no meaningful information), then the uninformative universe $\{0,1\}^n$ is the minimal sufficient statistics of small complexity. To analyze the question better we need a technical notion.

Define the *randomness deficiency* of an object x with respect to a finite set S containing it as the amount by which the complexity of x as an element of S falls short of the maximal possible complexity of an element in S when S is known explicitly (say, as a list):

$$\delta_S(x) = \log|S| - K(x \mid S). \tag{11}$$

The meaning of this function is clear: most elements of S have complexity near $\log |S|$, so this difference measures the amount of compressibility in x compared to the generic, typical, random elements of S. This is a generalization of the sufficiency notion in that it measures the discrepancy with typicality and hence sufficiency: if a set S is a sufficient statistic for x then $\delta_S(x) \stackrel{+}{=} 0$.

Kolmogorov Structure Function: We first consider the relation between the minimal unavoidable randomness deficiency of x with respect to a set S containing it, when the complexity of S is upper bounded by α. Such functional relations are known as *Kolmogorov structure functions*. He did not specify what is meant by $K(S)$ but it was noticed immediately, as the paper [15] points out, that the behavior of $h_x(\alpha)$ is rather trivial if $K(S)$ is taken to be the complexity of a program that lists S without necessarily halting. Section 3.4 elaborates this point. So, this section refers to explicit descriptions only. For technical reasons, we introduce the following variant of randomness deficiency (11):

$$\delta_S^*(x) = \log |S| - K(x \mid S, K(S)).$$

The function $\beta_x(\alpha)$ measuring the minimal unavoidable randomness deficiency of x with respect to every finite set S of complexity $K(S) < \alpha$. Formally, we define

$$\beta_x(\alpha) = \min_S \{ \delta_S(x) : K(S) < \alpha \},$$

and its variant β_x^* defined in terms of δ_S^*. Note that $\beta_x(K(x)) \stackrel{+}{=} \beta_x^*(K(x)) \stackrel{+}{=} 0$.

Optimal Non-Stochastic Objects: We are now able to formally express the notion of non-stochastic ojects using the Kolmogorov structure functions $\beta_x(\alpha), \beta_x^*(\alpha)$. For every given $k < n$, Shen constructed in [14] a binary string x of length n with $K(x) \leq k$ and $\beta_x(k - O(1)) > n - 2k - O(\log k)$.

Here, we improve on this result, replacing $n - 2k - O(\log k)$ with $n - k$ and using β^* to avoid logarithmic terms. This is the best possible, since by choosing $S = \{0,1\}^n$ we find $\log |S| - K(x \mid S, K(S)) \stackrel{+}{=} n - k$, and hence $\beta_x^*(c) \stackrel{+}{<} n - k$ for some constant c, which implies $\beta_x^*(\alpha) \leq \beta_x(c) \stackrel{+}{<} n - k$ for every $\alpha > c$. The proof is relegated to the full version of this paper [6].

Theorem 4. *For any given $k < n$, there are constants c_1, c_2 and a binary string x of length n with $K(x \mid n) \leq k$ such that for all $\alpha < k - c_1$ we have*

$$\beta_x^*(\alpha \mid n) > n - k - c_2.$$

Let x be one of the non-stochastic objects of which the existence is established by Theorem 4. Substituting $k \stackrel{+}{=} K(x|n)$ we can contemplate the set $S = \{x\}$ with complexity $K(S|n) \stackrel{+}{=} k$ and x has randomness deficiency $\stackrel{+}{=} 0$ with respect to S. This yields $0 \stackrel{+}{=} \beta_x^*(K(x|n)) \stackrel{+}{>} n - K(x|n)$. Since it generally holds that $K(x|n) \stackrel{+}{<} n$, it follows that $K(x|n) \stackrel{+}{=} n$. That is, these non-stochastic objects have complexity $K(x|n) \stackrel{+}{=} n$ and are *not random, typical, or in general position* with respect to every set S containing them with complexity $K(S|n) \not\stackrel{+}{=} n$, but they are random, typical, or in general position only for sets S with complexity $K(S|n) \stackrel{+}{>} n$ like $S = \{x\}$ with $K(S|n) \stackrel{\pm}{=} n$. That is, every explicit sufficient statistic S for x has complexity $K(S|n) \stackrel{\pm}{=} n$, and $\{x\}$ is such a statistic.

References

1. A.R. Barron, J. Rissanen, and B. Yu, The minimum description length principle in coding and modeling, *IEEE Trans. Inform. Theory*, IT-44:6(1998), 2743–2760.

2. T.M. Cover, Kolmogorov complexity, data compression, and inference, pp. 23–33 in: *The Impact of Processing Techniques on Communications*, J.K. Skwirzynski, Ed., Martinus Nijhoff Publishers, 1985.

3. T.M. Cover and J.A. Thomas, *Elements of Information Theory*, Wiley, New York, 1991.

4. R. A. Fisher, On the mathematical foundations of theoretical statistics, *Philosophical Transactions of the Royal Society of London, Ser. A*, 222(1922), 309-368.

5. Q. Gao, M. Li and P.M.B. Vitányi, Applying MDL to learn best model granularity, *Artificial Intelligence*, To appear. http://xxx.lanl.gov/abs/physics/0005062

6. P. Gács, J. Tromp, P. Vitányi, Algorithmic statistics, Submitted. http://xxx.lanl.gov/abs/math.PR/0006233

7. M. Li and P.M.B. Vitányi, *An Introduction to Kolmogorov Complexity and its Applications*, Springer-Verlag, New York, 2nd Edition, 1997.

8. A.N. Kolmogorov, Three approaches to the quantitative definition of information, *Problems Inform. Transmission* 1:1 (1965) 1-7.

9. A.N. Kolmogorov, On logical foundations of probability theory, Pp. 1–5 in: *Probability Theory and Mathematical Statistics*, Lect. Notes Math., Vol. 1021, K. Itô and Yu.V. Prokhorov, Eds., Springer-Verlag, Heidelberg, 1983.

10. A.N. Kolmogorov and V.A. Uspensky, Algorithms and Randomness, *SIAM Theory Probab. Appl.*, 32:3(1988), 389–412.

11. L.A. Levin, Laws of information conservation (nongrowth) and aspects of the foundation of probability theory, *Problems Inform. Transmission* 10:3(1974), 206–210.

12. L.A.Levin Randomness conservation inequalities: information and independence in mathematical theories, *Information and Control* 61 (1984) 15-37.

13. P. Martin-Löf, The definition of random sequences, *Inform. Contr.*, 9(1966), 602-619.

14. A.Kh. Shen, The concept of (α, β)-stochasticity in the Kolmogorov sense, and its properties, *Soviet Math. Dokl.*, 28:1(1983), 295-299.

15. A.Kh. Shen, Discussion on Kolmogorov complexity and statistical analysis, *The Computer Journal*, 42:4(1999), 340–342.

16. P.M.B. Vitányi and M. Li, Minimum Description Length Induction, Bayesianism, and Kolmogorov Complexity, *IEEE Trans. Inform. Theory*, IT-46:2(2000), 446–464.

17. V.V. V'yugin, On the defect of randomness of a finite object with respect to measures with given complexity bounds, *SIAM Theory Probab. Appl.*, 32:3(1987), 508–512.

18. V.V. V'yugin, Algorithmic complexity and stochastic properties of finite binary sequences, *The Computer Journal*, 42:4(1999), 294–317.

Minimum Message Length Grouping of Ordered Data

Leigh J. Fitzgibbon, Lloyd Allison, and David L. Dowe

School of Computer Science and Software Engineering
Monash University, Clayton, VIC 3168 Australia
{leighf,lloyd,dld}@csse.monash.edu.au

Abstract. Explicit segmentation is the partitioning of data into homogeneous regions by specifying cut-points. W. D. Fisher (1958) gave an early example of explicit segmentation based on the minimisation of squared error. Fisher called this *the grouping problem* and came up with a polynomial time Dynamic Programming Algorithm (DPA). Oliver, Baxter and colleagues (1996,1997,1998) have applied the information-theoretic Minimum Message Length (MML) principle to explicit segmentation. They have derived formulas for specifying cut-points imprecisely and have empirically shown their criterion to be superior to other segmentation methods (AIC, MDL and BIC). We use a simple MML criterion and Fisher's DPA to perform numerical Bayesian (summing and) integration (using message lengths) over the cut-point location parameters. This gives an estimate of the number of segments, which we then use to estimate the cut-point positions and segment parameters by minimising the MML criterion. This is shown to have lower Kullback-Leibler distances on generated data.

1 Introduction

Grouping is defined as the partitioning, or explicit segmentation, of a set of data into homogeneous groups that can be explained by some stochastic model [8]. Constraints can be imposed to allow only contiguous partitions over some variable or on data-sets that are ordered a priori. For example, time series segmentation consists of finding homogeneous segments that are contiguous in time.

Grouping theory has applications in inference and statistical description problems and there are many practical applications. For example, we wish to infer when and how many changes in a patient's condition have occurred based on some medical data. A second example is that we may wish to describe Central Processor Unit (CPU) usage in terms of segments to allow automatic or manager-based decisions to be made.

In this paper, we describe a Minimum Message Length (MML) [18, 22, 19] approach to explicit segmentation for data-sets that are ordered a priori. Fisher's original Maximum Likelihood solution to this problem was based on the minimisation of squared error. The problem with Maximum Likelihood approaches is that they have no stopping criterion, which means that unless the number of

H. Arimura, S. Jain and A. Sharma (Eds.): ALT 2000, LNAI 1968, pp. 56-70, 2000.

groups is known a priori, the optimal grouping would consist of one datum per group. Maximum Likelihood estimates for the cut-point positions are also known to be inaccurate [11] and have a tendency to place cut-points in close proximity of each other. MML inference overcomes both these problems by encoding the model and the data as a two-part message.

The MML solution we describe is based on Fisher's polynomial time Dynamic Programming Algorithm (DPA), which has several advantages over commonly used graph search algorithms. It is able to handle adjacent dependencies, where the cost of segment i is dependent on the model for segment $i-1$. The algorithm is exhaustive and can be made to consider all possible segmentations, allowing for numerical (summing and) integration. Computing the optimal segmentation of data into G groups results in the solution of all optimal partitions for $1..G$ over $1..K$, where K is the number of elements in the data-set.

Oliver, Baxter, Wallace and Forbes [3, 11, 10] have implemented and tested a MML based solution to the segmentation of time series data and compared it with some other techniques including Bayes Factors [9], AIC [1], BIC [15], and MDL [12]. In their work, they specify the cut-point to a precision that the data warrants. This creates dependencies between adjacent segments and without knowledge of Fisher's DPA they have used heuristic search strategies. They have empirically shown their criterion to be superior to AIC, BIC and MDL over the data-sets tested. However, the testing was only performed on data with fixed parameter values and equally spaced cut-points.

We use a simple MML criterion and Fisher's DPA to perform Bayesian (summing and) integration (using message lengths) over the cut-point parameter(s). This gives an estimate of the number of segments, which we then use to estimate the cut-point positions and segment parameters by minimising the MML criterion. This unorthodox[1] coding scheme has the advantage that because we do not state the cut-point positions, we do not need to worry about the precision to which they are stated and therefore reduce the number of assumptions and approximations involved. We compare our criterion with Oliver and Baxter's [11] MML, MDL and BIC criteria over a number of data-sets with and without randomly placed cut-points and parameters.

This paper is structured as follows. Section 2 contains background information on Fisher's grouping problem and his algorithm. It also contains an overview of the MML segmentation work by Oliver, Baxter and others [3, 11, 10] and an introduction to Minimum Message Length inference. Section 3 contains a re-statement of the segmentation problem using our terminology. In Section 4, we describe the message length formula that we use to segment the data and the approximate Bayesian integration technique we use to remove the cut-point parameter. In Section 5, we perform some experiments and compare with the previous work of Oliver, Baxter and others [10]. The concluding Sections, 6 and 7, summarize the results and suggest future work.

---

[1] Unorthodox in terms of the Minimum Message Length framework [18, 22, 19], where parameters that are to be estimated should be stated in the first part of the message.

2   Background

2.1   The Grouping Problem

An ordered set of K numbers $\{a_i : i = 0..K - 1\}$ can be partitioned into G contiguous groups in $\binom{K-1}{G-1}$ ways. We only consider contiguous partitions since we assume that the data has been ordered a priori[2]. For a given G, Fisher's solution to the grouping problem was to search for the contiguous partition determined by $G - 1$ cut-points that minimised the distance, D:

$$D = \sum_{i=0}^{K-1} (a_i - \overline{a}_i)^2 \tag{1}$$

where $\overline{a}_i$ represents the arithmetic mean of the a's assigned to the group in which i is assigned. For a given G, the partition which minimises D is called an optimal or least squares partition. Whilst Fisher was concerned with grouping normally distributed data (fitting piecewise constants), his techniques, and the techniques derived in this paper can be applied to other models.

The exhaustive search algorithm used to find the optimal partition is based on the following "Sub-optimisation Lemma"[8, page 795]:

Lemma 1. *If $A_1 : A_2$ denotes a partition of set A into two disjoint subsets A_1 and A_2, if P_1* denotes a least squares partition of A_1 into G_1 subsets and if P_2* denotes a least squares partition of A_2 into G_2 subsets; then, of the class of sub-partitions of $A_1 : A_2$ employing G_1 subsets over A_1 and G_2 subsets over A_2 a least squares sub-partition is $P_1* : P_2*$.*

This lemma is possible due to the additive nature of the distance measure. The algorithm based on this lemma is an example of a Dynamic Programming Algorithm (DPA) and is computable in polynomial time. The DPA is a general class of algorithm that is used in optimisation problems where the solution is the sum of sub-solutions. Fisher's algorithm can easily be expressed in pseudo-code. In Figure 1 the pseudo-code for a function $D(G)$ which returns the distance, D, for a number of groups, G, up to an upper bound G_{max} is shown.

The time complexity of Fisher's DPA is:

$$\forall_{k=1..G_{max}-1} \forall_{i=k..K-1} min_{j=k}^{i} D[k-1, j-1] + sumsqr(j, i) = O(G_{max} \cdot K^2) \tag{2}$$

In practice, $G_{max} \ll K$.

2.2   The Problem with the Maximum Likelihood Partition

How many segments? Given some data, where G is unknown, a practitioner must view a range of least square partition solutions and then select one. For easy

---

[2] This is what W. D. Fisher called the *restricted problem*.

Lookup functions:

$sum(i, j) = sum[j + 1] - sum[i]$

$sumsqr(i, j) = sumsqr[j + 1] - sum[i]$

$D(i, j) = sumsqr(i, j) - \frac{\text{sum}(i,j)^2}{j-i+1}$

$D(G) = D[G - 1, K - 1]$

Boundary conditions:

$sum[0] := 0$

$sumsqr[0] := 0$

Initial Step:

$sum[i] := sum[i - 1] + a_{i-1}, \forall_{i=1..K}$

$sumsqr[i] := sumsqr[i - 1] + a_{i-1}^2, \forall_{i=1..K}$

$D[0, i] := D(0, i), \forall_{i=0..K-1}$

General Step:

$D[k, i] := min_{j=k}^{i} D[k - 1, j - 1] + sumsqr(j, i),$

$\forall_{k=1..G_{max}-1} \forall_{i=k..K-1}$

Fig. 1. A Dynamic Programming Algorithm based on Fisher's Sub-optimisation Lemma.

data this may be satisfactory. However, for difficult data a human cannot detect subtle differences between the solutions. Consider the least square partitions for $G = \{2, 3, 4, 5\}$ of some generated data in Figures 3 to 6. From inspection of these four hypotheses, it is difficult to determine the true number of segments.

Poor parameter estimates Even when we know the number of segments in a data-set, the least squares partition may give poor estimates for the cut-point positions, and segment parameters. Oliver and Forbes [11] found that the Maximum Likelihood estimates for the cut-point position are unreliable. In their experiments the Maximum Likelihood technique that was given the correct number of segments had, on average, a higher Kullback-Leibler distance than a MML based technique that did not know the correct number of segments. An example of this can be seen in the least squares partitions in Figures 5 and 6. The least squares and MDL methods tend to place cut-points in close proximity of each other.

2.3   The Minimum Message Length Principle

The MML principle [18, 22, 19] is based on compact coding theory. It provides a criterion for comparing competing hypotheses (models) by encoding both the hypothesis and the data in a two-part message. For a hypothesis, H, and data, D, Bayes's theorem gives the following relationship between the probabilities:

$$Pr(H\&D) = Pr(H) \cdot Pr(D|H) = Pr(D) \cdot Pr(H|D), \qquad (3)$$

which can be rearranged as:

$$Pr(H|D) = \frac{Pr(H) \cdot Pr(D|H)}{Pr(D)} \qquad (4)$$

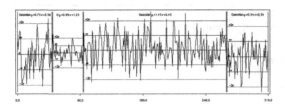

Fig. 2. Some generated data.

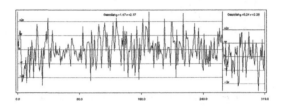

Fig. 3. Two segment least squares partition of Fig. 2.

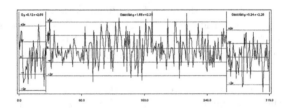

Fig. 4. Three segment least squares partition of Fig. 2.

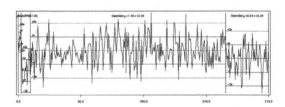

Fig. 5. Four segment least squares partition of Fig. 2.

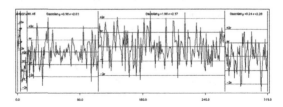

Fig. 6. Five segment least squares partition of Fig. 2.

After observing some data D, it follows that $Pr(H|D)$ is maximised when $Pr(H) \cdot Pr(D|H)$ is maximised. We know from coding theory that an event with probability P can be transmitted using an optimal code in a message of $-\log_2(P)$ bits[3] in length. Therefore the length of a two-part message (MessLen) conveying the parameter estimates (based on some prior) and the data encoded based on these estimates can be calculated as:

$$MessLen(H\&D) = -\log_2(Pr(H)) - \log_2(Pr(D|H)) \text{ bits} \qquad (5)$$

The receiver of such a hypothetical message must be able to decode the data without using any other knowledge. Minimising $MessLen(H\&D)$ is equivalent to maximising $Pr(H|D)$, the latter being a *probability* and *not* a density [20, section 2] [21, section 2] [5]. The model with the shortest message length is considered to give the best explanation of the data. This interpretation of inductive inference problems as coding problems has many practical and theoretical advantages over dealing with probabilities directly. A survey of MML theory and its many successful applications is given by Wallace and Dowe [19].

2.4   MML Precision of Cut-point Specification

We can encode the cut-point positions in $\log\binom{K-1}{G-1}$ nits. However, using this coding scheme can be inefficient for small sample sizes and noisy data. Consider two segments whose boundaries are not well-defined: the posterior distribution will not have a well defined mode, but there may be a region around the boundary with high probability. The MML principle states that we should use this region to encode the data - we should only state the cut-point to an accuracy that the data warrants, for otherwise we risk under-fitting.

Oliver, Baxter and others [3, 11, 10] studied the problem of specifying the cut-point imprecisely. They derived equations to calculate the optimal precision with which to specify the cut-point. Where the boundary between two segments is not well-defined, it is cheaper to use less precision for the cut-point specification. This reduces the length of the first part of the message but may increase the length of the second part. Where the boundary is well-defined, it pays to use a higher precision to save in the second part of the message. Empirical results [3, 11, 10] have shown that specifying cut-points imprecisely gives better estimates of the number of segments and lower Kullback-Leibler distances. Similar success with MML imprecise cut-point specification has been found by Viswanathan, Wallace, Dowe and Korb [17] for binary sequences.

3   Problem Re-Statement

We consider a process which generates an ordered data-set. The process can be approximated by, or is considered to consist of, an exhaustive concatenation of contiguous sub-sets that were generated by sub-processes. We consider a

---

[3] In the next sections of the paper we use the natural logarithm and the unit is nits.

sub-process to be homogeneous and the data generated by a process to consist entirely of one or more homogeneous sequences.

Let y be a univariate ordered data-set of K numbers generated by some process:

$$y = (y_0, y_1, ..., y_{K-1}) \tag{6}$$

which consists of G contiguous, exhaustive and mutually exclusive sub-sets:

$$s = (s_0, s_1, ..., s_{G-1}), \tag{7}$$

where the members of each s_i were generated by sub-process i, which can be modelled with parameters θ_i:

$$\theta = (\theta_0, \theta_1, ..., \theta_{G-1}), \tag{8}$$

and likelihood:

$$f(y \in s_i | \theta_i) \tag{9}$$

In some cases, the number of distinct sub-processes may be less than G. This is most likely to occur in processes that have discrete states. For example, a process that alternates between two discrete states would be better modelled as coming from two, rather than G, sub-processes since parameters would be estimated over more data. This is a common approach with implicit segmentation, where segments are modelled implicitly by a Markov Model [16, 7]. However, the use of G sub-processes results in a more tractable problem and is what is generally used for explicit segmentation. Moreover, in some cases we may wish to model data which can be considered as coming from a drifting process rather than a process with distinct states. In these cases, segmentation can be used to identify approximately stationary regions and is best modelled as coming from G distinct sub-processes.

The inference problem is to estimate some or all of : G, s, θ and $f(y \in s_i | \theta_i)$.

4   Calculating the Message Length with Gaussian Segments

In this section we describe the message length formula used to calculate the expected length of a message which transmits the model and the data. Assume that the size, K, of the data-set is known and given. In order for a hypothetical receiver to decode the message and retrieve the original data, we must encode the following: G, the number of segments; the cut-point positions, $c|s$; the parameter estimates, θ_i, for each segment s_i; and finally the data for each segment using the parameter estimates stated. We specify G using the universal log* code [13, 2], although we re-normalise the probabilities because we know that $G \leq K$. This simplifies the problem to the specification of:

- the cut-point positions $c|s$,
- the parameter estimates θ_i and data for each segment.

From Wallace and Freeman [22], the formula for calculating the length of a message where the model consists of several continuous parameters $\theta = (\theta_1, \ldots, \theta_n)$ is:

$$MessLen(H\&D) = -\log\left(\frac{h(\theta)f(y|\theta)}{\sqrt{F(\theta)}}\right) + \frac{n}{2}(1 + \log\kappa_n) \text{ nits} \qquad (10)$$

where $h(\theta)$ is a prior distribution over the n parameter values, $f(y|\theta)$ is the likelihood function for the model, $F(\theta)$ is the determinant of the Fisher Information matrix and κ_n is a lattice constant which represents the saving over the quantised n-dimensional space.

In this paper we consider Gaussian segments with two continuous parameters μ and σ: $y \in s_j \sim N[\mu_j, \sigma_j]$ so, $\theta_j = (\mu_j, \sigma_j)$. The lattice constant $\kappa_2 = \frac{5}{36\sqrt{3}}$ [4], the Fisher Information, $F(\theta)$, for the Normal distribution [10] is:

$$F(\mu, \sigma) = \frac{2n^2}{\sigma^4} \qquad (11)$$

and the negative log-likelihood is:

$$-\log f(y|\mu, \sigma) = \frac{n}{2}\log 2\pi + n\log\sigma + \frac{1}{2\sigma^2}\sum_{i=1}^{n}(x_i - \bar{x})^2 \qquad (12)$$

The prior distribution we use is non-informative based on the population variance, $\sigma_{pop}^2 = \frac{1}{K-1}\sum_{i=0}^{K-1}(y_i - \mu_{pop})^2$ where $\mu_{pop} = \frac{1}{K}\sum_{i=0}^{K-1} y_i$:

$$\forall_j \ h(\mu_j, \sigma_j) = \frac{1}{2\sigma_{pop}^2} \qquad (13)$$

This is the prior used by Oliver, Baxter and others [11, section 3.1.3] [3, 10], although the prior $\forall_j \ h(\mu_j, \sigma_j) = \frac{1}{4\sigma_{pop}^2}$ from [18, section 4.2] or other priors could also be considered. We use this prior, from Equation 13, to allow for a fair comparison with their criterion [3, 11, 10].

We use Equation 10 to send the parameters $\theta_j = (\mu_j, \sigma_j)$ and data for each segment. To encode the cut-point positions we use a simple coding scheme assuming that each combination is equally likely:

$$MessLen(c|K, G) = \log\binom{K-1}{G-1} \text{ nits} \qquad (14)$$

Based on Equation 10, the expected total length of the message is:

$$MessLen(H\&D) = \log^*(G) + MessLen(c|K, G) \qquad (15)$$
$$+ \sum_{j=1}^{G}\left(-\log\left(\frac{h(\theta_j)f(y \in s_j|\theta_j)}{\sqrt{F(\theta_j)}}\right) + \frac{n}{2}(1 + \log\kappa_n)\right) \text{ nits}$$

If we were to optimise the values of G, s and θ to minimise Equation 15, we would under-estimate G since c is being stated to maximum precision (see Section 2.4). We avoid this problem by summing the probabilities of the various MML estimates of $\theta_j = (\mu_j, \sigma_j)_{j=0,..,G-1}$ over all possible sub-partitions:

$$Prob'(G) = \sum_{i=1}^{\binom{K-1}{G-1}} e^{-MessLen(H\&D)_i} \qquad (16)$$

where $MessLen(H\&D)_i$ is the message length associated with the ith sub-partition from the $\binom{K-1}{G-1}$ possible sub-partitions and the values of the $\hat{\theta}_j$ associated with each such ith sub-partition. $Prob'$ gives unnormalised probabilities for the number of segments. The 'probabilities' are unnormalised because, for each ith sub-partition, the 'probabilities' consider only that part of the posterior density of the θ_j contained in the MML coding block[4].

We optimise Equation 16 to estimate G. This can be implemented by modifying Fisher's DPA given in Figure 1 by replacing the distance function with Equation 10 and changing the general step to sum over all sub-partitions:

$$D[k,i] := LOGPLUS(D[k-1, j-1], sumsqr(j,i)) \qquad (17)$$
$$\forall_{k=1..G_{max}-1} \forall_{i=k..K-1} \forall_{j=k..i}$$

where the $LOGPLUS$ function is used to sum the log-probabilities:

$$LOGPLUS(x,y) = -\log_e(e^{-x} + e^{-y}) \qquad (18)$$

Using Equation 16 to estimate G we then optimise Equation 15 to estimate the remaining parameters.

5   Experimental Evaluation

5.1   Generated Data

We now use Fisher's DPA to infer the number of segments G, the cut-point positions $c|s$ and segment parameters θ_i of some generated Gaussian data. The criteria to be compared are:

- MML-I, Equations 15 and 16 from the previous section.
- MMLOB, MML Equation (6) from the paper Oliver and Baxter [10].
- BIC, using $-\log f(x|\theta) + \frac{numberparams}{2} \log K$.
- MDL, using $-\log f(x|\theta) + \frac{continuousparams}{2} \log n + \log \binom{K}{G}$.

---

[4] However, normalising these 'probabilities' will give a reasonable approximation [5, sections 4 and 4.1] [19, sections 2 and 8] to the marginal/posterior probability of G which would be obtained by integrating out over all the $\theta_j = (\mu_j, \sigma_j)$.

The BIC and MDL criteria[5] were included since these were investigated and compared by Oliver and Baxter [10, page 8], but not over the range of data that we consider. AIC was omitted due to its poor performance in previous papers [3, 11, 10]. We expect our criterion, MML-I, to perform better where the data is noisy, the sample size is small or where the approximations break down in MMLOB.

We have generated three different data-sets S_0, S_1 and S_2:

- S_0 has fixed μ's and σ's and evenly-spaced cut-points; similar to Oliver and Baxter [10].
- S_1 has fixed μ's and σ's and (uniformly) randomly chosen cut-points (minimum segment size of 3).
- S_2 has random μ's and σ's drawn uniformly from $[0..1]$, and (uniformly) randomly chosen cut-points (minimum segment size of 3).

For each data-set, 100 samples were generated of sizes 20, 40, 80, 160 and 320 and with each of 1..7 segments. For S_0 and S_1, the variance of each segment is 1.0, and the means of the segments are monotonically increasing by 1.0.

5.2   Experimental Results

We have collated the data collected during the experiments to report: a count of the number of times the correct number of cut-points were inferred (score test); the average number of cut-points inferred; and the Kullback-Leibler (KL) distance between the true and inferred distribution. The KL distance gives an indication of how well the parameters for each segment are being estimated. This will be affected by the inferred number of cut-points and their placement.

MDL and BIC were generally out-performed by the two MML methods (MML-I and MMLOB) in all measures. The interesting comparison is between MML-I and MMLOB.

Not all of the results could be included due to space limitations. The KL distance and average number of cut-points for S_0 and S_1 were omitted. For these two data-sets, the average number of inferred cut-points was slightly better for MML-I, and the KL distances for MML-I and MMLOB were both very similar.

The score test results have been included for all data-sets and can be seen in Tables 1 to 2. Each table shows the number of times the correct number of cuts k was inferred from the 100 trials for each of the sample sizes under investigation (20,40,80,160 and 320). MML-I is more accurate than the other criteria for both S_0 and S_1 on the score test. The strange exception is for S_2, where MMLOB is not only more accurate than the other criteria, but has improved a seemingly disproportionate amount over its results for S_0 and S_1.

Table 3 shows the average number of inferred cuts for data-set S_2. None of the criteria appear to be excessively over-fitting.

---

[5] We also note that MDL has been refined [14] since the 1978 MDL paper [12]. For a general comparison between MDL and MML, see, e.g., [14, 19, 20] and other articles in that special issue of the *Computer Journal*.

Table 4 shows the average Kullback-Leibler (KL) distances and standard deviations for data-set S_2. The KL distance means and standard deviations for MML-I are consistent for all sample sizes and are overall best, performing exceptionally well on sample sizes $K \leq 40$. MMLOB, MDL and BIC appear to break down for small samples in terms of both the mean and standard deviation.

MML-I has consistently low KL distances over all data-sets and is generally able to more accurately infer the number of cut-points for S_0 and S_1 than the other criteria. MMLOB is more accurate at inferring the number of cuts for data-set S_2 but has substantially higher KL distances than MML-I, but slightly better KL distances than BIC and MDL.

5.3   Application to Lake Michigan-Huron Data

We have used the MML-I criterion developed in this paper to segment the lake Michigan-Huron data that was posed as a problem in W. D. Fisher's original 1958 paper [8]. The DPA using our criterion was implemented in Java 2 (JIT) and was able to consider the over 10^{12} possible segmentations (for $G \leq 10$) of the lake data, with $K = 96$ in 2.1 seconds on a Pentium running at 200 mega-hertz. It inferred that there are five segments; $G = 5$. A graph of the segmentation can be seen in Figure 7. In Figure 8 we have segmented the lake data up to the year 1999. We can see that the segmentation identified in Figure 7 has been naturally extended in Figure 8.

Fisher's original least squares program was written for the "Illiac" digital computer at the University of Illinois and could handle data-sets with $K \leq 200$ and $G \leq 10$ with running time up to approximately 14 minutes.

6   Conclusion

We have applied numerical Bayesian (summing and) integration for cut-point parameters in the grouping or segmentation problem. Using W. D. Fisher's polynomial time DPA, we were able to perform approximations to numerical Bayesian integration using a Minimum Message Length criterion (MML-I) to estimate the number of segments. Having done that, we then minimize the MML-I criterion (Equation 15) to estimate the segment boundaries and within-segment parameter values. This technique, MML-I, was compared with three other criteria: MMLOB [11], MDL and BIC. The comparison was based on generated data with fixed and random parameter values. Using the Fisher DPA, we were able to experiment over a larger range of data than previous work [3, 11, 10]. The MMLOB and MML-I criteria performed well and were shown to be superior to MDL and BIC. The MML-I criterion, using Bayesian integration, was shown to have overall lower Kullback-Leibler distances and was generally better at inferring the number of cut-points than the other criteria.

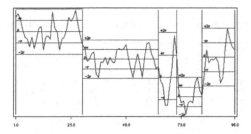

Fig. 7. Lake Michigan-Huron monthly mean water levels from 1860 to 1955 segmented by MML-I. This is the data that W. D. Fisher originally considered in 1958.

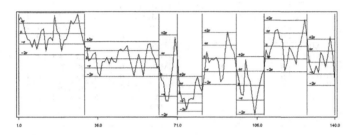

Fig. 8. Lake Michigan-Huron monthly mean water levels from 1860 to 1999 segmented by MML-I.

Table 1. Positive inference counts for data-set S_0.

$\hat{k}$	Criterion	20	40	80	160	320	Total
0	MML-I	86	93	93	100	95	467
	MMLOB	93	94	93	100	84	464
	MDL	89	96	99	100	99	483
	BIC	76	88	95	98	96	453
1	MML-I	43	69	76	83	89	360
	MMLOB	28	57	86	89	77	337
	MDL	24	35	62	96	98	315
	BIC	42	55	83	89	96	365
2	MML-I	3	21	63	74	91	252
	MMLOB	6	12	46	84	81	229
	MDL	4	10	13	52	98	177
	BIC	11	23	35	68	92	229
3	MML-I	0	3	17	51	79	150
	MMLOB	1	3	10	61	68	143
	MDL	2	5	5	14	76	102
	BIC	2	9	9	34	88	142
4	MML-I	0	0	6	44	77	127
	MMLOB	0	0	2	22	65	89
	MDL	0	1	1	2	45	49
	BIC	0	4	7	11	58	80
5	MML-I	0	0	0	19	66	85
	MMLOB	0	0	0	7	64	71
	MDL	0	0	0	2	9	11
	BIC	0	1	0	9	21	31
6	MML-I	0	0	0	5	49	54
	MMLOB	0	0	0	0	56	56
	MDL	0	0	0	0	3	3
	BIC	0	0	0	1	8	9

Table 2. Positive inference counts for data-sets S_1 and S_2 respectively.

k	Criterion	20	40	80	160	320	Total
1	MML-I	32	45	64	74	77	292
	MMLOB	22	40	62	72	78	274
	MDL	19	23	38	67	79	226
	BIC	35	38	57	78	81	289
2	MML-I	5	18	34	50	65	172
	MMLOB	5	6	27	43	58	139
	MDL	4	2	12	27	48	93
	BIC	14	9	23	37	54	137
3	MML-I	0	1	8	29	48	86
	MMLOB	0	1	9	16	50	76
	MDL	2	4	3	4	20	33
	BIC	3	8	13	14	32	70
4	MML-I	0	0	4	14	32	50
	MMLOB	0	0	3	12	30	45
	MDL	0	0	0	1	2	3
	BIC	0	2	2	6	12	22
5	MML-I	0	0	0	5	17	22
	MMLOB	0	0	0	1	24	25
	MDL	0	1	1	0	2	4
	BIC	0	1	1	1	9	12
6	MML-I	0	0	0	0	7	7
	MMLOB	0	0	0	0	9	9
	MDL	0	1	0	0	0	1
	BIC	0	1	0	0	2	3

k	Criterion	20	40	80	160	320	Total
1	MML-I	37	46	55	60	79	277
	MMLOB	44	56	65	68	82	315
	MDL	42	49	54	68	82	295
	BIC	49	51	59	69	85	313
2	MML-I	11	26	27	50	43	157
	MMLOB	16	33	35	57	57	198
	MDL	19	27	28	41	45	160
	BIC	30	37	37	52	53	209
3	MML-I	0	9	19	38	41	107
	MMLOB	2	12	30	37	51	132
	MDL	3	7	16	24	33	83
	BIC	5	11	27	30	40	113
4	MML-I	0	0	11	23	24	58
	MMLOB	0	5	10	24	27	66
	MDL	0	4	7	10	20	41
	BIC	0	6	14	15	25	60
5	MML-I	0	0	8	14	19	41
	MMLOB	0	1	9	13	28	51
	MDL	0	1	4	8	7	20
	BIC	0	1	4	12	12	29
6	MML-I	0	0	4	9	18	31
	MMLOB	0	0	3	9	20	32
	MDL	0	1	0	2	4	7
	BIC	0	1	1	5	9	16

Table 3. Average inferred number of cuts for data-set S_2.

k	Criterion	20	40	80	160	320
0	MML-I	0.150 ± 0.39	0.100 ± 0.39	0.090 ± 0.38	0.000 ± 0.00	0.130 ± 0.77
	MMLOB	0.080 ± 0.31	0.100 ± 0.41	0.010 ± 0.41	0.000 ± 0.00	0.450 ± 1.50
	MDL	0.130 ± 0.39	0.040 ± 0.20	0.010 ± 0.10	0.000 ± 0.00	0.010 ± 0.10
	BIC	0.340 ± 0.67	0.210 ± 0.64	0.070 ± 0.33	0.030 ± 0.22	0.060 ± 0.34
1	MML-I	0.490 ± 0.61	0.640 ± 0.64	0.890 ± 0.82	0.960 ± 0.78	1.040 ± 0.85
	MMLOB	0.480 ± 0.54	0.660 ± 0.57	0.800 ± 0.65	0.880 ± 0.61	1.020 ± 0.67
	MDL	0.560 ± 0.62	0.570 ± 0.57	0.630 ± 0.60	0.720 ± 0.49	0.840 ± 0.39
	BIC	0.730 ± 0.66	0.830 ± 0.68	0.800 ± 0.64	0.820 ± 0.56	0.870 ± 0.37
2	MML-I	0.530 ± 0.69	0.980 ± 0.89	1.360 ± 1.04	1.640 ± 0.94	1.870 ± 1.28
	MMLOB	0.730 ± 0.76	1.100 ± 0.86	1.170 ± 0.79	1.580 ± 0.77	1.760 ± 0.91
	MDL	0.750 ± 0.80	1.010 ± 0.88	1.020 ± 0.82	1.220 ± 0.75	1.380 ± 0.71
	BIC	1.110 ± 0.82	1.270 ± 0.87	1.270 ± 0.87	1.440 ± 0.73	1.490 ± 0.72
3	MML-I	0.460 ± 0.64	1.060 ± 0.94	1.880 ± 1.26	2.510 ± 1.27	2.830 ± 1.43
	MMLOB	0.790 ± 0.87	1.260 ± 1.04	1.950 ± 1.10	2.170 ± 0.89	2.750 ± 0.99
	MDL	0.890 ± 0.91	1.100 ± 0.96	1.620 ± 1.06	1.780 ± 0.95	2.090 ± 0.84
	BIC	1.220 ± 0.91	1.440 ± 1.09	2.010 ± 1.11	2.000 ± 0.92	2.320 ± 0.85
4	MML-I	0.400 ± 0.60	1.010 ± 0.94	2.180 ± 1.27	3.050 ± 1.79	3.590 ± 1.54
	MMLOB	0.750 ± 0.86	1.360 ± 1.24	2.410 ± 1.16	2.750 ± 1.39	3.600 ± 1.38
	MDL	0.860 ± 0.96	1.130 ± 1.12	1.980 ± 1.08	2.080 ± 1.18	2.620 ± 1.03
	BIC	1.120 ± 0.97	1.540 ± 1.10	2.350 ± 1.10	2.370 ± 1.12	2.900 ± 1.08
5	MML-I	0.330 ± 0.62	1.080 ± 1.17	2.260 ± 1.46	3.500 ± 1.85	3.970 ± 1.62
	MMLOB	0.640 ± 0.92	1.690 ± 1.33	2.510 ± 1.49	3.210 ± 1.37	4.310 ± 1.53
	MDL	0.880 ± 1.02	1.510 ± 1.34	1.970 ± 1.37	2.490 ± 1.38	2.980 ± 1.14
	BIC	1.170 ± 1.02	1.910 ± 1.31	2.310 ± 1.33	2.870 ± 1.30	3.300 ± 1.14
6	MML-I	0.340 ± 0.61	1.200 ± 1.30	2.530 ± 1.69	3.660 ± 1.75	5.420 ± 1.96
	MMLOB	0.640 ± 0.86	1.810 ± 1.46	2.910 ± 1.56	3.610 ± 1.46	5.010 ± 1.56
	MDL	0.730 ± 0.90	1.550 ± 1.48	2.060 ± 1.26	2.820 ± 1.43	3.530 ± 1.23
	BIC	1.100 ± 0.96	1.930 ± 1.39	2.680 ± 1.28	3.280 ± 1.36	3.900 ± 1.21

Table 4. Kullback-Leibler distances for data-set S_2.

k	Criterion	20	40	80	160	320
0	MML-I	0.218 ± 0.65	0.056 ± 0.13	0.023 ± 0.05	0.007 ± 0.01	0.013 ± 0.07
	MMLOB	0.422 ± 1.69	0.283 ± 2.08	0.034 ± 0.11	0.007 ± 0.01	0.049 ± 0.28
	MDL	0.716 ± 2.40	0.288 ± 2.10	0.016 ± 0.03	0.007 ± 0.01	0.007 ± 0.04
	BIC	1.159 ± 3.08	0.820 ± 3.24	0.132 ± 1.05	0.064 ± 0.52	0.046 ± 0.27
1	MML-I	0.588 ± 2.14	0.261 ± 0.29	0.154 ± 0.23	0.173 ± 0.55	0.072 ± 0.48
	MMLOB	4.650 ± 39.11	0.312 ± 0.90	0.389 ± 2.41	0.234 ± 1.56	0.070 ± 0.48
	MDL	5.633 ± 39.70	0.410 ± 1.36	0.538 ± 2.94	0.076 ± 0.24	0.137 ± 0.84
	BIC	5.841 ± 39.69	0.698 ± 2.04	0.725 ± 3.21	1.133 ± 9.52	0.136 ± 0.84
2	MML-I	0.542 ± 0.55	0.334 ± 0.30	0.244 ± 0.36	0.159 ± 0.30	0.227 ± 1.13
	MMLOB	0.835 ± 1.62	0.447 ± 1.22	0.248 ± 0.74	0.119 ± 0.21	0.145 ± 1.05
	MDL	1.590 ± 4.13	1.255 ± 7.05	0.260 ± 0.70	0.086 ± 0.14	0.035 ± 0.05
	BIC	1.625 ± 3.45	0.759 ± 1.70	1.022 ± 4.76	0.196 ± 0.59	0.045 ± 0.07
3	MML-I	0.620 ± 0.45	0.444 ± 0.40	0.266 ± 0.23	0.186 ± 0.22	0.116 ± 0.25
	MMLOB	1.181 ± 3.24	0.761 ± 2.61	0.322 ± 0.57	0.122 ± 0.22	0.097 ± 0.31
	MDL	1.323 ± 3.27	0.455 ± 0.61	0.470 ± 0.99	0.132 ± 0.27	0.085 ± 0.31
	BIC	1.650 ± 3.62	0.754 ± 1.18	0.909 ± 1.93	0.154 ± 0.32	0.169 ± 0.67
4	MML-I	0.670 ± 0.48	0.507 ± 0.48	0.361 ± 0.28	0.274 ± 0.43	0.176 ± 0.28
	MMLOB	5.499 ± 40.13	1.141 ± 4.70	0.454 ± 1.30	0.854 ± 6.52	0.542 ± 3.08
	MDL	6.013 ± 40.21	1.077 ± 4.64	0.518 ± 1.29	0.873 ± 6.51	0.279 ± 1.91
	BIC	3.710 ± 13.51	1.188 ± 3.30	0.760 ± 1.72	0.753 ± 4.09	1.255 ± 7.69
5	MML-I	0.671 ± 0.38	0.562 ± 0.33	0.441 ± 0.41	0.231 ± 0.20	0.202 ± 0.27
	MMLOB	3.826 ± 25.00	1.424 ± 6.27	0.572 ± 1.18	1.181 ± 9.36	0.133 ± 0.15
	MDL	2.096 ± 4.69	4.298 ± 25.49	0.755 ± 3.86	1.173 ± 9.36	0.118 ± 0.15
	BIC	2.476 ± 4.78	4.554 ± 25.49	0.803 ± 3.89	0.722 ± 3.49	0.240 ± 0.87
6	MML-I	0.722 ± 0.36	0.618 ± 0.48	0.386 ± 0.24	0.247 ± 0.19	0.299 ± 0.43
	MMLOB	5.688 ± 41.22	3.733 ± 24.12	0.674 ± 1.57	0.383 ± 1.03	0.259 ± 0.62
	MDL	5.756 ± 41.21	4.930 ± 28.90	0.816 ± 1.81	0.994 ± 4.87	0.169 ± 0.42
	BIC	4.375 ± 22.72	3.160 ± 10.83	1.206 ± 2.49	1.223 ± 4.92	0.294 ± 1.23

7   Further Work and Acknowledgments

We have not directly investigated how well the various criteria are placing the cut-points. The Kullback-Leibler distance gives an indirect measure since it is affected by the cut-point positions. We intend to perform a more explicit investigation into the placement of cut-points.

As well as the Gaussian distribution, MML formulas have been derived for discrete multi-state [17], Poisson, von Mises circular, and spherical Fisher distributions [21,6]. Some of these distributions and other models will be incorporated in the future.

We thank Dean McKenzie for introducing us to the W. D. Fisher (1958) paper and Rohan Baxter and Jonathan Oliver for providing access to the C code used in Baxter, Oliver and Wallace [10].

References

1. H. Akaike. Information theory and an extension of the maximum likelihood principle. In B. N. Petrov and F. Csaki, editors, *Proceeding 2nd International Symposium on Information Theory*, pages 267–281. Akademia Kiado, Budapest, 1973.
2. R. A. Baxter and J. J. Oliver. MDL and MML: Similarities and differences. Technical report TR 207, Dept. of Computer Science, Monash University, Clayton, Victoria 3168, Australia, 1994.

3. R. A. Baxter and J. J. Oliver. The kindest cut: minimum message length segmentation. In S. Arikawa and A. K. Sharma, editors, *Proc. 7th Int. Workshop on Algorithmic Learning Theory*, volume 1160 of *LCNS*, pages 83–90. Springer-Verlag Berlin, 1996.

4. J.H. Conway and N.J.A Sloane. *Sphere Packings, Lattices and Groups*. Springer-Verlag, London, 1988.

5. D. L. Dowe, R. A. Baxter, J. J. Oliver, and C. S. Wallace. Point estimation using the Kullback-Leibler loss function and MML. In *Pacific-Asia Conference on Knowledge Discovery and Data Mining (PAKDD98)*, volume 1394 of *LNAI*, pages 87–95, 1998.

6. D. L. Dowe, J. J. Oliver, and C. S. Wallace. MML estimation of the parameters of the spherical Fisher distribution. In S. Arikawa and A. K. Sharma, editors, *Proc. 7th Int. Workshop on Algorithmic Learning Theory*, volume 1160 of *LCNS*, pages 213–227. Springer-Verlag Berlin, 1996.

7. T. Edgoose and L. Allison. MML markov classification of sequential data. *Statistics and Computing*, 9:269–278, 1999.

8. W. D. Fisher. On grouping for maximum homogeneity. *Jrnl. Am. Stat. Soc.*, 53:789–798, 1958.

9. R. E. Kass and A. E. Raftery. Bayes factors. *Journal of the American Statistical Association*, 90(430):773–795, 1995.

10. J. J. Oliver, R. A. Baxter, and C. S. Wallace. Minimum message length segmentation. In X. Wu, R. Kotagiri, and K. Korb, editors, *Research and Development in Knowledge Discovery and Data Mining (PAKDD-98)*, pages 83–90. Springer, 1998.

11. J. J. Oliver and C. S. Forbes. Bayesian approaches to segmenting a simple time series. Technical Report 97/336, Dept. Computer Science, Monash University, Australia 3168, December 1997.

12. J. J. Rissanen. Modeling by shortest data description. *Automatica*, 14:465–471, 1978.

13. J. J. Rissanen. A universal prior for integers and estimation by minimum description length. *Annals of Statistics*, 11(2):416–431, 1983.

14. J. J. Rissanen. Hypothesis selection and testing by the MDL principle. *Computer Jrnl.*, 42(4):260–269, 1999.

15. G. Schwarz. Estimating the dimension of a model. *The Annals of Statistics*, 6:461–464, 1978.

16. S. Sclove. Time-series segmentation: A model and a method. *Information Sciences*, 29:7–25, 1983.

17. M. Viswanathan, C.S. Wallace, D.L. Dowe, and K. Korb. Finding cutpoints in noisy binary sequences - a revised empirical evaluation. In *12th Australian Joint Conference on Artificial Intelligence*, 1999. A sequel has been submitted to Machine Learning Journal.

18. C. S. Wallace and D. M. Boulton. An information measure for classification. *Computer Jrnl.*, 11(2):185–194, August 1968.

19. C. S. Wallace and D. L. Dowe. Minimum message length and Kolmogorov complexity. *Computer Jrnl.*, 42(4):270–283, 1999.

20. C. S. Wallace and D. L. Dowe. Rejoinder. *Computer Jrnl.*, 42(4):345–357, 1999.

21. C. S. Wallace and D. L. Dowe. MML clustering of multi-state, Poisson, von Mises circular and Gaussian distributions. *Statistics and Computing*, 10:73–83, 2000.

22. C. S. Wallace and P. R. Freeman. Estimation and inference by compact encoding (with discussion). *Journal of the Royal Statistical Society series B*, 49:240–265, 1987.

Learning From Positive and Unlabeled Examples[*]

Fabien Letouzey, François Denis, and Rémi Gilleron
{letouzey,denis,gilleron}@lifl.fr

Équipe Grappa,
LIFL, UPRESA 8022 CNRS, Université de Lille 1
and Université Charles de Gaulle, Lille 3,
FRANCE

Abstract. In many machine learning settings, examples of one class (called positive class) are easily available. Also, unlabeled data are abundant. We investigate in this paper the design of learning algorithms from positive and unlabeled data only. Many machine learning and data mining algorithms use examples for estimate of probabilities. Therefore, we design an algorithm which is based on positive statistical queries (estimates for probabilities over the set of positive instances) and instance statistical queries (estimates for probabilities over the instance space). Our algorithm guesses the weight of the target concept (the ratio of positive instances in the instance space) with the help of a hypothesis testing algorithm. It is proved that any class learnable in the Statistical Query model [Kea93] such that a lower bound on the weight of any target concept f can be estimated in polynomial time is learnable from positive statistical queries and instance statistical queries only. Then, we design a decision tree induction algorithm POSC4.5, based on C4.5 [Qui93], using only positive and unlabeled examples. We also give experimental results for this algorithm.

1 Introduction

In *Supervised Learning*, the learner relies on labeled training examples. Thus, for binary problems, positive examples and negative examples are mandatory for machine learning and data mining algorithms such as decision tree induction or neural networks. But, for many learning tasks, labeled examples are rare while numerous unlabeled examples are easily available. Under specific hypotheses, the problem of learning with the help of unlabeled data given a small set of labeled examples was studied by Blum and Mitchell [BM98]. Supposing two views of examples that are redundant but not correlated, they proved that unlabeled examples can boost accuracy. Learning situations for which the assumption is satisfied are described in [Mit99].

---

[*] This research was partially supported by "Motricité et Cognition : Contrat par objectifs région Nord/Pas-de-Calais"

H. Arimura, S. Jain and A. Sharma (Eds.): ALT 2000, LNAI 1968, pp. 71-84, 2000.
© Springer-Verlag Berlin Heidelberg 2000

Labeled examples are expensive to obtain because they require human effort. A "human expert" classifies each example in the teaching set as positive or negative. We argue that, in many machine learning settings, examples of one of the two classes are abundant and cheap. From now on, we call this class the positive class. A first example is web-page classification. Suppose we want a program that classifies web sites as "interesting" for a web user. Positive examples are freely available: it is the set of web pages corresponding to web sites in his bookmarks. Moreover unlabeled web pages are abundant. Other examples are:

- diagnosis of diseases: positive data are patients who have the disease, unlabeled data are all patients;
- marketing: positive data are clients who buy the product, unlabeled data are all clients in the database.

Our hypothesis is true for all settings where it is expensive or difficult to label a set of instances in order to obtain a learning sample. Therefore, we address the problem of learning with positive data and unlabeled data only. In a previous paper [DDGL99], we have given evidence – with both theoretical and empirical arguments – that positive examples and unlabeled examples can boost accuracy of many machine learning algorithms. It was noted that learning with positive and unlabeled data is possible as soon as the weight of the target concept (i.e. the ratio of positive examples) is known by the learner. An estimate of the weight can be obtained from a small set of labeled examples. Here with a hypothesis testing algorithm, we present learning algorithms which only use positive and unlabeled data.

The theoretical framework is presented in Section 2. Our learning algorithm is defined and proved in Section 3. It is applied to tree induction in Section 4

2   Learning Models of Learning from Positive and Unlabeled Examples

2.1   Learning models from labeled examples

First, let us recall the *probably approximately correct model* (PAC model for short) defined by Valiant [Val84]. In the PAC model, an adversary chooses a hidden $\{0,1\}$-valued function from a given concept class and a distribution over the instance space. The goal of the learner is to output in polynomial time, with high probability, a hypothesis with the following property: the probability is small that the hypothesis disagrees with the target function on an example randomly chosen according to the distribution. The learner gets information about the target function and the hidden distribution from an example oracle. The PAC model is the basic model in Computational Learning Theory [KV94]. Many variants of the model have been considered (see the fundamental paper of Haussler, Kearns, Littlestone and Warmuth [HKLW91]). For instance, in the *two-button model*, there are separate distributions and example oracles for positive and negative examples of a concept. It was proved equivalent to the PAC model.

One criticism of the PAC model is that it is a noise free model. There-fore extensions, in which the label provided with each random example may be corrupted with random noise, were studied. The *classification noise model* CN model for short) was first defined by Angluin and Laird [AL88]. In order to define and study learning algorithms which are robust to classification noise, Kearns [Kea93] has defined the *statistical query model* (SQ model for short). In this model, the example oracle is replaced by a weaker oracle which provides estimates for probabilities over the sample space. It is clear that given access to the example oracle, it is easy to simulate the statistics oracle by drawing a sufficiently large set of labeled examples, i.e. any class learnable from statistical queries is PAC learnable. There is a general scheme which transforms any SQ learning algorithm into a PAC learning algorithm. It is also proved in [Kea93] that the class of parity functions is learnable in the PAC model but cannot be learned from statistical queries. Also any class learnable from statistical queries is learnable with classification noise. The SQ model allows to define noise-tolerant learning algorithms because there is a general method which transforms any SQ learning algorithm into a CN learning algorithm. Many machine learning algo-rithms only use examples in order to estimate probabilities, thus they may be viewed as SQ learning algorithms. This is the case for induction tree algorithms such as C4.5 [Qui93] and CART [BFOS84].

Also interesting for our purpose is a variant of the CN model, namely the *constant-partition classification noise model* (CPCN model for short) which was defined by Decatur [Dec97]. In this model, the labeled example space is parti-tioned into a constant number of regions, each of which may have a different noise rate. An interesting example is the case where the rate of false positive ex-amples differs from the rate of false negative examples. Following the results of Kearns, it was proved by Decatur that any class learnable from statistical queries is also learnable with constant-partition classification noise. The proof uses the *hypothesis testing property*: a hypothesis with small error can be selected from a set of hypotheses by selecting the one with the fewest errors on a set of CPCN corrupted examples.

If we confuse in the notations the name of the model and the set of learnable classes, we can write the following inclusions:

$$SQ \subseteq CPCN \subseteq CN \subseteq PAC \tag{1}$$

$$SQ \subset PAC \tag{2}$$

To our knowledge, the equivalences between the models CN and SQ or be-tween the models CN and PAC remain open despite recent insights [BKW00] and [Jac00].

2.2 Learning models from positive and unlabeled examples

The *learning model from positive examples* (POSEX for short) was defined by Denis [Den98]. The model is similar to the PAC model with the following dif-ference: the learner gets information about the target function and the hidden distribution from two oracles, namely a *positive example oracle* and an *instance oracle*. At each request by the learner, the instance oracle draws an element of the instance space X, i.e. an unlabeled example, according to the hidden distribution D. At each request by the learner, the positive example oracle draws a positive example according to the hidden distribution D_f where f is the target concept and D_f is defined by:

$$D_f(x) = \begin{cases} D(x)/D(f) & \text{if } x \in f, \\ 0 & \text{otherwise.} \end{cases} \tag{3}$$

It was shown in [Den98] that any class learnable in the CPCN model is learnable in the POSEX model. The hint of the proof is to draw examples from the positive oracle with probability 2/3 with a positive label and examples from the instance oracle with probability 1/3 with a negative label, and then to use a CPCN algorithm. We will use such a scheme in our hypothesis testing algorithm in the next section.

The *learning model from positive queries* (POSQ for short) was also defined in [Den98]. In the SQ model, the oracle provides estimates for probabilities according to statistical queries. We slightly modify definitions of queries, but it is easy to show that it is equivalent to considering a statistical oracle which provides, within a given tolerance τ, estimates for probabilities $D(f \cap A)$ and $D(\overline{f} \cap A)$ where f is the target concept, $\overline{f}$ its complement and A any subset – for which membership is decidable in polynomial time – of the instance space. In the POSQ model, there are a positive statistical oracle which provides estimates for probabilities $D_f(A)$ and an instance statistical oracle which provides estimates for probabilities $D(A)$ within a given tolerance. It was shown that any class learnable in the SQ model such that the weight $D(f)$ of any target concept f can be estimated in polynomial time with these two oracles is learnable in the POSQ model. It was also shown that the class of k-DNF and the class of k-DL are learnable in the POSQ model. To summarize, the following inclusions hold:

$$POSQ \subseteq SQ \subseteq CPCN \subseteq POSEX \subseteq PAC \tag{4}$$

$$CPCN \subseteq CN \subseteq PAC \tag{5}$$

$$SQ \subset POSEX \subseteq PAC \tag{6}$$

The inequality between SQ and POSEX is because the class of parity functions is in POSEX but not in SQ. The equivalences between POSQ and SQ and between POSEX and PAC remain open. We conjectured that the class of complementary sets of lattices is PAC learnable but not POSEX learnable.

3   Learning Algorithm from Positive and Unlabeled Queries

We address in the present paper, the design of machine learning algorithms with positive and unlabeled examples that can be derived, using a general scheme, from learning algorithms in the SQ model. We transform our algorithm into a decision tree induction algorithm in the next section.

3.1   Introduction of the algorithm

In a previous paper [DDGL99], we considered the problem of learning with the help of positive and unlabeled data, given either a small number of labeled examples, or an estimate of the weight of the target concept. We presented experimental results showing that positive examples and unlabeled data can efficiently boost accuracy of the statistical query learning algorithm for monotone conjunctions in the presence of classification noise, and experimental results for decision tree induction.

Let us suppose that a concept class C is learnable in the SQ model by a learning algorithm L and let f be the target concept. A statistical query made by the learner provides estimates of probabilities $D(f \cap A)$ and $D(\overline{f} \cap A)$ for some subset A of the instance space chosen by the learner. Basic probabilities allow to write the following equations:

$$\begin{cases} D(f \cap A) = D(f) \times D_f(A) \\ D(\overline{f} \cap A) = D(A) - D(f \cap A) \end{cases} \tag{7}$$

$D_f(A)$ can be estimated with the positive statistical oracle, $D(A)$ can be estimated with the instance statistical oracle. Consequently, given an SQ algorithm, it is quite easy to modify it in order to obtain a POSQ algorithm provided an estimate of the weight of the target concept $D(f)$. This estimate can be obtained, either by extra information, or with the help of a small set of labeled examples.

Here, we suppose that the weight of the target concept is not known by the learner. The problem is to calculate an estimate of it. This can be done in the POSQ model for some specific classes of concept: k-DNF, k-DL (see [Den98]) but our aim is to define a generic method that transforms an SQ algorithm into a POSQ algorithm. Our solution, which is detailed in the next section, is an algorithm which guesses the weight of the target concept and then selects a hypothesis. The difficulty is that the hypothesis testing algorithm can only use information via the positive statistical oracle and the instance statistical oracle.

3.2   Learning algorithm from positive statistical queries and instance statistical queries

Let us consider a concept class C learnable in the SQ model by a learning algorithm L and let f be the target concept. We design a POSQ learning algorithm based on algorithm L. In the POSQ model, for any subset A of the instance space, we can calculate estimate $\hat{D}_f(A)$ of $D_f(A)$ with the positive statistical oracle $PSTAT$ and estimate $\hat{D}(A)$ of $D(A)$ with the instance statistical oracle $ISTAT$ within a given tolerance. Moreover, we suppose that $D(f) \in (0, 1]$ and that a minimal bound γ is known for $D(f)$, that is $0 < \gamma \leq D(f) \leq 1$. Let ϵ be the desired accuracy for the algorithm and let τ_{min} be a quantity smaller than any of the tolerances τ needed by L (but still an inverse polynomial in the learning problem parameters). The POSQ learning algorithm is given in Figure 1.

A consequence of this result is that whenever a *lower bound* on the weight of the target concept is known a priori, a class learnable in the SQ model is learnable in the POSQ model.

POSQ learning algorithm
parameters: SQ learning algorithm L; γ such that $0 < \gamma \leq D(f) \leq 1$
input: ϵ
   Construction of a hypothesis set
   Set ϵ' to $\frac{1}{2} \times \frac{\gamma}{2-\gamma} \times \epsilon$
   set N to $\lceil \frac{2}{\tau_{min}} \rceil$; set α to $\frac{1}{2N}$
   for $i = 1$ **to** N
      the current estimate of $D(f)$ is $\hat{p}_i = (2i-1)\alpha$
      run L with accuracy ϵ' using oracles $PSTAT$, $ISTAT$ within accuracy $\frac{\tau_{min}}{4}$
      and equations 7 ; output h_i
   Hypothesis testing algorithm
   for $i = 1$ **to** N
      call $PSTAT$ with input $\overline{h_i}$ within accuracy $\frac{\epsilon}{12}$
      call $ISTAT$ with input h_i within accuracy $\frac{\epsilon}{12}$
      set $\hat{e}(h_i)$ to $2\hat{D}_f(\overline{h_i}) + \hat{D}(h_i)$
output: $h = \underset{h_i}{\operatorname{argmin}}\ \hat{e}(h_i)$

Fig. 1. learning algorithm from positive and unlabeled queries

The algorithm iterates over larger guesses for $D(f)$. At each guess, the statistical query learning algorithm is called. But only positive and instance queries are available, thus when L makes a query, equations 7 are used with the current estimate $\hat{p}_i$ of $D(f)$ and the estimates returned by the oracles $PSTAT$ and $ISTAT$.

The hypothesis testing part of the algorithm selects the hypothesis which minimizes the quantity $\hat{e}(h_i)$. Minimizing $\hat{e}(h_i)$ is equivalent to minimizing an estimate of the error rate according to the following distribution: with probability $2/3$ draw a positive example and label it as positive; with probability $1/3$ draw an unlabeled example and label it as negative. This can be seen as: choosing a hypothesis h approximately consistent with positive data – when minimizing the first term of the sum – while avoiding over-generalization – when minimizing the second term.

3.3 Proof of the algorithm

Lemma 1. *There exists $i \in \{1, \ldots, N\}$ such that $error(h_i) \leq \epsilon'$.*

Proof. There exists i such that $D(f) \in [\hat{p}_i - \alpha, \hat{p}_i + \alpha]$ because, by definition of $\hat{p}_i$, $\bigcup_i [\hat{p}_i - \alpha, \hat{p}_i + \alpha] = [0, 1]$. For that value, $\hat{p}_i$ is an estimate of $D(f)$ within accuracy $\frac{\tau_{min}}{4}$ because $\alpha \leq \frac{\tau_{min}}{4}$. For all queries made by L, the oracles $PSTAT$ and $ISTAT$ are called with accuracy $\frac{\tau_{min}}{4}$ and equations 7 are used. It is easy to prove that estimates for algorithm L are made within accuracy τ_{min}. Consequently, by hypothesis on L, L outputs some h_i such that $error(h_i) \leq \epsilon'$.

Lemma 2. *Let h and h' be two hypotheses such that $error(h) \leq \frac{1}{2} \times \frac{\gamma}{2-\gamma} \times \epsilon$ and $error(h') > \epsilon$, then $e(h') - e(h) > \frac{\epsilon}{2}$, where, for any concept g, $error(g) = D(f \Delta g)$ is the (classical) error and $e(g)$ is defined by $e(g) = 2D_f(\overline{g}) + D(g)$.*

Proof. By hypothesis on h and h', $error(h) < \frac{1}{2} \times \frac{\gamma}{2-\gamma} \times error(h')$. The weight of the target concept satisfies: $0 < \gamma \leq D(f) \leq 1$; let $r(x) = \frac{x}{2-x}$, r is increasing, therefore: $error(h) < \frac{1}{2} \times \frac{D(f)}{2-D(f)} \times error(h')$. We obtain the following inequality:

$$\frac{2 - D(f)}{D(f)} \times error(h) < \frac{1}{2} \times error(h') \tag{8}$$

Now, for any concept g, $error(g) = D(f \cap \overline{g}) + D(\overline{f} \cap g)$ which leads to the following equation:

$$error(g) = D(f) \times D_f(\overline{g}) + (1 - D(f)) \times D_{\overline{f}}(g) \tag{9}$$

Using inequation 8 and equation 9, we obtain:

$$\frac{2 - D(f)}{D(f)}[D(f)D_f(\overline{h}) + (1 - D(f))D_{\overline{f}}(h)] < \frac{1}{2}[D(f)D_f(\overline{h'}) + (1 - D(f))D_{\overline{f}}(h')] \tag{10}$$

Now, with $2 - D(f) \geq D(f)$ and $1 - D(f) \leq (1 - D(f))(2 - D(f))/D(f)$ and inequation 10, we obtain:

$$(2 - D(f))D_f(\overline{h}) + (1 - D(f))D_{\overline{f}}(h) < \frac{1}{2}[(2 - D(f))D_f(\overline{h'}) + (1 - D(f))D_{\overline{f}}(h')] \tag{11}$$

Also, let us denote $2D_f(\overline{g}) + D(g)$ by $e(g)$, it is easy to prove that

$$e(g) = (2 - D(f)) \times D_f(\overline{g}) + (1 - D(f)) \times D_{\overline{f}}(g) + D(f) \tag{12}$$

Inequation 11, and equation 12 allow to prove the following inequality:

$$e(h) - D(f) < \frac{1}{2} \times (e(h') - D(f)) \tag{13}$$

As a consequence of this last inequality and because of the inequality $e(g) \geq error(g) + D(f)$, we get: $e(h') - e(h) > \frac{1}{2} \times (e(h') - D(f)) \geq \frac{1}{2} \times error(h') > \frac{1}{2}\epsilon$.

Proposition 1. *The output hypothesis satisfies $error(h) \leq \epsilon$ and the running time is polynomial in $1/\epsilon$ and $1/\gamma$.*

Proof. all estimates $\hat{e}(h_i)$ of $e(h_i)$ are done within accuracy $\frac{\epsilon}{4}$ and lemmas 1 and 2 ensure that the output hypothesis satisfies $error(h) \leq \epsilon$.

The number of hypotheses is N which is linear in $1/\tau_{min}$. We have supposed for sake of clarity in the definition of the algorithm that τ_{min} was fixed and known to the learner. Actually, τ_{min} is polynomial in the input accuracy of L, therefore τ_{min} is polynomial in ϵ' that is also polynomial in ϵ and γ. It is easy to verify that all queries are made within a tolerance polynomial in ϵ and γ.

3.4   Comments on the statistical queries models

Whether or not any SQ algorithm can be transformed into a POSQ algorithm remains an open question. It has been proved in [Den98] that this transformation is possible when the weight of the target concept can be estimated from the oracles PSTAT and ISTAT in polynomial time. We improve this result showing that it is possible when a lower bound on the weight of the target concept is given to the learner. But, the running time of the algorithm is polynomial in the inverse of this lower bound.

Let us consider a concept class $\mathcal{C}$ which is SQ learnable. $\mathcal{C}$ satisfies the property *Lowerbound* if there exists an algorithm W which, for any f in $\mathcal{C}$, for any distribution D on X, W with input ϵ, given access to PSTAT, ISTAT, then W outputs *yes* if $D(f) < \frac{\epsilon}{2}$, *no* if $D(f) > \epsilon$, *?* if $\frac{\epsilon}{2} \leq D(f) \leq \epsilon$ in time polynomial in $1/\epsilon$. Then we have the following result:

Proposition 2. *Any SQ learnable class which satisfies Lowerbound is POSQ learnable.*

Proof. Consider the following algorithm:

input: ϵ
   if W outputs yes
      output function 0
   else
      run the POSQ learning algorithm with parameter $\gamma = \frac{\epsilon}{2}$ and input ϵ

It is easy to prove that this algorithm is a learning algorithm from positive and instance statistical queries using Proposition 1 and definition of W.

Proving the property *Lowerbound* for every SQ learnable concept class would imply the equality between SQ and POSQ.

4   Decision Tree Learning with only Positive and Unlabeled Examples

4.1   C4.5POSUNL

In a previous paper [DDGL99], we presented an algorithm called C4.5POSUNL. It is a decision tree induction algorithm based on C4.5 with the following differences:

- only binary classification problems are considered. The classes are denoted by 0 and 1; an example is said to be positive if its label is 1.
- C4.5POSUNL takes as input:
  1. a (small) set of labeled examples LAB
     or
     an estimate $\hat{D}(f)$ of the weight of the target concept $D(f)$;

  2. a set of positive examples POS;
  3. a set of unlabeled examples UNL.
- the splitting criterion used by C4.5 is based on the information gain (or the gain ratio), itself based on the entropy. The gain is calculated from ratio of examples satisfying some property, thus it is calculated from statistical queries. The calculation of the gain in C4.5POSUNL is derived from classical formulas using equations 7. Let POS^n (respectively UNL^n) be the set of positive (respectively unlabeled) examples associated with the current node n, and let $\hat{D}(f)$ be an estimate of the weight of the target concept $D(f)$, we obtain the following equations:

$$\begin{cases} p_1 = \frac{|POS^n|}{|POS|} \times \frac{|UNL|}{|UNL^n|} \times \hat{D}(f) \\ p_0 = 1 - p_1 \\ Entropy(n) = -p_1 \log_2 p_1 - p_0 \log_2 p_0 \\ Gain(n,t) = Entropy(n) - \sum_{v \in Values(t)} \frac{|UNL^n_v|}{|UNL^n|} Entropy(nv) \end{cases} \tag{14}$$

where the cardinality of set A is denoted by $|A|$, $Values(t)$ is the set of every possible value for the attribute test t, UNL^n_v is the set of examples in UNL^n for which t has value v, and nv is the node below n corresponding to the value v for the attribute test t.

4.2 POSC4.5: An induction tree algorithm from positive and unlabeled examples only

As for C4.5POSUNL, we only consider binary classification problems and we suppose that one target class has been specified as positive. The learning algorithm is described in Figure 2. The algorithm takes as input a set POS of examples of the target class and a set UNL of unlabeled examples. The algorithm splits the set POS (respectively UNL) into two sets POS_L and POS_T (respectively UNL_L and UNL_T) using the usual values 2/3 and 1/3. The POSQ learning algorithm is called with the following modifications:

- the estimate $\hat{D}(f)$ of $D(f)$ takes the successive values 0.1, ... , 0.9;
- the SQ-like algorithm is C4.5POSUNL with inputs the current estimate of $D(f)$, the learning sets POS_L and UNL_L;
- the best value of $\hat{D}(f)$ is chosen according to the minimal estimate $\hat{e}(h)$ of $e(h)$ where the estimate is done with the test sets POS_T and UNL_T;
- run C4.5POSUNL with inputs the best value of $\hat{D}(f)$ and the sets POS and UNL.

4.3 Experiments with Decision Lists

A *decision list* over $x_1, \ldots, x_n$ is an ordered sequence $L = (m_1, b_1), \ldots, (m_p, b_p)$ of terms, in which each m_j is a monomial over $x_1, \ldots, x_n$, and each $b_j \in \{0,1\}$. The last monomial is always $m_p = 1$. For any input $a \in \{0,1\}^n$, the value $L(a)$

POSC4.5

input: POS and UNL

Split POS and UNL with ratios 2/3, 1/3 into POS_L, POS_T, UNL_L and UNL_T

for $i = 1$ **to** 9

the current estimate of $D(f)$ is $\frac{i}{10}$

run $C4.5POSUNL$ with input $\frac{i}{10}$, POS_L and UNL_L and output h_i

set $\hat{e}(h_i)$ to $2\frac{|\{x \in POS_T | h_i(x)=0\}|}{|POS_T|} + \frac{|\{x \in UNL_T | h_i(x)=1\}|}{|UNL_T|}$

$j = \underset{i}{\operatorname{argmin}}\ \hat{e}(h_i)$

run $C4.5POSUNL$ with input $\frac{j}{10}$, POS and UNL and **output** h

---

Fig. 2. learning algorithm from positive and unlabeled queries

is defined as b_j, where j is the smallest index satisfying $m_j(a) = 1$. We only consider 1-decision list where each monomial is a variable x_i or its negation $\overline{x_i}$. We set p to 11 and n to 20. The random choice of target f, weight $D(f)$ and distribution D are done as follows:

- a target decision list f is chosen randomly;
- For any $a \in \{0,1\}^n$, a weight w_a is chosen randomly in $[0,1)$;
- a normalization procedure is applied to the two sets of weights $\{w_a \mid f(a) = 1\}$ and $\{w_a \mid f(a) = 0\}$. Thus we get two distributions D_1 on f and D_2 on $\overline{f}$;
- a weight p for the target concept is chosen (depending on the experiment);
- D is defined by: for every a, $D(a) = pD_1(a) + (1 - p)D_2(a)$. Note that $D(f) = p$.

We compare three algorithms:

- C4.5POSUNL(LAB) which takes as input a set LAB of labeled examples – in order to compute an estimate of $D(f)$ – a set POS of positive examples and a set UNL of unlabeled examples;
- C4.5POSUNL($D(f)$) which takes as input the exact value of $D(f)$, a set POS of positive examples and a set UNL of unlabeled examples;
- POSC4.5 which takes as input a set POS of positive examples and a set UNL of unlabeled examples.

In the plots, the error rates and target weights are expressed in percent.

Experiment 1. We set $D(f)$ to 0.5, the size of POS is equal to the size of UNL and ranges from 50 to 1000 by step 50, the size of LAB is fixed to 25. For a given size of POS, we iterate 100 times the experiment EXP: a target f is drawn, a distribution D is chosen, sets LAB, POS and UNL are drawn randomly, we run the three algorithms and calculate the error rate of the output hypothesis on a large test set of 10000 examples. We average the error rates over the 100 experiments. The results are given in Figure 3. The learning algorithm POSC4.5 performs as well as C4.5POSUNL($D(f)$) where the exact value of $D(f)$ is given to the learner.

Experiments 2 and 3. The only difference is the size of POS: 1000 for experiment 2 and 100 for experiment 3. For both experiments, the size of UNL is fixed to 1000, $D(f)$ ranges from 0 to 1 by step 0.05, the size of LAB is fixed to 25. For a given value of $D(f)$, we average the error rates over the 100 experiments EXP. The results are given in Figs. 4 and 5. The learning algorithm POSC4.5 performs as well as C4.5POSUNL($D(f)$) only for values of $D(f)$ which are not close from 0 or 1. The problem when D(f) is close to 1 is that positive and unlabelled examples are drawn from similar distributions, whereas they are associated with opposit labels (1 for positive examples and 0 for unlabelled examples); this brings noise.

Experiment 4. The only difference with Experiment 2 is that classification noise with a noise rate 0.2 is applied. The results are given in Figure 6. The learning algorithm POSC4.5 performs as well as C4.5POSUNL($D(f)$) for values for $D(f)$ greater than 0.45. We comment this problem in the conclusion of the paper.

The reason why POSC4.5 can sometimes outperform C4.5POSUNL($D(f)$) is that it can select an inexact estimate $\widehat{D}(f)$ of $D(f)$ during the hypothesis selection phase because it brings a lower error rate due to biases in C4.5 internal heuristics (with this value C4.5 will make different choices).

4.4   Experiments with UCI problems

We consider two data sets from the *UCI Machine Learning Database* [MM98]: kr-vs-kp and adult. The majority class is chosen as positive. The size of LAB is fixed to 25. We let the number of positive and unlabeled examples vary, and compare the error rate of C4.5POSUNL(LAB), C4.5POSUNL($D(f)$) and POSC4.5. The results can be seen in Figs. 7 and 8. For kr-vs-kp, the plots are similar, the least good results are obtained by POSC4.5. This seems natural because it uses less information. Surprisingly, POSC4.5 obtains the best results for the data set adult. One reason is the number of examples. The reader should note that the results on the same data set are disappointing when the positive class is the minority class.

5   Conclusion

Experimental results show that the criterion used in the hypothesis testing algorithm is biased in favor of large values of $D(f)$. For small values of $D(f)$, the theoretical results of the present paper show that a large (but polynomial) number of examples is required.

Using a different weighting in the selection criterion leads to a bias in favor of different values of $D(f)$. So we search for improvements of our algorithm following the next ideas:

- If a lower bound and an upper bound for $D(f)$ are given to the learner, the estimates for $D(f)$ are chosen between this bounds and a better criterion for our hypothesis testing algorithm could be selected.

– The algorithm could find an estimate of $D(f)$ by successive approximations obtained by iterations of the POSQ algorithm, using either the weight $D(h)$ of the selected hypothesis h or the target weight estimate which was used to produce that hypothesis.

References

[AL88]   D. Angluin and P. Laird. Learning from noisy examples. *Machine Learning*, 2(4):343–370, 1988.

[BFOS84]   L. Breiman, J. H. Friedman, R. A. Olshen, and C. J. Stone. Classification and regression trees. Technical report, Wadsworth International, Monterey, CA, 1984.

[BKW00]   A. Blum, A. Kalai, and H. Wasserman. Noise-tolerant learning, the parity problem, and the statistical query model. In *Proceedings of the 32nd Annual ACM Symposium on Theory of Computing*, 2000. To appear.

[BM98]   A. Blum and T. Mitchell. Combining labeled and unlabeled data with co-training. In *Proc. 11th Annu. Conf. on Comput. Learning Theory*, pages 92–100. ACM Press, New York, NY, 1998.

[DDGL99]   F. DeComité, F. Denis, R. Gilleron, and F. Letouzey. Positive and unlabeled examples help learning. In *ALT 99, 10th International Conference on Algorithmic Learning Theory*, volume 1720 of *LNAI*, pages 219–230, 1999.

[Dec97]   S. E. Decatur. Pac learning with constant-partition classification noise and applications to decision tree induction. In *Proceedings of the Fourteenth International Conference on Machine Learning*, 1997.

[Den98]   F. Denis. PAC learning from positive statistical queries. In Michael M. Richter, Carl H. Smith, Rolf Wiehagen, and Thomas Zeugmann, editors, *Proceedings of the 9th International Conference on Algorithmic Learning Theory (ALT-98)*, volume 1501 of *LNAI*, pages 112–126, Berlin, October 8–10 1998. Springer.

[HKLW91]   D. Haussler, M. Kearns, N. Littlestone, and M. K. Warmuth. Equivalence of models for polynomial learnability. *Inform. Comput.*, 95(2):129–161, December 1991.

[Jac00]   J. Jackson. On the efficiency of noise-tolerant pac algorithms derived from statistical queries. In *Proceedings of the 13th Annual Conference on Computational Learning Theory*, 2000. To appear.

[Kea93]   M. Kearns. Efficient noise-tolerant learning from statistical queries. In *Proceedings of the 25th ACM Symposium on the Theory of Computing*, pages 392–401. ACM Press, New York, NY, 1993.

[KV94]   M. J. Kearns and U. V. Vazirani. *An Introduction to Computational Learning Theory*. MIT Press, 1994.

[Mit99]   Tom Mitchell. The role of unlabeled data in supervised learning. In *Proceedings of the Sixth International Colloquium on Cognitive Science*, 1999.

[MM98]   C.J. Merz and P.M. Murphy. UCI repository of machine learning databases, 1998.

[Qui93]   J. R. Quinlan. *C4.5: Programs for Machine Learning*. Morgan Kaufmann, San Mateo, CA, 1993.

[Val84]   L.G. Valiant. A theory of the learnable. *Commun. ACM*, 27(11):1134–1142, November 1984.

A   Experimental results

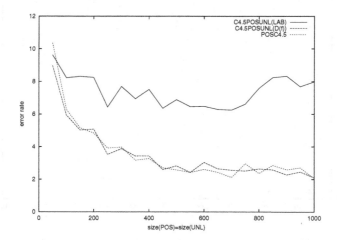

Fig. 3. $size(LAB) = 25$; $size(POS) = size(UNL)$ ranges from 50 to 1000 by step 50; $D(f) = 0.5$

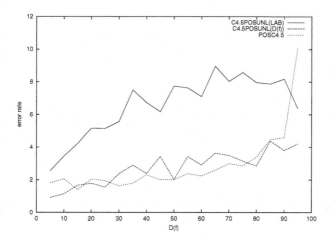

Fig. 4. $size(LAB) = 25$; $size(POS) = size(UNL) = 1000$; $D(f)$ ranges from 0 to 1 by step 0.05

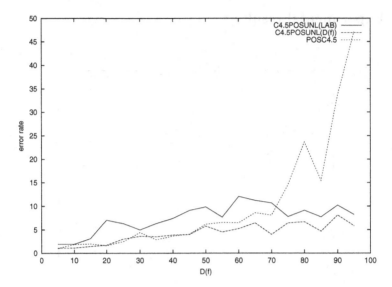

Fig. 5. $size(LAB) = 25$; $size(POS) = 100$; $size(UNL) = 1000$; $D(f)$ ranges from 0 to 1 by step 0.05

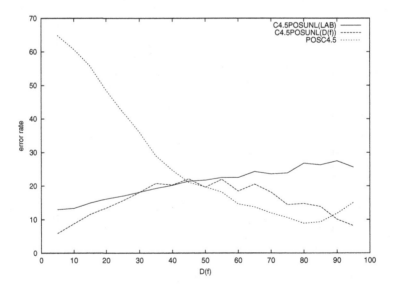

Fig. 6. $size(LAB) = 25$; $size(POS) = size(UNL) = 1000$; $D(f)$ ranges from 0 to 1 by step 0.05; a noise rate of 0.2 is applied

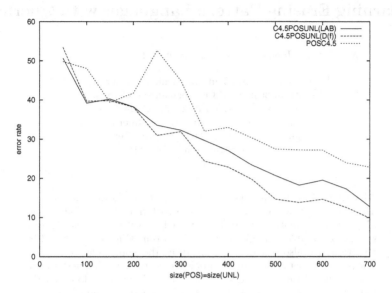

Fig. 7. `kr-vs-kp` data set; $size(LAB) = 25$; $size(POS) = size(UNL)$ ranges from 50 to 700 by step 50; $D(f) \approx 0.5$

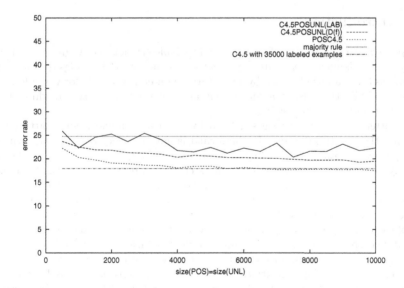

Fig. 8. `adult` data set; $size(LAB) = 25$; $size(POS) = size(UNL)$ ranges from 500 to 10000 by step 500; $D(f) \approx 0.75$

Learning Erasing Pattern Languages with Queries

Jochen Nessel[1] and Steffen Lange[2]

[1] Universität Kaiserslautern, Fachbereich Informatik
Postfach 3049, 67653 Kaiserslautern, Germany
nessel@informatik.uni-kl.de
[2] Universität Leipzig, Institut für Informatik
Augustusplatz 10–11, 04109 Leipzig, Germany
slange@informatik.uni-leipzig.de

Abstract. A pattern is a finite string of constant and variable symbols. The non-erasing language generated by a pattern is the set of all strings of constant symbols that can be obtained by substituting non-empty strings for variables. In order to build the erasing language generated by a pattern, it is also admissible to substitute the empty string.

The present paper deals with the problem of learning erasing pattern languages within Angluin's model of learning with queries. Moreover, the learnability of erasing pattern languages with queries is studied when additional information is available. The results obtained are compared with previously known results concerning the case that non-erasing pattern languages have to be learned.

1 Introduction

A pattern is a finite string of constant and variable symbols (cf. Angluin [1]). The non-erasing language generated by a pattern is the set of all strings of constant symbols that can be obtained by substituting non-empty strings for variables. In order to build the erasing language generated by a pattern, it is also admissible to substitute the empty string.

Patterns and the languages defined by them have found a lot of attention within the last two decades. In the formal language theory community, formal properties of both erasing and non-erasing pattern languages have carefully been analyzed (cf., e.g., Salomaa [15,16], Jiang *et al.* [7]). In contrast, in the learning theory community, mainly the learnability of non-erasing pattern languages has been studied (cf., e.g., Angluin [1], Marron and Ko [10], Angluin [3], Kearns and Pitt [8], Lange and Wiehagen [9]). The learning scenarios studied include Gold's [5] model of learning in the limit, Valiant's [20] model of probably approximately correct learning, and Angluin's [3] model of learning with queries. Moreover, interesting applications of pattern inference algorithms have been outlined. For example, learning algorithms for non-erasing pattern languages have been applied in an intelligent text processing system (cf. Nix [14]) and have been used to solve problems in molecular biology (cf., e.g., Shinohara and Arikawa [18]).

However, there is not so much known concerning the learnability of erasing pattern languages (cf. Shinohara [17], Mitchell [13]). A lot of interesting and

H. Arimura, S. Jain and A. Sharma (Eds.): ALT 2000, LNAI 1968, pp. 86–100, 2000.

quite easy to formulate problems are still open. The most challenging problem is the question of whether or not the class of all erasing pattern languages is Gold-style learnable from only positive data. In contrast, the affirmative answer to the analogue question for non-erasing pattern languages has already been given in the pioneering paper Angluin [1]. Thus, one may expect that things become generally more complicated when dealing with erasing pattern languages.

In the present paper, we study the learnability of erasing pattern languages in Angluin's [3] model of learning with queries. In contrast to Gold's [5] model of learning in the limit, Angluin's [3] model deals with 'one-shot' learning. Here, a learning algorithm (henceforth called query learner) receives information about a target language by asking queries which will truthfully be answered by an *oracle*. After asking at most finitely many queries, the learner is required to make up its mind and to output its one and only hypothesis. If this hypothesis correctly describes the target language, learning took place.

Furthermore, we address the problem of learning erasing pattern languages with additional information using queries, a refinement of Angluin's [3] model which has its origins in Marron [11]. In this setting, the query learner initially receives a string that belongs to the target language before starting the process of asking queries. As it turns out, this extra information may allow for a considerable speeding up of learning.

Although, there is a rich reservoir on results concerning the problem of learning non-erasing pattern languages with queries (cf. e.g., Angluin [3], Lange and Wiehagen [9], Erlebach *et al.* [4], Matsumoto and Shinohara [12]), to our knowledge, there is only one paper that addresses the erasing case. In Erlebach *et al.* [4], the authors pointed out that erasing one-variable pattern languages can be learned using polynomially many supersets queries. In the present paper, we mainly deal with the problem to which extent, if at all, the known results for the non-erasing case have their analogue when erasing pattern languages have to be learned. We hope that this and similar studies help to widen our understanding of the peculiarities of learning erasing pattern languages, in general, which, in the long term, may produce insights being of relevance to successfully attack the longstanding problem of whether or not positive examples suffice to learn erasing pattern languages in Gold's [5] model.

In former studies (cf., e.g., Angluin [3], Marron [11]), mainly the following types of queries have been considered:

Membership queries. The input is a string w and the answer is 'yes' and 'no', respectively, depending on whether w belongs to the target language L.

Equivalence queries. The input is a language L'. If $L = L'$, the answer is 'yes'. Otherwise, together with the answer 'no' a counterexample from the symmetrical difference of L and L' is supplied.

Subset queries. The input is a language L'. If $L' \subseteq L$, the answer is 'yes'. Otherwise, together with the answer 'no' a counterexample from $L' \setminus L$ is supplied.

Superset queries. The input is a language L'. If $L \subseteq L'$, the answer is 'yes'. Otherwise, together with the answer 'no' a counterexample from $L \setminus L'$ is supplied.

For equivalence, subset, and superset queries, also a *restricted form* has been studied. In the corresponding case, the answer "no" is no longer supplemented by a counterexample.

The following table summarizes the results obtained and compares them to the corresponding results concerning the learnability of non-erasing pattern languages with queries. The types of queries are identified according to the following scheme: (1) membership queries, (2) equivalence queries, (3) subset queries, and (4) restricted superset queries. (5) indicates the fact that additional information is available. The items in the table have to be interpreted as follows. The item 'No' indicates that queries of the specified type are insufficient to exactly learn the corresponding language class. The item 'YES' indicates that the corresponding class is learnable using queries of this type. Furthermore, if the add-on 'POLY' appears, it is known that polynomially many queries will do, while, otherwise, it has been shown that polynomially many queries do not suffice. The table items that are superscripted with a [†] refer to results from Angluin [3], while those superscripted with a [‡] refer to recent results from Matsumoto and Shinohara [12].

Type of queries	Arbitrary patterns		Regular patterns	
	non-erasing	erasing	non-erasing	erasing
(1)	YES[†]	No	YES[†]	YES
(4)	YES+POLY[†]	No	YES+POLY[†]	YES+POLY
(1) + (5)	YES[†]	No	YES+POLY[‡]	YES+POLY
(1) + (2) + (3)	YES[†]	YES	YES[†]	YES
(1) + (2) + (3) + (5)	YES	YES	YES+POLY[‡]	YES+POLY

2   Preliminaries

2.1   Patterns and their languages

In the following, knowledge of standard mathematical and recursion theoretic notations and concepts is assumed (cf., e.g., Rogers [19]). Furthermore we assume familiarity with basic language theoretic concepts (cf., e.g., Hopcroft and Ullman [6]). Patterns and pattern languages have been formally introduced in Angluin [1].

We assume a finite alphabet Σ such that $|\Sigma| \geq 2$ and a countable, infinite set of variables $\mathcal{X} = \{x, y, z, x_1, y_1, z_1, \ldots\}$. The elements from Σ are called *constants*. A *word* is any string – possibly empty – formed by elements from Σ. The empty string is denoted by ε.

A *pattern* is any non-empty string over $\Sigma \cup \mathcal{X}$. The set of all patterns is denoted by π. Of course π depends on Σ, but it will always be clear from the context, which alphabet is being used. Let α, β and the like range over pattern. Two patterns α and β are *equal*, written $\alpha = \beta$, if they are the same up to renaming of variables. For instance, $xy = yz$, whereas $xyx \neq xyy$.

Moreover, let α be a pattern that contains k distinctive variables. Then α is in normal form, if the variables occurring in α are precisely $x_1, \ldots, x_k$ and for every j with $1 \leq j < k$, the leftmost occurrence of x_j in α is left to the leftmost occurrence of x_{j+1}.

A pattern α is *homeomorphically embedded* in pattern β, if α can be obtained by deleting symbols from β. Obviously, it is decidable whether or not α is homeomorphically embedded in β.

By $vars(\alpha)$ we denote the set of variables appearing in pattern α. Let $|\alpha|$ stand for the number of symbols in α. By $|\alpha|_x$ we denote how many times the symbol x appears in α.

Let α be a pattern and let $|\alpha| = m$. Then, for all $j \in \mathbb{N}$ with $1 \leq j \leq m$, $\alpha[j]$ denotes the symbol at position j in pattern α. Moreover, for all $j, z \in \mathbb{N}$ with $1 \leq j \leq z \leq m$, we let $\alpha[j : z]$ denote the subpattern of α which starts at position j and ends at position z, i.e., $\alpha[j : z] = \alpha[j] \cdots \alpha[z]$.

If, for all $x \in vars(\alpha)$, $|\alpha|_x = 1$, the pattern α is said to be a *regular* pattern (i.e., every variable in α appears at most once). The set of all regular patterns is denoted by π_r. If $vars(\alpha) = \{x\}$ for some $x \in \mathcal{X}$, then α is said to be a *one-variable* pattern.

A *substitution* is a mapping from $\mathcal{X}$ to Σ^*. For a pattern α, $\alpha\sigma$ is the word that results from replacing all variables in α by their image under σ. For $x \in \mathcal{X}$, $w \in \Sigma^*$ and $\alpha \in \pi$, let $\alpha[x \leftarrow w]$ denote the result of replacing x by w in α.

For a pattern α, let $seqterm(\alpha)$ be the sequence of all non-variable parts of α. For example, $seqterm(xabybbzba) = (ab, bb, ba)$.

For a pattern α, the *erasing pattern language* $L_e(\alpha)$ generated by α is the set of all strings in Σ^* that one obtains by substituting strings from Σ^* for variables in α. We let α_ε denote the word that one obtains if one substitutes the empty string for all variables in α. Obviously, α_ε is the one and only shortest string in the language $L_\varepsilon(\alpha)$.

A pattern is called *proper*, if it contains at least one variable. It is easy to see that $L_\varepsilon(\alpha)$ is infinite if and only if α is proper. Therefore, the main objective of our studies are proper patterns.

For $\alpha, \beta \in \pi$, by $L_\varepsilon(\alpha)L_\varepsilon(\beta)$ we denote the set of all words uv with $u \in L_\varepsilon(\alpha)$ and $v \in L_\varepsilon(\beta)$. This notation extends to more than two patterns in the obvious way.

For a pattern α, the *non-erasing pattern language* $L(\alpha)$ generated by α is the set of all strings in Σ^+ that one obtains by substituting strings from Σ^+ for variables in α. The only difference between erasing and non-erasing languages is the additional option to substitute variables by the empty string. But this seemingly small detail makes a big difference. In the erasing case, things become generally much harder (cf., e.g., Salomaa [15,16], Jiang *et al.* [7]).

Finally, two patterns α and β are said to be *equivalent*, written $\alpha \equiv \beta$, provided that $L_\varepsilon(\alpha) = L_\varepsilon(\beta)$.

2.2   Models of learning with queries

The learning model studied in the following is called *learning with queries*. Angluin [3] is the first comprehensive study of this learning model. In this model, the learner has access to an oracle that truthfully answers queries of a specified kind. A *query learner* M is an algorithmic device that, depending on the reply on the queries previously made, either computes a new query or a hypothesis and halts. M *learns a target language L using a certain type of queries* provided that it eventually halts and that its one and only hypothesis correctly describes L. Furthermore, M *learns a target language class C using a certain type of queries*, if it learns every $L \in C$ using queries of the specified type. As a rule, when learning a target class C, M is not allowed to query languages not belonging to C (cf. Angluin [3]).

Moreover, we study *learning with additional information using queries*. In this setting, a query learner M receives, before starting to ask queries, one string that belongs to the target language. Then, similarly as above, M *learns a target language L with additional information using a certain type of queries* provided that, no matter which string $w \in L$ is initially presented, it eventually halts and the hypothesis which it outputs correctly describes L. Furthermore, M *learns a target language class C with additional information using a certain type of queries*, if it learns every $L \in C$ with additional information using queries of the specified type. As above, M is not allowed to query languages not belonging to the target class.

The *complexity* of a query learner is measured by the total number of queries to be asked in the worst-case. The relevant parameters are the length of the minimal description for the target language and, in case learning with additional information is studied, the length of the minimal description for the target language and the length of the initial example presented.

Since we deal with the learnability of (non-)erasing pattern languages, it seems to be appropriate to require that a query learner M uses just patterns to formulate its queries. It will become clear from the context whether a query α refers to the non-erasing language $L(\alpha)$ or the erasing language $L_\varepsilon(\alpha)$. Moreover, we generally assume that a query learner outputs patterns as hypotheses.

The following lemmata provide a firm basis to derive lower bounds on the number of queries needed.

Lemma 1. (Angluin [3]) *Assume that the target language class C contains at least n different elements $L_1, \ldots, L_n$, and there exists a language $L_\cap \notin C$ such that, for any pair of distinct indices i, j, $L_i \cap L_j = L_\cap$. Then any query learner that learns each of the languages L_i using equivalence, membership, and subset queries must make $n - 1$ queries in the worst case.*

Lemma 1 can easily be modified to handle the case that learning with additional information using queries is considered.

Lemma 2. *Assume that the target language class C contains at least n different elements $L_1, \ldots, L_n$, and there exists a non-empty language $L_\cap \notin C$ such that, for any pair of distinct indices i, j, $L_i \cap L_j = L_\cap$. Then any query learner that learns each of the languages L_i with additional information using equivalence, membership, and subset queries must make $n - 1$ queries in the worst case.*

PROOF. The initial example is simply taken from the non-empty language $L_\cap$. This example gives no real information, since it belongs to all languages L_i. The rest of the proof can literally be done as in Angluin [3]. ☒

3 Results

3.1 Learning of erasing pattern languages

Proposition 1 summarizes some first results that can easily be achieved.

Proposition 1.

(a) The class of all erasing pattern languages is not learnable using membership queries.

(b) The class of all erasing pattern languages is learnable using restricted equivalence queries.

(c) The class of all erasing pattern languages is not polynomially learnable using membership, equivalence, and subset queries.

PROOF. Assertion (b) is rather trivial, since the class of all erasing pattern languages constitutes an indexable class of recursive languages.

Assertion (c) follows directly from Lemma 1. To see this note that, for all $n \in \mathbb{N}$, there are $|\Sigma|^n$ many distinctive patterns of form xw, where $w \in \Sigma^+$ with $|w| = n$. Moreover, since, for all $w, w' \in \Sigma^+$, $|w| = |w'|$ and $w \neq w'$ imply $L_\varepsilon(xw) \cap L_\varepsilon(xw') = \emptyset$, we are immediately done.

It remains to verify Assertion (a). So, let $\alpha = ayy$. Moreover, for all $i \in \mathbb{N}$, let $\alpha_i = ax^{2i+1}yy$. Assume to the contrary that there is a query learner M that learns all erasing pattern languages using membership queries. Let $W = \{w_1, \ldots, w_n\}$ be the set of strings that M queries when learning α. Let $m = max(\{|w_i| \mid w_i \in W\})$. It is easy to see that, for all $w \in \Sigma^*$ with $|w| \leq m$, $w \in L_\varepsilon(\alpha)$ iff $w \in L_\varepsilon(\alpha_m)$. However, $L_\varepsilon(\alpha_m) \neq L_\varepsilon(\alpha)$, and thus M cannot learn α and α_m, a contradiction. ☒

As our next result shows, Assertion (c) remains valid if additional information is available. Note that, in contrast to all other results presented above and below, Theorem 1 comprises the non-erasing case, too.

Let $n \in \mathbb{N}$, let π^n be the class of all patterns having length n, and let $L_\varepsilon(\pi^n) = \{L_\varepsilon(\alpha) \mid \alpha \in \pi^n\}$ as well as $L(\pi^n) = \{L(\alpha) \mid \alpha \in \pi^n\}$.

Theorem 1. *The class of all erasing pattern languages in $L_\varepsilon(\pi^n)$ and of all non-erasing pattern languages in $L(\pi^n)$, respectively, is not polynomially learnable with additional information using membership, equivalence, and subset queries, even in case that n is a priori known.*

PROOF. Due to the limitations of space, we only handle the erasing case. For the sake of simplicity, assume that n is even. So, let $n = 2m$ and let $\pi_x^m \subseteq \pi^n$ be the set of all patterns α that fulfill Conditions (1) to (3), where

(1) $\alpha = xX_1aX_2a \cdots X_ma$, where $x \in \mathcal{X}$, $X_1 \in \{x\}^*$, $\ldots$, and $X_m \in \{x\}^*$.
(2) $|\alpha|_a = m$.
(3) $|\alpha|_x = m$.

The main ingredient of the proof is the following claim.

Claim. For all $\alpha, \beta \in \pi_x^m$, if $\alpha \neq \beta$, then $L_\varepsilon(\alpha) \cap L_\varepsilon(\beta) = \{a^{tm} \mid t \geq 1\}$.

Let α and β be given. Clearly, $\{a^{tm} \mid t \geq 1\} \subseteq L_\varepsilon(\alpha) \cap L_\varepsilon(\beta)$ follows directly from Conditions (2) and (3). Therefore, it remains to verify that $L_\varepsilon(\alpha) \cap L_\varepsilon(\beta) \subseteq$

$\{a^{tm} \mid t \geq 1\}$. So, let $w \in L_\varepsilon(\alpha)$ and let $w \notin \{a^{tm} \mid t \geq 1\}$. By Conditions (2) and (3), there has to be some σ with $x\sigma \notin \{a\}^*$ such that $\alpha\sigma = w$. Suppose to the contrary that $w \in L_\varepsilon(\beta)$. Hence there is some σ' with $x\sigma' \notin \{a\}^*$ such that $w = \beta\sigma'$.

By Conditions (2) and (3), we know that $|x\sigma'| = |x\sigma|$. Moreover, since α and β both start with x, we may conclude that $x\sigma' = x\sigma$. Now, choose the least index i such that $X_i \neq Y_i$. Note that i exists, since $\alpha \neq \beta$. Moreover, note that $i \neq n$, since $|\alpha| = |\beta|$ and i was chosen to be the least index with $X_i \neq Y_i$. By the choice of i, we obtain $(xX_1aX_2 \cdots X_{i-1}a)\sigma = (xY_1aY_2 \cdots Y_{i-1}a)\sigma'$.

Finally, pick the first position r in $x\sigma$ that is different from a. Note that such a position exists, since $x\sigma \notin \{a\}^*$. Let b be the rth letter in $x\sigma$. Without loss of generality we assume that $|X_i| < |Y_i|$. (Otherwise α is replaced by β and vice versa.) Let $|X_i| = k$ and $|Y_i| = \ell$. Hence $(X_ia)\sigma = (x\sigma)^k a$ and $Y_i\sigma = (x\sigma)^\ell = (x\sigma)^k x\sigma(x\sigma)^{\ell-k-1}$. Since $i \neq n$, X_i cannot form the end of α. But then $\alpha\sigma$ and $\beta\sigma$ must differ at position $z + k|x\sigma| + r$, where $z = |xX_1aX_2 \cdots X_{i-1}a\sigma|$. Hence $\alpha\sigma \neq \beta\sigma'$, a contradiction. This completes the proof of the claim.

By the latter claim, we may conclude that, for all $\alpha, \beta \in \pi_x^m$, $\alpha \neq \beta$ implies $L_\varepsilon(\alpha) \neq L_\varepsilon(\beta)$. To see this, note that, for all $\alpha \in \pi_x^m$, $L_\varepsilon(\alpha) \setminus \{a\}^+ \neq \emptyset$. Moreover, one easily verifies that $\{a^{tm} \mid t \geq 1\} \notin \pi_x^m$.

In order to apply Lemma 2, we have to estimate the number of patterns that belong to π_x^m. For $m \geq 1$, there are $\binom{2m-2}{m-1}$ possibilities to distribute the remaining $m - 1$ occurrences of x over the (possibly empty) strings X_1 to X_m. An easy and very rough calculation shows that, for all $m \geq 4$, $\binom{2m-2}{m-1} \geq 2^m$.

Hence, by Lemma 2, we may conclude that that any query learner that identifies π_x^m with additional information must make at least $2^m - 1$ membership, equivalence or subset queries. Finally, since, by assumption, $m = 2n$, and $\pi_x^m \subseteq \pi^n$, we are done. ☒

By Lemma 2, Theorem 1 allows for the following corollary.

Corollary 2. *The class of all erasing pattern languages is not polynomially learnable with additional information using membership, equivalence, and subset queries.*

In contrast to the non-erasing case (cf. Angluin [3]), restricted superset queries do not suffice the learn all erasing pattern languages. Recall that, for non-erasing pattern languages, even polynomially many restricted superset queries are enough. Surprisingly, the announced non-learnability result for erasing pattern languages remains valid, if additional information is provided.

Theorem 3. *The class of all erasing one-variable pattern languages is not learnable with additional information using restricted superset queries.*

PROOF. For all $j \geq 1$, we let $\alpha_j = x^j a$. Now, assume to the contrary that there exists a query learner M that finitely learns all one-variable pattern languages with additional information using restricted superset queries. Moreover, assume that M is allowed to use arbitrary erasing pattern languages as input to its restricted superset queries.

First, provide the string $w' = a$ to the learner. Note that w' belongs to all erasing pattern languages $L_\varepsilon(\alpha_j)$. The queries of the learner will be answered as follows:

Let β be the pattern queried by M. Depending on the minimal string β_ε in $L_\varepsilon(\beta)$, we distinguish the following cases:

Case 1. $\beta_\varepsilon = a$.

Now, there are $\beta', \beta'' \in \mathcal{X}^*$ such that $\beta = \beta' a \beta''$. If $vars(\beta') \setminus vars(\beta'') \neq \emptyset$, the reply is 'yes'; otherwise the reply is 'no'.

Case 2. $\beta_\varepsilon = \varepsilon$.

If there is some $x \in vars(\beta)$ with $|\beta|_x = 1$, then the reply is 'yes'. Otherwise, the reply is 'no'.

Case 3. Otherwise.

Then, the reply is 'no'.

Let π be the pattern which M outputs as its final hypothesis.

We claim that there is a pattern α_i such that (i) $L_\varepsilon(\alpha_i) \neq L_\varepsilon(\pi)$ and (ii) the reply to all the queries posed by M is correct, and therefore M must fail to learn $L_\varepsilon(\alpha_i)$.

The formal verification is as follows.

First, let β be a pattern for which the reply received was 'no'. Now, it is not hard to see that, for all α_j, this reply is correct, i.e., $L_\varepsilon(\alpha_j) \not\subseteq L_\varepsilon(\beta)$. (* In each case, either a or $b^j a$ witnesses $L_\varepsilon(\alpha_j) \setminus L_\varepsilon(\beta_{i_z}) \neq \emptyset$. *)

Second, let β be a pattern for which, in accordance with Case 2, the reply received was 'yes'. Clearly, $L_\varepsilon(\beta) = L_\varepsilon(x)$, and thus, for all α_j, $L_\varepsilon(\alpha_j) \subseteq L_\varepsilon(\beta)$.

Third, let $\beta_{k_1}, \ldots, \beta_{k_m}$ be the patterns for which, in accordance with Case 1, the reply received was 'yes'. Hence, there are patterns $\beta'_{k_1}, \ldots, \beta'_{k_m} \in \mathcal{X}^+$ and $\beta''_{k_1}, \ldots, \beta''_{k_m} \in \mathcal{X}^*$ such that, for all $z \leq m$, $\beta_{j_z} = \beta'_{j_z} a \beta''_{j_z}$. For every $z \leq m$, let x_z be the variable in $vars(\beta'_{j_z}) \setminus vars(\beta''_{j_z})$ for which $|\beta'_{j_z}|_{x_z}$ is maximal.

Finally, set $j = (|\pi| + 1) \cdot \prod_{z \leq m} |\beta'_{j_z}|_{x_z}$. Obviously, $L_\varepsilon(\alpha_j) \neq L_\varepsilon(\pi)$, since $L_\varepsilon(\pi)$ contains a string having the same length as π, while $L_\varepsilon(\alpha_j)$ does not. It remains to show that, for all $z \leq m$, $L_\varepsilon(\alpha_j) \subseteq L_\varepsilon(\beta_{k_z})$. So, let $w \in L_\varepsilon(\alpha_j)$ and let $z \leq m$. Hence, there is some $v \in \Sigma^*$ such that $v^j a = w$. By the choice of j, there is some $r \in \mathbb{N}$ such that $r = \frac{j}{|\beta'_{j_z}|_{x_z}}$. Now, select the substitution σ that assigns the string v^r to the variable x_z and the empty string ε to all other variables. Since $|\beta'_{j_z}|_{x_z} \cdot r = j$, we get $\beta_{j_z} \sigma = w$, and thus $w \in L_\varepsilon(\beta_{k_z})$. This completes the proof of the theorem. $\boxtimes$

Having a closer look at the demonstration of Theorem 3, we may immediately conclude:

Corollary 4. *The class of all erasing pattern languages is not learnable with additional information using restricted superset queries.*

3.2   Learning regular erasing pattern languages

As we have seen, in the general case, it is much more complicated to learn erasing pattern languages instead of non-erasing ones. Surprisingly, the observed differences vanish when regular erasing and regular non-erasing pattern languages constitute the subject of learning.

Proposition 2. *The class of all regular erasing pattern languages is not polynomially learnable using equivalence, membership and subset queries.*

PROOF. The proposition follows via Lemma 1. To see this, note that all pattern languages used in the demonstration of Proposition 1, Assertion (c) constitute regular erasing pattern languages. ⊠

As we will see, even polynomially many membership queries suffice to learn regular erasing pattern languages, if additional information is available. Hence, the corresponding result from Matsumoto and Shinohara [12] for regular non-erasing pattern languages translates in our setting of learning regular erasing pattern languages.

In order to prove Theorem 5, we define a procedure called *sshrink* (see Figure 1 below) that can be used to determine the shortest string in a target regular erasing pattern language $L_\varepsilon(\alpha)$. The input to the procedure *sshrink* is any string from $L_\varepsilon(\alpha)$. Moreover, *sshrink* requires access to a membership oracle for the target language $L_\varepsilon(\alpha)$. Note that *sshrink* is a modification of the procedure *shrink* in Matsumoto and Shinohara [12]. Moreover, *sshrink* is an abbreviation for the term 'solid shrink'.

In the formal definition of *sshrink* we make use of the following notation. Let $w \in \Sigma^+$ with $|w| = m$. For all $j \in \mathbb{N}$ with $1 \leq j \leq m$, $w[j \hookleftarrow \varepsilon]$ is the string which one obtains, if one erases $w[j]$, i.e., the constant at position j in w.

On input $w \in L_\varepsilon(\alpha)$, execute Instruction (A):

(A) Fix $m = |w|$ and goto (B).
(B) For $j = 1, \ldots, m$, ask the membership query $w[j \hookleftarrow \varepsilon]$. If the answer is always 'no', then output w. Otherwise, determine the least j, say $\hat{j}$, for which the answer is 'yes' and goto (C).
(C) Set $w = w[\hat{j} \hookleftarrow \varepsilon]$ and goto (A).

Figure 1: Procedure *sshrink*

The following lemma is quite helpful when verifying the correctness of the procedure *sshrink* (cf. Lemma 4 below).

Lemma 3. *Let $\alpha \in \pi_r$ and $w \in L_\varepsilon(\alpha)$. Then $w = \alpha_\varepsilon$ iff $v \notin L_\varepsilon(\alpha)$ for all proper subwords of w.*

PROOF. Necessity: Obviously, since α_ε is the shortest string in $L_\varepsilon(\alpha)$.

Sufficiency: Now, let $w \in L_\varepsilon(\alpha)$. Hence, there is a substitution σ such that $\alpha\sigma = w$. Suppose that there is a variable x in α such that $\sigma(x) \neq \varepsilon$. Now, modify σ to σ' by assigning the empty string ε to x. Since α is a regular pattern, we know that $\alpha\sigma'$ forms a subword of w. By definition, $\alpha\sigma' \in L_\varepsilon(\alpha)$. Therefore, if no proper subword of w belongs to $L_\varepsilon(\alpha)$, w must equal α_ε. ⊠

Lemma 4. *Let $\alpha \in \pi_r$ and $w \in L_\varepsilon(\alpha)$. On input w, sshrink outputs the string α_ε. Moreover, sshrink asks $O(|w|^2)$ membership queries.*

PROOF. The lemma follows immediately from Lemma 3 and the definition of the procedure *sshrink* (cf. Figure 1). ☒

Theorem 5. *The class of all regular erasing pattern languages is polynomially learnable with additional information using membership queries.*

PROOF. The proof is relatively easy for the case that $|\Sigma| \geq 3$. It becomes pretty hard if the underlying alphabet exactly contains two constant symbols, even though the underlying idea is the same. The main reason is, that the following fundamental lemma holds only in case that $|\Sigma| \geq 3$.

Lemma 5. (Jiang *et al.* [7]) *Let $\alpha, \beta \in \pi$ and $|\Sigma| \geq 3$. If $L_\varepsilon(\alpha) = L_\varepsilon(\beta)$, then seqterm($\alpha$) = seqterm($\beta$).*

To see the point, assume for a moment that $\Sigma = \{a, b\}$. As some quick calculation shows, $L_\varepsilon(xabyaz) = L_\varepsilon(xaybaz)$, but obviously seqterm($xabyaz$) $\neq$ seqterm($xaybaz$).

To proof the theorem, we start with the case of $|\Sigma| \geq 3$. Let $\alpha \in \pi_r$ and $w \in L_\varepsilon(\alpha)$ be given. Remember that *sshrink* uses $O(|w|^2)$ membership queries for a given w. Let $\alpha_\varepsilon = a_1 \cdots a_n$ be the word returned by *sshrink*. For all i with $1 \leq i \leq n - 1$, there is a constant $c \in \Sigma$ such that $c \neq a_i$ and $c \neq a_{i+1}$. Now, Lemma 5 and the regularity of α imply $a_1 \cdots a_i c a_{i+1} \cdots a_n \in L_\varepsilon(\alpha)$ iff, in pattern α, there is a variable between a_i and a_{i+1}. Hence, $n + 1$ additional membership queries suffices to find the positions at which variables appear in α, and therefore we can easily construct a pattern that defines the same erasing language as α.

Next, let $|\Sigma| = 2$. Now, the main obstacle is that there is no longer a "third letter", and therefore, as the above example shows, Lemma 5 remains no longer valid. However, we have been able to derive a couple of lemmata that allows us to show that there is kind of "normal form" to represent regular erasing pattern languages. Applying this insight, the theorem can be shown. The interested reader is referred to the appendix, where a short sketch of the proof can be found. ☒

In case that there is no additional information available, membership queries suffice to learn the class of all regular erasing pattern languages, contrasting the general case (cf. Proposition 1, Assertion (a)). However, Proposition 2 directly implies that membership queries cannot be used to find *one* element from the target regular erasing pattern languages *sufficiently fast*.

Corollary 6. *The class of all regular erasing pattern languages is learnable using membership queries.*

Again, in contrast to the general case (cf. Proposition 1, Assertion (c)), restricted superset queries suffice to learn regular erasing pattern languages *fast*.

One main ingredient of the proof of Theorem 7 is the following lemma which shows that polynomially many restricted superset queries can be used to find the shortest string in an unknown regular erasing pattern language.

Note that, in general, superset queries are undecidable for erasing pattern languages (cf. Jiang *et al.* [7]). However, since every regular erasing pattern language constitutes a regular language, the query learners used in the demonstration of Lemma 6 and Theorem 7 exclusively ask decidable restricted superset queries. Note that, for regular languages, the superset relation is decidable (cf., e.g, Hopcroft and Ullman [6]).

Lemma 6. *Let $|\Sigma| \geq 2$. For all $\alpha \in \pi$, it is possible to find α_ε with polynomially many restricted superset queries.*

PROOF. We briefly sketch the underlying idea, only. So, let α be the unknown pattern.

For all constants $a \in \Sigma$ and all $n = 1, 2, \ldots$, one asks restricted superset queries of the form $x_1 a x_2 a \cdots a x_{n+1}$, until the reply is 'no' for the first time. As a result, the first 'yes' allows one to determine how often the constant a appears in α_ε, i.e., the constant a occurs exactly n times.

Once the multiplicity of each constant is known, one simply selects the constant with the largest one. Now, let a have multiplicity n. Moreover, let $b_1, \ldots, b_k$ be the list of (possibly equivalent) constants different from a that must occurs in α. Now, one asks restricted superset queries for $x_1 b_1 x_2 a x_3 \cdots x_n a x_{n+1}$, $x_1 a x_2 b_1 x_3 \cdots x_n a x_{n+1}$, and so on, until 'yes' is returned for the first time. This gives the leftmost occurrence of b_1 with respect to the a's. By iterating this procedure for b_2 to b_k, all respective positions of the constants in α can be determined. Clearly, at the very end, this gives α_ε. It is not hard to see that at most $O(|\alpha|^2)$ restricted superset queries are sufficient to determine α_ε. ⊠

Theorem 7. *The class of all regular erasing pattern languages is polynomially learnable using restricted superset queries.*

PROOF. First, consider the case of $|\Sigma| \geq 3$. Let α be the unknown pattern and let $\alpha_\varepsilon = a_1 \cdots a_n$. Without loss of generality we may assume that α does not contain variables at consecutive positions.

Initially, query $a_1 x_1$. If the answer is yes, set $\beta = a_1$; else set $\beta = x_1 a_1$. Set $j = 2$ and execute Instruction (A).

(A) For all $i = j, \ldots, n$, query $\beta a_j \cdots a_i x_j$ until the answer is 'no'. If the answer is always 'yes', goto (B). Otherwise, goto (C).

(B) Query $\beta a_j \cdots a_n$. If the answer is 'yes', output $\beta = \beta a_j \cdots a_n$. Otherwise set $\beta = \beta a_j \cdots a_n x_j$.

(C) Let k be the least index such that reply is 'no'. Set $\beta = \beta a_j \cdots a_{k-1} x_j a_k$ and $j = k + 1$ and goto (A).

Obviously, the whole process requires $|\alpha_\varepsilon| + 2$ queries. Moreover, one easily verifies that $\beta_\varepsilon = \alpha_\varepsilon$. As above, note that all queries asked are indeed uniformly recursive, since they only require to compute the homeomorphic embedding relation.

It remains to show that $L_\varepsilon(\beta) = L_\varepsilon(\alpha)$.

In the remainder of this proof, we assume that α and β are in normal form. Hence, either the patterns are variable-free or there are $r, r' \in \mathbb{N}$ such that

$vars(\alpha) = \{x_1, \ldots, x_r\}$ and $vars(\beta) = \{x_1, \ldots, x_{r'}\}$. We claim that $\beta = \alpha$. Suppose the contrary and let p be the least position with $\beta[p] \neq \alpha[p]$.

Case 1. $p = 1$.

Obviously, if $\beta[1] = x_1$, then $L_\varepsilon(a_1 x) \not\supseteq L_\varepsilon(\alpha)$, and therefore $\alpha[1] = x_1$, a contradiction. Otherwise, let $\beta[1] = a_1$. But then, by construction, $\alpha[1] = a_1$, again a contradiction.

Case 2. $p > 1$.

By assumption, $\beta[1 : p - 1] = \alpha[1 : p - 1]$. Clearly, if β and α have a letter at position p, then $\beta[p] = \alpha[p]$ because of $\beta_\varepsilon = \alpha_\varepsilon$. Hence, it suffices to distinguish the following subcases.

Subcase 2.1. $\alpha[p] = x_j$ for some $j \leq r$.

Clearly, if $\alpha[1 : p - 1] = a_1 \cdots a_{p-1}$, then we are directly done. To see this note that every σ with $x_j \sigma \neq a_p$ defines a word $w = \alpha\sigma$ with $w \in L_\varepsilon(\alpha) \setminus L_\varepsilon(\beta)$, a contradiction. Next, suppose that $\alpha[1 : p - 1]$ contains at least one variable. By the choice of α, we know that $\alpha[p - 1] \notin \mathcal{X}$. Now, select a substitution σ that meets $x_j \sigma = c$, where $c \in \Sigma$, $c \neq \beta[p - 1]$, and $c \neq \beta[p]$. Since $|\Sigma| \geq 3$ such a constant must exist. Moreover, for all $x \in \mathcal{X} \setminus \{x_j\}$, set $\sigma(x) = \varepsilon$. Now, one easily verifies that $\alpha\sigma \in L_\varepsilon(\alpha) \setminus L_\varepsilon(\beta)$.

Subcase 2.2. $\beta[p] = x_j$ for some $j \leq r'$.

If $\alpha[1 : p] = a_1 \cdots a_{p-1} a_p$, we are directly done. To see this, note that $L_\varepsilon(a_1 \cdots a_{p-1} a_p x) \supseteq L_\varepsilon(\alpha)$, and therefore, by construction, $\beta[p] = a_p$, a contradiction. Next, consider the case that $\alpha[1 : p - 1]$ contains at least one variable. Let $a_z = \alpha[p]$. Hence, by construction, $L_\varepsilon(\beta[1 : p - 1]x) \supseteq L_\varepsilon(\alpha)$ and $L_\varepsilon(\beta[1 : p - 1]a_z x) \not\supseteq L_\varepsilon(\alpha)$, where x is a variable not occurring in $\beta[1 : p - 1]$. Let $w \in L_\varepsilon(\alpha)$. Then, by definition, there is some substitution σ such that $w = \alpha[1 : p-1]\sigma a_z \alpha[p+1 : m]\sigma$, where $m = |\alpha|$. Since $\beta[1 : p-1]) = \alpha[1 : p-1]$, this directly implies $w \in L_\varepsilon(\beta[1 : p - 1]a_z x)$, a contradiction.

Subcase 2.3. $\beta[p] = \varepsilon$.

Hence, $|\alpha| > |\beta|$. Let $|\beta| = m$. Since $\alpha_\varepsilon = \beta_\varepsilon$, we know that $\alpha[m+1] = x_{r'+1}$. Next, by the choice of α, we get $\alpha[m] \notin \mathcal{X}$, and therefore $\beta[m] = a_n$. However, this contradicts $L_\varepsilon(\beta) \supseteq L_\varepsilon(\alpha)$.

Subase 2.4. $\alpha[p] = \varepsilon$.

Hence, $|\beta| > |\alpha|$. Now, let $|\alpha| = m$. First, let $\alpha[m] = x_r$. Since $\alpha_\varepsilon = \beta_\varepsilon$, this yields $\beta[m+1] = x_{r+1}$. Because of $\beta[m] = \alpha[m]$, β must contain two consecutive variables which violates the construction of β. Second, let $\alpha[m] = a_n$. Again, since $\alpha_\varepsilon = \beta_\varepsilon$, we obtain $\beta[m + 1] = x_{r+1}$. But clearly, $L_\varepsilon(\alpha) \supseteq L_\varepsilon(\alpha)$, and since, $\beta[1 : m] = \alpha$, we obtain, by construction, $\beta = \alpha$, a contradiction.

Clearly, there are no other cases to consider, and therefore $\alpha = \beta$.

Finally, we discuss the case of $|\Sigma| = 2$. The underlying idea is as follows. The required query learner simulates the query learner from the demonstration of Theorem 5 (see also the appendix). As one can show, the membership query posed by the latter learner can equivalently replaced by restricted superset query. Note that this approach works only in case that, regular erasing pattern languages have to be learned. $\boxtimes$

4   Conclusion

In the present paper, we studied the learnability of erasing pattern languages within Angluin's [3] model of learning with queries. We mainly focused our attention on the following problem: Which of the known results for non-erasing pattern languages have their analogue when erasing pattern languages have to be learned and which of them have not? As it turns out, concerning regular pattern languages, there are no difference at all, while, in the general case, serious differences have been observed.

References

1. Angluin, D. (1980), Finding pattern common to a set of strings, *Journal of Computer and System Sciences 21*, 46–62. 86, 87, 88
2. Angluin, D. (1980), Inductive inference of formal languages from positive data, *Information and Control 45*, 117–135.
3. Angluin, D. (1988), Queries and concept learning, *Machine Learning 2*, 319–342. 86, 87, 88, 89, 90, 92, 98
4. Erlebach, T., Rossmanith, P., Stadtherr, H., Steger, A., Zeugmann, T. (1997), Learning one-variable pattern languages very efficiently on average, in parallel, and by asking questions, *In: Proc. Int. Conference on Algorithmic Learning Theory (ALT'97)*, Lecture Notes in Artificial Intelligence 1316, pages 260–276, Springer-Verlag. 87
5. Gold, M. (1967), Language identification in the limit, *Information and Control 10*, 447–474. 86, 87
6. Hopcroft, J. E., Ullman J. D. (1979), *Introduction to Automata Theory, Languages, and Computation*, Addison-Wesley Publishing Company. 88, 96
7. Jiang, T., Salomaa, A., Salomaa, K., Yu, S. (1995), Decision problems for patterns, *Journal of Computer and System Sciences 50*, 53–63. 86, 89, 95, 96
8. Kearns, M., Pitt, L. (1989), A polynomial-time algorithm for learning k-variable pattern languages from examples, *In: Proc. Workshop on Computational Learning Theory (COLT'89)*, pages 57–71, Morgan Kaufmann Publ. 86
9. Lange, S., Wiehagen, R. (1991), Polynomial-time inference of arbitrary pattern languages, *New Generation Computing 8*, 361–370. 86, 87
10. Marron, A., Ko, K. (1987), Identification of pattern languages from examples and queries, *Information and Computation 74*, 91–112. 86
11. Marron, A. (1988), Learning pattern languages from a single initial example and from queries, *In: Proc. Workshop on Computational Learning Theory (COLT'88)*, pages 1–23, Morgan Kaufmann Publ. 87
12. Matsumoto, S., Shinohara, A. (1997), Learning pattern languages using queries, *In: Proc. European Conference on Computational Learning Theory (EuroCOLT'97)*, Lecture Notes in Artificial Intelligence 1208, pages 185–197, Springer Verlag. 87, 88, 94
13. Mitchell, A. (1998), Learnability of a subclass of extended pattern languages, *In: Proc. ACM Workshop on Computational Learning Theory (COLT'98)*, pages 64–71, ACM-Press. 86
14. Nix, R. P. (1983), Editing by examples, PhD Thesis, Technical Report 280, Yale University, Dept. Computer Science. 86
15. Salomaa, A. (1994), Patterns (the formal language theory column), *EATCS Bulletin 54*, 46–62. 86, 89

16. Salomaa, A. (1994), Return to patterns (the formal language theory column), *EATCS Bulletin 55*, 144–157. 86, 89
17. Shinohara, T. (1983), Polynomial-time inference of extended regular pattern languages, *In: Proc. RIMS Symposia on Software Science and Engineering*, Lecture Notes in Computer Science 147, pages 115–127, Springer-Verlag. 86
18. Shinohara, T., Arikawa, S. (1995), Pattern inference, *In: Algorithmic Learning for Knowledge-Based Systems*, Lecture Notes in Artificial Intelligence 961, pages 259–291, Springer-Verlag. 86
19. Rogers, H. Jr. (1987), *Theory of Recursive Functions and Effective Computability*, MIT Press. 88
20. Valiant, L. G. (1984), A theory of the learnable, *Communications of the ACM 27*, 1134–1142. 86

A   Appendix

Next, we provide some more details concerning the problem of how to prove Theorem 5 in case that the underlying alphabet Σ contains exactly two constants.

Theorem. *Let $|\Sigma| = 2$. The class of all regular erasing pattern languages over Σ is polynomial learnable with additional information using membership queries.*

PROOF. Because of the lack of space, we only sketch the general idea, thereby skipping most of the details.

Suppose that $\Sigma = \{a, b\}$. Let $\alpha \in \Pi_r$ and $w \in L_\varepsilon(\alpha)$ be given. Applying the procedure *sshrink*, $O(|w|^2)$ membership queries suffices to determine α_ε (cf. Lemma 4, for the relevant details).

Hence, we may assume that $\alpha_\varepsilon = a_1 \cdots a_n$ is given, too. Now, based on α_ε, the variables in α can be determined as follows.

First, if $a_i = a_{i+1}$, it can easily be determined whether or not there is a variable between a_i and a_{i+1}. For that purpose, it suffice to ask of whether or not $a_1 \cdots a_{i-1} a_i b a_{i+1} \cdots a_n \in L_\varepsilon(\alpha)$, where $b \neq a_i$. Second, by asking of whether or not $b\alpha_\varepsilon \in L_\varepsilon(\alpha)$ $(\alpha_\varepsilon b \in L_\varepsilon(\alpha))$, it can be determined whether or not α begins (ends) with a variable, again assuming $b \neq a_1$ $(b \neq a_n)$.

Let α' be the resulting pattern. If α_ε contains only a's, for instance, we are already done. Otherwise, α_ε contains a's and b's. Now, one has to determine of whether or not there are variables in α' at the changes of form 'ab' and 'ba'.

There are a lot of cases to distinguish. In order to construct a pattern β with $L_\varepsilon(\beta) = L_\varepsilon(\alpha)$, the following procedure has to be implemented.

(0) All changes 'ab' and 'ba' in α' are marked 'needs attention'.
(1) If there is a change of form 'ab' and 'ba', respectively, that needs attention, then pick one and goto (2). Otherwise, set $\beta = \alpha'$ and return β.
(2) Determine to which of the relevant cases the change fixed in (2) belongs. Ask the corresponding queries and replace the change fixed in α' by the corresponding subpattern.
(3) Mark the selected/corresponding change as 'attended'.
(4) Goto (1).

The missing details are specified in a way such that Conditions (i) to (iii) are fulfilled, where

(i) In none of the relevant cases, a new change of form 'ab' and 'ba', respectively, is introduced.

(ii) In each of the relevant cases, at most three membership queries are necessary to determine the subpattern which hast to be substituted.

(iii) In each of the relevant cases, the subpattern which is substituted is equivalent to the corresponding subpattern in the unknown pattern α.

Obviously, (i) guarantees that this procedure terminates. By (ii), we know that $O(|\alpha'|)$ additional membership queries will do. Moreover, combing (iii) with Lemma 7 below, one may easily conclude that $L_\varepsilon(\beta) = L_\varepsilon(\alpha)$.

It remains to specify the relevant cases.

As a prototypical example, we discuss the following simple cases in detail.

Subsequently, let σ_ε be the substitution that assigns the empty word ε to all variables in $\mathcal{X}$.

Case 1. $\alpha' = \alpha_1 aabb\alpha_2$, *where the change of form 'ab' is marked.*

Ask whether or not $\alpha_1 aababb\alpha_2\sigma_\varepsilon \in L_\varepsilon(\alpha)$. If the answer is 'no', no variable appears in the target pattern at this change of form 'ab'. If the answer is 'yes', replace $aabb$ by $aaxbb$. It is not hard to see that Condition (iii) is fulfilled.

Case 2. $\alpha' = \alpha_1 xab^j y\alpha_2$, *where the change of form 'ab' is marked.*

Now, there is no need to ask any membership query at all. By Lemma 8 below, we know that a new variable between a and b does not change the erasing pattern language generated by the corresponding pattern.

Due to the space constraints, further details concerning the remaining cases are omitted. ☒

Lemma 7. *Let* $\alpha_1, \ldots, \alpha_n \in \pi_r$ *and let* $\alpha = \alpha_1, \ldots, \alpha_n$. *Moreover, let* $\beta \in \pi_r$ *such that* $L_\varepsilon(\alpha_i) = L_\varepsilon(\beta)$ *and, for all* $j \neq i$, *vars*$(\alpha_j) \cap$ *vars*$(\beta) = \emptyset$. *Then,* $L_\varepsilon(\alpha) = L_\varepsilon(\alpha_1) \cdots L_\varepsilon(\alpha_{i-1}) L_\varepsilon(\beta) L_\varepsilon(\alpha_{i-1}) \cdots L_\varepsilon(\alpha_n)$.

PROOF. Since α is regular, we have *vars*$(\alpha_i) \cap$ *vars*$(\alpha_j) = \emptyset$ for all j with $j \neq i$. This gives $L_\varepsilon(\alpha) = L_\varepsilon(\alpha_1) L_\varepsilon(\alpha_2) \cdots L_\varepsilon(\alpha_n)$. The remainder is obvious. ☒

Lemma 8. *Let* $j \in \mathbb{N}$. *Moreover, let* $\alpha_j = x_1 ab^j x_2$ *and* $\beta_j = y_1 a y_2 b^j y_3$. *Then,* $L_\varepsilon(\alpha_j) = L_\varepsilon(\beta_j)$.

PROOF. Let $j \in \mathbb{N}$ be given. Obviously, $L_\varepsilon(\alpha_j) \subseteq L_\varepsilon(\beta_j)$. It remains to show that $L_\varepsilon(\beta_j) \subseteq L_\varepsilon(\alpha_j)$.

Let σ be any substitution. We distinguish the following cases.

Case 1. $y_2\sigma \in \{a\}^*$.

Hence, $y_2\sigma = a^i$ for some $i \in \mathbb{N}$. Define σ' by setting $x_1\sigma' = y_1\sigma a^i$ and $x_2\sigma' = y_3\sigma$. Clearly, we get $\alpha_j\sigma' = y_1\sigma a^i ab^j y_3\sigma = y_1\sigma aa^i b^j y_3\sigma = \beta_j\sigma$.

Case 2. $y_2\sigma \in \{b\}^+$.

Hence, $y_2\sigma = b^i$ for some $i \in \mathbb{N}$. Define σ' by setting $x_1\sigma' = y_1\sigma$ and $x_2\sigma' = b^i y_3\sigma$. Obviously, we get $\alpha_j\sigma' = y_1\sigma ab^j b^i y_3\sigma = y_1\sigma ab^i b^j y_3\sigma = \beta_j\sigma$.

Case 3. Otherwise.

Hence, $y_2\sigma = wab^i$ for some $i \in \mathbb{N}$ and some $w \in \Sigma^*$. Define σ' by setting $x_1\sigma' = y_1\sigma aw$ and $x_2\sigma' = b^i y_3\sigma$. Obviously, we get $\alpha_j\sigma' = y_1\sigma awab^j b^i y_3\sigma = y_1\sigma awab^i b^j y_3\sigma = \beta_j\sigma$. ☒

Learning Recursive Concepts with Anomalies

Gunter Grieser[1], Steffen Lange[2], and Thomas Zeugmann[3]

[1] Technische Universität Darmstadt, Fachbereich Informatik, Alexanderstr. 10
64283 Darmstadt, Germany, e-mail: grieser@informatik.tu-darmstadt.de

[2] Universität Leipzig, Institut für Informatik, Augustusplatz 10–11
04109 Leipzig, Germany, e-mail: slange@informatik.uni-leipzig.de

[3] Medizinische Universität Lübeck, Institut für Theoretische Informatik, Wallstr. 40
23560 Lübeck, Germany, e-mail: thomas@tcs.mu-luebeck.de

Abstract. This paper provides a systematic study of inductive inference of indexable concept classes in learning scenarios in which the learner is successful if its final hypothesis describes a finite variant of the target concept – henceforth called learning with anomalies. As usual, we distinguish between learning from only positive data and learning from positive and negative data.

We investigate the following learning models: finite identification, conservative inference, set-driven learning, and behaviorally correct learning. In general, we focus our attention on the case that the number of allowed anomalies is finite but not *a priori* bounded. However, we also present a few sample results that affect the special case of learning with an *a priori* bounded number of anomalies. We provide characterizations of the corresponding models of learning with anomalies in terms of finite tell-tale sets. The varieties in the degree of recursiveness of the relevant tell-tale sets observed are already sufficient to quantify the differences in the corresponding models of learning with anomalies.

In addition, we study variants of incremental learning and derive a complete picture concerning the relation of all models of learning with and without anomalies mentioned above.

1   Introduction

Induction constitutes an important feature of learning. The corresponding theory is called inductive inference. Inductive inference may be characterized as the study of systems that map evidence on a target concept into hypotheses about it. The investigation of scenarios in which the sequence of hypotheses stabilizes to an accurate and finite description of the target concept is of some particular interest. The precise definitions of the notions evidence, stabilization, and accuracy go back to Gold [10] who introduced the model of learning in the limit.

The present paper deals with inductive inference of indexable classes of recursive concepts (indexable classes, for short). A concept class is said to be an indexable class if it possesses an effective enumeration with uniformly decidable membership. Angluin [2] started the systematic study of learning indexable concept classes. [2] and succeeding publications (cf., e.g., [20], for an overview)

H. Arimura, S. Jain and A. Sharma (Eds.): ALT 2000, LNAI 1968, pp. 101-115, 2000.

found a lot of interest, since most natural concept classes form indexable classes. For example, the class of all context sensitive, context free, regular, and pattern languages as well as the set of all boolean formulas expressible as monomial, k-CNF, k-DNF, and k-decision list constitute indexable classes.

As usual, we distinguish learning from positive data and learning from positive and negative data, synonymously called learning from text and informant, respectively. A text for a target concept c is an infinite sequence of elements of c such that every element from c eventually appears. Alternatively, an informant is an infinite sequence of elements exhausting the underlying learning domain that are classified with respect to their membership to the target concept.

An algorithmic learner takes as input larger and larger initial segments of a text (an informant) and outputs, from time to time, a hypothesis about the target concept. The set of all admissible hypotheses is called hypothesis space. When learning of indexable classes is considered, it is natural to require that the hypothesis space is an effective enumeration of a (possibly larger) indexable concept class. This assumption underlies almost all studies (cf., e.g., [2, 20]).

Gold's [10] original model requires the sequence of hypotheses to converge to a hypothesis correctly describing the target concept. However, from a viewpoint of potential applications, it suffices in most cases that the final hypothesis approximates the target concept sufficiently well. Blum and Blum [5] introduced a quite natural refinement of Gold's model that captures this aspect. In their setting of learning recursive functions with anomalies, it is admissible that the learner's final hypothesis may differ from the target function at finitely many data points. Case and Lynes [6] adapted this model to language learning.

Learning with anomalies has been studied intensively in the context of learning recursive functions and recursively enumerable languages (cf., e.g., [11]). Preliminary results concerning the learnability of indexable classes with anomalies can be found in Tabe and Zeugmann [17]. Note that Baliga *et al.* [3] studied the learnability of indexable classes with anomalies, too. However, unlike all other work on learning indexable classes, [3] allows the use of *arbitrary* hypothesis spaces (including those not having a decidable membership problem). Therefore, the results from [3] do not directly translate into our setting.

The present paper provides a systematic study of learning indexable concept classes with anomalies. We investigate the following variants of Gold-style concept learning: finite identification, conservative inference, set-driven inference, behaviorally correct learning, and incremental learning. We relate the resulting models of learning with anomalies to one another as well as to the corresponding versions of learning without anomalies. In general, we focus our attention to the case that the number of allowed anomalies is finite but not *a priori* bounded. However, we also present a few sample results that affect the special case that the number of allowed anomalies is *a priori* bounded.

Next, we mention some prototypical results. In the setting of learning with anomalies, the learning power of set-driven learners, conservative learners, and unconstrained IIMs does coincide. In contrast, when anomaly-free learning is considered, conservative learners and set-driven learners are strictly less powerful. Moreover, a further difference to learning without anomalies is established by showing that behaviorally correct learning with anomalies is strictly more powerful than learning in the limit with anomalies. Furthermore, in case the number of allowed anomalies is finite but not *a priori* bounded, it is proved that there is no need to use arbitrary hypothesis spaces in order to design superior behaviorally correct learners, thus refining the corresponding results from [3]. However, if the number of anomalies is *a priori* bounded, it is advantageous to use arbitrary hypothesis spaces. In order to establish these results, we provide characterizations of the corresponding models of learning with anomalies in terms of finite tell-tale sets (cf. [2]). As it turns out, the observed varieties in the degree of recursiveness of the relevant tell-tale sets are already sufficient to quantify the differences in the corresponding models of learning with anomalies.

Moreover, we derive a complete picture concerning the relation of the different models of incremental learning with and without anomalies.

2   Preliminaries

2.1   Basic notions

Let $\mathbb{N} = \{0, 1, 2, \ldots\}$ be the set of all natural numbers. By $\langle ., . \rangle \colon \mathbb{N} \times \mathbb{N} \to \mathbb{N}$ we denote Cantor's pairing function. Let A and B be sets. As usual, $A \triangle B$ denotes the symmetrical difference of A and B, i.e., $A \triangle B = (A \setminus B) \cup (B \setminus A)$. We write $A \# B$ to indicate that $A \triangle B \neq \emptyset$. For all $a \in \mathbb{N}$, $A =^a B$ iff $card(A \triangle B) \leq a$, while $A =^* B$ iff $card(A \triangle B) < \infty$. We let $\sigma \diamond \tau$ denote the concatenation of two possibly infinite sequences σ and τ.

Any recursively enumerable set $\mathcal{X}$ is called a *learning domain*. By $\wp(\mathcal{X})$ we denote the power set of $\mathcal{X}$. Let $\mathcal{C} \subseteq \wp(\mathcal{X})$ and let $c \in \mathcal{C}$. We refer to $\mathcal{C}$ and c as to a *concept class* and a *concept*, respectively. Sometimes, we will identify a concept c with its characteristic function, i.e., we let $c(x) = +$, if $x \in c$, and $c(x) = -$, otherwise. What is actually meant will become clear from the context.

We deal with the learnability of indexable concept classes with uniformly decidable membership defined as follows (cf. [2]). A class of non-empty concepts $\mathcal{C}$ is said to be an *indexable concept class with uniformly decidable membership* if there are an effective enumeration $(c_j)_{j \in \mathbb{N}}$ of all and only the concepts in $\mathcal{C}$ and a recursive function f such that, for all $j \in \mathbb{N}$ and all $x \in \mathcal{X}$, it holds $f(j, x) = +$, if $x \in c_j$, and $f(j, x) = -$, otherwise. We refer to indexable concept classes with uniformly decidable membership as to *indexable classes*, for short, and let $\mathcal{IC}$ denote the collection of all indexable classes.

2.2   Gold-style concept learning

Let $\mathcal{X}$ be the underlying learning domain, let $c \subseteq \mathcal{X}$ be a concept, and let $t = (x_n)_{n \in \mathbb{N}}$ be an infinite sequence of elements from c such that $\{x_n \mid n \in \mathbb{N}\} = c$. Then, t is said to be a *text* for c. By $Text(c)$ we denote the set of all texts for c. Let t be a text and let y be a number. Then, t_y denotes the initial segment of t of length $y + 1$. Furthermore, we set $content(t_y) = \{x_n \mid n \leq y\}$.

Let $\mathcal{C}$ be an indexable class. Then, we let $Text(\mathcal{C})$ be the collection of all texts in $\bigcup_{c \in \mathcal{C}} Text(c)$.

As in [10], we define an *inductive inference machine* (abbr. *IIM*) to be an algorithmic mapping from initial segments of texts to $\mathbb{N} \cup \{?\}$. Thus, an IIM either outputs a hypothesis, i.e., a number encoding a certain computer program, or it outputs "?," a special symbol representing the case the machine outputs "no conjecture." Note that an IIM, when learning some target class $\mathcal{C}$, is required to produce an output when processing any *admissible* information sequence, i.e., any initial segment of any text in $Text(\mathcal{C})$.

The numbers output by an IIM are interpreted with respect to a suitably chosen *hypothesis space* $\mathcal{H} = (h_j)_{j \in \mathbb{N}}$. Since we exclusively deal with the learnability of indexable classes $\mathcal{C}$, we always assume that $\mathcal{H}$ is also an indexing of some possibly larger indexable class. Hence, membership is uniformly decidable in $\mathcal{H}$, too. If $\mathcal{C} \subseteq \{h_j \mid j \in \mathbb{N}\}$ ($\mathcal{C} = \{h_j \mid j \in \mathbb{N}\}$), then $\mathcal{H}$ is said to be a *class comprising* (*class preserving*) hypothesis space for $\mathcal{C}$ (cf. [20]). When an IIM outputs some number j, we interpret it to mean that it hypothesizes h_j.

We define convergence of IIMs as usual. Let t be a text and let M be an IIM. The sequence $(M(t_y))_{y \in \mathbb{N}}$ of M's hypotheses *converges* to a number j iff all but finitely many terms of it are equal to j.

Now, we are ready to define *learning in the limit*.

Definition 1 ([6, 10]). *Let $\mathcal{C} \in \mathcal{IC}$, let c be a concept, let $\mathcal{H} = (h_j)_{j \in \mathbb{N}}$ be a hypothesis space, and let $a \in \mathbb{N} \cup \{*\}$.*

An IIM M $Lim^a Txt_{\mathcal{H}}$–identifies c iff, for every $t \in Text(c)$, there is a $j \in \mathbb{N}$ with $h_j =^a c$ such that the sequence $(M(t_y))_{y \in \mathbb{N}}$ converges to j.

M $Lim^a Txt_{\mathcal{H}}$–identifies $\mathcal{C}$ iff, for all $c' \in \mathcal{C}$, M $Lim^a Txt_{\mathcal{H}}$–identifies c'.

$Lim^a Txt$ denotes the collection of all indexable classes $\mathcal{C}'$ for which there are a hypothesis space $\mathcal{H}' = (h'_j)_{j \in \mathbb{N}}$ and an IIM M such that M $Lim^a Txt_{\mathcal{H}'}$–identifies $\mathcal{C}'$.

Subsequently, we write $LimTxt$ instead of $Lim^0 Txt$. We adopt this convention to all learning types defined below.

In general, it is not decidable whether or not an IIM has already converged on a text t for the target concept c. Adding this requirement to the above definition results in *finite learning* (cf. [10]). The resulting learning type is denoted by $Fin^a Txt$, where again $a \in \mathbb{N} \cup \{*\}$.

Next, we define *conservative* IIMs. Intuitively speaking, conservative IIMs maintain their actual hypothesis at least as long as they have not seen data contradicting it.

Definition 2 ([2]). *Let $\mathcal{C} \in \mathcal{IC}$, let c be a concept, let $\mathcal{H} = (h_j)_{j \in \mathbb{N}}$ be a hypothesis space, and let $a \in \mathbb{N} \cup \{*\}$.*

An IIM M $Consv^a Txt_{\mathcal{H}}$–identifies c iff M $Lim^a Txt_{\mathcal{H}}$–identifies c and, for every $t \in Text(c)$ and for any two consecutive hypotheses $k = M(t_y)$ and $j = M(t_{y+1})$, if $k \in \mathbb{N}$ and $k \neq j$, then $content(t_{y+1}) \not\subseteq h_k$.

M $Consv^a Txt_{\mathcal{H}}$–identifies $\mathcal{C}$ iff, for all $c' \in \mathcal{C}$, M $Consv^a Txt_{\mathcal{H}}$–identifies c'.

For every $a \in \mathbb{N} \cup \{*\}$, the resulting learning type $Consv^a Txt$ is defined analogously to Definition 1.

Next, we define *set-driven* learning. Intuitively speaking, the output of a set-driven IIM depends exclusively on the content of its input, thereby ignoring the order as well as the frequency in which the examples occur.

Definition 3 ([18]). *Let* $C \in \mathcal{IC}$, *let* c *be a concept, let* $\mathcal{H} = (h_j)_{j \in \mathbb{N}}$ *be a hypothesis space, and let* $a \in \mathbb{N} \cup \{*\}$.

An IIM M $Sdr^a Txt_\mathcal{H}$*–identifies* c *iff* M $Lim^a Txt_\mathcal{H}$*–identifies* c *and, for every* $t, t' \in Text(C)$ *and for all* $n, m \in \mathbb{N}$, *if* $content(t_n) = content(t'_m)$ *then* $M(t_n) = M(t'_m)$.

M $Sdr^a Txt_\mathcal{H}$*–identifies* C *iff, for all* $c' \in C$, M $Sdr^a Txt_\mathcal{H}$*–identifies* c'.

For every $a \in \mathbb{N} \cup \{*\}$, the resulting learning type $Sdr^a Txt$ is defined analogously to Definition 1.

At the end of this subsection, we provide a formal definition of *behaviorally correct learning*.

Definition 4 ([4, 6]). *Let* $C \in \mathcal{IC}$, *let* c *be a concept, let* $\mathcal{H} = (h_j)_{j \in \mathbb{N}}$ *be a hypothesis space, and let* $a \in \mathbb{N} \cup \{*\}$.

An IIM M $Bc^a Txt_\mathcal{H}$*–identifies* c *iff, for every* $t \in Text(c)$ *and for all but finitely many* $y \in \mathbb{N}$, $h_{M(t_y)} =^a c$.

M $Bc^a Txt_\mathcal{H}$*–identifies* C *iff, for all* $c' \in C$, M $Bc^a Txt_\mathcal{H}$*–identifies* c'.

For every $a \in \mathbb{N} \cup \{*\}$, the resulting learning type $Bc^a Txt$ is defined analogously to Definition 1.

2.3   Incremental concept learning

Now, we formally define the different models of incremental learning. An ordinary IIM M has always access to the whole history of the learning process, i.e., it computes its actual guess on the basis of the whole initial segment of the text t seen so far. In contrast, an *iterative* IIM is only allowed to use its last guess and the next element in t. Conceptually, an iterative IIM M defines a sequence $(M_n)_{n \in \mathbb{N}}$ of machines each of which takes as its input the output of its predecessor.

Definition 5 ([19]). *Let* $C \in \mathcal{IC}$, *let* c *be a concept, let* $\mathcal{H} = (h_j)_{j \in \mathbb{N}}$ *be a hypothesis space, and let* $a \in \mathbb{N} \cup \{*\}$.

An IIM M $It^a Txt_\mathcal{H}$*–identifies* c *iff, for every* $t = (x_n)_{n \in \mathbb{N}} \in Text(c)$, *the following conditions are fulfilled:*

(1) *for all* $n \in \mathbb{N}$, $M_n(t)$ *is defined, where* $M_0(t) = M(x_0)$ *and* $M_{n+1}(t) = M(M_n(t), x_{n+1})$.

(2) *the sequence* $(M_n(t))_{n \in \mathbb{N}}$ *converges to a number* j *with* $h_j =^a c$.

M $It^a Txt_\mathcal{H}$*–identifies* C *iff, for each* $c' \in C$, M $It^a Txt_\mathcal{H}$*–identifies* c'.

For every $a \in \mathbb{N} \cup \{*\}$, the resulting learning type $It^a Txt$ is defined analogously to Definition 1.

Let M be an iterative IIM as defined in Definition 5 and t be a text. Then, $M_*(t_n)$ denotes the last hypothesis output by M when processing t_n, i.e., $M_*(t_n) = M_n(t)$. We adopt this convention to all versions of incremental learners defined below.

Next, we consider a natural relaxation of iterative learning, named k-*bounded example-memory* inference. Now, an IIM M is allowed to memorize at most k of the elements in t which it has already seen, where $k \in \mathbb{N}$ is *a priori* fixed. Again, M defines a sequence $(M_n)_{n \in \mathbb{N}}$ of machines each of which takes as input the output of its predecessor. A k-bounded example-memory IIM outputs a hypothesis along with the set of memorized data elements.

Definition 6 ([15]). *Let $C \in \mathcal{IC}$, let c be a concept, let $\mathcal{H} = (h_j)_{j \in \mathbb{N}}$ be a hypothesis space, let $a \in \mathbb{N} \cup \{*\}$, and let $k \in \mathbb{N}$.*

An IIM M $Bem_k^a Txt_\mathcal{H}$–identifies c iff, for every $t = (x_n)_{n \in \mathbb{N}} \in Text(c)$, the following conditions are satisfied:

(1) *for all $n \in \mathbb{N}$, $M_n(t)$ is defined, where $M_0(t) = M(x_0) = \langle j_0, S_0 \rangle$ such that $S_0 \subseteq \{x_0\}$ and $card(S_0) \leq k$ and $M_{n+1}(t) = M(M_n(t), x_{n+1}) = \langle j_{n+1}, S_{n+1} \rangle$ such that $S_{n+1} \subseteq S_n \cup \{x_{n+1}\}$ and $card(S_{n+1}) \leq k$.*

(2) *the j_n in the sequence $(\langle j_n, S_n \rangle)_{n \in \mathbb{N}}$ of M's guesses converge to a number j with $h_j =^a c$.*

M $Bem_k^a Txt_\mathcal{H}$–identifies C iff, for each $c' \in C$, M $Bem_k^a Txt_\mathcal{H}$–identifies c'.

For every $k \in \mathbb{N}$ and every $a \in \mathbb{N} \cup \{*\}$, the resulting learning type $Bem_k^a Txt$ is defined analogously to Definition 1. By definition, $Bem_0^a Txt = It^a Txt$.

Next, we define learning by *feedback* IIMs. Informally speaking, a feedback IIM M is an iterative IIM that is additionally allowed to make a particular type of queries. In each learning stage $n + 1$, M has access to the actual input x_{n+1} and its previous guess j_n. Moreover, M computes a query from x_{n+1} and j_n which concerns the history of the learning process. That is, the feedback learner computes a data element x and receives a "YES/NO" answer $A(x)$ such that $A(x) = 1$, if $x \in content(t_n)$, and $A(x) = 0$, otherwise. Hence, M can just ask whether or not the particular data element x has already been presented in previous learning stages.

Definition 7 ([19]). *Let $C \in \mathcal{IC}$, let c be a concept, let $\mathcal{H} = (h_j)_{j \in \mathbb{N}}$ be a hypothesis space, let $a \in \mathbb{N} \cup \{*\}$, and let $Q \colon \mathbb{N} \times \mathcal{X} \to \mathcal{X}$ be a total computable function. An IIM M, with a computable query asking function Q, $Fb^a Txt_\mathcal{H}$–identifies c iff, for every $t = (x_n)_{n \in \mathbb{N}} \in Text(c)$, the following conditions are satisfied:*

(1) *for all $n \in \mathbb{N}$, $M_n(t)$ is defined, where $M_0(t) = M(x_0)$ as well as $M_{n+1}(t) = M(M_n(t), A(Q(M_n(t), x_{n+1})), x_{n+1})$.*

(2) *the sequence $(M_n(t))_{n \in \mathbb{N}}$ converges to a number j with $h_j =^a c$ provided A truthfully answers the questions computed by Q.*

M $Fb^a Txt_\mathcal{H}$–identifies C iff, for each $c' \in C$, M $Fb^a Txt_\mathcal{H}$–identifies c'.

For every $a \in \mathbb{N} \cup \{*\}$, the resulting learning type $Fb^a Txt$ is defined analogously to Definition 1.

3   Learning from positive data only

In this section, we study the power and the limitations of the various models of learning with anomalies. We relate these models to one another as well as to the different models of anomaly-free learning. We are mainly interested in the case that the number of allowed anomalies is finite but not *a priori* bounded. Nevertheless, in order to give an impression of how the overall picture changes when the number of allowed anomalies is *a priori* bounded, we also present selected results for this case.

3.1   Gold-style learning with anomalies

Proposition 1 summarizes the known relations between the considered models of anomaly-free learning from text.

Proposition 1 ([10, 14, 16]).
$FinTxt \subset ConsvTxt = SdrTxt \subset LimTxt = BcTxt \subset \mathcal{IC}.$

In the setting of learning recursive functions the first observation made when comparing learning in the limit with anomalies to behaviorally correct inference was the *error correcting power* of Bc-learners, i.e., $Ex^* \subseteq Bc$ (cf., e.g., [4, 7]). Interestingly enough, this result did not translate into the setting of learning recursively enumerable languages from positive data (cf. [6]). But still, a certain error correcting power is preserved in this setting, since $Lim^a Txt \subseteq Bc^b Txt$ provided $a \leq 2b$ (cf. [6]).

When comparing learning with and without anomalies in our setting of learning indexable classes, it turns out that even finite learners may become more powerful than Bc-learners.

Theorem 1. $Fin^1 Txt \setminus BcTxt \neq \emptyset.$

However, the opposite is also true. For instance, PAT, the well-known class of all pattern languages (cf. [2]), witnesses the even stronger result:

Theorem 2. $ConsvTxt \setminus Fin^* Txt \neq \emptyset.$

As we will see, the relation between the standard learning models changes considerably, if it is no longer required that the learner must almost always output hypotheses that describe the target concept correctly. The following picture displays the established coincidences and differences by relating the models of learning with anomalies to one another and by ranking them in the hierarchy of the models of anomaly-free learning.

$$Fin^* Txt \subset Consv^* Txt = Sdr^* Txt = Lim^* Txt \subset Bc^* Txt \subset \mathcal{IC}$$
$$\cup \qquad\qquad \cup \qquad\qquad\quad \cup \qquad\qquad \cup \qquad\qquad \cup$$
$$FinTxt \subset ConsvTxt = SdrTxt \subset LimTxt = BcTxt$$

To achieve the overall picture, we establish characterizations of all models of learning with a finite but not *a priori* bounded number of anomalies. On the one hand, we present characterizations in terms of finite tell-tale sets. On the other hand, we prove that some of the learning models coincide.

Proposition 2 ([17]). *For all $C \in \mathcal{IC}$ and all $a \in \mathbb{N} \cup \{*\}$: $C \in Lim^a Txt$ iff there is an indexing $(c_j)_{j \in \mathbb{N}}$ of C and a recursively enumerable family $(T_j)_{j \in \mathbb{N}}$ of finite sets such that*

(1) *for all $j \in \mathbb{N}$, $T_j \subseteq c_j$,*
(2) *for all $j, k \in \mathbb{N}$, if $T_j \subseteq c_k \subseteq c_j$, then $c_k =^a c_j$.*

The characterization of Fin^*Txt is similar to the known characterization of $FinTxt$ (cf. [13]).

Theorem 3. *For all $C \in \mathcal{IC}$: $C \in Fin^*Txt$ iff there is an indexing $(c_j)_{j \in \mathbb{N}}$ of C and a recursively generable family $(T_j)_{j \in \mathbb{N}}$ of finite sets such that*

(1) *for all $j \in \mathbb{N}$, $T_j \subseteq c_j$,*
(2) *for all $j, k \in \mathbb{N}$, if $T_j \subseteq c_k$, then $c_k =^* c_j$.*

In contrast to Proposition 1, when a finite number of errors in the final hypothesis is allowed, conservative IIMs become exactly as powerful as unconstrained IIMs.

Theorem 4. $Lim^*Txt = Consv^*Txt$.

Proof. Let $C \in Lim^*Txt$, let $\mathcal{H} = (h_j)_{j \in \mathbb{N}}$ be a hypothesis space, and let M be an IIM that $Lim^*Txt_{\mathcal{H}}$–identifies C. Moreover, assume that M never outputs "?." The conservative IIM M' uses the following hypothesis space $\mathcal{H}'$. For all $j \in \mathbb{N}$ and $x \in \mathcal{X}$, we let $h'_{j,x} = h_j \setminus \{x\}$. Moreover, we let $\mathcal{H}'$ be the canonical enumeration of all those concepts $h'_{j,x}$.

Let $c \in C$, let $t = (x_j)_{j \in \mathbb{N}}$ be a text for c, and let $y \in \mathbb{N}$. On input t_y, M' determines $j = M(t_y)$, and outputs the canonical index of h'_{j,x_0} in $\mathcal{H}'$.

It is straightforward to verify that M is a conservative IIM that witnesses $C \in Lim^*Txt$.   □

As it turns out, when learning with anomalies is considered, set-driven learners become exactly as powerful as unconstrainted IIMs, again nicely contrasting Proposition 1.

Theorem 5. $Sdr^*Txt = Lim^*Txt$.

However, there is a difference between conservative inference and set-driven learning, on the one hand, and learning in the limit, on the other hand, which we want to point out next. While learning in the limit is invariant to the choice of the hypothesis space (cf. [17]), conservative inference and set-driven learning, respectively, is not. Moreover, in order to design a superior conservative and a set-driven learner, respectively, it is sometimes inevitable to select a hypothesis space that contains concepts which are not subject to learning.

Theorem 6.
(1) *There is an indexable class $C \in Consv^*Txt$ such that, for all class preserving hypothesis spaces $\mathcal{H}$ for C, there is no IIM M that $Consv^*Txt_{\mathcal{H}}$–identifies C.*
(2) *There is an indexable class $C \in Sdr^*Txt$ such that, for all class preserving hypothesis spaces $\mathcal{H}$ for C, there is no IIM M that $Sdr^*Txt_{\mathcal{H}}$–identifies C.*

For conservative learning and set-driven inference without anomalies, the analogue of Theorem 6 holds, as well (cf. [14, 16]).

Next, we study behaviorally correct identification. As we will see, finite tell-tale sets form a conceptual basis that is also well-suited to characterize the collection of all Bc^*Txt–identifiable indexable classes. Surprisingly, the existence of the corresponding tell-tale sets is still sufficient.

Theorem 7. *For all $C \in IC$: $C \in Bc^*Txt$ iff there is an indexing $(c_j)_{j \in \mathbb{N}}$ of C and a family $(T_j)_{j \in \mathbb{N}}$ of finite sets such that*

(1) *for all $j \in \mathbb{N}$, $T_j \subseteq c_j$,*
(2) *for all $j, k \in \mathbb{N}$, if $T_j \subseteq c_k \subseteq c_j$, then $c_k =^* c_j$.*

Proof. Due to the space constraint we sketch the sufficiency part, only. First, we define an appropriate hypothesis space $\mathcal{H} = (h_{\langle j,k \rangle})_{j,k \in \mathbb{N}}$. Let $(F_j)_{j \in \mathbb{N}}$ be an effective enumeration of all finite subsets of $\mathcal{X}$ and let $(w_j)_{j \in \mathbb{N}}$ be the lexicographically ordered enumeration of all elements in $\mathcal{X}$.

We subsequently use the following notions and notations. For all $c \subseteq \mathcal{X}$ and all $z \in \mathbb{N}$, we let $c^z = \{w_r \mid r \leq z, w_r \in c\}$. Moreover, for all $j, k, z \in \mathbb{N}$, we let $S_{\langle j,k,z \rangle}$ be the set of all indices $r \leq k$ that meet (i) $F_j \subseteq c_r$ and (ii), for all $r' < r$ with $c_{r'} \supseteq F_j$, $c_r^z \subset c_{r'}^z$.

Now, we are ready to define the required hypothesis space $\mathcal{H}$. For all $j, k \in \mathbb{N}$ we define the characteristic function of $h_{\langle j,k \rangle}$ as follows. If $S_{\langle j,k,z \rangle} = \emptyset$, we set $h_{\langle j,k \rangle}(w_z) = -$. If $S_{\langle j,k,z \rangle} \neq \emptyset$, we let $n = max\, S_{\langle j,k,z \rangle}$ and set $h_{\langle j,k \rangle}(w_z) = c_n(w_z)$.

Since membership is uniformly decidable in $(c_j)_{j \in \mathbb{N}}$, we know that $\mathcal{H}$ constitutes an admissible hypothesis space.

The required IIM M is defined as follows. Let $c \in C$, $t \in Text(c)$, and $y \in \mathbb{N}$.
IIM M: "On input t_y proceed as follows:
Determine $j \in \mathbb{N}$ with $F_j = content(t_y)$ and output $\langle j, y \rangle$."

Due to lack of space, the verification of M'c correctness is omitted. $\square$

Note that Baliga *et al.* [3] have recently shown that the same characterizing condition completely describes the collection of all indexable classes that are Bc^*Txt–identifiable with respect to *arbitrary* hypothesis spaces (including hypothesis space not having a decidable membership problem). Hence, our result refines the result from [3] in that it shows that, in order to Bc^*Txt–identify an indexable class, it is always possible to select a hypothesis space with uniformly decidable membership. However, as we see next, it is inevitable to select the actual hypothesis space appropriately.

Theorem 8. *There is an indexable class $C \in Bc^*Txt$ such that, for all class preserving hypothesis spaces $\mathcal{H}$ for C, there is no IIM M that $Bc^*Txt_{\mathcal{H}}$-learns C.*

In contrast, $BcTxt$ is invariant to the choice of the hypothesis space.

To be complete, note that it is folklore that there are indexable classes which are not Bc^*Txt-identifiable. Furthermore, applying the stated characterizations of the learning types Fin^*Txt, Lim^*Txt, and Bc^*Txt, the following hierarchy can be shown.

Theorem 9. $Fin^*Txt \subset Lim^*Txt \subset Bc^*Txt \subset IC$.

At the end of this subsection, we turn our attention to the case that the number of allowed anomalies is *a priori* bounded. On the one hand, Case and Lynes' [6] result that $Lim^{2a}Txt \subseteq Bc^aTxt$ nicely translates into our setting.

Surprisingly, the opposite is also true, i.e., every IIM that Bc^aTxt–identifies a target indexable class can be simulated by a learner that $Lim^{2a}Txt$–identifies the same class, as expressed by the following theorem.

Theorem 10. *For all $a \in \mathbb{N}$: $Bc^aTxt = Lim^{2a}Txt$.*

Proof. Let $a \in \mathbb{N}$. As mentioned above, $Lim^{2a}Txt \subseteq Bc^aTxt$ can be shown by adapting the corresponding ideas from [6] (see also [11], for the relevant details).

Next, we verify that $Bc^aTxt \subseteq Lim^{2a}Txt$. Let $\mathcal{C} \in Bc^aTxt$, let $\mathcal{H}$ be a hypothesis space, and let M be an IIM that $Bc^aTxt_\mathcal{H}$–identifies $\mathcal{C}$. Since membership is uniformly decidable in $\mathcal{H}$, the set $\{(j,k) \mid h_j \neq^{2a} h_k\}$ is recursively enumerable. Hence, without loss of generality, we may assume that there is a total recursive function $f: \mathbb{N} \to \mathbb{N} \times \mathbb{N}$ such that $\{f(n) \mid n \in \mathbb{N}\} = \{(j,k) \mid h_j \neq^{2a} h_k\}$.

The required IIM M' also uses the hypothesis space $\mathcal{H}$. Let $c \in \mathcal{C}$, $t \in Text(c)$, and $y \in \mathbb{N}$.

IIM M': "On input t_y proceed as follows:

If $y = 0$, set $z = 0$, determine $j_0 = M(t_0)$, and output j_0. If $y \geq 1$, determine $j = M'(t_{y-1})$. For all $s = z, \ldots, y$, determine $j_s = M(t_s)$, and test whether or not $(j, j_s) \in \{f(n) \mid n \leq y\}$. In case there is no such pair, then output j. Otherwise, set $z = y$ and output j_y."

Since M $Bc^aTxt_\mathcal{H}$–identifies c from t, there has to be a least y such that, for all $y' \geq y$, $h_{M(t_{y'})} =^a c$, and therefore, for all $y', y'' \geq y$, $h_{M(t_{y'})} =^{2a} h_{M(t_{y''})}$. Hence, M' converges on t to a hypothesis j that meets $h_j =^{2a} c$. □

Applying Theorem 2, we may conclude:

Corollary 11. *For all $\mathcal{C} \in \mathcal{IC}$ and all $a \in \mathbb{N}$: $\mathcal{C} \in Bc^aTxt$ iff there is an indexing $(c_j)_{j \in \mathbb{N}}$ of $\mathcal{C}$ and a recursively enumerable family $(T_j)_{j \in \mathbb{N}}$ of finite sets such that*

(1) *for all $j \in \mathbb{N}$, $T_j \subseteq c_j$, and*
(2) *for all $j, k \in \mathbb{N}$, if $T_j \subseteq c_k$ and $c_k \subseteq c_j$, then $c_k =^{2a} c_j$.*

The latter corollary nicely contrasts the results in [3]. When arbitrary hypothesis spaces are admissible (including hypothesis space not having a decidable membership problem), there is no need to add any recursive component, i.e., the existence of the corresponding tell-tale sets is again sufficient.

Moreover, the relation between set-driven learners and conservative inference changes completely, if the number of allowed anomalies is *a priori* bounded.

Theorem 12. $Consv^1Txt \setminus \bigcup_{a \in \mathbb{N}} Sdr^aTxt \neq \emptyset$.

Theorem 13. *For all $a \in \mathbb{N}$: $Sdr^aTxt \subset Consv^aTxt$.*

The relation between conservative learners and unconstrained IIMs is also affected, if the number of allowed anomalies is *a priori* bounded.

Theorem 14. *For all $a \in \mathbb{N}$: $Lim^aTxt \subset Consv^{a+1}Txt \subset Lim^{a+1}Txt$.*

Proof. Let $a \in \mathbb{N}$. By definition, we get $Consv^{a+1}Txt \subseteq Lim^{a+1}Txt$. Moreover, $Consv^{a+1}Txt \setminus Lim^aTxt \neq \emptyset$ follows via Theorem 15 below. Furthermore, $Lim^{a+1}Txt \setminus Consv^{a+1}Txt \neq \emptyset$ can be shown by diagonalization.

It remains to show that $Lim^aTxt \subseteq Consv^{a+1}Txt$. To see this, recall the definition of the conservative IIM M' from the demonstration of Theorem 4. It is easy to see that the final hypothesis of M' differs at most at one data point from the final hypothesis of the unconstrained IIM M which M' simulates. $\square$

Finally, when learning with an *a priori* bounded number of allowed anomalies is considered, the existence of infinite hierarchies of more and more powerful *Fin*-learners, *Consv*-learners, *Lim*-learners, and *Bc*-learners, parameterized in the number of allowed anomalies, can be shown. The following theorem provides the missing piece to establish these infinite hierarchies.

Theorem 15. *For all $a \in \mathbb{N}$: $Fin^{2a+1}Txt \setminus Bc^a Txt \neq \emptyset$.*

3.2 Incremental learning with anomalies

Proposition 3 summarizes the known results concerning incremental learning.

Proposition 3 ([15]).

(1) $ItTxt \subset FbTxt$.

(2) $ItTxt \subset Bem_1 Txt$.

(3) *For all $k \in \mathbb{N}$, $Bem_k Txt \subset Bem_{k+1} Txt$.*

(4) $Bem_1 Txt \setminus FbTxt \neq \emptyset$.

(5) $FbTxt \setminus \bigcup_{k \in \mathbb{N}} Bem_k Txt \neq \emptyset$.

The overall picture remains unchanged for incremental learning with a finite number of allowed anomalies.

More specifically, iterative learners that have the freedom to store *one* additional example may outperform feedback learners that are allowed to make up to finitely many errors in their final hypothesis.

Theorem 16. $Bem_1 Txt \setminus Fb^* Txt \neq \emptyset$.

Proof. The separating class $\mathcal{C}$ is defined as follows. $\mathcal{C}$ contains $c_0 = \{a\}^+$ and, for all $j \geq 1$, $c_j = \{a^\ell \mid 1 \leq \ell \leq 2j\} \cup \{b\}^+$. Moreover, for all $j, k, m \geq 1$, $\mathcal{C}$ contains the concept $c'_{j,k,m} = \{a^\ell \mid 1 \leq \ell \leq 2j\} \cup \{a^{2\langle j,k \rangle + 1}\} \cup \{b^\ell \mid 1 \leq \ell \leq m\}$.

Claim 1. $\mathcal{C} \in Bem_1 Txt$.

The required IIM M updates its example-memory as follows. As long as no element from $\{b\}^+$ occurs, M memorizes the maximal element from $\{a\}^+$ seen so far. Otherwise, it memorizes the maximal element from $\{b\}^+$ that has been presented so far. In addition, M updates its hypotheses in accordance with the following cases.

Case 1. M has never received an element from $\{b\}^+$.

Then, M guesses c_0.

Case 2. M receives an element x from $\{b\}^+$ for the first time.

Let $x = b^m$. If M has memorized an element of type a^{2j}, M guesses c_j. If it has memorized an element of type $a^{2\langle j,k \rangle + 1}$, M guess $c'_{j,k,m}$. If x is the first element presented at all, M simply guesses c_1.

Case 3. Otherwise.

Let x be the new element presented, let c' be M's actual guess, and let b^m be the element memorized by M.

First, if $x \in \{b\}^+$ and c' is of type $c'_{j,k,m}$, M guesses $c'_{j,k,m'}$, where $m' = max \{m, |x|\}$. If $x \in \{b\}^+$ and c' is of type c_j, M guesses c'.

Second, if $x \in \{a\}^+$ and $x \in c'$, M guesses c'. If $x \in \{a\}^+$, $x \notin c'$, and x is of type a^{2j}, M guesses c_j. Otherwise, i.e., $x \in \{a\}^+$, $x \notin c'$, and x is of type $a^{2\langle j,k\rangle+1}$, M guesses $c'_{j,k,m}$

The verification of M's correctness is straightforward.

Claim 2. $C \notin Fb^*Txt$.

Suppose to the contrary that there is a feedback learner M' that witnesses $C \in Lim^*Txt$. Hence, there is a locking sequence σ for c_0, i.e., σ is a finite sequence with $content(\sigma) \subseteq c_0$ and, for all finite sequences ρ with $content(\rho) \subseteq c_0$, $M'_*(\sigma \diamond \rho) = M'_*(\sigma)$.

Let j be the least index with $content(\sigma) \subseteq c_j$. Consider M when fed the text $t = \sigma \diamond a, \ldots, a^{2j} \diamond b \diamond b, b^2 \diamond b, b^2, b^3 \diamond \cdots \diamond b, b^2, \ldots, b^n \diamond \cdots$ for c_j. Since M' learns c_j, M' converges on t. Hence, there is a y such that (i) the last element in t_y equals b and (ii), for all $r \in \mathbb{N}$, $M'_*(t_y) = M'_*(t_{y+r})$.

Finally, fix τ such that $t_y = \sigma \diamond a, \ldots, a^{2j} \diamond \tau$. Let k, m be the least indices such that $content(t_y) \subseteq c'_{j,k,m}$ and $a^{2\langle j,k\rangle+1}$ is an element from c_0 which M' has never asked for when processing t_y. Consider M' when fed the text $t' = \sigma \diamond a, \ldots, a^{2j} \diamond a^{2\langle j,k\rangle+1} \diamond \tau \diamond b, b, \ldots$ for $c'_{j,k,m}$. By the choice of σ und y, M' converges on t and t' to the same hypothesis. (To see this note that the b's at the end of t' guarantee that M' almost always ask the same question as in case it is fed t_y, thereby, due to choice of $a^{2\langle j,k\rangle+1}$, always receiving the same answer.) Since $c_j \neq^* c'_{j,k,m}$, M' cannot learn both concepts, a contradiction. $\square$

The opposite holds, as well. Feedback queries may compensate the ability of a bounded-example memory learner to memorize any *a priori* fixed number of examples *and* to make finitely many errors in its final hypothesis.

Theorem 17. $FbTxt \setminus \bigcup_{k \in \mathbb{N}} Bem_k^*Txt \neq \emptyset$

Proof. We define the separating class C as follows. We set $C = \bigcup_{k \in \mathbb{N}} C_k$, where, for all $k \in \mathbb{N}$, the subclass C_k is defined as follows.

Let $(F_j)_{j \in \mathbb{N}}$ be a repetition-free enumeration of all finite sets of natural numbers. By convention, let $F_0 = \emptyset$. Moreover, we let $P_0 = \{b\}^+$ and $P_{j+1} = P_j \setminus \{b^{n p_j} \mid n \geq 1\}$, where, for all $j \in \mathbb{N}$, p_j is the $j+1$-st prime number.

Let $k \in \mathbb{N}$. Then, C_k contains the concept $c_0 = \{a\}^+$ as well as, for all $j, m \geq 1$ and all $l_0, \ldots, l_k$ with $j < l_0 < \cdots < l_k$, the concept $c_{(j,m,l_0,\ldots,l_k)} = \{a^\ell \mid 1 \leq \ell \leq j\} \cup \{a^{l_0}, \ldots, a^{l_k}\} \cup \{b^{j+1} \mid j \in F_m\} \cup P_{(l_0,\ldots,l_k)} \cup \{d^j\}$.

By definition, C contains exclusively infinite concepts, and thus $C \in FbTxt$ (cf. [8], for the relevant details).

For proving $C \notin \bigcup_{k \in \mathbb{N}} Bem_k^*Txt$, it suffices to show that, for every $k \in \mathbb{N}$, $C_k \notin Bem_k^*Txt$. The corresponding verification is part of the demonstration of Theorem 18 below. $\square$

Our next result illustrates the error-correcting power of bounded example-memories. As it turns out, every additional example which an incremental learner can memorize may help to correct up to finitely many errors.

Theorem 18. *For all* $k \in \mathbb{N}$, $Bem_{k+1}Txt \setminus Bem_k^*Txt \neq \emptyset$.

Proof. Let $k \in \mathbb{N}$. We claim that C_k (cf. the demonstration of Theorem 17 above) separates the learning types $Bem_{k+1}Txt$ and Bem_k^*Txt.

Claim 1. $C_k \in Bem_{k+1}Txt$.

The required bounded example-memory learner M behaves as follows. As a rule, M memorizes the $k + 1$ longest elements from $\{a\}^+$ which it has seen so far. Moreover, M updates its hypotheses in accordance with the following cases.

Case 1. M has never received an element from $\{d\}^+$.

Then, M outputs an index for the concept c_0 that allows M to determine all elements from $\{b\}^+$ that have been presented so far.

Case 2. M receives an element x from $\{d\}^+$ for the first time.

Let $x = d^j$ and let S' be the set of all elements from $\{b\}^+$ seen so far. M outputs an index for the concept $\{a^\ell \mid 1 \leq \ell \leq j\} \cup \{d^j\} \cup S'$ that allows M to determine the elements in S'.

Case 3. Otherwise.

We distinguish the following subcases.

Case 3.1. M has memorized $k + 1$ elements s with $|s| > j$.

Let x be the new element presented, let $S = \{a^{l_0}, \ldots, a^{l_k}\}$ be the set of elements memorized by M, and let S' be the set of elements from $\{b^+\}$ that are encoded in M's last hypothesis. If $x \in \{b\}^+ \setminus P_{\langle l_0, \ldots, l_k \rangle}$, we let $S' = S' \cup \{x\}$. Otherwise, S' remains unchanged. Moreover, M outputs an index for the concept $\{a^\ell \mid 1 \leq \ell \leq j\} \cup S \cup S' \cup P_{\langle l_0, \ldots, l_k \rangle} \cup \{d^j\}$ that allows M to recompute the elements in S'.

Case 3.2. Not Case 3.1.

As above, M outputs an index of the concept $\{a^\ell \mid 1 \leq \ell \leq j\} \cup \{d^j\} \cup S'$ that allows M to determine the elements in S', where S' is again the set of all elements from $\{b\}^+$ seen so far.

The verification of M's correctness is straightforward.

Claim 2. $C_k \notin Bem_k^*Txt$.

Suppose to the contrary that there is a k-bounded example-memory learner M' that witnesses $C \in Lim^*Txt$. Hence, there is a locking sequence σ for c_0, i.e., σ is a finite sequence with $content(\sigma) \subseteq c_0$ and, for all finite sequences ρ with $content(\rho) \subseteq c_0$, $\pi_1(M_*'(\sigma \diamond \rho)) = \pi_1(M_*'(\sigma))$.[1] Now let $j = max\{|x| \mid x \in content(\sigma)\}$. Similarly as in the demonstration of Theorem 6 in [15], one may use counting arguments to show that there are indices $l_0, l_0', \ldots, l_k, l_k'$ such that Conditions (a) to (d) are fulfilled, where

(a) $j < l_0 < l_1 < \cdots < l_k$.
(b) $j < l_0' < l_1' < \cdots < l_k'$.
(c) $\{l_0, l_1, \ldots, l_k\} \neq \{l_0', l_1', \ldots, l_k'\}$.
(d) $M_*'(\sigma \diamond a^{l_0}, \ldots, a^{l_k}) = M_*'(\sigma \diamond a^{l_0'}, \ldots, a^{l_k'})$.

Assume that $\langle l_0, \ldots, l_k \rangle < \langle l_0', \ldots, l_k' \rangle$. Let t_1 and t_1' be the lexicographically ordered text for $P_{\langle l_0, \ldots, l_k \rangle}$ and $P_{\langle l_0', \ldots, l_k' \rangle}$, respectively. Moreover, we set $\sigma' = \sigma \diamond a, a^2, \ldots, a^j$. Since M' infers $c_{\langle j, 0, l_0, \ldots, l_k \rangle}$, there is a finite sequence τ with $content(\tau) \subseteq P_{\langle l_0, \ldots, l_k \rangle}$ such that, for all finite sequences ρ with $content(\rho) \subseteq P_{\langle l_0, \ldots, l_k \rangle}$, $\pi_1(M_*'(\sigma' \diamond a^{l_0}, \ldots, a^{l_k} \diamond d^j \diamond \tau)) = \pi_1(M_*'(\sigma' \diamond a^{l_0}, \ldots, a^{l_k} \diamond d^j \diamond \tau \diamond \rho))$.

---

[1] Recall that M outputs pairs $\langle j, S \rangle$. By convention, we let $\pi_1(\langle j, S \rangle) = j$.

Now, fix $m' \in \mathbb{N}$ with $F_{m'} = \{\ell \mid b^\ell \in content(\tau)\}$ and consider M' when successively fed the text $t = \sigma' \diamond a^{l_0}, a^{l_1}, \ldots, a^{l_k} \diamond d^j \diamond \tau \diamond t_1$ for $c_{(j,0,l_0,\ldots,l_k)}$ and the text $t' = \sigma' \diamond a^{l'_0}, a^{l'_1}, \ldots, a^{l'_k} \diamond d^j \diamond \tau \diamond t'_1$ for $c_{(j,m',l'_0,\ldots,l'_k)}$, respectively. By the choice of σ and τ and since, by definition, $P_{(l'_0,\ldots,l'_k)} \subset P_{(l_0,\ldots,l_k)}$, we may conclude that M' converges to the same hypothesis when fed t and t', respectively. Since $c_{(j,0,l_0,\ldots,l_k)} \neq^* c_{(j,m',l'_0,\ldots,l'_k)}$, M' cannot learn both concepts, a contradiction. $\square$

For incremental learning with anomalies, Proposition 3 rewrites as follows.

Corollary 19.
(1) $It^*Txt \subset Fb^*Txt$.
(2) $It^*Txt \subset Bem_1^*Txt$.
(3) For all $k \in \mathbb{N}$, $Bem_k^*Txt \subset Bem_{k+1}^*Txt$.
(4) $Bem_1^*Txt \setminus Fb^*Txt \neq \emptyset$.
(5) $Fb^*Txt \setminus \bigcup_{k \in \mathbb{N}} Bem_k^*Txt \neq \emptyset$.

4   Learning from positive and negative data

In the section, we briefly summarize the results that can be obtained when studying learning with anomalies from positive and negative data.

Let $\mathcal{X}$ be the underlying learning domain, let $c \subseteq \mathcal{X}$ be a concept, and let $i = ((x_n, b_n))_{n \in \mathbb{N}}$ be any sequence of elements of $\mathcal{X} \times \{+, -\}$ such that $content(i) = \{x_n \mid n \in \mathbb{N}\} = \mathcal{X}$, $content^+(i) = \{x_n \mid n \in \mathbb{N}, b_n = +\} = c$ and $content^-(i) = \{x_n \mid n \in \mathbb{N}, b_n = -\} = \mathcal{X} \setminus c = \bar{c}$. Then, we refer to i as an informant. By $Info(c)$ we denote the set of all informants for c.

For all $a \in \mathbb{N} \cup \{*\}$, the standard learning models Fin^aInf, $Consv^aInf$, Lim^aInf and Bc^aInf are defined analogously as their text counterparts by replacing text by informant. Moreover, we extend the definitions of all variants of iterative learning in the same manner and denote the resulting learning types by It^aInf, Fb^aInf, and Bem_k^aInf, where $k \in \mathbb{N}$.

Since $\mathcal{IC} = ConsvInf$ (cf. [10]), we may easily conclude:

Corollary 20.
For all $a \in \mathbb{N} \cup \{*\}$: $ConsvInf = Consv^aInf = Lim^aInf = Bc^aInf$.

Moreover, one can easily show that the known inclusions $FinTxt \subset FinInf$ and $FinInf \subset ConsvTxt$ (cf. [13]) rewrite as follows:

Theorem 21. $Fin^*Txt \subset Fin^*Inf \subset Consv^*Txt$.

Concerning incremental learning, it has recently be shown that $\mathcal{IC} = FbInf = Bem_1Inf$ (cf. [12]). Clearly this allows for the following corollary.

Corollary 22. For all $a \in \mathbb{N} \cup \{*\}$: $ConsvInf = Fb^aInf = Bem_1^aInf$.

Moreover, it is folklore that $\mathcal{IC} = It^*Inf$. In contrast, if the number of allowed anomalies is a priori bounded, an infinite hierarchy of more and more powerful iterative learners can be observed.

Theorem 23. $ItInf \subset It^1Inf \subset It^2Inf \subset \cdots \subset It^*Inf = ConsvInf$.

Finally, it is not hard to verify that the results obtained so far prove the existence of an infinite hierarchy of more and more powerful finite learners parameterized in the number of allowed anomalies.

References

1. D. Angluin. Finding patterns common to a set of strings. *Journal of Computer and System Sciences*, 21:46–62, 1980.
2. D. Angluin. Inductive inference of formal languages from positive data. *Information and Control*, 45:117–135, 1980.
3. G.R. Baliga, J. Case, and S. Jain. The synthesis of language learners. *Information and Computation*, 152:16–43, 1999.
4. J. Bārzdiņš. Two theorems on the limiting synthesis of functions. In *Theory of Algorithms and Programs Vol. 1*, pages 82–88, Latvian State University, 1974, (Russian).
5. L. Blum and M. Blum. Toward a mathematical theory of inductive inference. *Information and Control*, 28:122–155, 1975.
6. J. Case and C. Lynes. Machine inductive inference and language identification. In *Proc. 9th International Colloquium on Automata, Languages and Programming*, Lecture Notes in Computer Science 140, pages 107–115. Springer-Verlag, Berlin, 1982.
7. J. Case and C.H. Smith. Comparison of identification criteria for machine inductive inference. *Theoretical Computer Science* 25:193–220, 1983.
8. J. Case, S. Jain, S. Lange, and T. Zeugmann, Incremental concept learning for bounded data mining. *Information and Computation* 152:74–110, 1999.
9. M. Fulk. Prudence and other restrictions in formal language learning. *Information and Computation*, 85:1–11, 1990.
10. E.M. Gold. Language identification in the limit. *Information and Control*, 10:447–474, 1967.
11. S. Jain, D. Osherson, J. Royer, and A. Sharma. *Systems that Learn - 2nd Edition, An Introduction to Learning Theory*. MIT Press, Cambridge, Mass., 1999.
12. S. Lange and G. Grieser. On the strength of incremental learning. In *Proc. 10th International Conference on Algorithmic Learning Theory*, Lecture Notes in Artificial Intelligence 1720, pages 118–131. Springer-Verlag, Berlin, 1999.
13. S. Lange and T. Zeugmann. Types of monotonic language learning and their characterization. In *Proc. 5th Annual ACM Workshop on Computational Learning Theory*, pages 377–390. ACM Press, New York, 1992.
14. S. Lange and T. Zeugmann. Language learning in dependence on the space of hypotheses. In *Proc. 6th Annual ACM Conference on Computational Learning Theory*, pages 127–136. ACM Press, New York, 1993.
15. S. Lange and T. Zeugmann. Incremental learning from positive data. *Journal of Computer and System Sciences*, 53:88–103, 1996.
16. S. Lange and T. Zeugmann. Set-driven and rearrangement-independent learning of recursive languages. *Mathematical Systems Theory*, 29:599–634, 1996.
17. T. Tabe and T. Zeugmann. Two variations of inductive inference of languages from positive data. Technical Report RIFIS-TR-CS-105, Kyushu University, 1995.
18. K. Wexler and P. Culicover. *Formal Principles of Language Acquisition*. MIT Press, Cambridge, Mass., 1980.
19. R. Wiehagen. Limes-Erkennung rekursiver Funktionen durch spezielle Strategien. *Journal of Information Processing and Cybernetics (EIK)*, 12:93–99, 1976.
20. T. Zeugmann and S. Lange. A guided tour across the boundaries of learning recursive languages. In K.P. Jantke and S. Lange, editors, *Algorithmic Learning for Knowledge-Based Systems*, Lecture Notes in Artificial Intelligence 961, pages 190–258. Springer-Verlag, Berlin, 1995.

Identification of Function Distinguishable Languages

Henning Fernau

Wilhelm-Schickard-Institut für Informatik, Universität Tübingen
Sand 13, D-72076 Tübingen, Germany
fernau@informatik.uni-tuebingen.de

Abstract. We show how appropriately chosen functions which we call *distinguishing* can be used to make deterministic finite automata backward deterministic. These ideas can be exploited to design regular language classes identifiable in the limit from positive samples. Special cases of this approach are the k-reversible and terminal distinguishable languages as discussed in [1,8,10,17,18].

1 Introduction

The learning model we use is *identification in the limit from positive samples* as proposed by Gold [13]. In this well-established model, a language class $\mathcal{L}$ (defined via a class of language describing devices $\mathcal{D}$ as, e.g., grammars or automata) is said to be *identifiable* if there is a so-called *inference machine* I to which as input an arbitrary language $L \in \mathcal{L}$ may be enumerated (possibly with repetitions) in an arbitrary order, i.e., I receives an infinite input stream of words $E(1)$, $E(2)$, ..., where $E : \mathbb{N} \to L$ is an enumeration of L, i.e., a surjection, and I reacts with an output device stream $D_i \in \mathcal{D}$ such that there is an $N(E)$ so that, for all $n \geq N(E)$, we have $D_n = D_{N(E)}$ and, moreover, the language defined by $D_{N(E)}$ equals L.

Recently, Rossmanith [19] defined a probabilistic variant of Gold's model which he called *learning from random text*. In fact, the only languages that are learnable in this variant are those that are also learnable in Gold's model. In that way, our results can also transferred into a stochastic setting.

This model is rather weak (when considering the descriptive capacity of the device classes which can be learned in this way), since Gold already has shown [13] that any language class which contains all finite languages and one infinite language is not identifiable in the limit from positive samples. On the other hand, the model is very natural, since in most applications, negative samples are not available. There are several ways to deal with this sort of weakness:

1. One could allow certain imprecision in the inference process; this has been done in a model proposed by Wiehagen [25] or within the PAC model proposed by Valiant [24] and variants thereof as the one suggested by Angluin [2] where membership queries are admissible, or, in another sense, by several

H. Arimura, S. Jain and A. Sharma (Eds.): ALT 2000, LNAI 1968, pp. 116–130, 2000.

heuristic approaches to the learning problem (including genetic algorithms or neural networks).

2. One could provide help to the learner by a teacher, see [2].

3. One could investigate how far one could get when maintaining the original deterministic model of learning in the limit.

The present paper makes some steps in the third direction.

The main point of this paper is to give a unified view on several identifiable language families through what we call f-distinguishing functions. In particular, this provides, to our knowledge, the first complete correctness proof of the identifiability of some language classes proposed to be learnable, as, e.g., in the case of terminal distinguishable languages. Among the language families which turn out to be special cases of our approach are the k-reversible languages [1] and the terminal-distinguishable languages [17,18], which belong, according to Gregor [14], to the most popular identifiable regular language classes. Moreover, we show how to the ideas underlying the well-known identifiable language classes of k-testable languages, k-piecewise testable languages and threshold testable languages transfer to our setting.

The paper is organized as follows: In Section 2, we provide both the necessary background from formal language theory and introduce the central concepts of the paper, namely the so-called distinguishing functions and the function distinguishable grammars, automata and languages. Furthermore, we introduce function canonical automata which will become the backbone of several proofs later on. In Section 3, several characteristic properties for function distinguishable languages are established. Section 4 shows the inferrability of the class of f-distinguishable languages (for each distinguishing function f), while Section 5 presents a concrete inference algorithm which is quite similar to the one given by Angluin [1] in the case of 0-reversible languages. Section 6 exhibits several interesting special cases of the general setting, relating to k-testable languages, k-piecewise testable languages and threshold testable languages. Section 7 concludes the paper, indicating practical applications of our method and extensions to non-regular language families.

2   Definitions

2.1   Formal language prerequisites

Σ^* is the set of words over the alphabet Σ. Σ^k ($\Sigma^{<k}$) collects the words whose lengths are equal to (less than) k. λ denotes the empty word. Pref(L) is the set of prefixes of L and $u^{-1}L = \{\, v \in \Sigma^* | uv \in L \,\}$ is the quotient of $L \subseteq \Sigma^*$ by u.

We assume that the reader knows that regular languages can be characterized either (1) by left-linear grammars $G = (N, T, P, S)$, where N is the set of nonterminal symbols, T is the set of terminal symbols, $P \subset N \times (N \cup \{\lambda\})T^*$ is the rule set and $S \in N$ is the start symbol, or (2) by (deterministic) finite automata $A = (Q, T, \delta, q_0, Q_F)$, where Q is the state set, $\delta \subseteq Q \times T \times Q$ is the transition relation, $q_0 \in Q$ is the initial state and $Q_F \subseteq Q$ is the set of final states. As usual, δ^* denotes the extension of the transition relation to arbitrarily long input words. The language defined by a grammar G (or an automaton A) is written $L(G)$ (or $L(A)$, respectively). An automaton is called *stripped* iff all states are accessible from the initial state and all states lead to some final state. Observe that the transition function of a stripped deterministic finite automaton is not total in general.

Let $A = (Q, T, \delta, q_0, Q_F)$ be a finite automaton. We call an automaton $A' = (Q', T, \delta', q_0, Q'_F)$ *general subautomaton* if $Q' \subseteq Q$, $\delta' \subseteq \delta$ and $Q'_F \subseteq Q_F$. The *stripped subautomaton* of some finite automaton $A = (Q, T, \delta, q_0, Q_F)$ is obtained by removing all states from Q which are not accessible from the initial state and all states which do not lead to some final state, together with all triples from δ which contain states which have to be removed according to the formulated rules.

We denote the minimal deterministic automaton of the regular language L by $A(L)$. Recall that $A(L) = (Q, T, \delta, q_0, Q_F)$ can be described as follows: $Q = \{u^{-1}L | u \in \mathrm{Pref}(L)\}$, $q_0 = \lambda^{-1}L = L$; $Q_F = \{u^{-1}L | u \in L\}$; and $\delta(u^{-1}L, a) = (ua)^{-1}L$ with $u, ua \in \mathrm{Pref}(L)$, $a \in T$. According to our definition, any minimal deterministic automaton is stripped.

Furthermore, we need two automata constructions in the following:

The *product automaton* $A = A_1 \times A_2$ of two automata $A_i = (Q_i, T, \delta_i, q_{0,i}, Q_{F,i})$ for $i = 1, 2$ is defined as $A = (Q, T, \delta, q_0, Q_F)$ with $Q = Q_1 \times Q_2$, $q_0 = (q_{0,1}, q_{0,2})$, $Q_F = Q_{F,1} \times Q_{F,2}$, $((q_1, q_2), a, (q'_1, q'_2)) \in \delta$ iff $(q_1, a, q'_1) \in \delta_1$ and $(q_2, a, q'_2) \in \delta_2$.

A *partition* of a set S is a collection of pairwise disjoint nonempty subsets of S whose union is S. If π is a partition of S, then, for any element $s \in S$, there is a unique element of π containing s, which we denote $B(s, \pi)$ and call the *block* of π containing s. A partition π is said to *refine* another partition π' iff every block of π' is a union of blocks of π. If π is any partition of the state set Q of the automaton $A = (Q, T, \delta, q_0, Q_F)$, then the *quotient automaton* $\pi^{-1}A = (\pi^{-1}Q, T, \delta', B(q_0, \pi), \pi^{-1}Q_F)$ is given by $\pi^{-1}\hat{Q} = \{B(q, \pi) | q \in \hat{Q}\}$ (for $\hat{Q} \subseteq Q$) and $(B_1, a, B_2) \in \delta'$ iff $\exists q_1 \in B_1 \exists q_2 \in B_2 : (q_1, a, q_2) \in \delta$.

2.2   Distinguishing functions

In order to avoid cumbersome case discussions, let us fix now T as the terminal alphabet of the left-linear grammars and as the input alphabet of the finite automata we are going to discuss.

Definition 1. *Let F be some finite set. A mapping $f : T^* \to F$ is called a distinguishing function if $f(w) = f(z)$ implies $f(wu) = f(zu)$ for all $u, w, z \in T^*$.*

In the literature, we can find the terminal function [18]

$$\mathrm{Ter}(x) = \{a \in T \mid \exists u, v \in T^* : uav = x\}$$

and, more generally, the k-terminal function [10]

$$\mathrm{Ter}_k(x) = (\pi_k(x), \mu_k(x), \sigma_k(x)), \quad \text{where}$$
$$\mu_k(x) = \{a \in T^{k+1} \mid \exists u, v \in T^* : uav = x\}$$

and $\pi_k(x)$ $[\sigma_k(x)]$ is the prefix [suffix] of length k of x if $x \notin T^{<k}$, and $\pi_k(x) = \sigma_k(x) = x$ if $x \in T^{<k}$. The example $f(x) = \sigma_k(x)$ leads to the k-reversible languages, confer [1,10]. We will discuss these and other distinguishing functions in Section 6. Other examples of distinguishing functions in the context of even linear languages can be found in [9].

Observe that every regular language R induces, via its Nerode equivalence classes a distinguishing function f_R, where $f_R(w)$ maps w to the equivalence class containing w. Especially, T^* leads to a trivial distinguishing function $f_{T^*} : T^* \to \{q\}$, and the class of f_{T^*}-distinguishable languages coincides with the class of 0-reversible languages [1] over the alphabet T. In fact, many assertions, as well as their proofs, which we state in the following for f-distinguishable automata and languages correspond to similar assertions for 0-reversible language as exhibited by Anglam.

In some sense, these are the only distinguishing functions, since one can associate to every distinguishing function f a finite automaton $A_f = (F, T, \delta_f, f(\lambda), F)$ by setting $\delta_f(q, a) = f(wa)$, where $w \in f^{-1}(q)$ can be chosen arbitrarily, since f is a distinguishing function.

Definition 2. *Let* $G = (N, T, P, S)$ *be a left-linear grammar with*

$$P \subseteq (N \setminus \{S\}) \times ((N \setminus \{S\})T \cup \{\lambda\}) \cup \{S\} \times (N \setminus \{S\}).$$

This means that rules in G *are of the forms* $S \to A$, $A \to Ba$, *or* $A \to \lambda$ *for* $A, B \in N \setminus \{S\}$ *and* $a \in T$. *Let* $f : T^* \to F$ *be a distinguishing function. We will say that* G *is* f-distinguishable *if:*

1. G *is backward deterministic, i.e., for all* $A, B \in N$, $A \to w$ *and* $B \to w$ *imply* $A = B$.
2. *For all* $A \in N \setminus \{S\}$ *and for all* $x, y \in L(G, A)$,[1] *we have* $f(x) = f(y)$. *(In other words, for* $A \in N \setminus \{S\}$, $f(A) := f(x)$ *for some* $x \in L(G, A)$ *is well-defined.)*
3. *For all* $A, B, C \in N \setminus \{S\}$ *with* $B \neq C$ *and for all* $a \in T$, *if (a)* $S \to B$ *and* $S \to C$ *are in* P *or if (b)* $A \to Ba$ *and* $A \to Ca$ *are in* P, *then* $f(B) \neq f(C)$.

A language is called f-distinguishable *iff it can be generated by an* f-distinguishable left-linear grammar.*

The family of f-distinguishable languages is denoted by f-DL.*

Observe that the class f-DL formally fixes the alphabet of the languages by the range of f. As we have already seen by the examples for distinguishing functions listed above, f can oftenly defined for *all* alphabets. Taking this generic point of view, for example, Ter-DL is just the class of (reversals of) terminal distinguishable languages [9,18], where the alphabet is left unspecified.

Remark 1. Our notation is adapted from the so-called terminal distinguishable languages introduced by Radhakrishnan and Nagaraja in [18]. We use left-linear

---

[1] We will denote by $L(G, A)$ the language obtained by the grammar $G_A = (N, T, P, A)$.

grammars, while they use right-linear grammars in their definitions. This means that, e.g., the class Ter-DL coincides with the reversals (mirror images) of the class of terminal distinguishable languages, as exhibited in [9].[2]

Definition 3. *Let $A = (Q, T, \delta, q_0, Q_F)$ be a finite automaton. Let $f : T^* \to F$ be a distinguishing function. A is called f-distinguishable if:*

1. *A is deterministic.*
2. *For all states $q \in Q$ and all $x, y \in T^*$ with $\delta^*(q_0, x) = \delta^*(q_0, y) = q$, we have $f(x) = f(y)$.*
   (In other words, for $q \in Q$, $f(q) := f(x)$ for some x with $\delta^*(q_0, x) = q$ is well-defined.)
3. *For all $q_1, q_2 \in Q$, $q_1 \neq q_2$, with either (a) $q_1, q_2 \in Q_F$ or (b) there exist $q_3 \in Q$ and $a \in T$ with $\delta(q_1, a) = \delta(q_2, a) = q_3$, we have $f(q_1) \neq f(q_2)$.*

For example, for each distinguishing function f, the associated automaton A_f is f-distinguishable.

Remark 2. Our aim is to show the identifiability of each language class f-DL, where f is a distinguishing function. To this end, the notion of distinguishing function was tailored, and we do not see how to provide a simpler notion to ensure identifiability of the corresponding language classes. For example, it is easily seen that, for each distinguishing function $f : T^* \to F$, any f-distinguishing automaton has at most $|F|$ accepting states. This conceptual simple property is not useful to define an identifiable language class, since already the class of regular languages having a single accepting state is not identifiable in the limit, as this class contains all languages $L_m = \{\, a^n b \mid n < m \,\}$ for $m = 1, 2, \ldots, \infty$, see [13].

We need a suitable notion of a canonical automaton in the following.

Definition 4. *Let $f : T^* \to F$ be a distinguishing function and let $L \subseteq T^*$ be a regular set. Let $A(L, f)$ be the stripped subautomaton of the product automaton $A(L) \times A_f$, i.e., delete all states that are not accessible from the initial state or do not lead into a final state of $A(L) \times A_f$. $A(L, f)$ is called f-canonical automaton of L.*

Remark 3. 1. Observe that an f-canonical automaton trivially obeys the first two restrictions of an f-distinguishing automaton.
2. Clearly, $L(A(L, f)) = L$. □

---

[2] Note that their definition of terminal distinguishable right-linear grammar does not completely coincide with ours, but in order to maintain their results, their definition should be changed accordingly.

3   Characteristic Properties

We start this section with a sequence of rather straightforward remarks which turn out to be useful in the proof of the main theorem of this section which is Theorem 1. There, we derive six equivalent characterizations for regular languages to be f-distinguishable. In particular, the characterization by f-canonical automata will be needed in Section 4 in order to prove the inferrability of f-distinguishable languages, as well as in Section 5 for proving the correctness of the inference algorithm stated there.

In order to simplify the discussions below, we will always consider only the case of non-empty languages.

Remark 4. Let $f : T^* \to F$ be a distinguishing function. Consider $L \subseteq T^*$. Then, L is f-distinguishable iff L is accepted by an f-distinguishing automaton.

Proof. This easily follows via the standard proof showing the equivalence of left-linear grammars and finite automata.   □

More precisely, the ith ($i = 1$, $i = 2$, $i = 3a$, $i = 3b$) condition for f-distinguishable left-linear grammars "corresponds" to the ith condition for f-distinguishable finite automata. In particular, this means that backward deterministic left-linear grammars correspond to deterministic finite automata. Since it is well-known that the state-transition function δ of a finite automaton can be extended to a (partial) function mapping a state and a word over T into some state, this observation immediately yields the following:

Remark 5. Let $f : T^* \to F$ be a distinguishing function and let G be an f-distinguishable left-linear grammar. Then, for all nonterminals A, B, $A \Rightarrow^* w$ and $B \Rightarrow^* w$ imply $A = B$. [3]   □

Remark 6. Let $f : T^* \to F$ be a distinguishing function. Let $A = (Q, T, \delta, q_0, Q_F)$ be an f-distinguishing automaton accepting L. Then, we find: If $u_1 v, u_2 v \in L \subseteq T^*$ and $f(u_1) = f(u_2)$, then $\delta^*(q_0, u_1) = \delta^*(q_0, u_2)$.

Proof. Consider the final states $q_i = \delta^*(q_0, u_i v)$ of A for $i = 1, 2$. Since $f(q_i) = f(u_i v)$ and since $f(u_1) = f(u_2)$ implies that $f(u_1 v) = f(u_2 v)$, condition 3a. in the definition of f-distinguishing automata yields $q_1 = q_2$.

By induction, and using condition 3b. in the induction step argument, one can show that $\delta^*(q_0, u_1 v') = \delta^*(q_0, u_2 v')$ for every prefix v' of v. This yields the desired claim.   □

We are now presenting the main result of this section.

Theorem 1 (Characterization theorem). *The following conditions are equivalent for a regular language $L \subseteq T^*$ and a distinguishing function $f : T^* \to F$:*

1. L is f-distinguishable.

---

[3] This condition has been called *strongly backward deterministic* in [22].

2. For all $u, v, w, z \in T^*$ with $f(w) = f(z)$, we have $zu \in L \iff zv \in L$ whenever $\{wu, wv\} \subseteq L$.

3. For all $u, v, w, z \in T^*$ with $f(w) = f(z)$, we have $u \in z^{-1}L \iff v \in z^{-1}L$ whenever $u, v \in w^{-1}L$.

4. The f-canonical automaton of L is f-distinguishable.

5. L is accepted by an f-distinguishable automaton.

6. For all $u_1, u_2, v \in T^*$ with $f(u_1) = f(u_2)$, we have $u_1^{-1}L = u_2^{-1}L$ whenever $\{u_1 v, u_2 v\} \subseteq L$.

Proof. '1. → 2.:' Assume firstly that L is generated by an f-distinguishable left-linear grammar $G = (N, T, P, S)$. Consider $\{wu, wv\} \subseteq L$. Due to Remark 5 there will be a unique nonterminal A that will generate w, and both $S \Rightarrow^* Au$ and $S \Rightarrow^* Av$. More specifically, let $u = a_r \ldots a_1$ and let

$$S \Rightarrow X_0 \Rightarrow X_1 a_1 \Rightarrow X_2 a_2 a_1 \Rightarrow \ldots \Rightarrow X_{r-1} a_{r-1} \ldots a_1 \Rightarrow X_r a_r \ldots a_1 = Au \quad (1)$$

be the first of the above-mentioned derivations. Consider now a word $z \in T^*$ with $f(z) = f(w)$. By definition of distinguishing functions, we have $f(zu) = f(wu)$. This means that any derivation of zu via G must start with $S \Rightarrow X_0$, since otherwise the third condition (part (a)) of f-distinguishable grammars would be violated. By repeating this argument, taking now part (b) of the third part of the definition, we can conclude that any derivation of zu via G must start as depicted in Equation (1). Similarly, one can argue that any derivation of zv must start as any derivation of wv for the common suffix v. This means that any possible derivation of zu via G leads to the nonterminal A after processing the suffix u, and any possible derivation of zv via G leads to the nonterminal A after processing the suffix v, as well. Hence, $zu \in L$ iff $A \Rightarrow^* z$, and $zv \in L$ iff $A \Rightarrow^* z$. Therefore, $zu \in L$ iff $zv \in L$, as required.

'2. ↔ 3.' is trivial.

'3. → 4.:' Due to Remark 3, we have to consider only cases 3a. and 3b. of the definition of f-distinguishable automaton. We will prove that the f-canonical automaton $A = A(L, f) = (Q, T, \delta, q_0, Q_F)$ of L is indeed f-distinguishable by using two similar contradiction arguments.

Assume firstly that there exist two different final states q_1, q_2 of A, i.e., $q_i = (w_i^{-1}L, X_i)$ with $w_1^{-1}L \neq w_2^{-1}L$ and $X = X_1 = X_2$. We may assume that $X = f(w_1) = f(w_2)$. Consider two strings $u, v \in w_1^{-1}L$. Since we may assume property 3., we know that either $u, v \in w_2^{-1}L$ or $u, v \notin w_2^{-1}L$. Since q_1 and q_2 are final states, $u = \lambda \in w_1^{-1}L \cap w_2^{-1}L$. This means that $v \in w_1^{-1}L$ implies $v \in w_2^{-1}L$. Interchanging the roles of w_1 and w_2, we obtain $w_1^{-1}L = w_2^{-1}L$, a contradiction.

Secondly, consider two different states q_1, q_2 of A such that there is a third state q_3 with $\delta(q_1, a) = \delta(q_2, a) = q_3$. We have to treat the case that $q_i = (w_i^{-1}L, X_i)$ (where $i = 1, 2$) with $w_1^{-1}L \neq w_2^{-1}L$ and $X = X_1 = X_2$. We may assume that $X = f(w_1) = f(w_2)$. Since A is stripped by definition, there exists a suffix s such that $w_1 as, w_2 as \in L$. Hence, $as \in w_1^{-1}L \cap w_2^{-1}L$. This means that $v \in w_1^{-1}L$ implies $v \in w_2^{-1}L$. Interchanging the roles of w_1 and w_2, we obtain $w_1^{-1}L = w_2^{-1}L$, a contradiction.

'4. → 5.' is trivial.

'5. ↔ 1.' see Remark 4.

'4. → 6.' follows immediately by using Remark 6.

'6. → 4.': Let the regular language $L \subseteq T^*$ satisfy condition 6. Consider $A = A(L, f) = (Q, T, \delta, q_0, Q_F)$. Due to Remark 3, we have to verify only condition 3. in the definition of f-distinguishing automata for A. If $u_1, u_2 \in L$ with $f(u_1) = f(u_2)$, then $u_1^{-1}L = u_2^{-1}L$. Hence, $\delta^*(q_0, u_1) = \delta^*(q_0, u_2)$, i.e., A satisfies condition $3a$.

Consider two states $u_1^{-1}L$, $u_2^{-1}L$ of $A(L)$ with $f(u_1) = f(u_2)$. Assume that $(u_1a)^{-1}L = (u_2a)^{-1}L$ for some $a \in T$. Since $A(L, f)$ is stripped by definition, there is some $v' \in T^*$ such that $\{u_1av', u_2av'\} \subseteq L$. Hence, $\delta^*(q_0, u_1) = \delta^*(q_0, u_2)$, i.e., A satisfies condition $3b$.   □

Observe that the characterization theorem yields new characterizations for the special cases of both k-reversible and terminal distinguishable languages. More precisely, the first three characterizing conditions are new in the case of k-reversible languages, and the last three conditions are new in the case of terminal distinguishable languages.

We end this section with providing two further lemmas which will be useful in the following sections.

Lemma 1. *Let f be a distinguishing function. Any general subautomaton of an f-distinguishable automaton is f-distinguishable.*

Proof. By definition.   □

Lemma 2. *Let f be a distinguishing function. The stripped subautomaton of an f-distinguishable automaton is isomorphic to the f-canonical automaton.*

Proof. Denote by $A' = (Q', T, \delta', q_0, Q'_F)$ the stripped subautomaton of some f-distinguishable automaton $A = (Q, T, \delta, q_0, Q_F)$. According to Lemma 1, A' is f-distinguishable. We have to show that, for all $q_1, q_2 \in Q'$ with $f(q_1) = f(q_2)$,

$$\{v \in T^* \mid \delta^*(q_1, v) \in Q'_F\} = \{v \in T^* \mid \delta^*(q_2, v) \in Q'_F\} \Rightarrow q_1 = q_2,$$

since then the mapping $q \mapsto (w^{-1}L(A), f(q))$ for some $w \in T^*$ with $\delta'^*(q_0, w) = q$ in A' will supply the required isomorphism.

Since A' is stripped, there exist strings $u_1, u_2, v \in T^*$ with $q_1 = \delta'^*(q_0, u_1)$, $q_2 = \delta'^*(q_0, u_2)$ and $\{u_1v, u_2v\} \subseteq L(A)$. Since $f(q_1) = f(q_2)$ implies $f(u_1) = f(u_2)$, we can apply Remark 6 in order to conclude that q_1 equals q_2.   □

4   Inferrability

According to a theorem due to Angluin [15, Theorem 3.26], a language class $\mathcal{L}$ is inferable if any language $L \in \mathcal{L}$ has a characteristic sample, i.e., a finite subset $\chi(L) \subseteq L$ such that L is a minimal language from $\mathcal{L}$ containing $\chi(L)$.

For the language class f-DL and some language $L \in f$-DL, consider the corresponding f-canonical automaton $A(L, f) = (Q, T, \delta, q_0, Q_F)$ and define

$$\chi(L, f) = \{ u(q)v(q) \mid q \in Q \}$$
$$\cup \{ u(q)av(\delta(q, a)) \mid q \in Q, a \in T \},$$

where $u(q)$ and $v(q)$ are words of minimal length with $\delta^*(q_0, u(q)) = q$ and $\delta^*(q, v(q)) \in Q_F$. Naturally, a finite automaton for $\chi(L, f)$ may be computed by some Turing machine which is given A_L and A_f as input.

Theorem 2. *For each distinguishing function f and each $L \in f$-DL, $\chi(L, f)$ is a characteristic sample of L.*

Proof. Consider an arbitrary language $L' \in f$-DL with $\chi(L, f) \subseteq L'$. Set $A = A(L, f) = (Q, T, \delta, q_0, Q_F)$ and $A' = A(L', f) = (Q', T, \delta', q_0', Q_F')$, cf. Theorem 1. We have to show $L \subseteq L'$. Therefore, we will prove:

(*) for all $w \in \text{Pref}(L)$,

$$q = \delta^*(q_0, w) = (w^{-1}L', f(w)) = ((u(q))^{-1}L', f(u(q))).$$

(*) implies: If $w \in L$, i.e., $q_f = \delta^*(q_0, w)$ is final state of A, then, since $u(q_f) \in \chi(L, f) \subseteq L'$, $(u(q_f))^{-1}L'$ is an accepting state of the minimal automaton $A(L')$ of L'. This means that $(u(q_f)^{-1}L', f(u(q_f)))$ is an accepting state of A', i.e., $w \in L'$, since $f(w) = f(u(q))$. Hence, L is a minimal f-distinguishable language containing $\chi(L, f)$.

We prove (*) by induction over the length of the prefix w we have to consider. If $|w| = 0$, then $w = u(q_0) = \lambda$. Hence, (*) is trivially verified.

We assume that (*) holds for all $w \in T^{<n+1}$, $n \geq 0$. We discuss the case where $w \in T^n$, $a \in T$ and $wa \in \text{Pref}(L)$. Since $w \in \text{Pref}(L)$, the induction hypothesis yields $(w^{-1}L', f(q)) = ((u(q))^{-1}L', f(q))$, where $q = \delta^*(q_0, w)$ and $f(w) = f(q) = f(u(q))$. Therefore, $(wa)^{-1}L' = (u(q)a)^{-1}L'$ and $f(wa) = f(u(q)a)$, since f is a distinguishing function. Consider $q' = \delta(q, a) = \delta^*(q_0, wa)$.

Since $\{u(q)av(q'), u(q')v(q')\} \subseteq \chi(L, f) \subseteq L'$ and $f(u(q)a) = f(u(q')) = f(wa)$, $\delta'^*(q_0', u(q)a) = \delta'^*(q_0', u(q'))$ due to Remark 6 and, hence, we can conclude that $(u(q'))^{-1}L' = (u(q)a)^{-1}L'$. The induction of (*) is finished. $\square$

5   Inference algorithm

We sketch an algorithm which receives an input sample set $I_+ = \{w_1, \ldots, w_M\}$ (a finite subset of the language $L \in f$-DL to be identified) and finds a minimal language $L' \in f$-DL which contains I_+. In order to specify that algorithm more precisely, we need the following notions.

The *prefix tree acceptor* $PTA(I_+) = (Q, T, \delta, q_0, Q_F)$ of a finite sample set $I_+ = \{w_1, \ldots, w_M\} \subset T^*$ is a deterministic finite automaton which is defined as follows: $Q = \text{Pref}(I_+)$, $q_0 = \lambda$, $Q_F = I_+$ and $\delta(v, a) = va$ for $va \in \text{Pref}(I_+)$.

A simple merging state inference algorithm f-`Ident` for f-DL now starts with the automaton A_0 which is the stripped subautomaton of $PTA(I_+) \times A_f{}^4$ and merges two arbitrarily chosen states q and q' which cause a conflict to the first or the third of the requirements for f-distinguishing automata. (One can show that the second requirement won't be violated ever when starting the merging process with A_0 which trivially satisfies that condition.) This yields an automaton A_1. Again, choose two conflicting states p, p' and merge them to obtain an automaton A_2 and so forth, until one comes to an automaton A_t which is f-distinguishable. In this way, we get a chain of automata $A_0, A_1, \ldots, A_t$. Speaking more formally, each automaton A_i in this chain can be interpreted as a quotient automaton of A_0 by the partition of the state set of A_0 induced by the corresponding merging operation. Observe that each A_i is stripped, since A_0 is stripped.

Completely analogous to [1, Lemma 1], one can prove:

Lemma 3. *Consider a distinguishing function f and some $L \in f$-DL. Let $I_+ \subseteq L \subseteq T^*$ be a finite sample. Let π be the partition of states of A_0 (the stripped subautomaton of $PTA(I_+) \times A_f$) given by: $(q_1, f(q_1))$, $(q_2, f(q_2))$ belong to the same block iff $q_1^{-1}L = q_2^{-1}L$ and $f(q_1) = f(q_2)$.[5] Then, the quotient automaton $\pi^{-1}A_0$ is isomorphic to a subautomaton of $A(L, f)$.* $\square$

Theorem 3. *Let f be a distinguishing function. Consider a chain of automata $A_0, A_1, \ldots, A_t$ obtained by applying the sketched algorithm f-`Ident` on input sample I_+, where A_0 is the stripped subautomaton of $PTA(I_+) \times A_f$. Then, we have:*

1. *$L(A_0) \subseteq L(A_1) \subseteq \cdots \subseteq L(A_t)$.*
2. *A_t is f-distinguishable and stripped.*
3. *The partition π_t of the state set of A_0 corresponding to A_t is the finest partition π of the state set of A_0 such that the quotient automaton $\pi^{-1}A_0$ is f-distinguishable.*

Proof. 1. is clear, since f-`Ident` is a merging states algorithm.
2. follows almost by definition.
3. can be shown by induction, proving that each π_i corresponding to A_i refines π. Since this proof is analogous to [1, Lemma 25], we omit it; see also [6, Propriété 1.1]. $\square$

Theorem 4. *In the notations of the previous theorem, $L(A_t)$ is a minimal f-distinguishable language containing I_+.*

Proof. The previous theorem states that $L(A_t) \in f$-DL and $I_+ = L(A_0) \subseteq L(A_t)$. Consider now an arbitrary language L containing I_+. We consider the quotient automaton $\pi^{-1}A_0$ defined in Lemma 3. This Lemma shows that

$$L(\pi^{-1}A_0) \subseteq L = L(A(L, f)).$$

---

[4] Of course, this automaton is equivalent to $PTA(I_+)$.
[5] Note that states of $PTA(I_+)$ are words over T.

By Lemma 1, $\pi^{-1}A_0$ is f-distinguishable, because $A(L, f)$ is f-distinguishable due to Theorem 1. Theorem 3 yields that π_t refines π, so that

$$L(A_t) = L(\pi_t^{-1}A_0) \subseteq L(\pi^{-1}A_0) = L. \quad \Box$$

Theorem 5. *If $L \in f\text{-}DL$ is enumerated as input to the algorithm f-Ident, it converges to the f-canonical automaton $A(L, f)$.*

Proof. At some point N of the enumeration process, the characteristic sample $\chi(L, f)$ will have been given to f-Ident. By combining Theorems 2 and 4, for all $n \geq N$, and all automata A_n output by f-Ident, we have $L(A_n) = L$. The argument of Theorem 4 shows that each A_n (with $n \geq N$) is isomorphic to a subautomaton of $A(L, f)$ generating $L = L(A(L, f))$. Since each A_n is stripped, it must be isomorphic to $A(L, f)$ for $n \geq N$. $\quad \Box$

We refrain from giving details of particular cases of f-Ident, since good implementations of f-Ident will depend on the choice of the distinguishing function f. We refer to [1,10,18] for several specific algorithms, including their time analysis. We only remark that the performance of the general algorithm f-Ident sketched above depends on the size of A_f (since the characteristic sample $\chi(L, f)$ we defined above depends on this size) and is in this sense "scalable", since "larger" A_f permit larger language families to be identified. More precisely:

Proposition 1. *Let f and g be distinguishing functions. If A_f is a homomorphic image of A_g, then $f\text{-}DL \subseteq g\text{-}DL$.*

Proof. In order to show the inclusion, we can restrict our argument to the f- (g)-canonical automata. Let $L \in f\text{-}DL$. Consider $A(L, f)$. Recall that $A(L, f)$ is the stripped version of the product automaton $A(L) \times A_f$, where also $L(A(L) \times A_f) = L$. Now, it is easy to extend the assumed automata homomorphism mapping A_f onto A_g to a homomorphism mapping $A(L) \times A_f$ onto $A(L) \times A_g$, i.e., $L = L(A(L) \times A_g) \in g\text{-}DL$. $\quad \Box$

We will discuss special cases below.

Remark 7. As regards the time complexity, let us mention briefly that the f-Ident algorithm can be implemented to run in time $O(\alpha(|F|n)|F|n)$, where α is the inverse Ackermann function and n is the total length of all words in I_+ from language L, when L is the language presented to the learner for f-DL.

Proof. This observation follows from the fact that f-Ident can be implemented similarly to the algorithm for 0-reversible languages exhibited by Angluin [1]. Moreover, her time analysis carries over to our situation. $\quad \Box$

Observe that this leads to an $O((\alpha(|T|^k n)|T|^k n)$ algorithm for k-reversible languages, even if we output the deterministic minimal automaton as canonical object (instead of $A(L, f)$ as would be done by our algorithm), since $A(L)$ can be obtained by $A(L, f)$ by computationally simple projection. On the other hand,

Angluin [1] presented an $O(kn^3)$ algorithm for the inference of k-reversible languages. When k is small compared to n (as it would be in realistic applications, where k could be considered even as a fixed parameter), our algorithm would turn out to be superior compared with Angluin's. Recall that this feature is prominent in so-called fixed-parameter algorithms, see [3,4,16].

We mention that f-Ident can be easily converted into an incremental algorithm, as sketched in the case of reversible languages in [1].

6   Special cases

Already in Section 2.2, we gave several examples of distinguishing functions, which, due to the results in the preceding sections, lead to identifiable language classes. We will discuss these and other distinguishing functions and the corresponding classes here.

In [10], we claimed the inferrability of the k-terminal distinguishable languages without proof. This fact follows from our general results together with the following lemma.

Lemma 4. *For all $k \in \mathbb{N}$, Ter_k is a distinguishing function.*

Proof. Consider three strings $u, w, z \in T^*$ with $\mathrm{Ter}_k(w) = \mathrm{Ter}_k(z)$. It is clear that $\pi_k(w) = \pi_k(z)$ implies $\pi_k(wu) = \pi_k(zu)$ and that $\sigma_k(w) = \sigma_k(z)$ implies $\sigma_k(wu) = \sigma_k(zu)$. Now, if $\mu_k(w) = \mu_k(z)$ and $\sigma_k(w) = \sigma_k(z)$, then consider some word $x \in \mu_k(wu)$. If $x \in \mu_k(w)$, then clearly $x \in \mu_k(z) \subseteq \mu_k(zu)$. If $x \in \mu_k(u)$, then trivially $x \in \mu_k(zu)$. The only remaining case is $x = x_1 x_2$, $x_1 \neq \lambda$ and $x_2 \neq \lambda$, where x_1 is a suffix of w and x_2 is a prefix of u. Hence, x_1 is also a suffix of $\pi_k(w)$, i.e., x_1 is also a suffix of z. Therefore, $x \in \mu_k(zu)$. This yields $\mu_k(wu) \subseteq \mu_k(zu)$. Interchanging the roles of w and z, we obtain $\mu_k(wu) = \mu_k(zu)$ as desired.   □

This leads to an $O((\alpha(|T|^{2k} 2^{|T|^k} n)|T|^{2k} 2^{|T|^k} n)$ algorithm for k-terminal distinguishable languages, where n is the total length of all words in a positive sample I_+.

We can also supply a proof of the following theorem stated in [10] in this place:

Theorem 6 (Hierarchy theorem). $\forall k \geq 0 : \mathrm{Ter}_k\text{-}DL \subset \mathrm{Ter}_{k+1}\text{-}DL$.

Proof. As indicated in [10], $\{a^k, a^{k+1}\}$ is in Ter_{k+1}-DL but not in Ter_k-DL. We like to apply Proposition 1 in order to prove the inclusion. To this end, we have to show how to map states of $A_{\mathrm{Ter}_{k+1}}$, which are of the form (x, Y, z) with $x, z \in T^{<k+2}$ and $Y \subseteq 2^{T^{k+2}}$, into states of A_{Ter_k}. This can be done by

$$(x, Y, z) \mapsto (\pi_k(x), (\bigcup_{y \in Y} \mu_k(y)) \cup \mu_k(x) \cup \mu_k(z), \sigma_k(z)).$$

The reader may verify that this mapping is indeed a homomorphism.   □

Since every k-testable language (in the strict sense) [12] is easily seen to be generatable by a general subautomaton of the Ter_k-distinguishable automaton A_{Ter_k}, it follows that every k-testable language is in Ter_k-DL due to Lemma 1.

Ruiz and García discussed another family of language classes which they called k-piecewise testable languages [21] and showed that each member of this family is identifiable. In the following, we show how these ideas can be adapted in order to create identifiable language classes within our setting.

Given $x, y \in T^*$, we say that $x = a_1 a_2 \ldots a_n$, with $a_i \in T$, $i = 1, \ldots, n$, is a *sparse subword* of y iff $y \in T^*\{a_1\}T^*\{a_2\}T^* \ldots T^*\{a_n\}T^*$. We will write $x|y$ in this case. $\cdot|\cdot$ is also called *division (ordering)*. Let $\Delta_k(w) = \{x \in T^{<k} \mid x|w\}$.

Without proof, we state:

Lemma 5. *For all $k \in \mathbb{N}$, Δ_k is a distinguishing function.* $\square$

Observe in this place that $w \mapsto \{x \in T^k \mid x|w\}$ is not a distinguishing function in general.

Completely analogous to the hierarchy theorem shown for Ter_k-DL, one can prove:

Theorem 7 (Hierarchy theorem). $\forall k \geq 0 : \Delta_k\text{-}DL \subset \Delta_{k+1}\text{-}DL$. $\square$

Another related distinguishing function is

$$w \mapsto (pi_k(w), \{x \in T^{<k} \mid x|w\}, \sigma_k(w)).$$

Finally, Ruiz, España and García [20] discussed a generalization of k-testable languages, where they allowed to count the multiplicities of (forbidden) subwords defining the so-called threshold testable languages. This counting feature can be incorporated both in Ter_k, as well as in Δ_k in order to obtain other possibly interesting classes of distinguishing functions. For reasons of space, we only discuss how to generalize Δ_k and leave all the details to the reader. Let $\#(x, y)$ be the number of positions at which x occurs as sparse subword of y. Then define, for every $k, \ell \in \mathbb{N}$:

$$\Delta_{k,\ell}(w) = \{(x, \#(x, w)) \mid x \in T^{<k}, \#(x, w) < \ell\}.$$

Again, we state without proof.

Lemma 6. *For all $k, \ell \in \mathbb{N}$, $\Delta_{k,\ell}$ is a distinguishing function.* $\square$

This section might have convinced the reader that there are indeed a number of interesting language classes which are shown to be identifiable by using our setting.

7   Discussion

We have proposed a large collection of families of languages, each of which is identifiable in the limit from positive samples, hence extending previous works.

As the main technical contribution of the paper, we see the introduction of new canonical objects, namely the automata $A(L, f)$. This also simplifies correctness proofs of inference algorithms for k-reversible languages, $k > 0$, to some extent. It seems to be interesting to study these canonical automata also in the search-space framework of Dupont and Miclet [5,7,6].

We feel that deterministic methods (such as the one proposed in this paper) are quite important for practical applications, since they could be understood more precisely than mere heuristics, so that one can prove certain properties about the algorithms. Moreover, the approach of this paper allows one to make the bias (which each identification algorithm necessarily has) explicit and transparent to the user: The bias consists in (1) the restriction to regular languages and (2) the choice of a particular distinguishing function f.

We will provide a publicly accessible prototype learning algorithm for (each of the families) f-DL in the future. A user can then firstly look for an appropriate f by making learning experiments with typical languages he expects to be representative for the languages in his particular application. After this "bias training phase", the user may then use the such-chosen learning algorithm (or better, an improved implementation for the specific choice of f) for his actual application.

If the application suggests that the languages which are to be inferred are non-regular, methods such as those suggested in [17] can be transferred. This is done most easily by using the concept of *control languages* as undertaken in [8,9] or [23, Section 4] or by using the related concept of *permutations*, see [11].

Acknowledgments: We gratefully acknowledge discussions with J. Alber and J. M. Sempere. Moreover, the comments of the unknown referees were very helpful for improving the paper.

References

1. D. Angluin. Inference of reversible languages. *Journal of the Association for Computing Machinery*, 29(3):741–765, 1982. 116, 117, 119, 125, 126, 127
2. D. Angluin. Learning regular sets from queries and counterexamples. *Information and Computation*, 75:87–106, 1987. 116, 117
3. R. G. Downey and M. R. Fellows. *Parameterized Complexity*. Springer, 1999. 127
4. R. G. Downey, M. R. Fellows, and U. Stege. Parameterized complexity: A framework for systematically confronting computational intractability. In *Contemporary Trends in Discrete Mathematics: From DIMACS and DIMATIA to the Future*, volume 49 of *AMS-DIMACS*, pages 49–99. AMS Press, 1999. 127
5. P. Dupont. Incremental regular inference. In L. Miclet and C. de la Higuera, editors, *Proceedings of the Third International Colloquium on Grammatical Inference (ICGI-96): Learning Syntax from Sentences*, volume 1147 of *LNCS/LNAI*, pages 222–237. Springer, 1996. 129
6. P. Dupont and L. Miclet. Inférence grammaticale régulière: fondements théoriques et principaux algorithmes. Technical Report RR-3449, INRIA, 1998. 125, 129
7. P. Dupont, L. Miclet, and E. Vidal. What is the search space of the regular inference? In R. C. Carrasco and J. Oncina, editors, *Proceedings of the Second International Colloquium on Grammatical Inference (ICGI-94): Grammatical Inference and Applications*, volume 862 of *LNCS/LNAI*, pages 25–37. Springer, 1994. 129

8. H. Fernau. Learning of terminal distinguishable languages. Technical Report WSI–99–23, Universität Tübingen (Germany), Wilhelm-Schickard-Institut für Informatik, 1999. Short version published in the proceedings of AMAI 2000, see http://rutcor.rutgers.edu/~amai/AcceptedCont.htm. 116, 129, 130

9. H. Fernau. Identifying terminal distinguishable languages. Submitted revised version of [8]. 119, 120, 129

10. H. Fernau. *k*-gram extensions of terminal distinguishable languages. In *Proc. International Conference on Pattern Recognition*. IEEE/IAPR, 2000. To appear. 116, 118, 119, 126, 127

11. H. Fernau and J. M. Sempere. Permutations and control sets for learning non-regular language families. In *Proc. International Conference on Grammatical Inference*. Springer, 2000. To appear. 129

12. P. García and E. Vidal. Inference of *k*-testable languages in the strict sense and applications to syntactic pattern recognition. *IEEE Transactions on Pattern Analysis and Machine Intelligence*, 12:920–925, 1990. 128

13. E. M. Gold. Language identification in the limit. *Information and Control (now Information and Computation)*, 10:447–474, 1967. 116, 120

14. J. Gregor. Data-driven inductive inference of finite-state automata. *International Journal of Pattern Recognition and Artificial Intelligence*, 8(1):305–322, 1994. 117

15. S. Jain, D. Osherson, J. S. Royer, and A. Sharma. *Systems That Learn*. MIT Press, 2nd edition, 1999. 123

16. R. Niedermeier. Some prospects for efficient fixed parameter algorithms (invited paper). In B. Rovan, editor, *SOFSEM'98*, volume 1521 of *LNCS*, pages 168–185. Springer, 1998. 127

17. V. Radhakrishnan. *Grammatical Inference from Positive Data: An Effective Integrated Approach*. PhD thesis, Department of Computer Science and Engineering, Indian Institute of Technology, Bombay (India), 1987. 116, 117, 129

18. V. Radhakrishnan and G. Nagaraja. Inference of regular grammars via skeletons. *IEEE Transactions on Systems, Man and Cybernetics*, 17(6):982–992, 1987. 116, 117, 118, 119, 126

19. P. Rossmanith. Learning from random text. In O. Watanabe and T. Yokomori, editors, *Algorithmic Learning Theory (ALT'99)*, volume 1720 of *LNCS/LNAI*, pages 132–144. Springer, 1999. 116

20. J. Ruiz, S. España and P. García. Locally threshold testable languages in strict sense: application to the inference problem In V. Honavar and G. Slutski, editors, *Proceedings of the Fourth International Colloquium on Grammatical Inference (ICGI-98)*, volume 1433 of *LNCS/LNAI*, pages 150–161. Springer, 1998. 128

21. J. Ruiz and P. García. Learning *k*-piecewise testable languages from positive data. In L. Miclet and C. de la Higuera, editors, *Proceedings of the Third International Colloquium on Grammatical Inference (ICGI-96): Learning Syntax from Sentences*, volume 1147 of *LNCS/LNAI*, pages 203–210. Springer, 1996. 128

22. J. M. Sempere and G. Nagaraja. Learning a subclass of linear languages from positive structural information. In V. Honavar and G. Slutski, editors, *Proceedings of the Fourth International Colloquium on Grammatical Inference (ICGI-98)*, volume 1433 of *LNCS/LNAI*, pages 162–174. Springer, 1998. 121

23. Y. Takada. A hierarchy of language families learnable by regular language learning. *Information and Computation*, 123:138–145, 1995. 129

24. L. G. Valiant. A theory of the learnable. *Communications of the ACM*, 27:1134–1142, 1984. 116

25. R. Wiehagen. Identification of formal languages. In *Mathematical Foundations of Computer Science (MFCS'77)*, volume 53 of *LNCS*, pages 571–579. Springer, 1977. 116

A Probabilistic Identification Result

Eric McCreath

Basser Department of Computer Science
University of Sydney NSW 2006 Australia
ericm@cs.usyd.edu.au

Abstract. The approach used to assess a learning algorithm should reflect the type of environment we place the algorithm within. Often learners are given examples that both contain noise and are governed by a particular distribution. Hence, probabilistic identification in the limit is an appropriate tool for assessing such learners. In this paper we introduce an exact notion of probabilistic identification in the limit based on Laird's thesis. The strategy presented incorporates a variety of learning situations including: noise free positive examples, noisy independently generated examples, and noise free with both positive and negative examples. This yields a useful technique for assessing the effectiveness of a learner when training data is governed by a distribution and is possibly noisy. An attempt has been made to give a preliminary theoretical evaluation of the Q-heuristic. To this end, we have shown that a learner using the Q-heuristic stochastically learns in the limit any finite class of concepts, even when noise is present in the training examples. This result is encouraging, because with enough data, there is the expectation that the learner will induce a correct hypothesis. The proof of this result is extended to show that a restricted infinite class of concepts can also be stochastically learnt in the limit. The restriction requires the hypothesis space to be *g-sparse*.

H. Arimura, S. Jain and A. Sharma (Eds.): ALT 2000, LNAI 1968, pp. 131-141, 2000.

1   Introduction

The type of training examples provided to a learner has a significant effect on the class of concepts that may be learnt. For example, in the identification in the limit framework, by restricting the training examples to positive only examples we severely restrict the class of concepts that may be identified. However, by attaching a distribution to the instance space, providing the positive examples to the learner according to this distribution, the class of concepts that may be learnt is extended [12]. Also, the environment in which we assess a learning system should reflect the environment in which we expect the learner to operate. We often expect learners to operate in domains that both contain noise and training examples which are governed by some distribution. This provides a strong motivation for probabilistic identification in the limit, introduced by Laird [7,8], where training examples are possibly noisy. Laird's approach, although embracing noise in the training examples, assumes both positive and negative examples are provided to the learner. Whereas, the approach taken in this paper uses an oracle to determine if an example will be positive or negative. This generalizes the type of training examples given to a learner, permitting probabilistic identification results to encompass a larger variety of learning situations. The stochastic process used to generate example texts and the definition of probabilistic identification is presented in section 2.

The Q heuristic was designed for an ILP system, LIME. This system learns from possibly noisy data where the number of positive and negative training examples are fixed and independent from the concept provided[11, 10]. The heuristic simply uses Bayes rule[1] given the assumptions regarding the training examples. We show that a learner which employs the Q heuristic will stochastically learn in the limit:

- any finite class of concepts, and
- a restricted infinite classes of concepts.

Of course, a finite class of concepts is trivially learnable from positive only data in the identification in the limit setting [6]. Hence, it is also learnable in the stochastic identification in the limit setting. What keeps our result from being trivial is the presence of noise in the data. Having presented this result, we explore conditions under which the result can be extended to an infinite class of concepts. The proof techniques for the infinite case, which introduces the notion of g-sparse hypothises spaces, builds on that of the finite case. These results are presented in section 3.

Section 4 contains two example concepts classes which may be shown to be g-sparse. We finally discuss possible future direction in section 5.

2   Probabilistic Identification in the Limit

Probabilistic identification in the limit extends identification in the limit by replacing the teacher that presents all the examples to the learner with a teacher

---

[1] $P(H|E) = \frac{P(E|H)P(H)}{P(E)}$

that uses a distribution to present examples to the learner. The criterion of success is correspondingly altered requiring that with probability 1 the learner induces a correct hypothesis all but finitely many times.

Let X be the instance space and D_X be a probability measure over X. Note, D_X is a mapping from 2^X to $[0,1]$ and $D_X(\{x\})$ is simply written $D_X(x)$. We also assume X to be a countable set. Recall that members of 2^X are concepts. Let C be a class of concepts. The probability cover of a concept c, defined $\theta(c)$, is $D_X(c) = \sum_{x \in c} D_X(x)$.

The error or difference between two concepts c_1 and c_2 with respect to the probability measure D_X is defined as $\mathrm{error}(c_1, c_2) = \theta(c_1 \Delta c_2)$. By using *error* to evaluate a hypothesis the hypothesis only needs to be correct on instances which have nonzero probability in the instance space distribution. This is reasonable as the learner will never be presented with an instance with zero probability.

We let $\mathbb{E} = X \times \{\mathrm{Pos}, \mathrm{Neg}\}$ be the set of all labelled instances of the instance space X. We usually refer to labelled instances as examples. An example text $E \in \mathbb{E}^\infty$ is an infinite sequence of examples. The learner conjectures a hypothesis from an initial finite sequence of E. This initial finite sequence of E of length m is denoted $E[m]$. We let SEQ denote the set of all initial finite sequences, $\{E[m] | E \in \mathbb{E}^\infty \wedge m \in \mathbb{N}\}$.

Let h be a hypothesis. In the present work, h is a computer program. The extension of a hypothesis h, denoted $ext(h)$, is the concept which h represents. A hypothesis space is a sequence (usually infinite) of hypothesis. We assume that the hypothesis space H under consideration is enumerable. Let $h_0, h_1, \ldots$ be an enumeration of H. We further assume that H is uniformly decidable, i.e., there exists a computable function $f : \mathbb{N} \times X \to \{0, 1\}$ defined below:

$$f(i, x) = \begin{cases} 1 & \text{if } x \in ext(h_i), \\ 0 & \text{otherwise.} \end{cases}$$

We say that a hypothesis space H is complete with respect to a concept class C if for each $c \in C$, there is a hypothesis h in the space H such that $c = ext(h)$.

We define a learner M to be a computable machine that implements a mapping from SEQ into H.

We also assume the learner is able to compute $\theta(ext(h))$ for any h in the hypothesis space H. Note that such a capability is unlikely to be available to any computable learner, however, $\theta(ext(h))$ may always be estimated and its exact value is not critical to induce the hypothesis with the largest Q-value[2].

Definition 1 (Convergence). *Learner M converges to hypothesis h on E just in case for all but finitely many $m \in \mathbb{N}$, $M(E[m]) = h$. This is denoted $M(E){\downarrow} = h$.*

A stochastic process GEN is used to generate these example texts. This process may be formulated in a variety of ways depending on the kind of tests against which the learner is to be benchmarked. The example texts generated

---

[2] Note that, the Q-value is the value use to compare competing hypotheses.

will reflect the target concept, although it may not be an exact or complete representation of the target concept. As the text may contain examples which have opposite labelling to that which would reflect the concept. Also, there is no explicit requirement that the text contain a complete set of instances.

We now introduce a general stochastic process for generating example texts, this process is denoted $\text{GEN}^{O}_{\langle \mu_p, \mu_n \rangle}$. The parameters $\langle \mu_p, \mu_n \rangle$ governs the amount of noise in the texts generated. μ_p gives the level of noise in the positive examples and correspondingly μ_n for the negative examples. In most cases $\mu_p = \mu_n$, however, it is useful to allow these parameters to be different in some cases. By setting $\mu_p = \mu_n = 0$ the process will generate noise free example texts. The parameter $O \in \{\text{Pos}, \text{Neg}\}^{\infty}$ is an oracle which determines which elements will be positive and negative in the sequence generated by $\text{GEN}^{O}_{\langle \mu_p, \mu_n \rangle}$ prior to any instance being selected. The n'th element in the oracle O is denoted $O(n)$. By using an oracle we may model a variety of situations. For example, the oracle may determine all examples in the example text to be negative, hence we will model learning from only negative examples. We show the stochastic convergence results for any oracle, thus proving the result for a variety of situations. We may also place a probability measure over $\{\text{Pos}, \text{Neg}\}^{\infty}$ and assume O is stochastically generated by such a measure. As the stochastic learning result is shown for any $O \in \{\text{Pos}, \text{Neg}\}^{\infty}$ the result will be also true for an oracle generated by any stochastic process.

The algorithm for $\text{GEN}^{O}_{\langle \mu_p, \mu_n \rangle}(c, X, D_X)$ works as follows. In each cycle of the main loop the next example in the example text is generated. The oracle O is used to determine if the next example will be positive or negative. If the oracle decides that the next example will be positive, the following process is used: a biased coin is flipped where the probability of the coin coming up "Heads" is μ_p and "Tails" is $1 - \mu_p$; if the coin comes up "Heads" then any instance is randomly selected from X using D_X and output as a positive example, if the coin is "Tails" then any instance is randomly selected from c using the distribution J^c_X where:

$$
J^c_X(x) = \begin{cases} D_X(x)/\theta(c) & \text{if } x \in c, \\ 0 & \text{otherwise.} \end{cases}
$$

A similar process is used if the oracle decides that the next example will be negative. This algorithm generates a text which reflects the concept c, where the sign of each example in the text matches the sign of the corresponding element in O and the parameters $\langle \mu_p, \mu_n \rangle$ determine the levels of noise introduced into the example text.

We now calculate the probability measure over $\mathbb{E}$ for each example generated by $\text{GEN}^{O}_{\langle \mu_p, \mu_n \rangle}$. There are two possible probability measures an example may have, either G^+ or G^-. The n'th element of the example text will have probability measure G^+ if $O(n) = \text{Pos}$, otherwise it will have probability measure G^- when $O(n) = \text{Neg}$.

So when the oracle O determines the n'th example to be labelled "Pos", that is $O(n) = $ Pos, example $\langle x, s \rangle$ is governed by:

$$G^+(\langle x, s \rangle) = \begin{cases} \mu_p D_X(x) + (1 - \mu_p)(J_X^c(x)) & \text{if } s = \text{Pos}, \\ 0 & \text{if } s = \text{Neg}. \end{cases}$$

Correspondingly, for the examples where $O(n) = $ Neg:

$$G^-(\langle x, s \rangle) = \begin{cases} \mu_n D_X(x) + (1 - \mu_n)(J_X^{\bar{c}}(x)) & \text{if } s = \text{Neg}, \\ 0 & \text{if } s = \text{Pos}. \end{cases}$$

As D_X, $J_X^{\bar{c}}$, and J_X^c are probability measures on X it is straightforward to show that G^+ and G^- are probability measures on $\mathbb{E}$.

Note $G^+(\mathbb{E}) = 1$ and $G^-(\mathbb{E}) = 1$. These measures are used to define the probability measure $\text{Prob}_{\text{GEN}^O_{\langle \mu_p, \mu_n \rangle}(c, X, D_X)}$ on the σ-field $\mathcal{F} \subset 2^{(\mathbb{E}^\infty)}$, where $\mathcal{F}$ is the σ-field generated from the prefix sets of $2^{(\mathbb{E}^\infty)}$. Note that for every prefix set $B_\sigma = \{E \in \mathbb{E}^\infty | \sigma = E[|\sigma|]\}$ where $\sigma = \langle e_0, e_1, \ldots, e_n \rangle$ we have $\text{Prob}_{\text{GEN}^O_{\langle \mu_p, \mu_n \rangle}(c, X, D_X)}(B_\sigma) = \prod_{n < |\sigma|} f(e_n, O(n))$, where

$$f(\langle x, s \rangle, o) = \begin{cases} G^+(\langle x, s \rangle) & \text{if } o = \text{Pos}, \\ G^-(\langle x, s \rangle) & \text{if } o = \text{Neg}. \end{cases}$$

We refer the reader to *Measure Theory and Probability* by Adam and Guillemin [1] or *Probability and Measure* by Billingsley [3] for further information on measure theory.

Using $\text{GEN}^O_{\langle \mu_p, \mu_n \rangle}$ provides a flexible way of modelling different forms of training data. We now provide a list of common models for training data and show how these are specializations of $\text{GEN}^O_{\langle \mu_p, \mu_n \rangle}$.

Noise free, positive examples: If we set $\mu_p = \mu_n = 0$ and set $O = \langle \text{Pos}, \text{Pos}, \text{Pos}, \ldots \rangle$ the training data will be noise free and positive. The distribution of this training data will reflect a normalized version of the instance space distribution, where elements outside the target concept have probability zero of appearing in a text. This is identical to the assumption about the training data used by Montagna and Simi [12] who showed that whatever may be learnt in the limit from both positive and negative data may also be stochastically learnt in the limit from only positive data. This result assumes D_X is approximately computable. This is also similar to the model used by Angluin [2] when she considered TXTEX-identification. Angluin allows a null or empty element, denoted $\star$, to be part of the text, to facilitate modelling a text for the empty language.

Noisy, independently generated examples: Laird's [7, 8] classification noise process assumes that instances are chosen according to some distribution and then correctly labelled according to the target concept. After this a demon with probability ξ flips the class label from positive to negative or from negative to positive, thereby creating noise in the training data[3]. This process generates an example text where each example is independent and has the following distribution:

$$P_{\text{Laird}}(\langle x, s \rangle) = \begin{cases} (1 - \xi)D_X(x) & \text{if } s = \text{Pos} \wedge x \in c, \\ \xi D_X(x) & \text{if } s = \text{Pos} \wedge x \notin c, \\ \xi D_X(x) & \text{if } s = \text{Neg} \wedge x \in c, \\ (1 - \xi)D_X(x) & \text{if } s = \text{Neg} \wedge x \notin c. \end{cases}$$

Now let us see how this distribution can be modelled in our framework. We now place a probability measure over $\{\text{Pos}, \text{Neg}\}^\infty$ such that each element is the sequence is independent and is "Pos" with probability w and "Neg" with probability $1 - w$. We denote an oracle produced by such a distribution O_w.

Now, each element in the example text produced by $\text{GEN}^{O_w}_{\langle \mu_p, \mu_n \rangle}$ will be independent and have the following distribution:

$$P(\langle x, s \rangle) = \begin{cases} w(\mu_p + (1 - \mu_p)/\theta(c))D_X(x) & \text{if } s = \text{Pos} \wedge x \in c, \\ w\mu_p D_X(x) & \text{if } s = \text{Pos} \wedge x \notin c, \\ (1 - w)\mu_n D_X(x) & \text{if } s = \text{Neg} \wedge x \in c, \\ (1 - w)(\mu_n + (1 - \mu_n)/(1 - \theta(c)))D_X(x) & \text{if } s = \text{Neg} \wedge x \notin c. \end{cases}$$

Now, let $w = \theta(c) + \xi - 2\theta(c)\xi$, $\mu_p = \frac{\xi}{\theta(c) + \xi - 2\theta(c)\xi}$, and $\mu_n = \frac{\xi}{1 - \theta(c) - \xi + 2\theta(c)\xi}$. Then the distribution for each example in the example text generated by $\text{GEN}^{O_w}_{\langle \mu_p, \mu_n \rangle}$ will be identical to P_{Laird}. It follows, their probability measures over $\mathbb{E}^\infty$ will also be identical. Hence, by showing a result for stochastic learning with $\text{GEN}^{O}_{\langle \mu_p, \mu_n \rangle}$ we correspondingly show the result for Laird's model of training data.

Noise free, with both positive and negative examples: Learning with both positive and negative examples is the same as EX-identification where the functions in question have range restricted to either "Pos" or "Neg". Angluin [2] when considering EX-identification in a probabilistic setting assumes that each example is independent in the text and the probability of an example appearing is based on a distribution from the range of the function. This gives us the following distribution over the examples:

$$P(\langle x, s \rangle) = \begin{cases} D_X(x) & \text{if } s = \text{Pos} \wedge x \in c, \\ 0 & \text{if } s = \text{Pos} \wedge x \notin c, \\ 0 & \text{if } s = \text{Neg} \wedge x \in c, \\ D_X(x) & \text{if } s = \text{Neg} \wedge x \notin c. \end{cases}$$

If the oracle O_w, as defined in the previous model, where $w = \theta(c)$ and $\mu_p = \mu_n = 0$, then $\text{GEN}^{O_w}_{\langle \mu_p, \mu_n \rangle}$ gives the same distribution over each of the generated examples in the text.

---

[3] Laird [7] uses μ for the noise parameter, however, as it different to the noise parameter used here, we use ξ to refer to Laird's noise parameter.

By showing a learner to stochastically identify a class of concepts C when examples are provided by $\text{GEN}^0_{\langle \mu_p, \mu_n \rangle}$, we also show that the learner will stochastically identify C when examples are provided by distributions used in the other models.

Definition 2, of probabilistic identification in the limit, is based on the definition given in Laird's thesis [7,8].

Definition 2 (Probabilistic identification in the limit). *Given an instance space X and a probability measure D_X over X. A learner M is said to identify the class of concepts C stochastically in the limit, with respect to a hypothesis space H, if and only if*

(a) *examples are provided by GEN, and*

(b) $(\forall c \in C)\ Prob_{GEN(c,X,D_X)}\left\{ E \in \mathbb{E}^\infty \middle| M(E){\downarrow} = h \wedge error(ext(h), c) = 0 \right\} = 1.$

This setting has the expected property that any subset of a class that is stochastically learnable in the limit is also stochastically learnable in the limit with respect to the same hypothesis space.

Laird [7] shows that any class of concepts that has a recursively enumerable set of hypotheses may be stochastically identified in the limit.[4] This assumes both positive and negative examples are presented to the learner according to the distribution. This result is then extended by Laird to include noise in the training examples. Both the Borel-Cantelli[5] and Hoeffding's probability inequality [5], used in the proofs by Laird, are also central to the results given in this paper.

3   Probabilistic Identification with the Q-heuristic

Let m be the total number of examples presented to the learner, so $m = n + p$, where p is the number of positive examples and n is the number of negative examples. Let $\text{GEN}^O_{\langle \mu_p, \mu_n \rangle}$ generate the example text E. The learner M, given initial sequence $E[m]$ induces the hypothesis $M(E[m])$.

The order of presentation of examples, the sign of examples, and the proportion of positive and negative examples is dependent on the choice of oracle O. Since these aspects of the example presentation are not crucial for the learning algorithm, we assume that the learner is provided with a multiset of positive examples (of cardinality p) a multiset of negative examples (of cardinality n).

The algorithm simply works by choosing the hypothesis with the maximum[6] Q value [7] given the current examples. In general there may be a set of hypotheses with equal Q values. To stop the algorithm alternating between them, the

---

[4] Note that, if hypotheses are total Turing programs then a recursively enumerable set of hypotheses is the same as a uniform recursive set of hypotheses.

[5] The reader is directed to an introductory text on measure theory such as, *Measure Theory and Probability* [1] for more information.

[6] The notation $\text{argmax}_{h \in H} Q(h)$ denotes the set $\{ h \in H \mid (\forall h' \in H)\ Q(h) \geq Q(h')) \}$.

[7] $Q_\sigma(h) = \lg(P(h)) + |\text{TP}_\sigma| \lg\left(\frac{1-\epsilon}{\theta(ext(h))} + \epsilon \right) + |\text{TN}_\sigma| \lg\left(\frac{1-\epsilon}{1-\theta(ext(h))} + \epsilon \right) + |\text{FPN}_\sigma| \lg(\epsilon)$
where TP_σ, TN_σ, and FPN_σ are respectively the true positive, true negatives, and

hypothesis with the minimum index[8] is chosen. If this minimum index selection is removed then the algorithm will still learn stochastically in the limit, although only in the behaviourally correct sense. Note that the algorithm is computable as it only must consider a finite initial portion of the possibly infinite hypothesis space [9, proposition 4.3.2].

Input :
  An indexed hypothesis space H.
  A prior probability distribution over H.
  A function θ for evaluating the theta value of a hypothesis.
  A sequence $\sigma = E[m]$ of m examples from the example text E.
  The noise parameter $\epsilon \in [0,1)$ such that $\mu_p \leq \epsilon$ and $\mu_n \leq \epsilon$.
Output :
  A hypothesis h.
$h := \text{minindex}(\text{argmax}_{h \in H} Q_\sigma(h))$
output h

Algorithm 1: Stochastic Identification using the Q heuristic

3.1   A finite concept class

Theorem 1. *Let C be any finite concept class and let H be any hypothesis space which is complete for C. Then for any noise parameter ϵ, there exists a learning algorithm that stochastically identifies C in the limit with respect to H when examples are provided by $GEN^O_{\langle \mu_p, \mu_n \rangle}$ for any oracle O and any $\mu_p \leq \epsilon$ and $\mu_n \leq \epsilon$.*

Proof. Due to space limitations we only briefly outline the proof here, a full version may be obtained in the authors thesis [9]. The proof compares h_t, a hypothesis that correctly classifies the target concept, with h_δ, a hypothesis that is in error. The value of $Q(h_t) - Q(h_\delta)$ is partitioned into three parts: a fixed constant, a sum of a list of random variables each corresponding to a positive example, and a sum of a list of random variables each corresponding to a negative example. The expected value for each of these random variables is shown to be positive. Assuming that the sum of these random variable is at least half the expected sum, we will have $Q(h_t) > Q(h_\delta)$ at some point, even when the fixed constant is negative. Applying Hoeffding's inequality, we compute a bound on the failure of this assumption. This bound is then used in conjunction with the Borel-Cantelli lemma to show that the class of concepts can be stochastically identified in the limit. □

---

false negatives or positives where the initial sequence is evaluated using hypothesis h.

[8] The notation minindex(S) denotes the hypothesis $h \in S$ such that $(\forall h' \in S - \{h\})\ h < h'$, where $<$ is a total ordering on H.

3.2   A restricted infinite concept class

The problem with extending the above result to an infinite concept class is when the hypotheses, with respect to their priors, converge on the target concept too quickly. When this occurs over an infinite set of concepts the bound on inducing an incorrect hypothesis is not finite. To address this problem a restriction is placed on the rate any hypothesis may be converged on.

Definition 3 (g-sparse with respect to a concept). *Let $g : \mathbb{N} \to \mathbb{R}$. Let c be a concept. A hypothesis space, $H = \{h_i | i \in \mathbb{N}\}$, is said to be g-sparse with respect to concept c if there exists $m_c \in \mathbb{N}$ and $w_c \in \mathbb{R}$ such that for all $j > m_c$, we have:*

$$error(c, ext(h_j)) \neq 0 \Rightarrow error(c, ext(h_j)) \geq w_c g(j).$$

Definition 4 (g-sparse). *A hypothesis space H is said to be g-sparse if H is g-sparse with respect to concepts $\emptyset$, the instance space X, and $ext(h_i)$ for all $h_i \in H$.*

Theorem 2. *Let C be any concept class and H be any hypothesis space which is complete for C. Let $\epsilon \in [0, 1)$ be the noise parameter. Assuming H is g-sparse where $g(i) = \frac{1}{i^\alpha}$ for $\alpha < 1$, there exists an algorithm that stochastically identifies C in the limit with respect to H when examples are provided by $GEN^O_{\langle \mu_p, \mu_n \rangle}$ for any oracle O and any $\mu_p \leq \epsilon$ and $\mu_n \leq \epsilon$.*

Proof. Similarly we only briefly outline the proof here, see [9] for the full version. This proof extends the previous proof. The learner once again uses Algorithm 1.

Given the g-spares constraint we may apply Hoeffdings inequality to find a bound on the probability of inducing an incorrect hypothesis. This bound is then used in conjunction with the Borel-Cantelli lemma to show that the class of concepts can be stochastically identified in the limit. □

4   Example Concept Classes

The learnability results presented in the previous two sections are interesting because our model incorporates noise in the data and a stochastic criterion of success. We feel that our approach is more realistic because although the classes discussed previously are learnable in the limit (in the traditional Gold [4] sense), they are not learnable in the Gold setting if noise is present. We next consider a class that is not learnable in the limit from positive only data in Gold's setting, but is learnable in our stochastic setting from only positive data even in the presence of noise.

The proofs of Propositions 1 and 2 work by showing that the hypothesis spaces in question are *g-sparse* with respect to a instance space distribution and then applying Theorem 2. The reader is directed to [9] for these proofs.

Proposition 1. *Let $H = \{h_1, h_2, h_3, \dots\} = \{\mathbb{N}, \emptyset, \{1\}, \{2\}, \{1, 2\}, \{3\}, \{1, 3\}, \dots\}$. The concept class consisting of all the finite subsets of $\mathbb{N}$ together with $\mathbb{N}$ is stochastically learnable in the limit with respect to H.*[9]

The g-sparse constraint is not a strong restriction as most enumerations of a hypotheses would generally not "target" a particular hypothesis "quickly".

We now consider the classes of concepts that consists of the empty set, the set of naturals and sets of the form $\{1, 2, \dots, k\}$, this class is a subset of the class shown to be stochastically learnable in the limit in the previous proposition, hence, the class will also be stochastically learnable in the limit.[10] However, we include this result as it may be proved using a restricted hypothesis space and a different instance space distribution which forms a tighter bound on the g-sparse restriction, and hence a more difficult concept to learn.

Proposition 2. *Let the instance space X be $\mathbb{N}$. Let the instance space distribution $D_X(x) = \frac{s_1}{x^{3/2}}$ where s_1 is the normalizing constant. Let $H = \{h_1, h_2, h_3, \dots\} = \{\mathbb{N}, \emptyset, \{1\}, \{1, 2\}, \{1, 2, 3\}, \{1, 2, 3, 4\}, \dots\}$. The concept class consisting of $\mathbb{N}$ and $\emptyset$ together with $\{\{1, 2, \dots, k\} | k \in \mathbb{N}\}$ is stochastically learnable in the limit with respect to H.*

5 Discussion

The results of stochastic identification in the limit in this paper are preliminary. An open question is whether these results could be extended to take into account complexity issues. This would give some idea of the the expected number of training examples provided to the learner, before the correct hypothesis is induced. In this case both the distribution of concepts presented to the learner and the prior probability used become critical. Another open question is what are the characteristics of *g-sparse* hypothesis spaces.

6 Acknowledgements

I thank Arun Sharma for his insight and advice. I also thank him for his encouragement to extend the initial finite result. I would also like to thank the reviewers for their helpful comments.

References

1. M. Adams and V. Guillemin. *Measure Theory and Probability*. Birkhäuser Boston, 1996.
2. D. Angluin. Identifying languages from stochastic examples. Technical Report TR–614, University of Yale, 1988.

---

[9] Since the data presentation could be guided by any oracle, this result holds for positive only data, too.

[10] See Proposition 7.1.1 of [9].

3. P. Billingsley. *Probability and Measure.* John Wiley & Sons, 1995.
4. E. M. Gold. Language identification in the limit. *Information and Control,* 10:447–474, 1967.
5. W. Hoeffding. Probability inequalities for sums of bounded random variables. *Journal of the American statistical association,* 58:13–30, 1963.
6. S. Jain, D. Osherson, J. Royer, and A. Sharma. *Systems That Learn: An Introduction to Learning Theory.* MIT Press, second edition edition, 1999.
7. P. Laird. *Learning from Good Data and Bad.* PhD thesis, Yale University, 1987.
8. P. Laird. *Learning from Good and Bad Data.* Kluwer Academic Publishers, Boston, MA, 1988.
9. E. McCreath. *Induction in First Order Logic from Noisy Training Examples and Fixed Example Set Sizes.* PhD thesis, The University of New South Wales, 1999.
10. E. McCreath and A. Sharma. ILP with noise and fixed example size: A Bayesian approach. In *Fifteenth International Joint Conference on Artificial Intelligence,* volume 2, pages 1310–1315, 1997.
11. E. McCreath and A. Sharma. Lime: A system for learning relations. In *The 9th International Workshop on Algorithmic Learning Theory.* Springer-Verlag, October 1998.
12. F. Montagna and G. Simi. Paradigms in measure theoretic learning and in informant learning. Unpublished Draft.

A New Framework for Discovering Knowledge from Two-Dimensional Structured Data Using Layout Formal Graph System

Tomoyuki Uchida[1], Yuko Itokawa[1], Takayoshi Shoudai[2], Tetsuhiro Miyahara[1], and Yasuaki Nakamura[1]

[1] Faculty of Information Sciences, Hiroshima City University,
Hiroshima 731-3194, Japan
{uchida@cs,yuko@toc.cs,miyahara@its,nakamura@cs}.hiroshima-cu.ac.jp
[2] Department of Informatics, Kyushu University 39, Kasuga 816-8580, Japan
shoudai@i.kyushu-u.ac.jp

Abstract. We present a new framework for discovering knowledge from two-dimensional structured data by using Inductive Logic Programming. Two-dimensional graph structured data such as image or map data are widely used for representing relations and distances between various objects. First, we define a layout term graph suited for representing two-dimensional graph structured data. A layout term graph is a pattern consisting of variables and two-dimensional graph structures. Moreover, we propose Layout Formal Graph System (LFGS) as a new logic programming system having a layout term graph as a term. LFGS directly deals with graphs having positional relations just like first order terms. Second, we show that LFGS is more powerful than Layout Graph Grammar, which is a generating system consisting of a context-free graph grammar and positional relations. This indicates that LFGS has the richness and advantage of representing knowledge about two-dimensional structured data.

Finally, we design a knowledge discovery system, which uses LFGS as a knowledge representation language and refutably inductive inference as a learning method. In order to give a theoretical foundation of our knowledge discovery system, we give the set of weakly reducing LFGS programs which is a sufficiently large hypothesis space of LFGS programs and show that the hypothesis space is refutably inferable from complete data.

1 Introduction

The purpose of this paper is to give a framework for discovering knowledge from two-dimensional graph structured data. A graph is one of the most common abstract structures and is widely used for representing relations between various data such as image, map, molecular, CAD or network data. In graph structures, a vertex represents an object, and an edge represents a relation between objects but not a distance between them. In representing two-dimensional structured data such as image or map data, it is needed to represent two-dimensional

H. Arimura, S. Jain and A. Sharma (Eds.): ALT 2000, LNAI 1968, pp. 141–155, 2000.

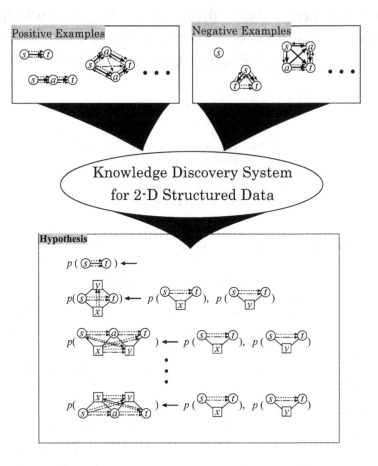

Fig. 1. A knowledge discovery system using LFGS

graph structured data with distances between objects and positional relations. As methods of expressing knowledge for various data, logic program, decision diagram using ID3 algorithm [12], and association rules are known. Especially, for graph structured data, Muggleton et al. produced the Inductive Logic Programming system PROGOL and applied it to biochemical and chemical data [3,10]. For graph structured data, we have already designed and implemented a knowledge discovery system KD-FGS [8,9]. The KD-FGS system uses Formal Graph System (FGS) as a knowledge representation language and refutably inductive inference as a learning method.

In [16], we presented a term graph as a hypergraph whose hyperedges are regarded as variables. By adding positional relations with distances between objects to the notion of a term graph, we define a layout term graph for representing two-dimensional structured data. By using layout term graphs, we have the advantage of solving the isomorphism problem of layout term graphs in polynomial time. And we propose Layout Formal Graph System (LFGS) as a new logic programming system which directly deals with layout term graphs instead of first order terms. By comparing LFGS with Layout Graph Grammar (LGG) [1], which is a generating system for two-dimensional graph structured data, we show that the sets of graphs generated by LGG are also definable by LFGS. This indicates that interesting sets of graphs such as the trees, the binary trees, the series parallel graphs, the partial k-trees for a positive fixed integer k, the maximal outerplanar graphs, and the complete graphs, are definable by LFGS.

From the above theoretical foundations, we can design a knowledge discovery system as follows. By employing a matching algorithm for layout term graphs, we can design various knowledge discovery systems, for example, a system based on Minimum Description Length principle [13] such as SUBDUE System [2] and a system whose hypotheses are association rules or decision diagrams over a layout term graph. In this paper, we design a knowledge discovery system based on Inductive Logic Programming in Fig. 1. Our system uses LFGS as a knowledge representation language and refutably inductive inference as a learning method. As inputs, our discovery system receives positive and negative examples about two-dimensional structured data. As an output, the system produces an LFGS program as a rule describing the given examples. In order to give a theoretical foundation of our system, we give the set of weakly reducing LFGS programs which is a sufficiently large hypothesis space of LFGS programs and show that the hypothesis space is refutably inferable from complete data.

This paper is organized as follows. In Section 2, we define a layout term graph as a pattern consisting of variables and positional relations in order to represent two-dimensional structured data. And we introduce LFGS as a new knowledge representation language suited for two-dimensional graph structured data. In Section 3, we show that LFGS is more powerful than LGG. In Section 4, we design our knowledge discovery system by giving a framework of refutably inductive inference of LFGS programs.

2   LFGS as a New Logic Programming System for Two-Dimensional Structured Data

In this section, we define a layout term graph, which is a new knowledge representation for two-dimensional structured data. And we present Layout Formal Graph System (LFGS), which is a logic programming system having a layout term graph as a term. This section gives a theoretical foundation for knowledge discovery systems using a layout term graph as a pattern and other systems using LFGS as a knowledge representation language.

Let Σ and Λ be finite alphabets and $\mathcal{X}$ an alphabet. An element in Σ, $\Lambda \cup \{x, y\}$ and $\mathcal{X}$ is called a *vertex label*, an *edge label*, and a *variable label*, respectively. Assume that $(\Sigma \cup \Lambda \cup \{x, y\}) \cap \mathcal{X} = \emptyset$ and $\Lambda \cap \{x, y\} = \emptyset$. Let $\mathcal{N}$ be the set of non-negative integers and $\mathcal{N}^+ = \mathcal{N} - \{0\}$. For a list or a set

S, the number of elements in S is denoted by $|S|$. Let V, E and H be a finite set, a subset of $V \times \Lambda \times V$, and a multi-set of lists of distinct vertices in V, respectively. An element in V, E and H is called a *vertex*, a *directed edge* (or simply an *edge*), and a *variable* (or a *hyperedge*), respectively. For a variable h, we denote the set of all elements in h by $V(h)$ and $V(H)$ denotes $\bigcup_{h \in H} V(h)$. We assume two functions, called *rank* and *perm*, for the variable label set $\mathcal{X}$. The first function $rank : \mathcal{X} \to \mathcal{N}^+$ assigns a positive integer for each variable label. A positive integer $rank(x)$ is called the *rank* of x. The second function *perm* assigns a permutation over $rank(x)$ elements for each variable label $x \in \mathcal{X}$.

That is, for a variable label $x \in \mathcal{X}$, $perm(x) = \begin{pmatrix} 1 & 2 & \cdots & i & \cdots & k \\ \xi(1) & \xi(2) & \cdots & \xi(i) & \cdots & \xi(k) \end{pmatrix}$ is an operation which change the i-th element to the $\xi(i)$-th element for each $1 \leq i \leq k$, where $k = rank(x)$ and $\xi : \{1, \ldots, k\} \to \{1, \ldots, k\}$ is a permutation. Applying a permutation $perm(x)$ to a variable $h = (v_1, v_2, \ldots, v_k)$ is defined as follows. $h \cdot perm(x) = (v_1, v_2, \ldots, v_k) \cdot perm(x) = (v_{\xi^{-1}(1)}, v_{\xi^{-1}(2)}, \ldots, v_{\xi^{-1}(k)})$. Each variable $h \in H$ is labeled with a variable label in $\mathcal{X}$ whose rank is $|h|$. Let F be a subset of $(V \cup H) \times \{x,y\} \times (V \cup H)$, whose elements are called *layout edges*. For E and F, we allow multiple edges and multiple layout edges but disallow self-loops. Let $dist : F \to \mathcal{N}$ be a function which gives a distance between two vertices, a vertex and a variable, or two variables. A layout edge (u, x, v) (resp. (u, y, v)) means that the vertex u must be placed in the left (resp. lower) side of the vertex v so that the distance between u and v is more than $dist((u, x, v))$ in the x-direction (resp. $dist((u, y, v))$ in the y-direction). Later we define a *substitution* which replaces variables with graphs. In order to specify the positions of the resulting graphs after applying a substitution, we give relations between a vertex and a variable, or two variables, in advance, by $dist$ and layout edges. A layout edge labeled with an edge label $s \in \{x,y\}$ is called an *s-edge*. For an edge label $s \in \{x,y\}$, an *s-path* is a sequence of layout edges $(u_1, s, u_2), (u_2, s, u_3), \ldots, (u_n, s, u_{n+1})$ such that $u_i \neq u_j$ for $1 \leq i < j \leq n+1$, where each u_i $(1 \leq i \leq n+1)$ is a vertex or a variable. If $u_1 = u_{n+1}$, the s-path is called an *s-cycle*.

Definition 1. A 4-tuple $g = (V, E, H, F)$ is called a *layout term graph* if it satisfies the following conditions.

(1) For any two distinct vertices in V, there exist an x-path and a y-path between them such that the paths consist of only vertices.
(2) For any two distinct variables in H, there exist an x-edge and a y-edge between them.
(3) For any variable $h \in H$ and any vertex $v \in V - V(h)$, there exist an x-path and a y-path between h and v.
(4) For any variable $h \in H$ and any vertex $v \in V(h)$, there exists no layout edge between h and v.
(5) There is no x-cycle and y-cycle in g.

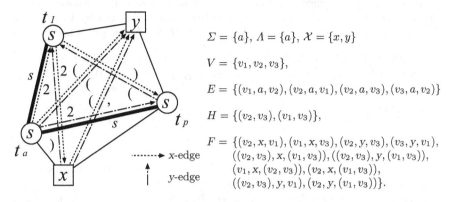

$$\Sigma = \{a\}, \ \Lambda = \{a\}, \ \mathcal{X} = \{x, y\}$$

$$V = \{v_1, v_2, v_3\},$$

$$E = \{(v_1, a, v_2), (v_2, a, v_1), (v_2, a, v_3), (v_3, a, v_2)\}$$

$$H = \{(v_2, v_3), (v_1, v_3)\},$$

$$F = \{(v_2, x, v_1), (v_1, x, v_3), (v_2, y, v_3), (v_3, y, v_1),$$
$$((v_2, v_3), x, (v_1, v_3)), ((v_2, v_3), y, (v_1, v_3)),$$
$$(v_1, x, (v_2, v_3)), (v_2, x, (v_1, v_3)),$$
$$((v_2, v_3), y, v_1), (v_2, y, (v_1, v_3))\}.$$

Fig. 2. A layout term graph $g = (V, E, H, F)$. A variable is represented by a box with thin lines to its elements and its variable label is in the box. An edge is represented by a thick line.

(6) For any variable $h = (v_1, \ldots, v_k) \in H$ whose variable label is x, there exist an x-path from v_i to v_{i+1} and a y-path from $v_{\xi^{-1}(i)}$ to $v_{\xi^{-1}(i+1)}$ for all
$$1 \leq i \leq k-1, \text{ where } perm(x) = \begin{pmatrix} 1 & 2 & \cdots & k \\ \xi(1) & \xi(2) & \cdots & \xi(k) \end{pmatrix}.$$

A layout term graph $g = (V, E, H, F)$ is *ground* if $H = \emptyset$. We note that a term graph defined in [16] is regarded as a layout term graph having no layout edge. If both (u, a, v) and (v, a, u) are in E, we treat the two edges as one undirected edge between u and v. A vertex labeling function and a variable labeling function of g are denoted by $\varphi_g : V \to \Sigma$ and $\lambda_g : H \to \mathcal{X}$, respectively.

Example 1. In Fig. 2, we give a layout term graph $g = (V, E, H, F)$. $rank(x) = rank(y) = 2$, $perm(x) = \begin{pmatrix} 1 & 2 \\ 1 & 2 \end{pmatrix}$ and $perm(y) = \begin{pmatrix} 1 & 2 \\ 2 & 1 \end{pmatrix}$. Then, $(v_2, v_3) \cdot perm(x) = (v_2, v_3) \begin{pmatrix} 1 & 2 \\ 1 & 2 \end{pmatrix} = (v_2, v_3)$ and $(v_1, v_3) \cdot perm(y) = (v_1, v_3) \begin{pmatrix} 1 & 2 \\ 2 & 1 \end{pmatrix} = (v_3, v_1)$. $dist((v_2, x, v_1)) = dist((v_1, x, (v_2, v_3))) = 2$, $dist((v_2, x, (v_1, v_3))) = dist(((v_2, v_3), x, (v_1, v_3))) = 3$, $dist((v_1, x, v_3)) = 4$, $dist((v_2, y, v_3)) = 2$, $dist((v_3, y, v_1)) = dist((v_2, y, (v_1, v_3))) = 3$, $dist(((v_2, v_3), y, v_1)) = 4$, and $dist((v_2, v_3), y, (v_1, v_3)) = 5$.

Let $g = (V, E, H, F)$ be a layout term graph. From the definition of a layout term graph, there exist an x-path which passes all vertices in V. This x-path is called a *Hamiltonian x-path*. The occurrence order of vertices is shown to be unique for all Hamiltonian x-paths. The occurrence order of a vertex $v \in V$ over a Hamiltonian x-path is denoted by $Ord_g^X(v) \in \mathcal{N}^+$. Inversely, for $1 \leq i \leq |V|$, the i-th vertex over a Hamiltonian x-path is denoted by $Ver_g^X(i) \in V$. Similarly, there is a y-path which passes all vertices in V and we call this y-path a *Hamiltonian y-path*. The occurrence order of vertices is shown to be unique for all Hamiltonian y-paths. The occurrence order of a vertex v in V over a Hamiltonian y-path is denoted by $Ord_g^Y(v) \in \mathcal{N}^+$ and the i-th vertex is denoted by $Ver_g^Y(i)$ for $1 \le i \le |V|$. For a layout term graph $g = (V, E, H, F)$, F can give a layout of g.

Example 2. Let $g = (V, E, H, F)$ be the layout term graph in Fig. 2. Sequences of layout edges $((v_2, x, v_1), (v_1, x, v_3))$ and $((v_2, y, v_3), (v_3, y, v_1))$ are the Hamiltonian x-path and the Hamiltonian y-path of g, respectively. $Ord_g^X(v_2) = 1$, $Ord_g^X(v_1) = 2$, $Ord_g^X(v_3) = 3$, $Ord_g^Y(v_2) = 1$, $Ord_g^Y(v_3) = 2$, and $Ord_g^Y(v_1) = 3$. $Ver_g^X(1) = v_2$, $Ver_g^X(2) = v_1$, $Ver_g^X(3) = v_3$, $Ver_g^Y(1) = v_2$, $Ver_g^Y(2) = v_3$, and $Ver_g^Y(3) = v_1$.

In the same way as logic programming system, an *atom* is an expression of the form $p(g_1, \ldots, g_n)$, where p is a predicate symbol with arity n and $g_1, \ldots, g_n$ are layout term graphs. Let $A, B_1, \ldots, B_m$ be atoms with $m \ge 0$. Then a *graph rewriting rule* or a *rule* is a clause of the form $A \leftarrow B_1, \ldots, B_m$.

Definition 2. A *program* of *Layout Formal Graph System* (an *LFGS program*, for short) is a finite set of graph rewriting rules.

For example, the LFGS program Γ_{TTSP} in Fig. 3 generates a family of two-terminal series parallel graphs (TTSP graphs, for short) with layouts. A series-parallel graph is a multiple directed acyclic graph obtained by recursively applying two composition rules, called a series composition rule and a parallel composition rule. A TTSP graph is a series parallel graph having two distinguished vertices s and t called source and sink, respectively.

Let $g = (V, E, H, F)$ be a layout term graph. Let P^X and P^Y be a longest Hamiltonian x-path and a longest Hamiltonian y-path, respectively. The *minimum layout edge set* of g is the subset F' of F such that $F' = F - \bigcup_{s \in \{x,y\}} \{(c, s, d) \in F \mid (c, s, d) \text{ is not in } P^s \text{ and the total of distances between } c \text{ and } d \text{ over } P^s \text{ is greater than or equal to } dist((c, s, d))\}$. Layout term graphs $g = (V_g, E_g, H_g, F_g)$ and $f = (V_f, E_f, H_f, F_f)$ are *isomorphic*, which is denoted by $g \simeq f$, if there exists a bijection $\pi : V_g \to V_f$ satisfying the following conditions (1)-(4). Let F_g' and F_f' be the minimum layout edge set of g and f, respectively. For a variable $(u_1, u_2, \ldots, u_k) \in H$, $\pi((u_1, u_2, \ldots, u_k))$ denotes $(\pi(u_1), \pi(u_2), \ldots, \pi(u_k))$.

(1) $\varphi_g(v) = \varphi_f(\pi(v))$ for any $v \in V_g$.
(2) $(u, a, v) \in E_g$ if and only if $(\pi(u), a, \pi(v)) \in E_f$.
(3) $h \in H_g$ if and only if $\pi(h) \in H_f$, and $\lambda_g(h) = \lambda_f(\pi(h))$.
(4) For each $s \in \{x, y\}$, $(c, s, d) \in F_g'$ if and only if $(\pi(c), s, \pi(d)) \in F_f'$ and $dist((c, s, d))$ of g is equal to $dist((\pi(c), s, \pi(d)))$ of f.

Theorem 1. *Let g and f be layout term graphs. The problem of deciding whether or not g and f are isomorphic is solvable in polynomial time.*

Proof For layout term graphs $g = (V_g, E_g, H_g, F_g)$ and $f = (V_f, E_f, H_f, F_f)$, we consider a mapping $\pi : V_g \to V_f$ which assigns the vertex v of f for a vertex u of g such that $Ord_g^X(u) = Ord_f^X(v)$. Since the occurrence order of any vertex

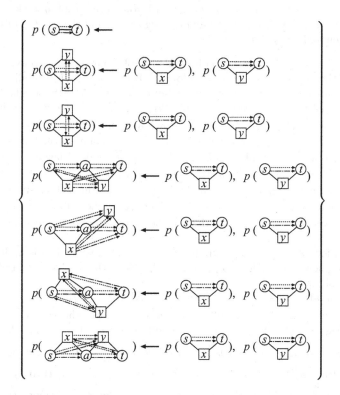

Fig. 3. An LFGS program Γ_{TTSP} which generates a family of TTSP graphs with layouts

of each layout term graph is unique for all Hamiltonian x-paths and $|V_g| = |V_f|$, the mapping π is a bijection from V_g to V_f. For a layout term graph, we can find a bijection π in polynomial time by using an algorithm for finding a Hamiltonian path for a directed acyclic graph in [4]. We can easily decide whether or not π satisfies the isomorphic conditions for g and f in polynomial time. (QED)

Let $g = (V, E, H, F)$ be a layout term graph, σ be a list $(v_1, v_2, \ldots, v_k)$ of k vertices in V, x be a variable label in $\mathcal{X}$ with $perm(x) = \begin{pmatrix} 1 & 2 & \cdots & k \\ \xi(1) & \xi(2) & \cdots & \xi(k) \end{pmatrix}$. The form $x := [g, \sigma]$ is called a *binding* of x if there are x-paths from v_i to v_{i+1} of g and there are y-paths from $v_{\xi^{-1}(i)}$ to $v_{\xi^{-1}(i+1)}$ of g for all $1 \leq i \leq k - 1$. For a list S of vertices, we denote by $S[m]$ the m-th element of S. A *substitution* θ is a finite collection of bindings $\{x_1 := [g_1, \sigma_1], \ldots, x_n := [g_n, \sigma_n]\}$, where x_i's are mutually distinct variable labels in $\mathcal{X}$ and each g_i ($1 \leq i \leq n$) has no variable label in $\{x_1, \ldots, x_n\}$. In the same way as logic programming system, we obtain a new layout term graph f, denoted by $g\theta$, by applying a substitution

$\theta = \{x_1 := [g_1, \sigma_1], \ldots, x_n := [g_n, \sigma_n]\}$ to a layout term graph $g = (V, E, H, F)$ in the following way. Let $N = |V|$ and $r_i = rank(x_i)$, and the number of vertices of g_i is denoted by N_i for all $1 \leq i \leq n$.

(1) First, for all $1 \leq i \leq n$, we replace all variables having the variable label x_i with the layout term graph g_i as follows. Let $h_i^1, h_i^2, \ldots, h_i^{k_i}$ be all variables which are labeled with the variable label x_i. And let C_i be the set of all layout edges incident to one of the variables $h_i^1, h_i^2, \ldots, h_i^{k_i}$. Then, we attach the k_i layout term graphs $g_i^1, g_i^2, \cdots, g_i^{k_i}$, which are copies of g_i, to g according to the k_i lists $\sigma_i^1, \sigma_i^2, \ldots, \sigma_i^{k_i}$, which are the k_i copies of σ_i in the following way. We remove all variables $h_i^1, h_i^2, \ldots, h_i^{k_i}$ from H and all layout edges in C_i from F, and identify the m-th element $h_i^j[m]$ of h_i^j and the m-th element $\sigma_i^j[m]$ of σ_i^j for all $1 \leq j \leq k_i$ and all $1 \leq m \leq r_i$. Then, the resulting graph is denoted by f_0. We assume that the vertex label of each vertex $h_i^j[m]$ $(1 \leq m \leq r_i)$ is used for f_0, that is, the vertex label of $\sigma_i^j[m]$ is ignored in f_0.

(2) Next, for all $i = 1, \ldots, n$ and all $j = 1, \ldots, k_i$, a layout of f_0 is updated by adding new layout edges to f_0 so that $g\theta$ satisfies the conditions in Definition 1 as follows.

(i) For all $u \in V - V(h_i^j)$ such that $Ord_g^X(u) < Ord_g^X(h_i^j[1])$, we add a new x-edge to f_0 as follows. If $(u, x, h_i^j) \in C_i$ (the vertex u_1 of g in Fig. 4 is an example of u), we add $(u, x, Ver_{g_i^j}^X(1))$ to f_0 (the layout edge $(u_1, x, Ver_{g_i^j}^X(1))$ is added in $g\theta$ of Fig. 4). If $(h_i^j, x, u) \in C_i$ and $Ord_{g_i^j}^X(\sigma_i^j[1]) > 1$, we add $(Ver_{g_i^j}^X(Ord_{g_i^j}^X(\sigma_i^j[1]) - 1), x, u)$ to f_0.

(ii) For all $u \in V - V(h_i^j)$ such that there exists $m < r_i$ satisfying the condition $Ord_g^X(h_i^j[m]) < Ord_g^X(u) < Ord_g^X(h_i^j[m+1])$ and $Ord_{g_i^j}^X(\sigma_i^j[m]) + 1 < Ord_{g_i^j}^X(\sigma_i^j[m+1])$, we add a new x-edge to f_0 as follows. If $(u, x, h_i^j) \in C_i$ (the vertex u_2 of g in Fig. 4 is an example of u), we add (u, x, v) to f_0, where v is $Ver_{g_i^j}^X(Ord_{g_i^j}^X(\sigma_i^j[m]) + 1)$ (the vertex v of g_i in Fig. 4 is given as an example and the layout edge (u_2, x, v) is added in $g\theta$). If $(h_i^j, x, u) \in C_i$, we add $(Ver_{g_i^j}^X(Ord_{g_i^j}^X(\sigma_i^j[m+1]) - 1), x, u)$ to f_0.

(iii) For all $u \in V - V(h_i^j)$ such that $Ord_g^X(h_i^j[r_i]) < Ord_g^X(u)$, we add a new x-edge to f_0 as follows. If $(u, x, h_i^j) \in C_i$ and the vertex $\sigma_i^j[r_i]$ is not the rightmost vertex in g_i^j (such as u_3 in Fig. 4), we add $(u, x, Ver_{g_i^j}^X(Ord_{g_i^j}^X(\sigma_i^j[r_i]) + 1))$ to f_0. If $(h_i^j, x, u) \in C_i$ (the vertex u_3 of g in Fig. 4 is an example of u), we add (w, x, u) to f_0 (the layout edge $(Ver_{g_i^j}^X(N_i), x, u_3)$ is added in $g\theta$ of Fig. 4). where w is the rightmost vertex of g_i^j.

For each added layout edge e, we set $dist(e)$ to the distance of the layout edge between u and h_i^j. For any $d \in V \cup (H - \{h_i^1, \ldots, h_i^{k_i}\})$ in g and any variable h in g_i^j, we add a new x-edge (d, x, h) with $dist((d, x, h)) = dist((d, x, h_i^j))$ to f_0 if $(d, s, h_i^j) \in C_i$ and there is not an x-path from h to d in f_0. And we add a new x-edge (h, x, d) with $dist((h, x, d)) = dist((h_i^j, x, d))$ to f_0 if $(h_i^j, x, d) \in C_i$ and there is not an x-path from d to h in f_0. In a similar way, we add new y-edges to f_0. Then, the resulting graph f is obtained from f_0.

When a layout is ignored, we note that the above operation of applying a substitution to a layout term graph is the same as that of a term graph in [16]. In Fig. 5, we give the layout term graph $g\theta$ obtained by applying the substitution $\theta = \{x := [g_1, (w_1, w_2)], y := [g_2, (u_1, u_4)]\}$ to the term graph g as an example.

A *unifier* of two layout term graphs g_1 and g_2 is a substitution θ such that $g_1\theta \simeq g_2\theta$. A unifier θ of g_1 and g_2 is a *most general unifier (mgu)* of g_1 and g_2, if for any unifier τ of g_1 and g_2, there exists a substitution γ such that $\tau = \theta\gamma$.

Lemma 1. *There exists no mgu of two layout term graphs, in general.*

Proof (Sketch) We can obtain this lemma by showing that two layout term graphs g_1 and g_2 in Fig. 6 have no mgu. Assume that g_1 and g_2 have a unifier $\theta = \{x := [g, (u_1, u_2)]\}$ and g has a variable. The leftmost vertex (the vertex u of g in Fig. 6) in $V(H)$ is at the k-th position in the x-path of $g = (V, E, H, F)$. Then the leftmost vertex (the vertex u of $g_1\theta$ in Fig. 6) in $V(H_{g_1\theta})$ is at the $(k+1)$-st position in the x-path of $g_1\theta = (V_{g_1\theta}, E_{g_1\theta}, H_{g_1\theta}, F_{g_1\theta})$. The leftmost vertex (the vertex u of $g_2\theta$ in Fig. 6) in $V(H_{g_2\theta})$ is at the k-th position in the x-path of $g_2\theta = (V_{g_2\theta}, E_{g_2\theta}, H_{g_2\theta}, F_{g_2\theta})$. Since $g_1\theta \simeq g_2\theta$, we have a contradiction. So any unifier of g_1 and g_2 is of the form $\theta = \{x := [g, (u_1, u_2)]\}$ for a ground layout term graph g. We can show that, for $n \geq 1$, a substitution $\{x := [f_n, (v_1, v_2)]\}$ for a ground layout term graph f_n in Fig. 6 is a unifier of g_1 and g_2. Thus any unifier of g_1 and g_2 is not an mgu of g_1 and g_2. (QED)

Notions of a *goal*, a *derivation* and a *refutation* are defined in a way similar to those in logic programming [7], except that a unifier instead of an mgu is used in a derivation and a refutation. Due to Lemma 1, in LFGS a derivation is based on an enumeration of unifiers and only ground goal is considered. We say that a ground layout term graph g is *generated* by an LFGS program Γ and its predicate symbol p if there exists a refutation in Γ from the goal $\leftarrow p(g)$. And the set of all ground layout term graphs generated by Γ and its predicate symbol p is said to be *definable* by Γ and p, and the set is denoted by $GL(\Gamma, p)$.

3   LFGS and Layout Graph Grammar

In [1], Brandenburg presented Layout Graph Grammar (LGG) consisting of an underlying context-free graph grammar and layout specifications. Its underlying context-free graph grammar is a vertex replacement system such as Node-Label Controlled Graph Grammar (NLCG) in [5]. LFGS is a logic programming system obtained by extending Formal Graph System (FGS) [16] for two-dimensional graph structured data. In [16], we gave an interesting subclass of FGS, which is called a regular FGS. And we showed that the set of graphs L is definable by a regular FGS program if and only if L is generated by a hyperedge replacement

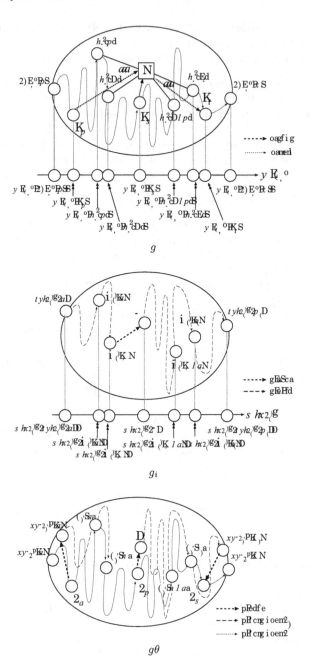

Fig. 4. Updating layout edges for $g\theta$, where $g = (V, E, H, F)$ is a layout term graph, $\theta = \{\cdots, x_i := [g_i, \sigma_i], \cdots\}$, $N = |V|$, $r_i = rank(x_i)$, and the number of vertices in g_i is N_i.

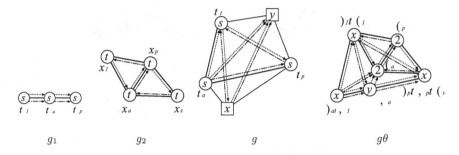

Fig. 5. Ground layout term graphs g_1 and g_2, a layout term graph g, a substitution $\theta = \{x := [g_1, (w_1, w_2)], y := [g_2, (u_1, u_4)]\}$ and the resulting layout term graph $g\theta$

grammar [5]. And in [15], we showed that for an NLCG G, there exist an FGS program Γ and its predicate symbol p such that the set of graphs generated by G is definable by Γ and p. In this section, we show that LFGS is more powerful than LGG w.r.t. the sets of generated graphs.

First of all, we introduce some notions of LGG. A *graph* $g = (V, E, m)$ over Σ and Λ consists of a finite set of vertices V, a vertex labeling function $m : V \to \Sigma$, and a finite set of edges $E = \{(u, a, w) \mid u, w \in V, u \neq w \text{ and } a \in \Lambda\}$. In the same way as a layout term graph, let $E^s = \{(u, s, w) \mid u, w \in V, u \neq w\}$, and $g^s = (V, E^s, m)$ for $s \in \{x, y\}$. In order to simplify the discussion in comparing LFGS with LGG, we consider $g^* = g^x \cup g^y$ satisfying the following conditions (1) and (2). And g^* is called a *drawing specification*.

(1) g^x and g^y are acyclic.
(2) For every pair of vertices (u, w) with $u \neq w$, there is a path over g^x from u to w, or conversely, And there is a path over g^y from u to w, or conversely.

Let N, T and Δ be alphabets such that $N \cap T = \emptyset$. An element of N, T and Δ is called a *nonterminal vertex label*, a *terminal vertex label* and a *terminal edge label*, respectively. A graph grammar employed in LGG is one of the vertex replacement systems such as node-label controlled graph grammars [6] defined as follows.

Definition 3. A *graph grammar* is a system $GG = (N, T \cup \Delta, P, S)$ defined as follows. P is a set of finitely many productions of the form $p = (A, R, C)$, where A is a nonterminal vertex label in N, R is a nonempty graph and C is a connection relation consisting of tuples (B, a, u) with $B \in N \cup T$, $a \in \Delta$ and u being the vertex of R. And S is the axiom and is regarded as a vertex having the vertex label S.

A direct *derivation step* $g \Rightarrow g'$ rewrites a graph $g = (V, E, m)$ into a graph $g' = (V', E', m')$ by applying a production $p = (A, R, C)$ to a vertex w having a nonterminal vertex label A as follows. Replace w by an isomorphic copy of

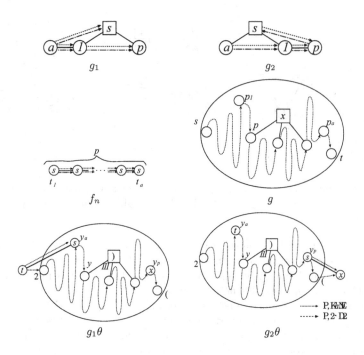

Fig. 6. Layout term graphs g_1 and g_2 which have no mgu

R that is disjoint with g. Then establish edges between the neighbors of w and the vertices of R as specified by C. That is, $V' = (V - \{w\}) \cup V(R)$, where $V(R)$ is the set of all vertices of R. And an edge $e = (s, a, t)$ is in E' if and only if $e \in E$ with $s \neq w$ and $w \neq t$ or $e \in E(R)$ or e is established by a connection from C as follows, where $E(R)$ is the set of all edges in R. If $(B, a, u) \in C$ and $u \in V(R)$, then (v, a, u) is an edge of g' if and only if v has a nonterminal vertex label B and (v, a, w) is an edge in g. The *graph language* generated by a graph grammar GG, denoted by $L(GG)$, is the set of all generated graphs with terminal vertex labels. That is, $L(GG) = \{g \mid S \Rightarrow^* g, m(w)$ is a terminal vertex label for every vertex $w \in V(g)\}$.

Definition 4. A *layout graph grammar* $LGG = (GG, LS)$ consists of a graph grammar GG and a layout specification LS associating finitely many drawing specifications with each production of GG.

We consider a derivation step of GG in which g' is obtained from g by replacing a vertex w of g by the graph R according to p. Then, the drawing specification is updated as follows. In g^X, the x-edges incoming to w are transferred to the vertex of R having no incoming x-edge, and the x-edges outgoing from w are transferred from the vertex of R having no outgoing x-edge. y-edges are treated similarly. The *language* $L(LGG)$ of a layout graph grammar $LGG = (GG, LS)$

consists of the set of all pairs $(g, \mathrm{DS}(g))$ such that $g \in L(GG)$ and $\mathrm{DS}(g)$ is constructed along a derivation $S \Rightarrow^* g$.

Theorem 2. *Let G be an LGG. Then there is an LFGS program Γ and its predicate symbol p such that $GL(\Gamma, p) = L(G)$.*

Proof (Sketch) We construct graph rewriting rules according to productions in LGG G and according to the operation of adding new edges in a derivation step. Then, we can obtain the LFGS program Γ from G. By simulating a derivation of G with a refutation of Γ and conversely, we can prove $L(G) = GL(\Gamma, p)$. (QED)

The interesting sets of graphs such as the trees and the binary trees, the series parallel graphs, the partial k-trees for fixed k, the maximal outerplanar graphs, and the complete graphs, are generated by a graph grammar which is employed by LGG [1]. From Theorem 2, these sets are also definable by LFGS. In [15], we showed that there exists a set of graphs L such that FGS can define L but not generated by any NLCG. This result and Theorem 2 suggest that LFGS is more powerful than LGG.

4   Refutably Inductive Inference of LFGS Programs

In this section, we introduce a sufficiently large hypothesis space of LFGS programs, the set of weakly reducing LFGS programs, and show that the hypothesis space is refutably inferable from complete data. Since Mukouchi and Arikawa [11] showed that refutably inductive inference is essential in machine discovery from facts, this result gives a theoretical foundation of our knowledge discovery system from two-dimensional structured data with such an LFGS program as a hypothesis.

We give our framework of refutably inductive inference of LFGS programs in a way based on our previous results [8,9]. In this section we assume that the distance of any layout edge is bounded by a constant. Let $g = (V, E, H, F)$ be a layout term graph. Then we denote the *size of g* by $\|g\|$ and define $\|g\| = |V| + |E| + |H|$. For example, $\|g\| = |V| + |E| + |H| = 3 + 4 + 2 = 9$ for the layout term graph $g = (V, E, H, F)$ in Fig. 2. For an atom $p(g_1, \ldots, g_n)$, we define $\|p(g_1, \ldots, g_n)\| = \|g_1\| + \cdots + \|g_n\|$.

Definition 5. A graph rewriting rule $A \leftarrow B_1, \ldots, B_m$ is said to be *weakly reducing* if $\|A\theta\| \geq \|B_i\theta\|$ for any $i = 1, \ldots, m$ and any substitution θ. An LFGS program Γ is *weakly reducing* if every graph rewriting rule in Γ is weakly reducing.

For example, the LFGS program Γ_{TTSP} in Fig. 3 is weakly reducing. The set of all ground atoms is called the *Herbrand base*, denoted by $\mathcal{HB}$, and is considered as the set of all training examples. A subset I of $\mathcal{HB}$ is called an *interpretation*, and is considered as a set of positive training examples. An LFGS program Γ is called a *correct program* for an interpretation I if the least Herbrand model of Γ, which is the set of all ground atoms proved from Γ, is equal to I. A *complete presentation* of an interpretation I is an infinite sequence $(w_1, t_1), (w_2, t_2), \cdots$ of elements in $\mathcal{HB} \times \{+, -\}$ such that $\{w_i \mid t_i = +, i \geq 1\} = I$ and $\{w_i \mid t_i = -, i \geq 1\} = \mathcal{HB} - I$.

A *refutably inductive inference algorithm* is a special type of inductive inference algorithm. The algorithm receives a complete presentation as an input. If the algorithm produces the sign "refute" and stops, we say that the algorithm *refutes* the hypothesis space. A refutably inductive inference algorithm produces hypotheses as outputs or refutes a given hypothesis space. A refutably inductive inference algorithm is said to *converge* to an LFGS program Γ for a presentation, if it produces the same LFGS program Γ after some finitely many times of hypothesis changes.

Definition 6. A refutably inductive inference algorithm is said to *refutably infer a hypothesis space $\mathcal{H}$ from complete data*, if it satisfies the following condition. For any interpretation $I \subseteq \mathcal{HB}$ and any complete presentation δ of I, (1) if there exists a correct program in $\mathcal{H}$ for I then the algorithm converges to a correct program in $\mathcal{H}$ for I from δ, (2) otherwise the algorithm refutes $\mathcal{H}$ from δ.

Theorem 3. *For any $n \geq 1$, the hypothesis space $\mathcal{WR}^{[\leq n]}$ of all weakly reducing LFGS programs with at most n graph rewriting rules has infinitely many hypotheses. And $\mathcal{WR}^{[\leq n]}$ is refutably inferable from complete data.*

This theorem can be shown in a way based on [11,14]. We can construct a machine discovery system for a refutably inferable hypothesis space. Thus Theorem 3 gives a theoretical foundation of our knowledge discovery system. By a simple enumeration of hypotheses, the hypothesis space $\mathcal{WR}^{[\leq n]}$ is inferable but not refutably inferable. If the number of graph rewriting rules is not bounded by a constant, then this hypothesis space is not refutably inferable. In case that the distance of a layout edge is not bounded by a constant, we need another learning method about distances of layout edges.

5   Concluding Remarks

We have given a framework of discovering knowledge from two-dimensional graph structured data with positional relations such as image or map data. We have defined a layout term graph for representing two-dimensional graph structured data. And we have proposed Layout Formal Graph System (LFGS) as a new logic programming system which is used as a knowledge representation language. Also we have shown that LFGS is more powerful than Layout Graph Grammar (LGG). Finally we have designed a knowledge discovery system using LFGS for two-dimensional graph structured data.

We have shown that the isomorphism problem for layout term graphs is solvable in polynomial time. However, in order to develop a knowledge discovery system, we must construct an efficient algorithm for finding a unifier of a ground layout term graph and a layout term graph.

References

1. F. J. Brandenburg. Designing graph drawings by layout graph grammars. *Proc. Graph Drawing '94*, Lecture Notes in Computer Science, Vol. 894:416–427, 1994. 143, 149, 153

2. D. J. Cook and L. B. Holder. Substructure discovery using minimum description length and background knowledge. *Journal of Artificial Intelligence Research*, 1:231–255, 1994. 143

3. P. Finn, S. Muggleton, D. Page, and A. Srinivasan. Pharmacophore discovery using the inductive logic programming system progol. *Machine Learning*, pages 241–270, 1998. 142

4. M. Garey and D. Johnson. *Computers and Intractability: A Guide to the Theory of NP-Completeness*. Freeman, 1979. 147

5. A. Habel and H.-J. Kreowski. May we introduce to you: hyperedge replacement. *Proceedings of the 3rd International Workshop on Graph-Grammars and Their Application to Computer Science, LNCS 291*, pages 15–26, 1987. 149, 151

6. D. Janssens and G. Rozenberg. On the structure of node-label-controlled graph languages. *Information Sciences*, 20:191–216, 1980. 151

7. J. W. Lloyd. *Foundations of Logic Programming, Second, Extended Edition.* Springer-Verlag, 1987. 149

8. T. Miyahara, T. Shoudai, T. Uchida, T. Kuboyama, K. Takahashi, and H. Ueda. Discovering new knowledge from graph data using inductive logic programming. *Proc. ILP-99, Springer-Verlag, LNAI 1634*, pages 222–233, 1999. 142, 153

9. T. Miyahara, T. Uchida, T. Kuboyama, T. Yamamoto, K. Takahashi, and H. Ueda. KD-FGS: a knowledge discovery system from graph data using formal graph system. *Proc. PAKDD-99, Springer-Verlag, LNAI 1574*, pages 438–442, 1999. 142, 153

10. S. Muggleton, A. Srinivasan, R.D. King, and M.J.E Sternberg. Biochemical knowledge discovery using inductive logic programming. *Proc. DS-98, Springer-Verlag, LNAI 1532*, pages 326–341, 1998. 142

11. Y. Mukouchi and S. Arikawa. Towards a mathematical theory of machine discovery from facts. *Theoretical Computer Science*, 137:53–84, 1995. 153, 154

12. L. R. Quinlan. Induction of decision trees. *Machine Learning 1*, pages 81–106, 1986. 142

13. J. Rissanen. Modeling by the shortest data description. *Automatica 14*, pages 465–471, 1978. 143

14. T. Shinohara. Rich classes inferable from positive data: length-bounded elementary formal systems. *Information and Computation*, 108:175–186, 1994. 154

15. T. Uchida, T. Miyahara, and Y. Nakamura. Formal graph systems and node-label controlled graph grammars. *Proc. 41st Inst. Syst. Control and Inf. Eng.*, pages 105–106, 1997. 151, 153

16. T. Uchida, T. Shoudai, and S. Miyano. Parallel algorithm for refutation tree problem on formal graph systems. *IEICE Transactions on Information and Systems*, E78-D(2):99–112, 1995. 142, 145, 149

Hypotheses Finding via Residue Hypotheses with the Resolution Principle

Akihiro Yamamoto[1,2] and Bertram Fronhöfer[3]

[1] Faculty of Technology and MemeMedia Laboratory, Hokkaido University
N 13 W 8, Kita-ku, Sapporo 060-8628 Japan
[2] "Information and Human Activity", PRESTO, JST
yamamoto@meme.hokudai.ac.jp
[3] Institut für Informatik, TU München
D–80290 München
fronhoef@informatik.tu-muenchen.de

Abstract. For given logical formulae B and E such that $B \not\models E$, hypothesis finding means the generation of a formula H such that $B \wedge H \models E$. Hypothesis finding constitutes a basic technique for fields of inference, like inductive inference and knowledge discovery. It can also be considered a special case of abduction. In this paper we define a hypothesis finding method which is a combination of residue hypotheses and anti-subsumption. Residue hypotheses have been proposed on the basis of the terminology of the Connection Method, while in this paper we define it in the terminology of resolution. We show that hypothesis finding methods previously proposed on the bases of resolution are embedded into our new method. We also point out that computing residue hypotheses becomes a lot more efficient under the restrictions required by the previous methods to be imposed on hypotheses, but that these methods miss some hypotheses which our method can find. Finally, we show that our method constitutes an extension of Plotkin's relative subsumption.

1 Introduction

For given logical formulae B and E such that $B \not\models E$, hypothesis finding means the generation of a formula H such that $B \wedge H \models E$. The formulae B, E, and H are intended to represent a *background theory*, a *positive example*, and a *hypothesis* respectively. Hypothesis finding constitutes a basic technique for fields of inference, like inductive inference and knowledge discovery. It can also be considered a special case of abduction. This paper treats hypothesis finding in clausal logic.

Various methods were developed for hypothesis finding on the basis of the resolution principle, but many of them imposed severe restrictions on the hypotheses to be generated. The abductive inference by Poole [12] and its improvement [6] require that every hypothesis should be a conjunction of literals. Some methods developed in the area of Inductive Logic Programming, e.g. *the bottom method* (or *the bottom generalization method*) [16], *inverse entailment* [9] [1], and *saturation* [13], generate hypotheses which consist of exactly one clause. As we pointed out in [19] some important hypotheses might be failed to generate under such restrictions.

---

[1] In previous works [15,16] by one of the authors, the bottom method was not well distinguished from inverse entailment.

H. Arimura, S. Jain and A. Sharma (Eds.): ALT 2000, LNAI 1968, pp. 156–165, 2000.
© Springer-Verlag Berlin Heidelberg 2000

In order to remove such restrictions and also in order to put hypothesis finding on general grounds, we have recently proposed a new concept : *residue hypotheses* [4,5]. Residue hypotheses are defined on the basis of the terminology of the Connection Method, which is a special method for theorem proving [2]. Based on the residue hypothesis concepts we have developed several hypothesis finding methods and shown that they are generalizations of the bottom method.

In this paper we define residue hypotheses in terminology of resolution. The definition gives at least two contributions. Firstly we show that residue hypotheses are useful in design and analysis of hypothesis finding even when we adopt the resolution principle as its basis. The second is to give a solution to a problem which we have left unsolved in the previous research.

Residue hypotheses were initially defined in propositional logic, and then lifted up to first-order logic by using anti-instantiation. We have mentioned that some method other than anti-instantiation should be employed for more flexible hypotheses, but did not give any proposal for it. As an answer to this problem, anti-subsumption is proposed in this paper. Subsumption is originally defined as a relation of two clauses. It can be extended in several manners to a relation of two sets of clauses. We adopt an extension, denoted by $\sqsupseteq$, which was proposed in a learning algorithm of logic programs [1]. In order to make our discussion general and simple, we define the residue hypothesis for any satisfiable set S of clauses and denote it by $\mathrm{Res}(S)$. The main theorem shows that

$$S \vdash T \implies \mathrm{Res}(T) \sqsupseteq \mathrm{Res}(S)$$

where $\vdash$ is provability by resolution, set inclusion, and subsumption. Since all of the resolution-based methods above make resolvents and subsumed clauses from $B \cup \overline{E}$, where $\overline{E}$ is a negation of (skolemized) E, any hypothesis derived by them can also be derived by the combination of residue hypotheses and the inverse of $\sqsupseteq$. This shows that anti-subsumption is appropriate for the replacement of anti-instantiation.

With the main theorem we show which type of hypotheses may be missed by resolution-based methods but can be found by our new method. Moreover, the theorem shows that our hypothesis finding method defines a new relation between sets of clauses, as an extension of Plotkin's relative subsumption [11]. These results are contribution to the first aim of this paper.

This paper is organized as follows: In the next section we define terminology and notation for our discussion. In Section 3 we define residue hypotheses in the terminology of resolution. In Section 4, we give the main result which shows how resolution proofs affect hypothesis finding, and in Section 5 we explain the relation between the main result and the bottom method and Poole's method for abduction. In the last section we give a view on the complexity of computing residue hypotheses.

2   Hypothesis Finding in Clausal Logic

We assume the readers to be familiar with first-order logic and clausal logic. When more precise definitions are needed, we refer them to textbooks on these areas (e.g. [2,3,8]).

Let $\mathcal{L}$ be a first-order language. As in the Prolog language, each variable is assumed to start with a capital letter. For each variable X we prepare a new constant symbol

c_X called the *Skolem constant* of X. We let $\mathcal{L}^s$ denote the language whose alphabet is obtained by adding all the Skolem constants to the alphabet of $\mathcal{L}$.

In this paper a *clause* is a formula of the form

$$C = \forall X_1 \ldots X_k(A_1 \vee A_2 \vee \ldots \vee A_n \vee \neg B_1 \vee \neg B_2 \vee \ldots \vee \neg B_m)$$

where $n \geq 0$, $m \geq 0$, A_i's and B_j's are all atoms, and $X_1, \ldots, X_k$ are all variables occurring in the atoms. We sometimes represent the clause C in the form of the implication

$$A_1, A_2, \ldots, A_n \leftarrow B_1, B_2, \ldots, B_m.$$

In this paper we define a clausal theory as follows:

Definition 1. A *clausal theory* is a finite set of clauses *without any tautological clauses* which represents the conjunction of clauses contained therein. The set of all clausal theories in $\mathcal{L}$ ($\mathcal{L}^c$) is denoted by $\mathrm{CT}(\mathcal{L})$ ($\mathrm{CT}(\mathcal{L}^c)$ resp.).

Let S be a clausal theory. We assume that no pair of clauses in S share variables. A substitution σ_S replaces each variable in S with its Skolem constant. The set of ground clauses which is an instance of some clause in S is denoted by $ground(S)$.

Definition 2. For a ground clausal theory $S = \{C_1, C_2, \ldots, C_m\}$ where

$$C_i = L_{i,1} \vee L_{i,2} \vee \ldots \vee L_{i,n_i} \quad \text{for } i = 1, 2, \ldots, m,$$

we define its *complement*[2] as the set of clauses

$$\overline{S} = \{\neg L_{1,j_1} \vee \neg L_{2,j_2} \vee \ldots \vee \neg L_{m,j_m} \mid 1 \leq j_1 \leq n_1, 1 \leq j_2 \leq n_2, \ldots, 1 \leq j_m \leq n_m\}.$$

When any variable occurs in S, we define $\overline{S} = \overline{S\sigma_S}$.

Definition 3. A *hypothesis finding problem* (*HFP*, for short) in clausal logic is defined as a pair (B, E) of satisfiable clausal theories such that $B \not\models E$. The theory B is called a *background theory*, and each clause in E is called a *positive example*. A solution to the $HFP(B, E)$ is given by any clausal theory H such that $B \cup H \models E$.

Because we do not consider any negative example, an *example* means a positive example in this paper.

Definition 4. A *fitting procedure* (or a *fitting*, for short) $\mathcal{F}$ is a procedure which generates hypotheses H from a given example E with the support of a background theory B. The set of all such hypotheses is denoted by $\mathcal{F}(E, B)$.

Each of the fittings we are now discussing can be represent as a main routine consisting of two sub-procedures. The first sub-procedure enumerates highly specific clausal theories and the second generalizes each of them. We give formal definitions.

Definition 5. A *base enumerator* Λ is a procedure which takes an example E and a background theory B as its input and enumerates ground clausal theories in $\mathcal{L}^s$. The set of clausal theories enumerated in the procedure is denoted by $\Lambda(E, B)$ and called a *base set*.

---

[2] Using the terminology of the Connection Method, the complement of S corresponds to *the set of negated paths* in the matrix representation of S.

Definition 6. A *generalizer* Γ takes a ground clausal theory K in $\mathcal{L}^s$ and generates clausal theories in $\mathcal{L}$. The set of clauses generated by Γ is denoted by $\Gamma(K)$.

Procedure $\mathrm{FIT}_{\Lambda,\Gamma}(E, B)$

1. Choose non-deterministically a ground clausal theory K from $\Lambda(E, B)$.
2. Return non-deterministically clausal theories in $\Gamma(K)$.

If either of the sets $\Lambda(E, B)$ and $\Gamma(K)$ is infinite, we must use some dovetailing method in order to enumerate all elements in these sets. In our discussion we need not mind about how the dovetailing is implemented.

3   Residue Hypotheses

In order to make our discussion simple, we put $S = B \cup \overline{E}$ and slightly modify some definitions in our previous work [4,5].

Definition 7. For an unsatisfiable and ground clausal theory S, the *residue hypothesis* for S is defined as a clausal theory which is obtained by deleting all tautological clauses from $\overline{S}$. The residue hypothesis is denoted by $\mathrm{Res}(S)$[3].

We can obtain $\mathrm{Res}(S)$ from a ground clausal theory S by deleting all clauses containing pairs of complementary literals.

Hypotheses finding with residue hypotheses is based on Herbrand's theorem, which is described in textbooks on Automated Theorem Proving (e.g. [2,3,8])[4].

Theorem 1 (Herbrand). *A finite set S of clauses is unsatisfiable if and only if there is a finite and unsatisfiable subset of* $ground(S)$.

For our aim we use the following corollary.

Corollary 1. *Let S be a clausal theory and T be a ground clausal theory such that $T \subseteq ground(S)$. Then $S \cup H$ is unsatisfiable for any clausal theory H such that $\mathrm{Res}(T) \subseteq ground(H)$.*

In [4,5] we used this corollary directly. That is, we considered an enumerator GT and a generalizer AI which satisfy the following specifications:

$$GT(S) = \{K \in \mathrm{CT}(\mathcal{L}^c) \mid K = \mathrm{Res}(T) \text{ for some } T \text{ such that } T \subseteq ground(S) \},$$
$$AI(K) = \{H \in \mathrm{CT}(\mathcal{L}) \mid H\theta = K \text{ for some substitution } \theta \}.$$

In the next example we apply the fitting $\mathrm{FIT}_{GT,AI}$ to a hypothesis finding problem.

---

[3] Each of clause in $\mathrm{Res}(S)$ corresponds to a *non-complementary path* in the Connection Method terminology. This definition via non-complementary paths was used in [4,5].

[4] Theorem 1 is called "Herbrand's Theorem, Version II" in Chang and Lee's textbook [3], which has two versions of "Herbrand's Theorem".

Example 1. Let us consider the background theory

$$B_1 = \{pet(X) \leftarrow dog(X), small(X)\}$$

and the positive example

$$E_1 = \{pet(c) \leftarrow\}.$$

Let $S_1 = B_1 \cup \overline{E_1}$. Then

$$ground(S_1) = \left\{ \begin{array}{l} pet(c) \leftarrow dog(c), small(c) \\ \leftarrow pet(c) \end{array} \right\},$$

and we put $T_1 = ground(S_1)$. The residue hypothesis for T_1 is

$$\text{Res}(T_1) = \left\{ \begin{array}{l} dog(c), pet(c) \leftarrow \\ small(c), pet(c) \leftarrow \end{array} \right\}.$$

By applying anti-instantiation to $\text{Res}(T_1)$, we get the hypothesis

$$H_1 = \left\{ \begin{array}{l} dog(Y), pet(Y) \leftarrow \\ small(Z), pet(Z) \leftarrow \end{array} \right\}$$

in $\text{FIT}_{GT,AI}(E_1, B_1)$. ∎

We define a weaker form of anti-instantiation using the subsumption relation between clauses.

Definition 8. A clause C *subsumes* a clause D, written as $C \succeq D$, if every literal in $C\theta$ occurs in D.

If a clausal theory S is unsatisfiable and a clause $D \in S$ is subsumed by C, then the clausal theory which is obtained by replacing D with C is also unsatisfiable. We extend subsumption to a relation between two sets of clauses in the following way:

Definition 9. Let H and K be clauses. We define $H \sqsupseteq K$ iff, for every clause D in K, there is a clause C in H such that $C \succeq D$.

Now we revise the fitting $\text{FIT}_{GT,AI}$ by replacing the generalizer AI with a generalizer AS which satisfies

$$AS(K) = \{H \in \text{CT}(\mathcal{L}) \mid H \sqsupseteq K\}.$$

Example 2. Consider the following background theory and example:

$$B_2 = \left\{ \begin{array}{l} even(0) \leftarrow \\ even(s(X)) \leftarrow odd(X) \end{array} \right\},$$
$$E_2 = \{odd(s^5(0)) \leftarrow\}.$$

The predicates *even* and *odd* are respectively intended to represent an even number and an odd number. The constant 0 means zero, and the function s is the successor function for natural numbers. The term which is an n-time application of s to 0 is written as $s^n(0)$. Then for $HFP(E_2, B_2)$ we may expect the hypothesis

$$H_2 = \{odd(s(X)) \leftarrow even(X)\}.$$

We show that $\text{FIT}_{GT,AS}$ derives the hypothesis. At first we make a clausal theory

$$T_2 = \left\{ \begin{array}{l} even(0) \leftarrow, \\ even(s^2(0)) \leftarrow odd(s(0)), \\ even(s^4(0)) \leftarrow odd(s^3(0)), \\ \leftarrow odd(s^5(0)) \end{array} \right\},$$

which is a subset of $ground(B_2 \cup \overline{E_2})$. The residue hypothesis for T_2 is

$$\text{Res}(T_2) = \left\{ \begin{array}{l} odd(s^5(0)) \leftarrow even(s^4(0)), even(s^2(0)), even(0), \\ odd(s^5(0)), odd(s(0)) \leftarrow even(s^4(0)), even(0), \\ odd(s^5(0)), odd(s^3(0)) \leftarrow even(s^2(0)), even(0), \\ odd(s^5(0)), odd(s^3(0)), odd(s(0)) \leftarrow even(0) \end{array} \right\}$$

Since $H_2 \sqsupseteq \text{Res}(T_2)$, H_2 is in $\text{FIT}_{GT,AS}(E_2, B_2)$.

4   Resolution and Anti-Subsumption

We show that deriving logical consequences from S reduces the search space for the generalizer AS. We need as preparation a definition and Lee's Theorem, which shows that deriving logical consequences of a clausal theory is accomplished by making resolvents and deriving subsumed clauses.

Definition 10. Let S and T be clausal theories. We write $S \vdash T$ if there is a sequence of clausal theories $U_0, U_1, \ldots, U_n$ such that $U_0 = S$, U_n is a variant of T, and one of the following holds for each U_i $(i = 1, 2, \ldots n)$:

1. $U_i \subseteq U_{i-1}$.
2. $U_i = U_{i-1} \cup \{C\}$ where C is subsumed by a clause in U_{i-1}.
3. $U_i = U_{i-1} \cup \{C\}$ where C is a resolvent of some two clauses in U_{i-1}.

Theorem 2 ([7]). *Let S and T be clausal theories. Then T is a logical consequence of T iff $S \vdash T$.*

The main theorem is now the following.

Theorem 3. *Let S be clausal theory and T be a ground clausal theory. Then $S \vdash T$ implies $\text{Res}(T) \sqsupseteq \text{Res}(S)$.*

Proof. There is a subset U of $ground(S)$ and a sequence $U_0 = U, U_1, \ldots, U_m = T$ which satisfies the conditions 1–3 of Definition 10. Then $\text{Res}(U_i) \sqsupseteq \text{Res}(U_{i-1})$, by Lemma 2, Lemma 3, and Lemma 4 which are proved below. Therefore $\text{Res}(T) \sqsupseteq \text{Res}(S)$. ∎

Before we will show that each operation for deriving U_i from U_{i-1} implies $\text{Res}(U_{i-1}) \sqsupseteq \text{Res}(U_i)$, we give a lemma on tautologies and subsumption.

Lemma 1. *If a clause C is subsumed by a tautological clause, then C is also a tautology.*

Lemma 2. *For ground clausal theories S and T, $S \supset T$ implies $\text{Res}(T) \sqsupseteq \text{Res}(S)$.*

Proof. From the definition, it is clear that $\overline{T} \sqsupseteq \overline{S}$. Then $\text{Res}(T) \sqsupseteq \text{Res}(S)$ by Lemma 1. ∎

Lemma 3. *Let S be a ground clausal theory. If a ground clause D is subsumed by a clause $C \in S$, then*

$$\text{Res}(S \cup \{D\}) \sqsupseteq \text{Res}(S).$$

Proof. Without loss of generality, we can assume that

$$C = L_1 \vee L_2 \vee \ldots \vee L_m,$$
$$D = L_1 \vee L_2 \vee \ldots \vee L_m \vee L_{m+1} \vee \ldots \vee L_n.$$

Then every clause F in $\overline{S}$ contains a literal $\neg L_i$ for some $i = 1, 2, \ldots, m$, and is subsumed by a clause F' in $\overline{S \cup \{D\}}$ which is obtained by adding $\neg L_i$ to F. This means that $\overline{S \cup \{D\}} \sqsupseteq \overline{S}$. If F is not a tautology, F' is not, either. Then $\text{Res}(S \cup \{D\}) \sqsupseteq \text{Res}(S)$ by Lemma 1. ∎

Lemma 4. *Let S be a ground clausal theory and C_1 and C_2 be clauses in S. Assume that C_1 has a literal L and C_2 has $\neg L$ and let D be the resolvent of C_1 and C_2 obtained by deleting L and $\neg L$ from $C_1 \vee C_2$. Then*

$$\text{Res}(S \cup \{D\}) \sqsupseteq \text{Res}(S).$$

Proof. We prove the theorem in the case when $S = \{C_1, C_2\}$. The proof can easily be extended if S has more clauses. Let

$$C_1 = L_{1,1} \vee L_{1,2} \vee \ldots \vee L_{1,n_1} \text{ and}$$
$$C_2 = L_{2,1} \vee L_{2,2} \vee \ldots \vee L_{2,n_2}$$

and we can assume, without loss of generality, that

$$L = L_{1,1} = L_{1,2} = \cdots = L_{1,m_1} = \neg L_{2,1} = \neg L_{2,2} = \cdots = \neg L_{2,m_2}$$

Then the resolvent D is

$$D = L_{1,m_1+1} \vee L_{1,m_1+2} \vee \ldots \vee L_{1,n_1} \vee L_{2,m_2+1} \vee L_{2,m_2+2} \vee \ldots \vee L_{2,n_2}.$$

From the definition we get the following set of clauses:

$$\overline{S} = \{\neg L_{1,i} \vee \neg L_{2,j} \mid 1 \leq i \leq n_1, 1 \leq j \leq n_2\},$$
$$\overline{D} = \{\neg L_{1,i} \mid i = m_1 + 1, m_1 + 2, \ldots, n_1\} \cup \{\neg L_{2,j} \mid j = m_2 + 1, m_2 + 2, \ldots, n_2\},$$
$$\overline{S \cup \{D\}} = \{C \vee L \mid C \in \overline{S}, L \in \overline{D}\}.$$

In order to show the result of the theorem, we consider three cases :

Case 1. When $m_1 + 1 \leq i \leq n_1$ and $1 \leq j \leq n_2$,

$$\neg L_{1,i} \vee \neg L_{2,j} \vee \neg L_{1,i} \succeq \neg L_{1,i} \vee \neg L_{2,j}.$$

Case 2. When $1 \leq i \leq n_1$ and $m_2 + 1 \leq j \leq n_2$,

$$\neg L_{1,i} \vee \neg L_{2,j} \vee \neg L_{2,j} \succeq \neg L_{1,i} \vee \neg L_{2,j}.$$

Case 3. When $1 \leq i \leq, m_1$ and $1 \leq j \leq m_2$, $L_{1,i} = \neg L_{2,j}$ and therefore $\neg L_{1,i} \vee \neg L_{2,j}$ is not in $\text{Res}(S)$.

Combining the analysis of these three cases and by Lemma 1, we get $\text{Res}(S \cup \{D\}) \sqsupseteq \text{Res}(S)$. ∎

5   Comparison to Other Work

Poole [12] formalized abductive inference based on resolution, by using the fitting $\text{FIT}_{AB,AS}$ where

$$AB(E, B) = \{\{H\} \mid H = \overline{C} \text{ for some a ground clause } C \text{ such that } B \cup \overline{E} \vdash C\}.$$

Theorem 3 shows that $\text{FIT}_{AB,AS}(E, B) \subseteq \text{FIT}_{GT,AS}(E, B)$, which means that the fitting $\text{FIT}_{GT,AS}$ is more powerful than Poole's method.

Now we will compare $\text{FIT}_{GT,AS}$ with the bottom method. Since we showed in [17] that the bottom method is equivalent or more powerful than hypothesis finding methods well-known in the ILP area, comparison with the bottom method is sufficient.

The bottom method generates hypotheses which consist of only one clause. In the terminology of this paper, it is $\text{FIT}_{BT,AS}$ where

$$BT(E, B) = \left\{ \{C\} \;\middle|\; \begin{array}{l} C \text{ is a ground clause such that } B \cup \overline{E} \vdash \neg L \\ \text{for every literal } L \text{ in } C \end{array} \right\}.$$

As mentioned in [16], $\text{FIT}_{BT,AI}$ does not differ from $\text{FIT}_{BT,AS}$. Off course, it is clear that the bottom method cannot derive any clausal theories consisting of more than one clause, like H_1 in Example 1. We showed in [17,18] that the hypothesis H_2 in Example 2 cannot be derived with the bottom method. We will give the difference between $\text{FIT}_{GT,AS}$ and $\text{FIT}_{BT,AS}$ more formally as follows:

Theorem 4. *For any $HFP(B, E)$, it holds that $FIT_{GT,AS}(E, B) \supseteq FIT_{BT,AS}(E, B)$.*

Proof. All that we have to show is $GT(E, B) \supseteq BT(E, B)$. Let $C = \neg L_1 \vee \neg L_2 \vee \ldots \vee \neg L_n$ be a ground clause in $BT(E, B)$. From the definition of $BT(E, B)$, it holds that $B \cup \overline{E} \vdash L_1 \wedge L_2 \wedge \ldots \wedge L_n$. Since $C = \text{Res}(L_1 \wedge L_2 \wedge \ldots \wedge L_n)$, we get a clausal theory U by Theorem 3 which is a subset of $ground(B \cup \overline{E})$ and $C \sqsupseteq \text{Res}(U)$.   ∎

The proof of Theorem 4 shows which hypotheses may be missed by the bottom method. Let U be the clausal theory in the proof and

$$U_0 = U, U_1, \ldots, U_m = L_1 \wedge L_2 \wedge \ldots \wedge L_n$$

be a sequence of clausal theories deriving $L_1 \wedge L_2 \wedge \ldots \wedge L_n$. Then $\text{FIT}_{BT,AS}(E, B)$ may not contain a hypothesis H such that $H \sqsupseteq U_i$ for some $i = 0, 1, \ldots, m - 1$ but $H \not\sqsupseteq U_m$. The hypothesis H_2 in Example 2 is such a hypothesis, and therefore is missed by the bottom method.

The results above can be analyzed from a semantical viewpoint. We showed in [16] that the bottom method is complete for deriving clauses H which subsume E relative to B. The definition of relative subsumption was given by Plotkin [11].

Definition 11. Let H and E be clauses and B be a clausal theory. Then H *subsumes E relative to B* iff $\forall(H\theta \rightarrow E)$ is a logical consequence of B for some θ.

The condition for the relative subsumption is equivalent to the condition that $\neg H\theta\sigma_E\mu$ is a logical consequence of $B \cup \overline{E}$ for some substitution μ which makes $H\theta\sigma_E$ ground. Then $B \cup \overline{E} \vdash \neg H\theta\sigma_E\mu$ by Lee's theorem. The proof of Theorem 4 shows that $H \in \text{FIT}_{GT,AS}$ if H subsumes E relative to B, which is consistent with our previous work [16]. In other words, the relation of two clausal theories H and E defined by $H \in \text{FIT}_{GT,AS}(E, B)$ is an extension of Plotkin's relative subsumption of two clauses.

6   Concluding Remarks

The problem of computing Res(S) from S is equivalent to the enumeration of all satisfiable interpretations of S. This problem is similar to counting such interpretations, which is denoted by ♯SAT and treated in a textbook on the computational complexity [10]. The problem ♯SAT is in the class ♯P. Therefore the complexity of computing the residue hypothesis is quite high in general.

This fact might explain why the abductive hypothesis finding method and the bottom method were discovered earlier than our method. Assuming severe restrictions on hypotheses, they derive clausal theories whose residue hypotheses are easily computed. In fact, the abductive method generates theories consisting of a clause $L_1 \vee \ldots \vee L_n$ and the bottom method derives theories of the form $L_1 \wedge \ldots \wedge L_n$. In both cases the residue hypotheses of derived theories are computed in linear time. But the comparison in the last section shows that the efficiency is obtained by missing hypotheses which might be important.

The generalizer we adopted in this paper is the inverse of subsumption. Resolution-based theorem proving uses subsumption, factoring and resolution as inference rules. Therefore the inverse of factoring and that of resolution might be considered as well. Using them as generalizers in Procedure FIT$_{\Lambda,\Gamma}(E, B)$ will be investigated in the near future.

Acknowledgments

The authors thank Prof. Taisuke Sato, Prof. Chiaki Sakama, Prof. Hiroki Arimura, and Prof. Koichi Hirata for fruitful discussions.

References

1. H. Arimura. Learning Acyclic First-order Horn Sentences From Implication, In *Proceedings of the 8th International Workshop on Algorithmic Learning Theory(LNAI 1316)*, pages 432–445, 1997. 157
2. W. Bibel. *Deduction: Automated Logic.* Academic Press, 1993. 157, 159
3. C.-L. Chang and R. C.-T. Lee. *Symbolic Logic and Mechanical Theorem Proving.* Academic Press, 1973. 157, 159
4. B. Fronhöfer and A. Yamamoto. Relevant Hypotheses as a Generalization of the Bottom Method. In Proceedings of the Joint Workshop of SIG-FAI and SIG-KBS, *SIG-FAI/KBS-9902*, pages 89–96. JSAI, 1999. 157, 159
5. B. Fronhöfer and A. Yamamoto. Hypothesis Finding with Proof Theoretical Appropriateness Criteria. Submitted to the AI journal, 2000. 157, 159
6. K. Inoue. Linear Resolution for Consequence Finding. *Artificial Intelligence*, 56:301–353, 1992. 156
7. R.C.T. Lee. A Completeness Theorem and Computer Program for Finding Theorems Derivable from Given Axioms. PhD thesis, University of California, Berkeley, 1967. 161
8. A. Leitsch. *The Resolution Calculus.* The Resolution Calculus, 1997. 157, 159
9. S. Muggleton. Inverse Entailment and Progol. *New Generation Computing*, 13:245–286, 1995. 156
10. C. H. Papadimitriou. *Computational Complexity.* Addison Wesley, 1993. 164
11. G. D. Plotkin. A Further Note on Inductive Generalization. In *Machine Intelligence 6*, pages 101–124. Edinburgh University Press, 1971. 157, 163

12. D. Poole. A Logical Framework for Default Reasoning. *Artificial Intelligence*, 36:27–47, 1988. 156, 163

13. C. Rouveirol. Extensions of Inversion of Resolution Applied to Theory Completion . In S. Muggleton, editor, *Inductive Logic Programming*, pages 63–92. Academic Press, 1992. 156

14. T. Sato and S. Akiba. Inductive Resolution. In *Proceedings of the 4th International Workshop on Inductive Logic Programming (LNAI 744)*, pages 101–110. Springer-Verlag, 1993.

15. A. Yamamoto. Representing Inductive Inference with SOLD-Resolution. In *Proceedings of the IJCAI'97 Workshop on Abduction and Induction in AI*, pages 59 – 63, 1997. 156

16. A. Yamamoto. Which Hypotheses Can Be Found with Inverse Entailment? In *Proceedings of the 7th International Workshop on Inductive Logic Programming (LNAI 1297)*, pages 296 – 308, 1997. The extended abstract is in *Proceedings of the IJCAI'97 Workshop on Frontiers of Inductive Logic Programming, pp.19–23 (1997)*. 156, 163

17. A. Yamamoto. Logical Aspects of Several Bottom-up Fittings. In *Proceedings of the 9th International Workshop on Algorithmic Learning Theory (LNAI 1501)*, pages 158–168, 1998. 163

18. A. Yamamoto. An Inference Method for the Complete Inverse of Relative Subsumption. *New Generation Computing*, 17(1):99–117, 1999. 163

19. A. Yamamoto. Revising the Logical Foundations of Inductive Logic Programming Systems with Ground Reduced Programs. New Generation Computing, 17(1):119–127, 1999. 156

Conceptual Classifications Guided by a Concept Hierarchy

Yuhsuke ITOH and Makoto HARAGUCHI

Division of Electronics and Information Engineering
Hokkaido University
N-13 W-8, Kita-ku, Sapporo 060-8628, JAPAN
makoto@db-ei.eng.hokudai.ac.jp

Abstract. Given a concept hierarchy and a set of instances of multiple concepts, we consider the revision problem that the primary concepts subsuming the instances are judged inadequate by a user. The basic strategy to resolve this conflict is to utilize the information the hierarchy involves in order to classify the instance set and to form a set of several intermediate concepts. We refer to the strategy of this kind as hierarchy-guided classification. For this purpose, we make a condition, Similarity Independence Condition, that checks similarities between the hierarchy and the instances so that the similarities are invariant even when we generalize those instances to some concept at the middle. Based on the condition, we present an algorithm for classifying instances and for modifying the concept hierarchy.

1 Introduction

We propose in this preliminary paper an algorithm to classify a set of instances and to form new concepts based on the classification. Such a classification task normally depends on what kinds of concepts and instances we concern. Both the concepts and instances which we consider here are conceptual structure represented by some knowledge representation languages. One of important issues about them seems related to the tasks for building and revising thesaurus or MRD, machine readable dictionary. It is generally convinced that building thesaurus is a hard task and needs much cost. Some support systems for reducing such a task have been designed. For instance, a computational system DODDLE [5] with the input WordNet, a kind of large MRD, has strategies to identify some anomalies we encounter in applying WordNet to some particular domain for which the MRD is not yet sufficiently developed. The anomalies found by DODDLE are inadequateness of the subsumption relationship between terms in a concept hierarchy involved in the dictionary. However, DODDLE does not contain semantic information, such as types and roles, on conceptual terms, so the detection of anomalies is much restricted.

This papaer is directly motivated by DODDLE, and tries to present a framework for those systems revising concept hierarchy, using the semantic information. For this purpose, we suppose a Classic [1, 2], particularly a CoreClassic [2], as a knowledge representation language. Although much efforts have been

H. Arimura, S. Jain and A. Sharma (Eds.): ALT 2000, LNAI 1968, pp. 166-177, 2000.

already paid for the studies on the learnabilities on those languages, the goal of this preliminary paper differs from them at the following points:

1. A concept hierarchy is itself a knowledge source. At the same time, it is the target of knowledge revision when we find some inadequateness in it. So some part of hierarchy may be utilizable to revise and resolve anomalies in the hierarchy itself. So a system we suppose in this paper revises knowledge and refers it at the same time.

2. Normally, a concept hierarchy has the root or top node, meaning "everything". Hence in the worst case, some individual concept may be classified to the top. However the classification has no information in this case. Similarly, when the hierarchy has only too abstract concepts subsuming very particular instances, the user also feels that something intermediate between them are missed, although the subsumption is logically valid.

Taking these points into account, we present a framework with the following invocation condition, a strategy and a key notion to solve the problem.

Given a concept hierarchy and a set of instances of multiple concepts, the primary concepts subsuming the instances are judged inadequate by a user.

The basic strategy to resolve this conflict is to utilize the information the hierarchy involves in order to classify the instance set and to form a set of severl intermediate concepts, each from each class. We refer to the strategy of this kind as hierarchy-guided classification.

For this purpose, we check similarities between concepts in the hierarchy and the instances so that the similarities are invariant even when we generalize those instances to some concept at the middle. This condition is called a Similarity Independence Condition (SIC).

This paper is organized as follows. First in Section2, we give some definitions about CoreClassic according to the literature [2]. In Section 3, we informally introduce a classification problem and exemplify it. In Section 4, we present Similarity Independence Condition and show some properties about it. In Section 5, we present a formal definition of classification task and a corresponding algorithm, and show what classifications it actually performs. In Section6, we summarize this paper.

2   Descriptions

We first define our language to describe concepts, CoreClassic, and introduce the standard lattice operations for computing the least common subsumer and unifications of two or more concepts, that are key to handle our space of concepts.

In CoreClassic, a description is formally a finite set of constraints for individual objects, and is used to denote a set of individuals satisfying all the constraints in the description, where we suppose descriptions in the form of conjunctive normal forms without loss of generality. To describe various relationships between individuals, CoreClassic provides three kinds of symbols: *primitive* class $p_1, p_2, ...,$ roles $r_1, r_2, ...,$ and attribute $a_1, a_2, ..., b_1, b_2, ...$ Given a domain of interpretation, p_j, r_k and a_ℓ are interpreted as a set of individuals, a binary relations and a function, respectively. Then the follwing two types of constraints can be asserted in the language:

Type Constraints:

$$(ALL \ (r_1...r_k) \ p_\ell) \tag{1}$$

meaning that an $r_1...r_k$ filler y of x should be a member of the set p_ℓ denotes, where $r_1...r_k$ is the composition of relations defined as $r_1...r_k(x,y) \Leftrightarrow$ there exist $x = z_1, z_2, ..., z_m = y$ such that $r_j(z_j, z_{j+1})$ holds for $1 \leq j \leq m-1$, and we say that y is a $r_1...r_k$ filler of x if $r_1...r_k(x,y)$ holds. As a first-order formula , (1) can be written as

$$r_1...r_k(x,y) \Rightarrow y \in p_\ell \tag{2}$$

Equality Constraints:

$$(ALL \ (r_1...r_k) \ (SAME\_AS \ (a_1...a_n) \ (b_1...b_m)) \tag{3}$$

meaning that, for any $r_1...r_k$ filler y of x, $a_1...a_n(y) = a_n(...(a_1(y)...) = b_m(...(b_1(y)...) = b_1...b_m(y)$ should hold. As in the case of constraint (1), (3) just corresponds to

$$r_1...r_k(x,y) \Rightarrow a_1...a_n(y) = b_1...b_m(y). \tag{4}$$

Note that just one free variable occurs in each constraint. Thus a description is given as a set of constraints for the unique free variable x:

$$D(x) = \{const_1(x), ..., const_k(x)\}.$$

For the free variable is clear from the syntax, $D(x)$ is simply written as D. Moreover, given an interpretation of first order logic, the extension of D is defined as $ext(D) = \{x | \text{for all } c \in D \ c(x) \text{ holds}\}$. For instance,

D(x)= { x ∈ person, spouse(x) ∈ person,
    spouse(spouse(x)) = x, address(x) ∈ address_name
    address(spouse(x)) = address(x) } ,

In addition to these constrains, we have another constrain, $address(spouse(x)) \in address\_name$, that is a logical consequence of $D(x)$. In what follows, $const(D) = \{const | D \models const\}$ denotes the set of all constraints, either type or equality constraint, derived from a description D.

In the case of descriptions with equality constraints, it is convenient to represent each description by a rooted directed graph, called a concept graph, for the reasonig about equalities is naturally realized by path structures in the graph. However, this paper is mainly concerned with an algebraic structure between descriptions, so we omit the details.

2.1   Subsumption and Least Common Subsumer

Now let us briefly introduce notions of subsumptions, least common subsumers and unifications. They are needed to analyze the relationships between descriptions and to form a new concept from instance descriptions.

For two descriptions D_2, D_1, we say that D_1 subsumes D_2 (written as $D_2 \Rightarrow D_1$) if

$$\forall x \ (\ \text{if}\ D_2(x)\ \text{then}\ D_1(x)\ ). \tag{5}$$

In what follows, the formula (5) is also denoted by $D_2 \models D_1$, and we say that D_2 entails D_1

Proposition 1. *The following four conditions are equivalent.*

(1) $D_2 \Rightarrow D_1$
(2) $ext(D_2) \subseteq ext(D_1)$ for every interpretation.
(3) $D_1 \subseteq const(D_2)$ (i.e. if $d \in D_1$ then $D_2 \models d$)
(4) $const(D_1) \subseteq const(D_2)$
    (i.e. if $D_1 \models d$ then $D_2 \models d$)

From the proposition, when D_1 subsumes D_2, every constraint for D_1 is also valid in D_2. Hence, in order to check if D_1 subsumes D_2, it suffices to check if every $d \in D_1$ is entailed by D_2. Although the concept graph representation quickly performs the theorem-proving task of this kind, as we have already explained, see the literature for details.

Based on the definition and analysis of subsumptions, we then define least common subsumer (LCS, for short) .

Definition 2. Given two or more descriptions D_j, we say that $D = \vee_j D_j$ is the least common subsumer of D_j if the following conditions are satisfied:

(1) For any j, $D_j \Rightarrow D$
(2) $D \Rightarrow D'$ holds whenever $D_j \Rightarrow D$ for any j.

The construction of $\vee D_j$ is very similar to finite automata synthesis for recognizing set intersection. However, it suffices to remind that $\vee D_j$ is really constructable form D_j. The proposition below is a direct consequence of the definition and Proposition 1.

Proposition 3. $const(D_1) \cap const(D_2) = const(D_1 \vee D_2)$

Compared with the join operation $D_1 \vee D_2$, the unification (meet) $D_1 \wedge D_2$ of D_j is more direct, for it suffices to consider a set union $D_1 \cup D_2$.

Proposition 4. $D_1 \cup D_2$ has the following property:

1. $D_1 \cup D_2 \Rightarrow D_j$ for $j = 1, 2$.
2. If $D \Rightarrow D_j$ $(j = 1, 2)$ then $D \Rightarrow D_1 \cup D_2$.

Thus $D_1 \cup D_2$ is greatest among descriptions subsumed by both D_j. Hence $D_1 \cup D_2 = D_1 \wedge D_2$.

3   Classification Problem and a Principle to Solve it

A concept hierarchy H is defined as a finite set of descriptions such that

(1) the empty description ϕ is in H.
(2) no two descriptions in H are equivalent.
(3) there exists a unique parent description $\Pi(D)$, defined below, for each $D \in H - \{\phi\}$

The empty description ϕ denotes "everything", since its extension always denotes an interpretation domain. In other words, it is simply asserting that there is no constraint to be checked. Moreover, two descriptions D_j are said equivalent if $D_1 \Rightarrow D_2$ and $D_2 \Rightarrow D_1$, and is normally written as $D_1 \equiv D_2$. However in this paper, we do not distinguish syntactic equality "$=$" and the equivalence $\equiv$ for notational convenience.

For two descriptions D_1 and D_2 in H, we say that D_1 is a predecessor of D_2 if D_1 subsumes D_2 . Moreover D_1 is called a parent of D_2 if D_1 is a predecessor of D_2 and if there exists no $D_3 \in H - \{D_1, D_2\}$ such that $D_2 \Rightarrow D_3 \Rightarrow D_1$. The parent of D is denoted by $\Pi(D)$.

A sequence $\phi, D_1, D_2, ..., D_k = D$ of descriptions such that $D_j = \Pi(D_{j+1})$ just corresponds to a path from root ϕ to a description D in the hierarchy H, and is written as $path(D)$. From Proposition 1, we have

$$\phi \subseteq const(D_1) \subseteq ...const(D_j) \subseteq const(D_{j+1})...$$

For no two descriptions in this sequence are equivalent, there exists at least one $d \in D_{j+1}$ such that D_j never entails d. Such d is understood as a new constraint to form a successor D_{j+1} from its parent D_j. Intuitively speaking, we regard a path from a root as a flow of constraint additions to form more specific concepts. In fact, we have the following proposition.

Proposition 5. *Suppose $D_2 \Rightarrow D_1$. Then $D_2 \equiv D_1 \cup \{c \in D_2 | D_1 \not\models c\}$*

As a terminal case, we will get to an instance description of some concept. One way to define a class of instances is to give a sublanguage to describe only individual descriptions . However, in this preliminary paper, we does not make such a restriction. So a (positive) training set ES is simply defined as a set of descriptions except those in H.

An incremental learning algorithm, receiving a training set ES of some single description in the above sense, has been already studied in [2]. Instead, we present here a classification problem to divide a given training set ES of descriptions to a partition $\{ES_j\}$. For each $ES_j \subseteq ES$, we computes $\vee E_j$. Thus it can be regarded as a kind of conceptual classification of training instances or a problem of learning multiple concepts from ES.

3.1   A Simple Example of Hierarchy-Guided Classification

This subsection presents a simple example to show why we consider hierarchy-guided classifications.

Our concept hierarchy H has ϕ as a top concept. Hence, when nothing in H except ϕ subsumes an instance $E \in ES$, E will be located under ϕ because of the trivial subsumption $E \Rightarrow \phi$. Even when we have non-ϕ description D subsuming E, one might think that D is not an adequate super concept to which E belongs. The situation really depends on one's intention and conceptual cognition about the subsumption between general and specific concepts. We consider that the hierarchy is inadequate for such a person when he/she has a doubt to the subsumption $E \Rightarrow D$, even though the subsumption is logically valid. So the purpose of classification of instances is to classify them and to generate an adequate general description according to the classification. Although we can have various criterion to search for a classification, we consider in this preliminary paper a hierarchy-guided classification.

For instance, suppose we have a concept hierarchy shown by Figure 1 in which the notion of (field) hockey is given. On the other hand, the notion of ice hockey is not presently registered in H. Suppose furthermore we have in our mind a description IH_H, "Ice Hockey in Hokkaido Island", which will be an instance description of ice hockey IH hidden in H. For the (field) hockey and ice hockey have different playing field, IH and IH_H as well are not subsumed by *(field) hockey*, but by *skating*.

The corresponding descriptions of skating, (field) hockey and ice hockey are given in Figure 2, where $A \Rightarrow B_1, ..., B_n$ and $term(x) \in p_1 \wedge ... \wedge p_k$ are abbreviations of $(A \Rightarrow B_1), ..., (A \Rightarrow B_n)$ and $term(x) \in p_1, ..., term(x) \in p_k$, respectively.

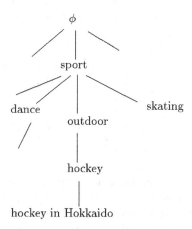

Fig. 1. A Sample Hierarchy

$\text{Sport}(x) = \{x \in \text{sport}\}$

$S(x) = \{\ x \in \text{sport}, \text{playing\_field}(x) \in \text{ice\_rink}, \text{wear\_shoe}(x) \in \text{skating\_shoe}\ \}$

$\text{FH}(x) = \{$
    $x \in \text{sport} \wedge \text{ball\_game}, \text{playing\_unit}(x) \in \text{team},$
    $\text{playing\_field}(x) \in \text{field}, \text{instrument}(\text{playing\_field}(x)) \in \text{goal\_net}$
    $\text{playing\_unit} \bullet \text{player}(x,y) \Rightarrow y \in \text{person}, \text{has\_in\_hand}(y) \in \text{stick}\}$

$\text{IH\_H}(x) = \{$
    $x \in \text{sport}, \text{playing\_unit}(x) \in \text{team},$
    $\text{activity\_area}(\text{playing\_unit}(x)) \in \text{Hokkaido\_Island}$
    $\text{playing\_field}(x) \in \text{ice\_rink}, \text{instrument}(\text{playing\_field}(x)) \in \text{goal\_net}$
    $\text{playing\_unit} \bullet \text{player}(x,y) \Rightarrow$
        $y \in \text{person}, \text{has\_in\_hand}(y) \in \text{stick}, \text{wear}(y) \in \text{protector},$
        $\text{wear\_shoe}(y) \in \text{skating\_shoe}\ \}$

Fig. 2. Sample Descriptions

Then our problem in this case is explained as follows:

Given a training set of instances including those of ice hockey in Hokkaido, our
classifier has to distinguish those from others like instances of "Ice Dance"
and so on, where the concept of ice dance is also invisible in H.

The training set ES can contain instances of "Ice Hockay in Kyushu Island".
Our hierarchy H specializes the notion of hockey to "hockey in Hokkaido".
According to Hierarchy-guided classification, the designation of Hokkaido
in the concept Hockay is regarded important, so our classifier should also
distinguish instances of ice hockay in hokkaido island from other including
those of ice hockay in Kyushu .

To solve the problem as in the above, a criterion we introduce here is a notion
of *Similarity Independence Condition* meaning that

a similarity between a concept in a hierarchy and instances of some target
class does not depend on each instance.

In the case of ice hockay in Hokkaido island, there may exist various individual descriptions subsumed by the class description *IH_H* in Figure 2. Each
has each individual constraint added to *IH_H*. However, from the viewpoint of
hockey in Hokkaido in the hierarchy illustrated in Figure 1, such an individual information disappears, and only a similarity determined by the class descriptions
becomes visible.

4 Similarity Independence Condition and a Classification Algorithm

First we define Similarity Independence Condition (SIC, for short) and then present an algorithm based on it.

Before introducing SIC, we have to answer what is a similarity between concepts. In this preliminary paper, we simply consider that a similarity is a set of constrains shared by two descriptions. Since $const(D_1 \vee D_2) = const(D_1) \cap const(D_2)$ holds, LCS, $D_1 \vee D_2$, is regarded to show the similarity.

Definition 6. (Similarity Independence Condition) For a description D_s and $ES_t \subseteq ES$, ES_t is said to satisfy SIC with respect to D_s, if $E \vee D_s = E' \vee D_s$ holds for any E and E' in ES_t.

Proposition 7.

(A) SIC is closed under generalizations. That is, if $D \Rightarrow D'$ and ES_t satisfies SIC w.r.t. D, then SIC is also valid for ES_t w.r.t. D'.

(B) The following two conditions are equivalent:

    (1) ES_t satisfies SIC w.r.t. D.

    (2) $(\vee ES_t) \vee D = E \vee D$ for any $E \in ES_t$

Proof. Part A: From the assumption, we have $const(D') \subseteq const(D)$ and $const(E_1) \cap const(D) = const(E_2) \cap const(D)$ for any $E_1, E_2 \in ES_t$. Hence the conclusion is a direct consequence of set operation.

Part B: (2) $\Rightarrow$ (1) is trivial. To prove (1) $\Rightarrow$ (2), let $J = D \vee E$. Then, clearly $D \Rightarrow J$ and $E \Rightarrow J$ for any $E \in ES_t$. Therefore $E \Rightarrow \vee ES_t \Rightarrow J$. Hence $J = E \vee D \Rightarrow (\vee ES_t) \vee D \Rightarrow J \vee D = J$. Thus we have $J = (\vee ES_t) \vee D$. Q.E.D.

4.1 Building new hierarchy from instance description set satisfying SIC

From the proposition, when ES_t satisfies SIC w.r.t. D, we can construct a new concept $\vee ES_t$ that has the same similarity with D as its instances ES_t have. When D appears in a concept hierarchy H, $\vee ES_t$, a new concept generated from ES_t satisfying SIC, is to be put in H based on the following analysis.

First recall that there exists a path from root ϕ to D.

$$D = D_k \Rightarrow D_{k-1} \Rightarrow ... \Rightarrow D_1 \Rightarrow D_0 = \phi \qquad (6)$$

$$\phi \subseteq const(D_1) \subseteq ... \subseteq const(D_k) \qquad (7)$$

Since $D_k = D \Rightarrow E \vee D = (\vee ES_t) \vee D$, we have

$$const(E \vee D) \subseteq const(D) = \cup_{j \leq k} const(D_j)$$

Then let us consider the most specific D_{ms} such that $const(D_{ms}) \subseteq const(E \vee D)$. That is, $\vee ES_t \Rightarrow E \vee D \Rightarrow D_{ms}$. From this simple argument, it follows that $\Pi(\vee ES_t) = D_{ms}$ whenever we add $\vee ES_t$ to our hierarchy H.

case1: $D_{ms} = \phi$. In this case, the remaining constraints in $\vee ES_t$ are spread over the series of constraints, and is not kept in one D_j as a "chunk" of constraints. Therefore, $\vee ES_t$ is a direct successor of root concept.

case2: D_{ms} is neither ϕ nor $D = D_k$. For both $D = D_k$ and $\vee ES_t$ has D_{ms} as the common predecessor, $\vee ES_t$ appears in $H \cup \{\vee ES_t\}$ as a "brother concept" of $D = D_k$. For instance, given D as the hockey concept and ES_t of some ice hockey instances, $\vee ES_t$ is located just under the sport concept in Figure 1, not under the concept *outdoor*, for it does not subsume $E \vee D$. Note that $\vee ES_t$ is not necessarily the ice hockey concept. If ES_t keeps some individual information incident to some subclass of ice hockey, then $\vee ES_t$ is the subclass located under the ice hockey concept which is still invisible in this case.

case3: $D_{ms} = D_k$. This case clearly put $\vee ES_t$ just under D. That is, $\vee ES_t$ is a "specialization" of D. As an example, suppose we have hockey concept as D and ES_t of some university hockey instances. Then $\vee ES_t$, a subclass of university hockey, is directly located under the hockey concept.

4.2   How to collect instances satisfying SIC

This subsection describe how to collect instances satisying SIC. For this purpose, suppose we have a description D in H and a set $\{ES_t\}$ of instances. It is often the case that each $E \in ES_t$ shows each similarity with respect to D. The similarity $D \vee E$ will represent some aspect of D which E is concerned with. So in order to keep the condition SIC, simply gather all such instances concerning the same aspect of D. Formaly we have the following definition.

Definition 8. Given a description $D \in H$, an equivalence relation $\sim_D$ is defined as:

$$E_1 \sim_D E_2 \Leftrightarrow D \vee E_1 = D \vee E_2$$

We use this equivalence relation to divide instance set showing the same similarity with a given description in the hierarchy.

4.3   Similarity Index

From the argument given in the preceding subsections, it turn out that, when every instance in ES have at least one shared constraint with D, we can classify ES into subgroups, compared with D. So the remaining problem is to find such a D in H.

As is shown in the series of constrains (7), a path from the root provides us a growing sets of constrains, the series of descriptions in H. So the corresponding similarities between descriptions on the path and a given instance E increase, as we go down H on the path:

$$\phi \subseteq const(E \vee D_1) \subseteq ... \subseteq const(E \vee D_{k-1}) \subseteq const(E \vee D_k)....$$

In the case of ice hockay in Hokkaido island, any instance of both ice hockey in Kyushu island and one in Hokkaido island will show the same similarity to the (field) hockey description. They are therefore classified into the same group according to SIC. However, H in Figure 1 further specializes the notion of hockey to its subconcept, hockey in Hokkaido island. Thus the hockey in Hokkaido and any instance of ice hockey in Hokkaido show the same and stronger similarity. This enables us to distinguish Hokkaido and other area even in the case of ice hockey. Formally we define s-index for each instance description to associate it with a concept in H so that the corresponding similarity is maximal.

Definition 9. s-index (similarity index) Given a concept hierarchy H and an instance description E, a description $D \in H$ is called a s-index of E if

(1) $D \vee E \neq \phi$,
(2) there exists at least one $d \in D \vee E$ such that $\neg(\Pi(D) \vee E \Rightarrow d)$, and
(3) no successor of D in H satisfies the condition (2).

The constraint $d \in D$ in the conditon (2) is a constraint that is newly added to form D from its parent description $\Pi(D)$. Clearly, $const(\Pi(D)) \neq const(D)$. In additon, the condition (3) requires that $const(D \vee E) = const(D' \vee E)$ for any successor D' of D in H.

4.4   Multiple occurrences of s-indices

Basically, for each instance $E \in ES$, s-index D of E is firstly calculated, and then equivalence relation $\sim_D$ is used to classify D-indexed instances.

However, in general, there may exist several s-indices for an instance description E. For such an E and its s-indices $D_1, ..., D_k$, we consider a system of similarities between the s-indices and the instance.

> **Weak Identity:** $E \vee D_1, ..., E \vee D_k$ can be a weak identity of things with respect to H in the following sense.
> 1. E is something showing the similarities $E \vee D_1, ..., E \vee D_k$ to H, and
> 2. $E \vee D_1, ..., E \vee D_k$ are all the similarities we can observe from H.
> Thus everything we can know from the viewpoint of H is described by the $E \vee D_1, ..., E \vee D_k$. Consequently, if there exists another E' with the same s-indices and the corresponding similarities $E \vee D_j = E' \vee D_j$ (for all j), there exists a strong evidence showing that E and E' are grouped into the same one.

Based on this intuition, we make the following definition.

Definition 10. Suppose we have a hierarchy H and an instance description set ES. For $E_1, E_2 \in ES$, E_1 and E_2 are said equivalent w.r.t. H, written as $E_1 \sim E_2$, if (1) $s\text{-}index(E_1) = s\text{-}index(E_2)$ and (2) for each $D \in s\text{-}index(E_1)$, $E_1 \sim_D E_2$ holds, where $s\text{-}index(E)$ denotes the set of all s-indices of E.

The following proposition just corresponds to Proposition 7.

Proposition 11. *Let $[E]$ be an equivalence class $\{E' \in ES | E' \sim E\}$. Then $\vee[E] \sim E'$ for any $E' \in [E]$. Thus, $[E]$ satisfies SIC for any shared s-index D of $[E]$.*

Proof. The conclusion directly follows from a fact that, for each shared s-index D of any E' in $[E]$, $\vee[E] \vee D = E' \vee D$ holds.

In the case with multiple s-indices $\{D_1, ..., D_k\}$, we have k paths from the root

$$D_\ell = D_\ell^{n_\ell} \Rightarrow D_\ell^{n_\ell - 1} \Rightarrow ... \Rightarrow D_\ell^1 \Rightarrow D_\ell^0 = \phi, \tag{8}$$

where $1 \le \ell \le k$. For each path (8), we can find the most specific description $D_\ell^{ms(\ell)}$ such that $const(D_\ell^{ms(\ell)}) \subseteq const(E_i)$ for any $E_i \in [E]$. Thus, new description $\vee[E]$ is subsumed by $D_\ell^{ms(\ell)}$. Since this argument holds for each ℓ, we have $\vee[E] \Rightarrow \wedge_\ell D_\ell^{ms(j)}$. Furthermore, for $D_\ell^{ms(j)}$ is a generalization of D_ℓ, we can conclude the argument by the following proposition.

Proposition 12. *Let $[E]$ be an equivalence class of ES with the s-indices $\{D_1, ..., D_k\}$. Then there exists a family of their generalizations $\{\overline{D_1}, ..., \overline{D_k}\}$ such that $\vee[E] \Rightarrow \overline{D_1} \wedge ... \wedge \overline{D_k}$.*

Proposition 13. *Given ES, the set of all training instances, Let $\{[E_1], ..., [E_n]\}$ be the partition determined by the equivalence relation $\sim$. Then, for any description $D \in H$ such that $D \vee (\vee[E_j]) \ne \phi$, $[E_j]$ satisfies SIC with respect to D.*

4.5   An Algorithm

Now an algorithm satisfying our requiement is clear. It simply calculates the equvalence classes $\{[E] | E \in ES\}$, and form a new description $\vee[E]$ for each equivalence class $[E]$. From the propositon 13, $[E]$ satisfies SIC.

To characterize the behavior of our algorithm, we first introduce the class of possible classifications guided by a hierarchy. Intuitively speaking, such a class is obtained by forgetting or removing some constraints added on paths in the hierarchy. For the generalization operation is considered to realize such an operation, we first define a *class descriptor* C as a finite set of generalizations of concepts in H. That is, C is defined as a finite set $\{\overline{D_1}, ..., \overline{D_n}\}$ such that $D_j \Rightarrow \overline{D_j}$ for some $D_j \in H$. Then, we have the following definition of classifications guided by a hierarchy.

Definition 14. *A classification guided by a hierarchy H is defined as a finite set $\{C_1, ..., C_m\}$ of class descriptors $C_j = \{\overline{D_{j1}}, ..., \overline{D_{jn_j}}\}$ such that, for any $E \in ES$, there exists a unique class descriptor C subsuming E, that is, $E \Rightarrow \wedge_{\overline{D}}\{\overline{D} \in C\}$.*

From the definition, we can classify $E \in ES$ according to which class descriptor subsumes E. In other word, E_1 and E_2 are regarded equivalent and classified into the same group whenever they are subsumed by the same and the unique descriptor in C. Note that we allow subsumptions between class descriptors. For instance, in the case of hockey example, the concept of ice hockey in Hokkaido island is subsumed by the concept of ice hockey and that any instances of ice hockey whose activity areas are not Hokkaido island are uniquely subsumed by the ice hockey concept.

Now we are ready to show what classification our algorithm computes.

Theorem 15. *Given a classification* $\{C_1, ..., C_n\}$ *guided by* H, E_1 *and* E_2 *are subsumed by the same descriptor* C_j *whenever* $E_1 \sim E_2$.

In other words, a partition $\{[E]|E \in ES\}$ obtained by $\sim$ is always a refinement of the partition defined by the classification $\{C_1, ..., C_n\}$ guided by H.

Proof. First let us define $wid(E)$, for each $E \in ES$, as

$$wid(E) = \{E \vee D_j | D_j \in s\text{-}index(E)\}.$$

Clearly, $E \Rightarrow \wedge wid(E)$ holds and $wid(E)$ is a class descriptor. Now, suppose that we have a classification guided by H and that two E_1 and E_2 in ES are subsumed by distinct descriptors C_1 and C_2 in the classification, respectively. Then, from the proposition 16 below,

$$E_j \Rightarrow \wedge wid(E_j) \Rightarrow \wedge C_j \tag{9}$$

holds for $j = 1, 2$.

To prove the theorem, it suffices to show that $E_1 \sim E_2$ never holds. Suppose to the contrary $E_1 \sim E_2$. This directly implies $\wedge wid(E_1) = \wedge wid(E_2)$. Then, by the subsumptions (9), $E_j \Rightarrow \wedge wid(E_i) \Rightarrow \wedge C_i$ holds for $i \neq j$. Clealy this contradict to the assumption that a class desciptor subsuming an instance description is unique. Q.E.D.

Proposition 16. *Suppose* $E \Rightarrow \wedge C$, *where* C *is a class descriptor. Then,* $\wedge wid(E) \Rightarrow \wedge C$ *holds.*

Proof. Suppose $E \Rightarrow \wedge C = \overline{D_1} \wedge ... \wedge \overline{D_n}$. This implies that, for any $\overline{D_j}$, there exists a s-index D of E such that $D \Rightarrow \overline{D_j}$. Thus, there exists $(E \vee D) \in wid(E)$ such that $\wedge wid(E) \Rightarrow (E \vee D) \Rightarrow \overline{D_j}$. For $\overline{D_j}$ is arbitrary chosen, we have $\wedge wid(E) \Rightarrow \wedge C$. Q.E.D.

4.6   Present experiment

An experimental system has been already implemented and tested for a small set of descriptions [4] under some restriction on CoreClassic. The hockey example has been tried, and the system successfully generates the right LCS and places it at an adequate position in the hierarchy.

The system uses some simple similarity measure to select the best s-index D when more than two s-indices are found for an instances E. This is because, the existence of multiple s-indices are troublesome both in its semantics and accountability to users. It is not an easy task to analyze and explain the class descriptor $wid(E)$ invisible in the hierarchy H. $wid(E)$ actually concerns both generalizations and multiple paths representing contexts in a sense. So it seems that we need more strong theory for the case of multiple s-indices.

On the other hand, the measure used in that experiment is designed so that it grows when $E \vee D$ becomes larger. Moreover it decreases when the number of descriptions in D not shared by instance E increases even when the shared part is large one. Although the measure is simple, it shows a good performance, provided the concepts in the hierarchy has adequate abstraction levels, compared with the instances.

5   Concluding Remarks

There still remain a lot of things to do. The most important thing seems related to the level of abstraction:

In the case of MRD, a lot of word concept are stored in it. It could be a case that an instance subsumes a concept. (Normally a concept subsumes instances.) Such a situation may happen when MRD contains a lot of words whose meaning is very concrete and when users feed the system instance descriptions at very abstract level. Thus it seems to make some parameter or to have a selection method to choose descriptions at some adequate level of abstractions or to cut off description that are too much concrete or abstract. Particularly, according to the definition of equivalence relation $\sim_D$ allows us to have a singleton group of instances. Such a case will happen if the individual descriptions have very particular properties that are also shared with some very concrete "concept" in our hierarchy. In such a case, we have too much refined partition that is almost of no use. Another way to cope with this problem seems to use k-MMG, an algorithm to find a minimal descriptive pattern to explain positive instances. For k-MMG has been originally designed so as to solve multiple covering problem, the technique will be also used for conceptual classifications of multiple concepts.

References

1. M.Frazier & L.Pitt: CLASSIC Learning, *Machine Learning*, Vol. 25, No. 2–3, pp 151–193, 1996.
2. W.W.Cohen & H.Hirsh: The Learnability of Description Logics with Equality Constraints, *Machine Learning*, Vol. 17, No. 2–3, pp 169–199, 1996.
3. H.Arimura, T.Shinohara & S.Otsuki: Polynomial Time Algorithm for Finding Finite Unions of Two Tree Pattern Languages, LNAI 659, pp 118–131 Springer, 1993.
4. Y.Itoh: Knowledge Revision of Conceptual Hierarchy base on a Classification Master Thesis, Hokkaido University, 1999 (in Japanese).
5. T.Yamaguchi: A Legal Ontology Refinement Environment using a General Ontology, Proc. Workshop on Application of Logic Programming to Legal Reasoning, pp 176–185, 1994.

This article was processed using the LaTeX macro package with LLNCS style

Learning Taxonomic Relation by Case-based Reasoning

Ken Satoh

Division of Electronics and Information, Hokkaido University
N13W8 Kita-ku, Sapporo, 060-8628, Japan
ksatoh@db-ei.eng.hokudai.ac.jp

Abstract. In this paper, we propose a learning method of minimal case-base to represent taxonomic relation in a tree-structured concept hierarchy. We firstly propose case-based taxonomic reasoning and show an upper bound of necessary positive cases and negative cases to represent a relation. Then, we give an learning method of a minimal casebase with sampling and membership queries. We analyze this learning method by sample complexity and query complexity in the framework of PAC learning.

1 Introduction

This paper proposes a method of learning a minimal casebase to represent a relation of objects in a tree-structured concept hierarchy. Suppose that we would like to learn "eat" relation between CARNIVORA and FOOD using the taxonomic structure in Fig. 1. We assume that once an instance of the leaf class in the above structure satisfies/dissatisfies a property, then it applies to all the instance in the class since the leaf class denotes the objects which satisfy the same property. Suppose that we observe that an instance of LEO eats CHICKEN. Since nothing prevents to believe that every instance of CARNIVORA eats every instance of FOOD, we believe so. Suppose that we observe that an instance of AILUROPODA does not eat PORK even if he is hungry. Then, this is a counterexample of our current belief. We need to revise our brief. One way of revising

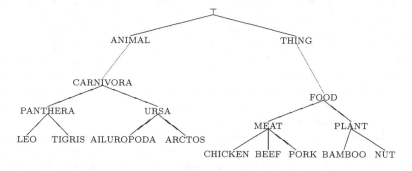

Fig. 1. Taxonomic Structure

H. Arimura, S. Jain and A. Sharma (Eds.): ALT 2000, LNAI 1968, pp. 179–193, 2000.

is to make an experiment for other instances. Since LEO is PANTHERA which is one hierarchy down from CARNIVORA, we check whether an instance of the other class of PANTHERA, which is, TIGRIS eats PORK. We find that the instance of TIGRIS eats PORK and therefore, we now believe that every instance of PANTHERA eats every instance of FOOD. By iterating this kind of observations and experiments, we can learn exact "eat" relation between CARNIVORA and FOOD.

In this paper, we formalize this phenomena by case-based reasoning. In order to perform classification task by case-based reasoning, we introduce a similarity measure and we accumulate negative cases and positive cases in a casebase. We can check a tuple of instances in the relation by deciding whether the nearest case to the new tuple belongs to the relation.

In [Satoh98] and [Satoh00], we use a set-inclusion based similarity for a case represented as a tuple of boolean-valued attributes.

In [Satoh98], we have shown that for every boolean function f, we can represent a boolean function f in a casebase whose size is bounded by $|DNF(f)| \cdot (1 + |CNF(f)|)$ where $|DNF(f)|(|CNF(f)|$, resp.) is the size of a minimal DNF(CNF resp.) representation of f. Specifically, we have shown that a boolean function defined by a casebase with our similarity measure is a complement of a *monotone extension* [Bshouty93, Khardon96] such that a set of positive cases in the casebase is called *basis* in [Bshouty93] and negative cases are assignments in the monotone extension.

In [Satoh00], we have proposed an approximation method of finding a critical casebase and analyze the approximation method in PAC (probably approximately correct) learning framework with membership query. Let n be a number of propositions and $\epsilon < 1, \delta < 1$ be arbitrary positive numbers. If $|DNF(f)|$ and $|CNF(f)|$ is small, then we can efficiently discover an approximate critical casebase such that the probability that the classification error rate by the discovered casebase is more than ϵ is at most δ. The sample size of cases is bound in polynomial of $\frac{1}{\epsilon}, \frac{1}{\delta}, |DNF(f)|$ and $|CNF(f)|$ and necessary number of membership queries is bound in polynomial of n, $|DNF(f)|$ and $|CNF(f)|$.

In this paper, we extend these results so that we learn a relation of objects in tree-structured concept hierarchy. Specifically, we analyze case-based representability of relations and propose an approximation method of a *critical casebase* which is a minimal casebase representing the considered relation.

There are works on applying case-based reasoning for taxonomic reasoning [Bareiss88, Edelson92]. [Bareiss88] takes a heuristic approach of learning a relation between objects. [Edelson92] uses case-based reasoning for computer-aided education to identify correct generalization. However, as far as we know, there are no theoretical results on computational complexity on these applications of case-based reasoning.

In this paper, we use the least common generalized concept to which two objects belong for similarity measure between these objects. Moreover, for similarity between two tuples of objects, we use set-inclusion based similarity over the least common generalized concepts. These similarity measure is not numerical-based similarity. The idea of non-numerical similarity has been suggested by various people [Ashley90, Ashley94, Osborne96, Matuschek97]. [Ashley90, Ashley94] firstly propose set-inclusion based similarity measure for legal case-based reasoning and [Osborne96] and [Matuschek97] pay attention to properties of these non-numerical similarity measure. This paper can be regarded as an application of these research to taxonomic reasoning.

The structure of this paper is as follows. In Section 2, we define taxonomic reasoning and in Section 3, we propose CBR which performs taxonomic reasoning in CBR and in Section 4, we discuss case-based representability of relations and in Section 5, we propose a learning method of a minimal casebase to represent a relation and in Section 6, we summarize our contributions and discuss future work. The proofs are found in Appendix.

2   Taxonomic Reasoning in Tree-structured Concepts

$\mathcal{O}$ is a set called a *set of objects*. $\mathcal{C}$ is a finite set called a *set of concepts*. We introduce a tree T called *concept tree* each of whose node is associated with an element in $\mathcal{C}$. The root of the tree is denoted as $top(T)$ and we define a function *parent* which maps an element c in $\mathcal{C}$ except $top(T)$ into another element in $\mathcal{C}$ which is a parent node of c in T. Conversely, a function *child* maps an element of c except leaf nodes into a set of child nodes of c. The height of the tree denoted as $height(T)$ is defined as the largest number of edges in a path between $top(T)$ to any leaf node in T and width of the tree denoted as $width(T)$ is defined as the number of leaf nodes.

We say that c_1 *is more general than* c_m (written as $c_m \prec c_1$) if there is a path between c_1 and c_m in a concept tree such that $parent(c_m) = c_{m-1}, parent(c_{m-1}) = c_{m-2}, parent(c_3) = c_2, parent(c_2) = c_1$. We write $c_m \preceq c_1$ if $c_m \prec c_1$ or $c_m = c_1$.

We call concepts associated with the leaf nodes of T *leaf concepts*. We define a function *class* from $\mathcal{O}$ to leaf concepts so that each object in $\mathcal{O}$ belongs to a leaf concept.

Let c_1 and c_2 be concepts. We define $lcgc(c_1, c_2)$ (called *the least common generalized concept w.r.t. c_1 and c_2*) as the concept c such that there is no less general node c' than c such that c' is more general than c_1 and c_2. We also define $gcgc(c_1, c_2)$ (called *the greatest common generalized concept w.r.t. c_1 and c_2*) as c_1 if $c_1 \preceq c_2$ and as c_2 if $c_2 \preceq c_1$ and undefined otherwise.

Let c_1, c_2 and c_3 be concepts. We say c_1 *is more or equally similar to c_2 than to c_3* if $lcgc(c_1, c_2) \preceq lcgc(c_1, c_3)$. For example, in Fig. 1, we have the following.

1. *LEO* is more or equally similar to *TIGRIS* than to *AILUROPODA*, since $lcgc(LEO, TIGRIS) = PANTHERA$ and $lcgc(LEO, AILUROPODA) = CARNIVORA$ and $PANTHERA \preceq CARNIVORA$.
2. *CHICKEN* is more or equally similar to *PORK* than to *BAMBOO*, since $lcgc(CHICKEN, PORK) = MEAT$ and $lcgc(CHICKEN, BAMBOO) = FOOD$ and $MEAT \preceq FOOD$.

Let o_1, o_2, o_3 be objects. We say o_1 *is more or equally similar to* o_2 *than to* o_3 denoted as $lcgc(o_1, o_2) \preceq lcgc(o_1, o_3)$ where $lcgc(o, o')$ denotes $lcgc(class(o), class(o'))$.

We call an n-ary tuple of objects in $\mathcal{O}^n$ a *case*. Let O be a case. We denote the i-th component of the tuple O as $O[i]$.

We define $lcgc(O_1, O_2)$ as

$$\langle lcgc(O_1[1], O_2[1]), lcgc(O_1[1], O_2[1]), ...lcgc(O_1[n], O_2[n]) \rangle$$

We also define $class(O)$ as $\langle class(O[1]), ..., class(O[n]) \rangle$.

Let O_1, O_2 and O_3 be cases. Then, we say O_1 *is more or equally similar to* O_2 *than to* O_3 denoted as $lcgc(O_1, O_2) \preceq lcgc(O_1, O_3)$ if for each i $(1 \le i \le n)$, $lcgc(O_1[i], O_2[i]) \preceq lcgc(O_1[i], O_3[i])$.

We have the following important property for $\preceq$.

Proposition 1. *Let* O, O_1, O_2 *be cases.* $lcgc(O_1, O) \preceq lcgc(O_2, O)$ *iff* $lcgc(O_1, O_2) \preceq lcgc(O, O_2)$.

We define a language which expresses a taxonomic relation. We introduce n variables $x_1, ..., x_n$ which represent the position of arguments in the relation. *An atomic formula* has the one of the following form:

- $x \preceq c$ where x is one of $x_1, ..., x_n$ and c is the name of a concept in $\mathcal{C}$ which means that x is less or equally general than c.
- a special symbol, $\mathbf{T}$ which means truth.
- a special symbol, $\mathbf{F}$ which means falsity.

A formula is the combination of an atomic formula and $\wedge$ and $\vee$ in the usual sense. We denote a set of all formulas as $\mathcal{L}$.

Let us regard an atomic formula as a proposition. Then, $\mathcal{L}$ can be regarded as negation-free propositional language. Then, we can define a disjunctive normal form (DNF) of a formula in $\mathcal{L}$ as a DNF form of the translated propositional language. Similarly, we also define a conjunctive normal form (CNF) of a formula in $\mathcal{L}$ as well.

We can also simplify a formula along with the following inference rules (together with usual propositional inference rules):

$$\frac{((x \preceq c_1) \wedge \Phi) \vee ... \vee ((x \preceq c_m) \wedge \Phi) \text{ and } child(C) = \{c_1, ..., c_m\}}{(x \prec c) \wedge \Phi}$$

$$\frac{((x \preceq top(T)) \wedge \Phi)}{\Phi}$$

$$\frac{(x \prec c) \wedge \Phi \text{ and } child(C) = \{c_1, ..., c_m\}}{((x \preceq c_1) \wedge \Phi) \vee ... \vee ((x \preceq c_m) \wedge \Phi)}$$

$$\frac{x \preceq c_1 \vee x \preceq c_2 \text{ and } lcgc(c_1, c_2) = c_1}{x \preceq c_1}$$

$$\frac{x \preceq c_1 \wedge x \preceq c_2 \text{ and } gcgc(c_1, c_2) \text{ is } c_1}{x \preceq c_1}$$

$$\frac{x \preceq c_1 \wedge x \preceq c_2 \text{ and } gcgc(c_1, c_2) \text{ is undefined}}{F}$$

For example, in the above "eat" relation, we would have the following cumbersome DNF representation:

$((x \preceq LEO) \wedge (y \preceq CHICKEN)) \vee ((x \preceq LEO) \wedge (y \preceq BEEF))$
$\vee ((x \preceq LEO) \wedge (y \preceq PORK))$
$\vee ((x \preceq TIGRIS) \wedge (y \preceq CHICKEN)) \vee ((x \preceq TIGRIS) \wedge (y \preceq BEEF))$
$\vee ((x \preceq TIGRIS) \wedge (y \preceq PORK))$
$\vee ((x \preceq AILUROPODA) \wedge (y \preceq BAMBOO))$
$\vee ((x \preceq ARCTOS) \wedge (y \preceq CHICKEN))$
$\vee ((x \preceq ARCTOS) \wedge (y \preceq BEEF))$
$\vee ((x \preceq ARCTOS) \wedge (y \preceq PORK))$
$\vee ((x \preceq ARCTOS) \wedge (y \preceq NUT)).$

or the following compact DNF representation:

$((x \preceq PANTHERA) \wedge (y \preceq MEAT))$
$\vee ((x \preceq AILUROPODA) \wedge (y \preceq BAMBOO))$
$\vee ((x \preceq ARCTOS) \wedge (y \preceq MEAT)) \vee ((x \preceq ARCTOS) \wedge (y \preceq NUT)).$

Let F be a formula in $\mathcal{L}$. We define $|DNF(F)|$ as the smallest number of disjuncts in logically equivalent DNF forms to F induced by the above inference rules and we define $|CNF(F)|$ as the smallest number of conjuncts in logically equivalent CNF forms to F as well.

Let O be a case and F be a formula of $\mathcal{L}$. We say that O *satisfies* F denoted as $O \models F$ if one of the following conditions hold.

1. If F is an atomic formula $x_i \preceq c$, then $class(O[i]) \preceq c$.
2. If F is of the form $G \wedge H$, then $O \models G$ and $O \models H$.
3. If F is of the form $G \vee H$, then $O \models G$ or $O \models H$.

We define $\phi(F) = \{O \in \mathcal{O}^n | O \models F\}$.

Definition 2. Let $\mathcal{R} \subseteq \mathcal{O}^n$. We call $\mathcal{R}$ *an n-ary relation over objects* if it satisfies the condition that a case O is in $\mathcal{R}$ if and only if every case $O' \in \mathcal{O}^n$ such that $class(O') = class(O)$ is in $\mathcal{R}$.

The above condition for $\mathcal{R}$ expresses that cases has the same properties if every class for each component of these cases belongs to the same leaf class.

Definition 3. We say that a set of cases S *consists of representatives* if for every $O \in S$, there is no $O' \in S$ such that $O \neq O'$ and $class(O) = class(O')$.

A subset of S, S', is a *representation set* of S if S satisfies the following conditions:

- S *consists of representatives.*
- S *is maximal in terms of set-inclusion among subsets of S consisting of representatives.*

We say that a formula $F \in \mathcal{L}$ represents $\mathcal{R}$ or F is a representation of $\mathcal{R}$ if $\phi(F) = \mathcal{R}$. Note that any relation over cases can be represented as a disjunctive normal form as follows.

Definition 4. Let $\mathcal{R}$ be an n-ary relation and S be a representation set for $\mathcal{R}$. We denote the formula $\bigvee_{O \in S}((x_1 \preceq class(O[1]))) \wedge \dots \wedge (x_n \preceq class(O[n])))$ as $DISJ(\mathcal{R})$.

We define $|DNF(\mathcal{R})|$ as $|DNF(DISJ(\mathcal{R}))|$ and $|CNF(\mathcal{R})|$ as $|CNF(DISJ(\mathcal{R}))|$.

It is obvious that for any relation $\mathcal{R}$, $DISJ(\mathcal{R})$ represents $\mathcal{R}$. Conversely, for any formula $F \in \mathcal{L}$, $\phi(F)$ expresses a relation.

3   Case-based Taxonomic Reasoning

Definition 5. Let CB be a set of cases which are divided into CB^+ and CB^-. We call CB a *casebase*, CB^+ a set of *positive cases* and CB^- a set of *negative cases* respectively.

We say *a case O is positive w.r.t. CB* if there is a case $O_{ok} \in CB^+$ such that for every negative case $O_{ng} \in CB^-$, $lcgc(O, O_{ng}) \npreceq lcgc(O, O_{ok})$.

Note that $lcgc(O, O_{ng}) \npreceq lcgc(O, O_{ok})$ does not imply $lcgc(O, O_{ok}) \prec lcgc(O, O_{ng})$ since $\preceq$ is a partial order relation.

In the above definition, "O is positive" means that there is a positive case such that O is not more or equally similar to any negative case than to the positive case.

Definition 6. Let CB be a casebase $\langle CB^+, CB^- \rangle$. We say that *$n$-ary relation $\mathcal{R}_{CB}$ is represented by a casebase CB* if $\mathcal{R}_{CB} = \{O \in \mathcal{O}^n | O \text{ is positive w.r.t. } CB\}$.

Conversely, any relation $\mathcal{R}$ can be represented by a casebase $\langle CB^+, CB^- \rangle$ where CB^+ is a representation set of $\mathcal{R}$ and CB^- is a representation set of $\mathcal{O}^n - \mathcal{R}$. Therefore, we can perform "taxonomic reasoning" by case-based reasoning.

From Proposition 1, the following holds.

Proposition 7. *Let CB be a casebase $\langle CB^+, CB^- \rangle$. A case O is positive if and only if there is a case $O_{ok} \in CB^+$ such that for every case $O_{ng} \in CB^-$, $lcgc(O_{ok}, O_{ng}) \npreceq lcgc(O_{ok}, O)$.*

Definition 8. Let S be a set of cases and O be a case. We say that *S is reduced w.r.t. O* if for every $O' \in S$, there is no $O'' \in S$ such that $O' \neq O''$ and $lcgc(O, O') = lcgc(O, O'')$.

Let S be a set of cases and S' be a subset of S and O be a case. S' is a *reduced subset of S w.r.t. O* if S' satisfies the following conditions:

- S' is reduced w.r.t. O.
- S' is maximal in terms of set-inclusion among subsets of S having reduced-ness w.r.t. O.

We say that *a subset of S, $NN(O,S)$, is a nearest reduced subset of S w.r.t. O* if it is a reduced subset of the following set w.r.t. O:

$$\{O' \in S| \text{ There is no } O'' \in S \text{ s.t. } lcgc(O,O'') \prec lcgc(O,O')\}$$

For a positive case O_{ok}, we only need the most similar negative cases to O_{ok} in order to represent a set of cases which O_{ok} makes to be positive. Furthermore, it is sufficient to have only one equally similar negative case among the most similar negative cases to represent a set of cases which O_{ok} makes to be positive.

Therefore, we only need any arbitrary nearest reduced subset of CB^- w.r.t. each positive case to represent the same relation as the following proposition shows.

Proposition 9. *Let CB be a casebase $\langle CB^+, CB^- \rangle$. Let $CB' = \langle CB^+, \bigcup_{O_{ok} \in CB^+} NN(O_{ok}, CB^-) \rangle$ where $NN(O_{ok}, CB^-)$ is any arbitrary nearest reduced subset of CB^- w.r.t. $O_{ok} \in CB^+$. Then, $\mathcal{R}_{CB} = \mathcal{R}_{CB'}$.*

4   Case-based Representability

In this section, we discuss an upper bound of minimal casebase size to represent a relation.

Lemma 10. *Let $\mathcal{R}$ be an n-ary relation over objects and CB^+ be a subset of $\mathcal{R}$ and $D_1 \vee ... \vee D_k$ be a DNF representation of $\mathcal{R}$. Suppose that for every D_i, there exists $O_{ok} \in CB^+$ such that $O_{ok} \in \phi(D_i)$. Then, $\mathcal{R} = \mathcal{R}_{CB}$ where $CB = \langle CB^+, \overline{\mathcal{R}} \rangle$.*

For the next lemma, we need the definition of $O\downarrow_{O'}^l$ and $PNN(O,\overline{\mathcal{R}})$ defined as follows:

Definition 11. *Let O and O' be cases. We define a set of cases $O\downarrow_{O'}^l$ for $l(1 \leq l \leq n)$ such that $class(O[l]) \neq class(O'[l])$ as follows. $O'' \in O\downarrow_{O'}^l$ if O'' satisfies the following condition:*

- $parent(lcgc(O'[l], O''[l])) = lcgc(O'[l], O[l])$
- $lcgc(O'[j], O''[j]) = lcgc(O'[j], O[j])$ *for* $j \neq l(1 \leq j \leq n)$.

$O\downarrow_{O'}^l$ is a set of the nearest cases to O' among cases whose $lcgc$ with O' differs from $lcgc(O', O)$ in the l-th concept. Note that the number of elements of a representation set of $O\downarrow_{O'}^l$ for l-th object is at most $width(T)$.

In the "eat" relation, if $O = \langle o_A, o_N \rangle$ where $class(o_A) = AILUROPODA$ and $class(o_N) = NUT$, and $O' = \langle o_L, o_C \rangle$ where $class(o_L) = LEO$ and $class(o_C) = CHICKEN$, then $O\downarrow_{O'}^1 = \{\langle o_T, o_{N\vee B} \rangle| \ class(o_T) = TIGRIS$ and $(class(o_{N\vee B}) = NUT$ or $class(o_{N\vee B}) = BAMBOO) \}$, and $O\downarrow_{O'}^2 = \{\langle o_{A\vee A}, o_{B\vee P} \rangle| \ (class(o_{A\vee A}) = AILUROPODA$ or $class(o_{A\vee A}) = ARCTOS)$ and $(class(o_{B\vee P}) = BEEF$ or $class(o_{B\vee P}) = PORK) \}$.

Definition 12. Let $\mathcal{R}$ be an n-ary relation over objects.

We say that *a subset of* $\overline{\mathcal{R}}$, $PNN(O', \overline{\mathcal{R}})$, *is a pseudo nearest reduced negative subset w.r.t.* O iff it is a reduced set of the following set w.r.t. O:

$$\{O \in \overline{\mathcal{R}}| \text{ For every } l(1 \leq l \leq n) \text{ s.t. } class(O[l]) \neq class(O'[l]),$$
$$\text{for every case } O'' \in O\downarrow_{O'}^{l}, O'' \in \mathcal{R}\}$$

Note that for every pseudo nearest reduced negative subset w.r.t. a case O', $PNN(O', \overline{\mathcal{R}})$, there is a nearest reduced set of $\overline{\mathcal{R}}$ w.r.t. O', $NN(O', \overline{\mathcal{R}})$ s.t. $NN(O', \overline{\mathcal{R}}) \subseteq PNN(O', \overline{\mathcal{R}})$, and conversely, for every nearest reduced set of $\overline{\mathcal{R}}$ w.r.t. O', $NN(O', \overline{\mathcal{R}})$, there is a pseudo nearest reduced negative subset w.r.t. a case O', $PNN(O', \overline{\mathcal{R}})$ s.t. $NN(O', \overline{\mathcal{R}}) \subseteq PNN(O', \overline{\mathcal{R}})$.

Lemma 13. *Let* $\mathcal{R}$ *be an n-ary relation over objects. Suppose that* $D_1 \wedge ... \wedge D_k$ *be a CNF representation of* $\mathcal{R}$ *and* O *be a case. Then, for every pseudo nearest reduced negative subset w.r.t. a case* O, $PNN(O, \overline{\mathcal{R}})$, $|PNN(O, \overline{\mathcal{R}})| \leq k$.

Corollary 14. *Let* $\mathcal{R}$ *be an n-ary relation over objects and* $D_1 \wedge ... \wedge D_k$ *be a CNF representation of* $\mathcal{R}$ *and* O *be a case and* $NN(O, \overline{\mathcal{R}})$ *be a nearest reduced subset of* $\overline{\mathcal{R}}$ *w.r.t.* O. *Then,* $|NN(O, \overline{\mathcal{R}})| \leq k$. *Especially,* $|NN(O, \overline{\mathcal{R}})| \leq |CNF(\mathcal{R})|$.

By Lemma 10, Proposition 9 and Corollary 14, we have the following theorem which gives an upper bound of representability of n-ary relations.

Theorem 15. *Let* $\mathcal{R}$ *be an n-ary relation over objects. Then, there exists a casebase* $\mathcal{CB} = \langle \mathcal{CB}^+, \mathcal{CB}^- \rangle$ *such that* $\mathcal{R}_{\mathcal{CB}} = \mathcal{R}$ $|\mathcal{CB}^+| \leq |DNF(\mathcal{R})|$, $|\mathcal{CB}^-| \leq |DNF(\mathcal{R})| \cdot |CNF(\mathcal{R})|$ *and* $|\mathcal{CB}| \leq |DNF(\mathcal{R})|(1 + |CNF(\mathcal{R})|)$.

5   Learning Critical Casebase

We firstly give a definition of a *critical casebase*.

Definition 16. Let $\mathcal{R}$ be an n-ary relation over $\mathcal{O}^n$ and $\mathcal{CB}$ be a casebase $\langle \mathcal{CB}^+, \mathcal{CB}^- \rangle$. $\mathcal{CB}$ is *critical* w.r.t. $\mathcal{R}$ if $\mathcal{CB}$ satisfies the following conditions:

- $\mathcal{R} = \mathcal{R}_{\mathcal{CB}}$
- *There is no casebase* $\mathcal{CB}' = \langle \mathcal{CB}'^+, \mathcal{CB}'^- \rangle$ *such that* $\mathcal{R} = \mathcal{R}_{\mathcal{CB}'}$ *and* $\mathcal{CB}'^+ \subseteq \mathcal{CB}^+$ *and* $\mathcal{CB}'^- \subseteq \mathcal{CB}^-$ *and* $\mathcal{CB}' \neq \mathcal{CB}$.

The above definition means that if we remove some of cases from $\mathcal{CB}$, the new casebase no longer represents $\mathcal{R}$.

The following results(Theorem 18 and Lemma 20) are related with a minimal set of negative cases and positive cases.

Definition 17. Let $\mathcal{R}$ be an n-ary relation and $\mathcal{CB}$ be a casebase $\langle \mathcal{CB}^+, \mathcal{CB}^- \rangle$ such that $\mathcal{R}_{\mathcal{CB}} = \mathcal{R}$. $\mathcal{CB}^-$ *is a set of minimal negative cases w.r.t.* $\mathcal{CB}^+$ *and* $\mathcal{R}$ if there is no casebase $\mathcal{CB}' = \langle \mathcal{CB}^+, \mathcal{CB}'^- \rangle$ such that $\mathcal{CB}'^- \subset \mathcal{CB}^-$ and $\mathcal{R}_{\mathcal{CB}'} = \mathcal{R}$.

The following theorem concerns about necessary and sufficient condition of a set of minimal negative cases given $\mathcal{CB}^+$ and $\mathcal{R}$.

Theorem 18. *Let $\mathcal{R}$ be an n-ary relation and $\mathcal{CB}$ be a casebase $\langle \mathcal{CB}^+, \mathcal{CB}^- \rangle$ such that $\mathcal{R}_{\mathcal{CB}} = \mathcal{R}$. $\mathcal{CB}^-$ is a set of minimal negative cases w.r.t. $\mathcal{CB}^+$ and $\mathcal{R}$ if and only if $\mathcal{CB}^- = \bigcup_{O_{ok} \in \mathcal{CB}^+} NN(O_{ok}, \overline{\mathcal{R}})$ where $NN(O_{ok}, \mathcal{CB}^-)$ is any arbitrary nearest reduced subset of $\mathcal{CB}^-$ w.r.t. $O_{ok} \in \mathcal{CB}^+$.*

The above theorem intuitively means that if $\mathcal{CB}^+$ and a set of negative case $\mathcal{CB}'^-$ represents a relation $\mathcal{R}$, we can reduce $\mathcal{CB}^-$ down to $\bigcup_{O_{ok} \in \mathcal{CB}^+} NN(O_{ok}, \overline{\mathcal{CB}^-})$.

Definition 19. *Let $\mathcal{R}$ be an n-ary relation and $\mathcal{CB}$ be a casebase $\langle \mathcal{CB}^+, \mathcal{CB}^- \rangle$ such that $\mathcal{R}_{\mathcal{CB}} = \mathcal{R}$. $\mathcal{CB}^+$ is a set of minimal positive cases w.r.t. $\mathcal{R}$ if there is no casebase $\mathcal{CB}' = \langle \mathcal{CB}'^+, \mathcal{CB}'^- \rangle$ such that $\mathcal{CB}'^+ \subset \mathcal{CB}^+$ and $\mathcal{CB}'^-$ is any arbitrary set of negative cases and $\mathcal{R}_{\mathcal{CB}'} = \mathcal{R}$.*

The following lemma shows a sufficient condition on a set of minimal positive cases.

Lemma 20. *Let $\mathcal{R}$ be an n-ary relation and $\mathcal{CB}$ be a casebase $\langle \mathcal{CB}^+, \mathcal{CB}^- \rangle$ such that $\mathcal{R}_{\mathcal{CB}} = \mathcal{R}$. Suppose for every $O_{ok} \in \mathcal{CB}^+$, $O_{ok} \notin \mathcal{R}_{\langle \mathcal{CB}^+ - \{O_{ok}\}, \overline{\mathcal{R}} \rangle}$. Then, $\mathcal{CB}^+$ is a set of minimal positive cases w.r.t. $\mathcal{R}$.*

Now, we propose an approximation method of discovering a critical casebase. In order to do that, we assume that there is a probability distribution $\mathcal{P}$ over $\mathcal{O}^n$. We would like to have a casebase such that the probability that the casebase produces more errors than we expect is very low.

The algorithm in Fig. 2 performs such an approximation. The algorithm is a modification of [Satoh00]. Intuitively, in the algorithm we try to find counter examples by sampling and if enough sampling is made with no counter examples, we are done. If we find a positive counter example then we add it to $\mathcal{CB}^+$ and if we find a negative counter example then we try to find a "nearest" negative case to a positive case from the found negative counter example.

In the algorithm, $O \in \mathcal{R}$? expresses a label whether $O \in \mathcal{R}$ or not. If $O \in \mathcal{R}$ then the label is "yes" and otherwise "no".

The following lemma gives an upper bound for a number of positive counter cases.

Lemma 21. *Let $\mathcal{R}$ be an n-ary relation and $D_1 \vee \ldots \vee D_{|DNF(\mathcal{R})|}$ be a DNF representation with a minimal size $|DNF(\mathcal{R})|$ of $\mathcal{R}$. Suppose that the situation that $O \in \mathcal{R}$ and $O \notin \mathcal{R}_{\mathcal{CB}}$ occurs during the execution of **FindCCB**(δ, ϵ). Then, for every $1 \leq k \leq |DNF(\mathcal{R})|$, if there exists $O_{ok} \in \mathcal{CB}^+$ such that $O_{ok} \in \phi(D_k)$ then $O \notin \phi(D_k)$. This situation happens at most $|DNF(\mathcal{R})|$ times.*

The following lemma gives an upper bound for a number of negative counter cases.

Lemma 22. *Let $\mathcal{R}$ be an n-ary relation over objects. Suppose that the situation that $O \notin \mathcal{R}$ and $O \in \mathcal{R}_{\langle \{O_{ok}\}, \mathcal{CB}^- \rangle}$ occurs for some $O_{ok} \in \mathcal{CB}^+$ during the execution of **FindCCB**(δ, ϵ). Then, there exists some $O' \in PNN(O_{ok}, \overline{\mathcal{R}})$ such that $lcgc(O', O_{ok}) \preceq lcgc(O, O_{ok})$ and $O' \notin \mathcal{CB}^-$. This situation happens at most $|CNF(\mathcal{R})|$ times for each $O_{ok} \in \mathcal{CB}^+$.*

FindCCB(δ, ϵ)
begin
  $\mathcal{CB}^+ := \emptyset$ and $\mathcal{CB}^- := \emptyset$ and $m := 0$

1. O is taken from $\mathcal{O}^n$ according to the probability distribution $\mathcal{P}$ and get $\langle O, O \in \mathcal{R}? \rangle$ as an oracle.
2. If $O \in \mathcal{R}$ and $O \notin \mathcal{R}_{\langle \mathcal{CB}+, \mathcal{CB}- \rangle}$, then
   (a) $\mathcal{CB}^+ := \mathcal{CB}^+ \cup \{O\}$
   (b) $m := 0$ and Goto 1.
3. If $O \notin \mathcal{R}$ and $O \in \mathcal{R}_{\langle \mathcal{CB}+, \mathcal{CB}- \rangle}$, then
   for every O_{ok} s.t. $O \in \mathcal{R}_{\langle \{O_{ok}\}, \mathcal{CB}- \rangle}$,
   (a) $O_{pmin} := \mathbf{pminNG}(O, O_{ok})$
   (b) $\mathcal{CB}^- := \mathcal{CB}^- \cup \{O_{pmin}\}$
   (c) $m := 0$ and Goto 1
4. $m := m + 1$
5. If $m >= \frac{1}{\epsilon} \ln \frac{1}{\delta}$ then
      output $\mathcal{CB}^+$ and $\bigcup_{O_{ok} \in \mathcal{CB}+} NN(O_{ok}, \mathcal{CB}^-)$
      where $NN(O_{ok}, \mathcal{CB}^-)$ is any set among the nearest reduced subsets of $\mathcal{CB}^-$ w.r.t. $O_{ok} \in \mathcal{CB}^+$.
   else Goto 1.

end

---

pminNG(O, O_{ok})
begin

1. For every $1 \leq l \leq n$ s.t. $O[l] \neq O_{ok}[l]$, we take any arbitrary representation set of $O \downarrow^l_{O_{ok}}$ and denote the representation set as S.
2. For every $O' \in S$,
   (a) Make a membership query for O'.
   (b) If $O' \notin \mathcal{R}$ then $O := O'$ and Goto 1.
3. output O'. /* $O' \in PNN(O_{ok}, \overline{\mathcal{R}})$ */

end

Fig. 2. Approximating a critical casebase

By the above two lemmas, an upper bound for a number of negative counter cases is $|DNF(\mathcal{R})| \cdot |CNF(\mathcal{R})|$.

Let $\mathcal{R}_1 \Delta \mathcal{R}_2$ be a difference set between $\mathcal{R}_1$ and $\mathcal{R}_2$ (that is, $(\overline{\mathcal{R}_1} \cap \mathcal{R}_2) \cup (\mathcal{R}_1 \cap \overline{\mathcal{R}_2})$).

The following theorem shows that we can efficiently find an approximation of a critical casebase with high probability if $|DNF(\mathcal{R})|, |CNF(\mathcal{R})|, width(T)$ and $height(T)$ is small.

Theorem 23. *Let $\mathcal{R}$ be an n-ary relation over objects and T be a concept tree. The above algorithm stops after taking at most $(\frac{1}{\epsilon} \ln \frac{1}{\delta}) \cdot |DNF(\mathcal{R})| \cdot (1 +$*

$|CNF(\mathcal{R})|$) *cases according to* $\mathcal{P}$ *and asking at most* $n^2 \cdot width(T) \cdot height(T) \cdot$ $|DNF(\mathcal{R})| \cdot |CNF(\mathcal{R})|$ *membership queries and produces* CB *with the probability at most* δ *such that* $\mathcal{P}(\mathcal{R} \Delta \mathcal{R}_{CB}) \geq \epsilon$.

The next theorem shows that output from **FindCCB**(δ, ϵ) is an approximation of a critical casebase.

Theorem 24. *Let* CB *be an output from* **FindCCB**(δ, ϵ). *If* $\mathcal{R}_{CB} = \mathcal{R}$, CB *is a critical casebase w.r.t.* $\mathcal{R}$.

6   Conclusion

The contributions of this paper are as follows.

1. We show that for every relation $\mathcal{R}$ with a concept tree T, in order to represent $\mathcal{R}$, an upper bound of necessary positive cases is $|DNF(\mathcal{R})|$ and the upper bound of necessary negative cases is $|DNF(\mathcal{R})| \cdot |CNF(\mathcal{R})|$.
2. We give an learning method of a critical casebase and we analyze computational complexity of the method in the PAC learning framework and show that the sample size of cases is at most $(\frac{1}{\epsilon} \ln \frac{1}{\delta}) \cdot |DNF(\mathcal{R})| \cdot (1 + |CNF(\mathcal{R})|)$ and necessary number of membership queries is at most $n^2 \cdot width(T) \cdot height(T) \cdot |DNF(\mathcal{R})| \cdot |CNF(\mathcal{R})|$.

We would like to pursue the following future work.

1. We would like to extend our method to handle multiple-inheritance.
2. We would like to extend our language to include negations and extend our method to learn a formula in an extended language.
3. We would like to generalize our results for more abstract form of case-based reasoning.

Acknowledgements I thank Prof. Akihiro Yamamoto from Hokkaido University on discussion of proofs and useful comments and anonymous referees for instructive comments of the paper. This research is partly supported by Grant-in-Aid for Scientific Research on Priority Areas, "Research Project on Discovery Science", The Ministry of Education, Japan.

References

[Ashley90] Ashley, K. D.: *Modeling Legal Argument: Reasoning with Cases and Hypotheticals* MIT press (1990) 181
[Ashley94] Ashley, K. D., and Aleven, V.: A Logical Representation for Relevance Criteria. S. Wess, K-D. Althoff and M. Richter (eds.) *Topics in Case-Based Reasoning, LNAI 837* (1994) 338–352 181
[Bareiss88] Bareis, R.: PROTOS; a Unified Approach to Concept Representation, Classification and Learning. Ph.D. Dissertation, University of Texas at Austin, Dep. of Computer Sciences (1988) 180

[Bshouty93] Bshouty, N. H.: Exact Learning Boolean Functions via the Monotone Theory. *Information and Computation* **123** (1995) 146–153   180

[Edelson92] When Should a Cheetah Remind you of a Bat? Reminding in Case-Based Teaching. *Proc. of AAAI-92* (1992) 667 – 672   180

[Matuschek97] Matuschek, D., and Jantke, K. P.: Axiomatic Characterizations of Structural Similarity for Case-Based Reasoning. *Proc. of Florida AI Research Symposium (FLAIRS-97)* (1997) 432–436   181

[Khardon96] Khardon, R., and Roth, D.: Reasoning with Models. *Artificial Intelligence* **87** (1996) 187–213   180

[Osborne96] Osborne, H. R., and Bridge, D. G.: A Case Base Similarity Framework. *Advances in Case-Based Reasoning, LNAI 1168* (1996) 309 – 323   181

[Satoh98] Satoh, K.: Analysis of Case-Based Representability of Boolean Functions by Monotone Theory. *Proceedings of ALT'98* (1998) 179–190   180

[Satoh00] Satoh, K., and Ryuich Nakagawa: Discovering Critical Cases in Case-Based Reasoning (Extended Abstract). *Online Proceedings of 6th Symposium on AI and Math*, http://rutcor.rutgers.edu/ amai/AcceptedCont.htm (2000)   180, 187

Appendix: Proof of Theorems

Proof of Proposition 1 Let $O[i], O_1[i], O_2[i]$ be i-th component of O, O_1, O_2. Suppose that $lcgc(O_1[i], O[i]) \preceq lcgc(O_2[i], O[i])$. Since $O_1[i] \preceq lcgc(O_1[i], O[i])$, $O_1[i] \preceq lcgc(O_2[i], O[i])$ by transitivity. Since $O_2[i] \preceq lcgc(O_2[i], O[i])$, $lcgc(O_1[i], O_2[i]) \preceq lcgc(O_2[i], O[i]) = lcgc(O[i], O_2[i])$. The converse holds in a similar way.

"$lcgc(O_1[i], O[i]]) \preceq lcgc(O_2[i], O[i]])$" iff $lcgc(O_1[i], O_2[i]) \preceq lcgc(O, O_2[i])$" holds for every $i(1 \le i \le n)$ and the proposition holds.

Proof of Proposition 7 By the original definition that O is positive and by Proposition 1.

Proof of Proposition 9 We need to prove the following lemma.

Lemma 25. *Let CB be a casebase $\langle CB^+, CB^- \rangle$. Let $O'_{ng} \in CB^-$ and $CB' = \langle CB^+, CB'^- \rangle$ where $CB'^- = CB^- - \{O'_{ng}\}$. If for all $O_{ok} \in CB^+$, there exists $O_{ng} \in CB'^-$ s.t. $lcgc(O_{ng}, O_{ok}) \preceq lcgc(O'_{ng}, O_{ok})$. Then $\mathcal{R}_{CB} = \mathcal{R}_{CB'}$.*

Proof: Clearly, $\mathcal{R}_{CB} \subseteq \mathcal{R}_{CB'}$. Suppose that $\mathcal{R}_{CB} \ne \mathcal{R}_{CB'}$. Then, there exists some O such that $O \notin \mathcal{R}_{CB}$ and $O \in \mathcal{R}_{CB'}$. This means:

- $\forall O'_{ok} \in CB^+ \exists O_{ng} \in CB^-$ s.t. $lcgc(O_{ng}, O) \preceq lcgc(O'_{ok}, O)$.
- $\exists O_{ok} \in CB^+ \forall O_{ng} \in CB'^-$ s.t. $lcgc(O_{ng}, O) \not\preceq lcgc(O_{ok}, O)$. Let O'_{ok} be such O_{ok}.

Then, $lcgc(O'_{ng}, O) \preceq lcgc(O'_{ok}, O)$.

By Proposition 1, this means $lcgc(O'_{ng}, O'_{ok}) \preceq lcgc(O, O'_{ok})$. However, since there exists $O_{ng} \in CB'^-$, $lcgc(O_{ng}, O'_{ok}) \preceq lcgc(O'_{ng}, O'_{ok})$ by the condition of O'_{ng}, there exists $O_{ng} \in CB'^-$, $lcgc(O_{ng}, O'_{ok}) \preceq lcgc(O, O'_{ok})$. This implies

$lcgc(O_{ng}, O) \preceq lcgc(O'_{ok}, O)$ again by Proposition 1 and leads to contradiction with $O \in \mathcal{R}_{\mathcal{CB}'}$.

Proof of Proposition 9 (continued)

Suppose $O_{ng} \notin \bigcup_{O_{ok} \in \mathcal{CB}^+} NN(O_{ok}, \mathcal{CB}^-)$. Then, for every $O_{ok} \in \mathcal{CB}^+$, $O_{ng} \notin NN(O_{ok}, \mathcal{CB}^-)$. This means that there exists $O'' \in \mathcal{CB}^-$ s.t. $lcgc(O_{ok}, O'') \preceq lcgc(O_{ok}, O_{ng})$. Therefore, by Lemma 25, $\mathcal{R}_{\mathcal{CB}} = \mathcal{R}_{\mathcal{CB}''}$ where $\mathcal{CB}'' = \langle \mathcal{CB}^+, (\mathcal{CB}^- - \{O_{ng}\}) \rangle$. Even after removing O_{ng} from $\mathcal{CB}^-$, $\bigcup_{O_{ok} \in \mathcal{CB}^+} NN(O_{ok}, (\mathcal{CB}^- - \{O_{ng}\})) = \bigcup_{O_{ok} \in \mathcal{CB}^+} NN(O_{ok}, \mathcal{CB}^-)$, since otherwise, O_{ng} was in $\bigcup_{O_{ok} \in \mathcal{CB}^+} NN(O_{ok}, \mathcal{CB}^-)$. Therefore, we can remove all O_{ng} such that $O_{ng} \notin \bigcup_{O_{ok} \in \mathcal{CB}^+} NN(O_{ok}, \mathcal{CB}^-)$ from $\mathcal{CB}^-$ without changing $\mathcal{R}_{\mathcal{CB}}$ and thus, $\mathcal{R}_{\mathcal{CB}} = \mathcal{R}_{\mathcal{CB}'}$.

Proof of Lemma 10 Since $\overline{\mathcal{R}} \subseteq \overline{\mathcal{R}_{\mathcal{CB}}}$ always holds, $\mathcal{R}_{\mathcal{CB}} \subseteq \mathcal{R}$. Therefore, to prove the Lemma, it is sufficient to show that for every $O \in \mathcal{R}$, there is some positive case $O_{ok} \in \mathcal{CB}^+$ such that for every $O_{ng} \in \overline{\mathcal{R}}$, $lcgc(O_{ng}, O_{ok}) \not\preceq lcgc(O, O_{ok})$.

Suppose $O \in \mathcal{R}$. Then, there exists a disjunct D of the DNF representation of $\mathcal{R}$ such that $O \in \phi(D)$. This means that for every $i(1 \leq i \leq n)$, if $x_i \preceq c$ appears in D, $class(O[i]) \preceq c$. Let $O_{ok} \in \mathcal{CB}^+$ be a case satisfying $O_{ok} \in \phi(D)$. This also means that every $i(1 \leq i \leq n)$, if $x_i \preceq c$ appears in D, $class(O_{ok}[i]) \preceq c$. Therefore, if $x_i \preceq c$ appears in D, $lcgc(class(O[i]), class(O_{ok}[i])) \preceq c$.

Suppose that there exists $O_{ng} \in \overline{\mathcal{R}}$ such that $lcgc(O_{ng}, O_{ok}) \preceq lcgc(O, O_{ok})$. This means that for every $i(1 \leq i \leq n)$,

$$lcgc(class(O_{ng}[i]), class(O_{ok}[i])) \preceq lcgc(class(O[i]), class(O_{ok}[i])).$$

Therefore, every $i(1 \leq i \leq n)$, if $x_i \preceq c$ appears in D, $lcgc(class(O_{ng}[i]), class(O_{ok}[i])) \preceq c$ and this implies $class(O_{ng}[i]) \preceq c$. Thus, $O_{ng} \in \mathcal{R}$ and this leads to contradiction. Therefore, for every $O \in \mathcal{R}$, there is some positive case $O_{ok} \in \mathcal{CB}^+$ such that for every $O_{ng} \in \overline{\mathcal{R}}$, $lcgc(O_{ng}, O_{ok}) \not\preceq lcgc(O, O_{ok})$. This means $\mathcal{R} \subseteq \mathcal{R}_{\mathcal{CB}}$.

Proof of Lemma 13 Let D be any clause in the above CNF representation. We define a case $O_{min}(D) \in \overline{\mathcal{R}}$ w.r.t. a clause D in the above CNF representation of $\mathcal{R}$ as follows. For every $j(1 \leq j \leq n)$,

- $lcgc(class(O_{min}(D)[j]), c) = parent(c)$ if $x_j \preceq c$ appears in D.
- $class(O_{min}(D)[j]) = class(O[j])$ if $x_j \preceq c$ does not appear in D.

Suppose that $O' \in \overline{\mathcal{R}}$, but O' is not equal to any of the above $O_{min}(D)$. Since $O' \in \overline{\mathcal{R}}$, there is some clause D in the above CNF representation such that $O' \notin \phi(D)$. Then, for every $j(1 \leq j \leq n)$, $class(O'[j]) \not\preceq c$ if $x_j \preceq c$ appears in D. In other words, for every $j(1 \leq j \leq n)$, $c \prec lcgc(class(O'[j]), c)$ if $x_j \preceq c$ appears in D.

Since O' is not equal to any of the above $O_{min}(D)$, at least either of the following is satisfied:

- there exists $j(1 \leq j \leq n)$ s.t. $parent(c) \prec lcgc(class(O'[j]), c)$ if $x_j \preceq c$ appears in D.

– there exists $j(1 \leq j \leq n)$ s.t. $class(O'[j]) \neq class(O[j])$ if $x_j \preceq c$ does not appear in D.

This means that $lgc(O_{min}(D),O) \prec lgc(O',O)$. Then, for any O'' s.t. $lgc(O_{min}(D),O) \preceq lgc(O'',O) \prec lgc(O',O)$, $O'' \notin \phi(D)$. Therefore, O' is not included in any of pseudo nearest negative subsets of w.r.t. O.

Let $PNN(O,\overline{\mathcal{R}})$ be a pseudo nearest negative subset w.r.t. O. Then, the above means that there exists a reduced subset S of $\{O_{min}(D)|D$ is a clause in the above CNF representation of $\mathcal{R}\}$ w.r.t. O such that $PNN(O,\overline{\mathcal{R}}) \subseteq S$. Since $|S| \leq k$, $|PNN(O,\overline{\mathcal{R}})| \leq k$.

Proof of Corollary 14   For every nearest reduced set of $\overline{\mathcal{R}}$ w.r.t. O', $NN(O_{ok},\overline{\mathcal{R}})$, there is a pseudo nearest reduced negative subset w.r.t. a case O', $PNN(O_{ok},\overline{\mathcal{R}})$ s.t. $NN(O_{ok},\overline{\mathcal{R}}) \subseteq PNN(O_{ok},\overline{\mathcal{R}})$. Therefore, by Lemma 13, $|NN(O_{ok},\overline{\mathcal{R}})| \leq |PNN(O_{ok},\overline{\mathcal{R}})| \leq k$.

Proof of Theorem 18   We need the following Lemma.

Lemma 26. Let $\mathcal{R}$ be an n-ary relation and CB be a casebase $\langle CB^+, CB^- \rangle$ such that $\mathcal{R}_{CB} = \mathcal{R}$. Then, $\bigcup_{O_{ok} \in CB^+} NN(O_{ok},\overline{\mathcal{R}}) \subseteq CB^-$.

Proof Suppose that $O_{ng} \in \bigcup_{O_{ok} \in CB^+} NN(O_{ok},\overline{\mathcal{R}})$, but $O_{ng} \notin CB^-$. Then, there is $O_{ok} \in CB^+$ such that $O_{ng} \in NN(O_{ok},\overline{\mathcal{R}})$. Since $O_{ng} \notin CB^-$ but $O_{ng} \in \overline{\mathcal{R}}$, there exists $O \in CB^-$ (therefore $O \in \overline{\mathcal{R}}$) such that $lgc(O,O_{ok}) \prec lgc(O_{ng},O_{ok})$. This contradicts that $O_{ng} \in NN(O_{ok},\overline{\mathcal{R}})$.

Proof of Theorem 18 (continued) By Lemma 26, $\bigcup_{O_{ok} \in CB^+} NN(O_{ok},\overline{\mathcal{R}}) \subseteq CB^-$. Suppose that CB^- contains some O_{ng} other than $\bigcup_{O_{ok} \in CB^+} NN(O_{ok},\overline{\mathcal{R}})$. We consider two disjoint situations.

– Suppose that for all $O_{ok} \in CB^+$, there exists $O'_{ng} \in CB^-$ s.t. $lgc(O'_{ng},O_{ok}) \preceq lgc(O_{ng},O_{ok})$. Then, by Lemma 25, $\mathcal{R}_{CB''} = \mathcal{R}$ where $CB'' = \langle CB^+, CB'^- - \{O_{ng}\} \rangle$. Therefore, it contradicts minimality of CB^-.
– Suppose that there exists $O_{ok} \in CB^+$ such that for every $O'_{ng} \in CB^-$, $lgc(O'_{ng},O_{ok}) \not\preceq lgc(O_{ng},O_{ok})$. This means that O_{ng} is in $NN(O_{ok},\overline{\mathcal{R}})$. This leads to contradiction and thus $CB^- = \bigcup_{O_{ok} \in CB^+} NN(O_{ok},\overline{\mathcal{R}})$.

Proof of Lemma 20   Suppose that there is a casebase $CB' = \langle CB'^+, CB'^- \rangle$ such that $\mathcal{R}_{CB'} = \mathcal{R}$ and $CB'^+ \subset CB^+$ and CB'^- is any arbitrary set of negative cases.

Then, $\mathcal{R}_{CB'} = \mathcal{R}_{\langle CB'+,\overline{\mathcal{R}} \rangle}$. Suppose that $O_{ok} \in CB^+$ and $O_{ok} \notin CB'^+$. Then, since $CB'^+ \subseteq CB^+ - \{O_{ok}\}$, $\mathcal{R}_{\langle CB'+,\overline{\mathcal{R}} \rangle} \subseteq \mathcal{R}_{\langle CB^+-\{O_{ok}\},\overline{\mathcal{R}} \rangle}$. Therefore, $O_{ok} \notin \mathcal{R}_{CB'}$ and $\mathcal{R}_{CB'} \neq \mathcal{R}$. Thus, it leads to contradiction.

Proof of Lemma 21   Suppose that $O \in \phi(D_k)$ for some D_k such that $O_{ok} \in CB^+$. Then, in order to make $O \notin \mathcal{R}$, we need to have a negative case $O_{ng} \in CB^-$ such that $lgc(O_{ok},O_{ng}) \preceq lgc(O_{ok},O)$. Since $O \in \phi(D_k)$ and $O_{ok} \in CB^+$, for every $i(1 \leq i \leq i)$ such that $x_i \preceq c$ appears in D_k, $O[i] \preceq c$ and $O_{ok}[i] \preceq c$. This means that $lcgc(O_{ok}[i], O[i]) \preceq c$. Thus, $lcgc(O_{ok}[i], O_{ng}[i]) \preceq c$ and $O_{ng}[i] \preceq c$ if $x_i \preceq c$ appears in D_k. This means $O_{ng} \in \phi(D_k)$ and thus $O_{ng} \in \mathcal{R}$ and it leads to contradiction. Therefore, $O \notin \phi(D_k)$.

Since every time the above O is found, we add O to $\mathcal{CB}^+$ at Step 2 in **FindCCB**(δ, ϵ), the number of unsatisfied D_k is reduced at least 1. Therefore, the above situation happens at most $|DNF(\mathcal{R})|$.

Proof of Lemma 22   Every time the above O finds, we search **pminNG**(O, O_{ok}). Let $O_{pmin} = $ **pminNG**(O, O_{ok}). Then, O_{pmin} is in $PNN(O_{ok}, \overline{\mathcal{R}})$. If O_{pmin} were in $\mathcal{CB}^-$ already, O could not be a negative counter example.

Since we add O_{pmin} to $\mathcal{CB}^-$ at Step 3b in **FindCCB**(δ, ϵ), the number of un-added $PNN(O_{ok}, \overline{\mathcal{R}})$ is reduced at least 1. Since $|PNN(O_{ok}, \overline{\mathcal{R}})| \leq |CNF(\mathcal{R})|$ by Lemma 13, the above situation happens at most $|CNF(\mathcal{R})|$ times for each O_{ok}.

Proof of Theorem 23   We only need to get at most $\frac{1}{\epsilon} \ln \frac{1}{\delta}$ examples according to $\mathcal{P}$ to check whether a counter example exists or not, in order to satisfy the accuracy condition. Since the number of counter examples (positive or negative) is at most $|DNF(\mathcal{R})| \cdot (1 + |CNF(\mathcal{R})|)$ by Lemma 21 and Lemma 22, we only need to get at most $(\frac{1}{\epsilon} \ln \frac{1}{\delta}) \cdot |DNF(\mathcal{R})| \cdot (1 + |CNF(\mathcal{R})|)$ samples as a total.

Let $\mathcal{CB}$ be $\langle \mathcal{CB}^+, \mathcal{CB}^- \rangle$. For each negative counter example O and for every O_{ok} such that $O \in \mathcal{R}_{\langle \{O_{ok}\}, \mathcal{CB}^- \rangle}$, we compute an element, O_{pmin}, in a pseudo nearest reduced negative subset w.r.t. O_{ok} by **pminNG**(O, O_{ok}).

Since the number of elements in a representation set of $O\downarrow_{O_{ok}}^l$ for each l such that $class(O[l]) \neq class(O_{ok}[l])$ is at most $width(T)$, the number of possible cases checked for one iteration in **pminNG**(O, O_{ok}) is at most $n \cdot width(T)$.

Since the number of iteration in **pminNG**(O, O_{ok}) is at most $n \cdot height(T)$, we will make a membership query at most $n^2 \cdot width(T) \cdot height(T)$ times to find O_{pmin}. Since the number of negative counter examples is at most $|CNF(\mathcal{R})| \cdot |DNF(\mathcal{R})|$, we need at most $n^2 \cdot width(T) \cdot heght(T) \cdot |CNF(\mathcal{R})| \cdot |DNF(\mathcal{R})|$ membership queries.

Proof of Theorem 24   Let $\mathcal{CB}$ be $\langle \mathcal{CB}^+, \mathcal{CB}^- \rangle$. Since we can guarantee that for every $O_{ok} \in \mathcal{CB}^+$, $O_{ok} \notin \mathcal{R}_{\langle \mathcal{CB}^- - \{O_{ok}\}, \mathcal{CB}^- \rangle}$, there is no subset $\mathcal{CB}'^+$ of $\mathcal{CB}^+$ such that $\mathcal{R}_{\mathcal{CB}'} = \mathcal{R}$ where $\mathcal{CB}' = \langle \mathcal{CB}'^+, \mathcal{CB}^- \rangle$ by Lemma 20.

If we can find all the $PNN(O_{ok}, \overline{\mathcal{R}})$ by using **pminNG**(c, O_{ok}), then we can get $NN(O_{ok}, \overline{\mathcal{R}})$ by choosing $O_{ng} \in PNN(O_{ok}, \overline{\mathcal{R}})$ such that there is no O'_{ng} such that $O'_{ng} \in PNN(O_{ok}, \overline{\mathcal{R}})$ and $lcgc(O'_{ng}, O_{ok}) \prec lcgc(O_{ng}, O_{ok})$. At the output step in **FindCCB**(δ, ϵ), we perform such a selection. Therefore, if $\mathcal{R} = \mathcal{R}_{\mathcal{CB}}$ then, $\mathcal{CB}^- = \bigcup_{O_{ok} \in \mathcal{CB}^+} NN(O_{ok}, \mathcal{CB}^-)$ and this is a minimal set of negative cases w.r.t. $\mathcal{CB}^+$ and $\mathcal{R}$ by Lemma 26.

Average-Case Analysis of Classification Algorithms for Boolean Functions and Decision Trees

Tobias Scheffer

University of Magdeburg, FIN/IWS
P.O. Box 4120, 39016 Magdeburg, Germany
scheffer@iws.cs.uni-magdeburg.de

Abstract. We conduct an *average-case analysis* of the generalization error rate of classification algorithms with finite model classes. Unlike *worst-case* approaches, we do not rely on bounds that hold for all possible learning problems. Instead, we study the behavior of a learning algorithm *for a given problem*, taking properties of the problem and the learner into account. The solution depends only on known quantities (*e.g.,* the sample size), and the histogram of error rates in the model class which we determine for the case that the sought target is a randomly drawn Boolean function. We then discuss how the error histogram can be estimated from a given sample and thus show how the analysis can be applied approximately in the more realistic scenario that the target is unknown. Experiments show that our analysis can predict the behavior of decision tree algorithms fairly accurately even if the error histogram is estimated from a sample.

1 Introduction

In the setting of *classification learning* which we study in this paper, the task of a *learner* is to approximate a joint distribution on *instances* and *class labels* as well as possible. A *hypothesis* is a mapping from instances to class labels; the (generalization, or true) *error rate* of a hypothesis h is the chance of drawing a pair of an instance x and a class label y (when drawing according to the sought target distribution) such that the hypothesis conjectures a class label $h(x)$ which is distinct from the "correct" class label y. While we would like to minimize this true error rate, it is only the empirical error on the training sample (*i.e.,* a set of pairs (x_i, y_i) of fixed size) which we can measure and thus minimize. A learner minimizes the empirical error within a prescribed model class (a set of potentially available hypotheses).

Most known *analyses* of classification algorithms give *worst-case* guarantees on the behavior of the studied algorithms. Typically, it is guaranteed that the performance of the learner is very unlikely to lie below some bound *for every possible underlying problem*. Consequently, such bounds tend to be pessimistic for all but very few underlying learning problems.

H. Arimura, S. Jain and A. Sharma (Eds.): ALT 2000, LNAI 1968, pp. 194-207, 2000.

In an attempt to close the gap between worst-case guarantees and experimental results, a number of *average-case* analyses have been presented which predict the expected behavior (over all possible samples) of a learning algorithm *for a given problem*. Average-case analyses have been presented for decision stump learners [7], k-nearest neighbor [11,12], and linear neural networks [3] as well as for one-variable pattern languages [13] and naive Bayesian classifiers [10,9].

PAC- and VC-style results impose mathematical constraints on the range of possible error rates of classification algorithms which hold for all possible learning problems. Complementing this *mathematical* view, average-case analyses can be seen as reflecting a *science*-oriented perspective. The learning agent is considered as a system the behavior of which is to be described as accurately as possible. The primary benefit of average-case analyses is their ability to predict the behavior of a learning algorithm in a specific scenario much better than worst-case analyses; their primary drawback is their dependence on properties of the learning algorithm and the learning problem which correspond to the the initial state of the system. In a typical classification setting, these properties are unknown.

In Sections 2 and 3, we present computationally efficient *average-case* analyses that predict the behavior of classification algorithms with finite hypothesis languages. In Section 2 we assume that the training set error of the returned hypothesis is known and quantify the expected generalization error of hypotheses with that empirical error. In Section 3 we assume that the learner finds the training set error minimizing hypothesis in the model class (but this least training set error does not have to be known) and quantify the expected generalization error of that hypothesis. Both analyses depend on the histogram of error rates in the model class. This joint property of model class and learning problem counts how often each possible error rate occurs in the model class.

In Section 4, we derive the exact error histogram for the case that the sought target is a randomly drawn function and the instances are governed by the uniform distribution. Similar settings are commonly studied in average-case analyses (*e.g.*, [7]). In Section 5, we discuss how the error histogram can be estimated from an available sample. We can then apply the analysis approximately for arbitrary targets. We present experiments that indicate that, even without any background knowledge on the target, we can still obtain fairly accurate results.

Let us clarify some notational details. Let H_i be some finite model class – *i.e.*, a set of available hypotheses. For instance, H_i could contain all decision trees with i leaf nodes. $h \in H_i$ is then a hypothesis and maps instances x to class labels y. A classification problem is given by an (unknown) density $p(x,y)$. The generalization error rate of h with respect to this problem (which we want to minimize) is then $\epsilon(h) = \int \sum_y \ell(h(x), y) p(x,y) dx$, where $\ell(\cdot, \cdot)$ is the zero-one loss function. Given a finite sample S consisting of m independent examples, drawn according to $p(x,y)$, the empirical (or sample) error rate of h is $e(h) = \frac{1}{m} \sum_{(x,y) \in S} \ell(h(x), y)$. It is important to distinguish between generalization error ϵ (which we really *want* to minimize) and empirical error e (which we *are able* to measure and minimize using the sample) throughout this paper.

2   Generalization Error Given the Empirical Error

Suppose that we have a given model class H_i and a sample size m. The model class H_i is the particular learning bias of the learning algorithm, the behavior of which we would like to predict. Every hypothesis $h \in H_i$ has a fixed but unknown generalization error $\epsilon(h)$ with respect to the (unknown) learning problem $p(x, y)$. When we draw a sample S governed by $p(x, y)^m$, then each hypothesis incurs an empirical error rate $e(h)$. Suppose that we put the hypotheses into boxes labeled with the possible empirical error rates $\frac{0}{m}, \frac{1}{m}, \ldots, \frac{m}{m}$. We call the set of hypotheses in box e H_i^e. Each box with label e has its own distribution of generalization error rates in it (over all possible samples S and over the hypotheses contained in the box). We will write this distribution $p(\epsilon(h_i^e)|e, H_i, m)$. We would expect most of the hypotheses with empirical error rate of $\frac{0}{m}$ to have fairly small generalization error rates, although the majority of them is likely to incur a nonzero generalization error. On the other hand, most hypotheses with empirical error rate $\frac{m}{m}$ will also incur a rather high true error (depending on the sample size and other factors) which will in most cases still be lower than one.

A learning algorithm conducts a search in the prescribed model class H_i and comes to some hypothesis h_i^L with empirical error e (not necessarily the globally smallest empirical error in H_i). If we assume that all hypotheses in H_i with identical empirical error e are equally likely to be found by the learner, then h_i^L can be treated as if it were drawn from H_i^e (the box of hypotheses with empirical error e) under uniform distribution. Consequently, $p(\epsilon(h_i^e)|e, H_i, m)$ governs the generalization error of our learning algorithm when the observed empirical error of the returned hypothesis is e. When we can quantify $p(\epsilon(h_i^e)|e, H_i, m)$, then we can also quantify the distribution which governs the generalization error of the hypothesis returned by our learner.

We can read $p(\epsilon(h_i^e)|e, H_i, m)$ as "P(generalization error | empirical error)". The intuition of our analysis (which is a simplified version of the analysis discussed in [15]) is that application of Bayes' rule implies "P(generalization error | empirical error) = P(empirical error | generalization error)P(generalization error)/ normalization constant". Note that P(empirical error | generalization error) is simply the binomial distribution. (Each example can be classified correctly or erroneously; the chance of the latter happening is ϵ; this leads to a binomial distribution.) We can interpret "P(generalization error)", the prior in our equation, as the histogram of error rates in H_i. This histogram counts, for every ϵ the fraction of the hypotheses in H_i which incur an error rate of ϵ. Let us now look at the analysis in more detail.

Let h_i^L be a hypothesis drawn from H_i^e at random under uniform distribution. In Equation 1, we only expand our definition of h_i^L. Then, in Equation 2, we decompose the expectation by integrating over all possible error rates ϵ. In Equation 3, we apply Bayes' rule. $\pi(\epsilon|H_i)$ is the histogram of error rates in H_i. It specifies the probability of drawing a hypothesis with error rate ϵ when drawing at random under uniform distribution from H_i.

$$E(\epsilon(h_i^L)|e, H_i, m)$$

$$= E(\epsilon(h)|e(h) = e, h \in H_i, m) \tag{1}$$

$$= \int \epsilon p(\epsilon(h) = \epsilon|e(h) = e, h \in H_i, m)d\epsilon \tag{2}$$

$$= \int \epsilon \frac{P(e(h) = e|\epsilon(h) = \epsilon, h \in H_i, m)\pi(\epsilon|H_i)}{P(e(h) = e|h \in H_i, m)}d\epsilon \tag{3}$$

Since, over all ϵ, the distribution $p(\epsilon(h) = \epsilon|e(h) = e, H_i, m)$ has to integrate to one (Equation 4), we can treat $P(e(h) = e|h \in H_i, m)$ as a normalizing constant which we can determine as in Equation 6.

$$\int p(\epsilon(h) = \epsilon|e(h) = e, h \in H_i, m)d\epsilon = 1 \tag{4}$$

$$\Leftrightarrow \int \frac{P(e(h) = e|\epsilon(h) = \epsilon, h \in H_i, m)\pi(\epsilon|H_i)}{P(e(h) = e|h \in H_i, m)}d\epsilon = 1 \tag{5}$$

$$\Leftrightarrow P(e(h) = e|h \in H_i, m) = \int P(e(h) = e|\epsilon(h) = \epsilon, h \in H_i, m)\pi(\epsilon|H_i)d\epsilon \tag{6}$$

Combining Equations 3 and 6 we obtain Equation 7. In this equation, we also state that, when the true error ϵ is given, the empirical error e is governed by the binomial distribution which we write as $B[\epsilon, m](e)$.

$$E(\epsilon(h_i^L)|e, H_i, m) = \frac{\int \epsilon B[\epsilon, m](e)\pi(\epsilon|H_i)d\epsilon}{\int B[\epsilon, m](e)\pi(\epsilon|H_i)d\epsilon} \tag{7}$$

We have now found a solution that quantifies $E(\epsilon(h_i^L)|e, H_i, m)$, the exact expected generalization error of a hypothesis from H_i with empirical error rate e for a given learning problem $p(x, y)$. Equation 7 specifies the actual error rate for the given learning problem rather than a worst-case bound that holds for all possible learning problems. The additional information of $\pi(\epsilon|H_i)$ makes this possible.

3   Analysis of Exhaustive Learners

In this section, we assume that the learner can be guaranteed to find the hypothesis in H_i that minimizes the empirical error (breaking ties by drawing at random). On the other hand, we do not require the empirical error rate of the resulting hypothesis to be known (so the learner does not have to be invoked before the analysis can be applied). We can predict both the resulting empirical error rate and the resulting generalization error from the histogram of error rates and the number of hypotheses. The analysis is a simplification of an analysis proposed by Scheffer and Joachims [19]. Let us first sketch how the resulting empirical error rate on the training set can be predicted without running the learning algorithm at all.

The empirical error rate of a single hypothesis with generalization error ϵ is governed by the binomial distribution $B[m, \epsilon]$. The least empirical error rate in H_i is e if no hypothesis achieves an empirical error which is lower than e. Let us make the simplifying assumption that the empirical error rates of two or more hypotheses are independent *given the corresponding true error rates*. Formally, $P(\bigwedge_{h_j \in H_i} e(h_j)|\epsilon(h_j)) = \prod_{h_j \in H_i} P(e(h_j)|\epsilon(h_j))$. Now we can approximate the chance that no hypothesis incurs an error of less than e as $\prod_{h \in H_i} P(e(h) \geq e|\epsilon(h), m)$. Note that the histogram $\pi(\epsilon|H_i)$ tells us how many hypotheses have error rates of ϵ (for each ϵ). Let us now look at the analysis in more detail.

In order to determine the expected true error (expected over all samples) of h_i^L (the hypothesis that minimizes the empirical error within H_i), we factorize the hypothesis h that the learner returns (Equation 8). Since we assume the learner to break ties between hypotheses with equally small empirical error at random, all hypotheses with equal true error rates ϵ have an exactly equal prior probability of becoming h_i^L. We re-arrange Equation 8 such that all hypotheses h_ϵ with true error ϵ are grouped together. $\pi(\epsilon|H_i)$ is again the density of hypotheses with error rate ϵ among all the hypotheses in H_i (with respect to the given learning problem). This takes us to Equation 9.

$$E(\epsilon(h_i^L)|H_i, m) = \int_h \epsilon(h)P(h_i^L = h|H_i, m)dh \qquad (8)$$

$$= \int_\epsilon \epsilon P(h_i^L = h_\epsilon|\epsilon, H_i, m)\pi(\epsilon|H_i)d\epsilon \qquad (9)$$

Let $H_i^* = \mathrm{argmin}_{h \in H_i}\{e(h)\}$ be the set of hypotheses in H_i which incur the least empirical error rate. Note that H_i^* is a random variable because only the sample size m is fixed whereas the sample S itself (on which H_i^* depends) is a random variable. In order to determine the chance that h_ϵ (an arbitrary hypothesis with true error rate ϵ) is selected as h_i^L, we first factorize the chance that h_ϵ lies in H_i^*, the empirical error minimizing hypotheses of H_i (Equation 10). A hypothesis that does not lie in H_i^* has a zero probability of becoming h_i^L (Equation 11). In Equation 12, we factorize the cardinality of $|H_i^*|$. When this set is of size n, then each hypothesis in H_i^* has a chance of $\frac{1}{n}$ of becoming h_i^L (the learner breaks ties at random) (Equation 13). In Equation 14, we factorize the least empirical error e and, in Equation 15, we simply split up the conjunction (like $p(a, b) = p(a)p(b|a)$).

$$P(h_i^L = h_\epsilon|\epsilon, H_i, m)$$
$$= P(h_i^L = h_\epsilon|H_i, m, h_\epsilon \in H_i^*)P(h_\epsilon \in H_i^*) \qquad (10)$$
$$+ P(h_i^L = h_\epsilon|H_i, m, h_\epsilon \notin H_i^*)(1 - P(h_\epsilon \in H_i^*))$$
$$= P(h_i^L = h_\epsilon|H_i, m, h_\epsilon \in H_i^*)P(h_\epsilon \in H_i^*) \qquad (11)$$
$$= \sum_n P(h_i^L = h_\epsilon|H_i, m, h_\epsilon \in H_i^*, |H_i^*| = n)P(h_\epsilon \in H_i^*, |H_i^*| = n) \qquad (12)$$

$$= \sum_n \frac{1}{n} P(h_\epsilon \in H_i^*, |H_i^*| = n) \tag{13}$$

$$= \sum_e \sum_n \frac{1}{n} P(h_\epsilon \in H_i^*, |H_i^*| = n | e(h_\epsilon) = e) P(e(h_\epsilon) = e | \epsilon, m) \tag{14}$$

$$= \sum_e \sum_n \frac{1}{n} P(h_\epsilon \in H_i^* | e(h_\epsilon) = e, m) P(|H_i^*| = n | h_\epsilon \in H_i^*, e(h_\epsilon) = e)$$
$$P(e(h_\epsilon) = e | \epsilon, m) \tag{15}$$

By inserting Equation 15 into Equation 9 we get Equation 16.

$$E(\epsilon(h_i^L) | H_i, m)$$
$$= \int \epsilon \left(\sum_e \sum_n \frac{1}{n} P(|H_i^*| = n | h_\epsilon \in H_i^*, e(h_\epsilon) = e) \right. \tag{16}$$
$$\left. P(h_\epsilon \in H_i^* | e(h_\epsilon) = e, m) P(e(h_\epsilon) = e | \epsilon, m) \pi(\epsilon | H_i) \right) d\epsilon$$

Assuming that the chance of the set of empirical error minimizing hypotheses H_i^* being of size n when h_ϵ is known to lie in this set does not depend on *which* hypothesis is known to lie in this set (formally, $P(|H_i^*| = n | h_1 \in H_i^*) = P(|H_i^*| = n | h_2 \in H_i^*)$ for all h_1, h_2) we can claim that $c = P(|H_i^*| = n | h_\epsilon \in H_i^*, e(h_\epsilon) = e)$ is constant for all h_ϵ.

Equation 16 specifies the expectation of $\epsilon(h_i^L)$. The density $p(\epsilon(h_i^L) | H_i, m)$ has to integrate to one (Equation 17). Equation 16 takes us from Equation 17 to Equation 18 in which we use the abbreviation c for $P(|H_i^*| = n | h_\epsilon \in H_i^*, e(h_\epsilon) = e)$. c is therefore determined uniquely by Equation 19.

$$\int p(\epsilon(h_i^L) = \epsilon | H_i, m) d\epsilon = 1 \tag{17}$$

$$\Leftrightarrow \int \sum_e \sum_n \frac{1}{n} c \, P(h_\epsilon \in H_i^* | e(h_\epsilon) = e, m)$$
$$P(e(h_\epsilon) = e | \epsilon, m) \pi(\epsilon | H_i) d\epsilon = 1 \tag{18}$$

$$\Leftrightarrow c = \left(\int \sum_e P(h_\epsilon \in H_i^* | e(h_\epsilon) = e, m) P(e(h_\epsilon) = e | \epsilon, m) \pi(\epsilon | H_i) d\epsilon \right)^{-1} \tag{19}$$

Combining Equations 16 and 19 and stating that the empirical error is governed by the binomial distribution (given the true error) we obtain Equation 20.

$$E(\epsilon(h_i^L) | H_i, m)$$
$$= \frac{\int \epsilon \left(\sum_e P(h_\epsilon \in H_i^* | e(h_\epsilon) = e, m) B[\epsilon, m](e) \pi(\epsilon | H_i) \right) d\epsilon}{\int \sum_e P(h_\epsilon \in H_i^* | e(h_\epsilon) = e, m) B[\epsilon, m](e) \pi(\epsilon | H_i) d\epsilon} \tag{20}$$

Let us now tackle the last unknown term, $P(h_\epsilon \in H_i^*|e(h_\epsilon) = e, m)$. A hypothesis h_ϵ (with true error rate ϵ) lies in H_i^* when no hypothesis in H_i achieves a lower empirical error rate. There are $|H_i|$ many hypotheses; their true error rates are fixed but completely arbitrary – $i.e.$, they are neither independent nor governed by some identical distribution. These $|H_i|$ error rates constitute the density $\pi(\epsilon|H_i)$ which measures how often each error rate ϵ occurs in H_i (we have already seen this density in Equation 9). Each of these hypotheses incurs an empirical error rate that is by itself governed by the binomial distribution $B[m, \epsilon]$. Let us assume that the empirical error rates of two or more hypotheses are independent $given~the~corresponding~true~error~rates$ as discussed earlier in this section. Formally, $P(\bigwedge_{h_j \in H_i} e(h_j)|\epsilon(h_j)) = \prod_{h_j \in H_i} P(e(h_j)|\epsilon(h_j))$. Now we can quantify the chance that no hypothesis incurs an error of less than e which makes our hypothesis h with $e(h) = e$ a member of H_i^*. For all but extremely small H_i (formally, $p^{|H_i|} \approx p^{|H_i|-1}$) we can write this chance as in Equation 21. Note again that the empirical error (given the true error) is governed by the binomial distribution (Equation 22).

$$P(h_\epsilon \in H_i^*|e(h_\epsilon) = e, m) = \prod_{\epsilon'} P(e(h) \geq e|\epsilon', m)^{|H_i|\pi(\epsilon'|H_i)} \tag{21}$$

$$= \prod_{\epsilon'} \left(\sum_{e' \geq e} B[\epsilon', m](e') \right)^{|H_i|\pi(\epsilon'|H_i)} \tag{22}$$

What have we achieved so far? Equations 20 and 22 quantify the expected generalization error of h_i^L for a given problem in terms of three quantities: the number of hypotheses in model class H_i (which can typically easily be computed), the sample size m (which is known), and the histogram of error rates in H_i, $\pi(\epsilon|H_i)$. Note that, for Equations 20 to give us the expected error $\epsilon(h_i^L)$, it is not necessary to actually run the learner and determine $e(h_i^L)$. Let us also emphasize that we are not talking about $bounds$ on the error rate for a class of possible problems. Subject to the mentioned independence assumptions, Equations 20 and 21 quantify the expected generalization error of an empirical error minimizing hypothesis $for~a~particular,~given~learning~problem$. When only the sample size m and $|H_i|$ are given, it is impossible to determine where in the interval specified by the Chernoff bound the actual error rate lies. Additionally given the density $\pi(\epsilon|H_i)$, however, we can determine the $actual$ density that governs the generalization error, and thereby also the expected generalization error.

4   Learning Boolean Functions

In order to apply the analysis, the histogram of error rates $\pi(\epsilon|H_i)$ has to be known. Let us determine $\pi(\epsilon|H_i)$ when the target is a randomly drawn Boolean function over attributes x_1 through x_k and the instances are governed by the uniform distribution. For each target function f_k the target distribution $p_k(x, y)$

is then $\frac{1}{|X|}$ when $f_k(x) = y$ and 0 otherwise. Let H_i contain all Boolean functions over the first i attributes. Model classes H_1 to H_{k-1} contain 1 through $k-1$ of the relevant attributes; the target function does usually not lie within the model class and the classifier can only approximate the target. Model class H_k contains all relevant attributes. Model classes H_{k+1} through H_n contain all relevant plus additional irrelevant attributes.

Each target function f_k (with corresponding target distribution $p_k(x,y)$) yields some error histogram $\pi_k(\epsilon|H_i, f_k) = \pi_k(\epsilon|H_i, p_k(x,y))$. When $P(f_k)$ is the uniform distribution as stated above, then the expected resulting error can be described by Equation 23, which is just Equation 20 averaged over all f_k. The subscript $E_{\{f_k,S\}}$ indicates that now both f_k and the sample S are random variables.

$$E_{\{f_k,S\}}(\epsilon(h_L)|H_i, m) \tag{23}$$
$$= \int \frac{\int \epsilon \left(\sum_e P(h_\epsilon \in H_i^*|e(h_\epsilon) = e, m)B[\epsilon, m](e)\pi(\epsilon|H_i, f_k) \right) d\epsilon}{\int \sum_e P(h_\epsilon \in H_i^*|e(h_\epsilon) = e, m)B[\epsilon, m](e)\pi(\epsilon|H_i, f_k)d\epsilon} P(f_k)df_k$$

$$\text{where } P(h_\epsilon \in H_i^*|e(h_\epsilon) = e, m) = \prod_{\epsilon'} \left(\sum_{e' \geq e} B[\epsilon', m](e') \right)^{|H_i|\pi(\epsilon'|H_i)} \tag{24}$$

In order to further reduce Equation 23 we need to distinguish two cases.

(1): $i < k$. f_k splits the Boolean instance space into 2^k instances whereas the hypotheses split the space only into 2^i subspaces each of which is assigned only one class label. Hence, 2^{k-i} instances with potentially distinct class labels fall into the same subspace. Since f_k is governed by the uniform distribution, assigning one class label (drawn uniformly from the set $\{0,1\}$ to 2^{k-i} instances will misclassify a number ν of instances governed by the binomial distribution $B[2^{k-i}, \frac{1}{2}]$. Let ν_1 through ν_{2^i} be the numbers of instances misclassified in subspaces 1 through 2^i when a randomly drawn class label is assigned to the whole subspace. The vector $(\nu_1, \ldots, \nu_{2^i})$ is governed by $(B[2^{k-i}, \frac{1}{2}])^{2^i}$ as specified more detailedly in Equation 25.

$$P(\nu = (\nu_1, \ldots, \nu_{2^i})) = \prod_{j=1}^{j=2^i} B\left[2^{k-i}, \frac{1}{2}\right](\nu_j) \tag{25}$$

Given a vector ν, the corresponding error rate is just the sum over all subspaces divided by the number of instances: $\epsilon = \sum_{j=1}^{2^i} \nu_j / 2^k$. Hence, we can characterize the distribution that governs this sum of errors ϵ recursively in Equation 26. The intuition of this equation is that an error of e instances is incurred in subspace j through 2^i when *either* an error of ν_j (class label 0) is incurred in subspace j and an error of $e - \nu_j$ is incurred in subspaces $j+1$ through k, *or* an error of $2^{k-i} - \nu_j$ is incurred in subspace j (class label 1) and the remaining error of $e - (2^{k-i} - \nu_j)$ is incurred in subspaces $j+1$ through k. The factor 2^k is used to convert error rates into absolute numbers of errors and vice versa. The intuition of Equation 27 is that, in the last subspace, ν_{2^i} instances are misclassified with certainty when $\nu_{2^i} = 2^{k-i} - \nu_{2^i}$ (equally many instances have class labels of zero and one), and ν_{2^i} and $2^{k-i} - \nu_{2^i}$ instances are misclassified with probability $\frac{1}{2}$ otherwise, and no other error rates are possible.

$$P\left(\epsilon = \frac{e}{2^k}\Big|\nu_j,\ldots,\nu_{2^i}\right) = \frac{1}{2}P\left(\epsilon = \frac{e-\nu_1}{2^k}\Big|\nu_{j+1},\ldots,\nu_{2^i}\right) \tag{26}$$

$$+\frac{1}{2}P\left(\epsilon = \frac{e-2^{k-i}+\nu_1}{2^k}\Big|\nu_{j+1},\ldots,\nu_{2^i}\right)$$

$$\text{where } P\left(\epsilon = \frac{e}{2^k}\Big|\nu_{2^i}\right) = \begin{cases} 1 & \text{iff } \nu_{2^i} = 2^{k-i} - \nu_{2^i} \\ \frac{1}{2} & \text{iff } \nu_{2^i} = e \\ \frac{1}{2} & \text{iff } \nu_{2^i} = 2^{k-i} - e \\ 0 & \text{otherwise} \end{cases} \tag{27}$$

Hence, over all functions f_k (with fixed k) and hypotheses h, Equation 28 gives the distribution of error histograms. In this equation, we simply factorize ν; $P(\epsilon \,|\nu = (\nu_1,\ldots,\nu_{2^i}))$ is quantified by Equation 26, and $P(\nu = (\nu_1,\ldots,\nu_{2^i}))$ by Equation 25.

$$\pi_k(\epsilon|H_i) = \sum_\nu P(\epsilon \,|\nu = (\nu_1,\ldots,\nu_{2^i}))P(\nu = (\nu_1,\ldots,\nu_{2^i})) \tag{28}$$

Finally, we can quantify the expected (over all samples S and target functions f_k) resulting error rate in Equation 29.

$$E_{\{f_k,S\}}(\epsilon(h_L)|H_i,m,k) \tag{29}$$

$$= \sum_\nu \left(\frac{\int \epsilon \left(\sum_e P(h_\epsilon \in H_i^*|e(h_\epsilon) = e,m)B[\epsilon,m](e)P(\epsilon|\nu)\right) d\epsilon}{\int \sum_e P(h_\epsilon \in H_i^*|e(h_\epsilon) = e,m)B[\epsilon,m](e)P(\epsilon|\nu)d\epsilon} \right.$$

$$\left. P(\nu = (\nu_1,\ldots,\nu_{2^i})) \right)$$

$P(h_\epsilon \in H_i^*|e(h_\epsilon) = e,m)$ is quantified by Equation 24, $P(\epsilon|\nu)$ by Equation 26, and $P(\nu = (\nu_1,\ldots,\nu_{2^i}))$ by Equation 25. We can evaluate Equation 29 easily as it refers only to the binomial distribution, the sample size and the numbers of attributes i and k.

(2): $i \geq k$. In this case, the target function assigns one class label to 2^{i-k} instances which can be distinguished by the hypothesis. The hypothesis distinguishes 2^i subspaces; a randomly drawn hypothesis will assign each of these subspaces the correct class label half the time. Hence, the distribution of error rates is governed by the binomial distribution as given in Equation 30.

$$\pi(\epsilon|H_i,f_k) = B\left[\frac{1}{2},2^i\right] \tag{30}$$

We can quantify the expected resulting error in Equation 31 by replacing π in Equation 20 by the binomial distribution.

$$E_{\{f_k,S\}}(\epsilon(h_L)|H_i,m,k) \tag{31}$$

$$= \frac{\int \epsilon \left(\sum_e P(h_\epsilon \in H_i^* | e(h_\epsilon) = e, m) P(e(h_\epsilon) = e | \epsilon, m) B[\frac{1}{2}, 2^i](\epsilon) \right) d\epsilon}{\int_\epsilon \sum_e P(h_\epsilon \in H_i^* | e(h_\epsilon) = e, m) P(e(h_\epsilon) = e | \epsilon, m) B[\frac{1}{2}, 2^i](\epsilon) d\epsilon}$$

$P(h_\epsilon \in H_i^* | e(h_\epsilon) = e, m)$ is given by Equation 24. Let us check whether Equations 29 and 31 predict the error rate of a learner accurately. In our experiments, we drew 200 Boolean functions with 3 relevant attributes and allowed model classes of between 1 and 6 attributes. Figure 1 shows the averaged error histograms for all model classes. Figure 2 compares theoretical and measured error rates $\epsilon(h_i^L)$ of hypotheses with least empirical error. We can see that the predicted error rates fit the measured rates fairly closely.

Note that the averaged error histograms of model classes 1 through 3 are equal. As long as the error histogram stays constant, increasing the number of hypotheses decreases the resulting error rate. As we add irrelevant attributes, the ratio of hypotheses with very low error rates decreases and the resulting error increases.

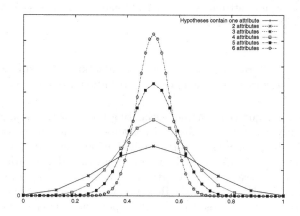

Fig. 1. Error histograms for models which contain Boolean attributes $x_1, \ldots x_i$ when the target function requires attributes x_1, x_2, x_3. The distributions are equal in the first three models; the variance then increases.

5   Decision Trees and Unknown Targets

In general, the error histogram is not known. However, we can estimate the error histogram from the sample and thus apply the analysis approximately for arbitrary target distributions. As an estimate of $\pi(\epsilon | H_i)$ we use the empirical counterpart $\pi(e | H_i)$ (the distribution of empirical error rates of hypotheses in H_i with respect to the sample S) which we can record when H_i is known and a sample S is available. We can obtain $\pi(e | H_i)$ by repeatedly drawing hypotheses

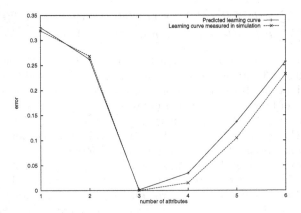

Fig. 2. (b) Learning curve: Expected error (theoretical and measured values) when the target function requires attributes x_1 through x_3 and model H_i (i is on the horizontal axis) uses attributes x_1 through x_i.

from H_i under uniform distribution, or by conducting a Markov random walk in the hypothesis space with the uniform distribution as stationary distribution [4].

This raises the question whether estimating the error histogram of a model class sufficiently accurately is any easier than estimating the error rate of all hypotheses in that model class. Fortunately, Langford and McAllester [8] have answered this question affirmatively. It is obvious that the empirical error histogram converges toward the true error histogram when m grows – in other words, $\lim_{m \to \infty} P(e|H_i) = \pi(\epsilon|H_i)$. However, when m goes to infinity, then all empirical error rates converge to their corresponding true error rates and the error prediction problem becomes trivial as we can treat the training sample error rates as true error rates. One of the main results of PAC theory (*e.g.*, [6]) is that we achieve uniform convergence (*i.e.*, *all* empirical error rates approximate their corresponding true error rates accurately) only when $\frac{\log |H_i|}{m}$ is sufficiently small. However, the empirical error histogram converges to the true histogram even if $\frac{\log |H_i|}{m}$ is arbitrarily large.

Consider a process in which both the sample size m_i and the size of the model class grow in parallel when $i \to \infty$, such that $\frac{\log |H_i|}{m_i}$ stays constantly large. Over this process, we are unable to estimate all error rates in H_i but $P(e|H_i)$ converges to $\pi(\epsilon|H_i)$ as i grows [8]. In this respect, estimating the histogram is much easier than estimating all error rates in H_i. For an extended discussion on the complexity and accuracy of estimating π, see [14].

The objective of the next experiment is to check whether our analysis can predict the error rate of a decision tree learner accurately for a set of problems from the UCI data set repository. For each problem and every number of leaf nodes i, we estimate the histogram of error rates $\pi(\epsilon|H_i)$ using 4000×2^i randomly drawn decision trees using an algorithm described in [14] running in $O(4000i)$. Using the estimate of π, we evaluate Equation 20. We also run a decision tree learner that minimizes the empirical error rate using exactly i leaf nodes [15]. We use the resulting empirical error to evaluate Equation 7. We then run a 10-fold cross validation loop (for each number i). In each fold, we run the exhaustive/greedy learner and estimate the generalization error using the holdout set.

Figure 3 compares the predicted to the measured generalization error rates (based on Equation 20) for the empirical error minimizing learner learner, and Figure 4 compares predicted error given the empirical error (Equation 7) to measured error. For most measurements, the predicted value lies within the standard deviation of the measured value which indicates that the predictions are relatively accurate. Only for the Cleveland and *E. Coli* problem we can see significant deviations.

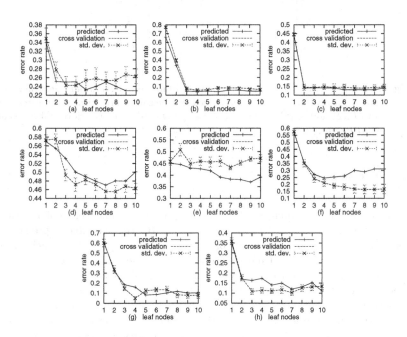

Fig. 3. Predicted (Equation 20) and measured (10-fold cross validation) generalization error rates of decision trees restricted to i leaf nodes. (a) diabetes, (b) iris, (c) crx, (d) cmc, (e) cleveland, (f) ecoli, (g) wine, (h) ionosphere.

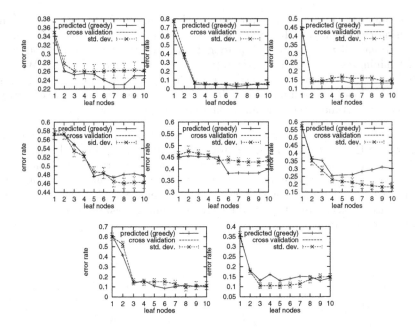

Fig. 4. Predicted (Equation 7) and measured (10-fold cross validation) generalization error rates of a decision tree learner (based on measured empirical error rates), restricted to i leaf nodes. (a) diabetes, (b) iris, (c) crx, (d) cmc, (e) cleveland, (f) ecoli, (g) wine, (h) ionosphere.

6   Discussion

Average-case analyses quantify the expected (over all samples) error of a learning algorithm for *a* given target function. Consequently, they are able to predict the behavior of a learning algorithm for a specific learning problem much better than worst-case analyses. Unfortunately, average-case analyses are not quite as easy to apply as worst-case analyses. The reason is their reference to specific properties of the underlying learning problems which typically are not known. In science, this corresponds to the initial state of a physical system that has to be known before the development of that system over time can be predicted.

In most cases, average-case analyses break the error rate only approximately into measurables and domain properties. This is clearly a drawback, but it does not automatically void the usefulness of such analyses. Since the strength of such approximations is often difficult to quantify, in most cases the only feasible way is to run learning algorithms and to measure the deviation between predicted and measured error rates. The experiments presented in this paper provide evidence for the usefulness of the approximate Equation 20. The analysis of the error rate given the empirical error (Equation 7) differs from most known analyses by not being approximate.

Average-case analyses have been discussed for various learners. Iba and Langley [7] have studied the behavior of decision stump learners. Okamoto and Yugami [11, 12] presented an analysis for k-nearest neighbor classifiers; Fukumizu [3] for linear neural networks. Reischuk and Zeugmann [13] analyzed the average time complexity of an algorithm that learns one-variable pattern languages. An analysis of Naive Bayesian classifiers has been presented by Langley et al. [10]; under some simplifying approximations [9] the analysis becomes computationally efficient. An average-case analysis of cross validation has been presented in [16].

A first version of the analysis class was presented by Scheffer and Joachims [18, 17] and later generalized [19] and applied to text categorization and decision tree regularization [15]. Independently, Domingos [1] presented a similar analysis which additionally assumes that all hypotheses incur equal error rates. Lifting the latter assumption [2] leads to an analysis that (besides making the additional assumption that the training set error is known) deviates from the first analysis [18] only in some technical details.

The histogram of error rates has been used to improve on *worst-case* error bounds. The idea of a worst-case analysis of [5] is that hypotheses with an error rate of much more than the desired error bound ε have a much smaller chance of incurring the least empirical error than hypotheses with an error rate that lies just slightly above ε. In contrast to the resulting *shell decomposition bounds*, we obtain the exact distribution that governs the resulting error rate (and therefore also the expected error).

An interesting question to pose is whether the estimated empirical error histogram can lead to a non-approximate claim on the resulting generalization error. Given the uncertainty that remains when the histogram has been estimated, it is not possible to determine the *exact expected* generalization error (which we are concerned about in this paper), but Langford and McAllester [8] have proven worst-case shell decomposition *bounds* that differ from those of [5] by taking into account that the histogram is only estimated.

We have shown that the error histogram for Boolean functions is a certain binomial distribution. A fundamental question is whether there is a more general link between the error histogram and measurable properties (such as the VC dimension) of the model class and the class of target functions.

References

1. P. Domingos. A process-oriented heuristic for model selection. In *Proceedings of the Fifteenth International Conference on Machine learning*, pages 127–135, 1998.
2. P. Domingos. Process-oriented estimation of generalization error. In *Proceedings of the Sixteenth International Joint Conference on Artificial Intelligenct*, 1999.
3. K. Fukumizu. Generalization error of linear neural networks in unidentifiable cases. In *Proceedings of the Tenth International Conference on Algorithmic Learning Theory*, 1999.

4. W. Gilks, S. Richardson, and D. Spiegelhalter, editors. *Markov Chain Monte Carlo in Practice*. Chapman & Hall, 1995.
5. D. Haussler, M. Kearns, S. Seung, and N. Tishby. Rigorous learning curve bounds from statistical mechanics. *Machine Learning*, 25, 1996.
6. David Haussler. Decision theoretic generalizations of the PAC model for neural net and other learning applications. *Information and Computation*, 100(1):78–150, September 1992.
7. W. Iba and P. Langley. Induction of one-level decision trees. In *Proceedings of the Ninth International Conference on Machine Learning*, pages 233–240, 1992.
8. J. Langford and D. McAllester. Computable shell decomposition bounds. In *Proceedings of the International Conference on Computational Learning Theory*, 2000.
9. P. Langley and S. Sage. Tractable average case analysis of naive bayes classifiers. In *Proceedings of the Sixteenth International Conference on Machine Learning*, pages 220–228, 1999.
10. Pat Langley, Wayne Iba, and Kevin Thompson. An analysis of bayesian classifiers. In *Proceedings of the Tenth National Conference on Artificial Intelligence*, pages 223–228, 1992.
11. S. Okamoto and Y. Nobuhiro. An average-case analysis of the k-nearest neighbor classifier for noisy domains. In *Proceedings of the Fifteenth International Joint Conference on Artificial Intelligence*, pages 238–243, 1997.
12. S. Okamoto and N. Yugami. Generalized average-case analysis of the nearest neighbor algorithm. In *Proceedings of the Seventeenth International Conference on Machine Learning*, pages 695–702, 2000.
13. Rüdiger Reischuk and Thomas Zeugmann. Learning 1-variable pattern languages in linear average time. In *Proceedings of the Eleventh Annual Conference on Computational Learning Theory*, pages 198–208, 1998.
14. T. Scheffer. *Error Estimation and Model Selection*. Infix Publisher, Sankt Augustin, 1999.
15. T. Scheffer. Nonparametric regularization of decision trees. In *Proceedings of the European Conference on Machine Learning*, 2000.
16. T. Scheffer. Predicting the generalization performance of cross validatory model selection criteria. In *Proceedings of the International Conference on Machine Learning*, 2000.
17. T. Scheffer and T. Joachims. Estimating the expected error of empirical minimizers for model selection. Technical Report TR 98-9, Technische Universitaet Berlin, 1998.
18. T. Scheffer and T. Joachims. Estimating the expected error of empirical minimizers for model selection (abstract). In *Proceedings of the Fifteenth National Conference on Artificial Intelligence*, 1998.
19. T. Scheffer and T. Joachims. Expected error analysis for model selection. In *Proceedings of the Sixteenth International Conference on Machine Learning*, 1999.

Self-duality of Bounded Monotone Boolean Functions and Related Problems

Daya Ram Gaur and Ramesh Krishnamurti

School of Computing Science, Simon Fraser University
B.C, V5A 1S6, Canada
{gaur,ramesh}@cs.sfu.ca

Abstract. In this paper we show the equivalence between the problem of determining self-duality of a boolean function in DNF and a special type of satisfiability problem called NAESPI. Eiter and Gottlob [8] use a result from [2] to show that self-duality of monotone boolean functions which have bounded clause sizes (by some constant) can be determined in polynomial time. We show that the self-duality of instances in the class studied by Eiter and Gottlob can be determined in time linear in the number of clauses in the input, thereby strengthening their result. Domingo [7] recently showed that self-duality of boolean functions where each clause is bounded by $(\sqrt{\log n})$ can be solved in polynomial time. Our linear time algorithm for solving the clauses with bounded size infact solves the $(\sqrt{\log n})$ bounded self-duality problem in $O(n^2 \sqrt{\log n})$ time, which is better bound then the algorithm of Domingo [7], $O(n^3)$.
Another class of self-dual functions arising naturally in application domain has the property that every pair of terms in f intersect in at most constant number of variables. The equivalent subclass of NAESPI is the c-bounded NAESPI. We also show that c-bounded NAESPI can be solved in polynomial time when c is some constant. We also give an alternative characterization of *almost self-dual* functions proposed by Bioch and Ibaraki [5] in terms of NAESPI instances which admit solutions of a 'particular' type.

1 Introduction

The problem of determining if a monotone boolean function in DNF containing n clauses, is self-dual is ubiquitous. It arises in distributed systems [1,10], artificial intelligence [16], databases [14], convex programming [11] and hypergraph theory [8], to name a few. The exact complexity of determining if a monotone boolean function is self-dual is open. Fredman and Khachiyan [9] provide an $O(n^{4o(\log n)+O(1)})$ algorithm for solving the problem. Bioch and Ibaraki [3] describe a host of problems which are equivalent to determining the self-duality. They also address the question of existence of incremental polynomial algorithms for solving the problem of determining the self-duality of monotone boolean functions. In a related paper [4] they define a decomposition of the problem and give an algorithm to determine a minimal canonical decomposition. Bioch

H. Arimura, S. Jain and A. Sharma (Eds.): ALT 2000, LNAI 1968, pp. 209–223, 2000.
© Springer-Verlag Berlin Heidelberg 2000

and Ibaraki [5] describe an incremental polynomial algorithm [15] for generating all monotone boolean functions of n variables. It has been shown that for *2-monotone* [6] boolean functions, it is possible to check the self-duality in polynomial time. Bioch and Ibaraki [5] define *almost self-dual* functions as an approximation to the class of self-dual functions. They describe an algorithm based on almost self-duality to determine if a function is self-dual. The complexity of their procedure is exponential in the worst case. Ibaraki and Kameda [12] show that every self-dual function can be decomposed into a set of majority functions over three variables. This characterization in turn gives an algorithm (though not polynomial) for checking self-duality. Makino and Ibaraki [13] define the latency of a monotone boolean function and relate it to the complexity of determining if a function is self-dual.

In this paper we show the equivalence between the problem of determining self-duality of a boolean function and a special type of satisfiability problem called NAESPI (to be defined later). We identify a subclass (denoted easily satisfiable) of NAESPI instances which can be solved in polynomial time. We show that *almost self-duality* [5] implies that the corresponding NAESPI is not easily solvable and vice-versa. Having established the equivalence between almost self-duality and not easily satisfiable instances of NAESPI, we show an NP-completeness result for determining the solution of a particular type of NAESPI. This result is interesting as it relates to the concept of almost self-duality. Eiter and Gottlob [8] use a result from [2] to show that self-duality of monotone boolean functions which have bounded clause sizes can be determined in polynomial time. We show that NAESPI which has clauses of size at most k (denoted k-NAESPI) can be solved in $O(n^{2k+2})$ time (this corresponds to self-duality of monotone boolean functions which have clauses of size at most k). Next, we reduce the complexity of the $O(n^{2k+2})$ algorithm for solving k-NAESPI to $O(2^{(k^2)}nk)$, which is linear in n for constant k. We show that for k-NAESPI where the intersection between pairs of clauses is bounded by c, the number of clauses is at most k^{c+1}. We also show that c-bounded NAESPI can be solved in $O(n^{2c+2})$ time, which is polynomial for constant c.

In Section 2, we introduce the problem of determining whether a monotone boolean function is self-dual. Next we introduce the not-all-equal satisfiability problem with only positive literals and with the intersection property (NAESPI), and establish the equivalence between the two problems. We also show that imposing certain restrictions to either the instances of NAESPI or solutions to NAESPI enables us to compute the solution in polynomial time. In Section 3, we provide an $O(n^{2k+2})$ algorithm for the NAESPI problem which has n clauses with at most k variables each. In Section 5. we modify the algorithm presented in Section 4. to obtain an algorithm for solving k-NAESPI in $O(2^{(k^2)}nk)$ time. In Section 5, we provide an upper bound on the number of clauses for the c-bounded k-NAESPI problem. In the same section, we show that c-bounded NAESPI can be solved in $O(n^{2c+2})$ time, which is polynomial for constant c.

2   Self-duality of monotone boolean functions and NAESPI

Given a boolean function $f(x_1, x_2, \ldots, x_n)$, we define its dual denoted by f^d as follows:

Definition 1 *Dual:* $f^d(x) = \bar{f}(\bar{x})$, *for all vectors* $x = (x_1, x_2, \ldots, x_n) \in \{0, 1\}^n$.

Next we define monotone boolean functions.

Definition 2 *Monotone boolean function: A boolean function f is monotone if* $\forall x, y \in \{0, 1\}^n \ f(x) \leq f(y)$. *A vector* $x \leq y$ *if* $x_i \leq y_i$, $i \in \{1..n\}$.

Equivalently, a boolean function is monotone if it can be represented by an expression which does not contain any negative literals. If a monotone function f is in disjunctive normal form (DNF) then f^d can be obtained by interchanging every *and* operator with an *or* operator and vice versa. f^d is then be in conjunctive normal form (CNF). Self-duality can now be defined as:

PROBLEM: Self-duality
INSTANCE: A boolean function $f(x_1, x_2, \ldots, x_n)$.
QUESTION: For every vector $x = (x_1, x_2, \ldots, x_n) \in \{0, 1\}^n$ is $f^d(x) = f(x)$?

From the definition of self-duality it follows that:

Property 1 A boolean function f is self-dual $\iff$ for all vectors $x \in \{0, 1\}^n$, $f(x) \neq f(\bar{x})$.

We can assume that the monotone function f is in DNF. Next we show that if there exists a pair of clauses in a monotone function f which do not intersect in any variable, then f is not self-dual. This observation is also implicit in [9].

Lemma 1 *If there exists a pair of non-intersecting clauses in a monotone function f, then f is not self-dual.*

Proof: Let C_1 and C_2 be two such clauses. We construct a vector $x \in \{0, 1\}^n$ such that all the variables occurring in C_1 are set to 1 and all the variables occurring in C_2 are set to 0. The remaining variables are arbitrarily set to 0 or 1. $f(x) = 1$ as the clause C_1 evaluates to 1. Also, $f(\bar{x}) = 1$ as C_2 evaluates to 0 on x. Hence by Proposition 2, f is not self-dual. $\square$

Lemma 1 allows us to focus only on those monotone boolean functions in which every pair of clauses intersect. Another assumption which we use throughout this paper is the following:

Property 2 Every variable in f belongs to at least 2 terms in f.

Property 2 coupled with Lemma 1 implies that each term has at most n variables where n is the total number of clauses in f. Therefore the total number of variables $m \leq n^2$ in f. Given such a function f, we now construct the NAESPI problem and show the equivalence of the two problems. Next we define the NAESPI problem.

PROBLEM: NAESPI
INSTANCE: Given a set of variables $V = (v_1, v_2, \ldots, v_m)$, and a collection of clauses $C_i, i = \{1, \ldots, n\}$, $C_i \subseteq V$, every pair of clauses C_i, C_j has a non-empty intersection.
QUESTION: Find a set $S \subseteq V$ such that S contains at least one variable from every clause, but no clause is contained in S.

We are given a monotone boolean function f in DNF form. P is obtained by interpreting the function as a CNF formula. In other words, if $f = (x_1 \wedge x_2) \vee (x_1 \wedge x_3) \vee (x_2 \wedge x_3)$ then $P = (x_1 \vee x_2) \wedge (x_1 \vee x_3) \vee (x_2 \vee x_3)$. Note that every pair of clauses in P intersect since every pair of clauses in f intersect. The next proposition states that the complement of a solution to a given NAESPI problem P is also a solution to P.

Proposition 1 *If S is solution to a given NAESPI problem P, then so is $\bar{S}$.*

We now show that the two problems are equivalent by showing that f is not self-dual if and only if P is satisfiable.

Theorem 1 *f is not self-dual $\iff$ P is satisfiable.*

Proof: $\Rightarrow$ Assume that f is not self-dual. By Proposition 2 we have a vector x such that $f(x) = f(\bar{x})$. There are two cases:

- $f(x) = f(\bar{x}) = 1$. Let C_i be the clause in f which evaluates to 1. For the vector $\bar{x}$, C_i evaluates to 0. As C_i intersects every other clause in f, all these clauses have at least one variable set to 0. This is a contradiction as $f(\bar{x})$ was supposed to be 1. Hence this case cannot happen. This also amounts to saying that the function is not dual-minor, hence it cannot be self-dual.
- $f(x) = f(\bar{x}) = 0$. Let S be the union of all the variables in f which are assigned 1 in the vector x. Each clause in f contains at least one 0 because $f(x) = 0$. Similarly, each clause in f contains at least one 1 as $f(\bar{x}) = 0$. This means that S contains at least one element from each clause in P and does not contain at least one element from each clause in P. Hence S intersects every clause in P but does not contain any clause in P. Therefore, S is a valid solution.

⟸ Given a solution S to P, construct the vector $x \in \{0,1\}^n$ as follows:

$$x_i = 1 \ if \ x_i \in S \ else \ x_i = 0$$

Clearly, $f(x) = 0$. Since $\bar{S}$ is also a solution to P (by Proposition 1), it follows that that $f(\bar{x}) = 0$. Hence by Proposition 2 f is not self-dual. □

We now describe two particular types of solutions to the NAESPI problem which can be computed in polynomial time.

Definition 3 *Easy solution: Given an NAESPI problem P, let S be a solution such that S is contained in some clause of P. We call S an easy solution to P.*

Given an easy solution S to the NAESPI problem P, we show that there exists a clause $C \in P$ such that C intersects S in $|C| - 1$ variables. We do this by showing that if this property does not hold, then we can augment S until the above mentioned property does hold. Given this fact, we devise an algorithm to try out all the possible valid subsets to see if any one of them is a solution. As the number of valid subsets is polynomial, the algorithm terminates in polynomial time. More formally we need the following lemma:

Lemma 2 *Let S be an easy solution to the NAESPI problem P. S can be extended to another easy solution S' such that for a clause $C \in P$, $|C \cap S| = |C| - 1$.*

Proof: Let C_0 be the clause which contains S. Let a be an element of C_0 not in S. Let $S = S \cup a$. If S is still a solution, we continue to add variables (which are not in C_0) to S until S is no longer a solution (it is easy to see that this process of adding variables must terminate). If S is not a solution to P then there is some clause $C \in P$, such that $C = S$. Let a be the last variable added to S. hen $|C \cap S - \{a\}| = |C| - 1$. But this implies that $|C \cap S| = |C| - 1$. □

Lemma 2 provides a simple polynomial algorithm that generates each *easy* candidate solution to the problem P, and verifies if it is indeed a solution. For clause $C \in P$, there are only $|C|$ subsets of size $|C| - 1$ which are candidates. For n clauses, there are at most $n \times |C| \le n^2$ candidates which need to be verified. Since verifying each candidate takes $O(n)$ time, the algorithm complexity is $O(n^3)$ time.

It should be noted that Lemma 2 is also valid for the NAESP problem (where we drop the requirement that all the pairs of clauses intersect). Next we show that if every pair of clauses in a given NAESPI problem P always intersects in at least two variables, then P is trivially satisfiable.

Definition 4 *Easily solvable: A NAESPI instance is said to be easily solvable if it admits an easy solution.*

Next we study the relationship between easily satisfiable instances of NAESPI and the *almost self-dual* functions proposed by Bioch and Ibaraki [5]. We give some definitions from [5] below. A monotone boolean function f is called *dual-minor* if $f \le f^d$. Given w a minterm of f, we represent by $\overline{w}$ all the variables which are not in w but in f.

Sub-dual of a function f, denoted $f^s = \sum_{w \in f} \overline{w} w^d$, where w is a minterm of f. A function f is defined to be *almost dual-major* if $f^s \leq f$. A function is satisfiable if there exists a vector $x \in \{0,1\}^n$ such that some clause evaluates to 1 (recall that f is in DNF). The set of variables set to 1 is referred to as the solution set S. f is easily satisfiable if the solution set S is properly contained inside some clause in f.

Definition 5 *Almost self-dual: A function f is called almost self-dual if $f^s \leq f$ and f is dual-minor.*

Theorem 2 *A monotone boolean function f is almost self-dual $\iff$ f^d is not easily satisfiable.*

Proof: $\Rightarrow$ Given an almost self-dual function f, we want to prove that f^d is easily satisfiable. As, f is self-dual, $f^s \leq f$, which implies $f^d \leq f^{sd}$. Suppose that f^d is easily satisfiable. This implies f^{sd} evaluates to 1 on some vector x. Let x be properly contained inside clause $C \in f^d$. But in f^{sd} we have $\overline{C}$ as a clause and as f^{sd} is in CNF, x is not a solution to f.

$\Leftarrow$ Given that f^d is not easily satisfiable, we want to show that $f^d \leq f^{sd}$. Suppose that $f^d(x) = 1$. We want to show that $f^{sd}(x) = 1$. As the solution to f^d is not an easy solution, it intersects every clause in f^{sd}. f is dual-minor because f^d has the intersection property. $\square$

Theorem 2 implies that f is almost self-dual $\iff$ the corresponding NAESPI is not easily satisfiable (corresponding NAESPI is structurally similar to f^d).

Lemma 3 *NAESPI with cardinality of intersection at least two has a trivial solution.*

Proof: Let C be the clause which does not properly contain any other clause (such a clause always exists). Let the cardinality of this clause be m. Let any $m - 1$ elements from this clause be denoted by set S. We claim that S is a solution. Since C intersects every other clause in at least two variables, S contains at least one variable from every clause. In addition, since every clause (other than C) contains a literal not in C, S cannot contain all the literals in a clause. $\square$

3 k-NAESPI

In this section we study the k-NAESPI problem, in which there are n clauses and every clause has at most k variables. We present an algorithm which solves the k-NAESPI problem in $O(n^{2k+2})$ time (where n is the number of clauses). For a given clause in the k-NAESPI problem, there are at most k assignments of boolean values to the variables which set exactly one of the variables in the clause to 1 and the remaining variables to 0. We call such an assignment a 10^* assignment. The algorithm operates in stages. For the subproblem in an intermediate stage, if B denotes the set of clauses which do not have any variable set to 1, the algorithm tries out all the k possible assignments of the type 10^* for the clauses in B. We show that at most k stages are needed by the algorithm, implying a running time of $O(n^{O(k)})$ for the algorithm.

In the following discussion, we assume that the problem has at least k distinct variables, else we can determine the satisfiability in $O(2^k)$ time.

Our algorithm is a recursive algorithm, which tries out all the possible 10* assignments for every clause in a stage. Let U denote the set of variables set to 1. Let B be the set of clauses that do not contain any variable in U. The algorithm tries out all possible 10* assignment for every clause in B. The subproblem obtained after choosing a clause is solved recursively. Sets U and B are updated in each stage. The algorithm terminates either after k stages or after all the variables are assigned a boolean value.

To prove the correctness of the algorithm we need the concept of minimal solutions.

Definition 6 *Minimal solution: A solution S to a k-NAESPI is minimal if no proper subset of S is a solution.*

Let S be a minimal solution to the given k-NAESPI problem instance. Then there is a clause C which contains at most one element from S. Suppose this were not true, then every clause contains at least two variables from S. Remove from S any element $s \in S$. $S - s$ is still a solution to the problem as every clause contains at least one element from S. Clearly this violates the minimality of S. The above argument holds for any intermediate stage in the algorithm. At any intermediate stage, note that U denotes the set of variables set to 1 so far in the partial assignment and B the set of clauses which do not contain any variable in U.

Theorem 3 *If the partial assignment U can be extended to a complete minimal solution U', then there exists a clause in B which contains at most one element from U'.*

Proof: Let A denote the set of clauses which contain one or more variables from the set U (the set of variables set to 1 in the partial assignment). Let W be the set of variables occurring in the set of clauses B (which do not contain any variable set to 1). Note that $U \cap W = \phi$. This means that setting any variable in W to 0 does not unsatisfy any clause in set A. To obtain a contradiction, assume that every clause in B contains at least two variables from the set U'. We can set any variable in U' to 0 without unsatisfying any of the previously satisfied clauses. This violates the fact that U' is minimal.   □

Next we show that the satisfiability of any subproblem when the algorithm terminates is easy to determine. Without loss of generality, we can assume that the algorithm terminates after k stages (else the satisfiability can be determined trivially). We argue that after k stages, there are at least k clauses of cardinality 2. Furthermore, the satisfiability of such an instance can be ascertained in polynomial time.

Lemma 4 *Let P be a k-NAESPI problem which contains at least k distinct clauses of size 2. Satisfiability of P can be determined in polynomial time.*

Proof: Without loss of generality, assume that the first k clauses are:

$$(a_1, b), (a_2, b), \ldots, (a_k, b)$$

Suppose that there exists a clause C which does not contain b. Then $a_i \in C, \forall i \in \{1, \ldots, n\}$, since every pair of clauses intersect. If such a clause C exists, then P is unsatisfiable, else P is satisfiable.   □

The algorithm moves from stage i to stage $i+1$ by picking a clause and setting some variable in it to 1 and every other variable to 0. The variable set to 1 is different from any of the variables set to 1 in stages 1 to i. This follows from the fact that at each stage the algorithm only considers clauses which do not have any variable set to 1.Thus after k stages, there are at least k clauses in which exactly one variable is set to 1 and the remaining variables set to 0. Also, the k variables which are set to 1 are all distinct. We next define the concept of contraction, and describe some properties of contractions. We use contraction to show that after k stages the problem has at least k distinct clauses of cardinality 2.

Let A be a subset of variables in the k-NAESPI problem.

Definition 7 *Contraction: For $A \subseteq V$ (V is the set of variables in problem P'), a contraction $A \to a$ occurs when every occurrence of a variable in A is replaced by a.*

The property of contractions stated in the proposition below follows from the definition.

Proposition 2 *Problem P' obtained by contraction $A \to a$ is satisfiable $\iff P$ has a solution S which contained all the variables in A.*

Contraction $A \to a$ implies that if P' has a solution, then all the variables in A (in P) can be forced to the same value. Lemma 5 below proves that after k stages, there are at least k clauses of cardinality 2 each.

Lemma 5 *After the algorithm has made k choices (and is in stage $k+1$) there exists a contraction such that the resulting problem P' has at least k clauses of cardinality 2.*

We have k clauses of the type:

$$(a_1, A_1), (a_2, A_2), \ldots, (a_k, A_k)$$

Each a_i, $i = 1, \ldots, k$, is a distinct variable that is set to 1. Each A_i, $i = 1, \ldots, k$, is the set of variables in a clause that are set to 0. As $A_1 = A_2 = \ldots = A_k = 0$, we can perform contraction $(A_1 \cup A_2 \cup \ldots \cup A_k) \to b$. We can therefore represent the k clauses as below:

$$(a_1, b), (a_2, b), \ldots, (a_k, b)$$

Each of the above k clauses is of cardinality 2.   □
We use Lemmas 4 and 5 to show that the algorithm terminates in $O(n^{2k+2})$ time.

Theorem 4 *The algorithm runs in $O(n^{2k+2})$ time.*

Proof: By Lemma 5 the algorithm needs at most k stages. In each stage the algorithm has to try at most n clauses., for each of which there are at most k assignments of type 10^* to be tried. Therefore the recurrence is:

$$T(k) = n \times k \times T(k-1)$$

which evaluates to $(n \times k)^k \le (n^2)^k$ as $k \le n$. As it takes $O(n^2)$ time to verify the solution, the time complexity is $O(n^{2k+2})$.   □

4   Linear Time algorithm for solving k-NAESPI

The algorithm is again recursive but instead of trying out every possible 10^* assignment for every clause, it tries out all the $2^k - 2$ contractions for each of some k clauses. The algorithm begins by choosing a clause of length greater than 2 and a contraction for it. It then removes all the clauses which are trivially satisfied (clauses which contain both the contracted variables). Suppose that we are in Stage $l+1$. The clauses which are of cardinality 2 are of the form shown below (Lemma 4). This is under the assumption that the contraction we made is extendible to a solution.

$$(a_1 \vee b) \wedge (a_2 \vee b) \wedge (. \vee b) \wedge (. \vee b) \wedge (a_l \vee b)$$

Without loss of generality, we assume that there is a clause which does not contain any of the variables from the set $\{a_1, \ldots, a_l\}$ else, we have a solution to the problem. This follows from the fact that each clause contains at least one of the variables from $\{a_1, \ldots, a_l\}$. Setting all the variables in $\{a_1, \ldots, a_l\}$ to 1 and rest of the variables to 0, results in a solution to the given instance. Let C be such a clause. For Stage $l+1$ we try out all the possible 2^k-2 contractions for Clause C. We need to argue that any contraction of C gives us a subproblem with $l+1$ distinct variables $a_1, a_2, \ldots, a_{l+1}$. Let A be the set of variables in C which are set to the same value and B the set of remaining variables in C (which are set to a value different from the value to which the variables in A are set). If $b \notin A$ then there exists a variable in B which is different from any of the $a_{i's}$. This is due to the fact that C does not contain any of the variables $a_1, a_2, \ldots, a_l$. Hence the clause obtained after the contraction is distinct. The case when $b \in A$ is symmetrical.

Formally the algorithm is stated below:

Algorithm

1. S is the set of distinct variables which belong to some clauses of size 2 and are forced to have the same value ($S = \{a_1, a_2, \ldots, a_l\}$ in the previous example). Initially $S = \Phi$.

2. Find a clause C such that C does not contain any variable in S. If no such clause exists then S intersects with all the clauses and we are done.
3. For each contraction (out of the $2^k - 2$ possible ones), update S, remove all the clauses which are trivially satisfied and goto Step 2.

Let us consider the projective plane example again.

Example 1.

$$(1 \vee 2 \vee 3) \wedge (3 \vee 4 \vee 5) \wedge (1 \vee 5 \vee 6) \wedge (1 \vee 4 \vee 7) \wedge (2 \vee 5 \vee 7) \wedge (3 \vee 6 \vee 7) \wedge (2 \vee 4 \vee 6)$$

Consider the first clause and a contraction in which $\{1, 2\}$ get the same value and 3 gets a value different from 1 and 2. Since $\{1, 2\}$ get the same value we can replace them with a new variable a. Hence, the modified problem is:

$$(a \vee 3) \wedge (3 \vee 4 \vee 5) \wedge (a \vee 5 \vee 6) \wedge (a \vee 4 \vee 7) \wedge (a \vee 5 \vee 7) \wedge (3 \vee 6 \vee 7) \wedge (a \vee 4 \vee 6)$$

and $S = \{a\}$. Let $(3 \vee 4 \vee 5)$ be the clause C (which does not contain a) for which we are going to try out all the possible contractions next. Possible contractions for C are $\{\{3, 4\}, \{3, 5\}, \{4, 5\}\}$. Let $\{3, 4\}$ be contracted to variable b. Then the subproblem obtained is;

$$(a \vee b) \wedge (b \vee 5) \wedge (a \vee 5 \vee 6) \wedge (a \vee b \vee 7) \wedge (a \vee 5 \vee 7) \wedge (b \vee 6 \vee 7) \wedge (a \vee b \vee 6)$$

S now is updated to $S \cup \{5\} = \{a, 5\}$. Also, the problem is not in minimal form as we have clauses which contain the clause $(a \vee b)$. The minimal subproblem is:

$$(a \vee b) \wedge (b \vee 5) \wedge (a \vee 5 \vee 6) \wedge (a \vee 5 \vee 7) \wedge (b \vee 6 \vee 7)$$

and so on.

The algorithm solves the subproblem recursively. If the subproblem is unsatisfiable then we try out the next contraction for the first clause. If all the contractions have been tried for the first clause then we return unsatisfiable.

Theorem 5 *The modified algorithm terminates in $O((2^k)^k \times n \times k)$ time.*

Proof: After k recursive calls we can use Lemma 5 to determine the satisfiability of the instance, as all the contracted clauses (of size 2) are distinct. Therefore the number of the times Lemma 5 is invoked is given by the following recurrence:

$$f(k) = 2^k f(k - 1)$$

As it takes $O(nk)$ time to determine the satisfiability in the invocation of Lemma 5, the running time of the algorithm is $O((2^k)^k \times n \times k)$ which is linear in n. □

5 c-bounded

In this section we describe polynomial time algorithms for the k-*NAESPI* and the NAESPI problem when any two pairs of clauses intersect in at most c variables. It should be noted that we treat k and c as constants.

Definition 8 (c-bounded NAESPI) *A (k-)NAESPI is c-bounded if every two clauses intersect in less than c+1 variables.*

As pointed out in Section 1. c-bounded k-NAESPI is of interest because this subclass of NAESPI arises naturally in designing coteries used to achieve mutual exclusion in distributed system with minimum number of messages.

For c-bounded k-NAESPI we show that there exists an algorithm which can determine the satisfiability of the input instance in $O(n^{c+1}k)$ time. We show an upper bound of k^{c+1} on the number of clauses (n) for c-bounded k-NAESPI which do not contain any solution of size strictly less than l. In this case the algorithm shown in Section 4. for solving k-NAESPI terminates in $O(k^{(c+1)k}n)$ time for c-bounded k-NAESPI. If there exists a solution of size at most c then we try out all the subsets of size c. As there are $O(n^c)$ subsets of size c and verifying the solution takes $O(nk)$ time, the total running time for this case is $O(n^{c+1}k)$. Since, $O(n^{c+1}k))$ dominates $O(k^{(c+1)k}n)$, c-bounded k-NAESPI can be solved in $O(n^{c+1}k))$ time.

For the c-bounded NAESPI we give an $O(n^{2c+2})$ algorithm for solving the problem. It should be noted that c-bounded k-NAESPI is a subclass of c-bounded NAESPI hence the latter results is weaker. Also, the techniques used in obtaining the respective results have no similarity whatsoever. Sections 5.1 and 5.2 describe the results for the c-bounded k-NAESPI and c-bounded NAESPI problems respectively.

5.1 c-bounded k-NAESPI

In this section we show that for a *c-bounded k-NAESPI*, the number of clauses $n \leq k^{c+1}$. The main tool used in obtaining the results is an auxiliary graph which is defined below.

Definition 9 (Auxiliary Graph) *An auxiliary graph is an edge labeled clique graph whose vertices are the clauses and the labels on edge (i,j) are the variables which are common to clauses i and j.*

Definition 10 (c-solvable) *A k-NAESPI is c-solvable if there exists a solution S such that $|S| \leq c$.*

Theorem 6 *For c-bounded k-NAESPI (which is not c-solvable) the number of clauses $n \leq k^{c+1}$.*

Proof: Let G be the auxiliary graph. For any c variables $x_1, \ldots, x_c$, let $K_1, \ldots, K_c$ be the corresponding cliques which contain labels $x_1, \ldots, x_c$. Let

$V_{1,c} = \cap_{i \in \{1..c\}} K_i$ be the set of vertices which are in cliques K_1 through K_c. We claim:

$$|V_{1,c}| \leq k$$

Let u be a vertex which is not in $K_1, \ldots, K_c$. Such a vertex should exist otherwise the given input is c-solvable. No two edges from u which are incident on any two vertices in $V_{1,c}$ can have the same label, else we have an edge which has $k+1$ labels on it. As $|u| \leq k$, we get $|V_{1,c}| \leq k$.

Now we bound the size of $\cap_{i \in \{1..c-1\}} K_i$. Let v be a vertex which does not belong to $\cap_{i \in \{1..c-1\}} K_i$ (v exists because the input is not $(c-1)$-solvable). Every edge from v onto $\cap_{i \in \{1..c-1\}} K_i$ has a label different from $x_1, \ldots, x_{c-1}$ (as $\cap_{i \in \{1..c-1\}} K_i$ is maximal). Let L be the set of labels on the edges incident from v onto $\cap_{i \in \{1..c-1\}} K_i$. Each label $l \in L$ can occur at most k times or we would have $|V_{1,c}| > k$.

Using the argument presented above, if $l \leq c$:

$$|\cap_{i \in \{1..l\}} K_i| \leq k^{c-l+1}$$

Now we are ready to bound the size of individual cliques K_i. Let u be the vertex not in K_i (such a vertex exists because the input is not 1-solvable). L is the set of labels on edges incident from u onto K_i. We know $|L| \leq k$ and $|K_i \cap K_j| \leq k^{c-1}$ for any label x_j. The maximum number of vertices in K_i is $\leq k^c$ (i.e. $l(x_i) \leq k^c$).

We also know that,

$$n \leq \sum_{x_i \in C} l(x_i)$$

Hence,

$$n \leq k^{c+1}$$

$\square$

In this section we have established that for instances of k-NAESPI which are c-bounded the number of clauses is $n \leq k^{c+1}$. Next we describe an $O(n^{2c+2})$ algorithm for c-bounded NAESPI.

5.2 c-bounded NAESPI

Definition 11 (c-bounded NAESPI) *An instance of NAESPI is called c-bounded if every pair of clauses intersect in at most c variables for some constant c.*

In this section we show that c-bounded NAESPI can be solved in $O(n^{2c+2})$ time. For a set of variables V an assignment of boolean values to the variables is called a 1^*0 assignment if all the variables in V except one are set to 1 and the remaining variable set to 0. If all but one variable are set to 0 then the assignment is called a 10^* assignment.

We use the following definitions in the subsequent subsections. A *solution* S to a given NAESPI is a subset of variables such that V intersects each clause in the input but does not contain any clause in the input. A solution S is called *minimal* if no proper subset of S is a solution. If V is the set of variables in the input instance then at times we refer to S as the set of variables which can be set to 1 and $V \setminus S$ is the set of variables which can be set to 0.

Given an instance of c-bounded NAESPI, without loss of generality, assume that the *minimal solution* contains $c+1$ variables at least, else the input instance is c-solvable and we can determine the solution in $O(n^{c+2})$ time. This follows because there are at most $O(n^c)$ hitting sets which could be defining the solution and it takes $O(n^2)$ time to verify if some subset is extendible to a solution.

Let $\{a_1, \ldots, a_c\}$ be the variables in the minimal solution. This implies the existence of c clauses $C_1 = (a_1 \vee A_1), C_2 = (a_2 \vee A_2), \ldots, C_c = (a_c \vee A_c)$, such that all the variables in the set $\cup_{i=1 \ldots c} A_i$ are set to 0 given the fact that the variables $a_1, a_2, \ldots, a_c$ have been set to 1. Once again we can partition the set of clauses in the input into two sets: P denotes the set of clauses which have at least one variable set to 1 and N denotes the set of clauses which have at least one variable set to 0 in our trial. Clauses which contain variables set to both 1 and 0 will be satisfied and are removed from further consideration. All the clauses in P contain every a_i as they have to intersect with every C_i. Clauses in N contain no variable set to 1.

Assume, $|P| \geq c + 2$, else we can try out all the $O(n^{c+1})$ possibilities and determine the solvability of the instance in $O(n^{2c+2})$ time. Once again, there are at most $O(n^{c+1})$ hitting sets and for each hitting set we spend $O(n^2)$ time to verify if the hitting set is indeed a solution.

Theorem 7 *Given N and P as defined above, the solvability of the input instance can be determined in polynomial time.*

Proof: It should be noted that all the uninstantiated variables in the set of clauses P are distinct. We are interested in finding a hitting set S of uninstantiated variables from P such that S does not contain any clause in N. If we have such a set S then, setting S to 0 and all the other variables to 1 leads to a solution.

Let l be the minimum number of uninstantiated variables in a clause in N. This implies that $|P| \leq l$, else there are two clauses in P which have an intersection in more than c variables. Furthermore every set of *(l-1)* uninstantiated variables from the set of variables in P does not contain any clause in N. This follows from the fact that l is the cardinality of the minimum-sized clause.

Let S_0, S_1 be two hitting sets of clauses in P, such that S_0 and S_1 differ in exacly one variable. If two such hitting sets do not exist, then all the variables are forced to have an assignment of values different from the variables a and b and the solvability of the instance can be determined easily. As S_0 and S_1 differ in only 1 variable and $|P| \geq c + 2$, $|S_0 \cap S_1| \geq c + 1$.

This implies that either S_0 or S_1 does not contain a clause in N. If both S_0 and S_1 contained a clause in N then there would be two clauses in N which intersect in more than c variables (note that each clause in N has at least $c+1$ variables). If S_0 is the hitting set which does not contain a clause in N, then setting all the variables in S_0 to 0 and the remaining variables to 1 leads to a solution to the input instance.

As there are n clauses of size at most n, determining the right set of clauses $C_1, \ldots, C_c$ and the 10^* assignments can take at most $\binom{n^2}{c} = O(n^{2c})$ time. As, it takes $O(n^2)$ time to verify a solution, the total running time for this case is $O(n^{2c+2})$.   □

The case where $|P| \leq c + 1$ is treated in the same way as, for the 2-bounded case. We try out all the $O(n^{c+1})$ minimal sets of variables in the set N which could be defining the solution. As it takes $O(n^2)$ time to verify if some subset of variables is a solution and given the fact that there are at most $O(n^{c+1})$ hitting sets, the total running time of the algorithm is $O(n^{2c+2})$. Hence, the running time of the algorithm is domainted by $O(n^{2c+2})$.

6   Conclusion

We established the equivalence of determining the satisfiability of the NAESPI problem and that of determining the self-duality of monotone boolean functions. We established the hardness of finding certain types of solutions to NAESPI. We also gave an alternate characterization of *almost self-dual* functions in terms of a subclass of NAESPI.

We provided an $O(2^{(k^2)}nk)$ algorithm for the NAESPI problem with n clauses and at most k variables per clause. We showed that the self-duality of instances in the class bounded by size studied by Eiter and Gottlob [8] can be determined in time linear in the number of clauses in the input, thereby strengthening their result. Domingo [7] recently showed that self-duality of boolean functions where each clause is bounded by $(\sqrt{\log n})$ can be solved in polynomial time. Our linear time algorithm for solving the clauses with bounded size infact solves the $(\sqrt{\log n})$ bounded self-duality problem in $O(n^2\sqrt{\log n})$ time, which is better bound then the algorithm of Domingo [7], $O(n^3)$.

For c-bounded k-NAESPI we showed that the number of clauses $n \leq k^{c+1}$. We also showed that c-bounded k-NAESPI can be solved in $O(n^{c+1}k)$ time. For c-bounded NAESPI we gave an $O(n^{2c+2})$ algorithm for determining the satisfiability of the problem. An open problem is to provide a polynomial time algorithm for the general NAESPI problem.

Acknowledgements: The authors would like to thank Tiko Kameda for helpful discussions and comments on an earlier version of this paper.

References

1. D. Barbara and H. Garcia-Molina. The vulnerability of vote assignments. *ACM Transactions on Computer Systems*, 4(3):187–213, Aug. 1986. 209
2. C. Berge. *Graphs and Hypergraphs*. North-Holland, 1973. 209, 210
3. J. Bioch and T. Ibaraki. Complexity of identification and dualization of positive boolean functions. *Information and Computation*, 123(1):50–63, 1995. 209
4. J. Bioch and T. Ibaraki. Decomposition of positive self-dual functions. *Discrete Mathematics*, 140:23–46, 1995. 209

5. J. C. Bioch and T. Ibaraki. Generating and approximating nondominated coteries. *IEEE Transactions on parallel and distributed systems*, 6(9):905–913, 1995. 209, 210, 213

6. E. Boros, P.L. Hammer, T. Ibaraki, and K. Kawakami. Identifying 2-monotonic positive boolean functions in polynomial time. In W.L. Hsu and R.C.T. Lee, editors, *Springer Lecture Notes in Computer Science 557*, International Symposium on Algorithms, Taipei, 104-115, 1991. 210

7. D. Carlos. Polynomial time algorithms for some self-duality problems. In *Proceedings of the Italian Conference on Algorithms*, March 1997. 209, 222

8. T. Eiter and G. Gottlob. Identifying the minimum transversals of a hypergraph and related problems. *Siam Journal of Computing*, 24(6):1278–1304, 1995. 209, 210, 222

9. Michael L. Fredman and Leonid Khachiyan. On the complexity of dualization of monotone disjunctive normal forms. *Journal of Algorithms*, 21(3):618–628, Nov. 1996. 209, 211

10. H. Garcia-Molina and D. Barbara. How to assign votes in a distributed system. *Journal of the ACM*, 32:841–860, 1985. 209

11. V. Gurvich and L. Khachiyan. Generating the irredundant conjunctive and disjunctive normal forms of monotone boolean functions. Technical Report LCSR-TR-251, Dept. of Computer Science, Rutgers Univ., Aug. 1995. 209

12. T. Ibaraki and T. Kameda. A boolean theory of coteries. *IEEE Transactions on Parallel and Distributed Systems*, pages 779–794, 1993. 210

13. K. Makino and T. Ibaraki. The maximum latency and identification of positive boolean functions. In D. Z. Du and X. S. Zhang, editors, *ISAAC 1994, Algorithms and Computation*, volume 834 of *Springer Lecture Notes in Computer Science*, pages 324–332. 210

14. H. Mannila and K. J. Räihä. An application of armstrong relations. *Journal of Computer and System Science*, 22:126–141, 1986. 209

15. C. Papadimitriou. *Computational Complexity*. Addison Wesley, 1994. 210

16. R. Reiter. A theory of diagnosis from first principles. *Artificial Intelligence*, 32:57–95, 1987. 209

Sharper Bounds for the Hardness of Prototype and Feature Selection

Richard Nock[1] and Marc Sebban[2]

[1] Université des Antilles-Guyane, Dépt Scientifique Interfacultaire, Campus de Schoelcher
97233 Schoelcher, France
Richard.Nock@martinique.univ-ag.fr
[2] Université des Antilles-Guyane, Dépt de Sciences Juridiques, Campus de Fouillole
97159 Pointe-à-Pitre, France
Marc.Sebban@univ-ag.fr

Abstract. As pointed out by Blum [Blu94], "nearly all results in Machine Learning [...] deal with problems of separating relevant from irrelevant information in some way". This paper is concerned with structural complexity issues regarding the selection of relevant Prototypes or Features. We give the first results proving that both problems can be much harder than expected in the literature for various notions of relevance. In particular, the worst-case bounds achievable by any efficient algorithm are proven to be very large, most of the time not so far from trivial bounds. We think these results give a theoretical justification for the numerous heuristic approaches found in the literature to cope with these problems.

1 Introduction

With the development and the popularization of new data acquisition technologies such as the World Wide Web (WWW), computer scientists have to analyze potentially huge data sets. The available technology to analyze data has been developed over the last decades, and covers a broad spectrum of techniques and algorithms. The overwhelming quantities of such easy data represent however a noisy material for learning systems, and filtering it to reveal its most informative content has become an important issue in the fields of Machine Learning (ML) and Data Mining.

In this paper, we are interested in two important aspects of this issue: the problem of selecting the most relevant examples (named prototypes), a problem to which we refer as "Prototype selection" (PS), and the problem of selecting the most relevant variables, a problem to which we refer as "Feature selection" (FS). Numerous works have addressed empirical results about efficient algorithms for PS and FS [Koh94, KS95, KS96, SN00a, SN00b, Ska94, WM97] and many others. However, in comparison, very few results have addressed the theoretical issues of

H. Arimura, S. Jain and A. Sharma (Eds.): ALT 2000, LNAI 1968, pp. 224–238, 2000.

both PS and FS, and more particularly have given insight into the hardness of FS and PS. This is an important problem because almost all efficient algorithms presented so far for PS or FS are heuristics, and no theoretical results are given for the guarantees they give on the selection process. The question of their behavior in the worst case is therefore of particular importance. Structural complexity theory can be helpful to prove lowerbounds valid for any time-efficient algorithm, and negative results for approximating optimization problems are important in that they may indicate we can stop looking for better algorithms [Bel96]. On some problems [KKLP97], they have even ruled out the existence of efficient approximation algorithms in the worst case.

In this paper, we are interested in PS and FS as optimization problems. So far, one theoretical result exists [BL97], which links the hardness of approximating FS and the hardness of approximating the MIN-SET-COVER problem. We are going to prove in that paper that PS and FS are very hard problems for various notions of what is "relevance", and our results go far beyond the negative results of [BL97]. The main difficulty in our approach is to capture the essential notions of relevance for PS and FS. As underlined in [BL97], there are many definitions for relevance, principally motivated by the question "relevant to what?", and addressing them separately would require large room space. However, these notions can be clustered according to different criteria, two of which seem to be of particular interest. Roughly speaking, relevance is generally to be understood with respect to a *distribution*, or with respect to a *concept*. While the former encompasses *information* measures, the latter can be concerned with the *target* concept (governing the labeling of the examples) or the *hypothesis* concept built by a further induction algorithm. In this work, we have chosen to address two notions of relevance, each representative of one cluster, for each of the PS and FS problems.

We prove for each of the four problems, that any time-efficient algorithm shall obtain very bad results in the worst case, much closer than expected to the "performances" of approaches consisting in *not* (or randomly) filtering the data ! From a practical point of view, we think our results give a theoretical justification to heuristic approaches of FS and PS. While these hardness results have the advantage of covering the basic notions of relevance found throughout the literature (of course by investigating four *particular* definitions of relevance), they have two technical commonpoints. First, the results are obtained by reduction from the same problem (MIN-SET-COVER), *but* they do *not* stem from a simple coding of the instance of MIN-SET-COVER. Second, the proofs are standardized: they all use the same reduction tool but in a different way. From a technical point of view, the reduction technique makes use of *blow-up reductions*, a class of reductions between optimization problems previously sparsely used in Computational Learning Theory [HJLT94, NJ98a, NJS98]. Informally, blow-up reductions (also related to *self-improving reductions*, [Aro94]) are reductions which can be made from a problem onto itself: the transformation is such that it depends on an integer d which is used to tune the hardness result: the higher d, the larger the inapproximability ratio obtained. Of course, there is a price to pay : the reduction time is also an increasing function of d; however, sometimes, it is possible to show that the inapproximability ratio can be blown-up *e.g.* up to *exponent* d, whereas the reduction time increases reasonably as a function of d [NJS98].

The remaining of this paper is organized as follows. After a short preliminary, the two remaining parts of the paper address separately PS and FS. Since all our results use reductions from the same problem, we detail one proof to explain the nature of *self-improving reductions*, and give proof sketches for the remaining results.

2   Preliminary

Let LS be some learning sample. Each element of LS is an example consisting of an observation and a class. We suppose that the observations are described using a set V of n Boolean $(0/1)$ variables, and there are only two classes, named "positive" (1) and "negative" (0) respectively. The basis for all our reductions is the minimization problem MIN-SET-COVER:

> NAME: MIN-SET-COVER.
> INSTANCE: a collection $C = \{c_1, c_2, ..., c_{|C|}\}$ of subsets of a finite set $S = \{s_1, s_2, ..., s_{|S|}\}$ ($|.|$ denotes the cardinality).
> SOLUTION: a set cover for S, *i.e.* a subset $C' \subseteq C$ such that every element of S belongs to at least one member of C.
> MEASURE: cardinality of the set cover, *i.e.* $|C'|$.

The central theorem which we use in all our results is the following one.

Theorem 1. *[ACG$^+$99, CK00] Unless $NP \subset DTIME[n^{\log\log n}]$, the problem* MIN-SET-COVER *is not approximable to within $(1 - \epsilon) \log |S|$ for any $\epsilon > 0$.*

By means of words, theorem 1 says that any (time) efficient algorithm shall not be able to break the logarithmic barrier $\log |S|$, that is, shall not beat significantly in the worst case the well-known *greedy set cover* approximation algorithm of [Joh74]. This algorithm guarantees to find a solution to any instance of MIN-SET-COVER whose cost, $|C'|$, is not larger than

$$\mathcal{O}(\log |S|) \times \text{opt}_{\text{MIN-SET-COVER}},$$

where opt$_{\text{MIN-SET-COVER}}$ is the minimal cost for this instance.
In order to state our results, we shall need particular complexity classes based on particular time requirement functions. We say that a function is *polylog(n)* if it is $\mathcal{O}(\log^c n)$ for some constant c, and quasi-polynomial, $QP(n)$, if it is $\mathcal{O}(n^{polylog(n)})$.

3   The Hardness of Approximating Prototype Selection

A simple and formal objective to prototype selection can be thought of as an information preserving problem as underlined in [BL97]. Fix some function f : $[0,1] \rightarrow [0,1]$ satisfying the following properties:

1. f is symmetric about $1/2$,
2. $f(1/2) = 1$ and $f(0) = f(1) = 0$,
3. f is concave.

Such functions are called *permissible* in [KM96]. Clearly, the binary entropy

$$H(x) = -x\log(x) - (1-x)\log(1-x),$$

the Gini criterion

$$G(x) = 4x(1-x)$$

[KM96] and the criterion

$$A(x) = 2\sqrt{x(1-x)}$$

used in [KM96, SS98] are all permissible. Define $p_1(LS)$ as the fraction of positive examples in LS, and $p_0(LS)$ as the fraction of negative examples in LS. Define $LS_{v=a}$ to be for some variable v the subset of LS in which all examples have value a ($\in \{0,1\}$) for v. Finally, define the quantity $I_f(v, LS)$ defined as

$$I_f(v, LS) = f(p_1(LS)) - \left(\frac{|LS_{v=1}|}{|LS|} f(p_1(LS_{v=1})) + \frac{|LS_{v=0}|}{|LS|} f(p_1(LS_{v=0})) \right)$$

This quantity, with f replaced by the functions $H(x), G(x)$ or $A(x)$, represents the common information measure to split the internal nodes of decision trees in all state-of-the-art decision tree learning algorithms (see for example [BFOS84, KM96, Mit97, Qui94, SS98]).

One objective in prototype selection can be to reduce the number of examples in LS while ensuring that any informative variable before will remain informative after the removal. The corresponding optimization problem, which we call MIN-PS$_f$ (for any f belonging to the category fixed above), is the following one:

NAME: MIN-PS$_f$
INSTANCE: a learning sample LS of examples described over a set of n variables $V = \{v_1, v_2, ..., v_n\}$.
SOLUTION: a subset LS' of LS such that $\forall 1 \leq i \leq n, I_f(v_i, LS) > 0 \Rightarrow I_f(v_i, LS') > 0$.
MEASURE: $|LS'|$.

There are two components in the self-improving reduction. The first one is to prove a basic inapproximability theorem. The second one, an *amplification lemma*, "blows-up" the result of the theorem. Then, we give some consequences illustrating the power of the amplification lemma.

Theorem 2. *Unless $NP \subset DTIME[n^{\log \log n}]$, MIN-PS$_f$ is not approximable to within $(1 - \epsilon) \log n$ for any $\epsilon > 0$.*

Proof. We show that MIN-PS$_f$ is as hard to approximate as MIN-SET-COVER: any solution to MIN-SET-COVER can be polynomially translated to a solution to MIN-PS$_f$ of the same cost, and reciprocally. Given an instance of MIN-SET-COVER, we build a set LS of $|C|$ positive examples and 1 negative example, each described over $|S|$ variables. We define a set $\{v_1, v_2, ..., v_{|S|}\}$ of Boolean variables, in one-to-one correspondence with the elements of S. The negative example is the all-0 example. Each positive example is denoted $e_1, e_2, ..., e_{|C|}$. We construct each positive example e_j so that it encodes the content of the corresponding set c_j of C. Namely, $e_j[k]$ is 1 iff $s_k \in c_j$, and 0 otherwise. Here we suppose obviously that each element of S is element of at least one element of C, which means that $\forall 1 \leq i \leq n, I_f(v_i, LS) > 0$. Suppose there exists a solution to MIN-SET-COVER of cost c. Then, we put in LS' the negative example, and all positive examples corresponding to the solution to MIN-SET-COVER. We see that for any variable v_j, there exists some positive example of LS' having 1 in its jth component, since otherwise the solution to MIN-SET-COVER would not cover the elements of S. It is straightforward to check that $\forall 1 \leq i \leq n, I_f(v_i, LS') > 0$, which means that LS' is a solution to MIN-PS$_f$ having cost $c + 1$.

Now, suppose that there exists a feasible solution to MIN-PS$_f$, of size c. There must be the negative example inside LS' since otherwise we would have $\forall 1 \leq i \leq n, I_f(v_i, LS') = 0$. Consider all elements of C corresponding to the $c - 1$ positive examples of LS'. If some element s_i of S were not covered, the variable v_i would be assigned to zero over all examples of LS', be they positive or negative. In other words, we would have $I_f(v_i, LS') = 0$, which is impossible. In other words, we have build a solution of MIN-SET-COVER of cost $c - 1$.

If we denote opt$_{\text{MIN-SET-COVER}}$ and opt$_{\text{MIN-PS}}$ the optimal costs of the problems, we have immediately opt$_{\text{MIN-PS}} =$ opt$_{\text{MIN-SET-COVER}} + 1$. A possible interpretation of theorem 1 is the following one [Aro94]: there exists some $\mathcal{O}(n^{\log \log n})$-time reduction from some NP-hard problem, say "SAT" for example, to MIN-SET-COVER, such that

- to any satisfiable instance of "SAT" corresponds a solution to MIN-SET-COVER whose cost is α,
- unsatisfiable instance of "SAT" are such that any feasible solution to MIN-SET-COVER will be of cost $> \alpha(1 - \epsilon) \log |S|$ for any $\epsilon > 0$.

This property is also called a *hard gap* in [Bel96].

If we consider the reduction from MIN-SET-COVER to MIN-PS$_f$, we see that the ratio between unsatisfiable and satisfiable instances of "SAT" is now

$$\rho = \frac{\alpha(1 - \epsilon) \log n + 1}{\alpha + 1}$$

For any $\epsilon' > 0$, if we choose $0 < \epsilon < \epsilon'$ (this is authorized by theorem 1), we have $\rho > (1 - \epsilon') \log n$ for MIN-PS$_f$, at least for sufficiently large instances of

"SAT". This concludes the proof of the theorem.   ∎

The amplification lemma is based on the following self-improving reduction. Fix some integer value $d > 1$. Suppose we take again the instance of MIN-SET-COVER, but we create $|S|^d$ variables instead of the initial $|S|$. Each variable represents now a d-tuple of examples. Suppose we number the variables $v_{i_1,i_2,\dots,i_d}$ with $i_1, i_2, \dots, i_d \in \{1, 2, \dots, |S|\}$, to represent the corresponding examples. The $|C| + 1$ old examples are replaced by $|C|^d + 1$ examples described over these variables, as follows:

- for any possible d-tuple $(c_{j_1}, c_{j_2}, \dots, c_{j_d})$ of elements of C, we create a positive example $e_{j_1, j_2, \dots, j_d}$, having ones in variable $v_{i_1, i_2, \dots, i_d}$ iff

$$\forall k \in \{1, 2, \dots, d\}, s_{i_k} \in c_{j_k},$$

and zeroes everywhere else. Thus, the Hamming weight of the example's description is exactly $\prod_{k=1}^{d} |c_{j_k}|$. By this procedure, we create $|C|^d$ positive examples,
- we add the all-zero example, having negative class.

We call LS_d this new set of examples. Note that the time made for the reduction is no more than $\mathcal{O}(|S|^d |C|^d)$. The following lemma exhibits that the inapproximability ratio for MIN-PS$_f$ actually grows as a particular function of d provided d is confined to reasonable values, in order to keep an overall reduction time not greater than $\mathcal{O}(n^{\log \log n})$. Informally, this assumption allows to use the inapproximability ratio of theorem 1 for our reduction. For the sake of simplicity in stating the lemma, we say that the reduction is *feasible* to state that this assumption holds.

Lemma 1. *Unless* $NP \subset DTIME[n^{\log \log n}]$, *provided the reduction is feasible, then* MIN-PS$_f$ *is not approximable to within*

$$\left(\frac{(1 - \epsilon) \log n}{d} \right)^d$$

for any $\epsilon > 0$.

Proof. Again, we suppose obviously that each element of S is element of at least one element of C, which means that each variable $v_{i_1, i_2, \dots, i_d}$ has

$$I_f(v_{i_1, i_2, \dots, i_d}, LS_d) > 0$$

Note that any feasible solution to MIN-PS$_f$ contains the negative example (same reason as for theorem 2). Also, in any solution $C' = \{c'_1, c'_2, \dots, c'_{|C'|}\}$ to MIN-SET-COVER, the following property **P** is satisfied without loss of generality: any element of C belonging to it has at least one element (of S) which is present in no other element of C', since otherwise the solution could be transformed in polynomial time into a solution of lower cost (simply remove arbitrarily elements in C' to satisfy **P** while keeping a cover of S). As **P** is satisfied, we call any subset of cardinality $|C'|$ of S containing one such distinguished element for each element of C' a *distinguished* subset of S. Finally, remark that MIN-PS$_f$ is equivalent to the problem of covering the set S^d using elements of C^d, and the minimal number of positive examples in LS_d is exactly the minimal cost c' of the instance of this generalization of MIN-SET-COVER. But, since **P** holds, covering C^d requires to cover any d-tuple of distinguished subsets of S and because property **P** holds, c' is at least c^d where c is the optimal cost of the instance of MIN-SET-COVER. Also, if we take all d-tuples of elements of C' feasible solution to MIN-SET-COVER, we get a feasible solution to the generalization of MIN-SET-COVER, which leads to the equality $c' = c^d$.

If we denote opt$_{\text{MIN-PS}}$ the optimal cost of MIN-PS$_f$ on the new set of examples LS_d, we obtain that

$$\text{opt}_{\text{MIN-PS}} = (\text{opt}_{\text{MIN-SET-COVER}})^d + 1$$

Given that $n = |S|^d$, and using the same ideas as for theorem 2, we obtain the statement of the lemma. □

What can we hope to gain by using lemma 1, which was not already proven by theorem 2 ? It is easy to show that the largest inapproximability ratio authorized by the same complexity assumption is

$$\rho = \log^{\log\left(\frac{\log n^{1-\epsilon}}{\log\log n}\right)} n \qquad (1)$$

(by taking $d = \mathcal{O}(\log\log n)$), which implies the simpler one:

Theorem 3. *Unless* $NP \subset DTIME[n^{\log\log n}]$, MIN-PS$_f$ *is not approximable to within*

$$\log^{(1-\epsilon)\log\log n} n$$

for any $\epsilon > 0$.

Another widely encountered complexity hypothesis, stronger than the one of theorem 3, is that $NP \not\subset QP$ [CK00]. In that case, the result of theorem 3 becomes stronger:

Theorem 4. *Unless* $NP \subset QP$, $\exists \delta > 0$ *such that* MIN-PS$_f$ *is not approximable to within* n^δ.

Proof. We prove the result for $\delta < 1/e$, and take $d = (1-\delta)\log n$. A good choice of ϵ in theorem 2 proves the result. □

The preceeding model takes into account the information of the variables to select relevant prototypes. We now give a model for prototype selection based on the notion of relevance with respect to a concept. For any set of examples LS, denote as $\mathcal{C}_{opt}(LS)$ the set of concept representations having minimal size, and consistent with LS. The notion of size can be e.g. the overall number of variables of the concept (if a variable appears i times, it is counted i times). The nature of the concepts is not really important: these could be decision trees, decision lists, disjunctive normal form formulas, linear separators, as well as simple clauses. Our negative results will force the concepts of $\mathcal{C}_{opt}(LS)$ to belong to a particularly simple subclass, expressible in each class. This notion of relevance is closely related to a particular kind of ML algorithms in which we seek consistent formulas with limited size: Occam's razors [KV94, NJS98]. Formulated as an optimization problem, the MIN-PS problem is the following one:

NAME: MIN-PS.
INSTANCE: a learning sample LS of examples described over a set of variables $\{v_1, v_2, ..., v_n\}$.
SOLUTION: a subset LS' of LS such that $\mathcal{C}_{opt}(LS') \subseteq \mathcal{C}_{opt}(LS)$.
MEASURE: $|LS'|$.

By means of words, PS is a problem of reducing the number of examples while ensuring that concepts consistent and minimal with respect to the subset of prototypes will also be valid for the whole set of examples. Our first result on the inapproximability of this new version of MIN-PS is the following one.

Theorem 5. *Unless $NP \subset DTIME[n^{\log \log n}]$, MIN-PS is not approximable to within $(1 - \epsilon) \log n$ for any $\epsilon > 0$.*

Proof. (*sketch*) The proof resembles the one of theorem 2. Given an instance of MIN-SET-COVER, we build a set LS of $|S|$ positive examples and 1 negative example, each described over $|C|$ variables. We define a set $\{v_1, v_2, ..., v_{|C|}\}$ of Boolean variables, in one-to-one correspondence with the elements of C. The negative example is the all-0 example. Each positive example is denoted $e_1, e_2, ..., e_{|S|}$. We construct each positive example e_j so that it encodes the membership of s_j into each element of C. Namely, $e_j[k]$ is 1 iff $s_j \in c_k$, and 0 otherwise. Similarly to theorem 2, the least number of examples which can be kept is exactly the cost of the optimal solution to MIN-SET-COVER, plus one.

The proof is similar to that of theorem 2, with the following remark on the minimal concepts. It can be shown that minimal concepts belonging to each of the classes cited before (trees, lists, etc.) will contain a number of variables equal to the minimal solution to MIN-SET-COVER, and each will be present only once. The reduction is indeed very generic and similar results were previously obtained by e.g. [NG95] (for linear separators and even multilinear polynomials), [NJ98b] (for decision lists), [HR76, HJLT94] (for decision trees), [Noc98] (for Disjunctive Normal Form formulas and simple clauses). From that, all minimal concepts will be equivalent to a simple clause whose variables correspond to C'. Property **P** in lemma 1 can still be used. $\qquad\square$

The amplification lemma follows from a particular self-improving reduction. Again, fix some integer value $d > 1$. Suppose we take again the instance of MIN-SET-COVER, but we create $d|C|$ variables instead of the initial $|C|$. Each variable is written $v_{i,j}$ to denote the jth copy of initial variable i, with $i = 1, 2, ..., |C|$ and $j = 1, 2, ..., d$. The $|S| + 1$ old examples are replaced by $|S|^d + 1$ examples described over these variables, as follows:

- for any possible d-tuple $(s_{j_1}, s_{j_2}, ..., s_{j_d})$ of elements of S, we create a positive example $e_{j_1, j_2, ..., j_d}$, having ones in variable $v_{k,l}$ iff $s_{j_i} \in c_k$, and zeroes everywhere else. By this procedure, we create $|C|^d$ positive examples,
- we add the all-zero example, having negative class.

We call LS_d this new set of examples. Note that the time made for the reduction is no more than $\mathcal{O}(|S|^d |C|^d)$. The following lemma is again stated under the hypothesis that the reduction is *feasible*, that is, takes no more time than $\mathcal{O}(n^{\log \log n})$, to keep the same complexity assumption as in theorem 1 (proof omitted).

Lemma 2. *Unless* $NP \subset DTIME[n^{\log \log n}]$, *provided the reduction is feasible, then* MIN-PS *is not approximable to within*

$$\left((1 - \epsilon) \log \left\lceil \frac{n}{d} \right\rceil \right)^d$$

for any $\epsilon > 0$.

What can we hope to gain by using lemma 2, which was not already proven by theorem 5 ? It is easy to show that the largest inapproximability ratio authorized by the same complexity assumption is now

$$\rho = \log^{\log \log \left(\frac{n}{\log \log n} \right)^{1-\epsilon}} n \tag{2}$$

which in turn implies the following one (greater than eq. 1):

Theorem 6. *Unless* $NP \subset DTIME[n^{\log \log n}]$, MIN-PS *is not approximable to within*

$$\log^{\log \log(n^{1-\epsilon})} n$$

for any $\epsilon > 0$.

With a slightly stronger hypothesis (and using $d = \mathcal{O}(polylog(n))$), we obtain

Theorem 7. *Unless* $NP \subset QP$, $\forall c > 0$, MIN-PS *is not approximable to within* $n^{\log^c n \log \log \log n}$.

With respect to 1, lemma 2 brings results much more negative provided stronger complexity assumptions are made. [PR94] make the very strong complexity assumption $NP \not\subset DTIME(2^{n^{\Omega(1)}})$. This is the strongest complexity assumption, since NP is definitely contained in $DTIME(2^{poly(n)})$. Using this hypothesis with $d = n^{\Omega(1)}$, we obtain the following, very strong result:

Theorem 8. *Unless* $NP \subset DTIME(2^{n^{\Omega(1)}})$, $\exists \gamma > 0$ *such that* MIN-PS *is not approximable to within*

$$2^{n^\gamma \log \log n}$$

What theorem 8 says is that approximating prototype selection up to exponential ratios

$$2^{n^{\gamma+o(1)}}$$

will be hard. Note that storing the examples would require 2^n examples in the worst case. Up to what is precisely hidden in the γ notation, approximating MIN-PS might not be efficient at all with respect to the storing of all examples.

4 The Hardness of Approximating Feature Selection

The first model of feature selection is related to the distribution of the examples in LS. Let V_i be the set of all variables except v_i, $i.e.$

$$V_i = \{v_1, v_2, ..., v_{i-1}, v_{i+1}, ..., v_n\}$$

Denote by $v_{\backslash i}$ a value assignment to all variables in V_i.

Definition 1. *[JKP94] A variable v_i is **strongly** relevant iff there exists some v, y and $v_{\backslash i}$ for which $\mathbf{Pr}(v_i = v, V_i = v_{\backslash i}) > 0$ such that*

$$\mathbf{Pr}(Y = y|v_i = v, V_i = v_{\backslash i}) \neq \mathbf{Pr}(Y = y|V_i = v_{\backslash i})$$

Definition 2. *[JKP94] A variable v_i is **weakly** relevant iff it is not strongly relevant, and there exists a subset of features V_i' of V_i for which there exists some v, y and $v_{\backslash i}'$ with $\mathbf{Pr}(v_i = v, V_i' = v_{\backslash i}') > 0$ such that*

$$\mathbf{Pr}(Y = y|v_i = v, V_i' = v_{\backslash i}') \neq \mathbf{Pr}(Y = y|V_i' = v_{\backslash i}')$$

In other words, a feature is weakly relevant if it becomes strongly relevant after having deleted some subset of features. We now show that under these two definitions are hidden algorithmic problems of very different complexities. We formulate the selection of relevant features as an optimization problem by focusing on the class conditional probabilities, following the definition of *coherency* which we give below:

Definition 3. *Given a whole set V of features with which LS is described, a subset V' of V is said to be **coherent** iff for any class y and any observation s described with V whose restriction to V' is noted s', we have*

$$\mathbf{Pr}(Y = y|V = s) = \mathbf{Pr}(Y = y|V' = s')$$

By means of words, coherency aims at keeping the class conditional probabilities between the whole set of variables and the selected subset. Formulated as an optimization problem, the MIN-S-FS problem is the following one:

- NAME: MIN-S-FS.
- INSTANCE: a learning sample LS of examples described over a set of variables $V = \{v_1, v_2, ..., v_n\}$.

- SOLUTION: a coherent subset V' of V containing strongly relevant features w.r.t. LS.
- MEASURE: $|V'|$.

The MIN-W-FS problem is the following one:

- NAME: MIN-W-FS.
- INSTANCE: a learning sample LS of examples described over a set of variables $V = \{v_1, v_2, ..., v_n\}$.
- SOLUTION: a coherent subset V' of V containing weakly relevant features w.r.t. LS.
- MEASURE: $|V'|$.

Since strong relevance for a variable is not influenced by its peers, we easily obtain the following theorem

Theorem 9. *Minimizing* MIN-S-FS *is polynomial.*

We now show that MIN-W-FS is much more difficult to approximate.

Theorem 10. *Unless* $NP \subset DTIME[n^{\log \log n}]$, MIN-W-FS *is not approximable to within* $(1 - \epsilon) \log n$ *for any* $\epsilon > 0$.

Proof. The reduction is the same as for theorem 5.   □

The result of theorem 10 shows that MIN-W-FS is hard, but it does not rule out the possibility of efficient feature selection algorithms, since the ratio of inapproximability is quite far from critical bounds of order n^γ (given that the number of features is n). We now show that theorem 10 is also subject to be amplified so that we can effectively remove the possibility of efficient feature selection. Fix some integer value $d > 1$. Suppose we take again the instance of MIN-SET-COVER of theorem 5, but we create $|C|^d$ variables instead of the initial $|C|$. Each variable represents now a d-tuple of elements of C. Suppose we number the variables $v_{i_1, i_2, ..., i_d}$ with $i_1, i_2, ..., i_d \in \{1, 2, ..., |C|\}$, to represent the corresponding elements of C. The $|S| + 1$ old examples are replaced by $|S|^d + 1$ examples described over these variables, as follows:

- for any possible d-tuple $(s_{j_1}, s_{j_2}, ..., s_{j_d})$ of elements of S, we create a positive example $e_{j_1, j_2, ..., j_d}$, having ones in variable $v_{i_1, i_2, ..., i_d}$ iff

$$\forall k \in \{1, 2, ..., d\}, s_{j_k} \in c_{j_k},$$

and zeroes everywhere else. By this procedure, we create $|S|^d$ positive examples,
- we add the all-zero example, having negative class.

We call LS_d this new set of examples. The reduction time is no more than $\mathcal{O}(|S|^d |C|^d)$. The following lemma is stated under the same hypothesis as for lemma 2.

Lemma 3. *Unless* $NP \subset DTIME[n^{\log\log n}]$, *provided the reduction is feasible,* MIN-W-FS *is not approximable to within*

$$\left(\frac{(1-\epsilon)\log n}{d}\right)^d$$

for any $\epsilon > 0$.

An immediate consequence is the following.

Theorem 11. *Unless* $NP \subset QP$, $\exists \delta > 0$ *such that* MIN-W-FS *is not approximable to within* n^δ.

In other words, up to what is be the maximal δ, theorem 11 shows that any non trivial algorithm cannot achieve a significant worst-case approximation of the MIN-W-FS problem, with respect to the simple keeping of all variables.

Our second model for feature relevance defines it with respect to the target concept [BL97].

Definition 4. *[BL97] A variable* v_i *is said to be relevant to the target concept* c *iff there exists a pair of examples* e_A *and* e_B *in the instance space such that their observations differ only in their assignment to* v_i *and they have a different class.*

From this, [BL97] define the following complexity measure.

Definition 5. *[BL97] Given a sample* LS *and a set of concept* $\mathcal{C}$, $r(LS,\mathcal{C})$ *is the number of features relevant using definition 4 to a concept in* C *that, out of all those whose error over* LS *is least, has the fewest relevant features.*

We call $\mathcal{C}_{min}(LS)$ to be the set of concepts from $\mathcal{C}$ whose error on LS is least. It is straightforward to check that in definition 5, $r(LS,\mathcal{C})$ defines the optimum of the following minimization problem.

NAME: MIN-FS.
INSTANCE: a learning sample LS of examples described over a set of variables $V = \{v_1, v_2, ..., v_n\}$, a class of concept $\mathcal{C}$.
SOLUTION: a subset V' of V such that there exists a concept in $\mathcal{C}_{min}(LS)$ which is described over V'.
MEASURE: the cardinality of the subset of V' consisting of relevant features according to definition 4.

A result stated in the paper of [BL97] says that MIN-FS is at least as hard to approximate as the MIN-SET-COVER problem (thus, we get the inapproximability ratio of theorem 1). On the other hand, the greedy set cover algorithm of [Joh74] can be used to approximate $r(LS,\mathcal{C})$ when $\mathcal{C}$ is chosen to be the set of monomials. If we follow [KV94] using a comment of [BL97], the number of variables chosen is no more than

$$r(LS, \text{monomials}) \times \log|LS|,$$

but $|LS|$ can theoretically be as large as 2^n. The question is therefore to what extent we can increase the inapproximability ratio to come as close as possible to the trivial barrier n (we keep all variables). Actually, it can easily be shown that the amplification result of lemma 1 still holds with the reduction allowing to prove the equivalence of MIN-SET-COVER and MIN-FS. Therefore, we get

Lemma 4. *Unless $NP \subset DTIME[n^{\log \log n}]$, provided the reduction is feasible, then* MIN-FS *is not approximable to within*

$$\left(\frac{(1 - \epsilon) \log n}{d} \right)^d$$

for any $\epsilon > 0$.

Similarly to theorem 4, we also get as a consequence:

Theorem 12. *Unless $NP \subset QP$, $\exists \delta > 0$ such that* MIN-FS *is not approximable to within n^δ.*

References

[ACG+99] G. Ausiello, P. Crescenzi, G. Gambosi, V. Kann, Marchetti Spaccamela A., and Protasi M. *Complexity and Approximation. Combinatorial Optimization Problems and their Approximability Properties*. Springer-Verlag, Berlin, 1999. 226

[Aro94] S. Arora. Probabilistic checking of proofs and hardness of approximation problems. Technical Report CS-TR-476-94, Princeton University, 1994. 225, 228

[Bel96] M. Bellare. Proof checking and Approximation: towards tight results. *SIGACT news*, 1996. 225, 228

[BFOS84] L. Breiman, J. H. Freidman, R. A. Olshen, and C. J. Stone. *Classification and Regression Trees*. Wadsworth, 1984. 227

[BL97] A. Blum and P. Langley. Selection of relevant features and examples in machine learning. *Artificial Intelligence*, pages 245–272, 1997. 225, 227, 235

[Blu94] A. Blum. Relevant examples and relevant features: Thoughts from computational learning theory. In *AAAI Fall Symposium (survey paper)*, 1994. 224

[CK00] P. Crescenzi and V. Kann. *A Compendium of NP-Optimization problems*. WWW-Available at http://www.nada.kth.se/~viggo/wwwcompendium/, 2000. 226, 230

[HJLT94] T. Hancock, T. Jiang, M. Li, and J. Tromp. Lower bounds on learning decision lists and trees. In *Proc. of the Symposium on Theoretical Aspects of Computer Science*, 1994. 225, 231

[HR76] L. Hyafil and R. Rivest. Constructing optimal decision trees is np-complete. *Inform. Process. Letters*, pages 15–17, 1976. 231

[JKP94] George H. John, Ron Kohavi, and Karl Pfleger. Irrelevant features and the subset selection problem. In *Proc. of the 11th International Conference on Machine Learning*, pages 121–129, 1994. 233

[Joh74]   D. S. Johnson. Approximation algorithms for combinatorial problems. *Journal of Computer and System Sci.*, pages 256–278, 1974. 226, 235

[KKLP97]   V. Kann, S. Khanna, J. Lagergren, and A. Panconesi. On the hardness of approximating MAX k-CUT and its dual. *Chicago Journal of Theoretical Computer Science*, 2, 1997. 225

[KM96]   M.J. Kearns and Y. Mansour. On the boosting ability of top-down decision tree learning algorithms. *Proceedings of the Twenty-Eighth Annual ACM Symposium on the Theory of Computing*, pages 459–468, 1996. 227

[Koh94]   R. Kohavi. Feature subset selection as search with probabilistic estimates. In *AAAI Fall Symposium on Relevance*, 1994. 224

[KS95]   R. Kohavi and D. Sommerfield. Feature subset selection using the wrapper model: overfitting and dynamic search space topology. In *First International Conference on Knowledge Discovery and Data Mining*, 1995. 224

[KS96]   D. Koller and R. M. Sahami. Toward optimal feature selection. In *Proc. of the 13 th International Conference on Machine Learning*, 1996. 224

[KV94]   M. J. Kearns and U. V. Vazirani. *An Introduction to Computational Learning Theory*. M.I.T. Press, 1994. 231, 235

[Mit97]   T. Mitchell. *Machine Learning*. McGraw-Hill, 1997. 227

[NG95]   R. Nock and O. Gascuel. On learning decision committees. In *Proc. of the 12 th International Conference on Machine Learning*, pages 413–420, 1995. 231

[NJ98a]   R. Nock and P. Jappy. Function-free horn clauses are hard to approximate. In *Proc. of the Eighth International Conference on Inductive Logic Programming*, pages 195–204, 1998. 225

[NJ98b]   R. Nock and P. Jappy. On the power of decision lists. In *Proc. of the 15 th International Conference on Machine Learning*, pages 413–420, 1998. 231

[NJS98]   R. Nock, P. Jappy, and J. Sallantin. Generalized Graph Colorability and Compressibility of Boolean Formulae. In *Proc. of the 9 th International Symp. on Algorithms and Computation*, pages 237–246, 1998. 225, 226, 231

[Noc98]   R. Nock. *Learning logical formulae having limited size : theoretical aspects, methods and results*. PhD thesis, Université Montpellier II, 1998. Also available as techreport RR-LIRMM-98014. 231

[PR94]   K. Pillaipakkamnatt and V. Raghavan. On the limits of proper learnability of subclasses of DNF formulae. In *Proc. of the 7 th International Conference on Computational Learning Theory*, pages 118–129, 1994. 232

[Qui94]   J. R. Quinlan. *C4.5 : programs for machine learning*. Morgan Kaufmann, 1994. 227

[Ska94]   D. B. Skalak. Prototype and feature selection by sampling and random mutation hill-climbing algorithms. In *Eleventh International Conference on Machine Learning*, pages 293–301, 1994. 224

[SN00a]   M. Sebban and R. Nock. Combining feature and prototype pruning by uncertainty minimization. In *Proc. of the 16 th International Conference on Uncertainty in Artificial Intelligence*, 2000. to appear. 224

[SN00b]   M. Sebban and R. Nock. Prototype selection as an information-preserving problem. In *Proc. of the 17 th International Conference on Machine Learning*, 2000. to appear. 224

[SS98]   R. E. Schapire and Y. Singer. Improved boosting algorithms using confidence-rated predictions. In *Proceedings of the Eleventh Annual ACM Conference on Computational Learning Theory*, pages 80–91, 1998. 227

[WM97]   D. Wilson and T. Martinez. Instance pruning techniques. In *Proc. of the 14 th International Conference on Machine Learning*, pages 404–411, 1997. 224

On the Hardness of Learning
Acyclic Conjunctive Queries

Kouichi Hirata *

Department of Artificial Intelligence
Kyushu Institute of Technology
Kawazu 680-4, Iizuka 820-8502, Japan
hirata@ai.kyutech.ac.jp

Abstract. A *conjunctive query problem* in relational database theory is a problem to determine whether or not a tuple belongs to the answer of a conjunctive query over a database. Here, a tuple and a conjunctive query are regarded as a ground atom and a nonrecursive function-free definite clause, respectively. While the conjunctive query problem is NP-complete in general, it becomes efficiently solvable if a conjunctive query is *acyclic*. Concerned with this problem, we investigate the learnability of *acyclic conjunctive queries* from an *instance* with a *j-database* which is a finite set of ground unit clauses containing at most *j*-ary predicate symbols. We deal with two kinds of instances, a *simple instance* as a set of ground atoms and an *extended instance* as a set of pairs of a ground atom and a *description*. Then, we show that, for each $j \geq 3$, there exist a *j*-database such that acyclic conjunctive queries are not polynomially predictable from an extended instance under the cryptographic assumptions. Also we show that, for each $n > 0$ and a polynomial p, there exists a $p(n)$-database of size $O(2^{p(n)})$ such that predicting Boolean formulae of size $p(n)$ over n variables reduces to predicting acyclic conjunctive queries from a simple instance. This result implies that, if we can ignore the size of a database, then acyclic conjunctive queries are not polynomially predictable from a simple instance under the cryptographic assumptions. Finally, we show that, if either $j = 1$, or $j = 2$ and the number of element of a database is at most l (≥ 0), then acyclic conjunctive queries are pac-learnable from a simple instance with *j*-databases.

1 Introduction

From the viewpoints of both computational/algorithmic learning theory and inductive logic programming, Džeroski *et al.* [11] have first shown the learnability of (first-order) definite programs, called *ij-determinate*. Furthermore, the series of their researches, Cohen [5–7, 9], Džeroski [11, 12, 21], Kietz [20–22] and Page [9, 26] have placed the theoretical researches for the learnability of logic programs in one of the main research topics in inductive logic programming. Recently, it has been deeply developed as [1, 18, 23, 24, 29, 30].

* This work is partially supported by Japan Society for the Promotion of Science, Grants-in-Aid for Encouragement of Young Scientists (A) 11780284.

H. Arimura, S. Jain and A. Sharma (Eds.): ALT 2000, LNAI 1968, pp. 238-250, 2000.
© Springer-Verlag Berlin Heidelberg 2000

On the other hand, a *conjunctive query problem* in relational database theory [2, 4, 14, 16, 34] is a problem to determine whether or not a *tuple* belongs to the answer of a *conjunctive query* over a *database*. Here, a tuple, a conjunctive query, and a database in relational database theory are regarded as a ground atom $e = p(t_1, \ldots, t_n)$, a nonrecursive function-free definite clause $C = p(x_1, \ldots, x_n) \leftarrow A_1, \ldots, A_m$, and a finite set B of ground unit clauses in inductive logic programming. Then, we can say that it is a problem to determine whether or not e is provable from C over B, i.e., $\{C\} \cup B \vdash e$.

Since database schemes in relational database theory can be viewed as *hypergraphs*, many researchers such as [2, 4, 13, 14, 16, 34] have widely investigated the properties of database schemes or hypergraphs, together with the *acyclicity* of them[1]. It is known that the acyclicity frequently makes intractable problems in cyclic cases tractable. The conjunctive query problem is such an example: While the conjunctive query problem is NP-complete in general [15], Yannakakis has shown that it becomes solvable in polynomial time if a conjunctive query is acyclic [34]. Recently, Gottlob *et al.* have improved the Yannakakis's result that it is LOGCFL-complete [16].

The above acyclicity of a conjunctive query C is formulated by the *associated hypergraph* $H(C) = (V, E)$ *to* C. Here, V consists of all variables occurring in C and E contains the set $var(A)$ of all variables in A for each atom A in C. Then, a conjunctive query C is *acyclic* if $H(C)$ is acyclic, and a hypergraph is *acyclic* if it is reduced to an empty hypergraph by *GYO-reduction* (see Section 2 below).

Concerned with the conjunctive query problem, in this paper, we investigate the learnability of *acyclic conjunctive queries* from an *instance* with a *j-database* which is a database containing at most *j*-ary predicate symbols.

According to Cohen [5–7], we deal with two kinds of instances, a *simple instance* and an *extended instance*. A simple instance, which is a general setting in learning theory, is a set of ground atoms. On the other hand, an extended instance, which is a proper setting for inductive logic programming, is a set of pairs of a ground atom and a *description*. Note that, if an extended instance is allowed, then many programs that are usually written with function symbols can be rewritten as function-free programs. Furthermore, some experimental learning systems such as FOIL [28] also impose a similar restriction.

The acyclic conjunctive query problem, which is LOGCFL-complete mentioned above, is corresponding to the *evaluation* problem of our learning problem. Schapire [32] has shown that, if the corresponding evaluation problem is NP-hard, then the learning problem is not pac-learnable unless NP⊆P/Poly. Then, we cannot apply Schapire's result to our problem. Furthermore, since all of the Cohen's hardness results are based on the prediction preserving reductions to *cyclic* conjunctive queries [6, 7], we cannot apply them to our problem directly, while our prediction preserving reduction is motivated by them.

In this paper, first we prepare some notions and definitions due to Cohen [5–7]. Then, we show that, for each $j \geq 3$, there exist a *j*-database such that acyclic conjunctive queries are not polynomially predictable from an *extended*

---

[1] Note here that the concept of acyclicity is different from one in [1, 29].

instance under the cryptographic assumptions. In contrast, we show that, for each $n > 0$ and a polynomial p, there exists a $p(n)$-ary database of size $O(2^{p(n)})$ such that predicting Boolean formulae of size $p(n)$ over n variables reduces to predicting acyclic conjunctive queries from a *simple instance*. This result implies that if *we can ignore the size of a database*, then acyclic conjunctive queries are not polynomially predictable from a *simple instance* under the cryptographic assumptions. Finally, we show that, if either $j = 1$, or $j = 2$ and the number of element of a database is at most l (≥ 0), then acyclic conjunctive queries are pac-learnable from a *simple instance* with j-databases.

Our hardness of learning acyclic conjunctive queries implies that they become a typical example that collapses the equivalence between pac-learnability and subsumption-efficiency. In general, the subsumption problem for nonrecursive function-free definite clauses is NP-complete [3, 15]. It is also known that, for both famous *ij-determinate* and *k-local* clauses, the subsumption problems for them are solvable in polynomial time [22] and they are pac-learnable from a simple (also an extended) instance [7, 9, 11]. In contrast, for acyclic conjunctive queries, while the subsumption problem is LOGCFL-complete [16], it is not polynomially predictable from an extended instance under the cryptographic assumptions.

2   Preliminaries

In this paper, a *term* is either a constant symbol or a variable. An *atom* is of the form $p(t_1, \ldots, t_n)$, where p is an n-ary predicate symbol and each t_i is a term. A *literal* is an atom or the negation of an atom. A *positive literal* is an atom and a *negative literal* is the negation of an atom. A *clause* is a finite set of literals. A *definite clause* is a clause containing one positive literal. A *unit clause* is a clause consisting of just one positive literal. By the definition of a term, a clause is always *function-free*.

A definite clause C is represented as

$$A \leftarrow A_1, \ldots, A_m \text{ or } A \leftarrow A_1 \wedge \ldots \wedge A_m,$$

where A and A_i ($1 \leq i \leq m$) are atoms. Here, an atom A is called the *head* of C and denoted by $hd(C)$, and a set $\{A_1, \ldots, A_m\}$ is called the *body* of C and denoted by $bd(C)$.

A definite clause C is *ground* if C contains no variables. A definite clause C is *nonrecursive* if each predicate symbol in $bd(C)$ is different from one of $hd(C)$, and *recursive* otherwise. Furthermore, a finite set of ground unit clauses is called a *database*. A database is called a *j-database* if the arity of predicate symbols in it is at most j.

According to the convention of relational database theory [2, 14, 16, 34], in this paper, we call a nonrecursive definite clause containing no constant symbols a *conjunctive query*.

Next, we formulate the concept of acyclicity. A hypergraph $H = (V, E)$ consists of a set V of vertices and a set $E \subseteq 2^V$ of hyperedges. For a hypergraph

$H = (V, E)$, the *GYO-reduct* $GYO(H)$ [2, 13, 14, 16] of H is the hypergraph obtained from H by repeatedly applying the following rules as long as possible:

1. Remove hyperedges that are empty or contained in other hyperedges;
2. Remove vertices that appear in ≤ 1 hyperedges.

Definition 1. A hypergraph H is called *acyclic* if $GYO(H)$ is the empty hypergraph, i.e., $GYO(H) = (\emptyset, \emptyset)$, and *cyclic* otherwise.

The *associated hypergraph* $H(C)$ to a conjunctive query C is a hypergraph $(var(C), \{var(L) \mid L \in C\})$, where $var(S)$ denotes the set of all variables occurring in S. Each hyperedge $\{var(L)\}$ is sometimes labeled by the predicate symbol of L.

Definition 2 (Gottlob *et al.* [16]). A conjunctive query C is called *acyclic* (*resp.*, *cyclic*) if the associated hypergraph $H(C)$ to C is acyclic (*resp.*, cyclic).

Example 1. Let C_1, C_2 and C_3 be the following conjunctive queries:

$$C_1 = p(x_1, x_2, x_3) \leftarrow q(x_1, y_1, \underline{y_2}), r(x_2, y_2, y_3), q(x_3, z_1, z_2), r(x_1, x_2, z_3),$$
$$C_2 = p(x_1, x_2, x_3) \leftarrow q(x_1, y_1, \underline{x_3}), r(x_2, y_2, y_3), q(x_3, z_1, z_2), r(x_1, x_2, z_3),$$
$$C_3 = p(x_1, x_2, x_3) \leftarrow s(x_1, x_2), s(x_2, x_3), s(x_3, x_1).$$

Then, the associated hypergraphs $H(C_1)$, $H(C_2)$ and $H(C_3)$ to C_1, C_2 and C_3 are described as Fig. 1. By the GYO-reduction, we can show that

$$GYO(H(C_1)) = (\{x_1, x_2, y_2\}, \{\{x_1, x_2\}, \{x_1, y_2\}, \{x_2, y_2\}\}) \neq \emptyset,$$

but $GYO(H(C_2)) = (\emptyset, \emptyset)$, so C_1 is cyclic but C_2 is acyclic. Furthermore, C_3 is acyclic, because the GYO-reduction first removes all hyperedges labeled by s from $H(C_3)$.

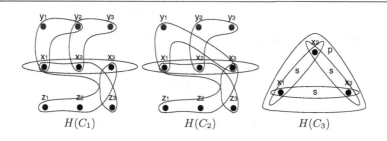

$$H(C_1) \qquad\qquad H(C_2) \qquad\qquad H(C_3)$$

Fig. 1. The associated hypergraphs $H(C_1)$, $H(C_2)$ and $H(C_3)$ to C_1, C_2 and C_3.

In this paper, the relation $\vdash$ denotes a usual provability relation; For a conjunctive query $C = A \leftarrow A_1, \ldots, A_m$, a database B and a ground atom e, $\{C\} \cup B \vdash e$ holds iff

1. $e \in B$ or
2. there exists a substitution θ such that $e = A\theta$ and $\{A_1\theta, \ldots, A_m\theta\} \subseteq B$.

Then, consider the following decision problem[2]:

ACQ (Acyclic Conjunctive Query) [16]
INSTANCE: An acyclic conjunctive query $C = p(x_1, \ldots, x_n) \leftarrow A_1, \ldots, A_m$, a database B, and a ground atom $e = p(t_1, \ldots, t_n)$.
QUESTION: Does $\{C\} \cup B \vdash e$ hold?

Theorem 1 (Gottlob *et al.* **[16]).** *The problem* **ACQ** *is LOGCFL-complete.*

The relationship between LOGCFL and other relevant complexity classes is summarized in the following chain of inclusions:

$$AC^0 \subseteq NC^1 \subseteq LOG \subseteq NLOG \subseteq LOGCFL \subseteq AC^1 \subseteq NC^2 \subseteq NC \subseteq P \subseteq NP,$$

where LOG denotes logspace and NLOG denotes nondeterministic logspace.

3   Models of Learnability

In this section, we introduce the models of learnability. The definitions and notations in this section are due to Cohen [5–7].

Let C be a conjunctive query and B be a database. A ground atom e is a *fact* of C if the predicate symbol of e is same as one of $hd(C)$. In this paper, assume that there exists no element of B of which predicate symbol is same as $hd(C)$.

For a conjunctive query C and a database B, the following set is called a *simple instance* of (C, B):

$$\{e \mid \{C\} \cup B \vdash e, e \text{ is a fact of } C\}.$$

For an element e of a simple instance of (C, B), we say that e is *covered by* (C, B).

Furthermore, we introduce a *description* D, which is a finite set of ground unit clauses. Then, the following set of pairs is called an *extended instance* of (C, B):

$$\{(e, D) \mid \{C\} \cup D \cup B \vdash e, e \text{ is a fact of } C\}.$$

For an element (e, D) of an extended instance of (C, B), we say that (e, D) is *covered by* (C, B).

In his learnability results, Cohen has adopted both the simple instance [7] and the extended instance [5, 6]. If the extended instance is allowed, then many programs that are usually written with function symbols can be rewritten as

---

[2] Gottlob *et al.* [16] have called the problem **ACQ** "Acyclic Conjunctive Query Output Tuple (ACQOT)".

function-free programs. There is also a close relationship between extended instances and "flattening" [10, 17, 24, 31]; Some experimental learning systems such as FOIL [28] also impose a similar restriction. See the papers [5, 6] for more detail.

In the following, we introduce some definitions and notions of learning theory.

Let X be a set, called a domain. Define a concept c over X to be a representation of some subset of X, and a language L to be a set of concepts. Associated with X and L are two *size complexity measures*. We will write the size complexity of some concept $c \in L$ or instance $e \in X$ as $|c|$ or $|e|$, and we will assume that this complexity measure is polynomially related to the number of bits needed to represent c or e. We use the notation X_n (*resp.*, L_n) to stand for the set of all elements of X (*resp.*, L) of size complexity no greater than n.

An *example* of c is a pair (e, b), where $b = 1$ if $e \in c$ and $b = 0$ otherwise. If D is a probability distribution function, a *sample of c from X drawn according to D* is a pair of multisets S^+, S^- drawn from the domain X according to D, S^+ containing only positive examples of c, and S^- containing only negative examples of c.

Definition 3. A language L is *polynomially predictable* if there exists an algorithm PACPREDICT and a polynomial function $m(1/\varepsilon, 1/\delta, n_e, n_t)$ so that for every $n_t > 0$, every $n_e > 0$, every $c \in L_{n_t}$, every ε ($0 \leq \varepsilon \leq 1$), every δ ($0 \leq \delta \leq 1$), and every probability distribution function D, PACPREDICT has the following behavior:

1. given a sample S^+, S^- of c from X_{n_e} drawn according to D and containing at least $m(1/\varepsilon, 1/\delta, n_e, n_t)$ examples, PACPREDICT outputs a hypothesis h such that

$$prob(D(h - c) + D(c - h) > \varepsilon) < \delta,$$

where the probability is taken over the possible samples S^+ and S^-.
2. PACPREDICT runs in time polynomial in $1/\varepsilon$, $1/\delta$, n_e, n_t, and the number of examples.
3. h can be evaluated in polynomial time.

The algorithm PACPREDICT is called a *prediction algorithm* for L and the function $m(1/\varepsilon, 1/\delta, n_e, n_t)$ is called the *sample complexity* of PACPREDICT.

Definition 4. A language L is *pac-learnable* if there exists an algorithm PACLEARN so that

1. PACLEARN satisfies all the requirements in Definition 3, and
2. on inputs S^+ and S^-, PACLEARN always outputs a hypothesis $h \in L$.

If L is pac-learnable, then L is polynomially predictable, but the converse does not hold in general; If L is not polynomially predictable, then L is not pac-learnable.

In this paper, a language L is regarded as some set of conjunctive queries. Furthermore, for a database B, $L[B]$ denotes the set of pairs of the form (C, B)

such that $C \in L$. Semantically, such a pair will denote either a simple or an extended instance.

For some set $\mathcal{B}$ of databases, $L[\mathcal{B}]$ denotes the set $\{L[B] \mid B \in \mathcal{B}\}$. Such a set of languages is called a *language family*. In particular, the set of j-databases is denoted by j-$\mathcal{B}$, and the set of databases consisting of at most l atoms by $\mathcal{B}_l$.

Definition 5. A language family $L[\mathcal{B}]$ is *polynomially predictable* if for every $B \in \mathcal{B}$ there exists a prediction algorithm PacPredict_B for $L[B]$. The pac-learnability of a language family is defined similarly.

We will deal with the language ACQ as the set of all acyclic conjunctive queries.

Schapire [32] has shown that, if the evaluation problem is NP-hard, then the learning problem is not pac-learnable unless $\text{NP} \subseteq \text{P/Poly}$. Since the problem **ACQ** is corresponding to an evaluation problem for $\text{ACQ}[\mathcal{B}]$ and it is LOGCFL-complete, we cannot apply Schapire's result to our learning problem $\text{ACQ}[\mathcal{B}]$.

Pitt and Warmuth [27] have introduced a notion of reducibility between prediction problems. *Prediction-preserving reducibility* is essentially a method of showing that one language is no harder to predict than another.

Definition 6 (Pitt & Warmuth [27]). Let L_i be a language over domain X_i ($i = 1, 2$). We say that *predicting L_1 reduces to predicting L_2*, denoted by $L_1 \unlhd L_2$, if there exists a function $f : X_1 \to X_2$ (called an *instance mapping*) and a function $g : L_1 \to L_2$ (called a *concept mapping*) satisfying the following conditions:

1. $x \in c$ iff $f(x) \in g(c)$;
2. the size complexity of g is polynomial in the size complexity of c;
3. $f(x)$ can be computed in polynomial time.

Theorem 2 (Pitt & Warmuth [27]). *Suppose that $L_1 \unlhd L_2$.*

1. *If L_2 is polynomially predictable, then so is L_1.*
2. *If L_1 is not polynomially predictable, then neither is L_2.*

For some polynomial p, let $\text{BF}_n^{p(n)}$ be the class of Boolean formulae over n variables of size at most $p(n)$, and let $\text{BF}^{p(n)} = \bigcup_{n \geq 1} \text{BF}_n^{p(n)}$. Then:

Theorem 3 (Kearns & Valiant [19]). $\text{BF}^{p(n)}$ *is not polynomially predictable under the cryptographic assumptions that inverting the RSA encryption function, recognizing quadratic residues and factoring Blum integers are solvable in polynomial time.*

4   The Hardness of Predicting Acyclic Conjunctive Queries

In this section, we discuss the hardness of predicting acyclic conjunctive queries. Note that the following proofs are motivated by Cohen (Theorem 5 in [6] and Theorem 9 in [7]).

If we can receive an example as a *ground clause*, Kietz [20, 21] implicitly has shown that acyclic conjunctive queries consisting of literals with at most j-ary predicate symbols ($j \geq 2$) are not pac-learnable unless RP = PSPACE, without databases as background knowledge. Under the same setting, Cohen [8] has strengthened this result that they are not polynomially predictable under the cryptographic assumptions.

On the other hand, by using Cohen's result (Theorem 3 in [6]), we can claim that, for each $j \geq 3$, the recursive version of ACQ[j-B] is not polynomially predictable from an extended instance under the cryptographic assumptions. In contrast, we obtain the following theorem.

Theorem 4. *For each $n \geq 0$, there exists a database $B \in$ 3-B such that* $\mathrm{BF}_n^{p(n)} \trianglelefteq$ ACQ[B] *from an extended instance.*

Proof. Let $e = e_1 \ldots e_n \in \{0,1\}^n$ be a truth assignment and $F \in \mathrm{BF}_n^{p(n)}$ be a Boolean formula of size polynomial $p(n)$ over Boolean variables $\{x_1, \ldots, x_n\}$.
First, construct the following database $B \in$ 3-B:

$$B = \left\{ \begin{array}{l} and(0,0,0),\ and(0,1,0),\ or(0,0,0),\ or(0,1,1),\ not(0,1) \\ and(1,0,0),\ and(1,1,1),\ or(1,0,1),\ or(1,1,1),\ not(1,0) \end{array} \right\}.$$

By the definition of an extended instance, an instance mapping f must map e to a fact and a description. Then, construct the following instance mapping f:

$$f(e) = (p(1), \{bit_1(e_1), \ldots, bit_n(e_n)\}).$$

Note that F is represented as a tree of size polynomial $p(n)$ such that each internal node is labeled by $\wedge$, $\vee$ or $\neg$, and each leaf is labeled by a Boolean variable in $\{x_1, \ldots, x_n\}$. Each internal node n_i of F ($1 \leq i \leq p(n)$) has one (n_i is labeled by $\neg$) or two (n_i is labeled by $\wedge$ or $\vee$) input variables and one output variable y_i. Let L_i be the following literals:

$$L_i = \left\{ \begin{array}{ll} and(z_{i1}, z_{i2}, y_i) & \text{if } n_i \text{ is labeled by } \wedge, \\ or(z_{i1}, z_{i2}, y_i) & \text{if } n_i \text{ is labeled by } \vee, \\ not(z_{i1}, y_i) & \text{if } n_i \text{ is labeled by } \neg. \end{array} \right.$$

Here, z_{i1} and z_{i2} denote input variables of n_i. Construct the following concept mapping g:

$$g(F) = p(y) \leftarrow (\textstyle\bigwedge_{1 \leq j \leq n} bit_j(x_j)), (\textstyle\bigwedge_{1 \leq i \leq p(n)} L_i),$$

where y is a variable in $(\bigwedge_{1 \leq i \leq p(n)} L_i)$ corresponding to an output of F.

Since F is represented as a tree, $g(F)$ is an acyclic conjunctive query. Furthermore, it holds that e satisfies F iff $f(e)$ is covered by $(g(F), B)$. In other words, e satisfies F iff

$$\{g(F)\} \cup \{bit_1(e_1), \ldots, bit_n(e_n)\} \cup B \vdash p(1).$$

Hence, the statement holds. $\square$

By incorporating Theorem 4 with Theorem 3, we obtain the following theorem:

Theorem 5. *For each $j \geq 3$, ACQ[j-$\mathcal{B}$] is not polynomially predictable from an extended instance under the cryptographic assumptions.*

Hence, we can conclude that not only the recursive version but also the non-recursive version of ACQ[j-$\mathcal{B}$] ($j \geq 3$) is not polynomially predictable from an extended instance under the cryptographic assumptions.

On the other hand, consider the predictability of ACQ[$\mathcal{B}$] from a simple instance.

Theorem 6. *For each $n \geq 0$, there exists a database $B \in p(n)$-$\mathcal{B}$ of size $O(2^{p(n)})$ such that $\mathrm{BF}_n^{p(n)} \unlhd \mathrm{ACQ}[B]$ from a simple instance.*

Proof. Let e and F be the same as Theorem 4. Also let B be the same as Theorem 4. Then, construct the following database B':

$$B' = B \cup \{ext(0,\ldots,0),\ldots,ext(1,\ldots,1)\}.$$

Here, *ext* is a new $p(n)$-ary predicate symbol. Note that the size of B' is $O(2^{p(n)})$.

By using the same literals L_i ($1 \leq i \leq p(n)$) as Theorem 4, construct an instance mapping f and a concept mapping g as follows:

$$f(e) = p(e_1,\ldots,e_n,1),$$
$$g(F) = p(x_1,\ldots,x_n,y) \leftarrow (\textstyle\bigwedge_{1\leq i\leq p(n)} L_i), ext(\overline{Y}).$$

Here, $\overline{Y}$ denotes the tuple of all $p(n)$ variables occurring in $\bigwedge_{1\leq i\leq p(n)} L_i$ and y is a variable in $(\bigwedge_{1\leq i\leq p(n)} L_i)$ corresponding to an output of F.

The GYO-reduct of the associated hypergraph $H(g(F))$ of $g(F)$ first removes all hyperedges except the hyperedge labeled by *ext* from $H(g(F))$, so $GYO(H(g(F))) = (\emptyset, \emptyset)$ (see Fig. 2). Then, $g(F)$ is an acyclic conjunctive query. Furthermore, it is obvious that e satisfies F iff $\{g(F)\} \cup B' \vdash f(e)$. Hence, the statement holds. $\qquad\square$

Hence, we can conclude that, if *we can ignore the size of a database*, then ACQ[$\mathcal{B}$] is not polynomially predictable from a simple instance under the cryptographic assumptions.

Let B be a database and f be an instance mapping in the proof of Theorem 6. Consider the following concept mapping g' similar as g:

$$g'(F) = p(x_1,\ldots,x_n,y) \leftarrow \textstyle\bigwedge_{1\leq i\leq p(n)} L_i.$$

Then, it holds that e satisfies F iff $\{g'(F)\} \cup B \vdash f(e)$.

Furthermore, consider the following instance mapping f'', concept mapping g'' and database B'':

$$f''(e) = p(e_1,\ldots,e_n),$$
$$g''(F) = p(x_1,\ldots,x_n) \leftarrow (\textstyle\bigwedge_{1\leq i\leq p(n)} L_i), true(y),$$
$$B'' = B \cup \{true(1)\}.$$

Here, y is a variable in $(\bigwedge_{1\leq i\leq p(n)} L_i)$ corresponding to an output of F. Then, it also holds that e satisfies F iff $\{g''(F)\} \cup B'' \vdash f''(e)$.

However, both $g'(F)$ and $g''(F)$ are *cyclic* as Fig. 2. In order to avoid to the cyclicity, we need to introduce a new $p(n)$-ary predicate symbol *ext* and a database B' of size $O(2^{p(n)})$ in the proof of Theorem 6.

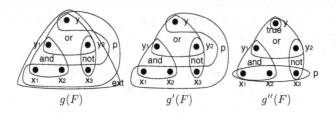

Fig. 2. The associated hypergraphs to $g(F)$, $g'(F)$ and $g''(F)$, where $F = (x_1 \wedge x_2) \vee \neg x_3$. Note that $g(F)$ is acyclic but $g'(F)$ and $g''(F)$ are cyclic.

5 Simple Learnable Subclasses of Acyclic Conjunctive Queries

Since the assumption of Theorem 6 is too strong, in this section, we discuss the learnable subclass of ACQ[j-$\mathcal{B}$] from a simple instance. First, the following theorem holds:

Theorem 7. ACQ[1-$\mathcal{DB}$] *is pac-learnable from a simple instance.*

Proof. We can assume that a target conjunctive query has no variables that occur in the body but not in the head. Let n be an arity of a target predicate p, and m be the number of distinct predicate symbols in $B \in$ 1-$\mathcal{DB}$, where m predicate symbols are denoted by $q_1, \ldots, q_m$. We set an initial hypothesis C as:

$$C = p(x_1, \ldots, x_n) \leftarrow \bigwedge_{1 \leq i \leq n} \bigwedge_{1 \leq j \leq m} q_j(x_i).$$

Then, by applying Valiant's technique of learning monomials [33] to C, the statement holds. □

Consider the case that $j = 2$. In the following, we discuss the learnability of ACQ[2-$\mathcal{B}_l$], where $\mathcal{B}_l$ denotes the set of databases consisting of at most l atoms.

We prepare some notions of *k-local conjunctive queries* according to [7,9]. A variable x is *adjacent to* a variable y if they appear in the same literal of the conjunctive query, and *connected to* y if either x is adjacent to y or there exists a variable z such that x is adjacent to z and z is connected to y. The *locale* of a variable x is the set of literals that contain either x or some variable connected to x. The *locality* of a variable is the cardinality of the largest locale of it. The *locality* of a conjunctive query is the cardinality of the largest locale of any variable in it. A conjunctive query is *k-local* if the locality of it is at most k, and we denote the set of all k-local conjunctive queries by k-LOCAL.

Theorem 8 (Cohen [7], Cohen & Page [9]). *For any fixed $k \geq 0$ and $j \geq 0$, k-LOCAL[j-$\mathcal{B}$] is pac-learnable from a simple instance.*

For $B \in 2\text{-}\mathcal{B}$, let G_B denote the labeled directed multigraph (V_B, E_B) such that V_B is a set of constant symbols in B and E_B is a set of pairs (a, b) labeled by q if there exists an atom $q(a, b) \in B$. Furthermore, we denote the length of longest path in G_B in which each edge occurs at most once by $len(G_B)$.

Lemma 1. *Let $B \in 2\text{-}\mathcal{B}$ and suppose that the predicate symbol p does not occur in B. Also let C be the following acyclic conjunctive query:*

$$C = p(x) \leftarrow q_1(x, y_1), q_2(y_1, y_2), \ldots, q_m(y_{m-1}, y_m),$$

where q_i occurs in B and $y_j \neq y_k$ $(j \neq k)$. For a ground atom $p(a)$, if $\{C\} \cup B \vdash p(a)$ and $m \geq len(G_B)$, then there exists an acyclic conjunctive query C':

$$C' = p(x) \leftarrow r_1(x, y_1), r_2(y_1, y_2), \ldots, r_{m'}(y_{m'-1}, y_{m'}),$$

such that r_i occurs in B, $y_j \neq y_k$ $(j \neq k)$, $\{C'\} \cup B \vdash p(a)$, and $m' \leq len(G_B)$.

Proof. By removing the literals corresponding to the cycle in G_B accessible from a in C, and by applying an adequate renaming substitution, we can obtain the above C'. Such a cycle does exist because $m \geq len(G_B)$. □

Theorem 9. *For a fixed $l \geq 0$, $ACQ[2\text{-}\mathcal{B}_l]$ is pac-learnable from a simple instance.*

Proof. For each $B \in \mathcal{B}_l$, let m_1 and m_2 be the number of atoms in B with unary and binary predicate symbols, respectively. Note that $m_1 + m_2 = l$. Let $C \in ACQ[B]$ be a target acyclic conjunctive query with the head $p(x_1, \ldots, x_n)$.

Since C is acyclic, there exist no two literals $q(y_1, y_2)$ and $r(z_1, z_2)$ in $bd(C)$ such that both q and r occur in B, y_1 and y_2 are connected to x_i $(1 \leq i \leq r)$, z_1 and z_2 are connected to x_j $(1 \leq j \leq r)$, $x_i \neq x_j$, and one of $y_1 = z_1$, $y_1 = z_2$, $y_2 = z_1$ or $y_2 = z_2$ holds. Then, for each variable x_i, any locale of x_i consisting of atoms with binary predicate symbols whose arguments' variables are distinct is regarded as a tree such that the root is labeled by x_i.

For each x_i, consider a complete m_2-ary tree T_i such that the root is labeled by x_i, each node is labeled by a mutually distinct new variable, each edge is labeled by possible binary predicate symbol in B (at most m_2), and the depth is at most $len(G_B)$ (by Lemma 1). Then, each locale of x_i is corresponding to a subtree of T_i rooted by x_i. Since $len(G_B) \leq m_2$, each locale contains at most $m_2^{m_2} \left((m_1 + m_2)^{m_2^{m_2}} \right) \leq l^{l^l+1}$ atoms. Here, the first and the second $m_2^{m_2}$ represent the maximum number of atoms with binary predicate symbols and one of nodes in a subtree of T associated with a locale. Also m_1 and m_2 in $m_1 + m_2$ represent the maximum number of atoms with unary predicate symbols and one of atoms with binary predicate symbols such that the first argument's variable is equal to the second one, respectively. Note here that the number of all locales of x_i, which is the total number of subtrees of T_i rooted by x_i, is independent from n.

The above discussion holds for each x_i $(1 \leq i \leq n)$. Hence, the target acyclic conjunctive query is l^{l^l+1}-local, by considering all locales constructed from T_i for each x_i. Since the number of all locales is bounded by polynomial on n, the statement holds by Theorem 8. □

Theorem 9 is a similar result as pac-learnability of arbitrary conjunctive queries with a *forest* introduced by Horváth and Turán [18]. In Theorem 9, a target conjunctive query is restricted to be acyclic but a database is given as an arbitrary 2-database. In contrast, in [18], a database is restricted to be a forest but a target conjunctive query is arbitrary.

6   Learnability and Subsumption-Efficiency

We say that a clause C *subsumes* another clause D if there exists a substitution θ such that $C\theta \subseteq D$. The *subsumption problem for a language* L is the problem of whether or not C subsumes D for each $C, D \in L$. As the corollary of the LOGCFL-completeness of **ACQ**, Gottlob *et al.* [16] have discussed the *subsumption problem* for ACQ.

In general, the subsumption problem for nonrecursive function-free definite clauses is NP-complete [3, 15]. As the tractable cases for the subsumption problem, it is known the following theorem. Here, i-DEPTHDETERM denotes the set of all *determinate* clauses of which the variable depth is at most i [11].

Theorem 10 (Kietz & Lübbe [22]; Gottlob *et al.* **[16]).** *The subsumption problems for i-DEPTHDETERM and k-LOCAL ($i, j, k \geq 0$) are solvable in polynomial time [22]. Also the subsumption problem for ACQ is LOGCFL-complete [16].*

It is also known that both i-DEPTHDETERM[j-$\mathcal{B}$] [11] and k-LOCAL[j-$\mathcal{B}$] [7, 9] ($i, j, k \geq 0$) are pac-learnable from a simple instance, so from an extended instance with an empty description. On the other hand, ACQ[j-$\mathcal{B}$] ($j \geq 3$) is not polynomially predictable from an extended instance under the cryptographic assumptions by Theorem 5. Hence, the language ACQ is a typical example that collapses the equivalence between pac-learnability from an extended instance and subsumption-efficiency.

7   Conclusion

In this paper, we have discussed the learnability for acyclic conjunctive queries. First, we have shown that, for each $j \geq 3$, ACQ[j-$\mathcal{B}$] is not polynomially predictable from an *extended instance* under the cryptographic assumptions. Also we have shown that, for each $n \geq 0$ and a polynomial p, there exists a database $B \in p(n)$-$\mathcal{B}$ of size $O(2^{p(n)})$ such that $\mathrm{BF}_n^{p(n)} \trianglelefteq \mathrm{ACQ}[B]$ from a *simple instance*. This implies that, if *we can ignore the size of a database*, then ACQ[$\mathcal{B}$] is not polynomially predictable from a simple instance under the cryptographic assumptions. Finally, we have shown that ACQ[1-$\mathcal{B}$] and ACQ[2-$\mathcal{B}_l$] ($l \geq 0$) are pac-learnable from a *simple instance*. It remains open whether ACQ[j-$\mathcal{B}$] ($j \geq 2$) and ACQ[j-$\mathcal{B}_l$] ($j \geq 3, l \geq 0$) are pac-learnable or not polynomially predictable from a simple instance.

In Section 6, we have claimed that the language ACQ collapses the equivalence between pac-learnability from an *extended* instance and subsumption-efficiency. It also remains open whether or not pac-learnability from a *simple* instance and subsumption-efficiency are equivalent to any language.

Various researches have investigated the learnability by using equivalence and membership queries such as [1, 23, 24, 30, 29]. Note that our result in this paper implies that $ACQ[j\text{-}\mathcal{B}]$ $(j \geq 3)$ is not learnable using equivalence queries alone. It is a future work to analyze the learnability of $ACQ[j\text{-}\mathcal{B}]$ $(j \geq 3)$ by using membership and equivalence queries, and by extending to one containing function symbols or recursion. It is also a future work to analyze the relationship between our acyclicity and the acyclicity introduced by [1, 29].

Fagin [14] has given the *degree* of acyclicity; α-acyclic, β-acyclic, γ-acyclic and Berge-acyclic. In particular, he has shown the following chain of implication for any hypergraph H: H is Berge-acyclic $\Rightarrow$ H is γ-acyclic $\Rightarrow$ H is β-acyclic $\Rightarrow$ H is α-acyclic (none of the reverse implication holds in general). Acyclicity in the literature such as [2, 4, 13, 16, 34] and also in this paper is corresponding to Fagin's α-acyclicity [14]. Note that none of the results in this paper implies the predictability of the other degrees of acyclicity. It is a future work to investigate the relationship between the degree of acyclicity and the learnability.

Acknowledgment

The author would like to thank Hiroki Arimura in Kyushu University for a motivation of this paper and insightful comments. He also would like to thank Akihiro Yamamoto in Hokkaido University and Shinichi Shimozono in Kyushu Institute of Technology for constructive discussion. Finally, he would like to thank anonymous referees of ALT2000 for valuable comments.

References

1. Arimura, H.:   *Learning acyclic first-order Horn sentences from entailment*, Proc. 8th ALT, LNAI **1316**, 432–445, 1997.
2. Beeri, C., Fagin, R., Maier, D. and Yannakakis, M.: *On the desirability of acyclic database schemes*, Journal of the ACM **30**, 479–513, 1983.
3. Baxter, L. D.: *The complexity of unification*, Doctoral Thesis, Department of Computer Science, University of Waterloo, 1977.
4. Chekuri, C. and Rajaraman, A.: *Conjunctive query containment revisited*, Theoretical Computer Science **239**, 211–229, 2000.
5. Cohen, W. W.: *Pac-learning recursive logic programs: Efficient algorithms*, Journal of Artificial Intelligence Research **2**, 501–539, 1995.
6. Cohen, W. W.: *Pac-learning recursive logic programs: Negative results*, Journal of Artificial Intelligence Research **2**, 541–573, 1995.
7. Cohen, W. W.:   *Pac-learning non-recursive Prolog clauses*,   Artificial Intelligence **79**, 1–38, 1995.
8. Cohen, W. W.: *The dual DFA learning problem: Hardness results for programming by demonstration and learning first-order representations*, Proc. 9th COLT, 29–40, 1996.

9. Cohen, W. W. and Page Jr., C. D.: *Polynomial learnability and inductive logic programming: Methods and results*, New Generation Computing **13**, 369–409, 1995.
10. De Raedt, L. and Džeroski, S.: *First-order jk-clausal theories are PAC-learnable*, Artificial Intelligence **70**, 375–392, 1994.
11. Džeroski, S., Muggleton, S. and Russell, S.: *PAC-learnability of determinate logic programs*, Proc. 5th COLT, 128–135, 1992.
12. Džeroski, S., Muggleton, S. and Russell, S.: *Learnability of constrained logic programs*, Proc. 6th ECML, LNAI **667**, 342–347, 1993.
13. Eiter, T. and Gottlob, G.: *Identifying the minimal transversals of a hypergraph and related problems*, SIAM Journal of Computing **24**, 1278–1304, 1995.
14. Fagin, R.: *Degrees of acyclicity for hypergraphs and relational database schemes*, Journal of the ACM **30**, 514–550, 1983.
15. Garey, M. R. and Johnson, D. S.: *Computers and intractability: A guide to the theory of NP-completeness*, W. H. Freeman and Company, 1979.
16. Gottlob, G., Leone, N. and Scarcello, F.: *The complexity of acyclic conjunctive queries*, Proc. 39th FOCS, 706–715, 1998.
17. Hirata, K.: *Flattening and implication*, Proc. 10th ALT, LNAI **1720**, 157–168, 1999.
18. Horváth, T. and Turán, G.: *Learning logic programs with structured background knowledge*, in De Raedt, L. (ed.): *Advances in inductive logic programming*, 172–191, 1996.
19. Kearns, M. and Valiant, L.: *Cryptographic limitations on learning Boolean formulae and finite automata*, Journal of the ACM **41**, 67–95, 1994.
20. Kietz, J.-U.: *Some lower bounds for the computational complexity of inductive logic programming*, Proc. 6th ECML, LNAI **667**, 115–123, 1993.
21. Kietz, J.-U. and Džeroski, S.: *Inductive logic programming and learnability*, SIGART Bulletin **5**, 22–32, 1994.
22. Kietz, J.- U. and Lübbe, M: *An efficient subsumption algorithm for inductive logic programming*, Proc. 11th ICML, 130–138, 1994.
23. Khardon, R.: *Learning function-free Horn expressions*, Proc. 11th COLT, 154–165, 1998.
24. Khardon, R.: *Learning range-restricted Horn expressions*, Proc. EuroCOLT99, LNAI **1572**, 111–125, 1999.
25. Muggleton, S. (*ed.*): *Inductive logic programming*, Academic Press, 1992.
26. Page Jr., C. D. and Frisch, A. M: *Generalization and learnability: A study of constrained atoms*, in [25], 129–161.
27. Pitt, L. and Warmuth, M. K.: *Prediction preserving reduction*, Journal of Computer System and Science **41**, 430–467, 1990.
28. Quinlan, J. R.: *Learning logical definitions from relations*, Machine Learning **5**, 239–266, 1990.
29. Reddy, C. and Tadepalli, P.: *Learning first-order acyclic Horn programs from entailment*, Proc. 8th ILP, LNAI **1446**, 23–37, 1998.
30. Reddy, C. and Tadepalli, P.: Learning Horn definitions: Theory and application to planning, New Generation Computing **17**, 77–98, 1999.
31. Rouveirol, C.: *Extensions of inversion of resolution applied to theory completion*, in [25], 63–92.
32. Schapire, E.: *The strength of weak learning*, Machine Learning **5**, 197–227, 1990.
33. Valiant, L.: *A theory of learnable*, Communications of the ACM **27**, 1134–1142, 1984.
34. Yannakakis, M.: *Algorithms for acyclic database schemes*, Proc. 7th VLDB, 82–94, 1981.

Dynamic Hand Gesture Recognition Based On Randomized Self-Organizing Map Algorithm

Tarek El.Tobely[1], Yuichiro Yoshiki[2], Ryuichi Tsuda[2], Naoyuki Tsuruta[2], and Makoto Amamiy[1]

[1] Department of Intelligent Systems, Graduate School of Information Science and Electrical Engineering, Kyushu University, Fukuoka, Japan.
6-1, Kasuga-Koen, Kasuga, Fukuoka 816, Japan
(`tobely, amamiya`)`@al.is.kyushu-u.ac.jp`
[2] Department of Electronic Engineering, Graduate School of Electronics Engineering, Fukuoka University, Fukuoka, Japan. 8-19-1, Nanakuma, Jonan, Fukuoka, 814-0180, Japan (`yoshiki , rtsuda, tsuruta`)`@mdmail.tl.fukuoka-u.ac.j`

Abstract. Gesture recognition is an appealing tool for natural interface with computers especially for physically impaired persons. In this paper, it is proposed to use Self-Organized Map (SOM) to recognize the posture images of hand gestures. Since the competition algorithm of SOM allows alleviating many difficulties associated with gesture recognition. However, it is required to reduce the recognition time of one image in SOM network to the range of normal video camera rates, this permits the network to accept dynamic input images and to perform on-line recognition for hand gestures. To achieve this, the Randomized Self-Organizing Map algorithm (RSOM) is proposed as a new recognition algorithm for SOM. With RSOM algorithm, the recognition time of one image reduced to 12.4 % of the normal SOM competition algorithm with 100 % accuracy and allowed the network to recognize images within the range of normal video rates. The experimental results to recognize six dynamic hand gestures using RSOM algorithm is presented.

1 Introduction

The goal of gesture understanding research is to redefine the way people interact with computers. By providing computers with the ability to understand gestures, speech, and facial expressions, it is possible to bring human-computer interaction closer to human-human interaction. However, the research in gesture recognition can be divided into image-based systems and instrument glove-based systems. The image based gesture recognition systems is considered as passive input systems that usually employ one or more cameras to capture human motions. While in the glove-based systems, the user requires to wear glove-like instrument, which is equipped with sensors on the back of finger joints to detect the finger flex and extension [1]. In this work, image-based gesture recognition system is used to recognize different hand gestures using SOM network. Where, each gesture is treated as a set of consequence postures. These postures are used

H. Arimura, S. Jain and A. Sharma (Eds.): ALT 2000, LNAI 1968, pp. 252-263, 2000.

in constructing the features map of SOM network. Indeed, the competition algorithm of SOM network can easily be modified to alleviate some critical problems in gesture recognition systems such as gesture start-end points, temporal and spatial variances, and postures ambiguity. In image-based gesture recognition systems, visual methods using some images features are divided into two major techniques: the first uses the projected position, and the second uses the motion information [2]. Some other methods [3] can estimate human gestures from silhouettes using the idea of synthesis without extracting the features. With SOM, the recognition process can use a technique similar to silhouette recognition. However, the competition algorithm of SOM allows recognizing the images without modifying its gray levels. So, the input image will be applied to the network as it is, and the features map neuron that has maximum similarity between its codebook and this input will be selected as the winner neuron.

In SOM competition, the winner computation depends on the numbers of input neurons and feature map neurons. So, if the dimensionality n of input space is high and the number of feature map neurons m is large, the required computations to answer the winner category is very large, in the order of nm. Because of that, SOM is not easily affordable to most dynamic image recognition applications where the input images are taken from video camera. In this paper, it is proposed to apply new recognition algorithm to SOM network. The algorithm is called Randomized Self-Organizing Map (RSOM). In RSOM algorithm, the winner competition is applied in two phases, the first uses random subset of input image to select a primary winner, and the second search for the winner in the set of neurons neighbor to the primary winner. RSOM algorithm applied to recognize six-hand gestures of Jan-Ken-Pon game. The results showed that with RSOM algorithm, the recognition time of one image reduced to the range of normal video rate, and the network could recognize dynamic gesture images.

In the next section, our proposal to use SOM in gesture recognition is presented. Then, in sections 3 and 4, the RSOM competition algorithm and its statistical analysis are explained. In section 5, the application of RSOM algorithm to recognize dynamic hand gestures is presented. Finally, the conclusion and discussion are given in section 6.

2   SOM Gesture Recognition System

Self-Organizing neural networks are biologically motivated by the ability of the brain to map outside world into the cortex, where nearby stimuli are coded on nearby cortical areas. Kohonen (1982) has proposed a simple algorithm for the formation of such mapping. A sequence of inputs is presented to the network for which synaptic weights are then updated to eventually reproduce the input probability distribution as closely as possible [4]. SOM competition in Euclidean space runs as follow: Apply the input to the network. Then, measure the Euclidean distance between the input pattern and the codebooks of all features map neurons. Finally, the neuron with minimum distance is considered as the winner. During SOM learning scheme, the network can visualize or project high dimensional input space into two-dimensional feature map while preserving the topological relations. Moreover, the point density function of the feature map codebook approximates some monotonic function of the probability density function of the input learning data. Introducing SOM network to gesture recognition applications requires faster recognition algorithm so that it can accept dynamic gesture and implement on-line gesture recognition. Also, it is proposed to decompose each gesture into a sequence of postures. The postures can be recognized using SOM competition algorithm. After that, a pattern matching for each sequence of postures can be used to designate the meaning of the gesture given by the input images.

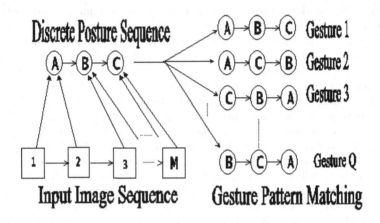

Fig. 1. SOM gesture recognition system, discrete posture recognition by SOM network, then gesture definition by pattern matching algorithm.

Figure 1 shows a complete SOM gesture system divided into two stages. The first convert the input images sequence into discrete posture states, and the second apply pattern matching algorithm for each set of discrete posture sequence to give the gesture meaning of the input image. The first stage can be implemented using SOM network, where the network is constructed to recognize the discrete postures of all gestures.

In general, any gesture recognition system has many critical problems such as gesture start-end points, temporal and spatial variance, and gesture ambiguity. The next subsections present how SOM gesture recognition system can overcome these difficulties.

2.1   Gesture Start-End Points

Start-end point problem is very important for continuos gestures recognition. It is required to discriminate between the gesture postures and the transition from the end point of one gesture to the start point of the next. Since, SOM select winner for any input images even if this image does not belong to any gesture. For that, the concept of competition threshold is proposed. Where, the input image is considered as posture if its competition distance is less than certain threshold value. This can filter out the transition images from gesture images.

2.2 Temporal and Spatial Variance

Temporal variance and spatial variance are two important factors in any gesture recognition system. Temporal variance is due to the varying period to perform the gesture. However, SOM gesture recognition system is insensitive to the speed of the gestures. Since the network accepts discrete input images and converts to discrete postures sequence. Therefore, if the same gesture is given to the network in fast or slow speed, SOM network will convert it into the same discrete posture sequence. Gesture spatial variance means the different scales or size of shape in the gestures. To avoid this problem, it is recommended to construct the network feature map using different variety for each posture. In this case, the network can tolerate the spatial variance between different users.

2.3 Posture Ambiguity

Some postures used in the system may be quite similar to another postures. To overcome this problem, it is recommended to associate prediction technique to the recognition process. The prediction process is controlled using different conditional probability equations as used in natural language processing systems [5] or speech recognition systems [6]. In this case, the network can give a sequence of three winners for each image, and the prediction system can select the neuron with maximum probability as the winner.

3 RSOM Competition

The winner searching in SOM networks depends on measuring the similarity between the input and the codebook of all features map neurons. Then, the neuron with maximum similarity is selected as the winner. Different competition scheme can be used to measure this similarity such as correlation, direction cosine, or Euclidean distance. However, the winner searching computation increases as the network size increases. This is the main motivation to modify the normal recognition algorithm of SOM network, the new proposed algorithm is called Randomized Self-Organizing Map (RSOM) algorithm. In this algorithm, the winner competition is less depending on the network size and spends shorter time in winner searching. However, RSOM is applied for winner searching on SOM networks that constructed using its normal competition algorithm.

During SOM learning scheme, similar inputs are mapped in a contiguous location on the network feature map. Therefore, it is possible to divide the feature map into subsets of contiguous clusters. Where the neighbor neurons with similar codebook are belong to the same cluster, this in fact the main foundation of RSOM algorithm.

Before implementing RSOM algorithm, it is required to apply the following off-line computations:

- Divide the network feature map into continuous subsets of clusters.
- From each cluster, select one neuron, usually in its center, as the cluster representative.

In gesture recognition applications, the division of feature map into different clusters can be applied manually. Since, in such applications, the codebook of SOM feature map is coded into the image it represents. Therefore, it is possible to define the set of neurons in each cluster by viewing the codebook of the feature map neurons as image. However, the automatic division of feature map into clusters is also possible by using algorithm similar to the LVQ algorithm [7].

The on-line competitions of RSOM are done in two phases: The first phase uses subset of the input image to estimate the position of the winner on the feature map; the winner in this phase is called the winner candidates, and its competition runs as follow:

- Select simple random sample S from the input image with size k and apply to the network.
- With any competition scheme, apply the competition between the pixels in S and the corresponding codebooks of each cluster representative in the network
- The cluster of the winner selected from this competition is considered as the cluster candidates.
- With the same competition scheme, apply the competition between the pixels in S and the corresponding codebooks of all neurons in the cluster candidate.
- The winner selected from this competition is called the winner candidates.

In the second phase, the entire input image pixels are used to search for the winner in the set of feature map neurons neighbor to the winner candidate. The winner selected from this phase is considered as the final SOM winner. The competition in this phase runs as follow:

- Input all the image pixels to the network.
- With the same competition scheme used in the first phase, apply the competition between the set of feature map neurons neighbor to the winner candidate.
- If the competition threshold condition is satisfied, consider the selected winner as the final SOM winner. Otherwise, neglect this winner and consider the input image as gesture transition image.

As will be explained in the next section, the size of the random subset S depends on the standard deviation and pixels distribution of the input image. In addition, the width of the winner candidate's neighbor neurons depends mainly on the sample size k.

4   Competition Parameters

The competition in RSOM algorithm depends on three main parameters, the Pixel Usage Ratio (PUR), the Neighborhood Range (NR), and the Competition Threshold (CT). The PUR represents the ratio between the randomly selected pixels to the total image pixels. Those selected pixels are used in the first phase of RSOM to find the winner candidate. While, the NR defines the size of the winner candidate neighborhood function. During the second phase competition of RSOM, the final winner is selected from this NR set. The winner selected from this phase is considered as gestures posture if the competition value satisfies the CT value, otherwise the winner will be neglected, and the input image is considered as gesture transition image.

In the first competition phase of RSOM, the similarity between the input image and the codebook of feature map neurons is measured using Euclidean distance for the subset of input image.

$$D_j = \sum_{i=1, i \in S}^{n} (\mu_{ij} - X_i)^2, \ \ j = 1, \ldots, m \tag{1}$$

Where, D_j represents the distance between the input image and the codebook of neuron j, S is the randomly selected subset of image pixels, μ_{ij} is the weight between the input neuron i and the output neuron j, n is the number of input pixels, m is the number of feature map neurons, and X_i is the gray level value of pixel i in the input image. The winner candidate WC is selected as the neuron with minimum Euclidean distance.

$$D_{WC} = \min_{j=1}^{m}(D_j), \ \ j = 1, \ldots, m \tag{2}$$

The question of how large the sample is required to select arises now. To select a larger sample than the requirements to achieve the desired results is wasteful of the recognition time. In our case, the number of pixels in the input image (the population) is statistically large, and the number of pixels in the subset S (the sample size) is calculated as the sample that could estimate the mean of the input image pixels. This will give the most accurate proportional calculation of $D_{j'}s$ in equation 1 compared to its values with the normal SOM competition. The calculation of the sample size deends on the standard deviation of the image pixels, the required sample confidence coefficient, and the sample estimation interval [8].

$$V = Z \times \frac{\sigma}{\sqrt{k}} \tag{3}$$

Where, V represents the required estimation interval of the selected sample, Z is the normal distribution curve area for the required confidence coefficient, σ is the standard deviation of the population, and k is the required sample size. When equation 3 solved for k, it gives:

$$k = \frac{Z^2 \sigma^2}{V^2} \tag{4}$$

If sampling without replacement from a finite population (n) is required, equation 3 becomes:

$$V = Z \times \frac{\sigma}{\sqrt{k}} \sqrt{\frac{n-k}{n-1}} \tag{5}$$

Which, when solved for k, gives:

$$k = \frac{nZ^2\sigma^2}{V^2(n-1) + Z^2\sigma^2} \tag{6}$$

So, the PUR can be calculated as:

$$PUR = \frac{k}{n} \tag{7}$$

For normal distribution population, the best choice for the estimation interval and the confidence coefficient are 5 and 0.95, respectively. Indexing this value of confidence coefficient on the table of normal curve areas yields $z = 1.96$. The above equations are also valid if the sample is selected from non-normal population. Since the central limit theory states that for large samples, the distribution of its mean is approximately normally distributed regardless of how the parent population is distributed [9]. In this case, it is recommended to decrease the estimation interval to 2, this will increase the sample size for the same standard deviation and confidence coefficient.

By SOM learning scheme, the locality of feature map neurons for the competition winner of each input pixel in the same image is preserved, since SOM maps similar inputs in a contiguous location on the network feature map. Therefor, the competition between any input pixel and the set of weights connected to that input would give the minimum difference in a small linear range near to the competition winner, as shown in figure 2. It is clear that, for different pixels of the input image, the location of best match neurons falls in a very narrow range around the winner.

Of course, there is no clear cut to consider the winner candidate selected from the first phase competition of RSOM algorithm as the normal SOM winner. However, as SOM keeps the locality of feature map neurons for the competition winner with different input pixel. In addition, the probability density functions (pdf) of the selected sample S is similar to the pdf of the sample population, and with SOM learning scheme the point density function of the feature map codebook approximates some monotonic function of the probability density function of the input learning images. Therefore, applying the competition using subset of input image will select the winner candidate in a very near position on the network feature map to SOM winner. Furthermore, as the number of elements in the randomly selected subset S increases, the winner candidate falls closer to SOM winner. The essence here is that, by using subset of image pixels instead of the entire pixels it is possible to reach a set of feature map neurons in which SOM winner lies. The task of the second phase competition is to reach SOM winner. Simply, in this phase, a set of neighborhood neurons around the winner candidates is defined. Then the competition between these neurons will be applied using the entire image pixels.

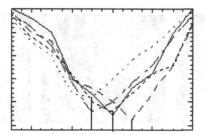

Fig. 2. The square of the difference between individual input pixels and the weights of feature map neurons connected to those pixels. The abscissa represents linear range of feature map neurons near to the competition winner, and the ordinate shows the difference. The best match for individual inputs falls in a very near location to the winner.

$$D_j = \sum_{i=1}^{n} (\mu_{ij} - X_i)^2, \ j \in NR \tag{8}$$

After that, neuron c with minimum distance D_c will be considered as the final SOM winner if CT condition is satisfied, otherwise this competition is neglected and the input image is considered as gesture transition image not posture image.

$$D_C = \min_{j}^{m}(D_j), \ j \in NR \tag{9}$$

$$if \ (D_c \leq CT) \ then \ C \ is \ the \ final \ SOM \ Winner \tag{10}$$

Of course, the value of CT differs from application to application, so it is better to calculate its value empirically. For example, it can be considered as the minimum D_c value for all postures in the given application. However, it is clear that the winner competition in RSOM algorithm can reduce the required computations to reach the winner. Since the computations in the first and second phase of the algorithm depend on the values of PUR and NR, respectively. Given that PUR<< 1 and NR<< m.

5   Dynamic Gesture Recognition

SOM network is implemented to recognize dynamic hand gestures of Jan-Ken-Pon game. The game includes three hand postures called GUU, CHUKI, and PAA as shown in figure 3 respectively. First, the network feature map is constructed using Kohonen competition algorithm. The training images are collected from different persons under the same lighting condition.

Fig. 3. Three learning images for the postures of Jan-Ken-Pon game.

After learning, the feature map of the network divided into three clusters, one for each posture. Also, the codebooks of the neurons in each cluster are coded very similar to the images of its posture. Figure 4 shows examples of three codebook images, one from each cluster.

Fig. 4. The codebook of three neurons from each cluster of SOM network.

During the recognition phase, the network is tested using new images that never see before. The input is given as a sequence of images that changes the hand gestures from posture to posture. For example, the images start from GUU posture and changes to PAA posture. In this case, the network input may be one of the following six different gestures: GUU-CHUKI, GUU-PAA, CHUKI-GUU, CHUKI-PAA, PAA-GUU, and PAA-CHUKI. However, for hand gesture of three postures, the system can accept 12 different gestures.

To test RSOM algorithm, the dynamic gesture images is given to the network as a sequence of 100 images representing the change of hand position from posture to another. At first, the recognition using the normal SOM competition algorithm is applied to show the correct correspondence between the input images and feature map neurons. After that, the same gesture images are used again to estimate the performance of RSOM algorithm. To implement RSOM algorithm, it is required to apply its off-line computations. So, the network feature map is divided into three clusters for GUU, CHUKI, and PAA postures.

Then, one neuron in the center of each cluster is designated for the cluster representative task. The experiments applied on Alpha 21164A / 600 MHz processor, with gcc compiler without optimization. Figure 5 shows the recognition time of a sequence of 100 images using normal SOM competition algorithm and RSOM algorithm with different values of PUR and NR.

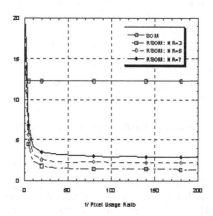

Fig. 5. The recognition time (in second)of 100 images using SOM and RSOM with different values of PUR and NR

The recognition accuracy of RSOM is considered as the rate of selecting the same winner selected by the normal SOM competition algorithm. The recognition accuracy of the experiments in figure 5 is shown in figure 6.

The recognition time of one image using normal SOM competition algorithm is constant and equal 0.124 second. With RSOM algorithm, the recognition time and accuracy of one image depends on the values of PUR and NR. As shown, decreasing the PUR decreases the recognition time and accuracy, while increasing the NR increases the recognition time and accuracy. Of course, the best choice for PUR and NR is the values that give the minimum recognition time with 100 % accuracy. By comparing the results of two graphs, it is founded that the minimum recognition time with 100 This means that the network can recognize more than 25 image-frame per second. Therefore, the network can apply on-line recognition for dynamic input gestures given from digital camera However, due to the nature of Jan-Ken-Pon problem, the start-end point's problem is not exist. Since, the end point in any gesture can be considered as the start point of the next. In addition, the network feature map is constructed using different images from each posture, so the recognition algorithm could avoid the gesture variance problem and posture ambiguity problem.

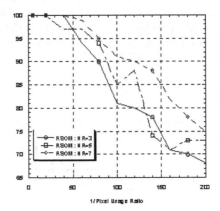

Fig. 6. The recognition accuracy of 100 images using SOM and RSOM with different values of PUR and NR.

The learning data are images with 120*160 pixels and 256 gray levels. The standard deviations for PAA, CHUKI, and GUU images were 17.80, 20.03, and 19.00, respectively. Also, the distribution of the gray levels in all images was approximately normal. The sample S is selected as simple random sample with replacement. From equation 4, for $V = 5$ and $Z = 1.96$, the sample size k should be greater than 308. Therefore, for recognition accuracy of 100%, the PUR should be greater than 0.016, which coincide with the experimental results.

6   Discussion

Gesticulation is doubtless an expressive way for human interaction with computers. In this paper, SOM gesture recognition system is proposed for hand gesture recognition applications. Where, each gesture is treated as a sequence of postures. SOM network is prompted to recognize the postures, then pattern matching technique associated with prediction system are used to recognize the gestures. However, to allow SOM network to catch the input images in its normal speed, it is required to reduce the recognition time of one image to the range of normal video rates, for that RSOM algorithm is proposed. RSOM algorithm uses random subset of input image to reference the feature map very near to SOM winner. The algorithm is less depending on the network size, since the size of the random input subset depends on the standard deviation of the input image. Also, it is possible to increase the number of feature map neurons and clusters. Since, whatever the number of neurons in the clusters, only one neuron from each cluster (the cluster representative) enters the winner candidate competition. The algorithm applied to recognize dynamic hand gestures of Jan-Ken-Pon game; the experimental results show that the recognition time of one image in RSOM algorithm is only 12.4 % of normal SOM recognition algorithm. In addition, the recognition time of each image reduced to the range of normal video rates, this means that the system can recognize dynamic gestures in its normal speed.

References

1. W. Freeman and M. Roth, "Orientation Histograms For Hand Gesture Recognition, " International Workshop on Automatic Face- and Gesture- Recognition, IEEE Computer Society, Zurich, Switzerland, June 1995.
2. J. Davis and M. Shah, "Recognizing Hand Gestures," ECCV'94, Pages 331-340, 1994.
3. Y. Kameda, M. Minoh, and K. Ikeda, "Three Dimension Pose Estimation Of An Articulated Object From Its Silhouette Image," In ACCV'93, pages 612-615, 1993
4. T. Kohonen, "Self-Organizing Maps," Springer Series in Information Science, 1997.
5. S. Russell and P. Norving, " Artificial Intelligence, A Modern Approach," Prentice-Hall, Inc., 1995.
6. W. Black, and A. Taylor, "Automatically Clustering Similar Units For Unit Selection In Speech Synthesis, " Proceedings of the Fifth European Conference on Speech Communication and Technology (Eurospeech 97), Greece, September 1997.
7. S. Kung, "Digital Neural Network," PTR Prentice Hall, 1995.
8. B. Gnedenko, I. Pavlov, and I. Ushakov, "Statistical Reliability Engineering, " John Wiely & Sons, Inc.,1999.
9. H. Frank and S. Altheon, "Statistics, Concepts and Applications," Cambradge University Press, 1994.

On Approximate Learning by Multi-layered Feedforward Circuits

Bhaskar DasGupta[*][1] and Barbara Hammer[2]

[1] Department of Computer Science, Rutgers University
Camden, NJ 08102, U.S.A.
bhaskar@crab.rutgers.edu
[2] Department of Mathematics/Computer Science, University of Osnabrück
D-49069 Osnabrück, Germany
hammer@informatik.uni-osnabrueck.de

Abstract. We consider the problem of efficient *approximate* learning by multi-layered feedforward circuits subject to two objective functions.

First, we consider the objective to *maximize* the ratio of correctly classified points compared to the training set size (e.g., see [3,5]). We show that for single hidden layer threshold circuits with n hidden nodes and varying input dimension, approximation of this ratio within a relative error c/n^3, for some positive constant c, is NP-hard *even if* the number of examples is *limited* with respect to n. For architectures with two hidden nodes (e.g., as in [6]), approximating the objective within some fixed factor is NP-hard *even if any* sigmoid-like activation function in the hidden layer and ε-separation of the output [19] is considered, or if the semilinear activation function substitutes the threshold function.

Next, we consider the objective to *minimize* the *failure ratio* [2]. We show that it is NP-hard to approximate the failure ratio within every *constant larger than* 1 for a multilayered threshold circuit provided the input biases are zero. Furthermore, even *weak* approximation of this objective is *almost* NP-hard.

1 Introduction

Feedforward circuits are a well established learning mechanism which offer a simple and successful method of learning an unknown hypothesis given some examples. However, the inherent complexity of training the circuits is till now an open problem for most practically relevant situations. Starting with the work of Judd [15,16] it turned out that training is NP-hard in general. However, most work in this area deals either with only very restricted architectures, activation functions not used in practice, or a training problem which is too strict compared to practical problems. In this paper we want to consider situations which are closer to the training problems as they occur in practice.

A *feedforward circuit* consists of nodes which are connected in a directed acyclic graph. The overall behavior of the circuit is determined by the *architecture* $\mathcal{A}$ and the circuit *parameters* w. Given a *pattern* or *example* set P consisting of points $(x_i; y_i)$, we want to learn the regularity with a feedforward circuit. Frequently, this is performed by

---

* Research supported by NSF grant CCR-9800086.

H. Arimura, S. Jain and A. Sharma (Eds.): ALT 2000, LNAI 1968, pp. 264–278, 2000.
© Springer-Verlag Berlin Heidelberg 2000

first choosing an architecture $\mathcal{A}$ which computes a function $\beta_\mathcal{A}(w, x)$ and then choosing the parameters w such that $\beta_\mathcal{A}(w, x_i) = y_i$ holds for every pattern $(x_i; y_i)$. The *loading problem* (or the *training problem*) is the problem to find weights w such that these equalities hold. The *decision version* of the loading problem is to decide (rather than to find the weights) whether such weights exist that load M onto $\mathcal{A}$.

Some previous results consider specific situations. For example, for every fixed architecture with threshold activation function or architectures with appropriately restricted connection graph loading is polynomial [8,10,15,20]. For some strange activation functions or a setting where the number of examples coincides with the number of hidden nodes loadability becomes trivial [25]. However, Blum and Rivest [6] show that a varying input dimension yields the NP-hardness of training threshold circuits with only two hidden nodes. Hammer [10] generalizes this result to multilayered threshold circuits. References [8,11,12,14,23,27] constitute generalizations to circuits with the sigmoidal activation function or other continuous activations. Hence finding an optimum weight setting in a concrete learning task may require a large amount of time.

Naturally, the constraint that all the examples must be correctly classified is too strict. In a practical situation, one would be satisfied if a large fraction (but not necessarily all) of the examples can be satisfied. Moreover, it may be possible that there are no choices for the weights which load a given set of examples. From these motivations, researchers have considered an approximate version of the learning problem where the number of correctly classified points is to be maximized. References [1,2,13] consider the complexity of training single threshold nodes with some error bounds. Bartlett and Ben-David [3] mostly deal with threshold architectures, whereas Ben-David et. al. [5] deals with other concept classes such as monomials, axis-aligned hyper-rectangles, monotone monomials and closed balls. We obtain NP-hardness results for the task of approximately minimizing the relative error of the success ratio for a correlated architecture and training set size, various more realistic activation functions, and training sets without multiple points. Another objective function is to approximately minimize the failure ratio. The work in [1,2] considers inapproximability of minimizing the failure ratio for a single threshold gate. We show that approximating this failure ratio for multilayered threshold circuits within every constant is NP-hard and even weak approximation of this objective function is almost NP-hard. Several proofs are omitted due to space limitations. They can be found in the long version of this paper.

2   The Basic Model and Notations

The architecture of a feedforward circuit $\mathcal{C}$ is described by a directed interconnection graph and the activation functions of $\mathcal{C}$. A node v of $\mathcal{C}$ computes a function

$$\gamma_v \left(\sum_{i=1}^{k} w_{v_i,v} u_{v_i} + b_v \right)$$

of its inputs $u_{v_1}, \ldots, u_{v_k}$. $\sum_{i=1}^{k} w_{v_i,v} u_{v_i} + b_v$ is called the *activation* of the node v. The inputs are either external, representing the input data, or internal, representing the outputs of the immediate predecessors of v. The coefficients $w_{v_i,v}$ (resp. b_v) are the *weights* (resp. *threshold*) of node v, and γ_v is the *activation function* of v. No cycles are allowed in the interconnection graph of C and the output of a designated node provides the output of the circuit. An *architecture* specifies the interconnection structure and the γ_v's, but not the actual numerical values of the weights or thresholds. The *depth* of a feedforward circuit is the length of the longest path of the interconnection graph. A *layered* feedforward circuit is one in which nodes at depth d are connected only to nodes at depth $d + 1$, and all inputs are provided to nodes at depth 1 only. A layered $(n_0, n_1, \ldots, n_h)$ circuit is a layered circuit with n_i nodes at depth $i \geq 1$ where n_0 is the number of inputs. We assume $n_h = 1$. Nodes at depth j, for $1 \leq j < h$, are called *hidden nodes*, and all nodes at depth j, for a particular j, constitute the jth *hidden layer*.

A Γ-circuit C is a feedforward circuit in which only functions in some set Γ are assigned to nodes. Hence each architecture $\mathcal{A}$ of a Γ-circuit defines a behavior function $\beta_{\mathcal{A}}$ that maps from the r real weights and the n inputs into an output value. We denote such a behavior as the function $\beta_{\mathcal{A}} : \mathbb{R}^{r+n} \mapsto \mathbb{R}$. Some popular choices of the activation functions are the perceptron activation function $H(x) = \begin{cases} 1 & \text{if } x \geq 0 \\ 0 & \text{otherwise} \end{cases}$ and the standard sigmoid $\text{sgd}(x) = 1/(1 + e^{-x})$.

The *loading problem* L is defined as follows (e.g., see [6,8]): Given an architecture $\mathcal{A}$ and a set of examples $P = \{(\boldsymbol{x}; y) \mid x \in \mathbb{R}^n, y \in \mathbb{R}\}$, find weights $\boldsymbol{w}$ so that for all $(\boldsymbol{x}; y) \in M$: $\beta_{\mathcal{A}}(\boldsymbol{w}, \boldsymbol{x}) = y$. In this paper we will deal with those classification tasks where $y \in \{0, 1\}$. Clearly, the hardness results obtained with this restriction will be valid in the unrestricted case also. An example $(\boldsymbol{x}; y)$ is a *positive example* if $y = 1$, otherwise it is a *negative example*. An example is *misclassified* by the circuit if $\beta_{\mathcal{A}}(\boldsymbol{w}, \boldsymbol{x}) \neq y$, otherwise it is *classified correctly*.

An *optimization* problem C is characterized by a non-negative objective function $m_C(x, y)$, where x is an input instance of the problem, y is a solution for x, and $m_C(x, y)$ is the cost of the solution y; the goal of the problem is to either maximize or minimize $m_C(x, y)$ for any particular x, depending on the problem. Denote by $\text{opt}_C(x)$ (or shortly $\text{opt}(x)$ if C is clear from the context) the optimum value of $m_C(x, y)$. For maximization, $(\text{opt}_C(x) - m_C(x, y))/\text{opt}_C(x)$ is the *relative error* of a solution y. The objective functions that are of relevance to this paper are as follows:

Success ratio function: $m_L(x, y) = |\{x \mid \beta_{\mathcal{A}}(\boldsymbol{w}, \boldsymbol{x}) = y\}| / |P|$ is the fraction of the correctly classified examples compared to the training set size (e.g., see [3]).

Failure ratio function: $m_C(x, y) = |\{x \mid \beta_{\mathcal{A}}(\boldsymbol{w}, \boldsymbol{x}) \neq y\}|$. If $\text{opt}_C(x) > 0$, $m_f(x, y) = m_C(x, y)/\text{opt}_C(x)$ is the ratio of the number of misclassified examples to the minimum possible number of misclassifications when at least one misclassification is unavoidable (e.g., see [2]).

3   Approximating the Success Ratio Function m_L

We want to show that in several situations it is difficult to approximate m_L for a loading problem L. These results would extend the results of [3] to more complex situations. For this purpose, the L-reduction from the so-called MAX-k-cut problem to a loading problem which is constructed in [3] is generalized such that it can be applied to several further situations as well. Since approximating the MAX-k-cut problem is NP-hard, the NP-hardness of approximability of the latter problems follows.

Definition 1. *Given an undirected graph $G = (V, E)$ and $k \geq 2$ in $\mathbb{N}$, the MAX-k-cut problem is to find a function $\psi : V \mapsto \{1, 2, \ldots, k\}$, such that $|\{(u, v) \in E \mid \psi(u) \neq \psi(v)\}| / |E|$ is maximized. The set of nodes in V which are mapped to i in this setting is called the ith* cut. *The edges (v_i, v_j) in the graph for which v_i and v_j are contained in the same cut are called monochromatic; all other edges are called bichromatic.*

Theorem 1. [17] *It is NP-hard to approximate the MAX-k-cut problem within relative error smaller than $1/(34(k-1))$ for $k \geq 2$, and within error smaller than c/k^3, c being some constant, $k \geq 3$, even if solutions without monochromatic edges exist.*

The concept of an *L-reduction* was defined in [21]. The definition stated below is a slightly modified version of [21] that will be useful for our purposes.

Definition 2. *An L-reduction from a maximization problem C_1 to a maximization problem C_2 consists of two polynomial time computable functions T_1 and T_2, two constants $\alpha, \beta > 0$, and a parameter $0 \leq a \leq 1$ with the following properties:*

(a) *For each instance I_1 of C_1, algorithm T_1 produces an instance I_2 of C_2.*
(b) *The maxima of I_1 and I_2, $\mathrm{opt}(I_1)$ resp. $\mathrm{opt}(I_2)$, satisfy $\mathrm{opt}(I_2) \leq \alpha \, \mathrm{opt}(I_1)$.*
(c) *Given any solution of the instance I_2 of C_2 with cost c_2 such that the relative error of c_2 is at most a, algorithm T_2 produces a solution I_1 of C_1 with cost c_1 satisfying $(\mathrm{opt}(I_1) - c_1) \leq \beta \, (\mathrm{opt}(I_2) - c_2)$.*

If C_1 is hard to approximate within relative error $a/(\alpha\beta)$ then C_2 is hard to approximate within relative error a.

Consider an L-reduction from the MAX-k-cut problem to the loading problem L with objective function m_L where the reductions performed by T_1 and T_2 have the following additional properties. Given an instance $I_1 = (V, E)$ of the MAX-k-cut problem, assume that T_1 produces in polynomial time an instance I_2, a specific architecture and an example set in $\mathbb{R}^n \times \{0, 1\}$ of the loading problem L with training set:

- $2|E|$ copies of each of some set of special points P_0 (e.g. the origin),
- for each node $v_i \in V$, d_i copies of one point e_i, where d_i is the degree of v_i,
- for each edge $(v_i, v_j) \in E$, one point e_{ij}.

Furthermore, assume that the following properties are satisfied:

(i) For an optimum solution for I_1 the algorithm T_1 finds an optimum solution of the instance I_2 of the corresponding loading problem L in which all special points P_0 and all points e_i are correct classified and exactly those points e_{ij} are misclassified which correspond to a monochromatic edge (v_i, v_j) in an optimal solution of I_1.
(ii) For any approximate solution of the instance I_2 of the loading problem L which classifies all special points in P_0 correctly, T_2 computes an approximate solution of the instance I_1 of the MAX-k-cut problem such that for every monochromatic edge (v_i, v_j) in this solution, either e_i, e_j, or e_{ij} is misclassified.

An analogous proof to [3] yields the following result:

Theorem 2. *Approximation of the above loading problem within relative error smaller than $((k-1)\epsilon)/(k(2|P_0|+3))$ is NP-hard since the above reduction is an L-reduction with $\alpha = k/(k-1)$, $\beta = 2|P_0|+3$, and $a = (k-1)/(k^2(2|P_0|+3))$.*

3.1 Application to Multi-layered Feedforward Circuits

First we consider H-circuits, $H(x)$ being the perceptron activation function. This type of architecture is common in theoretical study of neural networks (e.g., see [22,24]) as well as in their practical applications (e.g., see [28]). Assume that the first layer contains the input nodes $1, \ldots, n$, $h+1$ denotes the depth of the H-circuit, and n_i denotes the number of nodes at depth i. An instance of the loading problem will be represented by a tuple $(n, n_1, n_2, \ldots, n_h, 1)$ and by an example set with rational numbers. The following fact is an immediate consequence of Theorem 2 in [3]:

For any $h \geq 1$, constant $n_1 \geq 2$ and any $n_2, \ldots, n_h \in \mathbb{N}$, it is NP-hard to approximate the success ratio function m_L with instances (N, P), where N is the architecture of a layered $\{(n, n_1, \ldots, n_h, 1) \mid n \in \mathbb{N}\}$ H-circuit and P is a set of examples from $\mathbb{Q}^n \times \{0, 1\}$, with relative error at most $(68 n_1 2^{n_1} + 136 n_1^3 + 136 n_1^2 + 170 n_1)^{-1}$.

Correlated Architecture and Training Set Size The above training setting may be unrealistic in practical applications where one would allow larger architectures if a large amount of data is to be trained. One strategie would be to choose the size of the architecture such that valid generalization can be expected using well known bounds in the PAC setting [26]. Naturally the question arises about what happens to the complexity of training if one is restricted to situations where the number of examples is limited with respect to the number of hidden nodes. One extreme position would be to allow the number of training examples to be at most equal to the number of hidden nodes. Although this may not yield valid generalization, the decision version of the loading problem becomes trivial because of [25], or, more precisely:

If the number of hidden nodes in the first hidden layer is at least equal to the number of training examples and the threshold activation function, the standard sigmoidal function, or the semilinear activation function (or any function σ such that the class of σ-circuits possesses the universal approximation capability as defined in [25]) is used then the error of an optimum solution of the loading problem is determined by the number of contradictory training examples (i.e. $(x; y_1)$ and $(x; y_2)$ with $y_1 \neq y_2$.)

However, the following theorem yields an inapproximability result even if we restrict to situations where the number of examples and hidden nodes are correlated.

Theorem 3. *Approximtion of the success ratio function m_L with relative error smaller than c/k^3 (c is a constant, k is the number of hidden nodes) is NP-hard for the loading problem with instances $(\mathcal{A}, P)$ where $\mathcal{A}$ is a layered $(n, k, 1)$-H-architecture (n and k may vary) and $P \subset \mathbb{Q}^n \times \{0, 1\}$ is an example set with $k^{3.5} \leq |P| \leq k^4$ which can be loaded without errors.*

Proof. The proof is via L-reduction from the MAX-3-cut problem with a and β depending on k. The algorithms T_1 and T_2, respectively, will be defined in two steps: mapping an instance of the MAX-3-cut problem to an instance of the MAX-k-cut problem with appropriate k and size of the problem and to an instance of the loading problem, afterwards, or mapping a solution for the loading problem to a solution of the MAX-k-cut problem and then to a solution of the MAX-3-cut problem afterwards, respectively.

We first define T_1: given a graph (V, E) define $k = |V| \cdot |E|$ (w.l.o.g. $k \geq 3$) and (V', E') with $V' = V \cup \{v_{|V|+1}, \ldots, v_{|V|+k-3}\}$, $E' = E \cup \{(v_i, v_j) \mid i \in \{|V| + 1, \ldots, |V| + k - 3\}, j \in \{1, \ldots, |V| + k - 3\} \backslash \{i\}\}$ where the new edges in E' have the multiplicity $2|E|$. Reduce (V', E') to a loading problem for the architecture with $n = |V'| + 3$, k as above, and examples

(I) $2|E'|$ copies of the origin $(0^n; 1)$,

(II) d_i copies of the point e_i, i.e. $(0, \ldots, 0, 1, 0, \ldots, 0; 0)$ (the 1 is at the ith position from left) for each node $v_i \in V'$ where d_i is the degree of v_i,

(III) a vector e_{ij} for each edge $(v_i, v_j) \in E'$: $(0, \ldots, 0, 1, 0 \ldots, 0, 1, 0, \ldots, 0; 1)$ (the numbers 1 are at the ith and jth positions from left),

(IV) $2|E'|$ copies of each of the points $(0^{|V'|}, p^{ij}, 1; 1)$, $(0^{|V'|}, n^{ij}, 1; 0)$, where p^{ij} and n^{ij} are constructed as follows: define the points $x^{ij} = (4(i - 1) + j, j(i - 1) + 4((i - 2) + \ldots + 1))$ for $i \in \{1, \ldots, k\}$, $j \in \{1, 2, 3\}$. These $3k$ points have the property that if three of them lie on one line then we can find an i such that the three points coincide with x^{i1}, x^{i2}, and x^{i3}. Now we divide each point into a pair p^{ij} and n^{ij} of points which are obtained by a slight shift of x^{ij} in a direction that is orthogonal to the line $[x^{i1}, x^{i3}]$. Formally, $p^{ij} = x^{ij} + \epsilon N_i$ and $n^{ij} = x^{ij} - \epsilon N_i$, where N_i is a normal vector of the line $[x^{i1}, x^{i3}]$ with a positive second coefficient and ϵ is a small positive value. ϵ can be chosen such that the following holds:

Assume one line separates three pairs $(n^{i_1 j_1}, p^{i_1 j_1})$, $(n^{i_2 j_2}, p^{i_2 j_2})$, and $(n^{i_3 j_3}, p^{i_3 j_3})$, then necessarily $i_1 = i_2 = i_3$.

This property is fulfilled for $\epsilon \leq 1/(24 \cdot k(k - 1) + 6)$ due to Proposition 6 of [20], N being a vector of length 1. Consequently, the representation of the points n^{ij} and p^{ij} is polynomial in n and k.

Note that the number of points is $k^{3.5} \leq 5|E'| + 12k|E'| \leq k^4$ for large $|V|$. An optimum solution of the instance of the MAX-3-cut problem gives rise to a solution of the instance of the MAX-k-cut problem with the same number of monochromatic edges via mapping the nodes in $V \cap V'$ to the same three cuts as before and defining the ith cut by $\{v_{|V|+i}\}$ for $i \in \{1, \ldots, k - 3\}$. This solution can be used to define a solution of the instance of the loading problem as follows: The jth weight of node i in the hidden layer is chosen as $\begin{cases} -1 & \text{if } v_j \text{ is in the } i\text{th cut} \\ 2 & \text{otherwise,} \end{cases}$ and the bias is chosen as 0.5. The weights $(|V'| + 1, |V'| + 2, |V'| + 3)$ of the ith node are chosen as $(-i + 1, 1, -0.5 + 2 \cdot i(i - 1))$ which corresponds to the line through the points x^{i1}, x^{i2}, and x^{i3}. The output unit has the bias $-k + 0.5$ and weights 1, i.e. it computes an AND. With this choice of weights one can compute that all examples except the points e_{ij} corresponding to monochromatic edges are mapped correctly.

Conversely, an optimum solution of the loading problem classifies all points in **(I)**, **(II)**, and **(IV)** and all points e_{ij} corresponding to edges in $E' \backslash E$ correct because of the multiplicities of the respective points. We can assume that the activations of the nodes do not exactly coincide with 0 when the outputs on P are computed. Consider the restriction of the circuit mapping to the plane $\{(0, \ldots, 0, x_{n+1}, x_{n+2}, 1) \,|\, x_{n+1}, x_{n+2} \in \mathbb{R}\}$. The points $\boldsymbol{p}^{ij}$ and $\boldsymbol{n}^{ij}$ are contained in this plane. Because of the different outputs each pair $(\boldsymbol{p}^{ij}, \boldsymbol{n}^{ij})$ is to be separated by at least one line defined by the hidden nodes. A number $3k$ of such pairs exists. Therefore, each of the lines defined by the hidden nodes necessarily separates three pairs $(\boldsymbol{p}^{ij}, \boldsymbol{n}^{ij})$ with $j \in \{1, 2, 3\}$ and nearly coincides with the line defined by $[\boldsymbol{x}^{i1}, \boldsymbol{x}^{i3}]$. Denote the output weights of the circuit by $w_1, \ldots, w_k$ and the output bias by θ. We can assume that the ith node nearly coincides with the ith line and that the points $\boldsymbol{p}^{ij}$ are mapped by the node to the value 0. Otherwise we change all signs of the weights and the bias in node i, we change the sign of the weight w_i, and increase θ by w_i. But then the points $\boldsymbol{p}^{i2}$ are mapped to 0 by all hidden nodes, the points $\boldsymbol{n}^{i2}$ are mapped to 0 by all but one hidden node. This means that $\theta > 0$, $\theta + w_i < 0$ for all i and therefore $\theta + w_{i_1} + \ldots + w_{i_l} < 0$ for all $i_1, \ldots, i_l \in \{1, \ldots, k\}$ with $l \geq 1$. This means that the output unit computes the function NAND : $(x_1, \ldots, x_n) \mapsto \neg x_1 \wedge \ldots \wedge \neg x_n$ on binary values.

Define a solution of the instance of the MAX-k-cut problem by setting the ith cut c_i as $\{v_j \mid \text{the } i\text{th hidden node maps } e_j \text{ to } 1\} \setminus (c_1 \cup \ldots \cup c_{i-1})$. Assume some edge (v_i, v_j) is monochromatic. Then e_i and e_j are mapped to 1 by the same hidden node. Therefore e_{ij} is classified wrong. Note that all e_{ij} corresponding to edges in $E \setminus E'$ are correct, hence the nodes $v_{|V|+1}, \ldots, v_{|V|+k-3}$ each form one cut and the remaining nodes are contained in the remaining three cuts. Hence these three cuts define a solution of the instance of the MAX-3-cut problem such that almost edges corresponding to misclassified e_{ij} are monochromatic.

Denote by opt_1 the value of an optimum solution of the MAX-3-cut problem and by opt_2 the optimum value of the loading problem. We have shown that

$$\mathrm{opt}_2 = \frac{|E|\mathrm{opt}_1 + (|E'| - |E|) + 4|E'| + 12|E'|k}{5|E'| + 12|E'|k} \leq \frac{3}{2}\,\mathrm{opt}_1 \;.$$

Next we construct T_2. Assume that a solution of the loading problem with relative error smaller than c/k^3 is given. Then the points (I) and (IV) are correct due to their multiplicities. Otherwise the relative error of the problem would be at least $|E'|/(5|E'| + 12|E'|k) \geq c/k^3$ for appropriately small c and large k. As before we can assume that the output node computes the function $x \mapsto \neg x_1 \wedge \ldots \wedge \neg x_k$. Define opt_2 to be the value of an optimum solution of the loading problem and I_2 the value of the given solution. Assume some point e_{ij} corresponding to an edge in $E' \setminus E$ is misclassified. Then T_2 yields an arbitrary solution of the MAX-3-cut problem. For the quality I_1 of this solution compared to an optimum opt_1 we can compute

$$\mathrm{opt}_1 - I_1 \leq 1 \leq \frac{5|E'| + 12|E'|k}{|E|}(\mathrm{opt}_2 - I_2) \;.$$

This holds because an optimum solution of the loading problem classifies at least a number of $|E|$ points more correct than in the solution considered here.

If all e_{ij} corresponding to edges in $E' \setminus E$ are correct then we define a solution of the MAX-3-cut problem via the activation of the hidden nodes as above. Remaining nodes become members of the first cut. An argument as above shows that each monochromatic edge comes from a misclassification of either e_i, e_j, or e_{ij}. Hence

$$\text{opt}_1 - I_1 \leq \frac{5|E'| + 12|E'|k}{|E|}(\text{opt}_2 - I_2).$$

Setting $\alpha = 3/2$, $\beta = \tilde{c} \cdot k^3 \geq (5|E'| + 12|E'|k)/|E|$ for some constant $\tilde{c}$ and using Theorem 1 yields the result as stated above. $\square$

The $(n, 2, 1)$-$\{\text{sgd}, H_\epsilon\}$-net The above result deals with realistic circuit structures. However, usually a continuous and differentiable activation function is used in practice. A very common activation function is the standard sigmoid activation $\text{sgd}(x) = 1/(1 + e^{-x})$. Here we consider the loading problem with a feedforward architecture of the form $(n, 2, 1)$ where the input dimension n is allowed to vary. The sigmoidal activation function is used in the two hidden nodes. The output is the function

$$H_\epsilon(x) = \begin{cases} 0 & \text{if } x < -\epsilon, \\ \text{undefined} & \text{if } -\epsilon \leq x \leq \epsilon, \\ 1 & \text{otherwise}. \end{cases}$$

The purpose of this definition is to enforce that any classification is performed with a minimum separation accuracy ϵ. Furthermore, we restrict to solutions with output weights whose absolute values are bounded by some positive constant B. This setting is captured by the notion of so-called ϵ-separation (for example, see [19]). Formally, the circuit computes the function $\beta_A(w, x) = H_\epsilon(\alpha \, \text{sgd}(a^t x + a_0) + \beta \, \text{sgd}(b^t x + b_0) + \gamma)$ where $w = (\alpha, \beta, \gamma, a, a_0, b, b_0)$ are the weights and thresholds, respectively, of the output node and the two hidden nodes and $|\alpha|, |\beta| < B$ for some positive constant B.

Theorem 4. *It is NP-hard to approximate the m_L with relative error smaller than $1/2244$ for the architecture of a $\{(n, 2, 1) \mid n \in \mathbb{N}\}$-circuit with sigmoidal activation function for the hidden nodes, output activation function H_ϵ with $0 < \epsilon < 0.5$, weight restriction $B \geq 2$ of the output weights, and examples from $\mathbb{Q}^n \times \{0, 1\}$.*

The proof consists in an application of Theorem 2 and a careful examination of the geometric form of the classification boundary defined by those types of networks. It turns out that some argumentation can be transferred from the standard perceptron case since some geometrical situations merely correspond to the respective cases for perceptron networks. However, additional geometric situations may take place which are excluded in our setting with appropriate points in the set of special points P_0 in near optimum solutions. Due to the situation of ϵ-separation it turns out that the result transfers to more general activation functions:

Definition 3. *Two functions $f, g : \mathbb{R} \to \mathbb{R}$ are ϵ-approximates of each other if $|f(x) - g(x)| \leq \epsilon$ holds for all $x \in \mathbb{R}$.*

Corollary 1. *It is NP-hard to approximate the success ratio function m_L with relative error smaller than $1/2244$ for $\{(n, 2, 1) \mid n \in \mathbb{N}\}$-circuit architectures with activation function σ in the hidden layer and H_ϵ in the output, $\epsilon < 1/3$, weight restriction $B \geq 2$, and examples from $\mathbb{Q}^n \times \{0, 1\}$, provided $\sigma(x)$ is $\epsilon/(4B)$-approximate to $\text{sgd}(x)$.*

The $(n, 2, 1)$-$\{$lin, $H\}$-net In this section, we prove the NP-hardness of the approximability of the success ratio function with the semilinear activation function commonly used in the neural net literature [7,8]:

$$\text{lin}(x) = \begin{cases} 0 & \text{if } x \leq 0 \\ x & \text{if } 0 < x \leq 1 \\ 1 & \text{otherwise} \end{cases}.$$

This function captures the linearity of the sigmoidal activation at 0 as well as the asymptotic behavior. Note that the following result does not require ϵ-separation.

Theorem 5. *It is NP-hard to approximate m_L with relative error smaller than $1/2380$ for the architecture of $\{(n, 2, 1) \mid n \in \mathbb{N}\}$-circuit with the semilinear activation function in the hidden layer and the threshold activation function in the output.*

Again the proof consists in an application of Theorem 2 and an investigation of the geometrical form of the classification boundaries which enables us to define appropriate algorithms T_1 and T_2.

Avoiding Multiplicities In the reductions of previous sections, examples with multiplicities were contained in the training sets. In the practical relevant case of neural network training, patterns are often subject to noise. Hence the points do not come from a probability distribution with singletons, i.e. points with nonzero probability. As a consequence the question arises as to whether training sets where each point is contained at most once yield NP-hardness results for approximate training as well.

The reduction of the MAX-k-cut problem to a loading problem can be modified as follows: T_1 yields the *mutually different* points:

- a set P_0 of points p_i^j, $j = 1, \ldots, 3|E|$ for each i,
- for each node v_i, points e_i^j, $j = 1, \ldots, 2d_i$, where d_i is the degree of v_i,
- for each edge (v_i, v_j), two points e_{ij} and o_{ij}.

Assume, T_1 and T_2 satisfy the following properties:

(i') For an optimum solution of the MAX-k-cut problem one can find an optimum solution of the instance of the corresponding loading problem L in which the special points P_0 and all e_i^j points are correctly classified and exactly the monochromatic edges (v_i, v_j) lead to misclassified points e_{ij} or o_{ij}.

(ii') If for each i at least one p_l^j is correct, T_2 computes in polynomial time an approximate solution where, for each monochromatic edge (v_i, v_j), one of the points e_{ij} or o_{ij} or all points e_i^l ($l = 1, \ldots, 3|E|$) or all points e_j^l ($l = 1, \ldots, 3|E|$) are misclassified.

An analogous proof to [3] shows the following:

Theorem 6. *Under the assumptions stated above, an L-reduction with constants $\alpha = k/(k-1)$, $\beta = 3|P_0| + 6$, and $a = (k-1)/(k^2(3|P_0| + 6))$ arises.*

Corollary 2. *The reductions for general perceptron circuits and in Theorems 4 and 5 can be modified such that (i') and (ii') hold. Hence minimizing the relative error within some constant is NP-hard even for training sets without multiple points in these situations.*

4 Approximating the Failure Ratio Function m_f

Given an instance x of the loading problem, denote by $m_C(x, y)$ the number of examples in the training set misclassified by the circuit represented by y. Given c, we want to find weights such that $\mathrm{opt}_C(x) \leq m_C(x, y) \leq c \cdot \mathrm{opt}_C(x)$. The interesting case is *with errors*, i.e. $\mathrm{opt}_C(x) > 0$. Hence we restrict to the case with errors and investigate if the failure ratio $m_f = m_C(x, y)/\mathrm{opt}_C(x)$ can be bounded from above by a constant. We term this problem as *approximating the minimum failure ratio* within c while learning in the presence of errors [2]. It turns out that the approximation is NP-hard within a bound which is *independent* of the circuit architecture. For this purpose we use a reduction from the set-covering problem.

Definition 4 (Set Covering Problem [9]). *Given a set of points $S = \{s_1, \dots, s_p\}$ and a set of subsets $C = \{C_1, \dots, C_m\}$, find indices $I \subset \{1, \dots, m\}$ such that $\bigcup_{i \in I} C_i = S$. In this case the sets $C_i, i \in I$, are called a cover of S. A cover is called exact if the sets in a cover are mutually disjoint.*

For the set-covering problem the following result holds, showing that it is hard to approximate within every factor $c > 1$:

Theorem 7. *[4] For every $c > 1$ there is a polynomial time reduction that, given an instance φ of SAT, produces an instance of the set-covering problem and a number $K \in \mathbb{N}$ with the properties: if φ is satisfiable then there exists an exact cover of size K, if φ is not satisfiable then every cover has size at least $c \cdot K$.*

Using Theorem 7 Arora et.al. [2] show that approximating the minimum failure ratio function within a factor of c (for any constant $c > 1$) is NP-hard for a single threshold node if all the input thresholds are set to zero. We obtain the following result.

Theorem 8. *Assume that we are given a layered H-circuit where the thresholds of the nodes in the first hidden layer are fixed to 0 and let $c > 1$ be any given constant. Then the problem of approximating minimum failure ratio m_f while learning in the presence of errors within a factor of c is NP-hard.*

Proof. Without loss of generality, assume that the circuit contains at least one hidden layer. Assume that we are given a formula φ. Transform this formula with the given constant c to an instance $(S = \{s_1, \dots, s_p\}, C = \{C_1, \dots, C_m\})$ of the set-covering problem and a constant K such that the properties in Theorem 7 hold. Transform this instance of the set-covering problem to an instance of the loading problem for the given architecture with input dimension $n = |C| + 2 + n_1 + 1$ where n_1 denotes the number of hidden nodes in the first hidden layer and the following examples from $\mathbb{Q}^n \times \{0, 1\}$:

(I) $(\mathbf{e}_i, 0, 1, 0^{n_1+1}; 1)$, $(-\mathbf{e}_i, 0, 1, 0^{n_1+1}; 1)$, where $\mathbf{e}_i$ is the ith unit vector in $\mathbb{R}^{|C|}$,

(II) $c \cdot K$ copies of each of the points $(\mathbf{e}_{s_i}, -1, 1, 0^{n_1+1}; 1)$, $(-\mathbf{e}_{s_i}, 1, 1, 0^{n_1+1}; 1)$, where $\mathbf{e}_{s_i} \in \{0, 1\}^{|C|}$ is the vector with jth component as 1 if and only if $s_i \in C_j$, $i \in \{1, \dots, p\}$,

(III) $c \cdot K$ copies of each of $(0^{|C|}, 1, 0, 0^{n_1+1}; 1)$, $(0^{|C|}, 1/(2m), 1, 0^{n_1+1}; 1)$, and $(0^{|C|}, -1/(2m), 1, 0^{n_1+1}; 0)$, where the component $|C| + 1$ is nonzero in all three points and the component $|C| + 2$ is nonzero in the latter two points, $m = |C|$,

(IV) $c \cdot K$ copies of each of $(0^{|C|+2}, \boldsymbol{p}_i, 1; 0)$, $(0^{|C|+2}, \boldsymbol{p}_0, 1; 1)$, $(0^{|C|+2}, \tilde{\boldsymbol{z}}_i, 1; 1)$, $(0^{|C|+2}, \bar{\boldsymbol{z}}_i, 1; 0)$, where the points $\boldsymbol{p}_i$, $\tilde{\boldsymbol{z}}_i$, $\bar{\boldsymbol{z}}_i$ are constructed as follows: Choose $n_1 + 1$ points in each set $H_i = \{\boldsymbol{x} = (x_1, x_2, \dots, x_{n_1}) \in \mathbb{R}^{n_1} \mid x_i = 0, x_j > 0 \forall j \neq i\}$ (denote the points by $\boldsymbol{z}_1$, $\boldsymbol{z}_2$, ... and the entire set by Z) such that any given $n_1 + 1$ different points in Z lie on one hyperplane if and only if they are contained in one H_i. For $z_j \in H_i$ define $\tilde{\boldsymbol{z}}_j \in \mathbb{R}^{n_1}$ by $\tilde{\boldsymbol{z}}_j = (z_{j1}, \dots, z_{ji-1}, z_{ji} + \epsilon, z_{ji+1}, \dots, z_{jn_1})$, $\bar{\boldsymbol{z}}_j \in \mathbb{R}^{n_1}$ by $\bar{\boldsymbol{z}}_j = (z_{j1}, \dots, z_{ji-1}, z_{ji} - \epsilon, z_{ji+1}, \dots, z_{jn_1})$, for some small value ϵ which is chosen such that the following property holds: if one hyperplane in $\mathbb{R}^{n_1}$ separates at least $n_1 + 1$ pairs $(\tilde{\boldsymbol{z}}_i, \bar{\boldsymbol{z}}_i)$, these pairs coincide with the $n_1 + 1$ pairs corresponding to the $n_1 + 1$ points in some H_i, and the separating hyperplane nearly coincides with the hyperplane through H_i.

For an exact cover of size K, let the corresponding set of indices be $I = \{i_1, \dots, i_K\}$. Define the weights of a threshold circuit such that the ith node in the first hidden layer has the weights $(\mathbf{e}_I, 1, 1/(4m), \mathbf{e}_i, 0)$, where the jth component of $\mathbf{e}_I \in \{0, 1\}^{|S|}$ is 1 if and only if $j \in I$ and $\mathbf{e}_i$ is the ith unit vector in $\mathbb{R}^{n_1}$. The remaining nodes in the other layers compute the function $\boldsymbol{x} \mapsto x_1 \wedge \dots \wedge x_l$ of their inputs x_i. Since the cover is exact, this maps all examples correctly except K examples in **(I)**.

Conversely, assume that every cover has size at least $c \cdot K$. Assume some weight setting misclassifies less than $c \cdot K$ examples. We can assume that the activation of every node is different from 0 on the training set: for the examples in **(IV)** the weight w_n serves as a threshold, for the points in **(I)**, **(II)**, and **(III)** except for $(0^{|C|}, 1, 0^{n_1+2}; 1)$ the weight $w_{|C|+2}$ serves as a threshold, hence one can slightly change the respective weight which serves as a threshold without changing the classification of these examples such that the activation becomes nonzero. Assuming that the activation of $(0^{|C|}, 1, 0^{n_1+2}; 1)$ is zero we can slightly increase the weight $w_{|C|+1}$ such that the sign of the activation of all other points which are affected does not change. Because of the multiplicity of the examples the examples in **(II)**-**(IV)** are correctly classified. We can assume that the output of the circuit has the form $\beta_A(\boldsymbol{w}, \boldsymbol{x}) = f_1(\boldsymbol{x}) \wedge \dots \wedge f_{n_1}(\boldsymbol{x})$ where f_i is the function computed by the ith hidden node in the first hidden layer, because of the points in **(IV)**. This is due to the fact that the points $\tilde{\boldsymbol{z}}_i$ and $\bar{\boldsymbol{z}}_i$ enforce the respective weights of the nodes in the first hidden layer to nearly coincide with weights describing the hyperplane with ith coefficient zero. Hence the points $\boldsymbol{p}_i$ are mapped to the entire set $\{0, 1\}^{n_1}$ by the hidden nodes in the first hidden layer and determine the remainder of the circuit function. Hence all nodes in the first hidden layer classify all positive examples except less than $c \cdot K$ points of **(I)** correctly and there exists one node in the first hidden layer which classifies the negative example in **(III)** correctly as well. Consider this last node. Denote by $\boldsymbol{w}$ the weights of this node. Because of **(III)**, $w_{|C|+1} > 0$. Define $I = \{i \in \{1, \dots, |C|\} \mid |w_i| \geq w_{|C|+1}/(2m)\}$.

Assume $\{C_i \mid i \in I\}$ forms a cover. Because of **(III)** we find $w_{|C|+1}/(2m) + w_{|C|+2} > 0$ and $-w_{|C|+1}/(2m) + w_{|C|+2} < 0$. Hence one of the examples in **(I)** is classified wrong for every $i \in I$. Hence at least $c \cdot K$ examples are misclassified.

Assume that $\{C_i \mid i \in I\}$ does not form a cover. Then one can find for some $i \leq |S|$ and the point $(\mathbf{e}_{s_i}, -1, 1, 0^{n_1+1})$ in **(II)** an activation $< m \cdot w_{|C|+1}/(2m) - w_{|C|+1} + w_{|C|+2} = w_{|C|+2} - w_{|C|+1}/2$ which is negative because $-w_{|C|+1}/(2m) + w_{|C|+2} < 0$, $w_{|C|+1} > 0$ **(III)**. This yields a misclassified example with multiplicity $c \cdot K$. $\square$

One can obtain an even stronger result indicating that not only approximation within an arbitrary factor is NP hard but even approximation within a factor which is exponential in the input length is not possible unless NP $\subset$ DTIME($n^{poly(\log n)}$). For this purpose, we use a reduction from the so called label cover problem:

Definition 5 (Label Cover). *Given a bipartite graph $G = (V, W, E)$ with $E \subset V \times W$, labels B, D, and a set $\Pi \subset E \times B \times D$. A labeling consists of functions $P : V \to 2^B$ and $Q : W \to 2^D$ which assign labels to the nodes in the graph. The cost of a labeling is the number $\sum_{v \in V} |P(v)|$. An edge $e = (v, w)$ is covered if both, $P(v)$ and $Q(w)$ are not empty and for all $d \in Q(w)$ some $b \in P(v)$ exists with $(e, b, d) \in \Pi$. A total cover is a labeling such that each edge is covered.*

For the set-covering problem the following result holds, showing that it is almost NP-hard to obtain weak approximations:

Theorem 9. [2,18] *For every $\epsilon > 0$ there exists a quasipolynomial time reduction from the satisfiability problem to the label cover problem which maps an instance φ of size n to an instance (G, Π) of size $N \leq 2^{poly(\log n)}$ with the following properties: If φ is satisfiable then (G, Π) has a total cover with cost $|V|$. If φ is not satisfiable then every total cover has cost at least $2^{\log^{0.5-\epsilon} N}|V|$. Furthermore, (G, Π) has in both cases the property that for each edge $e = (v, w)$ and $b \in B$ at most one $d \in D$ exists with $(e, b, d) \in \Pi$.*

Via this Theorem and ideas of Arora et.al. [2] the following can be proved:

Theorem 10. *Assume that we are given a layered H-circuit where the thresholds of the nodes in the first hidden layer are fixed to 0 and let $\epsilon > 0$ be any given constant. If the problem of approximating minimum failure ratio m_f while learning in the presence of errors within a factor of $2^{\log^{0.5-\epsilon} N}$, N being the size of the respective input, is polynomial time, then NP $\subset$ DTIME($n^{poly(\log n)}$).*

Proof. Assume that we are given a formula φ. Transform this formula with the given constant ϵ to an instance (G, Π) of the label cover problem with the properties as described in Theorem 9. W.l.o.g. does the network contain at least one hidden layer.

First, we delete all $(e = (v, w), b, d)$ in Π such that for some edge e' incident to v no d' exists with $(e', b, d') \in \Pi$. Those labels are called *valid*. The costs for a total cover remain $|V|$ if φ is satisfiable. Otherwise, this can at most increase the costs. For each $e \in E$ and $b \in B$ a unique $d \in D$ exists such that $(e, b, d) \in \Pi$. We denote this element by $d(e, b)$. We can assume that a total cover exists, since this can be polynomially tested.

Now transform this instance to an instance of the loading problem. The input dimension is $n = n_2 + 2 + n_1 + 1$ where n_1 denotes the number of hidden nodes in the first hidden layer, $n_2 = |V||B| + |W||D|$, $E \subset V \times W$ are the edges, B and D are the labels. The following examples from $\mathbb{Q}^n \times \{0, 1\}$ are constructed: ($m = \max\{|B|, |D|\}$, $K = |B| \cdot |E|$, the first n_2 components are successively identified with the tuples in $V \times B$ and $W \times D$ and denoted via corresponding indices.)

(I) K copies of each of $(0^{n_2+2}, \boldsymbol{p}_i, 1; 0)$ ($i \geq 1$), $(0^{n_2+2}, \boldsymbol{p}_0, 1; 1)$, $(0^{n_2+2}, \tilde{\boldsymbol{z}}_i, 1; 1)$, $(0^{n_2+2}, \bar{\boldsymbol{z}}_i, 1; 0)$, where the points $\boldsymbol{p}_i, \tilde{\boldsymbol{z}}_i, \bar{\boldsymbol{z}}_i$ are the same points as in the proof of Theorem 8.

(II) K copies of $(0^{|n_2|}, 1, 0, 0^{n_1+1}; 1)$,

(III) K copies of $(0^{|n_2|}, 1/(16m^2), 1, 0^{n_1+1}; 1)$, $(0^{|n_2|}, -1/(16m^2), 1, 0^{n_1+1}; 0)$,

(IV) K copies of each of the points $(e_v, -1, 1, 0^{n_1+1}; 1)$, $(e_w, -1, 1, 0^{n_1+1}; 1)$, where e_v is 1 precisely at those places (v, b) such that b is a valid label for v and 0 otherwise, and e_w is 1 precisely at the places (w, d) such that $d \in D$ ($v \in V$, $w \in W$).

(V) K copies of each of the points $(-e_{v \to w,d}, 1, 1, 0^{n_1+1}; 1)$, where $-e_{v \to w,d}$ is -1 precisely at those places (v, b) such that b is a valid label for v and d is not assigned to $(v \to w, b)$ and at the place (w, d) and 0 otherwise ($v \to w \in E$).

(VI) $(-e_{v,b}, 0, 1, 0^{n_1+1}; 1)$, where $-e_{v,b}$ is -1 precisely at those places (v, b) such that b is a valid label for v.

Assume that a label cover with costs $|V|$ exists. Define the weights for the neurons in the first computation layer by $w_{(v,b)} = 1 \iff b$ is assigned to v, $w_{(w,d)} = 1 \iff d$ is assigned to w, $w_{n_2+1} = 1$, $w_{n_2+2} = 1/(32m^2)$. If a hidden layer is contained, the remaining coefficients of the ith hidden neuron in the first hidden layer are defined by $w_{n_2+2+i} = 1$, the remaining coefficients are 0. The neurons in other layers compute the logical function AND. This maps all points but at most $|V|$ points in **(VI)** to correct outputs. Note that the points in **(V)** are correct since each v is assigned precisely one b.

Conversely, assume that a solution of the loading problem is given. We show that it has at least a number of misclassified points which equals the costs of a cover, denoted by C. Assume for the sake of contradiction that less than C points are classified wrong. Since a cover has costs at most K we can assume that all points with multiplicities are mapped correctly. Because of the same argumentation as in 8 we can assume that the activation of every node is different from 0 on the training set. Additionally, we can assume that the output of the circuit has the form $\beta_A(w, x) = f_1(x) \wedge \ldots \wedge f_{n_1}(x)$ where f_i is the function computed by the ith hidden node in the first hidden layer, because of the points in **(I)**. Hence all nodes in the first hidden layer classify all positive examples except less than C points of **(V)** correctly and there exists one node in the first hidden layer which classifies the negative example in **(III)** correctly as well.

Denote by w the weights of this node. Because of **(II)**, $w_{|n_2|+1} > 0$. Label the node v with those valid labels b such that $w_{(v,b)} > w_{n_2+1}/(4m^2)$. Label the node w with those labels d such that $w_{(w,d)} > w_{n_2+1}/(2m)$. If this labeling forms a total cover, then we find for all b assigned to v in **(VI)** an activation smaller than $-w_{n_2+1}/(4m^2) + w_{n_2+2}$. Due to **(III)**, $w_{n_2+2} < 1/(16m^2) \cdot w_{n_2+1}$, hence the activation is smaller than 0 and leads to a number of misclassified points which is at least equal to the costs C.

Assume conversely that this labeling does not form a total cover. Then some v or w is not labeled, or for some label d for w and edge $v \to w$ no b is assigned to v with $(v \to w, b, d) \in \Pi$. Due to **(IV)** we find $\sum_{b \text{ valid for } v} w_{(v,b)} - w_{n_2+1} + w_{n_2+2} > 0$, hence together with **(III)** $\sum_{b \text{ valid for } v} w_{(v,b)} > w_{n_2+1} - w_{n_2+1}/(16m^2)$, hence at least one $w_{(v,b)}$ is of size at least $w_{n_2+1}/(2m)$. In the same way we find $\sum_d w_{(w,d)} - w_{n_2+1} + w_{n_2+2} > 0$, hence at least one $w_{(w,d)}$ is of size at least $w_{n_2+1}/(2m)$. Consequently, each node is assigned some label. Assume that the node w is assigned some d such that the edge $v \to w$ is not covered. Hence $w_{(w,d)} > w_{n_2+1}/(2m)$. Due to **(V)** we find $-\sum_{b \text{ valid for } v, d(v \to w, b) \neq d} w_{(v,b)} - w_{(w,d)} + w_{n_2+1} + w_{n_2+2} > 0$ and due to **(IV)** we find $\sum_{b \text{ valid for } v} w_{(v,b)} - w_{n_2+1} + w_{n_2+2} > 0$, hence $\sum_{b \text{ valid for } v, d(v \to w, b) = d} w_{(v,b)} > w_{n_2+1} - w_{n_2+2} - \sum_{b \text{ valid for } v, d(v \to w, b) \neq d} w_{(v,b)} > w_{n_2+1} - w_{n_2+2} + w_{(w,d)} - w_{n_2+1} -$

$w_{n_2+2} = w_{(w,d)} - 2w_{n_2+2} > w_{n_2+1}(1/(2m) - 1/(8m^2)) > w_{n_2+1}/(4m)$. Hence at least one weight corresponding to a label which can be used to cover this edge is of size at least $w_{n_2+1}/(4m^2)$. □

5 Conclusion

We have shown the NP-hardness of finding approximate solutions for the loading problem in several different situations. We have considered the question as to whether approximating the relative error of m_L within a constant factor is NP-hard. Compared to [3] we considered threshold circuits with correlated number of patterns and hidden neurons and the $(n, 2, 1)$-circuit with the sigmoidal (with ϵ-separation) or the semilinear activation function. Furthermore, we discussed how to avoid training using multiple copies of the example. We considered the case where the number of examples is correlated to the number of hidden nodes. Investigating the problem of minimizing the failure ratio in the presence of errors yields NP-hardness within every constant factor $c > 1$ for multi-layer threshold circuits with zero input biases, and even weak approximation of this ratio is hard under standard complexity-theoretic assumptions.

6 Acknowledgments

We would like to thank Eduardo Sontag for bringing the authors together, Peter Bartlett and Ben-David Shai for sending us their research work (references [3] and [5]) and pointing out the implications of Theorem 2 of [3], Elizabeth Sweedyk for sending details about reference [2], and NSF for providing financial support for this research.

References

1. E. Amaldi and V. Kann, The complexity and approximability of finding maximum feasible subsystems of linear relations, Theoretical Computer Science 147 (1-2), pp.181-210, 1995. 265
2. S. Arora, L. Babai, J. Stern, and Z. Sweedyk, The hardness of approximate optima in lattices, codes and systems of linear equations, Journal of Computer and System Sciences, 54, pp. 317-331, 1997. 264, 265, 266, 273, 275, 277
3. P. Bartlett and S. Ben-David, Hardness results for neural network approximation problems, to appear in Theoretical Computer Science (conference version in Fischer P. and Simon H. U. (eds.), Computational Learning Theory, Lecture Notes in Artificial Intelligence 1572, Springer, pp. 639-644, 1999). 264, 265, 266, 268, 272, 277
4. M. Bellare, S. Goldwasser, C. Lund, and A. Russell, Efficient multi-prover interactive proofs with applications to approximation problems, in Proceedings of the 25th ACM Symposium on the Theory of Computing, pp. 113-131, 1993. 273
5. S. Ben-David, N. Eiron and P. M. Long, On the difficulty of approximately maximizing agreements, 13th Annual ACM Conference on Computational Learning Theory (COLT), 2000. 264, 265, 277
6. A. Blum and R. L. Rivest, Training a 3-node neural network is NP-complete, Neural Networks 5, pp. 117-127, 1992. 264, 265, 266

7. J. Brown, M. Garber, and S. Vanable, Artificial neural network on a SIMD architecture, in Proc. 2nd Symposium on the Frontier of Massively Parallel Computation, Fairfax, VA, pp. 43-47, 1988. 272

8. B. DasGupta, H. T. Siegelmann, and E. D. Sontag, On the Intractability of Loading Neural Networks, in Roychowdhury V. P., Siu K. Y., and Orlitsky A. (eds.), Theoretical Advances in Neural Computation and Learning, Kluwer Academic Publishers, pp. 357-389, 1994. 265, 266, 272

9. M. R. Garey and D. S. Johnson, Computers and Intractability: A Guide to the Theory of NP-completeness, Freeman, San Francisco, 1979. 273

10. B. Hammer, Some complexity results for perceptron networks, in Niklasson L., Bodén M., and Ziemke, T. (eds.), ICANN'98, Springer, pp. 639-644, 1998. 265

11. B. Hammer, Training a sigmoidal network is difficult, in Verleysen M. (ed.), European Symposium on Artificial Neural Networks, D-Facto publications, pp. 255-260, 1998. 265

12. K.-U. Höffgen, Computational limitations on training sigmoid neural networks, Information Processing Letters 46(6), pp.269-274, 1993. 265

13. K.-U. Höffgen, H.-U. Simon, and K. S. Van Horn, Robust trainability of single neurons, Journal of Computer and System Sciences 50(1), pp.114-125, 1995. 265

14. L. K. Jones, The computational intractability of training sigmoidal neural networks, IEEE Transactions on Information Theory 43(1), pp. 167-713, 1997. 265

15. J. S. Judd, On the complexity of loading shallow networks, Journal on Complexity 4(3), pp.177-192, 1988. 264, 265

16. J. S. Judd, Neural network design and the complexity of learning, MIT Press, Cambridge, MA, 1990. 264

17. V. Kann, S. Khanna, J. Lagergren, and A. Panconesi, On the hardness of approximating max-k-cut and its dual, Technical Report CJTCS-1997-2, Chicago Journal of Theoretical Computer Science, 1997. 267

18. C. Lund and M. Yannakakis, On the hardness of approximate minimization problems, Journal of the ACM, 41(5), pp. 960-981, 1994. 275

19. W. Maass, G. Schnitger, and E. D. Sontag, A comparison of the computational power of sigmoid versus boolean threshold circuits, in Roychowdhury V. P., Siu K. Y., and Orlitsky A. (eds.), Theoretical Advances in Neural Computation and Learning, Kluwer Academic Publishers, pp. 127-151, 1994. 264, 271

20. M. Megiddo, On the complexity of polyhedral separability, Discrete Computational Geometry 3, pp. 325-337, 1988. 265, 269

21. C. H. Papadimtriou and M. Yannakakis. Optimization, Approximation and Complexity Classes, Journal of Computer & System Sciences 43, pp. 425-440, 1991. 267

22. I. Parberry and G. Schnitger, *Parallel computation with threshold functions*, Journal of Computer and System Sciences, 36, 3 (1988), pp. 278-302. 268

23. J. Šimà, Back-propagation is not efficient, Neural Networks 9(6), pp. 1017-1023, 1996. 265

24. K.-Y. Siu, V. Roychowdhury and T. Kailath, *Discrete Neural Computation: A Theoretical Foundation*, Englewood Cliffs, NJ: Prentice Hall, 1994. 268

25. E. D. Sontag, Feedforward nets for interpolation and classification, Journal of Computer and System Sciences 45, pp.20-48, 1992. 265, 268

26. M. Vidyasagar, A theory of learning and generalization, Springer, 1997. 268

27. V. H. Vu, On the infeasibility of training with small squared errors, in Jordan M. I., Kearns M. J., and Solla S. A. (eds.), Advances in Neural Information Processing Systems 10, MIT Press, pp. 371-377, 1998. 265

28. B. Widrow, R. G. Winter and R. A. Baxter, *Layered neural nets for pattern recognition*, IEEE Transactions on Acoustics, Speech and Signal Processing, 36 (1988), pp. 1109-1117. 268

The Last-Step Minimax Algorithm

Eiji Takimoto[1⋆] and Manfred K. Warmuth[2⋆⋆]

[1] Graduate School of Information Sciences, Tohoku University
Sendai, 980-8579, Japan.
t2@ecei.tohoku.ac.jp
[2] Computer Science Department, University of California, Santa Cruz
Santa Cruz, CA 95064, U.S.A.
manfred@cse.ucsc.edu

Abstract. We consider on-line density estimation with a parameterized density from an exponential family. In each trial t the learner predicts a parameter θ_t. Then it receives an instance x_t chosen by the adversary and incurs loss $-\ln p(x_t|\theta_t)$ which is the negative log-likelihood of x_t w.r.t. the predicted density of the learner. The performance of the learner is measured by the regret defined as the total loss of the learner minus the total loss of the best parameter chosen off-line. We develop an algorithm called the Last-step Minimax Algorithm that predicts with the minimax optimal parameter assuming that the current trial is the last one. For one-dimensional exponential families, we give an explicit form of the prediction of the Last-step Minimax Algorithm and show that its regret is $O(\ln T)$, where T is the number of trials. In particular, for Bernoulli density estimation the Last-step Minimax Algorithm is slightly better than the standard Krichevsky-Trofimov probability estimator.

1 Introduction

Consider the following repeated game based on density estimation with a family of probability mass functions $\{p(\cdot|\theta) \mid \theta \in \Theta\}$, where Θ denotes the parameter space. The learner plays against an adversary. In each trial t the learner produces a parameter θ_t. Then the adversary provides an instance x_t and the loss of the learner is $L(x_t, \theta_t) := -\ln p(x_t|\theta_t)$. Consider the following *regret* or *relative loss*

$$\sum_{t=1}^{T} L(x_t, \theta_t) - \inf_{\theta_B \in \Theta} \sum_{t=1}^{T} L(x_t, \theta_B).$$

This is the total on-line loss of the learner minus the total loss of the best parameter chosen off-line based on all T instances. The goal of the learner is to minimize the regret while the goal of the adversary is to maximize it. To get a finite regret we frequently need to restrict the adversary to choose instances from a bounded space (Otherwise the adversary could make the regret unbounded in

---

⋆ This work was done while the author visited University of California, Santa Cruz.
⋆⋆ Supported by NSF grant CCR-9821087

H. Arimura, S. Jain and A. Sharma (Eds.): ALT 2000, LNAI 1968, pp. 279-290, 2000.
© Springer-Verlag Berlin Heidelberg 2000

just one trial). So we let $\mathcal{X}_0$ be the instance space from which instances are chosen. Thus the game is specified by a parametric density and the pair $(\Theta, \mathcal{X}_0)$.

If the horizon T is fixed and known in advance, then we can use the optimal minimax algorithm. For a given history of play $(\boldsymbol{\theta}_1, \boldsymbol{x}_1, \ldots, \boldsymbol{\theta}_{t-1}, \boldsymbol{x}_{t-1})$ of the past $t-1$ trials, this algorithm predicts with

$$\boldsymbol{\theta}_t = \operatorname*{arginf}_{\boldsymbol{\theta}_t \in \Theta} \sup_{\boldsymbol{x}_t \in \mathcal{X}_0} \inf_{\boldsymbol{\theta}_{t+1} \in \Theta} \sup_{\boldsymbol{x}_{t+1} \in \mathcal{X}_0} \cdots \inf_{\boldsymbol{\theta}_T \in \Theta} \sup_{\boldsymbol{x}_T \in \mathcal{X}_0} \left(\sum_{t=1}^{T} L(\boldsymbol{x}_t, \boldsymbol{\theta}_t) - \inf_{\boldsymbol{\theta}_B \in \Theta} \sum_{t=1}^{T} L(\boldsymbol{x}_t, \boldsymbol{\theta}_B) \right).$$

The minimax algorithm achieves the best possible regret (called *minimax regret* or the *value* of the game). However this algorithm usually cannot be computed efficiently. In addition the horizon T of the game might not be known to the learner. Therefore we introduce a simple heuristic for the learner called the *Last-step Minimax Algorithm* that behaves as follows: Choose the minimax prediction assuming that the current trial is the last one (i.e. assuming that $T = t$). More precisely, the Last-step Minimax Algorithm predicts with

$$\boldsymbol{\theta}_t = \operatorname*{arginf}_{\boldsymbol{\theta}_t \in \Theta} \sup_{\boldsymbol{x}_t \in \mathcal{X}_0} \left(\sum_{q=1}^{t} L(\boldsymbol{x}_q, \boldsymbol{\theta}_q) - \inf_{\boldsymbol{\theta}_B \in \Theta} \sum_{q=1}^{t} L(\boldsymbol{x}_q, \boldsymbol{\theta}_B) \right).$$

This method for motivating learning algorithms was first used by Forster [4] for linear regression.

We apply the Last-step Minimax Algorithm to density estimation with one-dimensional exponential families. The exponential families include many fundamental classes of distributions such as Bernoulli, Binomial, Poisson, Gaussian, Gamma and so on. In particular, we consider the game $(\Theta, \mathcal{X}_0)$, where Θ is the exponential family that is specified by a convex[1] function F and $\mathcal{X}_0 = [A, B]$ for some $A < B$. We show that the prediction of the Last-step Minimax Algorithm is explicitly represented as

$$\boldsymbol{\theta}_t = \frac{t}{B - A} \Big(F(\alpha_t + B/t) - F(\alpha_t + A/t) \Big),$$

where $\alpha_t = \sum_{q=1}^{t-1} \boldsymbol{x}_q / t$. Moreover we show that its regret is $M \ln T + O(1)$, where

$$M = \max_{A \leq \alpha \leq B} \frac{F''(\alpha)(\alpha - A)(B - \alpha)}{2}.$$

In particular, for the case of Bernoulli, we show that the regret of the Last-step Minimax Algorithm is at most

$$\frac{1}{2} \ln(T + 1) + c, \tag{1}$$

where $c = 1/2$. This is very close to the minimax regret that Shtarkov showed for the fixed horizon game [7]. The minimax regret has the same form (1) but now $c = (1/2) \ln(\pi/2) \approx .23$.

---

[1] The function F is the dual of the cumulant function (See next section).

Another simple and efficient algorithm for density estimation with an arbitrary exponential family is the *Forward Algorithm* of Azoury and Warmuth [2]. This algorithm predicts with $\mu_t = (a + \sum_{q=1}^{t-1} x_q)/t$ for any exponential family. Here $a \geq 0$ is a constant that is to be tuned and the mean parameter μ_t is an alternate parameterization of the density. For a Bernoulli, the Forward Algorithm with $a = 1/2$ is the well-known Krichevsky-Trofimov probability estimator. The regret of this algorithm is again of the same form as (1) with $c = (1/2) \ln \pi \approx .57$ (See e.g. [5]). Surprisingly, the Last-step Minimax Algorithm is slightly better than the Krichevsky-Trofimov probability estimator ($c = .5$).

For general one-dimensional exponential families, the Forward Algorithm can be seen as a first-order approximation of the Last-step Minimax Algorithm. However, in the special case of Gaussian density estimation and linear regression, the Last-step Minimax Algorithm is identical to the Forward Algorithm[2] for some choice of a. For linear regression this was first pointed out by Forster [4].

In [2] upper bounds on the regret of the Forward Algorithm were given for specific exponential families. For all the specific families considered there, the bounds we can prove for the Last-step Minimax Algorithm are as good or better. In this paper we also give a bound of $M \ln T + O(1)$ that holds for a large class of one-dimensional exponential families. No such bound is known for the Forward Algorithm.

It is interesting to note that for Gaussian density estimation of unit variance, there exists a gap between the regret of the Last-step Minimax algorithm and the regret of the optimal minimax algorithm. Specifically, the former is $O(\ln T)$, while the latter is $O(\ln T - \ln \ln T)$ [10]. This contrasts with the case of Bernoulli, where the regret of the Last-step Minimax Algorithm is by a constant larger than the minimax regret.

Open Problems

There are a large number of open problems.

1. Is the regret of the Last-step Minimax Algorithm always of the form $O(\ln T)$ for density estimation with any member of the exponential family?
2. Does the Last-step Minimax Algorithm always have smaller regret than the Forward Algorithm?
3. For what density estimation and regression problems is the regret of the Last-step Minimax Algorithm "close to" the regret of the optimal minimax algorithm?
4. It is easy to generalize the Last-step Minimax Algorithm to the q-last-step Minimax algorithm where q is some constant larger than one. How does q affect the regret of the algorithm? How large should q be chosen so that the regret of the algorithm is essentially as good as the minimax algorithm.

---

[2] More strictly, for linear regression the Last-step Minimax Algorithm "'clips" the predictions of the Forward Algorithm so that the absolute value of the predictions is bounded.

Regret Bounds from the MDL Community

There is a large body of work on proving regret bounds that has its roots in the Minimum Description Length community [6, 11, 8, 9, 12, 13]. The definition of regret used in this community is different from ours in the following two parts.

1. The learner predicts with an arbitrary probability mass function q_t. In particular q_t does not need to be in the model class $\{p(\cdot|\theta) \mid \theta \in \Theta\}$. On the other hand, in our setting we require the predictions of the learner to be "proper" in the sense that they must lie in the same underlying model class.
2. The individual instances x_t does not need to be bounded. The adversary is instead required to choose an instance sequence $x_1, \ldots, x_T$ so that the best off-line parameter θ_B for the sequence belongs to a compact subset $K \subseteq \Theta$. For density estimation with an exponential family, this condition implies that $(1/T) \sum_{t=1}^{T} x_t \in K$.

In comparison with the setting in this paper, it is obvious that part 1 gives more choices to the learner while part 2 gives more choices to the adversary. Therefore the regret bounds obtained in the MDL setting are usually incomparable with those in our setting. In particular, Rissanen [6] showed under some condition on Θ that the minimax regret is

$$\frac{n}{2} \ln \frac{T}{2\pi} + \ln \int_K \sqrt{|I(\theta)|} \, d\theta + o(1), \tag{2}$$

where $\Theta \subseteq \mathbf{R}^n$ is of dimension n and

$$I(\theta) = (E_\theta(-\partial^2 \ln p(\cdot|\theta)/\partial\theta_i\partial\theta_j))_{i,j}$$

denotes the Fisher information matrix of θ. This bound is quite different from our bound $M \ln T + O(1)$.

2   On-line Density Estimation

We first give a general framework of the on-line density estimation problem with a parametric class of distributions. Let $\mathcal{X} \subseteq \mathbf{R}^n$ denote the instance space and $\Theta \subseteq \mathbf{R}^d$ denote the parameter space. Each parameter $\theta \in \Theta$ represents a probability distribution over $\mathcal{X}$. Specifically let $p(\cdot|\theta)$ denote the probability mass function that θ represents. An on-line algorithm called the *learner* is a function $\hat{\theta} : \mathcal{X}^* \to \Theta$ that is used to choose a parameter based on the past instance sequence. The protocol proceeds in trials. In each trial $t = 1, 2, \ldots$ the learner chooses a parameter $\theta_t = \hat{\theta}(x^{t-1})$, where $x^{t-1} = (x_1, \ldots, x_{t-1})$ is the instance sequence observed so far. Then the learner receives an instance $x_t \in \mathcal{X}$ and suffers a loss defined as the negative log-likelihood of x_t measured by θ_t, i.e.,

$$L(x_t, \theta_t) = -\ln p(x_t|\theta_t).$$

The total loss of the learner up to trial T is $\sum_{t=1}^{T} L(\boldsymbol{x}_t, \boldsymbol{\theta}_t)$. Let $\boldsymbol{\theta}_{B,T}$ be the best parameter in hindsight (off-line setting). Namely,

$$\boldsymbol{\theta}_{B,T} = \operatorname*{arginf}_{\boldsymbol{\theta} \in \Theta} \sum_{t=1}^{T} L(\boldsymbol{x}_t, \boldsymbol{\theta}).$$

If we regard the product of the probabilities of the individual instances as the joint probability (i.e., $p(\boldsymbol{x}^T | \boldsymbol{\theta}) = \prod_{t=1}^{T} p(\boldsymbol{x}_t | \boldsymbol{\theta})$), then the best parameter $\boldsymbol{\theta}_{B,T}$ can be interpreted as the maximum likelihood estimator of the observed instance sequence $\boldsymbol{x}^T$. We measure the performance of the learner for a particular instance sequence $\boldsymbol{x}^T \in \mathcal{X}^*$ by the *regret*, or the *relative loss*, defined as

$$R(\hat{\boldsymbol{\theta}}, \boldsymbol{x}^T) = \sum_{t=1}^{T} L(\boldsymbol{x}_t, \boldsymbol{\theta}_t) - \sum_{t=1}^{T} L(\boldsymbol{x}_t, \boldsymbol{\theta}_{B,T}).$$

The goal of the learner is to make the regret as small as possible. In this paper we are concerned with the worst-case regret and so we do not put any (probabilistic) assumption on how the instance sequence is generated. In other words, the preceding protocol can be viewed as a game of two players, the learner and the adversary, where the regret is the payoff function. The learner tries to minimize the regret, while the adversary tries to maximize it. In most cases, to get a finite regret we need to restrict the adversary to choose instances from a bounded space (Otherwise the adversary could make the regret unbounded in just one trial). So we let $\mathcal{X}_0 \subseteq \mathcal{X}$ be the set of instances from which instances are chosen. The choice of $\mathcal{X}_0$ is one of the central issues for analyzing regrets in our learning model.

3   Last-step Minimax Algorithm

If the horizon T of the game is fixed and known in advance, then we can use the minimax algorithm to obtain the optimal learner in the game theoretical sense. The value of the game is the best possible regret that the learner can achieve. In most cases, the value of the game has no closed form and the minimax algorithm is computationally infeasible. Also the number of trials T might not be known to the learner. For this reasons we suggest the following simple heuristic. Assume that the current trial t is the last one (in other words, assume $T = t$) and predict as the Minimax Algorithm would under this assumption. More precisely the Last-step Minimax Algorithm predicts with

$$\boldsymbol{\theta}_t = \operatorname*{arginf}_{\boldsymbol{\theta}_t \in \Theta} \sup_{\boldsymbol{x}_t \in \mathcal{X}_0} \left(\sum_{q=1}^{t} L(\boldsymbol{x}_q, \boldsymbol{\theta}_q) - \sum_{q=1}^{t} L(\boldsymbol{x}_q, \boldsymbol{\theta}_{B,t}) \right)$$

$$= \operatorname*{arginf}_{\boldsymbol{\theta}_t \in \Theta} \sup_{\boldsymbol{x}_t \in \mathcal{X}_0} \left(L(\boldsymbol{x}_t, \boldsymbol{\theta}_t) - \sum_{q=1}^{t} L(\boldsymbol{x}_q, \boldsymbol{\theta}_{B,t}) \right). \tag{3}$$

The last equality holds since the total loss up to trial $t-1$ of the learner is constant for the inf and sup operations.

3.1   Last-step minimax algorithm for exponential families

For a vector $\boldsymbol{\theta}$, $\boldsymbol{\theta}'$ denotes the transposition of $\boldsymbol{\theta}$. A class Θ_G of distributions is said to be an exponential family if parameter $\theta \in \Theta_G$ has density function

$$p(\boldsymbol{x}|\boldsymbol{\theta}) = p_0(\boldsymbol{x}) \exp(\boldsymbol{\theta}'\boldsymbol{x} - G(\boldsymbol{\theta})),$$

where $p_0(\boldsymbol{x})$ represents any factor of density which does not depend on $\boldsymbol{\theta}$. The parameter $\boldsymbol{\theta}$ is called the *natural* parameter. The function $G(\boldsymbol{\theta})$ is a normalization factor so that $\int_{\boldsymbol{x} \in \mathcal{X}} p(\boldsymbol{x}|\boldsymbol{\theta}) d\boldsymbol{x} = 1$ holds, and it is called the *cumulant function* that characterizes the family Θ_G. We first review some basic properties of the family. For further details, see [3, 1]. Let $g(\boldsymbol{\theta})$ denote the gradient vector $\nabla_{\boldsymbol{\theta}} G(\boldsymbol{\theta})$. It is well known that G is a strictly convex function and $g(\boldsymbol{\theta})$ equals the mean of $\boldsymbol{x}$, i.e. $g(\boldsymbol{\theta}) = \int_{\boldsymbol{x} \in \mathcal{X}} \boldsymbol{x} p(\boldsymbol{x}|\boldsymbol{\theta}) d\boldsymbol{x}$. We let $g(\boldsymbol{\theta}) = \boldsymbol{\mu}$ and call $\boldsymbol{\mu}$ the expectation parameter. Since G is strictly convex, the map $g(\boldsymbol{\theta}) = \boldsymbol{\mu}$ has an inverse: Let $f := g^{-1}$. Sometimes it is more convenient to use the expectation parameter $\boldsymbol{\mu}$ instead of its natural parameter $\boldsymbol{\theta}$. Define the second function F over the set of expectation parameters as

$$F(\boldsymbol{\mu}) = \boldsymbol{\theta}'\boldsymbol{\mu} - G(\boldsymbol{\theta}). \tag{4}$$

The function F is called the *dual* of G and strictly convex as well. It is easy to check that $f(\boldsymbol{\mu}) = \nabla_{\boldsymbol{\mu}} F(\boldsymbol{\mu})$. Thus the two parameters $\boldsymbol{\theta}$ and $\boldsymbol{\mu}$ are related by

$$\boldsymbol{\mu} = g(\boldsymbol{\theta}) = \nabla_{\boldsymbol{\theta}} G(\boldsymbol{\theta}), \tag{5}$$
$$\boldsymbol{\theta} = f(\boldsymbol{\mu}) = \nabla_{\boldsymbol{\mu}} F(\boldsymbol{\mu}). \tag{6}$$

For parameter $\boldsymbol{\theta}$, the negative log-likelihood of $\boldsymbol{x}$ is $G(\boldsymbol{\theta}) - \boldsymbol{\theta}'\boldsymbol{x} + \ln P_0(\boldsymbol{x})$. Since the last term is independent of $\boldsymbol{\theta}$ and thus does not affect the regret, we define the loss function simply as

$$L(\boldsymbol{x}, \boldsymbol{\theta}) := G(\boldsymbol{\theta}) - \boldsymbol{\theta}'\boldsymbol{x}. \tag{7}$$

It is easy to see that, for an instance sequence $\boldsymbol{x}^t$ up to trial t, the best off-line parameter $\boldsymbol{\mu}_{B,t}$ is given by $\boldsymbol{\mu}_{B,t} = \boldsymbol{x}_{1..t}/t$ (thus, $\boldsymbol{\theta}_{B,t} = f(\boldsymbol{x}_{1..t}/t)$), where $\boldsymbol{x}_{1..t}$ is shorthand for $\sum_{q=1}^{t} \boldsymbol{x}_q$. Moreover the total loss of $\boldsymbol{\theta}_{B,t}$ is

$$\sum_{q=1}^{t} L(\boldsymbol{x}_q, \boldsymbol{\theta}_{B,t}) = -tF(\boldsymbol{x}_{1..t}/t). \tag{8}$$

From (3), (7) and (8), it immediately follows that the Last-step Minimax Algorithm for the family Θ_G predicts with

$$\boldsymbol{\theta}_t = \operatorname*{arginf}_{\boldsymbol{\theta} \in \Theta_G} \ \sup_{\boldsymbol{x}_t \in \mathcal{X}_0} \ \left(G(\boldsymbol{\theta}) - \boldsymbol{\theta}'\boldsymbol{x}_t + tF(\boldsymbol{x}_{1..t}/t) \right). \tag{9}$$

3.2 For one dimensional exponential families

In what follows we only consider one dimensional exponential families. Let the instance space be $\mathcal{X}_0 = [A, B]$ for some reals $A < B$. Since F is convex, the supremum over x_t of (9) is attained at a boundary of $\mathcal{X}_0$, i.e., $x_t = A$ or $x_t = B$. So

$$\boldsymbol{\theta}_t = \arginf_{\boldsymbol{\theta} \in \Theta_G} \max \Big\{ G(\boldsymbol{\theta}) - A\boldsymbol{\theta} + tF(\alpha_t + A/t), G(\boldsymbol{\theta}) - B\boldsymbol{\theta} + tF(\alpha_t + B/t) \Big\}, \quad (10)$$

where $\alpha_t = x_{1..t-1}/t$. It is not hard to see that the minimax parameter $\boldsymbol{\theta}_t$ must satisfy $\boldsymbol{\mu}_t = g(\boldsymbol{\theta}_t) \in [A, B]$. So we can restrict the parameter space to

$$\Theta_{G, \mathcal{X}_0} = \{\boldsymbol{\theta} \in \Theta_G \mid g(\boldsymbol{\theta}) \in [A, B]\}.$$

Since for any $\boldsymbol{\theta} \in \Theta_{G, \mathcal{X}_0}$

$$\frac{\partial}{\partial \boldsymbol{\theta}} \Big(G(\boldsymbol{\theta}) - A\boldsymbol{\theta} + tF(\alpha_t + A/t) \Big) = g(\boldsymbol{\theta}) - A \geq 0,$$

the first term in the maximum of (10) is monotonically increasing in $\boldsymbol{\theta}$. Similarly the second term is monotonically decreasing. So the minimax parameter $\boldsymbol{\theta}_t$ must be the solution to the equation

$$G(\boldsymbol{\theta}) - A\boldsymbol{\theta} + tF(\alpha_t + A/t) = G(\boldsymbol{\theta}) - B\boldsymbol{\theta} + tF(\alpha_t + B/t).$$

Solving this, we have

$$\boldsymbol{\theta}_t = \frac{t}{B - A} \left(F(\alpha_t + B/t) - F(\alpha_t + A/t) \right). \quad (11)$$

Let us confirm that $\boldsymbol{\mu}_t = g(\boldsymbol{\theta}_t) \in [A, B]$. Since F is convex,

$$F(\alpha_t + B/t) = F(\alpha_t + A/t + (B - A)/t)$$
$$\geq F(\alpha_t + A/t) + f(\alpha_t + A/t)(B - A)/t.$$

Plugging this into (11), we have $\boldsymbol{\theta}_t \geq f(\alpha_t + A/t)$. Since g is monotonically increasing and $f = g^{-1}$,

$$\boldsymbol{\mu}_t = g(\boldsymbol{\theta}_t) \geq g(f(\alpha_t + A/t)) = \alpha_t + A/t \geq A. \quad (12)$$

Similarly we can show that

$$F(\alpha_t + A/t) \geq F(\alpha_t + B/t) - f(\alpha_t + B/t)(B - A)/t,$$

which implies

$$\boldsymbol{\mu}_t = g(\boldsymbol{\theta}_t) \leq g(f(\alpha_t + B/t)) = \alpha_t + B/t \leq B.$$

Hence we proved that $\boldsymbol{\mu}_t \in [A, B]$. Note that this argument also shows that

$$\alpha_t + A/t \leq \boldsymbol{\mu}_t \leq \alpha_t + B/t.$$

Therefore, the prediction $\boldsymbol{\mu}_t$ of the Last-step Minimax Algorithm (for the expectation parameter) converges $\alpha_t = x_{1..t-1}/t$, which is the prediction of the Forward Algorithm.

3.3   Analysis on the regret

Let

$$\delta_t = L(x_t, \theta_t) - \sum_{q=1}^{t} L(x_q, \theta_{B,t}) + \sum_{q=1}^{t-1} L(x_q, \theta_{B,t-1}).$$

Since

$$\sum_{t=1}^{T} \delta_t = \sum_{t=1}^{T} L(x_t, \theta_t) - \sum_{t=1}^{T} L(x_t, \theta_{B,T}) = R(\hat{\theta}, x^T),$$

bounding δ_t for all individual t's is a way to obtain an upper bound of the regret $R(\hat{\theta}, x^T)$. By (12) and (8), the prediction θ_t of the Last-step Minimax Algorithm (given by (11)) satisfies

$$L(x_t, \theta_t) - \sum_{q=1}^{t} L(x_q, \theta_{B,t}) \le G(\theta_t) - A\theta_t + tF(\alpha_t + A/t)$$

for any x_t. Moreover, applying (8) with t replaced by $t - 1$, we have

$$\sum_{q=1}^{t-1} L(x_q, \theta_{B,t-1}) = -(t-1)F(x_{1..t-1}/(t-1)) = -(t-1)F\left(\frac{t}{t-1}\alpha_t\right).$$

Hence we have

$$\delta_t \le G(\theta_t) - A\theta_t + tF(\alpha_t + A/t) - (t-1)F\left(\frac{t}{t-1}\alpha_t\right). \tag{13}$$

In the subsequent sections we will give an upper bound of the regret by bounding the right-hand-side of the above formula.

4   Density estimation with a Bernoulli

For a Bernoulli, an expectation parameter $\mu = g(\theta)$ represents the probability distribution over $\mathcal{X} = \{0, 1\}$ given by $p(0|\mu) = 1 - \mu$ and $p(1|\mu) = \mu$. In this case we have $\Theta_G = \mathbf{R}$, $\mathcal{X} = \mathcal{X}_0 = \{0, 1\}$, $G(\theta) = \ln(1 + e^\theta)$ and $F(\mu) = \mu \ln \mu + (1 - \mu) \ln(1 - \mu)$. From (11) it follows that in each trial t the Last-step Minimax Algorithm predicts with

$$\theta_t = t \ln \left[\frac{(\alpha_t + 1/t)^{\alpha_t + 1/t}(1 - \alpha_t - 1/t)^{1 - \alpha_t - 1/t}}{\alpha_t^{\alpha_t}(1 - \alpha_t)^{1 - \alpha_t}} \right], \tag{14}$$

where $\alpha_t = x_{1..t-1}/t$. In other words, the prediction for the expectation parameter is

$$\mu_t = \frac{(k+1)^{k+1}(t-k-1)^{t-k-1}}{k^k(t-k)^{t-k} + (k+1)^{k+1}(t-k-1)^{t-k-1}},$$

where $k = x_{1..t-1}$. This is different from the Krichevsky-Trofimov probability estimator (the Forward Algorithm with $a = \frac{1}{2}$) [5, 2] that predicts with $\mu_t =$

$(k + 1/2)/t$. The worst case regret of the standard algorithm was shown[3] to be $(1/2)\ln(T + 1) + (1/2)\ln\pi$. Surprisingly, the regret of the Last-step Minimax Algorithm is slightly better.

Theorem 1. *Let $\hat{\boldsymbol{\theta}}$ be the Last-step Minimax Algorithm that makes predictions according to (14). Then for any instance sequence $\boldsymbol{x}^T \in \{0,1\}^*$,*

$$R(\hat{\boldsymbol{\theta}}, \boldsymbol{x}^T) \leq \frac{1}{2}\ln(T + 1) + \frac{1}{2}.$$

Proof. Recall that the regret is $R(\hat{\boldsymbol{\theta}}, \boldsymbol{x}^T) = \sum_{t=1}^T \delta_t$ and δ_t is upper-bounded by (13), i.e.,

$$\delta_t \leq G(\boldsymbol{\theta}_t) + tF(\alpha_t) - (t-1)F\left(\frac{t}{t-1}\alpha_t\right).$$

(Note that for the case of Bernoulli the above inequality is an equality.) We can show that the r.h.s. of the above formula is concave in α_t and maximized at $\alpha_t = (t-1)/(2t)$. Plugging this into (14) we have $\boldsymbol{\theta}_t = 0$. So

$$\delta_t \leq G(0) + tF\left(\frac{t-1}{2t}\right) - (t-1)F(1/2)$$

$$= \ln 2 + \frac{t-1}{2}\ln\frac{t-1}{2t} + \frac{t+1}{2}\ln\frac{t+1}{2t} - (t-1)\ln(1/2)$$

$$= \frac{t-1}{2}\ln(t-1) + \frac{t+1}{2}\ln(t+1) - t\ln t$$

$$= \left(\frac{t+1}{2}\ln(t+1) - \frac{t}{2}\ln t\right) - \left(\frac{t}{2}\ln t - \frac{t-1}{2}\ln(t-1)\right).$$

Therefore

$$R(\hat{\boldsymbol{\mu}}, \boldsymbol{x}^T) = \sum_{t=1}^T \delta_t \leq \frac{T+1}{2}\ln(T+1) - \frac{T}{2}\ln T$$

$$= \frac{1}{2}\ln\left((T+1)(1+1/T)^T\right)$$

$$\leq \frac{1}{2}\ln(T+1) + \frac{1}{2}.$$

This completes the theorem.

5 Density Estimation with a General Exponential Family

In this section we give an upper bound of the regret of the Last-step Minimax Algorithm for a general exponential family, provided that the second and the third derivative of $F(\mu)$ is bounded for any $\mu \in [A, B]$. Note that the Bernoulli family do not satisfy this condition because the second derivative $F''(\mu) = 1/\mu + 1/(1-\mu)$ is unbounded when $\mu = 0$ and $\mu = 1$.

---

[3] This regret is achieved in the case where the sequence consists of all 0s or all 1s.

Theorem 2. *Assume that $|F''(\mu)|$ and $|F'''(\mu)|$ is upper-bounded by a constant for any $\mu \in [A, B]$. Then for any instance sequence $x^T \in [A, B]^T$, the regret of the Last-step Minimax Algorithm is upper-bounded by*

$$R(\hat{\theta}, x^T) \leq M \ln T + O(1),$$

where

$$M = \max_{A \leq \alpha \leq B} \frac{F''(\alpha)(\alpha - A)(B - \alpha)}{2}.$$

Proof. As in the case of the Bernoulli, we will bound

$$\delta_t \leq G(\theta_t) - A\theta_t + tF(\alpha_t + A/t) - (t-1)F(t\alpha_t/(t-1))$$

for each t to obtain an upper bound of the regret $R(\hat{\theta}, x^T) = \sum_{t=1}^{T} \delta_t$. The prediction θ_t of the Last-step Minimax Algorithm is given by (11), i.e.,

$$\theta_t = \frac{t}{B - A}\Big(F(\alpha_t + B/t) - F(\alpha_t + A/t)\Big),$$

where $\alpha_t = x_{1..t-1}/t$. Applying Taylor's expansion of F up to the third degree, we have

$$F(\alpha_t + B/t) = F(\alpha_t + A/t) + f(\alpha_t + A/t)\frac{B - A}{t} + \frac{f'(\alpha_t + A/t)}{2}\left(\frac{B - A}{t}\right)^2$$
$$+ O(1/t^3)$$
$$= F(\alpha_t + A/t) + f(\alpha_t + A/t)\frac{B - A}{t} + \frac{f'(\alpha_t)}{2}\left(\frac{B - A}{t}\right)^2$$
$$+ O(1/t^3).$$

Note that the last term $O(1/t^3)$ contains the hidden factors $f''(\alpha_t)$ and $f''(\alpha_t + A/t)$, which are assumed to be bounded by a constant. So the Last-step Minimax prediction is rewritten as

$$\theta_t = f(\alpha_t + A/t) + \frac{f'(\alpha_t)}{2}\frac{B - A}{t} + O(1/t^2).$$

The Taylor's expansion of G gives

$$G(\theta_t) = G(f(\alpha_t + A/t)) + g(f(\alpha_t + A/t))\frac{f'(\alpha_t)(B - A)}{2t} + O(1/t^2)$$
$$= (\alpha_t + A/t)f(\alpha_t + A/t) - F(\alpha_t + A/t)$$
$$+ \frac{\alpha_t f'(\alpha_t)(B - A)}{2t} + O(1/t^2). \tag{15}$$

Here we used the relations $f = g^{-1}$ and $G(f(\mu)) = f(\mu)\mu - F(\mu)$ (See (4) and (6)). Similarly

$$(t-1)F\left(\frac{t}{t-1}\alpha_t\right) = (t-1)F\Big((\alpha_t + A/t) + (\alpha_t/(t-1) - A/t)\Big)$$

$$= (t-1)\Big[F(\alpha_t + A/t) + f(\alpha_t + A/t)(\alpha_t/(t-1) - A/t)$$
$$+ \frac{1}{2}f'(\alpha_t + A/t)(\alpha_t/(t-1) - A/t)^2 + O(1/t^3)\Big]$$
$$= (t-1)F(\alpha_t + A/t) + (\alpha_t + A/t)f(\alpha_t + A/t) - Af(\alpha_t + A/t)$$
$$+ \frac{1}{2t}f'(\alpha_t)(\alpha_t - A)^2 + O(1/t^2). \tag{16}$$

Thus, $(15) - A\theta_t + tF(\alpha_t + A/t) - (16)$ gives

$$\delta_t \le \frac{f'(\alpha_t)(\alpha_t - A)(B - \alpha_t)}{2t} + O(1/t^2)$$
$$\le \frac{M}{t} + O(1/t^2).$$

This establishes the theorem.

5.1 Density estimation with a Gaussian of unit variance

For a Gaussian of unit variance, an expectation parameter μ represents the density

$$p(x|\mu) = \frac{1}{\sqrt{2\pi}} \exp\left(-\frac{1}{2}(x-\mu)^2\right).$$

Thus we have $\Theta_G = \mathbf{R}$, $\mathcal{X} = \mathbf{R}$, $\mathcal{X}_0 = [A, B]$, $G(\theta) = \frac{1}{2}\theta^2$ and $F(\mu) = \frac{1}{2}\mu^2$. In this case, the Last-step Minimax Algorithm predicts with

$$\theta_t = \mu_t = \alpha_t + \frac{A+B}{2t}.$$

Since $F''(\mu) = 1$ for all μ, Theorem 2 says that the regret of the Last-step Minimax Algorithm is

$$R(\hat{\theta}, x^T) \le \frac{(B-A)^2}{8} \ln T + O(1).$$

Note that for Gaussian density estimation the Last-step Minimax Algorithm predicts with the same value as the Forward Algorithm. So here we just have alternate proofs for previously published bounds [2].

5.2 Density estimation with a Gamma of unit shape parameter

For a Gamma of unit shape parameter, an expectation parameter μ represents the density

$$p(x|\mu) = \mu e^{-x\mu}.$$

In this case we have $\Theta_G = (-\infty, 0)$, $\mathcal{X} = (0, \infty)$, $\mathcal{X}_0 = [A, B]$, $G(\theta) = -\ln(-\theta)$ and $F(\mu) = -1 - \ln\mu$. The Last-step Minimax Algorithm predicts with

$$\theta_t = -1/\mu = -\frac{t}{B-A}\left(\ln(\alpha_t + B/t) - \ln(\alpha_t + A/t)\right).$$

Since $F''(\mu) = 1/\mu^2$, Theorem 2 says that the regret of the Last-step Minimax Algorithm is

$$R(\hat{\boldsymbol{\theta}}_t, \boldsymbol{x}^T) \leq \frac{(B-A)^2}{8AB} \ln T + O(1).$$

Previously, the $O(\ln T)$ regret bound is also shown for the Forward Algorithm [2]. However, the hidden constant in the order notation has not been explicitly specified.

Acknowledgments

The authors are grateful to Jun'ichi Takeuchi for useful discussions.

References

1. S. Amari. *Differential Geometrical Methods in Statistics.* Springer Verlag, Berlin, 1985.
2. K. Azoury and M. K. Warmuth. Relative loss bounds for on-line density estimation with the exponential family of distributions. In *Proceedings of the Fifteenth Conference on Uncertainty in Artificial Intelligence*, pages 31–40, San Francisco, CA, 1999. Morgan Kaufmann. To appear in Machine Learning.
3. O. Barndorff-Nielsen. *Information and Exponential Families in Statistical Theory.* Wiley, Chichester, 1978.
4. J. Forster. On relative loss bounds in generalized linear regression. In *12th International Symposium on Fundamentals of Computation Theory*, pages 269–280, 1999.
5. Y. Freund. Predicting a binary sequence almost as well as the optimal biased coin. In *Proc. 9th Annu. Conf. on Comput. Learning Theory*, pages 89–98. ACM Press, New York, NY, 1996.
6. J. Rissanen. Fisher information and stochastic complexity. *IEEE Transactions on Information Theory*, 42(1):40–47, 1996.
7. Y. M. Shtarkov. Universal sequential coding of single messages. *Prob. Pered. Inf.*, 23:175–186, 1987.
8. J. Takeuchi and A. Barron. Asymptotically minimax regret for exponential families. In *SITA '97*, pages 665–668, 1997.
9. J. Takeuchi and A. Barron. Asymptotically minimax regret by bayes mixtures. In *IEEE ISIT '98*, 1998.
10. E. Takimoto and M. Warmuth. The minimax strategy for Gaussian density estimation. In *To appear in COLT2000*, 2000.
11. Q. Xie and A. Barron. Asymptotic minimax regret for data compression, gambling, and prediction. *IEEE Trans. on Information Theory*, 46(2):431–445, 2000.
12. K. Yamanishi. A decision-theoretic extension of stochastic complexity and its applications to learning. *IEEE Transaction on Information Theory*, 44(4):1424–39, July 1998.
13. K. Yamanishi. Extended stochastic complexity and minimax relative loss analysis. In *Proc. 10th International Conference on Algorithmic Learning Theory - ALT'99*, volume 1720 of *Lecture Notes in Artificial Intelligence*, pages 26–38. Springer-Verlag, 1999.

Rough Sets and Ordinal Classification

Jan C. Bioch and Viara Popova

Dept. of Computer Science, Erasmus University Rotterdam
P.O. Box 1738, 3000 DR Rotterdam.
{bioch,popova}@few.eur.nl

Abstract. The classical theory of Rough Sets describes objects by discrete attributes, and does not take into account the ordering of the attributes values. This paper proposes a modification of the Rough Set approach applicable to monotone datasets. We introduce respectively the concepts of monotone discernibility matrix and monotone (object) reduct. Furthermore, we use the theory of monotone discrete functions developed earlier by the first author to represent and to compute decision rules. In particular we use monotone extensions, decision lists and dualization to compute classification rules that cover the whole input space. The theory is applied to the bankruptcy problem.

1 Introduction

Ordinal classification refers to the category of problems, in which the attributes of the objects to be classified are ordered. Ordinal classification has been studied by a number of authors, e.g. [1,16,5,18,12]. The classical theory of Rough Sets does not take into account the ordering of the attribute values. While this is a general approach that can be applied on a wide variety of data, for specific problems we might get better results if we use this property of the problem. This paper proposes a modification of the Rough Sets approach applicable to monotone datasets. Monotonicity appears as a property of many real-world problems and often conveys important information. Intuitively it means that if we increase the value of a condition attribute in a decision table containing examples, this will not result in a decrease in the value of the decision attribute. Therefore, monotonicity is a characteristic of the problem itself and when analyzing the data we get more appropriate results if we use methods that take this additional information into account. Our approach uses the theory of monotone discrete functions developed earlier in [2]. We introduce respectively monotone decision tables/datasets, monotone discernibility matrices and monotone reducts in section 2 and consider some issues of complexity. In section 3 we introduce monotone discrete functions and show the relationship with Rough Set Theory. As a corollary we find an efficient alternative way to compute classification rules. In section 4 we discuss a bankruptcy problem earlier investigated in [12]. It appears that our method is more advantageous in several aspects. Conclusions are given in section 5.

H. Arimura, S. Jain and A. Sharma (Eds.): ALT 2000, LNAI 1968, pp. 291–305, 2000.

2   Monotone Information Systems

An *information system* S is a tuple $S = \{U, A, V\}$ where: $U = \{x_1, x_2, \ldots, x_n\}$ is a non-empty, finite set of objects (observations, examples), $A = \{a_1, a_2, \ldots, a_m\}$ is a non-empty, finite set of attributes, and $V = \{V_1, V_2, \ldots, V_m\}$ is the set of domains of the attributes in A. A *decision table* is a special case of an information system where among the attributes in A we distinguish one called a *decision attribute*. The other attributes are called *condition attributes*. Therefore: $A = C \cup \{d\}$, $C = \{a_1, a_2, \ldots, a_m\}$ where a_i - condition attributes, d - decision attribute.

We call the information system $S = \{U, C \cup \{d\}, V\}$ *monotone* when for each couple $x_i, x_j \in U$ the following holds:

$$a_k(x_i) \geq a_k(x_j), \forall a_k \in C \Rightarrow d(x_i) \geq d(x_j) , \qquad (1)$$

where $a_k(x_i)$ is the value of the attribute a_k for the object x_i. The following example will serve as a running example for this paper.

Example 1. The following decision table represents a monotone dataset:

Table 1. Monotone decision table

U	a	b	c	d
1	0	1	0	0
2	1	0	0	1
3	0	2	1	2
4	1	1	2	2
5	2	2	1	2

2.1   Monotone Reducts

Let $S = \{U, C \cup \{d\}, V\}$ be a decision table. In the classical rough sets theory, the discernibility matrix (DM) is defined as follows:

$$(c_{ij}) = \begin{cases} \{a \in A : a(x_i) \neq a(x_j)\} & \text{for } i, j : d(x_i) \neq d(x_j) \\ \emptyset & \text{otherwise .} \end{cases} \qquad (2)$$

The variation of the DM proposed here is the *monotone discernibility matrix* $M_d(S)$ defined as follows:

$$(c_{ij}) = \begin{cases} \{a \in A : a(x_i) > a(x_j)\} & \text{for } i, j : d(x_i) > d(x_j) \\ \emptyset & \text{otherwise .} \end{cases} \qquad (3)$$

Based on the monotone discernibility matrix, the *monotone discernibility function* can be constructed following the same procedure as in the classical Rough Sets approach. For each non-empty entry of the monotone M_d $c_{ij} =$

$\{a_{k_1}, a_{k_2}, \ldots, a_{k_l}\}$ we construct the conjunction $C = a_{k_1} \wedge a_{k_2} \wedge \ldots \wedge a_{k_l}$. The disjunction of all these conjunctions is the monotone discernibility function:

$$f = C_1 \vee C_2 \vee \ldots \vee C_p . \qquad (4)$$

The *monotone reducts* of the decision table are the minimal transversals of the entries of the monotone discernibility matrix. In other words the monotone reducts are the minimal subsets of condition attributes that have a non-empty intersection with each non-empty entry of the monotone discernibility matrix. They are computed by dualizing the Boolean function f, see [3,2,15]. In section 3.3 we give another equivalent definition for a monotone reduct described from a different point of view.

Example 2. Consider the decision table from example 1. The general and *monotone* discernibility matrix modulo decision for this table are respectively:

Table 2. General decision matrix

	1	2	3	4	5
1	$\emptyset$				
2	a, b	$\emptyset$			
3	b, c	a, b, c	$\emptyset$		
4	a, c	b, c	$\emptyset$	$\emptyset$	
5	a, b, c	a, b, c	$\emptyset$	$\emptyset$	$\emptyset$

Table 3. Monotone decision matrix

	1	2	3	4	5
1	$\emptyset$				
2	a	$\emptyset$			
3	b, c	b, c	$\emptyset$		
4	a, c	b, c	$\emptyset$	$\emptyset$	
5	a, b, c	a, b, c	$\emptyset$	$\emptyset$	$\emptyset$

The general discernibility function is $f(a, b, c) = ab \vee ac \vee bc$. Therefore, the general reducts of table 1 are respectively: $\{a, b\}$, $\{a, c\}$ and $\{b, c\}$ and the core is empty. However, the *monotone* discernibility function is $g(a, b, c) = a \vee bc$. So the *monotone* reducts are: $\{a, b\}$ and $\{a, c\}$, and the *monotone* core is $\{a\}$. It can be proved that monotone reducts preserve the monotonicity property of the dataset.

Complexity Generating a reduct of minimum length is an NP-hard problem. Therefore, in practice a number of heuristics are preferred for the generation of only one reduct. Two of these heuristics are the "Best Reduct" method [13] and Johnson's algorithm [14]. The complexity of a total time algorithm for the problem of generating all minimal reducts (or dualizing the discernibility function) has been intensively studied in Boolean function theory, see [3,10,2]. Unfortunately, this problem is still unsolved, but a quasi-polynomial algorithm is known [11]. However, these results are not mentioned yet in the rough set literature, see e.g. [15].

2.2   Heuristics

As it was mentioned above, two of the more successful heuristics for generating one reduct are the Johnson's algorithm and the "Best reduct" heuristic.

Strictly speaking these methods do not necessarily generate reducts, since the minimality requirement is not assured. Therefore, in the *sequel* we will make the distinction between reducts vs *minimal* reducts. A good approach to solve the problem is to generate the reduct and then check whether any of the subsets is also a reduct. The *Johnson heuristic* uses a very simple procedure that tends to generate a reduct with minimal length (which is not guaranteed, however). Given the discernibility matrix, for each attribute the number of entries where it appears is counted. The one with the highest number of entries is added to the future reduct. Then all the entries containing that attribute are removed and the procedure repeats until all the entries are covered. It is logical to start the procedure with simplifying the set of entries (removing the entries that contain strictly or non strictly other elements). In some cases the results with and without simplification might be different. The *"Best reduct"* heuristic is based on the significance of attributes measure. The procedure starts with the core and on each step adds the attribute with the highest significance, if added to the set, until the value reaches one. In many of the practical cases the two heuristics give the same result, however, they are not the same and a counter example can be given. The dataset discussed in section 4, for example, gives different results when the two heuristics are applied (see [4]).

2.3 Rule Generation

The next step in the classical Rough Set approach [17,15] is, for the chosen reduct, to generate the *value (object) reducts* using a similar procedure as for computing the reducts. A contraction of the discernibility matrix is generated based only on the attributes in the reduct. Further, for each row of the matrix, the object discernibility function is constructed - the discernibility function relative to this particular object. The object reducts are the minimal transversals of the object discernibility functions.

Using the same procedure but on the monotone discernibility matrix, we can generate the monotone object reducts. Based on them, the classification rules are constructed. For the monotone case we use the following format:

$$\text{if } (a_{i_1} \geq v_1) \wedge (a_{i_2} \geq v_2) \wedge \ldots \wedge (a_{i_l} \geq v_l) \text{ then } d \geq v_{l+1} . \tag{5}$$

It is also possible to construct the classification rules using the dual format:

$$\text{if } (a_{i_1} \leq v_1) \wedge (a_{i_2} \leq v_2) \wedge \ldots \wedge (a_{i_l} \leq v_l) \text{ then } d \leq v_{l+1} . \tag{6}$$

This type of rules can be obtained by the same procedure only considering the columns of the monotone discernibility matrix instead of the rows. As a result we get rules that cover at least one example of class smaller than the maximal class value and no examples of the maximal class.

It can be proved that in the monotone case it is not necessary to generate the value reducts for all the objects - the value reducts of the minimal vectors of each class will also cover the other objects from the same class. For the rules with the dual format we consider respectively the maximal vectors of each class. Tables 4 and 5 show the complete set of rules generated for the whole table.

A set of rules is called a *cover* if all the examples with class $d \geq 1$ are covered, and no example of class 0 is covered. The minimal covers (computed by solving a set-covering problem) for the full table are shown in tables 6 and 7. In this case the minimal covers correspond to the unique minimal covers of the reduced tables associated with respectively the monotone reducts {a,b} and {a,c}.

Table 4. Monotone decision rules

class $d \geq 2$	class $d \geq 1$
$a \geq 2$	$a \geq 1$
$b \geq 2$	
$a \geq 1 \wedge b \geq 1$	
$c \geq 1$	

Table 5. The dual format rules

class $d \leq 0$	class $d \leq 1$
$a \leq 0 \wedge b \leq 1$	$b \leq 0$
$a \leq 0 \wedge c \leq 0$	$c \leq 0$

Table 6. mincover ab

class $d \geq 2$	class $d \geq 1$
$a \geq 1 \wedge b \geq 1$	$a \geq 1$
$b \geq 2$	

Table 7. mincover ac

class $d \geq 2$	class $d \geq 1$
$c \geq 1$	$a \geq 1$

Table 8. mincover ab (dual format)

class $d \leq 0$	class $d \leq 1$
$a \leq 0 \wedge b \leq 1$	$b \leq 0$

Table 9. mincover ac (dual format)

class $d \leq 0$	class $d \leq 1$
$a \leq 0 \wedge c \leq 0$	$c \leq 0$

The set of rules with dual format is not an addition but rather an alternative to the set rules of the other format. If used together they may be conflicting in some cases. It is known that the decision rules induced by object reducts in general do not cover the whole input space. Furthermore, the class assigned by these decision rules to an input vector is not uniquely determined. We therefore briefly discuss the concept of an *extension* of a discrete data set or decision table in the next section.

3   Monotone Discrete Functions

The theory of monotone discrete functions as a tool for data-analysis has been developed in [2]. Here we only briefly review some concepts that are crucial for our approach. A discrete function of n variables is a function of the form:

$$f : X_1 \times X_2 \times \ldots \times X_n \rightarrow Y ,$$

where $X = X_1 \times X_2 \times \ldots \times X_n$ and Y are finite sets. Without loss of generality we may assume: $X_i = \{0, 1, \ldots, n_i\}$ and $Y = \{0, 1, \ldots, m\}$. Let $x, y \in X$ be two discrete vectors. Least upper bounds and greatest lower bounds will be defined as follows:

$$x \vee y = v, \text{ where } v_i = \max\{x_i, y_i\} \tag{7}$$

$$x \wedge y = w, \text{ where } w_i = \min\{x_i, y_i\} . \tag{8}$$

Furthermore, if f and g are two discrete functions then we define:

$$(f \vee g)(x) = \max\{f(x), g(x)\} \tag{9}$$

$$(f \wedge g)(x) = \min\{f(x), g(x)\} . \tag{10}$$

(Quasi) complementation for X is defined as: $\overline{x} = (\overline{x}_1, \overline{x}_2, \ldots, \overline{x}_n)$, where $\overline{x}_i = n_i - x_i$. Similarly, the complement of $j \in Y$ is defined as $\overline{j} = m - j$. The complement of a discrete function f is defined by: $\overline{f}(x) = \overline{f(x)}$. The *dual* of a discrete function f is defined as: $f^d(x) = \overline{f}(\overline{x})$. A discrete function f is called *positive (monotone non-decreasing)* if $x \leq y$ implies $f(x) \leq f(y)$.

3.1   Representations

Normal Forms Discrete variables are defined as:

$$x_{ip} = \text{if } x_i \geq p \text{ then } m \text{ else } 0, \text{ where } 1 \leq p \leq n_i, \; i \in (n] = \{1, \ldots, n\} . \tag{11}$$

Thus: $\overline{x}_{ip+1} = $ if $x_i \leq p$ then m else 0. Furthermore, we define $x_{in_i+1} = 0$ and $\overline{x}_{in_i+1} = m$. *Cubic* functions are defined as:

$$c_{v,j} = j.x_{1v_1} x_{2v_2} \cdots x_{nv_n} . \tag{12}$$

Notation: $c_{v,j}(x) = $ if $x \geq v$ then j else 0, $\; j \in (m]$.
Similarly, we define *anti-cubic* functions by:

$$a_{w,i} = i \vee x_{1w_1+1} \vee x_{2w_2+1} \cdots \vee x_{nw_n+1} . \tag{13}$$

Notation: $a_{w,i}(x) = $ if $x \leq w$ then i else m, $i \in [m) = \{0, \ldots, m-1\}$. Note, that $j.x_{ip}$ denotes the conjunction $j \wedge x_{ip}$, where $j \in Y$ is a constant, and $x_{ip}x_{jq}$ denotes $x_{ip} \wedge x_{iq}$. A cubic function $c_{v,j}$ is called a *prime implicant* of f if $c_{v,j} \leq f$ and $c_{v,j}$ is maximal w.r.t. this property. The DNF of f:

$$f = \bigvee_{v,j}\{c_{v,j} \mid v \in \; j \in (m]\} , \tag{14}$$

is a unique representation of f as a disjunction of all its prime implicants (v is a minimal vector of class $d \geq j$).

If x_{ip} is a discrete variable and $j \in Y$ a constant then $x_{ip}^d = x_{i\overline{p}+1}$ and $j^d = \overline{j}$. The dual of the positive function $f = \bigvee_{v,j} j.c_{v,j}$ equals $f^d = \bigwedge_{v,j} \overline{j} \vee a_{\overline{v},\overline{j}}$.

Example 3. Let f be the function defined by table 6 and let e.g. x_{11} denote the variable: if $a \geq 1$ then 2 else 0, etc. Then $f = 2.(x_{11}x_{21} \vee x_{22}) \vee 1.x_{11}$, and $f^d = 2.x_{12}x_{21} \vee 1.x_{22}$.

Decision Lists

In [2] we have shown that monotone functions can effectively be represented by decision lists of which the minlist and the maxlist representations are the most important ones. We introduce these lists here only by example. The minlist representation of the functions f and f^d of example 2 are respectively:

$f(x) =$ if $x \geq 11, 02$ then 2   else if $x \geq 10$ then 1   else 0, and
$f^d(x) =$ if $x \geq 21$ then 2   else if $x \geq 02$ then 1   else 0.

The meaning of the minlist of f is given by:

if $(a \geq 1 \wedge b \geq 1) \vee b = 2$ then 2   else if $a \geq 1$ then 1   else 0.

The maxlist of f is obtained from the minlist of f^d by complementing the minimal vectors as well as the function values, and by reversing the inequalities. The maxlist representation of f is therefore:

$f(x) =$ if $x \leq 01$ then 0   else if $x \leq 20$ then 1   else 2, or equivalently:

if $a = 0 \wedge b \leq 1$ then 0   else if $b = 0$ then 1   else 2.

The two representations are equivalent to the following table that contains respectively the minimal and maximal vectors for each decision class of f. Each representation can be derived from the other by dualization.

Table 10. Two representations of f

minvectors	maxvectors	class
11, 02		2
10	20	1
	01	0

3.2 Extensions of Monotone Datasets

A *partially defined discrete function* (pdDf) is a function: $f : D \mapsto Y$, where $D \subseteq X$. We assume that a pdDf f is given by a decision table such as e.g. table 1. Although pdDfs are often used in practical applications, the theory of pdDfs is only developed in the case of pdBfs (partially defined Boolean functions). Here we discuss monotone pdDfs, i.e. functions that are monotone on D. If the function $\hat{f} : X \mapsto Y$, agrees with f on D: $\hat{f}(x) = f(x)$, $x \in D$, then $\hat{f}$ is called an *extension* of the pdDf f. The collection of all extensions forms a lattice: for, if f_1 and f_2 are extensions of the pdDf f, then $f_1 \wedge f_2$ and $f_1 \vee f_2$ are also extensions of f. The same holds for the set of all monotone extensions. The lattice of all *monotone* extensions of a pdDf f will be denoted here by $\mathcal{E}(f)$. It is easy to see that $\mathcal{E}(f)$ is universally bounded: it has a greatest and a smallest element. The maxlist of the maximal element called the *maximal monotone extension* can be directly obtained from the decision table.

Definition 1 *Let f be a monotone pdDf. Then the functions $f_{\min}$ and $f_{\max}$ are defined as follows:*

$$f_{\min}(x) = \begin{cases} \max\{f(y): y \in D \cap \downarrow x\} & \text{if } x \in \uparrow D \\ 0 & \text{otherwise} \end{cases} \quad (15)$$

$$f_{\max}(x) = \begin{cases} \min\{f(y): y \in D \cap \uparrow x\} & \text{if } x \in \downarrow D \\ m & \text{otherwise} . \end{cases} \quad (16)$$

Lemma 1 *Let f be a monotone pdDf. Then*
  a) $f_{\min}, f_{\max} \in \mathcal{E}(f)$.
  b) $\forall \hat{f} \in \mathcal{E}(f): f_{\min} \leq \hat{f} \leq f_{\max}$.

Since $\mathcal{E}(f)$ is a distributive lattice, the minimal and maximal monotone extension of f can also be described by the following expressions:

$$f_{\max} = \bigvee \{ \hat{f} \mid \hat{f} \in \mathcal{E}(f) \} \text{ and } f_{\min} = \bigwedge \{ \hat{f} \mid \hat{f} \in \mathcal{E}(f) \} . \quad (17)$$

Notation: Let $T_j(f) := \{x \in D : f(x) = j\}$. A minimal vector v of class j is a vector such that $f(v) = j$ and no vector strictly smaller than v is also in $T_j(f)$. Similarly, a maximal vector w is a vector maximal in $T_j(f)$, where $j = f(w)$. The sets of minimal and maximal vectors of class j are denoted by $minT_j(f)$ and $maxT_j(f)$ respectively.

According to the previous lemma $f_{\min}$ and $f_{\max}$ are respectively the minimal and maximal monotone extension of f. Decision lists of these extensions can be directly constructed from f as follows. Let $D_j := D \cap T_j(f)$, then $minT_j(f_{\min}) = minD_j$ and $maxT_j(f_{\max}) = maxD_j$.

Example 4. Consider the pdDf given by table 1, then its maximal extension is:

$f(x) = $ if $x \leq 010$ then 0
      else if $x \leq 100$ then 1
        else 2 .

As described in the last subsection, from this maxlist representation we can deduce directly the minlist representation of the dual of f and finally by dualization we find that f is:

$$f = 2.(x_{12} \vee x_{11}x_{21} \vee x_{22} \vee x_{31}) \vee 1.x_{11} . \quad (18)$$

However, f can be viewed as a representation of table 4! This suggests a close relationship between minimal monotone decision rules and the maximal monotone extension f_{max}. This relationship is discussed in the next section. The relationship with the methodology LAD (Logical Analysis of Data) is briefly discussed in subsection 3.5.

3.3   The relationship between monotone decision rules and f_{max}

We first redefine the concept of a monotone reduct in terms of discrete functions. Let $X = X_1 \times X_2 \times \ldots \times X_n$ be the input space, and let $A = [1, \ldots, n]$ denote the set of attributes. Then for $U \subseteq A$, $x \in X$ we define the set $U.x$ respectively the vector $x.U$ by:

$$U.x = \{i \in U : x_i > 0\} \tag{19}$$

and

$$(x.U)_i = \begin{cases} x_i & \text{if } i \in U \\ 0 & \text{if } i \notin U \ . \end{cases} \tag{20}$$

Furthermore, the characteristic set U of x is defined by $U = A.x$.

Definition 2 *Suppose $f : D \to Y$ is a monotone pdDf, $w \in D$ and $f(w) = j$. Then $V \subseteq A$ is a monotone w-reduct iff $\forall x \in D : (f(x) < j \Rightarrow w.U \nleq x.U)$.*

Note, that in this definition the condition $w.U \nleq x.U$ is equivalent to $w.U \nleq x$. The following lemma is a direct consequence of this definition.

Lemma 2 *Suppose f is a monotone pdDf, $w \in T_j(f)$. Then $V \subseteq A$ is a monotone w-reduct $\Leftrightarrow \forall x(f(x) < j \Rightarrow \exists i \in V$ such that $w_i > x_i)$.*

Corollary 1 *V is a monotone w-reduct iff $V.w$ is a monotone w-reduct. Therefore, w.l.o.g. we may assume that V is a subset of the characteristic set W of w: $V \subseteq W$.*

Monotone Boolean functions

We first consider the case that the dataset is Boolean: so the objects are described by condition and decision attributes taking one of two possible values $\{0, 1\}$. The dataset represents a *partially defined Boolean function* (pdBf) $f : D \to \{0, 1\}$ where $D \subseteq \{0, 1\}^n$. As we have only two classes, we define the set of true vectors of f by $T(f) := T_1(f)$ and the set of false vectors of f by $F(f) := T_0(f)$.

Notation: In the Boolean case we will make no distinction between a set V and its characteristic vector v.

Lemma 3 *Let $f : D \to \{0, 1\}$ be a monotone pdBf, $w \in D$, $w \in T(f)$. Suppose $v \leq w$. Then v is a w-reduct $\Leftrightarrow v \in T(f_{max})$.*

Proof: Since $v \leq w$, we have
v is a w-reduct $\Leftrightarrow \forall x(x \in D \cap F(f) \Rightarrow v \nleq x) \Leftrightarrow v \in T(f_{max})$.

Theorem 1 *Suppose $f : D \to \{0, 1\}$ is a monotone pdBf, $w \in D$, $w \in T(f)$. Then, for $v \leq w$, $v \in minT(f_{max}) \Leftrightarrow v$ is a minimal monotone w-reduct.*

Proof: Let $v \in minT(f_{max})$ and $v \leq w$ for some $w \in D$. Then v is a monotone w-reduct. Suppose $\exists u < v$ and u is a monotone w-reduct. Then by definition 2 we have: $u \in T(f_{max})$, which contradicts the assumption that $v \in minT(f_{max})$.

Conversely, let v be a minimal monotone w-reduct. Then by lemma 3 we have: $v \in T(f_{max})$. Suppose $\exists u < v : u \in T(f_{max})$. However, $v \leq w \Rightarrow u < w \Rightarrow U$ is a monotone w-reduct, which contradicts the assumption that v is a minimal w-reduct.

The results imply that the irredundant (monotone) decision rules that correspond to the object reducts are just the prime implicants of the maximal extension.

Corollary 2 *The decision rules obtained in rough set theory can be obtained by the following procedure: a) find the maximal vectors of class 1 (positive examples) b) determine the minimal vectors of the dual of the maximal extension and c) compute the minimal vectors of this extension by dualization. The complexity of this procedure is the same as for the dualization problem.*

Although the above corollary is formulated for monotone Boolean functions, results in [9] indicate that a similar statement holds for Boolean functions in general.

Monotone discrete functions

Lemma 4 *Suppose f is a monotone pdDf, $w \in T_j(f)$ and $v \leq w$. If $v \in T_j(f_{max})$ then the characteristic set V of v is a monotone w-reduct.*

Proof: $f_{max}(v) = j$ implies $\forall x(f(x) < j \Rightarrow v \nleq x)$. Since $w \geq v$ we therefore have $\forall x(f(x) < j \Rightarrow \exists i \in V$ such that $w_i \geq v_j > x_i)$.

Remark: Even if in lemma 4 the vector v is minimal: $v \in minT_j(f_{max})$, then still $V = A.v$ is not necessarily a minimal monotone w-reduct.

Theorem 2 *Suppose f is a monotone pdDf and $w \in T_j(f)$. Then $V \subseteq A$ is a monotone w-reduct $\Leftrightarrow f_{max}(w.V) = j$.*

Proof: If V is a monotone w-reduct, then by definition $\forall x(f(x) < j \Rightarrow w.V \nleq x)$. Since $w.V \leq w$ and $f(w) = j$ we therefore have $f_{max}(w.V) = j$.

Conversely, let $f_{max}(w.V) = j$, $V \subseteq A$. Then, since $w.V \leq w$ and the characteristic set of $w.V$ is equal to V, lemma 4 implies that V is a monotone w-reduct.

Theorem 3 *Let f be a monotone pdDf and $w \in T_j(f)$. If $V \subseteq A$ is a minimal monotone w-reduct, then $\exists u \in minT_j(f_{max})$ such that $V = A.u$.*

Proof: Since V is a monotone w-reduct, theorem 2 implies that $f_{max}(w.V) = j$. Therefore, $\exists u \in minT_j(f_{max})$ such that $u \leq w.V$. Since $A.u \subseteq V$ and $A.u$ is a monotone w-reduct (by lemma 4), the minimality of V implies $A.u = V$.

Theorem 3 implies that the minimal decision rules obtained by monotone w-reducts are not shorter than the minimal vectors (prime implicants) of f_{max}. This suggests that we can optimize a minimal decision rule by minimizing the attribute values to the attribute values of a minimal vector of f_{max}. For example, if V is a minimal monotone w-reduct and $u \in minT_j(f_{max})$ such that $u \leq w.V$ then the rule: 'if $x_i \geq w_i$ then j', where $i \in V$ can be improved by using the rule: 'if $x_i \geq u_i$ then j', where $i \in V$. Since $u_i \leq w_i$, $i \in V$, the second rule is applicable to a larger part of the input space X.

The results so far indicate the close relationship between minimal monotone decision rules obtained by the rough sets approach and by the approach using f_{max}. To complete the picture we make the following observations:

Observation 1: The minimal vector u (theorem 3) is not unique.

Observation 2: Lemma 4 implies that the length of a decision rule induced by a minimal vector $v \leq w$, $v \in minT_j(f_{max})$ is not necessarily smaller than that of a rule induced by a minimal w-reduct. This means that there may exist an $x \in X$ that is covered by the rule induced by v but not by the decision rules induced by the minimal reducts of a vector $w \in D$.

Observation 3: There may be minimal vectors of f_{max} such that $\forall w \in D$ $v \nleq w$. In this case if $x \geq v$ then $f_{max}(x) = m$ but x is not covered by a minimal decision rule induced by a minimal reduct.

In the next two subsections we briefly compare the rough set approach and the discrete function approach with two other methods.

3.4   Monotone Decision Trees

Ordinal classification using decision trees is discussed in [1,5,18]. A decision tree is called monotone if it represents a monotone function. A number of algorithms are available for generating and testing the monotonicity of the tree [5,18]. Here we demonstrate the idea with an example.

Example 5. A monotone decision tree corresponding to the pdDf given by table 1 and example 3 is represented in figure 1.

It can be seen that the tree contains information both on the corresponding extension and its complement (or equivalently its dual). Therefore the decision list representation tends to be more compact since we only need the information about the extension - the dual can always be derived if necessary.

3.5   Rough Sets and Logical Analysis of Data

The Logical Analysis of Data methodology (LAD) was presented in [9] and further developed in [8,6,7]. LAD is designed for the discovery of structural

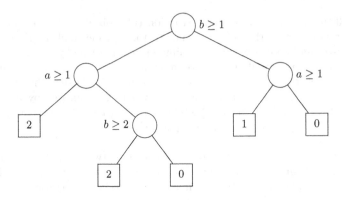

Fig. 1. Monotone decision tree representation of f

information in datasets. Originally it was developed for the analysis of Boolean datasets using partially defined Boolean functions. An extension of LAD for the analysis of numerical data is possible through the process of binarization. The building concepts are the supporting set, the pattern and the theory.

A set of variables (attributes) is called a *supporting set* for a partially defined Boolean function f if f has an extension depending only on these variables. A *pattern* is a conjunction of literals such that it is 0 for every negative example and 1 for at least one positive example. A subset of the set of patterns is used to form a *theory* - a disjunction of patterns that is consistent with all the available data and can predict the outcome of any new example. The theory is therefore an extension of the partially defined Boolean function.

Our research suggests that the LAD and the RS theories are similar in several aspects (for example, the supporting set corresponds to the reduct in the binary case and a pattern with the induced decision rule). The exact connections will be a subject of future research.

4   Experiments

4.1   The Bankruptcy Dataset

The dataset used in the experiments is discussed in [12]. The sample consists of 39 objects denoted by $F1$ to $F39$ - firms that are described by 12 financial parameters (see [4]). To each company a decision value is assigned - the expert evaluation of its category of risk for the year 1988. The condition attributes denoted by $A1$ to $A12$ take integer values from 0 to 4.

The decision attribute is denoted by d and takes integer values in the range 0 to 2 where: 0 means *unacceptable*, 1 means *uncertainty* and 2 means *acceptable*.

The data was first analyzed for monotonicity. The problem is obviously monotone (if one company outperforms another on all condition attributes then it should not have a lower value of the decision attribute). Nevertheless, one noisy example was discovered, namely $F24$. It was removed from the dataset and was not considered further.

4.2   Reducts and Decision Rules

The minimal reducts have been computed using our program 'the Dualizer'. There are 25 minimal general reducts (minimum length 3) and 15 monotone reducts (minimum length 4), see [4]. We have also compared the heuristics to approximate a minimum reduct: the best reduct method (for general reducts) and the Johnson strategy (for general and monotone reducts), see [4].

Table 11 shows the two sets of decision rules obtained by computing the object (value)- reducts for the monotone reduct $(A1, A3, A7, A9)$. Both sets of rules have minimal covers, of which the ones with minimum length are shown in table 12. A minimum cover can be transformed into an extension if the rules are considered as minimal/maximal vectors in a decision list representation. In this sense the minimum cover of the first set of rules can be described by the following function:

$$f = 2.x_{73}x_{93} \vee 1.(x_{33} \vee x_{73} \vee x_{11}x_{93} \vee x_{32}x_{72}) . \tag{21}$$

The maximal extension corresponding to the monotone reduct $(A1, A3, A7, A9)$ is represented in table 13.

Table 11. The rules for $(A1, A3, A7, A9)$

class $d \geq 2$	class $d \geq 1$
$A1 \geq 3$	$A1 \geq 3$
$A7 \geq 4$	$A3 \geq 3$
$A9 \geq 4$	$A7 \geq 3$
$A1 \geq 2 \wedge A7 \geq 3$	$A9 \geq 4$
$A3 \geq 2 \wedge A7 \geq 3$	$A1 \geq 1 \wedge A3 \geq 2$
$A7 \geq 3 \wedge A9 \geq 3$	$A1 \geq 1 \wedge A9 \geq 3$
	$A3 \geq 2 \wedge A7 \geq 2$
	$A3 \geq 2 \wedge A7 \geq 1 \wedge A9 \geq 3$
class $d \leq 0$	class $d \leq 1$
$A7 \leq 0$	$A7 \leq 2$
$A9 \leq 1$	$A9 \leq 2$
$A1 \leq 0 \wedge A3 \leq 0$	
$A1 \leq 0 \wedge A3 \leq 2 \wedge A7 \leq 1$	
$A1 \leq 0 \wedge A3 \leq 1 \wedge A7 \leq 2$	
$A1 \leq 0 \wedge A3 \leq 2 \wedge A9 \leq 2$	
$A3 \leq 0 \wedge A9 \leq 2$	
$A3 \leq 1 \wedge A7 \leq 2 \wedge A9 \leq 2$	
$A3 \leq 2 \wedge A7 \leq 1 \wedge A9 \leq 2$	

The function f or equivalently its minlist we have found consists of only 5 decision rules (prime implicants). They cover the whole input space. Moreover,

Table 12. The minimum covers for $(A1, A3, A7, A9)$

class $d \geq 2$	class $d \geq 1$
$A7 \geq 3 \wedge A9 \geq 3$	$A3 \geq 3$
	$A7 \geq 3$
	$A1 \geq 1 \wedge A9 \geq 3$
	$A3 \geq 2 \wedge A7 \geq 2$
class $d \leq 0$	class $d \leq 1$
$A1 \leq 0 \wedge A3 \leq 2 \wedge A7 \leq 1$	$A7 \leq 2$
$A1 \leq 0 \wedge A3 \leq 1 \wedge A7 \leq 2$	$A9 \leq 2$
$A3 \leq 1 \wedge A7 \leq 2 \wedge A9 \leq 2$	

Table 13. The maximal extension for $(A1, A3, A7, A9)$

class $d = 2$	class $d = 1$
$A1 \geq 3$	$A3 \geq 3$
$A3 \geq 4$	$A7 \geq 3$
$A7 \geq 4$	$A1 \geq 1 \wedge A3 \geq 2$
$A9 \geq 4$	$A1 \geq 1 \wedge A9 \geq 3$
$A1 \geq 2 \wedge A7 \geq 3$	$A3 \geq 2 \wedge A7 \geq 2$
$A3 \geq 2 \wedge A7 \geq 3$	$A3 \geq 2 \wedge A7 \geq 1 \wedge A9 \geq 3$
$A7 \geq 3 \wedge A9 \geq 3$	

each possible vector is classified as $d = 0, 1$ or 2 and not as $d \geq 1$ or $d \geq 2$ like in [12]. The latter paper uses both the formats shown in table 11 to describe a minimum cover, resulting in a system of 11 rules. Using both formats at the same time can result in much (possibly exponential) larger sets of rules. Another difference between our approach and [12] is our use of the monotone discernibility matrix. Therefore, we can compute all the monotone reducts and not only a generalization of the 'best reduct' as in [12].

5   Discussion and Further Research

Our approach using the concepts of monotone discernibility matrix/function and monotone (object) reduct and using the theory of monotone discrete functions has a number of advantages summarized in the discussion on the experiment with the bankruptcy dataset in section 4. Furthermore, it appears that there is close relationship between the decision rules obtained using the rough set approach and the prime implicants of the maximal extension. Although this has been shown for the monotone case this also holds at least for non-monotone *Boolean* datasets. We have discussed how to compute this extension by using dualization. The relationship with two other possible approaches for ordinal classification is discussed in subsections 3.4 and 3.5. We also computed monotone decision trees [5,18] for the datasets discussed in this paper. It appears that monotone decision trees are larger because they contain the information of both an extension and its dual! The generalization of the discrete function approach to non-monotone datasets and the comparison with the theory of rough sets is a topic of further research. Finally, the sometimes striking similarity we have found between Rough Set Theory and Logical Analysis of Data remains an interesting research topic.

References

1. Ben-David, A.: Monotonicity Maintenance in Information-Theoretic Machine Learning Algorithms. Machine Learning 19 (1995) 29–43 291, 301
2. Bioch, J. C.: Dualization, Decision Lists and Identification of Monotone Discrete Functions. Annals of Mathematics and Artificial Intelligence 24 (1998) 69–91 291, 293, 295, 297
3. Bioch, J. C., Ibaraki, T.: Complexity of Identification and Dualization of Positive Boolean Functions. Information and Computation 123 (1995) 50–63 293
4. Bioch, J. C., Popova, V.: The Rough Set and Ordinal Classification: The Bankruptcy Problem. Technical Report Dept. of Computer Science, eur-few-cs-0600, Erasmus University Rotterdam (2000) 294, 302, 303
5. Bioch, J. C., Potharst, R.: Decision Trees for Monotone Classification. in: K. van Marcke and W. Daelmans (eds), Proceedings of the Dutch Artificial Conference on Artificial Intelligence (NAIC'97), Antwerpen (1997) 361–369 291, 301, 304
6. Boros, E., Hammer, P. L., Ibaraki, T., Kogan, A.: Logical Analysis of Numerical Data. RUTCOR Research Report RRR 04-97, RUTCOR, Rutgers University (1997) 301
7. Boros, E., Hammer, P. L., Ibaraki, T., Kogan, A., Logical Analysis of Numerical Data. Mathematical Programming 79 (1997) 165–190 301
8. Boros, E., Hammer, P. L., Ibaraki, T., Kogan, A., Mayoraz, E., Muchnik, I.:An Implementation of Logical Analysis of Data. RUTCOR Research Report RRR 22-96, RUTCOR, Rutgers University (1996) 301
9. Crama, Y., Hammer, P. L., Ibaraki, T.: Cause-Effect Relationships and Partially Defined Boolean Functions. Annals of Operations Research 16 (1988) 299–326 300, 301
10. Eiter, T., Gottlob, G.: Identifying the Minimal Transversals of a Hypergraph and Related Problems. SIAM Journal on Computing 24 (1995) 1278–1304 293
11. Fredman, M., Khachiyan, L.: On the Complexity of Dualization of Monotone Disjunctive Normal Forms. Journal of Algorithms 21 (1996) 618–628 293
12. Greco, S., Matarazzo, B., Slowinski, R.: A New Rough Set Approach to Evaluation of Bankruptcy Risk. in: C. Zopounidis (ed.), Operational Tools in the Management of Financial Risks, Kluwer, Dordrecht (1998) 121–136 291, 302, 304
13. Hu, X., Cercone, N.: Learning in Relational Databases: a Rough Set Approach. Computational Intelligence 11 (1995) 323–338 293
14. Johnson, D. S.: Approximation Algorithms for Combinatorial Problems. Journal of Computer and System Sciences 9 (1974) 256–278 293
15. Komorowski, J., Polkowski, L., Skowron, A.: Rough Sets: A Tutorial. http://www.esslli.let.uu.nl/Courses/skowron/skowron.ps 293, 294
16. Makino, K., Suda, T., Yano, K., Ibaraki, T.: Data Analysis by Positive Decision Trees. In: Proceedings International symposium on cooperative database systems for advanced applications (CODAS), Kyoto (1996) 282–289 291
17. Pawlak, Z.: Rough Sets: Theoretical Aspects of Reasoning about Data. Kluwer Academic Publishers (1991) 294
18. Potharst, R., Bioch, J. C.: Decision Trees for Ordinal Classification. Intelligent Data Analysis 4 (2000) 1–15 291, 301, 304

A note on the generalization performance of kernel classifiers with margin.

Theodoros Evgeniou and Massimiliano Pontil

Center for Biological and Computational Learning, MIT
45 Carleton Street E25-201, Cambridge, MA 02142, USA
{theos,pontil}@ai.mit.edu

Abstract. We present distribution independent bounds on the generalization misclassification performance of a family of kernel classifiers with margin. Support Vector Machine classifiers (SVM) stem out of this class of machines. The bounds are derived through computations of the V_γ dimension of a family of loss functions where the SVM one belongs to. Bounds that use functions of margin distributions (i.e. functions of the slack variables of SVM) are derived.

1 Introduction

Deriving bounds on the generalization performance of kernel classifiers has been an important theoretical topic of research in recent years [4, 8–10, 12]. We present new bounds on the generalization performance of a family of kernel classifiers with margin, from which Support Vector Machines (SVM) can be derived. The bounds use the V_γ dimension of a class of loss functions, where the SVM one belongs to, and functions of the margin distribution of the machines (i.e. functions of the slack variables of SVM - see below).

We consider classification machines of the form:

$$\min \ \sum_{i=1}^{m} V(y_i, f(\mathbf{x}_i))$$
$$\text{subject to} \quad \|f\|_K^2 \le A^2 \tag{1}$$

where we use the following notation:

- $D_m = \{(\mathbf{x}_1, y_1), \ldots, (\mathbf{x}_m, y_m)\}$, with $(\mathbf{x}_i, y_i) \in R^n \times \{-1, 1\}$ sampled according to an unknown probability distribution $P(\mathbf{x}, y)$, is the training set.
- $V(y, f(\mathbf{x}))$ is the loss function measuring the distance (error) between $f(\mathbf{x})$ and y.
- f is a function in a Reproducing Kernel Hilbert Space (RKHS) $\mathcal{H}$ defined by kernel K, with $\|f\|_K^2$ being the norm of f in $\mathcal{H}$ [11, 2]. We also call f a hyperplane, since it is such in the feature space induced by the kernel K [11, 10].
- A is a constant.

H. Arimura, S. Jain and A. Sharma (Eds.): ALT 2000, LNAI 1968, pp. 306–315, 2000.

Classification of a new test point $\mathbf{x}$ is always done by simply considering *the sign* of $f(\mathbf{x})$.

Machines of this form have been motivated in the framework of statistical learning theory. We refer the reader to [10, 6, 3] for more details. In this paper we study the generalization performance of these machines for choices of the loss function V that are relevant for classification. In particular we consider the following loss functions:

- Misclassification loss function:

$$V(y, f(\mathbf{x})) = V^{msc}(yf(\mathbf{x})) = \theta(-yf(\mathbf{x})) \tag{2}$$

- Hard margin loss function:

$$V(y, f(\mathbf{x})) = V^{hm}(yf(\mathbf{x})) = \theta(1 - yf(\mathbf{x})) \tag{3}$$

- Soft margin loss function:

$$V(y, f(\mathbf{x})) = V^{sm}(yf(\mathbf{x})) = |1 - yf(\mathbf{x})|_+, \tag{4}$$

where θ is the Heavyside function and $|x|_+ = x$, if x is positive and zero otherwise. Loss functions (3) and (4) are "margin" ones because the only case they do not penalize a point $(\mathbf{x}, y)$ is if $yf(\mathbf{x}) \geq 1$. For a given f, these are the points that are correctly classified *and* have distance $\frac{|f(\mathbf{x})|}{\|f\|^2} \geq \frac{1}{\|f\|^2}$ from the surface $f(\mathbf{x}) = 0$ (hyperplane in the feature space induced by the kernel K [10]). For a point $(\mathbf{x}, y)$, quantity $\frac{yf(\mathbf{x})}{\|f\|}$ is its margin, and the probability of having $\frac{yf(\mathbf{x})}{\|f\|} \geq \delta$ is called the *margin distribution* of hypothesis f. For SVM, quantity $|1 - y_i f(\mathbf{x}_i)|_+$ is known as the *slack variable* corresponding to training point $(\mathbf{x}_i, y_i)$ [10].

We will also consider the following family of margin loss functions (nonlinear soft margin loss functions):

$$V(y, f(\mathbf{x})) = V^\sigma(yf(\mathbf{x})) = |1 - yf(\mathbf{x})|_+^\sigma. \tag{5}$$

Loss functions (3) and (4) correspond to the choice of $\sigma = 0, 1$ respectively. In figure 1 we plot some of the possible loss functions for different choices of the parameter σ.

To study the statistical properties of machines (1) we use some well known results that we now briefly present. First we define some more notation, and then state the results from the literature that we will use in the next section.

We use the following notation:

- $R_{emp}^V(f) = \sum_{i=1}^m V(y_i, f(\mathbf{x}_i))$ is the empirical error made by f on the training set D_m, using V as the loss function.

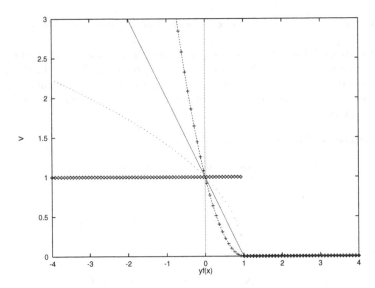

Fig. 1. Hard margin loss (line with diamond-shaped points), soft margin loss (solid line), nonlinear soft margin with $\sigma = 2$ (line with crosses), and $\sigma = \frac{1}{2}$ (dotted line)

- $R^V(f) = \int_{R^n \times \{-1,1\}} V(y, f(\mathbf{x})) \, P(\mathbf{x}, y) \, d\mathbf{x} \, dy$ is the expected error of f using V as the loss function.
- Given a hypothesis space of functions $\mathcal{F}$ (i.e. $\mathcal{F} = \{f \in \mathcal{H} : \|f\|^2 \le A^2\}$), we note by $h_\gamma^{V_{\mathcal{F}}}$ the V_γ dimension of the loss function $V(y, f(\mathbf{x}))$ in $\mathcal{F}$, which is defined as follows [1]:

Definition 1. *Let* $A \le V(y, f(\mathbf{x})) \le B$, $f \in \mathcal{F}$, *with* A *and* $B < \infty$. *The* V_γ-*dimension of* V *in* $\mathcal{F}$ *(of the set of functions* $\{V(y, f(\mathbf{x})) \mid f \in F\}$*) is defined as the the maximum number* h *of vectors* $(\mathbf{x}_1, y_1) \dots, (\mathbf{x}_h, y_h)$ *that can be separated into two classes in all* 2^h *possible ways using rules:*

$$\text{class 1 if: } V(y_i, f(\mathbf{x}_i)) \ge s + \gamma$$
$$\text{class -1 if: } V(y_i, f(\mathbf{x}_i)) \le s - \gamma$$

for $f \in \mathcal{F}$ *and some* $s \ge 0$. *If, for any number* m, *it is possible to find* m *points* $(\mathbf{x}_1, y_1) \dots, (\mathbf{x}_m, y_m)$ *that can be separated in all the* 2^m *possible ways, we will say that the* V_γ-*dimension of* V *in* $\mathcal{F}$ *is infinite.*

If instead of a fixed s for all points we use a different s_i for each $(\mathbf{x}_i, y_i)$, we get what is called the *fat-shattering* dimension fat$_\gamma$ [1]. Notice that definition (1) includes the special case in which we directly measure the V_γ dimension of the space of functions F, i.e. $V(y, f(\mathbf{x})) = f(\mathbf{x})$. We will need such a quantity in theorem 2.2 below.

Using the V_γ dimension we can study the statistical properties of machines of the form (1) based on a standard theorem that characterizes the generalization performance of these machines.

Theorem 1 (Alon et al., 1997). *Let $A \leq V(y, f(\mathbf{x})) \leq B$, $f \in \mathcal{F}$, $\mathcal{F}$ be a set of bounded functions. For any $\epsilon \geq 0$, for all $m \geq \frac{2}{\epsilon^2}$ we have that if $h_\gamma^{V_\mathcal{F}}$ is the V_γ dimension of V in $\mathcal{F}$ for $\gamma = \alpha\epsilon$ ($\alpha \geq \frac{1}{48}$), $h_\gamma^{V_\mathcal{F}}$ finite, then:*

$$Pr\left\{\sup_{f \in \mathcal{F}} \left| R_{\mathrm{emp}}^V(f) - R^V(f) \right| > \epsilon \right\} \leq \mathcal{G}(\epsilon, m, h_\gamma^{V_\mathcal{F}}), \tag{6}$$

where $\mathcal{G}$ is an increasing function of $h_\gamma^{V_\mathcal{F}}$ and a decreasing function of ϵ and m, with $\mathcal{G} \to 0$ as $m \to \infty$.

In [1] the fat-shattering dimension was used, but a close relation between that and the V_γ dimension [1] make the two equivalent for our purpose[1]. Closed forms of $\mathcal{G}$ can be derived (see for example [1]) but we do not present them here for simplicity of notation. Notice that since we are interested in classification, we only consider $\epsilon < 1$, so we will only discuss the case $\gamma < 1$ (since γ is about $\frac{1}{48}\epsilon$).

In "standard" statistical learning theory the VC dimension is used instead of the V_γ one [10]. However, for the type of machines we are interested in the VC dimension turns out not to be appropriate: it is not influenced by the choice of the hypothesis space $\mathcal{F}$ through the choice of A, and in the case that $\mathcal{F}$ is an infinite dimensional RKHS, the VC-dimension of the loss functions we consider turns out to be infinite (see for example [5]). Instead, scale-sensitive dimensions (such as the V_γ or fat-shattering one [1]) have been used in the literature, as we will discuss in the last section.

2   Main results

We study the loss functions (2 - 5). For classification machines the quantity we are interested in is the expected misclassification error of the solution f of problem 1. With some abuse of notation we note this with R^{msc}. Similarly we will note with R^{hm}, R^{sm}, and R^σ the expected risks using loss functions (3), (4) and (5), respectively, and with R_{emp}^{hm}, R_{emp}^{sm}, and R_{emp}^σ, the corresponding empirical errors. We will not consider machines of type (1) with V^{msc} as the loss function, for a clear reason: the solution of the optimization problem:

$$\min \ \sum_{i=1}^m \theta(-y_i f(\mathbf{x}_i))$$
$$\text{subject to} \quad \|f\|_K^2 \leq A^2$$

is independent of A, since for any solution f we can always rescale f and have the same cost $\sum_{i=1}^m \theta(-y_i f(\mathbf{x}_i))$.

For machines of type (1) that use V^{sm} or V^σ as the loss function, we prove the following:

---

[1] In [1] it is shown that $V_\gamma \leq \mathrm{fat}_\gamma \leq \frac{1}{\gamma} V_{\frac{\gamma}{2}}$.

Theorem 2. *The V_γ dimension h for $|1 - yf(\mathbf{x})|_+^\sigma$ in hypothesis spaces $\mathcal{F}_A = \{f \in \mathcal{H} | \|f\|_K^2 \leq A^2\}$ (of the set of functions $|1 - yf(\mathbf{x})|_+^\sigma \mid f \in \mathcal{F}_A\}$) and $y \in \{-1, 1\}$, is finite for $\forall\, 0 < \gamma$. If D is the dimensionality of the RKHS $\mathcal{H}$, R^2 is the radius of the smallest sphere centered at the origin containing the data $\mathbf{x}$ in the RKHS, and $B > 1$ is an upper bound on the values of the loss function, then h is upper bounded by:*

- $O(min(D, \frac{R^2 A^2}{\gamma^{\frac{2}{\sigma}}}))$ *for $\sigma < 1$*
- $O(min(D, \frac{(\sigma B^{\frac{\sigma-1}{\sigma}})^2 R^2 A^2}{\gamma^2}))$ *for $\sigma \geq 1$*

Proof

The proof is based on the following theorem [7] (proved for the fat-shattering dimension, but as mentioned above, we use it for the "equivalent" V_γ one).

Theorem 2.2 [Gurvits, 1997] The V_γ dimension h of the set of functions[2] $\mathcal{F}_A = \{f \in \mathcal{H} | \|f\|_K^2 \leq A^2\}$ is finite for $\forall\, \gamma > 0$. If D is the dimensionality of the RKHS, then $h \leq O(min(D, \frac{R^2 A^2}{\gamma^2}))$, where R^2 is the radius of the smallest sphere in the RKHS centered at the origin here the data belong to.

Let $2N$ be the largest number of points $\{(\mathbf{x}_1, y_1), \ldots, (\mathbf{x}_{2N}, y_{2N})\}$ that can be shattered using the rules:

$$
\begin{aligned}
\text{class } 1 \text{ if } |1 - y_i f(\mathbf{x}_i)|_+^\sigma &\geq s + \gamma \\
\text{class } -1 \text{ if } |1 - y_i f(\mathbf{x}_i)|_+^\sigma &\leq s - \gamma
\end{aligned}
\tag{7}
$$

for some s with $0 < \gamma \leq s$. After some simple algebra these rules can be decomposed as:

$$
\begin{aligned}
\text{class } 1 \text{ if } f(\mathbf{x}_i) - 1 &\leq -(s+\gamma)^{\frac{1}{\sigma}} \text{ (for } y_i = 1 \text{)} \\
\text{or } f(\mathbf{x}_i) + 1 &\geq (s+\gamma)^{\frac{1}{\sigma}} \text{ (for } y_i = -1 \text{)} \\
\text{class } -1 \text{ if } f(\mathbf{x}_i) - 1 &\geq -(s-\gamma)^{\frac{1}{\sigma}} \text{ (for } y_i = 1 \text{)} \\
\text{or } f(\mathbf{x}_i) + 1 &\leq (s-\gamma)^{\frac{1}{\sigma}} \text{ (for } y_i = -1 \text{)}
\end{aligned}
\tag{8}
$$

From the $2N$ points at least N are either all class -1, or all class 1. Consider the first case (the other case is exactly the same), and for simplicity of notation let's assume the first N points are class -1. Since we can shatter the $2N$ points, we can also shatter the first N points. Substituting y_i with 1, we get that we can shatter the N points $\{\mathbf{x}_1, \ldots, \mathbf{x}_N\}$ using rules:

$$
\begin{aligned}
\text{class } 1 \text{ if } f(\mathbf{x}_i) + 1 &\geq (s+\gamma)^{\frac{1}{\sigma}} \\
\text{class } -1 \text{ if } f(\mathbf{x}_i) + 1 &\leq (s-\gamma)^{\frac{1}{\sigma}}
\end{aligned}
\tag{9}
$$

Notice that the function $f(\mathbf{x}_i) + 1$ has RKHS norm bounded by A^2 plus a constant C (equal to the inverse of the eigenvalue corresponding to the constant

---

[2] As mentioned above, in this case we can consider $V(y, f(\mathbf{x})) = f(\mathbf{x})$.

basis function in the RKHS - if the RKHS does not include the constant functions, we can define a new RKHS with the constant and use the new RKHS norm). Furthermore there is a "margin" between $(s+\gamma)^{\frac{1}{\sigma}}$ and $(s-\gamma)^{\frac{1}{\sigma}}$ which we can lower bound as follows.

For $\sigma < 1$, assuming $\frac{1}{\sigma}$ is an integer (if not, we can take the closest lower integer),

$$\frac{1}{2}\left((s+\gamma)^{\frac{1}{\sigma}} - (s-\gamma)^{\frac{1}{\sigma}}\right) = \tag{10}$$

$$= \frac{1}{2}((s+\gamma) - (s-\gamma))\left(\sum_{k=0}^{\frac{1}{\sigma}-1}(s+\gamma)^{\frac{1}{\sigma}-1-k}(s-\gamma)^k\right) \geq \gamma\gamma^{\frac{1}{\sigma}-1} = \gamma^{\frac{1}{\sigma}}. \tag{11}$$

For $\sigma \geq 1$, σ integer (if not, we can take the closest upper integer) we have that:

$$2\gamma = \left((s+\gamma)^{\frac{1}{\sigma}}\right)^{\sigma} - \left((s-\gamma)^{\frac{1}{\sigma}}\right)^{\sigma} = \tag{12}$$

$$= ((s+\gamma)^{\frac{1}{\sigma}} - (s-\gamma)^{\frac{1}{\sigma}})\left(\sum_{k=0}^{\sigma-1}((s+\gamma)^{\frac{1}{\sigma}})^{\sigma-1-k}((s-\gamma)^{\frac{1}{\sigma}})^k\right) \leq$$

$$\leq ((s+\gamma)^{\frac{1}{\sigma}} - (s-\gamma)^{\frac{1}{\sigma}})\sigma B^{\frac{\sigma-1}{\sigma}}$$

from which we obtain:

$$\frac{1}{2}\left((s+\gamma)^{\frac{1}{\sigma}} - (s-\gamma)^{\frac{1}{\sigma}}\right) \geq \frac{\gamma}{\sigma B^{\frac{\sigma-1}{\sigma}}} \tag{13}$$

Therefore N cannot be larger than the V_γ dimension of the set of functions with RKHS norm $\leq A^2 + C$ and margin at least $\gamma^{\frac{1}{\sigma}}$ for $\sigma < 1$ (from eq. (11)) and $\frac{\gamma}{\sigma B^{\frac{\sigma-1}{\sigma}}}$ for $\sigma \geq 1$ (from eq. (13)). Using theorem 2.2, and ignoring constant factors (also ones because of C), the theorem is proved. $\square$

In figure 2 we plot the V_γ dimension for $R^2 A^2 = 1$, $B = 1$, $\gamma = 0.9$, and D infinite. Notice that as $\sigma \to 0$, the dimension goes to infinity. For $\sigma = 0$ the V_γ dimension becomes the same as the VC dimension of hyperplanes, which is infinite in this case. For σ increasing above 1, the dimension also increases: intuitively the margin γ becomes smaller relatively to the values of the loss function.

Using theorems 2 and 1 we can bound the expected error of the solution f of machines (1):

$$Pr\left\{\left|R_{\text{emp}}^V(f) - R^V(f)\right| > \epsilon\right\} \leq \mathcal{G}(\epsilon, m, h_\gamma), \tag{14}$$

where V is V^{sm} or V^σ. To get a bound on the expected misclassification error $R^{msc}(f)$ we use the following simple observation:

$$V^{msc}(y, f(\mathbf{x})) \leq V^\sigma(y, f(\mathbf{x})) \quad \text{for} \quad \forall \, \sigma, \tag{15}$$

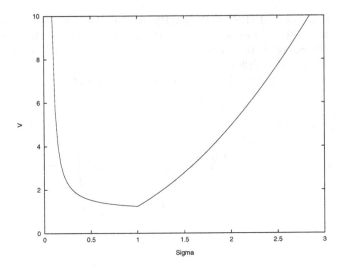

Fig. 2. Plot of the V_γ dimension as a function of σ for $\gamma = .9$

So we can bound the expected misclassification error of the solution of machine (1) under V^{sm} and V^σ using the V_γ dimension of these loss functions and the empirical error of f measured using again these loss functions. In particular we get that for $\forall \sigma$, with probability $1 - \mathcal{G}(\epsilon, m, h_\gamma^{V_\mathcal{F}^\sigma})$:

$$R^{msc}(f) \leq R^\sigma_{emp}(f) + \epsilon \tag{16}$$

where ϵ and γ are related as stated in theorem 1.

Unfortunately we cannot use theorems 2 and 1 for the V^{hm} loss function. For this loss function, since it is a binary-valued function, the V_γ dimension is the same as the VC-dimension, which, as mentioned above, is not appropriate to use in our case. Notice, however, that for $\sigma \to 0$, V^σ approaches V^{hm} pointwise (from theorem 2 the V_γ dimension also increases towards infinity). Regarding the empirical error, this implies that $R^\sigma \to R^{hm}$, so, theoretically, we can still bound the misclassification error of the solution of machines with V^{hm} using:

$$R^{msc}(f) \leq R^{hm}_{emp}(f) + \epsilon + \max(R^\sigma_{emp}(f) - R^{hm}_{emp}(f), 0), \tag{17}$$

where $R^\sigma_{emp}(f)$ is measured using V^σ for some σ. Notice that changing σ we get a family of bounds on the expected misclassification error. Finally, we remark that it could be interesting to extend theorem 2 to loss functions of the form $\theta(1 - yf(\mathbf{x}))h(1 - yf(\mathbf{x}))$, with h any continuous monotone function.

3   Discussion

In recent years there has been significant work on bounding the generalization performance of classifiers using scale-sensitive dimensions of real-valued functions out of which indicator functions can be generated through thresholding (see [4, 9, 8], [3] and references therein). This is unlike the "standard" statistical learning theory approach where classification is typically studied using the theory of indicator functions (binary valued functions) and their VC-dimension [10]. The work presented in this paper is similar in spirit with that of [3], but significantly different as we now briefly discuss.

In [3] a theory was developed to justify machines with "margin". The idea was that a "better" bound on the generalization error of a classifier can be derived by excluding training examples on which the hypothesis found takes a value close to zero (as mentioned above, classification is performed after thresholding a real valued function). Instead of measuring the empirical misclassification error, as suggested by the standard statistical learning theory, what was used was the number of misclassified training points *plus* the number of training points on which the hypothesis takes a value close to zero. Only points classified correctly with some "margin" are considered correct. In [3] a different notation was used: the parameter A in equation (1) was fixed to 1, while a margin ψ was introduced inside the hard margin loss, i.e $\theta(\psi - yf(x))$. Notice that the two notations are equivalent: given a value A in our notation we have $\psi = A^{-1}$ in the notation of [3]. Below we adapt the results in [3] to the setup of this paper, that is, we set $\psi = 1$ and let A vary. Two main theorems were proven in [3].

Theorem 3 (Bartlett, 1998). *For a given A, with probability $1 - \delta$, every function f with $\|f\|_K^2 \le A^2$ has expected misclassification error $R^{msc}(f)$ bounded as:*

$$R^{msc}(f) < R_{emp}^{hm}(f) + \sqrt{\frac{2}{m}(d \ln(34em/d)\log_2(578m) + \ln(4/\delta)}, \qquad (18)$$

where d is the fat-shattering dimension fat_γ of the hypothesis space $\{f : \|f\|_K^2 \le A^2\}$ for $\gamma = \frac{1}{16A}$.

Unlike in this paper, in [3] this theorem was proved without using theorem 1. Although practically both bound (18) and the bounds derived above are not tight and therefore not practical, bound (18) seems easier to use than the ones presented in this paper.

It is important to notice that, like bounds (14), (16), and (17), theorem 3 holds for a fixed A [3]. In [3] theorem 3 was extended to the case where the parameter A (or ψ in the notations of [3]) is not fixed, which means that the bound holds for all functions in the RKHS. In particular the following theorem gives a bound on the expected misclassification error of a machine that holds *uniformly* over all functions:

Theorem 4 (Bartlett, 1998). *For any f with $\|f\|_K < \infty$, with probability $1 - \delta$, the misclassification error $R^{mcs}(f)$ of f is bounded as:*

$$R^{msc}(f) < R_{emp}^{hm}(f) + \sqrt{\frac{2}{m}(d \ln(34em/d)\log_2(578m) + \ln(8\|f\|/\delta)}, \qquad (19)$$

where d is the fat-shattering dimension fat_γ of the hypothesis space consisting of all functions in the RKHS with norm $\le \|f\|_K^2$, and with $\gamma = \frac{1}{32\|f\|}$.

Notice that the only differences between (18) and (19) are the $ln(8\|f\|/\delta)$ instead of $ln(4/\delta)$, and that $\gamma = \frac{1}{32\|f\|}$ instead of $\gamma = \frac{1}{16A}$.

So far we studied machines of the form (1), where A is fixed *a priori*. In practice learning machines used, like SVM, do not have A fixed a priori. For example in the case of SVM the problem is formulated [10] as minimizing:

$$\min \ \textstyle\sum_{i=1}^{m} |1 - y_i f(\mathbf{x}_i)|_+ + \lambda \|f\|_K^2 \tag{20}$$

where λ is known as the *regularization parameter*. In the case of machines (20) we do not know the norm of the solution $\|f\|_K^2$ before actually solving the optimization problem, so it is not clear what the "effective" A is. Since we do not have a fixed upper bound on the norm $\|f\|_K^2$ a priori, we **cannot** use the bounds of section 2 or theorem 3 for machines of the form (20). Instead, we need to use bounds that hold uniformly for *all* A (or ψ if we follow the setup of [3]), for example the bound of theorem 4, so that the bound also holds for the solution of (20) we find. In fact theorem 4 has been used directly to get bounds on the performance of SVM [4]. A straightforward applications of the methods used to extend theorem 3 to 4 can also be used to extend the bounds of section 2 to the case where A is not fixed (and therefore hold for all f with $\|f\| < \infty$), and we leave this as an exercise.

There is another way to see the similarity between machines (1) and (20). Notice that the formulation (1) the regularization parameter λ of (20) can be seen as the *Lagrange multiplier* used to solve the constrained optimization problem (1). That is, problem (1) is equivalent to:

$$\max_\lambda \min_f \ \sum_{i=1}^{m} V(y_i, f(\mathbf{x}_i)) + \lambda(\|f\|_K^2 - A^2) \tag{21}$$

for $\lambda \geq 0$, which is similar to problem (20) that is solved in practice. However in the case of (21) the Lagrange multiplier λ is not known before having the training data, unlike in the case of (20).

So, to summarize, for the machines (1) studied in this paper, A is fixed a priori and the "regularization parameter" λ is not known a priori, while for machines (20) the parameter λ is known a priori, but the norm of the solution (or the effective A) is not known a priori. As a consequence we can use the theorems of this paper for machines (1) but not for (20). To do the second we need a technical extension of the results of section 2 similar to the extension of theorem 3 to 4 done in [3]. On the practical side, the important issue for both machines (1) and (20) is how to choose A or λ. We believe that the theorems and bounds discussed in sections 2 and 3 cannot be practically used for this purpose. Criteria for the choice of the regularization parameter exist in the literature - such as cross validation and generalized cross validation - (for example see [10, 11],[6] and references therein), and is the topic of ongoing research. Finally, as our results indicate, the generalization performance of the learning machines can be bounded using any function of the slack variables and therefore of the margin distribution. Is it, however, the case that the slack variables (margin distributions or any functions of these) are *the* quantities that control the generalization performance of the machines, or there are other important geometric quantities involved? Our results suggest that there are many quantities related to the generalization performance of the machines, but it is not clear that these are the most important ones.

Acknowledgments:
We wish to thank Peter Bartlett for useful comments.

References

1. N. Alon, S. Ben-David, N. Cesa-Bianchi, and D. Haussler. Scale-sensitive dimensions, uniform convergnce, and learnability. *J. of the ACM*, 44(4):615–631, 1997.
2. N. Aronszajn. Theory of reproducing kernels. *Trans. Amer. Math. Soc.*, 686:337–404, 1950.
3. P. Bartlett. The sample complexity of pattern classification with neural networks: the size of the weights is more important that the size of the network. *IEEE Transactions on Information Theory*, 1998.
4. P. Bartlett and J. Shawe-Taylor. Generalization performance of support vector machine and other patern classifiers. In C. Burges B. Scholkopf, editor, *Advances in Kernel Methods–Support Vector Learning*. MIT press, 1998.
5. T. Evgeniou and M. Pontil. On the V-gamma dimension for regression in Reproducing Kernel Hilbert Spaces. In Proceedings of Algorithmic Learning Theory, Tokyo, Japan, 1999.
6. T. Evgeniou, M. Pontil, and T. Poggio. Regularization Networks and Support Vector Machines. Advances in Computational Mathematics Vol. 13, No. 1, pp. 1–50, 2000.
7. L. Gurvits. A note on scale-sensitive dimension of linear bounded functionals in banach spaces. In *Proceedings of Algorithm Learning Theory*, 1997.
8. J. Shawe-Taylor, P. L. Bartlett, R. C. Williamson, and M. Anthony. Structural risk minimization over data-dependent hierarchies. *IEEE Transactions on Information Theory*, 1998. To appear. Also: NeuroCOLT Technical Report NC-TR-96-053, 1996, ftp://ftp.dcs.rhbnc.ac.uk/pub/neurocolt/tech_reports.
9. J. Shawe-Taylor and N. Cristianini. Robust bounds on generalization from the margin distribution. Technical Report NeuroCOLT2 Technical Report NC2-TR-1998-029, NeuroCOLT2, 1998.
10. V. N. Vapnik. *Statistical Learning Theory*. Wiley, New York, 1998.
11. G. Wahba. *Splines Models for Observational Data*. Series in Applied Mathematics, Vol. 59, SIAM, Philadelphia, 1990.
12. R. Williamson, A. Smola, and B. Scholkopf. Generalization performance of regularization networks and support vector machines via entropy numbers. Technical Report NC-TR-98-019, Royal Holloway College University of London, 1998.

On the Noise Model of Support Vector Machines Regression

Massimiliano Pontil, Sayan Mukherjee, and Federico Girosi

Center for Biological and Computational Learning, MIT
45 Carleton Street E25-201, Cambridge, MA 02142, USA
{pontil,sayan,girosi}@ai.mit.edu

Abstract. Support Vector Machines Regression (SVMR) is a learning technique where the goodness of fit is measured not by the usual quadratic loss function (the mean square error), but by a different loss function called the ϵ-Insensitive Loss Function (ILF), which is similar to loss functions used in the field of robust statistics. The quadratic loss function is well justified under the assumption of Gaussian additive noise. However, the noise model underlying the choice of the ILF is not clear. In this paper the use of the ILF is justified under the assumption that the noise is additive and Gaussian, where the variance and mean of the Gaussian are random variables. The probability distributions for the variance and mean will be stated explicitly. While this work is presented in the framework of SVMR, it can be extended to justify non-quadratic loss functions in any Maximum Likelihood or Maximum A Posteriori approach. It applies not only to the ILF, but to a much broader class of loss functions.

1 Introduction

Support Vector Machines Regression (SVMR) [8,9] has a foundation in the framework of statistical learning theory and classical regularization theory for function approximation [10,1]. The main difference between SVMR and classical regularization is the use of the ϵ-Insensitive Loss Function (ILF) to measure the empirical error. The quadratic loss function commonly used in regularization theory is well justified under the assumption of Gaussian, additive noise. In the case of SVMR it is not clear what noise model underlies the choice of the ILF. Understanding the nature of this noise is important for at least two reasons: 1) it can help us decide under which conditions it is appropriate to use SVMR rather than regularization theory; and 2) it may help to better understand the role of the parameter ϵ, which appears in the definition of the ILF, and is one of the two free parameters in SVMR.

In this paper we demonstrate the use of the ILF is justified under the assumption that the noise affecting the data is additive and Gaussian, where the variance and mean are random variables whose probability distributions can be explicitly computed. The result is derived by using the same Bayesian framework which can be used to derive the regularization theory approach, and it is an extension of existing work on noise models and "robust" loss functions [2].

H. Arimura, S. Jain and A. Sharma (Eds.): ALT 2000, LNAI 1968, pp. 316-324, 2000.

The plan of the paper is as follows: in section 2 we briefly review SVMR and the ILF; in section 3 we introduce the Bayesian framework necessary to prove our main result, which is shown in section 4. In section 5 we show some additional results which relate to the topic of robust statistics.

2   The ϵ-Insensitive Loss Function

Consider the following problem: we are given a data set $g = \{(\mathbf{x}_i, y_i)\}_{i=1}^{N}$, obtained by sampling, with noise, some unknown function $f(\mathbf{x})$ and we are asked to recover the function f, or an approximation of it, from the data g. A common strategy consists of choosing as a solution the minimum of a functional of the following form:

$$H[f] = \sum_{i=1}^{l} V(y_i - f(\mathbf{x}_i)) + \alpha \Phi[f], \tag{1}$$

where $V(x)$ is some loss function used to measure the interpolation error, α is a positive number, and $\Phi[f]$ is a smoothness functional. SVMR correspond to a particular choice for V, that is the ILF, plotted below in figure (1):

$$V(x) \equiv |x|_\epsilon \equiv \begin{cases} 0 & \text{if } |x| < \epsilon \\ |x| - \epsilon & \text{otherwise.} \end{cases} \tag{2}$$

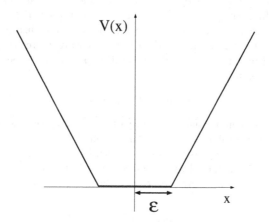

Fig. 1. The ILF $V_\epsilon(x)$.

Details about minimizing the functional (1) and the specific form of the smoothness functional (1) can be found in [8, 1, 3].

The ILF is similar to some of the functions used in robust statistics [5], which are known to provide robustness against outliers. However the function (2) is not only a robust cost function, because of its linear behavior outside the interval $[-\epsilon, \epsilon]$, but also assigns zero cost to errors smaller then ϵ. In other words, for the cost function V_ϵ any function closer than ϵ to the data points is a perfect interpolant.

It is important to notice that if we choose $V(x) = x^2$, then the functional (1) is the usual regularization theory functional [11, 4], and its minimization leads to models which include Radial Basis Functions or multivariate splines. The ILF represents therefore a crucial difference between SVMR and more classical models such as splines and Radial Basis Functions. What is the rationale for using the ILF rather than a quadratic loss function like in regularization theory? In the next section we will introduce a Bayesian framework that will allow us to answer this question.

3   Bayes Approach to SVMR

In this section, the standard Bayesian framework is used to justify the variational approach in equation (1). Work on this topic was originally done by Kimeldorf and Wahba, and we refer to [6, 11] for details.

Suppose that the set $g = \{(\mathbf{x}_i, y_i) \in R^n \times R\}_{i=1}^N$ of data has been obtained by randomly sampling a function f, defined on R^n, in the presence of additive noise, that is

$$f(\mathbf{x}_i) = y_i + \delta_i, \quad i = 1, \ldots, N \tag{3}$$

where δ_i are random independent variables with a given distribution. We want to recover the function f, or an estimate of it, from the set of data g. We take a probabilistic approach, and regard the function f as the realization of a random field with a known prior probability distribution. We are interested in maximizing the a posteriori probability of f given the data g, which can be written, using Bayes' theorem, as following:

$$\mathcal{P}[f|g] \propto \mathcal{P}[g|f] \, \mathcal{P}[f], \tag{4}$$

where $\mathcal{P}[g|f]$ is the conditional probability of the data g given the function f and $\mathcal{P}[f]$ is the a priori probability of the random field f, which is often written as $\mathcal{P}[f] \propto e^{-\alpha \Phi[f]}$, where $\Phi[f]$ is usually a smoothness functional. The probability $\mathcal{P}[g|f]$ is essentially a model of the noise, and if the noise is additive, as in equation (3) and i.i.d. with probability distribution $P(\delta)$, it can be written as:

$$\mathcal{P}[g|f] = \prod_{i=1}^N P(\delta_i). \tag{5}$$

Substituting equation (5) in equation (4), it is easy to see that the function that maximizes the posterior probability of f given the data g is the one that minimizes the following functional:

$$H[f] = -\sum_{i=1}^N \log P(f(\mathbf{x}_i) - y_i) + \alpha \Phi[f] . \tag{6}$$

This functional is of the same form as equation (1), once we identify the loss function $V(x)$ as the log-likelihood of the noise. If we assume that the noise in equation (3) is Gaussian, with zero mean and variance σ, then the functional above takes the form:

$$H[f] = \frac{1}{2\sigma^2} \sum_{i=1}^{N} (y_i - f(\mathbf{x}_i))^2 + \alpha\Phi[f],$$

which corresponds to the classical regularization theory approach [11, 4]. In order to obtain SVMR in this approach one would have to assume that the probability distribution of the noise is $P(\delta) = e^{-|\delta|_\epsilon}$. Unlike an assumption of Gaussian noise, it is not clear what motivates in this Bayesian framework such a choice. The next section will address this question.

4   Main Result

In this section we build on the probabilistic approach described in the previous section and on work done by Girosi [2], and derive a novel class of noise models and loss functions.

4.1   The Noise Model

We start by modifying equation (5), and drop the assumption that noise variables have all identical probability distributions. Different data points may have been collected at different times, under different conditions, so it is more realistic to assume that the noise variables δ_i have probability distributions P_i which are not necessarily identical. Therefore we write:

$$\mathcal{P}[g|f] = \prod_{i=1}^{N} P_i(\delta_i). \tag{7}$$

Now we assume that the noise distributions P_i are actually Gaussians, *but do not have necessarily zero mean*, and define P_i as:

$$P_i(\delta_i) \propto e^{-\beta_i(\delta_i - t_i)^2}. \tag{8}$$

While this model is realistic, and takes into account the fact that the noise could be biased, it is not practical because it is unlikely that we know the set of parameters $\beta \equiv \{\beta_i\}_{i=1}^{N}$ and $\mathbf{t} = \{t_i\}_{i=1}^{N}$. However, we may have some information about β and $\mathbf{t}$, for example a range for their values, or the knowledge that most of the time they assume certain values. It is therefore natural to model the uncertainty on β and $\mathbf{t}$ by considering them as i.i.d. random variables, with probability distributions $\mathcal{P}(\beta, \mathbf{t}) = \prod_{i=1}^{N} P(\beta_i, t_i)$. Under this assumption, equation (8) can be interpreted as $P_i(\delta_i|\beta_i, t_i)$, the conditional probability of δ_i *given* β_i and t_i. Taking this in account, we can rewrite equation (4) as:

$$\mathcal{P}[f|g, \beta, \mathbf{t}] \propto \prod_{i=1}^{N} P_i(\delta_i|\beta_i, t_i)\mathcal{P}[f]. \tag{9}$$

Since we are interested in computing the conditional probability of f given g, independently of $\boldsymbol{\beta}$ and $\mathbf{t}$, we compute the marginal of the distribution above, integrating over $\boldsymbol{\beta}$ and $\mathbf{t}$:

$$\mathcal{P}^*[f|g] \propto \int d\boldsymbol{\beta} \int d\mathbf{t} \prod_{i=1}^{N} P_i(\delta_i|\beta_i, t_i)\mathcal{P}[f]\mathcal{P}(\boldsymbol{\beta}, \mathbf{t}). \tag{10}$$

Using the assumption that $\boldsymbol{\beta}$ and $\mathbf{t}$ are i.i.d., so that $\mathcal{P}(\boldsymbol{\beta}, \mathbf{t}) = \prod_{i=1}^{N} P(\beta_i, t_i)$, we can easily see that the function that maximizes the a posteriori probability $\mathcal{P}^*[f|g]$ is the one that minimizes the following functional:

$$H[f] = \sum_{i=1}^{N} V(f(\mathbf{x}_i) - y_i) + \alpha\Phi[f], \tag{11}$$

where V is given by:

$$V(x) = -\log \int_0^\infty d\beta \int_{-\infty}^\infty dt \sqrt{\beta} e^{-\beta(x-t)^2} P(\beta, t), \tag{12}$$

where the factor $\sqrt{\beta}$ appears because of the normalization of the Gaussian (other constant factors have been disregarded). Equations (11) and (12) define a novel class of loss functions, and provide a probabilistic interpretation for them: using a loss function V with an integral representation of the form (12) is equivalent to assuming that the noise is Gaussian, but the mean and the variance of the noise are random variables with probability distribution $P(\beta, t)$. The classical quadratic loss function can be recovered by choosing $P(\beta, t) = \delta(\beta - \frac{1}{2\sigma^2})\delta(t)$, which corresponds to standard Gaussian noise with variance σ and zero mean.

The class of loss functions defined by equation (12) is an extension of the model discussed in [2], where only unbiased noise distributions are considered:

$$V(x) = -\log \int_0^\infty d\beta \sqrt{\beta} e^{-\beta x^2} P(\beta). \tag{13}$$

Equation (13) can be obtained from equation (12) by setting $P(\beta, t) = P(\beta)\delta(t)$. In this case, the class of loss functions can be identified as follows: given a loss function V in the model, the probability function $P(\beta)$ in equation (13) in the inverse Laplace transform of $\exp(-V(\sqrt{x}))$. So $V(x)$ verifies equation (13) if the inverse Laplace transform on $\exp(-V(\sqrt{x}))$ is nonnegative and integrable. In practice this is very difficult to check directly. Alternative approaches are discussed in [2]. A simple example of loss functions of type (13) is $V(x) = |x|^a, a(0, 2]$. When $a = 2$ we have the classical quadratic loss function for which $P(\beta) = \delta(\beta)$. The case $a = 1$ corresponds to the L_1 loss and equation (13) is solved by: $P(\beta) = \beta^2 \exp -\frac{1}{4\beta}$.

4.2   The Noise Model for the ILF

In order to provide a probabilistic interpretation the ILF we need to find a probability distribution $P_\epsilon(\beta, t)$ such that equation (12) is verified when we set

$V(x) = |x|_\epsilon$. This is a difficult problem, which requires the solution of an integral equation. Here we state a solution, but we do not know whether this solution is unique. The solution was found by extending work done by Girosi in [2] for the case where $\epsilon = 0$, which corresponds to the function $V(x) = |x|$. The solution we found has the form $P(\beta, t) = P(\beta)\lambda_\epsilon(t)$ where we have defined

$$P(\beta) = \frac{C}{\beta^2} e^{-\frac{1}{4\beta}}, \tag{14}$$

and

$$\lambda_\epsilon(t) = \frac{1}{2(\epsilon + 1)} \left(\chi_{[-\epsilon,\epsilon]}(t) + \delta(t - \epsilon) + \delta(t + \epsilon) \right), \tag{15}$$

where $\chi_{[-\epsilon,\epsilon]}$ is the characteristic function of the interval $[-\epsilon, \epsilon]$ and C is a normalization constant. Equations (14) and (15) arederived in the appendix. The shape of the functions in equations (14) and (15) is shown in figure (2). The above model has a simple interpretation: using the ILF is equivalent to assuming that the noise affecting the data is Gaussian. However, the variance and the mean of the Gaussian noise are random variables: the variance ($\sigma^2 = \frac{1}{2\beta}$) has a unimodal distribution that does not depend on ϵ, and the mean has a distribution which is uniform in the interval $[-\epsilon, \epsilon]$, (except for two delta functions at $\mp\epsilon$, which ensure that the mean is occasionally exactly equal to $\mp\epsilon$). The distribution of the mean is consistent with the current understanding of the ILF: errors smaller than ϵ do not count because they may be due entirely to the bias of the Gaussian noise.

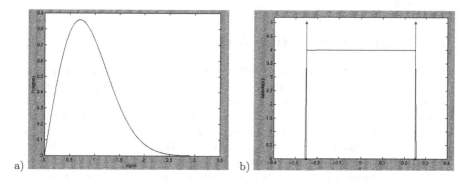

Fig. 2. a) The probability distribution $P(\sigma)$, where $\sigma^2 = \frac{1}{2\beta}$ and $P(\beta)$ is given by equation 14 ; b) The probability distribution $\lambda_\epsilon(x)$ for $\epsilon = .25$ (see equation 15).

5   Additional Results

While it is difficult to state the class of loss functions with an integral representation of the type (12), it is possible to extend the results of the previous section to a particular sub-class of loss functions, ones of the form:

$$
V_\epsilon(x) = \begin{cases} h(x) \text{ if } |x| < \epsilon \\ |x| \quad \text{otherwise,} \end{cases} \tag{16}
$$

where $h(x)$ is some symmetric function, with some restriction that will become clear later. A well known example is one of Huber's robust loss functions [5], for which $h(x) = \frac{x^2}{2\epsilon} + \frac{\epsilon}{2}$ (see figure (3.a)). For loss functions of the form (16), it can be shown that a *function* $P(\beta, t)$ that solves equation (12) always exists, and it has a form which is very similar to the one for the ILF. More precisely, we have that $P(\beta, t) = P(\beta)\lambda_\epsilon(t)$, where $P(\beta)$ is given by equation (14), and $\lambda_\epsilon(t)$ is the following compact-support distribution:

$$
\lambda_\epsilon(t) = \begin{cases} P(t) - P''(t) \text{ if } |t| < \epsilon \\ 0 \qquad\qquad \text{otherwise,} \end{cases} \tag{17}
$$

where we have defined $P(x) = e^{-V_\epsilon(x)}$. This result does not guarantee, however, that λ_ϵ is a measure, because $P(t) - P''(t)$ may not be positive on the whole interval $[-\epsilon, \epsilon]$, depending on h. The positivity constraint defines the class of "admissible" functions h. A precise characterization of the class of admissible h, and therefore the class of "shapes" of the functions which can be derived in this model is currently under study [7]. It is easy to verify that the Huber's loss function described above is admissible, and corresponds to a probability distribution for which the the mean is equal to $\lambda_\epsilon(t) = (1 + \frac{1}{\epsilon} - (\frac{t}{\epsilon})^2)e^{-\frac{t^2}{2\epsilon}}$ over the interval $[-\epsilon, \epsilon]$ (see figure (3.b)).

6   Conclusion and Future Work

An interpretation of the ILF for SVMR was presented. This will hopefully lead to a better understanding of the assumptions that are implicitly made when using SVMR. This work can be useful for the following two reasons: 1) it makes more clear under which conditions it is appropriate to use the ILF rather than the square error loss used in classical regularization theory; and 2) it may help to better understand the role of the parameter ϵ. We have shown that the use of the ILF is justified under the assumption that the noise affecting the data is additive and Gaussian, but not necessarily zero mean, and that its variance and mean are random variables with given probability distributions. Similar results can be derived for some other loss functions of the "robust" type. However, a clear characterization of the class of loss functions which can be derived in this framework is still missing, and it is the subject of current work. While we present this work in the framework of SVMR, similar reasoning can be applied

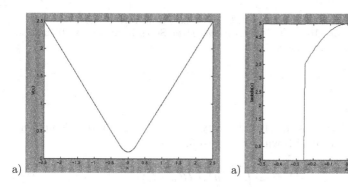

Fig. 3. a) The Huber loss function; b) the corresponding $\lambda_\epsilon(x)$, $\epsilon = .25$. Notice the difference between this distribution and the one that corresponds to the ILF: while for this one the mean of the noise is zero most of the times, in the ILF all the values of the mean are equally likely.

to justify non-quadratic loss functions in any Maximum Likelihood or Maximum A Posteriori approach. It would be interesting to explore if this analysis can be used in the context of Gaussian Processes to compute the average Bayes solution.

Acknowledgments
Federico Girosi wish to thank Jorg Lemm for inspiring discussions.

References

1. T. Evgeniou, M. Pontil, and T. Poggio. Regularization networks and support vector machines. *Advances in Computational Mathematics*, 13:1–50, 2000.
2. F. Girosi. Models of noise and robust estimates. A.I. Memo 1287, Artificial Intelligence Laboratory, Massachusetts Institute of Technology, 1991. ftp://publications.ai.mit.edu/ai-publications/1000-1499/AIM-1287.ps.
3. F. Girosi. An equivalence between sparse approximation and Support Vector Machines. *Neural Computation*, 10(6):1455–1480, 1998.
4. F. Girosi, M. Jones, and T. Poggio. Regularization theory and neural networks architectures. *Neural Computation*, 7:219–269, 1995.
5. P.J. Huber. *Robust Statistics*. John Wiley and Sons, New York, 1981.
6. G.S. Kimeldorf and G. Wahba. A correspondence between Bayesian estimation on stochastic processes and smoothing by splines. *Ann. Math. Statist.*, 41(2):495–502, 1971.
7. M. Pontil, S. Mukherjee, and F. Girosi. On the noise model of support vector machine regression. A.I. Memo 1651, MIT Artificial Intelligence Lab., 1998. ftp://publications.ai.mit.edu/ai-publications/1500-1999/AIM-1651.ps.
8. V. Vapnik. *The Nature of Statistical Learning Theory*. Springer, New York, 1995.
9. V. Vapnik, S.E. Golowich, and A. Smola. Support vector method for function approximation, regression estimation, and signal processing. In M. Mozer, M. Jordan, and T. Petsche, editors, *Advances in Neural Information Processing Systems 9*, pages 281–287, Cambridge, MA, 1997. The MIT Press.

10. V. N. Vapnik. *Statistical Learning Theory.* Wiley, New York, 1998.
11. G. Wahba. *Splines Models for Observational Data.* Series in Applied Mathematics, Vol. 59, SIAM, Philadelphia, 1990.

Appendix

Proof of eq. 14

We look for a solution of eq. (12) of the type $P(\beta, t) = P(\beta)\lambda(t)$. Computing the integral in equation (12) with respect to β, we obtain:

$$e^{-V(x)} = \int_{-\infty}^{+\infty} dt \lambda(t) G(x - t,) \tag{18}$$

where we have defined:

$$G(t) = \int_0^\infty d\beta P(\beta) \sqrt{\beta} e^{-\beta t^2}. \tag{19}$$

Notice that the function G is, modulo a normalization constant, a density distribution, because both the functions in the r.s.h. of equation (19) are overlapping densities. In order to compute G we observe that for $\epsilon = 0$, the function $e^{-|x|_\epsilon}$ becomes the Laplace distribution which belongs to the model in equation (13). Then, $\lambda_{\epsilon=0}(t) = \delta(t)$ and from equation (18) we have:

$$G(t) = e^{-|t|}. \tag{20}$$

Then, in view of the example discussed at the end of section 4.1 and equation (20), the function $P(\beta)$ in equation (19) is:

$$P(\beta) = \beta^2 e^{-\frac{1}{4\beta}},$$

which (modulo a constant factor) is equation (14). To derive equation (15), we rewrite equation (18) in Fourier space:

$$\tilde{F}[e^{-|x|_\epsilon}] = \tilde{G}(\omega)\tilde{\lambda}_\epsilon(\omega), \tag{21}$$

with:

$$\tilde{F}[e^{-|x|_\epsilon}] = \frac{sin(\epsilon\omega) + \omega cos(\epsilon\omega)}{\omega(1 + \omega^2)}, \tag{22}$$

and:

$$\tilde{G}(\omega) = \frac{1}{1 + \omega^2}. \tag{23}$$

Plugging equation (22) and (23) in equation (21), we obtain:

$$\tilde{\lambda}_\epsilon(\omega) = \frac{sin(\epsilon\omega)}{\omega} + cos(\epsilon\omega).$$

Finally, taking the inverse Fourier Transform and normalizing we obtain equation (15).

Computationally Efficient Transductive Machines

Craig Saunders, Alex Gammerman, and Volodya Vovk

Royal Holloway, University of London
Egham, Surrey, England, TW20 0EX
{craig,alex,vovk}@dcs.rhbnc.ac.uk

Abstract. In this paper we propose a new algorithm for providing confidence and credibility values for predictions on a multi-class pattern recognition problem which uses Support Vector machines in its implementation. Previous algorithms which have been proposed to achieve this are very processing intensive and are only practical for small data sets. We present here a method which overcomes these limitations and can deal with larger data sets (such as the US Postal Service database). The measures of confidence and credibility given by the algorithm are shown empirically to reflect the quality of the predictions obtained by the algorithm, and are comparable to those given by the less computationally efficient method. In addition to this the overall performance of the algorithm is shown to be comparable to other techniques (such as standard Support Vector machines), which simply give flat predictions and do not provide the extra confidence/credibility measures.

1 Introduction

Many risk-sensitive applications such as medical diagnosis, or financial analysis require predictions to be qualified with some measure of confidence. Indeed in general, any predictive machine-learning algorithm which requires human-computer interaction, often benefits from giving qualified predictions. The usability of the system is improved, and predictions with low confidence can be filtered out and processed in a different manner.

In this paper we have two aims: firstly, we wish to provide confidence and credibility values for our predictions, rather than the simple "flat" answer given by many Machine Learning techniques (such as a standard Support Vector Machine [10]); secondly we want to obtain these values in an efficient manner so that the algorithm is practical for large data sets, and does not suffer the time penalties of previously proposed algorithms (e.g. those in [1,7]).

To achieve the confidence and credibility measures, we build on ideas of algorithmic information theory (see [12]). By using these ideas, we are able to provide confidence measures with a strong theoretical foundation, and which do not rely on stronger assumptions than the standard i.i.d. one (we actually make a slightly weaker assumption, that of *exchangeability*). This is in contrast to many alternative methods (such as the Bayesian approach), which often require

H. Arimura, S. Jain and A. Sharma (Eds.): ALT 2000, LNAI 1968, pp. 325–337, 2000.

a prior probability (which is not known and has to be estimated), and confidence measures are given on the assumption that this prior is the correct one. In order to compute these values we use Support Vector Machines and the statistical notion of p-values, in an extension of the ideas presented in [7]. The multi-class method presented in that exposition however, was processing-intensive, and the length of time required meant that the algorithm was not practical for medium to large datasets. The method presented here (and originated in [11]) however, overcomes these difficulties, and in section 4 experiments are conducted on much larger data sets (e.g. 7900 training, 2000 test).

The layout of this paper is as follows. In section 2 we describe the theoretical motivation for the algorithm, then in section 3 we concentrate on a specific implementation which uses Support Vector machines. In this section we briefly describe a previous method of qualifying Support Vector method predictions, and extend the technique to the multi-class case. The inefficiencies of this method are presented, and a new algorithm is proposed. Experimental evidence is presented in section 4 which indicates that as well as providing confidence and credibility values, the algorithm's predictive performance is comparable to a standard Support Vector machine when using the same kernel function. Specifically, experiments were carried out on the US Postal Service digit database, and a comparison is made between the new algorithm, the algorithm presented in [7], and a standard Support Vector Machine. In section 5 we discuss the merits of this approach and suggest future directions of research.

2   Randomness

In [12] it was shown that approximations to universal confidence measures can be computed, and used successfully as a basis for machine learning. In this section we present a summary of the relevant ideas, which will provide a motivation for the technique described in section 3. What we are principally interested in is the randomness of a sequence $z = (z_1, \ldots, z_n)$ of elements of $z_i \in Z$ where Z is some sample space (for the applications presented in this paper, z is a sequence $(\mathbf{x}_1, y_1), \ldots, (\mathbf{x}_l, y_l), (\mathbf{x}_{l+1}, y_{l+1})$ where $\mathbf{x}_i \in \mathbb{R}^n, y \in \mathbb{Z}$, containing l training examples and one test example along with some provisional classification). Let $\mathcal{P} = \mathcal{P}_1, \mathcal{P}_2, \ldots$ be a sequence of statistical models such that, for every $n = 1, 2, \ldots$, $\mathcal{P}_n$ is a set of probability distributions in Z^n. In this paper we will only be interested in specific computable $\mathcal{P}$ (namely, the iid and exchangeability models). We say that a function $t : Z^* \to \mathbb{N}$ (where $\mathbb{N}$ is the set $\{0, 1, \ldots\}$ of non-negative integers) is a *log-test for $\mathcal{P}$-typicalness* if

1. for all $n \in \mathbb{N}$ and $m \in \mathbb{N}$ and all $P \in \mathcal{P}_n$, $P\{z \in Z^n : t(z) \geq m\} \leq 2^{-m}$.
2. t is semi-computable from below.

As proven by Kolmogorov and Martin-Löf (1996) (see also [4]), there exists a largest, to within an additive constant, log-test for $\mathcal{P}$-randomness, which is called $\mathcal{P}$-*randomness deficiency*. When $\mathcal{P}_n$ consists of all probability distributions of the type P^n, P being a probability distribution in Z, we omit "$\mathcal{P}$-" and speak of just *randomness deficiency.* If $d(z)$ is the randomness deficiency of a data sequence z, we call $\delta(z) = 2^{-d(z)}$ the *randomness level* of z. The randomness level δ is the smallest, to within a constant factor, p-value function; the latter notion is defined as follows: a function $t : Z^* \to [0, 1]$) is a *p-value function w.r.t. the iid model* if

1. for all $n \in \mathbb{N}$ and $r \in [0, 1]$ and all distributions $P \in Z$,
   $$P^n\{z \in Z^n : t(z) \leq r\} \leq r. \quad (1)$$
2. t must be semi-computable from above.

The randomness level is a universal measure of typicalness with respect to the class of iid distributions: if the randomness level of z is close to 0, z is untypical. Functions t which satisfy the above requirement are called *p-typicalness tests.*

2.1   Using Randomness

Unfortunately, this measure of typicalness is non-computable (and in practice one has to use particular, easily computable, p-value functions). If however one could compute the randomness deficiency of a sequence and we accept the iid assumption and ignore computation time, then the problem of prediction would become trivial. Assuming we have a training set $(\mathbf{x}_1, y_1), \ldots, (\mathbf{x}_l, y_l)$ and an unlabelled test example $\mathbf{x}_{l+1}$, we can do the following:

1. Consider all possible values Y for the label y_{l+1}, and compute the randomness level of every possible completion
   $$(\mathbf{x}_1, y_1), \ldots, (\mathbf{x}_l, y_l), (\mathbf{x}_{l+1}, Y)$$
2. Predict Y corresponding to the completion with the largest randomness level.
3. Output as the *confidence* in this prediction one minus the second largest randomness level.
4. Output as the *credibility* the randomness level of the prediction.

The intuition behind confidence can be described with the following example. Suppose we choose a "significance level" of 1%. If the confidence in our prediction exceeds 99% and we are wrong, then the actual data sequence belongs to the set of all data sequences with randomness level less than 1%, (which by (1) is a very rare event). Credibility can be seen as a measure of quality of our data set. Low credibility means that either the training set is non-random or the test example is not representative of the test set.

2.2   Use in Practice

In order to use these ideas in practice, we will associate a strangeness measure with each element in our extended training sequence (denoted α_i). If we have a strangeness measure which is invariant w.r.t. permutation of our data, the probability of our test example being the strangest in the sequence is $\frac{1}{l+1}$.

Because all permutations of strangeness measures are equiprobable, we can generalise this into a valid p-typicalness function :

$$t(z) = \frac{\#\{i : \alpha_i \geq \alpha_{l+1}\}}{l+1}.$$

This is the type of function we will use in order to approximate the randomness level of a sequence. In this paper, our strangeness measures (α_i) are constructed from the Lagrange multipliers of the SV optimisation problem, or the distances of examples from a hyperplane.

3   SV Implementation

In this section we describe a way of computing confidence and credibility values which uses Support Vector Machines. We first describe and extend the method outlined in [7] to the multi-class case. The new method presented later in this section is more computationally efficient than the one presented in [7] (for timings see section 4), allowing much larger datasets to be used.

3.1   Original Method

In [7], a method for two-class classification problems was presented. The method involved adding a test example to the training set, along with a provisional classification (say -1). A Support Vector machine was then trained on this extended set, and the resultant Lagrange multipliers were used as a strangeness measure. That is the following optimisation problem was solved :

$$\max \sum_{i=1}^{l} \alpha_i - \frac{1}{2} \sum_{i,j=1,\ldots,l+1} \alpha_i \alpha_j y_i y_j \mathcal{K}(\mathbf{x}_i, \mathbf{x}_j),$$

subject to the constraints,

$$\sum_{i=1,\ldots,l+1} \alpha_i = 0, \; \alpha_i \geq 0, \; i = 1,\ldots,l+1. \tag{1}$$

The p-typicalness function took the form :

$$p_- = \frac{\#\{i : \alpha_i \geq \alpha_{l+1}\}}{l+1}.$$

The test example was then added to the training set with a provisional classification of $+1$, and p_+ was calculated in a similar fashion. Confidence and credibility were then calculated as outlined in section 2.1.

Extension to Multi-Class Problems The method above can easily be extended to the multi-class case. Consider an n-class pattern recognition problem. This time, for each test example, n optimisation problems have to be solved (one for each possible classification). We generate n "one against the rest" classifiers, each time using the resultant α-values to calculate p-typicalness as follows. For each class $m \in \{1, \ldots, n\}$, train an m-against-the-rest Support Vector machine, and calculate p_m as :

$$p_m = \frac{\#\{i : (\alpha_i \geq \alpha_{l+1}) \wedge (y_i = m)\}}{|S_m|},$$

where

$$S_m = \{(\mathbf{x}_i, y_i) : y_i = m\}.$$

That is, for each classifier, we only use the α-values which correspond to the provisional classification given, in our calculation of p-typicalness. Unfortunately, although this method works in practice, it is rather inefficient and can only be used on small data sets. Consider as an example of a medium-large problem, the well known 10-class digit recognition problem of the US Postal Service data set. To train a single "one vs. the rest" SV machine on this data set takes approximately 2 minutes. Therefore, to use the above method to classify a test set of 2000 examples, it would take approximately $2 \times 10 \times 2007 = 40140$ minutes. Which is roughly 1 month! Clearly this is unacceptable, and an improvement has to be found.

3.2 New Method

The general idea is as follows; we create a hash function $f_h : \mathbb{R}^d \to \{1, \ldots, h\}$, which when given a training vector $\mathbf{x}_i$, returns a value in the range $\{1, \ldots, h\}$. This is used to create a total of $h * n$ subsets of our training data (where n is the number of classes in our training set). For each class in the training set, a Support Vector Machine is trained in the following way. For every possible output of the hash function j, train a Support Vector Machine each time leaving out of the training process those examples which both are a member of the class being considered, and return a value of j from the hash function.

More formally, we have the following. We are given a training set T which consists of l examples and their labels $(\mathbf{x}_1, y_1), \ldots, (\mathbf{x}_l, y_l)$, where $\mathbf{x}_k \in \mathbb{R}^d$ and $y_k \in \{1, \ldots, n\}$. We also have a hash function $f_h : \mathbb{R}^d \to \{1, \ldots, h\}$. Note that the hash function should be chosen so that it is "pseudo-random" and splits the training set into roughly equal portions. The hash function used in the experiments in this paper simply computed the sum of all attribute values modulo h plus 1.

First of all we create nh sets $S_{i,j}$ from our training set

$$S_{i,j} = \{(\mathbf{x}_k, 1) : y_k = i, f_h(\mathbf{x}_k) \neq j\} \cup \{(\mathbf{x}_k, -1) : y_k \neq i\}, \qquad (2)$$

where $i = 1, \ldots, n$ and $j = 1, \ldots, h$. On each of these sets we train a Support Vector Machine. That is, we obtain hn functions of the form

$$F_{i,j}(\mathbf{x}) = \sum_{k:(\mathbf{x}_k, y_k) \in S_{i,j}} \alpha_k y_k \mathcal{K}(\mathbf{x}_k, \mathbf{x}),$$

where $\mathcal{K}$ is some kernel function, and the α_i's are obtained by solving the following optimisation problems; maximise

$$\sum_{k=1}^{l} \alpha_k - \frac{1}{2} \sum_{k,m:(\mathbf{x}_k, y_k),(\mathbf{x}_m, y_m) \in S_{i,j}} \alpha_k \alpha_m y_k y_m \mathcal{K}(\mathbf{x}_k, \mathbf{x}_m),$$

subject to the constraints,

$$\sum_{k:(\mathbf{x}_k, y_k) \in S_{i,j}} y_k \alpha_k = 0, \quad \alpha_k \geq 0, \quad k = 1, \ldots, |S_{i,j}|.$$

This is similar to the "one against the rest" method which is often used in multi-class Support Vector Machines [9]. For our purposes though, we create several "one against the rest" classifiers for every class, each time only including positive examples which have a particular value when the hash function is applied.

3.3 Classification, Confidence, and Credibility

The procedure for classifying a new test example is given by Algorithm 1. In a nutshell the procedure simply applies the hash function to some new example $\mathbf{x}_{\text{new}}$, then for each class identifies a working set (denoted W_i) and a particular function $F_{i,j}$ (which did not use any element of the working set in its creation). The function $F_{i,j}$ is then used to obtain the distance to the hyperplane for each element of the working set, and our new example (these distances are denoted by $d_1, \ldots, d_{|W_i|}, d_{\text{new}}$). Note that "distance" here is defined as the output of a function $F_{i,j}(\mathbf{x})$, and therefore can be negative (if the point $\mathbf{x}$ lies on a specific side of the hyperplane). In order to give confidence and credibility values for the new example, we compute the example's p-value for each possible classification. Once the distances $d_1, \ldots, d_{|W_i|}, d_{\text{new}}$ to the hyperplane for a particular working set W_i (including our new test example) have been calculated, the p-value is simple to compute. The ideal situation is where our new example is the "strangest" example of the working set. For this algorithm the strangest example is the one with the smallest distance to the hyperplane (recall that "distance" in this sense can be negative, so the smallest d_k is either the example furthest on the "wrong" side of the hyperplane for classification c, or if all examples are on the positive side, the example closest to the hyperplane). The probability that our example $\mathbf{x}_{\text{new}}$ has the smallest valued distance to the hyperplane out of all examples in the working set is simply

$$P\left\{ d_{\text{new}} < \min_{1 \leq k \leq |W_i|} d_k \right\} \leq \frac{1}{|W_i| + 1},$$

Algorithm 1 Classifying a new test sample $\mathbf{x}_{new}$

Obtain $j_{new} = f_h(\mathbf{x}_{new})$.
for Each class i in training set **do**
    Create a working set W_i which includes all examples in the training set with $y_k = i$
    and $f_h(\mathbf{x}_k) = j_{new}$ (i.e. $W_i = \{x : f_h(\mathbf{x}_k) = j_{new}, y_k = i, k = 1, \dots, l\}$).
    For every example in W_i and $\mathbf{x}_{new}$ use $F_{i,j_{new}}$ (see eq (2)) to get the distance d_k
    from the hyperplane.
    Compute p-value (p_i) for new example, where $p_i = \frac{\#\{k : d_k \leq d_{new}\}}{|W_i|+1}$
end for
Predicted classification is $\arg\max_i p_i$.
Confidence in prediction is $1 - \max_{j \neq i} p_j$.
Credibility of prediction is $\max_i p_i$.

(since all permutations of $d_1, \dots, d_{|W_i|}, d_{new}$ are equiprobable).

The distances from the hyperplane are a valid strangeness measure (i.e. they are invariant under permutation), so we can construct a valid p-typicalness function as follows :

$$p_i = \frac{\#\{k : d_k \leq d_{new}\}}{|W_i| + 1}.$$

As stated in Algorithm 1, our prediction for $\mathbf{x}_{new}$ is given by the classification which yielded the highest p-value. In an ideal case, the p-value associated with the correct classification will be high, say $\geq 95\%$, and for all other classifications it will be low, say $\leq 5\%$. In this case both confidence and credibility will be high and our prediction is deemed to be reliable. If however the example looks very strange when given all possible classifications (i.e. the highest p-value is low, e.g. $\leq 10\%$), then although confidence may be high (all other p-values may still be $\leq 5\%$), our credibility will be low. The intuition here would be: although we are confident in our prediction (the likelihood of it being another candidate is low), the quality of the data upon which we base this prediction is also low, so we can still make an error. This would concur with the intuition in section 2. In this situation our test example may not be represented by the training set (in our experiments this would correspond to a disfigured digit).

4   Experiments and Results

Experiments were conducted on the well known benchmark USPS database (see e.g. [3]), which consists of 7291 training examples and 2007 test examples, where each example is a 16×16 pixelated image of a digit in the range 0–9. For all these experiments, the following kernel was used

$$\mathcal{K}(\mathbf{x}, \mathbf{y}) = \frac{(\mathbf{x} \cdot \mathbf{y})^3}{256}.$$

Although this kernel does not give the best possible performance on the data set, it is comparable and is only meant to ensure that a comparison between the techniques presented here is a fair one.

4.1   Efficiency Comparison

In order to compare this method to the one presented in [7], we conducted an experiment on a subset of the USPS data set. All examples of the digits 2 and 7 were extracted from the data set creating a two-class pattern recognition problem with 1376 training examples and 345 test examples. Table 1 shows the timings and error rates for both methods[1]. Note that a normal Support Vector machine also has 3 errors on this data set (when trained with the same kernel function). Also in this case, the 3 errors produced by the SV machine and the two transductive methods were the same 3 examples. For the new method the range of values which the hash function can produce (h), can be changed. The value of h determines how many subsets each class in the training set is split into, and results are shown for $h = 2, 3,$ and 4. Even though the data set in this

Method	Time	Errors	ave -log p-value
Old	5 hrs 20 mins	3	3.06
2 Splits	39 secs	4	2.51
3 Splits	50 secs	3	2.33
4 Splits	1 min 4 secs	3	2.20

Table 1. Timings, errors (out of 345), and average -log (base 10) p-values for the different methods, on a 2-class subset of the USPS data set. Note that large average p-values are preferable (see section 4.2)

experiment would not normally be considered to be large, the previous method suffers a heavy time penalty. The table clearly shows that the method proposed in this paper is more efficient, whilst retaining the same level of performance. In order to interpret the last column of the table, notice that a -log p-value of 2 indicates a p-value of 1%.

The gap in efficiency between the two methods is due to the fact that the new method does not have to run two optimisation problems for each test point. If the number of test examples is increased, the time taken by the hashing method does not alter significantly. The old method however, scales badly with any such increase. In order to illustrate this in practice we used a subset of the data described above. A total of 400 examples were used for training, and two test set sizes were used: 100 examples and 345 examples. Table 1 shows the error rates and timings of the old method, and the hashing method with 3 hash sets. Notice the time penalty incurred by the old method as the test set is expanded.

---

[1] Note that for the experiments we used the SVM implementation from Royal Holloway. See [8] for details.

Method	Time (100 examples)	Time (345 examples)
Old	11 mins 37 secs (0 errors)	39 mins 16 secs (5 errors)
3 Splits	12 secs (0 errors)	13 secs (6 errors)

Table 2. Timings and error rates for the two methods. The training set size was 400, and two test sets of size 100 and 345 were used. The old algorithm suffers a heavy time penalty with the increase in test set size.

4.2   Predictive Performance of the Algorithm

Experiments were also conducted on the full USPS data set, and the performance of the algorithm was measured when each class was split into different numbers of subsets. Table 2 summarises these results. In the case of having 5 splits, the performance of the algorithm deteriorated. This could be due to the fact that although by having 5 splits the training set was larger and therefore one would expect a better decision function, the working set is greatly reduced in size. This led to the p-values for many classes being of the same magnitude and would therefore result in more misclassifications. As a point of comparison for

No of Splits	Error Rate	ave -log p-value
2	5.7%	2.46
3	5.5%	2.23
4	5.4%	2.04
5	6.0%	1.91

Table 3. Error rates for different numbers of splits of each class; the last column gives the average minus log p-value over all incorrect classifications. The data set used was the 10-class USPS data set.

the results shown in table 2, note that the Support Vector Machine when using the same kernel has an error rate of 4.3%. Although for the smaller data set used in the previous section the performance of the new method, the original transductive method, and the Support Vector machine was identical, our quest for efficiency on a large data set has resulted in a small loss in performance in this case. Our aim though is to produce valid confidence and credibility values whilst retaining good performance, we are not necessarily trying to outperform all other methods. The table shows that the performance of the algorithm does not suffer to a large extent, even though it provides the extra measures.

The last column in the table shows the average minus log of p-values calculated for the incorrect classifications of the new example. For relatively noise-free data sets we expect this figure to be high, and our predictive performance to be good. This can also be interpreted as a measure of the quality of our approximation to the actual level of randomness, the higher the number, the better our approximation. This is our main aim: to improve the p-values produced by the algorithm. We believe that good predictive performance will be achieved as our p-values improve. This can already be seen in the progression from the algorithm presented in [1]. Our algorithm provides better confidence and credibility[2] values, and our predictive performance is also higher.

When comparing p-values in the tables it is important to note that there is an upper bound on the ave -log p-value which can be obtained. This stems from the fact that even if every incorrect classification is highlighted by the algorithm as the strangest possible, then the p-value is restricted by the sample size from which it is obtained. As an example, consider the p-values obtained in table 1. For the old method, the strangeness measure was taken over the whole training set (approx. 1300 examples). This would yield a maximum average (-log p-value) of 3.11. For hashing however, we are restricted to computing p-typicalness functions over the hash set. For 3 splits, each hash set contains roughly 225 examples. This would yield a maximum average of 2.34. For larger data sets, we would therefore hope that this figure qould improve (as the hash set size would increase).

4.3 Confidence and Credibility Values

For the experiments, the confidence in our predictions was typically very high, 85–99%. This was due to the data set being relatively noise free. In a data set corrupted by noise, we would expect the prediction not to be so clear cut. That is, the noise in the data may make another classification (other than correct one) appear to be random. The correct classification may have a large p-value (95%), and therefore may clearly be one we predict. The confidence in the prediction however, will be lower.

Our intuition behind the measure of credibility was that it should reflect the "quality" of our predictions. If credibility is low, then the example looks strange for every possible classification, and so our prediction is not as reliable. It is therefore expected that the credibility associated with a prediction which is later found to be incorrect, should be low in a majority of cases. This has been observed experimentally and is illustrated by Figure 1, which displays histograms showing the number of incorrect predictions which have credibility within a certain range for 2,3 and 4 splits.

4.4 Rejecting Examples

It is possible to use the measures of confidence and credibility to obtain a rejection criteria for difficult examples. Suppose we pick a specific confidence threshold, say 95%, and reject all predictions which fall below this level. We can then expect that the error rate on the remaining predictions will not deviate significantly from at most 5%. Note that over randomisations of the training set and the test example, and over time, we would expect the error rate to be $\leq 5\%$ (over all examples). In this scenario however, we have a fixed (but large) training set. Also, we are measuring the error over the non-rejected examples and not the

---

[2] In the paper, the measure of credibility was referred to as possibility.

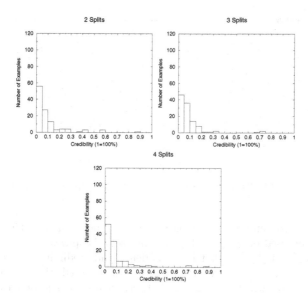

Fig. 1. Credibility values for incorrectly predicted examples, when run with different numbers of splits.

whole set. If a small number of examples are rejected however, we would not expect the error rate to deviate significantly from 5%. Unfortunately, it is not possible to say a-priori how many examples will be rejected. For our experiments have selected four possible rejection criteria, these are : Confidence, Credibility, Confidence × Credibility and (1 − Confidence) − Credibility.

The first measure is obvious - we want to reject all classifications which do not achieve a certain confidence value, therefore capping the generalisation error. The other measures however, also control generalisation error. We may wish to reject examples with low credibility; that is, those examples which look unlikely given any classification. Thirdly, by simply taking the product of the two measures, we end up with a single measure which is only high when both values are high. Finally, the difference between typicalness values of the two likeliest classifications can be used. Again, this is an attempt to reject samples which do not have a clear leading candidate for the correct classification. The rejection rate vs. generalisation error on non-rejected examples is plotted for hash sizes 2,3,4 and 5, and are shown in figure 2.

5   Discussion

In this paper we have presented an algorithm which gives both confidence and credibility values for its predictions, on a multi-class pattern recognition problem. This method overcomes the time penalties suffered by a previously proposed

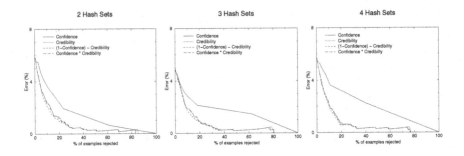

Fig. 2. Generalisation error on non-rejected examples vs. rejection rate.

algorithm, whilst retaining a comparable level of performance. This allows the method to be used on large real-world data sets. Empirical evidence has been presented which indicates that the confidence and credibility values produced by the algorithm correctly reflect confidence in the prediction and the quality of the data upon which it was based. Furthermore, in addition to providing confidence and credibility values, the performance of the algorithm has been shown to be comparable to that of Support Vector machines. The work here concentrates on pattern recognition problems, but can easily be extended to regression estimation. Both Support Vector Machine regression, and methods such as Ridge Regression (see e.g. [2], or [6] for the kernel-based version) can be extended to incorporate the ideas in this paper.

Acknowledgements

This work was partially supported by EPSRC GR/L35812 and GR/M15972, and EU INTAS-93-725-ext grants. In addition we are indebted to the support provided by IFR Ltd.

References

1. A. Gammerman, V. Vapnik, and V. Vovk. Learning by transduction. In *Uncertainty in Artificial Intelligence*, pages 148–155, 1998. 325, 334
2. A. Hoerl and R.W. Kennard. Ridge regression: Biased estimation for nonorthogonal problems. *Technometrics*, 12(1):55–67, 1970. 336
3. Y. LeCun, B. Boser, J. S. Denker, D. Henderson, R. E. Howard, W. Hubbard, and L. J. Jackel. "Handwritten digit recognition with back-propagation network". *Advances in Neural Information Processing Systems*, pages 396–404, 1990. 331
4. M. Li and P. Vitanyi. *An Introduction to Kolmogorov Compexity and Its Applications.* Springer, 1997. 326
5. P. Martin-Löf. The definition of random sequences. *Information and Control*, 1966.

6. C. Saunders, A. Gammerman, and V. Vovk. Ridge regression learning algorithm in dual variables. In *ICML '98. Proceedings of the 15th International Conference on Machine Learning*, pages 515–521. Morgan Kaufmann, 1998. 336
7. C. Saunders, A. Gammerman, and V. Vovk. Transduction with confidence and credibility. In *Proceedings of IJCAI'99*, volume 2, pages 722–726, 1999. 325, 326, 328, 332
8. C. Saunders, M.O. Stitson, J. Weston, L. Bottou, B. Schölkopf, and A. Smola. Support Vector machine - reference manual. Technical Report CSD-TR-98-03, Royal Holloway, University of London, 1998. 332
9. B. Schölkopf, C. Burges, and V. Vapnik. Extracting support data for a given task. In *Proceedings, First International Conference on Knowledge Discovery and Data Mining*, pages 252–257. AAAI Press, 1995. 330
10. V. N. Vapnik. *Statistical Learning Theory*. Wiley, 1998. 325
11. V. Vovk and A. Gammerman. Algorithmic randomness theory and its applications in computer learning. Technical Report CLRC-TR-00-02, Royal Holloway, University of London, 1999. 326
12. V. Vovk, A. Gammerman, and C. Saunders. Machine-learning applications of algorithmic randomness. In *Proceedings of ICML '99*, pages 444–453, 1999. 325, 326

Author Index

Lecture Notes in Artificial Intelligence (LNAI)

Lecture Notes in Computer Science